BANDITS AND PARTISANS

PITT SERIES IN RUSSIAN AND EAST EUROPEAN STUDIES

Jonathan Harris, Editor

BANDITS AND PARTISANS

THE ANTONOV MOVEMENT IN THE RUSSIAN CIVIL WAR

Erik C. Landis

UNIVERSITY OF PITTSBURGH PRESS

Published by the University of Pittsburgh Press, Pittsburgh PA 15260

Copyright © 2008, University of Pittsburgh Press

Manufactured in the United States of America

Printed on acid-free paper

10 9 8 7 6 5 4 3 2 1

Library of Congress Cataloging-in-Publication Data

Landis, Erik C.
Bandits and partisans : the Antonov movement in the Russian Civil War / Erik C. Landis.
    p. cm. — (Pitt series in russian and east european studies)
 Includes bibliographical references and index.
 ISBN-13: 978-0-8229-4343-3 (cloth : alk. paper)
 ISBN-10: 0-8229-4343-3 (cloth : alk. paper)
 1. Soviet Union—History—Revolution, 1917-1921—Protest movements. 2. Tambovskaia guberniia (R.S.F.S.R.)—History—20th century. 3. Peasant uprisings—Russia—Tambovskaia guberniia—History—20th century. 4. Antonov, Aleksandr Stepanovich. 5. Peasantry—Russia—Tambovskaia guberniia (R.S.F.S.R.) —Political activity—History—20th century . I. Title. II. Title: Antonov movement in the Russian Civil War.
 DK265.8.T3L36 2008
 947.084'1—dc22
             2007046148

FOR LISA AND HELENA, TRUE PARTISANS

CONTENTS

MAPS AND FIGURES

PREFACE

THIS BOOK IS a history of the Tambov rebellion, the second to appear in English and the first published since the breakup of the Soviet Union.[1] It is first and foremost a narrative account of the insurgency and its suppression, but it is also a study of the politics of civil war in Russia, a portrait of Soviet state building and Communist Party politics in their provincial setting, as well as an examination of popular politics in the village communities of Tambov. In touching upon these themes, I seek to contribute to developments in the historiography that have deepened and broadened our understanding of Russia's turbulent experience of the early twentieth century. Not only have more detailed studies of the central events of this period emerged since the breakup of the Soviet Union, utilizing recently unaccessible archival materials, but also the mosaic of local settings has similarly entered our descriptions of this period to provide a much deeper appreciation of the varieties of experience that often hinged upon central events.[2] Likewise, studies of the political culture of the early Soviet period have broadened scholars' appreciation of the context for understanding the strategies and practices of state building pursued by rival forces during the period of the Russian revolution and civil war.[3] The common critical focus of these studies has been on the outcomes of the revolution of 1917, explaining how many of the most salient contours of Soviet despotism emerged from these early years. While explanations have grown more sophisticated, new materials have also enriched the story of Russia's revolution and civil war with a personal perspective that deepens our understanding of this complex period.

To paraphrase Herbert Butterfield, the story has progressed far from the simple picture of good men fighting bad. This book aims to add to this development by presenting a portrait of an important rural rebellion that highlights many of the contingencies that ultimately defined and determined the course of events. The rural anti-Bolshevik rebellions that punctuated the civil war period became an area of particular interest among Russian and non-Russian historians alike, once restrictions on historical research and publishing in the USSR were loosened in the mid-1980s. For many, the story of the brave peasantry resisting the nascent dictatorship of the proletariat represented the resistance of the Russian people to an illegitimate, minority government that had usurped the democratic promise of the revolution of 1917. What emerged was a picture of village communities brutalized by the agents of the Bolshevik Party and driven to the brink of starvation by the exploitative policies of the Soviet state. Mounting grievances and desperation gave rise to armed rebellion, and the wave of insurgencies that confronted the regime in the final stage of the civil war conflict represented a violent plebiscite on the Bolsheviks' brand of revolution, one that nearly brought the Soviet experiment to an abrupt end. This overwhelming expression of opposition to the regime was ended only when the state used all the coercive resources at its disposal to suppress the popular will. The preponderance of contemporary research on this facet of the civil war era has been devoted to these bookends of the narrative—the nature of popular grievances with the Soviet regime and the extent and brutality of the regime-led suppression of popular resistance.

This study aims to provide a more complete picture of what was possibly the most important "front" of resistance to the Bolshevik regime in the late civil war period. In doing so, this study of the Antonov rebellion moves away from the basic grievance-suppression focus of much recent scholarship on civil war–era insurgencies and seeks to reveal the dynamic and contingent nature by which events unfolded in 1920 and 1921. In the broadest sense, this is a critical study of popular mobilization and counterinsurgency, one in which the collective identities of challengers and regime supporters alike are themselves objects of contention, where the simple labels of *bandit* and *partisan* formed the rhetorical focal point of a conflict in which rebels and their opponents struggled for popular support and solidarity with appeals regarding the worthiness of their cause and their legitimate prospects of success. The *antonovshchina* and its suppression did not take place in a "cognitive vacuum";[4] the themes and symbols that contending sides invoked were largely drawn from the context of Russia's revolution and civil war and their interpretation informed the armed conflict itself.

Further, the sense of what was possible for political actors, once again on both sides of the conflict, was informed by the unique conditions of state breakdown, the collapse of formal channels of communication and information, and the consequent political landscape, whose complexity has prompted several contemporary historians to refer to plural "civil wars" rather than impose an artificial coherence to the period following the Bolsheviks' seizure of power in October 1917.[5] Whatever the merits of this interpretation, the subsequent civil war did represent a discrete era for contemporaries, as the meanings and promise of the revolution that ended the Romanov dynasty were disputed and redefined, representing a symbolic touchstone as vital as it was elusive. This book seeks to situate the Antonov movement within the context of this brief but spectacular era of revolution and civil war in

Russia. Only against the backdrop of this peculiar era can one properly understand how an uprising in the autumn of 1920 could be transformed into an elaborate mass movement, and how that movement could just as rapidly collapse and be forgotten by the same communities that represented its former strength.

The puzzle that has informed this study from its very beginning can be summed up almost too simply: what are the conditions and mechanisms by which "bandits" become "partisans," only to return to being "bandits" once again? This is a puzzle that involves individual and collective identity, as well as questions relating to authenticity and memory. But it is also a puzzle that hinges on the context and the conditions that characterize particular eras. In this case, that era is the period of revolution and civil war in Russia, one that produced both heroism and tragedy, and one characterized by a heightened sense of anxiety as well as of possibility. The Antonov movement is best understood as belonging to this fascinating and peculiar era.

~

MANY PEOPLE have supported the research and the author through the completion of this book. Nearly all of the research was conducted while I was a postdoctoral fellow at All Souls College, Oxford. For this I would like to thank the then Warden of the College, John Davies, and the Fellows, whose generosity and patience were unparalleled. While in Oxford, I had the opportunity to brush shoulders with many learned people, and this book has benefited from the advice, feedback, and encouragement of many of them. Specifically, I would like to thank (and in no particular order) Orlando Figes, Diego Gambetta, Evan Mawdsley, Hew Strachan, Charles Webster, Judith Pallot, Marc Jansen, Carol Leonard, Stephen Lovell, Stathis Kalyvas, and the late Charles Feinstein. Special mention must be given to Steve Smith and Peter Holquist, both of whom have been exceptionally supportive colleagues.

In Russia, I would like to acknowledge the work of archivists in Tambov, especially Iurii Meshcheriakov, Tatiana Liapina, and Nina Logina at GATO, who were always friendly, knowledgeable, and helpful. Also in Tambov, my research over many months would have been impossible without the local knowledge and sincere friendship of Lilia Zhabina and Svetlana Reston.

This book also bears the intellectual influence of a brief time spent teaching in the Department of International Politics at the University of Wales in Aberystwyth, and mention should be given to the help and insight provided by Martin Alexander, Alistair Finlan, and Colin McInnes. I am also appreciative of the additional support provided by my current colleagues at Oxford Brookes University.

On a personal level, my parents, Richard and Toini, have been consistently encouraging since long before this book was begun. My wife, Lisa Sampson, has been not only loving and supportive but also intellectually curious and insightful, helping me through the grind of writing and opening my eyes to many more possibilities. It is to her and our daughter that this book is dedicated.

GLOSSARY AND ABBREVIATIONS

antonovshchina	the Antonov rebellion
Cheka	All-Russian Extraordinary Commission for Combating Sabotage and Counterrevolution (VChK)
druzhina, druzhiny	brotherhood, often a small squad of paramilitary soldiers
funt	unit of weight, equivalent to 0.9 lb.
glavkom	Red Army Headquarters
kombedy	committees of the poor
LSRs	Party of Left Socialist Revolutionaries
NEP	New Economic Policy
perelom	a decisive turning point or transformation
piaterka	five-man commission formed to execute orders no. 130 and 171
pood	unit of weight, equivalent to 36 lbs.
PSR	Party of Socialist Revolutionaries
razverstka	Soviet government policy of forced grain requisitioning (January 1919–March 1921)
revkom, revkomy	*revoliutsionnyi komitet*, revolutionary committee
RVSR	Revolutionary Military Council of the Soviet Republic
samosnabzhenie	self-provisioning; ad hoc food requisitioning by Red Army troops
sovkhozy	state collective farms
Sovnarkom	Council of People's Commissars
STK	Soiuz Trudovogo Krest'ianstva, Union of the Toiling Peasantry

uezd	level of Russian/Soviet administration between province and volost; equivalent to county
VChK	All-Russian Extraordinary Commission for Combating Sabotage and Counterrevolution (the Cheka)
verst	distance equivalent to 0.66 miles, like a kilometer (0.62 miles)
VNUS	Internal Security Service organized in September 1920 (incorporating VOKhR)
voensovety	local military councils
VOKhR	Internal Security Forces of the Soviet Republic, organized in May 1919
volost	level of Russian/Soviet administration, equivalent to district
VTsIK	All-Russian Central Executive Committee
zemstvo	institution of local self-government in postemancipation Russia

The provinces of European Russia, 1917

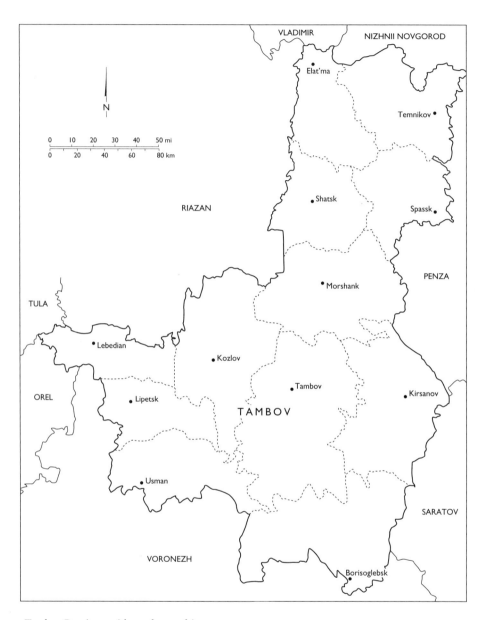

VLADIMIR   NIZHNII NOVGOROD

• Elat'ma

Temnikov •

RIAZAN

• Shatsk

Spassk •

PENZA

• Morshank

TULA

• Lebedian

OREL

• Kozlov

• Lipetsk

• Tambov

• Kirsanov

TAMBOV

• Usman

SARATOV

VORONEZH

• Borisoglebsk

N

0   10   20   30   40   50 mi

0   20   40   60   80 km

Tambov Province, with uezd townships

Southeastern Tambov Province, with railways and selected stations and villages

BANDITS AND PARTISANS

REVOLUTION AND RECALCITRANCE

WHEN THE ANTONOV brothers were finally killed in a shootout with Cheka agents in late June 1922 in the village of Nizhnii Shibriai, they had with them few personal possessions. After nearly one full year in hiding in the forests and swamps of southern Tambov Province, the former leaders of one of the largest rural insurgencies in modern Russian history were isolated in a forest hideaway, dependent upon a handful of sympathetic villagers and former comrades for food and, as proved critical to their discovery, medicines to treat the malaria that the elder brother, Aleksandr, had recently contracted. Although Aleksandr and Dmitrii had managed to evade capture in the very region that had for so long been considered their stronghold, and which had been the focus of all efforts by Soviet state authorities to locate them, they were only barely surviving, and if their presence near Nizhnii Shibriai was widely known among locals, it was hardly a source of inspiration and celebration for nearby village communities. It was rather one of curiosity and, perhaps, toleration.

The Cheka and other provincial party and state officials announced the deaths of the Antonovs in the local and central Soviet press, providing what details they could about the famous bandits who had, for nearly a year, from the autumn of

1920 to the summer of 1921, led an insurgency against the Soviet government in the profoundly agricultural province of Tambov, located some 350 miles southeast of Moscow, and home to a population of just over 3 million persons, over 90 percent of whom lived in the countryside and made their livelihoods through agriculture and small crafts. The rebellion in Tambov ended only after the concessionary measures of the New Economic Policy in the spring of 1921 and the deployment of tens of thousands of Red Army troops to the southern half of the province over the first months of that year. The Partisan Army, which at its height could boast a mounted force of 20,000–30,000 men, had been under the command of Aleksandr Antonov, and the network of village cells—called Unions of the Toiling Peasantry (known by the acronym STK, from Soiuz trudovogo krest'ianstva)—formed a civilian support structure for the insurgents that incorporated tens of thousands of people and hundreds of villages in a region where the Communist Party cells and institutions of the Soviet state had been rapidly and violently removed during the first weeks of the conflict. Yet, by the end of 1921, any vestiges of the rebellion and the ideas and ideals it sought to promote had been removed from the Tambov countryside, and the defiance of the Antonovs, when they were discovered by Cheka agents in the summer of 1922, was now supported by only four handguns and a briefcase full of ammunition.

Press reports in 1922 found it important to mention that two of their guns were monogrammed on the handle—"A. A." and "D. A.," respectively—and that the Antonovs were also reported to have in their possession a map of Tambov Province and a copy of a recent newspaper containing reports of starvation in the wider region. (At first glance, this latter detail is a somewhat odd inclusion in official press notices regarding their deaths.) If officials in the provincial administration and Communist Party were worried that their earlier failure to catch or kill the Antonovs left open the possibility of a return of the insurgency in southern Tambov, and with it the bloodshed that had taken the lives of hundreds of Red Army and Communist Party soldiers and of thousands—possibly even tens of thousands—of civilians in Tambov, then the marginal existence of the Antonovs upon their discovery in Nizhnii Shibriai must have been reassuring. Also among their possessions were notebooks that contained scattered writings, including what appeared to be the beginnings of a history of the Tambov rebellion written by Dmitrii Antonov. The central press in Moscow reported that Dmitrii had even penned an opening dedication to his brother, Aleksandr, recalling "every alcove (*ugol*), every bush, valley and forest that for us became familiar." This was, according to Dmitrii, the "best of times," when "during our ten-month-long war we defeated many Red Army forces and killed not a few Communist Party units."[1]

If there was confirmation that the Antonovs had no designs to renew their struggle with the Soviet state, then these few words from the pen of Dmitrii Antonov were that. However, they had long since been marginalized and defeated, and the village communities of southern Tambov, which had at one time mobilized for armed resistance to the Soviet state and which had paid a heavy price for their defiance in the summer of 1921, had actively distanced themselves from the experience and memory of the insurgency. The Antonov rebellion, part of the "petit-bourgeois counterrevolution" that Lenin had rather dramatically identified in March 1921 as "more dangerous than Denikin, Iudenich, and Kolchak combined,"[2] had been rapidly consigned to history as those same rural communities struggled to regain a normal life amid terrible material conditions and hardships at the close of the civil war era. The rebellion, and particularly its "heroic" pacification by the Red Army and Communist Party, would be far from simply "airbrushed" entirely out of official histories in the Soviet Union.[3] But if Dmitrii Antonov had completed his own account of the *antonovshchina*, as the rebellion became known, it would no doubt have dwelled on considerably different themes, no less heroic, drawn from the brief but spectacular time when the Partisan Army and STK dominated the countryside of southern Tambov Province and endeavored to instill and promote a collective identity for insurgents that rested upon the shared experience of injustice imposed by the Soviet state and on the prospects for positive change.

At the height of the Antonov rebellion, the support of the vast majority of village communities in the zone of the conflict was recognized by Soviet government and Red Army officials, and popular sympathy for the cause of the rebellion extended well beyond the immediate control of the Partisan Army. Yet no one in Tambov lamented the death of the "hero" Aleksandr Antonov in 1922, and the partisan leader did not survive in popular folk culture or local mythology. It was not until the very end of the century, after the Soviet Union had formally ceased to exist, that certain groups in Tambov began to champion the rehabilitation of the Antonovs as local heroes, and then it was principally ultranationalist and racist fringe groups that sought to rebrand the former "bandits" as true Russian patriots and no-nonsense "Tambov wolves."[4] While a memorial now stands near the site where the Antonovs were unceremoniously buried in the regional capital in 1922, the unveiling of the memorial (and the Orthodox church service that accompanied it) attracted relatively little attention, even from the local public. If the rebellion is remembered at all, it is as a tragedy in which countless innocent lives were lost, an episode in a wider tragedy of revolution and civil war in Russia.[5]

LOCAL GOVERNMENT, VILLAGE COMMUNITIES, AND DESERTION IN TAMBOV, 1918–1920

What came to define the political situation in Tambov Province during the civil war years was the weakness of local government. The province had always suffered from "underadministration" like all such territories in Russia in the late imperial period, and this characteristic was only exacerbated by the events of 1917 and the agrarian revolution against private estates in the countryside that continued into the early months of 1918. The inability of the Provisional Government to contain the land seizures was indicative of its own problems in this regard, and when the Bolshevik Party eventually assumed power in the province in 1918, problems with local administration hampered their own efforts to gain control over the villages and districts at a time when the Soviet government was beginning its mobilization for civil war.

For agrarian provinces such as Tambov, the contribution of the local population to the civil war effort against the various anti-Bolshevik forces in Soviet territory came down to supplying grain and army recruits from the countryside. This chapter seeks to describe these interrelated pursuits and the development of state relations with the village population by focusing on desertion and resistance to conscription. Desertion was one of the consistent problems for the Soviet government and Red Army throughout the civil war, and the Red Army deserter became not only emblematic of the failings of local administration, but also the principal enemy of the Soviet government as it confronted periodic resistance to its policies. In a very real sense, the Red Army deserter was the tangible face of so-called kulak resistance to Soviet authorities in the countryside.

Yet, as this chapter hopes to illustrate, the desertion problem was a complex and ambiguous one. Although significant as an indication of government failings, desertion arose for many reasons and from a variety of circumstances, and deserters themselves did not constitute a coherent political force in the Russian civil war. Nor, indeed, did they even represent a natural pool of support for opponents of the Soviet regime, as government officials feared and reported in the case of the Antonov rebellion after it began in the autumn of 1920.[6] Instead, to situate the Red Army deserter in the political landscape of civil war Tambov is to illustrate the potential and contingent, rather than existing and powerful, base of support for rural political opponents of the Soviet state, such as Antonov.

TESTING THE WATERS: THE FIRST CALL-UP OF 1918

The Red Army's desertion problem began in late May 1918, when the Soviet government made its first attempt at general conscription. The revolutionary government's reliance on the urban workers, Bolshevik Party members, and pro-Bolshevik volunteers was appearing insufficient for waging a war against the growing fronts of counterrevolution and foreign intervention facing the young Soviet state.[7] This first attempt at general mobilization was to be carried out in various towns and localities in Soviet Russia, not only in those areas with significant working-class populations, but also in those considered under threat from known counterrevolutionary fronts.[8] Soviet authorities in Tambov Province had already endeavored to create small military units for immediate dispatch to nearby areas where clashes had occurred with units of the Czechoslovak Legion, such as in neighboring Saratov Province, and Tambov was considered one of those territories facing immediate dangers and thus required to undertake a general mobilization.[9] The decree announcing the mobilization in Tambov declared that all adult men between the ages of twenty-one and twenty-five were to present themselves at muster points in their locality, where their suitability for service would be assessed and they would begin the process of assignment within the nascent Red Army.[10] The general outlook on the mobilization from the perspective of Moscow was to regard the exercise as experimental. Not only was this the Red Army's first attempt to conscript the peasants of central Russia, whose reliability was questioned principally on the grounds of class affiliation, but also the plan for general conscription was embarked upon with very little information on the number of young men of conscription age in the catchment area. Expectations may have been limited, but there was little or no concrete idea of what sort of turnout would constitute success.

As the announcement of the mobilization quickly filtered out to the rural localities, the response was not encouraging for government authorities in the province. The plans for conscription were received at a time when the village communities had already learned of the government's declaration of a state "monopoly" on grain, set out in decrees issued on 13 and 27 May 1918, and plans were already afoot for the requisition of those same foodstuffs for the task of alleviating the already desperate conditions affecting the urban population. Some efforts at food collection were already under way, and agents of the Food Commissariat—mostly groups of factory workers dispatched from the major industrial cities—had been greeted with partial confusion and almost uniform resistance, as villagers were still finding their way in a fluid political situation in the province and especially in the countryside.[11]

It was no surprise to provincial officials that village groups were hesitant to answer the call for military conscripts without strong reassurances for the safety of the village community at large. Two issues were most important in evaluating the initial responses of village communities: trust and security. The Bolshevik-led Soviet government did not take effective control of the provincial administration of Tambov until April 1918, and the Bolshevik Party's struggle to emulate their comrades in Petrograd by assuming control of the provincial administration had been largely conducted in the more substantial towns and the provincial capital, without the involvement of the rural localities.[12] Although "Soviet power" had been declared in individual uezds some months before the provincial government had made a similar break, such acts were largely a part of local political struggles within small municipalities. The declarations of Soviet authority were uniform on the surface, attaching local developments to a nationwide phenomenon, but they quickly revealed themselves to be expressions of local political assertion at the expense of provincial and central state authority, even where the local Bolshevik Party had assumed a leading role.[13]

While the Bolsheviks would hardly be an unknown commodity to those in the village communities of Tambov when conscription was to begin in June 1918, vocal opponents of the Bolsheviks only heightened the level of natural suspicion that greeted the mobilization order. Local soviet offices, charged with communicating and explaining the mobilization decree to village communities, reported to provincial officials that the reaction of the villagers did not inspire confidence. According to some reports, people had failed to comprehend the justification for conscription. In isolated reports, the need for a standing army was called into question. In other areas, though, the knowledge that civil war threatened inspired a mix of concern and outrage. Individual villagers decried the outbreak of a fratricidal war (*bratoubiistvennaia voina*); in the village of Mordovo, one local man snatched the firearm from the holster of a government representative sent to explain the conscription order and quickly rose before a village assembly, dramatically asking, "Look, comrades! For whom is this revolver loaded? Is it for our brother?!"[14] The slogans of antiwar sentiment—calls to resist both international war and civil war —were already quite familiar to those in the isolated villages of rural Russia.

Anxiety and skepticism were expressed in clearer terms in other localities. A familiar call reported by local soviet officials and representatives of the Military Commissariat was for the state to distribute firearms among the village population. The reasoning was simple: if the threats to security and well-being were so great, it is better to train the population at large to defend the homestead and native village.[15] In some places, this was made a condition for agreeing to mobilization—

losing able-bodied young men to the army could be compensated by the distribution of weapons to the community, possibly with arrangements for universal
military training.[16] In the village of Safonov (Usman uezd), nearly 400 locals
gathered to pass a resolution stating: "The mobilization of the people designated
[by the conscription decree] will take place only when weapons are delivered for
distribution among the citizens of all Safonov volost, and after a training center
is opened at the offices of the volost soviet, where all people can be taught how
to use these weapons . . . but until this is done, no mobilization will be allowed
to proceed.[17]

For Safonov volost, the mobilization order only heightened anxieties, for it
came at a time when such communities were reconciling the appearance of new
central state demands in what was, ostensibly, the postrevolutionary countryside.
Distrust of the state administration—its motives and intentions vis-à-vis the rural
population—combined with reports of counterrevolution to create a strong sense
of insecurity in the summer of 1918.[18] Despite the common reasoning popularized
in the Bolshevik press that the peasantry supported the Soviet government after
its decision to transfer all private lands to the peasants in November 1917, distrust
of state administration was much more concrete to peasants in mid-1918 than the
threat of counterrevolution.[19] The dependence of the Soviet administration upon
the "enthusiasm" of the working masses for the success of this first mobilization
was more an admission of weakness than of optimism.[20]

The first attempt at general conscription in Tambov was undone by even more
practical considerations than this. As happened with mobilizations during the 1904
conflict with Japan and in the weeks before the outbreak of hostilities in Europe
in 1914, provincial officials in Soviet Russia were unprepared to carry out the general conscription order.[21] With Military Commissariats organized in the provinces
and a limited number of localities beginning only in April, when, in the case of
Tambov, the Bolshevik Party was still only establishing itself at the head of government in the province, the test of military mobilization of the general population
was extremely daunting for provincial officials.[22] On 17 June, when young men eligible for conscription were to present themselves at the Military Commissariat in
the provincial capital and in other towns, very few preparations had been made
to process even the small number anticipated to respect the mobilization order. An
official sent by the Military Commissariat in Moscow to report on the preparations being made in Tambov, upon arriving only a couple of days before the mobilization was set to begin, was horrified to discover "that no work had been done,
except for that completed with a criminal sloppiness."[23] The chaos that resulted,
as groups arrived from the surrounding countryside and began to form a mob of

confused and anxious young men, was enough to temporarily overwhelm local administrators. Most spectacularly, in the provincial capital of Tambov, hundreds of men called up for military service set upon the local magazine, emptying it of rifles and machine guns. Opponents of the Bolshevik Party and the recently deposed provincial officials of the Provisional Government assumed brief control of the municipality, arresting leading members of the provincial soviet administration.

For nearly two days the Soviet regime in Tambov was overthrown. The brief reign of the reconstituted municipal Duma was more of appearance than substance, as its leaders were unable to control the mob. In fact, their reign was brought to a close when, abandoned by the mob of call-ups, whose taste for looting and joy-riding in the streets of the provincial capital was sated, the Duma leaders were unable to withstand the pressure of Red Army troops brought in to deal with the emergency. It was the last gasp of the Provisional Government in the province, but it was the beginning of another struggle for Soviet authorities to gain mastery over the rural population.[24]

While the events in Tambov city were uniquely serious in that the disorders took place at the political center of the province, similar disorders accompanied the June mobilization campaign in other provincial towns as well. Within Tambov Province, popular insecurity and distrust, combined with a lack of preparation for the mobilization, created disturbances in the uezd towns of Kirsanov and Borisoglebsk, and in the town of Kozlov, simultaneous disorders among the garrisoned soldier population—discontent with material conditions and anxious at the prospect of assignment to combat zones—resulted in a brief uprising similar to that in the capital, with the uezd administrators temporarily deposed and incarcerated by insurgents. These rebellious servicemen and call-ups were possibly emboldened by news of serious disturbances among soldiers in other provincial cities, notably in nearby Saratov, where Red Army soldiers in May 1918 resisted being transferred to the front lines by attacking the provincial soviet.[25] The mob of young men called to the muster point in Tambov were reported to be discussing precisely such precedents for rebellion, and their moves to escalate the defiance on 17 June were justified by other, less reliable reports of a wider political context informed by rumors, for example, of the assassinations of both Lenin and Trotsky in Moscow. Despite this effort to place measures of defiance into a wider frame of reference, and despite the best efforts of many of the remaining opponents of the Bolsheviks to exploit the public disorders in Tambov, the discontent among the mobilized villagers in the provincial capital was spectacular in effect but brief in duration.

ESTABLISHING A FOOTHOLD: STATE-VILLAGE RELATIONS, 1918

The shambles of the June mobilization campaign left the government with its own priorities regarding the reestablishment of authority in the provincial capital, while for the young men who had traveled from the villages to the muster points, their attention similarly returned to more domestic matters. The Bolsheviks' drive to reassert control over governmental affairs following the June uprisings was severe and wide-ranging, and many known supporters of the Duma opposition were executed in the weeks that followed. The consolidation of political control over the provincial government and bureaucracy became even more urgent following the spectacular break between the Bolshevik Party and their former coalition partners, the Left Socialist Revolutionaries (LSRs), although in the case of the LSRs, there was less a crackdown by provincial Bolshevik officials than a facilitated disengagement.[26] The experience of the uprising, then, may have helped the Bolshevik Party consolidate control over the government by eliminating known opponents, but it left the question of mobilizing the local population for war unresolved. To a small extent, the rebelliousness of the mob in the provincial capital was carried to the villages with the erstwhile military call-ups, but it similarly died down with the passage of time and attacks on village soviets and recently established cells of the Bolshevik Party were isolated occurrences. While distrust of the government still reigned throughout much of the countryside, there was nothing particularly cathartic about the uprising in the provincial capital for villagers whose experience with the new Soviet government was in its first weeks.[27]

The next round of mobilizations to the Red Army would not be ventured again in Tambov until the late autumn of 1918.[28] According to a senior Red Army official, S. S. Kamenev, writing in 1923, the Red Army remained a largely volunteer force until the end of 1918, consisting mainly of urban workers and Bolshevik Party members.[29] Membership in the Bolshevik Party expanded considerably as the first year under the Soviet government drew to a close, and in the province of Tambov this expansion proceeded only modestly. At the time of the October seizure of power in Petrograd, the Bolshevik contingent in Tambov numbered just over 1,000 members, and by August 1918, the party had still made little headway.[30] One of the few lessons drawn by officials in Moscow from the experience of the June uprising in Tambov was the need for strong Bolshevik leadership in the province.[31]

But even before this event, the Soviet government had recognized the need to forge an effective network of *local* institutions to manage the rural population. The network of volost and village soviets had taken shape with tremendous rapidity in the first half of 1918, but these were rarely more than ad hoc assemblies, often the former institutions of local administration (such as the zemstvos, the institutions of local self-government in postemancipation Russia) renamed in conformity with the changing national political situation.[32] These local soviets, serving as legitimate organizational representatives of the community, did more to frustrate the efforts of state representatives working in the countryside than to assist them, as they often identified principally with the interests of the locality in opposition to those of the central government. The Soviet government saw that it had to rely on the resources of the countryside in order to survive and to mount a credible war effort in its conflict with the Whites and their supporters in the West. This meant not only grain to feed the army and the urban population, but also manpower for the army and for maintaining a basic infrastructure in Soviet territory.

Toward this end, the government launched an initiative to replace the local network of soviets with institutions that would be more responsive to the needs of the Soviet government. These institutions, the committees of the poor (*kombedy*), were ideally to be class-based bodies, composed of members of the rural proletariat and working in the interests of the village poor at the expense of the wealthier members of the village communities. Because the village and volost soviets were believed to have promoted the interests of the wealthier and more powerful members of the village communities, the new committees of the poor were intended to redress that balance and bring the proletarian revolution to those rural communities. The official rhetoric advocated bringing a civil war to the villages that would end with the triumph of the powerless in the hierarchical peasant society.

Unlike the soviets, which had genuinely spread through the province of Tambov as communities united to embrace the revolution against the landed gentry and landholders operating outside the peasant commune, the kombedy were brought to the villages by agents of the Soviet state and Communist Party. Party activists by the hundred were brought into provinces such as Tambov to organize kombedy in the localities and to transfer village authority away from the village soviets.[33] A significant contribution was made by military servicemen from the garrisons in towns such as Kozlov and Usman, while in Borisoglebsk uezd, soldiers in the town of Borisoglebsk and at railway stations awaiting assignment to the southern front also played a central role in organizing kombedy in the surrounding countryside.[34] Groups of soldiers were dispatched to bring the kombedy to the villages. Some activists were more zealous than others, and some communities resisted the new institutions.

In many villages, the creation of the kombedy was as effortless as the previous creation of the village soviet: a matter of a name change and the formal election of the same individuals who had been serving in the soviet.[35] In other communities, the idea of a new institution to replace the soviet was resisted tooth and nail. This was hardly unexpected, given that the kombedy were conceived as institutional weapons in the class war. Where local communities were against the replacement of the village soviet by such a committee, state organizers resorted to a variety of means to establish such a committee. Finding people to serve as members of the kombedy was difficult in such cases, and organizers enlisted the involvement of the nonfarming peasantry and those who had only recently arrived in a locality, such as refugees from war-torn areas or in-migrants from the starving cities of Soviet territory. Often, service in the kombedy was the only source of income for such people who, at best, had only a tenuous membership in the local community. Organizers often had to resort to fixing elections—when elections were actually staged—to get such "outsiders" selected for membership to the kombedy. In many cases, the organizers themselves served in some capacity as members of the new kombedy, although they were not locally based and could be in a given village or volost only periodically. In the first instance, the principal task was getting kombedy organized in as many localities as possible. Some were organized clandestinely —not simply against the wishes of the local community, but under their noses, as well.[36]

The kombedy would be forced to find their feet in the autumn and early winter of 1918, when the provincial government was confronted with the twin tasks of procuring food from the countryside and conscripting local men from the villages for service in the Red Army. The timing for the former task was determined by the harvest, which began in August and extended through October. Tambov had already become a favored destination for the squads of workers and soldiers who scoured the countryside for grain to be purchased at government prices under the terms of the food monopoly established in May 1918. Despite the poor weather at harvest time, officials in Moscow encouraged these procurement squads to go to Tambov, where the harvest was believed to be "gigantic," according to Lenin, enough "to save the entire revolution."[37] The number of such procurement agents present in Tambov during the autumn was lower than during the more chaotic days of the summer of 1918, a reduction owing to the steady mobilization of Communist Party members and workers for service in the Red Army. But the overall number was still significant—just under 5,000—and Tambov was a principal destination for such procurement squads.[38] Armed with state decrees, portraits of Lenin the leader, as well as rifles and handguns, procurement agents became one of the more active groups in organizing local committees of the poor, and the greatest expansion in the network of kombedy occurred when these squads of procurement workers were at the peak of their activity, registering harvest totals and securing the delivery of "surpluses" to government collection points.[39] By the beginning of October 1918, there was a total of 315 volost-level committees of the poor, and some 2,576 such committees at the village level.[40]

For the task of mobilizing soldiers, the timing for a second attempt at general conscription was determined by the simple need for a larger army force, one that would require less preparation for combat. The Red Army's reliance on trade union and Communist Party members may have created an elite force of relative reliability and effectiveness, but it was always going to fall short of the requirements of a Soviet government facing threats on multiple fronts. When the Red Army achieved its most significant victory to date in early September—the recapture of Kazan from the forces of the Komuch government—this was achieved with units organized along traditional military lines and with the extensive use of officers who had served in the tsarist army. This victory effectively ended the threat posed by the Komuch government in the Volga region, but at no time did it appear to be the end of hostilities with anti-Bolshevik forces. Yet the victory at Kazan did demonstrate the effectiveness of a traditionally organized Red Army. Trotsky, as people's commissar for the army and navy and now chairman of the Revolutionary Military Council (RVSR), set to extending these principles to the Red Army as a whole. Ad hoc partisan units were to be integrated into formal regiments, and there would be fewer divisions of the Red Army, organized into army groups. What is more, a complementary system of reserves was required to reinforce these active units, but because of the developing threats facing the Soviet Republic in late 1918, there would be fewer strategic reserves in proportion to active front-line units.[41]

An overall expansion of the army was necessitated; for Lenin, the magical figure of 3 million represented the manpower target for the Soviet armed forces, faced with the threats of counterrevolution and the challenges of defending the coming world proletarian revolution.[42] On 11 September 1918, the Soviet government announced its intention to conscript a single age group—twenty-year-olds (born in 1898)—as well as to mobilize former officers and NCOs of the tsarist army, those born between 1890 and 1897.[43] This was quickly followed by the call-up of all men born between 1893 and 1897, precisely the same groups who had been among the last ones mobilized during the world war effort in 1916 and whom the Bolsheviks had initially sought to recall in selected localities in June 1918, with such disastrous results for the Tambov provincial government.[44]

As the system of kombedy expanded, so did the network of local military commissariats responsible for compiling lists of men eligible for military call-up.[45] The announced mobilization itself was to be undertaken in November and December, after such lists were drawn up and after the major work in the fields and preparations for the procurement campaign were completed. While the introduction of local military commissariats and kombedy was intended to improve the state's capacity to undertake measures such as a conscription drive, the upheaval brought by the changes connected with the introduction of the kombedy only served to complicate matters in the short term. Tensions were raised in villages where the kombedy had been introduced after a struggle with local supporters of the soviet, and these tensions were further heightened when the new kombedy were called upon to oversee the registration of harvest collection and surplus grain for procurement by state agents.

In addition, in certain communities where locals were polarized over the introduction of the kombedy, the "civil war" or "class war" within the village became a tangible component in consolidating the authority of the kombedy. The instructions issued by uezd officials concerning the duties of the new committees of the poor varied in certain nuances and in their emphasis, but in many localities the new byword of the Soviet regime—*terror*—represented a critical function of these new agents of the state in the villages.[46] The registration of "bourgeois" households— persons and property—and placing these individuals on the lowest level of rations (a status they shared with other members of the "exploiting classes" in the towns), was one facet of the class war the kombedy were intended to introduce into the villages. Because the kombedy were introduced on a shoestring budget, and often on no budget whatsoever, the mandatory "contributions" by these households and individuals became an important source of income for the new committees almost from the moment of their inception.[47] Once again, the experiences of individual communities varied considerably, according to how much resistance there had been to organizing a committee. But in those localities where the new committees were embattled and engaged in an increasingly polarized environment, the terror in the villages could be very real, rather than the stuff of reports and stories from the towns.

A Communist Party member from the region of Tokarevka and Abakumova in Tambov uezd, S. Bulgakov, described the developing situation in a report to VTsIK, based on his impressions following a brief trip home:

> In the villages now people are afraid of wearing clean clothes in public because they might be branded "bourgeois" and have their clothes confiscated. Anyone who owns a half-decent horse is at risk of being called "bourgeois," and God help you if your house is actually clean and tidy—even if you have a family of ten to fifteen persons living there and you slave day and night just to keep it moderately clean. It too can become a "contribution," or whatever they call a tax these days.[48]

Bulgakov further described the confrontational atmosphere that surrounded the kombedy and the fact that the Communist Party members who served on the volost committees of the poor in Tokarevka and Abakumovka were never seen on the street or in meetings without brandishing personal firearms. There was a siege mentality displayed by many members of the Communist Party and of the kombedy in the countryside. In the towns, Communist Party members behaved similarly. And the tasks set for these individuals by the Soviet state in late 1918 only accentuated this mind-set.

At the time of the call-up of the former officers, junior officers, and twenty-year-olds, the campaign to collect grain from the village farmers was also in full swing. Villagers were enticed to deliver their foodstuffs to collection points by promises of exchange for various necessary items, such as salt and kerosene, whose distribution the government controlled.[49] Despite these promises of goods exchange, the declared monopoly over grain surpluses remained controversial. The involvement of government agents and the kombedy in registering the harvests and evaluating consumption norms for individual households only made the policy that much more controversial and unpopular, even if the alternative, represented by the grain speculators who were so numerous in the late summer of 1918, was equally menacing and unpopular. Some localities, though, were more primed for confrontation with the government agents than others, and in these areas violence quickly erupted once demands for delivery of surpluses were issued.

The first major outbreak of hostilities occurred in an area already familiar to provincial officials. In Morshansk uezd, a conflict had developed within the soviet administration itself over the state's declaration of the food dictatorship in May 1918, and in June this resulted in a violent schism within the Communist Party and soviet administration. On 10 July 1918, the Morshansk uezd Congress of Soviets was forcibly dispersed by progovernment troops after the faction of delegates who were opposed to the provisions of the food dictatorship decree passed a protest resolution. Many delegates were arrested, but those opponents to the grain monopoly who managed to escape arrest took their struggle to the countryside, convening a dissident congress on 22 July that drew representation from a nine-volost region in southwest Morshansk uezd. This "extraordinary" congress was also forcibly dispersed by Cheka agents and progovernment troops, and the main dissidents were finally rounded up. But the opposition to the grain monopoly and planned campaign to requisition surpluses from the village farmers in the region was already primed for action.[50]

It would come as little surprise, then, to the embattled Communist Party and soviet administration in Morshansk uezd that when hostilities began over the requisitioning of grain in October 1918, it was principally in the region where the dissidents had made their final stand. Some clashes between government agents and local farmers had occurred in early August, but by early November clashes necessitated the intervention of government troops. The defiance began in the village of Ostrovka, where villagers began a march toward the uezd town of Morshansk following a prolonged dispute with a grain requisition detachment. Hoping to protest directly to uezd officials, the crowd gathered supporters as it moved from village to village. The marchers were finally met by armed troops some twenty miles outside Morshansk, and after several rounds were shot by both sides, the government forces made several arrests from among the marchers.[51] The spirit of defiance, though, had already spread through much of the region, as locals carried the news of the clashes from village to village, and in many cases the news was accompanied by calls for similar resistance to the government. In the village of Cherkino, locals took the occasion to disband its local committee of the poor and to restore the village soviet in its place. In the nearby village of Pavlovka, locals did much the same, disbanding the kombedy and restoring the institution of the soviet, electing Filipp Khromtsov as chairman. Khromtsov had been the chairman of the village committee of the poor, and before that he had been chairman of the village soviet.[52]

It was in the midst of such disturbances that general conscription was ventured, and clashes over military mobilization led to the overall crisis in public order facing provincial officials. In Morshansk, uezd officials were confronted with peasant marchers to the west and with rebellious military call-ups to the east. On 10 November, over 600 soldiers had to be brought in from Tambov uezd and from neighboring Penza Province to regain control over rebellious military conscripts who had already disarmed one unit of armed government soldiers and who threatened to bring their rebellion to the town of Morshansk and its sizable garrison population.[53] At the same time, conscripts in southwestern Tambov uezd were similarly resisting mobilization, requiring the eventual intervention of over 1,000 government troops armed with artillery and machine guns.[54]

In October and November 1918, seven out of twelve uezds in Tambov Province reported serious disturbances and clashes between village communities and government agents.[55] In many localities that experienced uprisings, the committees of the poor emerged as the principal targets, for the kombedy were the institutional embodiment of so many of the changes that were being brought to the countryside, and in most cases they were the agents of many of the new demands being made of the rural population. In many cases where local communities had been divided over the legitimacy of the kombedy, or where the kombedy had been fiercely resisted by the local community as a whole, committee members often met extremely violent ends, as the spirit of rebellion spread through the countryside. One kombedy member who was spared such a fate in the village of Levye Lamki, in Morshansk uezd, described events in the village in a letter to his brother:

> On 31 October, a delegation from a neighboring village arrived and began sounding the church bell. It was an awfully hazy day, but there was no fire to be seen. People assembled after the sounding of the bell, and there the delegation explained the situation. Then the assembled crowd seized two members of the committee of the poor, dispatching one of these out of the village, and the other they killed. The people at the assembly had arrived armed with staffs and pikes in order to do battle against the Soviet government. Orders from the assembly were to pick their own delegation and set off for another neighboring village and sound the alarm for an uprising there. . . . The spirit of the crowd was fabulous, and especially their grand designs, as they wanted to march all the way to Moscow, and from there, it seemed, their spirit would carry them all the way to New York. It seemed as if everything was complete. There was now a new government in place.[56]

The author of this letter, Victor Sakharov, survived the events uninjured, although the other five members were murdered by the crowd. Yet, in Sakharov's strangely bemused opinion, "if there had been no uprising [brought from the neighboring village], then our villagers would have just sat around and discussed matters. But, as it happened, there was an uprising, and there were no discussions, and quite simply, the lot of them ate a bit too much meat that day and they needed to go out and throw a few punches."[57]

Provincial officials publicly identified this and other village uprisings as the work of counterrevolutionary "whiteguardists" and agents of the Bolsheviks' socialist opponents, the Left and Right SRs.[58] But in their investigations into the disorders, and in their instructions to local administrations, they recognized that the failure to contain panic and rumor was the most important explanation for the seriousness and scale of the uprisings in the autumn of 1918.[59] Investigators in Tambov uezd found that a variety of rumors had fueled the disturbances across the countryside. "In general, we can ascertain the following," they wrote,

> The majority of peasants, including in part the poor peasants, were deluded and misled by various provocateurs and slanderers, who spread absurd, seditious rumors, such as that Krasnov and his bands were drawing close and had already taken Tambov city, that the Bolsheviks were forcibly removing religious icons from schools and private homes, that the soviets were going to require that each woman

hand over ten arshin of canvas, or that from those who did not have canvas, money would be collected, and that they were confiscating 3–6 funt of fleece per person, and money from those who did not keep a flock. The prohibition on teaching religious lessons in schools—it is rumors such as these that disturbed the peasants; …the majority of poor peasants did not know what or on whose behalf the uprisings were actually being fought.[60]

Many of the village communities in the province were aware of a general sense of anxiety surrounding the increasing presence of government agents in the countryside, as well as the demands connected with the civil war, such as the requisition of horses and the conscription of young men.[61] There was a strong element of desperation in the rebelliousness of the village groups who attacked the kombedy and who refused to give grain on demand or recruits to the Red Army. Much had changed in the lives of people in the countryside, and fear was combined with confusion over events both near and distant.[62] One village man who was involved in a local uprising told investigators: "No one has attempted to set right the views of myself and us peasants, for we live in a remote village. In our village, they don't read newspapers, and no one explains to us the truth about Soviet power."[63] This was a familiar refrain to the relatively new officials in the Soviet government, as it was to government officials in rural regions of Russia before the revolution. But the professed ignorance of individual peasants in the Tambov countryside was not simply strategic, designed to gain pardon. In a political environment fraught with risk, and with people still struggling to gain their bearings following a full year of upheaval, not everyone embraced the call to active resistance. Instead, many chose, as one villager explained, to "await their saviors," whoever those saviors might be.[64]

COUNTING THE COSTS: DESERTION, 1918–1919

The conscription drive in the final months of 1918 may have been beset with troubles in its execution, but the overall result for the Red Army was far from insignificant. Drafting former officers had resulted in over 20,000 experienced army personnel joining the Soviet armed forces. Over 81,000 junior officers also were drafted in the course of this November campaign.[65] Although by most accounts the mobilization of these military "specialists" had been the most troublesome for local military commissariats, trained military men were required for the continued expansion of the Red Army and its transformation into a regular military force drawing on the mass of the eligible population, rather than a limited enterprise dependent entirely upon Communist Party members and the urban population. Mobilizations of party members remained an important part of the contribution of soldiers from Tambov Province, as the local party organizations were first called to contribute one-fifteenth of their expanding membership to the Red Army and then quickly required to mobilize a further one-fifth.[66] While the overall effect of the mobilization drives in the autumn and winter of 1918 was to change the character of the Red Army irrevocably, from a force of largely urban volunteers to an army dominated by rural conscripts, the main combat duties were reserved for the most reliable volunteers and conscripts from the Communist Party and the cities of Soviet Russia.[67]

During the winter months, the actual fighting of the civil war briefly impinged on the southern territory of Tambov Province, sending the local administration into chaos as advance units of General Petr Krasnov's Don Army advanced into Borisoglebsk uezd. Left weakened by the diversion of Red Army forces to regain control in the Novokhoper region in Voronezh Province to the west, local Communist Party members quickly capitulated in Borisoglebsk when Cossack troops began their attack on 22 December 1918. It was later reported that the Cossacks were better equipped to deal with the freezing temperatures and high winds in the region, and several also wore seized Red Army uniforms to confuse the town's defenders. The evacuation by Soviet and Communist Party personnel was hasty and chaotic, and the subsequent occupation by the Don Cossacks, lasting over two weeks, was brutal and lacking in any long-term objective.[68] Abandoned by the main forces of the Don Army that were bogged down in Voronezh and Tsaritsyn, the Cossack occupiers in Borisoglebsk—isolated and dispirited—eventually succumbed to a small force of rapidly mobilized Red Army units composed of Communist Party and Komsomol members.[69]

While the threats to Tambov Province receded, and as attention shifted to the eastern front as the Red Army gained the upper hand in the south, the local military commissariats continued to grapple with the demands of general conscription and processing recruits brought into the ranks during the mobilization drive in the final months of 1918. The integration of rural conscripts was made more difficult by the army's inability to accommodate them and by the problems of the provincial administration and transport system in processing and delivering them to their new assignments. Some of the first reports from front-line commanders as the conscription campaign took shape spoke of reinforcements arriving unannounced in rail cars, without guns, boots, or adequate provisions. Local military commissariats, overwhelmed in some cases by the sheer number of recruits, hastily formed these young men into units and dispatched them on trains for the front. In many cases, particularly when soldiers were sent without guns, the recruits simply jumped off the trains and took flight, at the very least unwilling to go into battle without a firearm. The availability of rail cars to transport such newly formed units was rare enough; the majority of conscripts who absconded in 1918 and early 1919 did so while waiting—often for days—for transport to arrive. Every moderate-sized railway station in central Russia was also a temporary home to countless young soldiers who billeted in whatever shelter they could find, from derelict railcars to commandeered space in nearby villages (peasant huts, churches, abandoned houses). In the freezing winter, often lacking adequate provisions, the futility of military service often occurred to these new recruits well before they had seen battle or even boot camp. Given such ample opportunity, thousands of recruits simply disappeared, one by one or in groups.[70]

The haste with which local commissariats dispatched these new conscripts is partly explained by reports from division commanders of the urgent need for reinforcements on the front lines. But another major consideration for commissariats in charge of mobilizations was the desire to move newly formed units out of their jurisdiction. In the case of Tambov, the riots in June 1918 that accompanied the initial attempt at conscription served as an object lesson in the volatility of newly conscripted young men and in the fundamental weakness of Soviet administration in the provinces.[71] The shortage of barracks space for the newly mobilized men, as well as the problems caused by inadequate rations, left many local administrations wary of the potential public order problems that could result. Local commissariats were thus more than happy to transfer troops to the front or to other towns and provinces to cope with their predicament. However, while placing new conscripts on trains may have relieved some of the anxiety felt by local officials, it only contributed to the ongoing problem of desertion. Despite the efforts of the military commissariats to place armed guards on each railway carriage, one inspector believed that the rate of desertion among soldiers actually en route was between one-quarter and one-half of conscripts.[72]

INSTITUTING THE STRUGGLE WITH DESERTION, 1919

During the occupation of Borisoglebsk, the Soviet government was taking its first steps toward consolidating its commitment to general conscription. By decree of the Soviet Central Executive Committee (VTsIK), the All-Russian Antidesertion Commission was created in late December 1918.[73] The Central Antidesertion Commission was to be a part of the Defense Council, created in November 1918, and local bodies were to be established in parallel with the administrative system in the provinces. By the beginning of 1919, provincial antidesertion organizations were already being formed.[74]

The antidesertion commissions were established at a time when the Soviet countryside was once more undergoing an administrative shake-up. The committees of the poor were formally abandoned by the central government in November 1918, at the Sixth Congress of Soviets in Moscow, as part of a new emphasis in government policy that was designed, in essence, to be less antagonistic toward the peasantry. While the antipathy toward the village kulaks remained, the Soviet government, dependent upon the mass of the peasantry both for its soldiers and for grain, sought to broaden its base of support by embracing the poor and middle peasants.[75] The strict rhetoric of class war that had accompanied the introduction of the committees of the poor was reconsidered, and the committees themselves—which had become the target of so many violent attacks in the final months of the 1918—were to be phased out and replaced by newly elected soviets.[76] Electoral lists were intended to exclude individuals registered as belonging to the village bourgeoisie, or kulaks, and the local organizations did all they could to guarantee that the new soviet elections would return a favorable leadership composed of Communist Party members or individuals loyal to the Soviet government.

The elections took place mainly in January and February 1919, although some localities did not resolve their elections until the end of the summer. On the whole, the process of reelecting the soviets occurred without major incident.[77] The ability of the uezd administrations and Communist Party to influence the outcomes of village and volost elections was limited, especially in the case of the Communist Party itself, which had expanded considerably in the previous months but was steadily depleted by mobilizations to the Red Army, and with a great many withdrawing from the party before they too were mobilized for military service.[78] Not surprisingly, and particularly in the case of village-level soviets, the elections returned a vast majority of local officials with no party affiliation, meaning that they did not belong to the Communist Party.[79] At the next level in the administrative hierarchy, results for the volost soviets were significantly different, with a much higher proportion of Communist Party members serving on the all-important executive committees.[80]

These local institutions were vital to the government's efforts to combat desertion, for they were now the institution of governmental authority closest to the village communities. The chairman of a village soviet was made the military commissar for that locality and was given responsibility for maintaining accurate lists of male villagers eligible for service. These chairmen were also the first level of authority in regulating exemption from military service, and these responsibilities placed them at the heart of the struggle with desertion. Young men who refused to serve in the Red Army, whatever their motivation, often had to secure the consent (implicit or explicit) of the local soviet chairman if they were to carry on a relatively normal life in their native village. Through the soviet chairman, official exemption or temporary release from duty was secured from the military commissariat in the uezd.

The desertion problem in the first months of 1919 was still very much defined by the failure of soldiers to appear for mobilization. While significant numbers of conscripts did manage to desert after appearing for mobilization at military commissariat offices and at muster points, the vast majority of those considered deserters according to the definitions established by the Antidesertion Commission, were those who had failed to heed the call to duty issued by the mobilization officials of the Red Army in the previous year and in the first weeks of 1919. One inspector believed that in some areas of the Moscow military sector, as many as 95 percent of eligible men refused to appear for muster. Overall, the success rate was rarely better than 40 percent among eligible men in the winter of 1918–1919.[81]

This continued into the first half of 1919. The government attempted to correct this pattern by altering their conscription tactic with the volost-based mobilization campaign in April–May 1919, but it failed to change matters for the better. In their appeal to volost soviets to produce ten to twenty of their finest men for military service, the Soviet government was breaking with the familiar tradition of conscripting entire age groups. This break with custom resulted in some confusion as to whether the call for ten to twenty soldiers from each volost was a recruitment drive or a mobilization campaign. Was the government calling for volunteers, or was each volost required to produce on average fifteen new soldiers for the Red Army? Obviously, the government hoped that a spirit of voluntarism could be cultivated among the working peasantry. In mid-May 1919, the Central Committee even announced that any men enlisted during the volost mobilization drive would be officially considered "volunteers" and would receive correspondingly more advantageous benefits packages. But at no time did the government call the volost campaign a voluntary recruitment drive; it was a mobilization, and in some localities, strict instructions were delivered to volost soviet administrations detailing the required number of soldiers to be produced by each locality. Overall, however, considerable confusion blighted the April–May campaign, and the results were extremely unsatisfactory for the Defense Council and the Red Army. Only some 24,000 soldiers were enlisted as a result of the volost mobilization campaign—

less than one-fifth the total anticipated by officials.[82] Provincial military commissariats cited the continuing "petit-bourgeois" mentality of the great mass of the peasantry in Soviet Russia. The fact that the mobilization drive coincided with the spring sowing season and the intense field work this entailed, only served to bring that mentality to the fore, as young men obeyed the "higher calling" of responsibility to their fields and family.[83]

By the time the volost mobilization campaign came to close, the scale of the desertion problem was truly becoming apparent. People who had failed to appear for mobilization—draft dodgers—accounted for over three-quarters of all deserters. In some provinces, as much as 90 percent of young men registered as eligible for conscription had failed to appear for mobilization.[84] The ineffectiveness of the policy of general conscription was becoming clear just as the crisis on the eastern front was reaching its height. The Defense Council dispatched plenipotentiaries to the various provinces to inspect and report on the conduct of local administration that related to the desertion problem and other difficulties associated with the "rear guard" behind the front lines.[85] The individual sent to Tambov, V. N. Podbel'skii, was a native of the province who had long been a member of the Bolshevik Party and had held senior positions in the Soviet government from the time of the revolution in 1917. Podbel'skii's first telegrams back to Moscow reporting on the situation in Tambov concentrate on the desertion problem and on the weakness of local soviet administration that permitted the problem to worsen. Soviet executive committees, according to Podbel'skii, were often complicit in concealing known deserters, and the soviet chairmen regularly failed to respect the instruction concerning, in particular, the volost mobilization campaign. He attributed this to the shortage of Communist Party members in the countryside represented in the rural soviets.[86] The soviets were instruments of the community rather than of the Soviet government.[87]

The effective enforcement of conscription orders, and rounding up known or suspected deserters, required agents of the state who could bypass local administration. At the time of the volost mobilization campaign, such agents were only in a state of formation. Among the host of measures taken at the end of 1918 and in early 1919 to combat desertion was the formation of patrols of Communist Party members and Red Army soldiers that would scour the villages for recalcitrant men who had either failed to appear for mobilization or had actively deserted their units. The antidesertion patrols in Tambov in the late spring of 1919 were, as one local Communist Party official reported, "merely a drop in the ocean," but their appearance in the countryside had a swift effect on the local political environment.[88]

In his memoirs of life in Podgornoe village (Borisoglebsk uezd), Anton Okninskii described the first encounter of the local community and administration with an antidesertion patrol. At dawn one morning, the locals were drawn out of their homes by the sound of singing approaching the village. Upon seeing a group of Red Army soldiers singing revolutionary anthems, people initially believed that they were drunk. Others, however, were quickly aware that it was a patrol searching for deserters. News of their presence in the region had already reached Podgornoe, and those who had sons and husbands intent on evading military service reacted as if well prepared for this occurrence. Okninskii began questioning one peasant man who was helping his two sons cover their faces with black axle grease. Their plan, Okninskii was told, was to go through the fields to the neighboring volost. "By the time the soldiers make their way to [our] volost soviet and enjoy the gossip there, my boys will be nearly ten kilometers outside Podgornoe, over in the area where those soldiers have already searched."[89]

When he soon encountered the commander of the patrol—the sole member of the patrol on horseback—Okninskii introduced himself as the volost soviet accountant. "Very pleased to meet you," said the commander. "Your job must deal with statistics and so on. My duties are different altogether—my job is to shoot people! And it is for this purpose we have arrived here in your volost. No one from your volost presented himself for the last military call-up."[90] While one may be disinclined to take Okninskii's portrait of the commander at face value, the antidesertion patrols were authorized to conduct public trials of captured deserters within the villages. In addition to their role as agents of the developing propaganda campaign to discourage desertion, the patrols also acted as tribunals with the authority to execute the captured in exceptional cases.[91]

In Okninskii's account, the determined commander of the antidesertion squad resisted attempts by the local soviet officials in Podgornoe to "soften him up"— he refused offers of food and, especially, drink. Instead, he stuck to his task, demanding to see the soviet's lists of local men who were eligible for military service. While the squad commander was examining the list of "counterrevolutionaries," as he insisted on calling them, the chairman of the volost soviet was trying to dissuade him from targeting certain individuals whose names were on the list:

"This one's a good *muzhik,* reliable, always stood by the soviet."

"Comrade," inquired the squad commander, "are you a party member?"

"No, I'm nonparty."

"Then your opinion regarding these men holds no significance for me whatsoever."

The work of the antidesertion squad proceeded, following methods and strategies that had been honed in a short space of time through constant interaction with village communities intent on protecting their own. The first targets were men known to have served in the tsarist army who were still eligible for service in the Red Army. Their refusal to serve the Soviet cause was taken as a clear indication of counterrevolutionary sympathies, owing to their past association with the old regime, and the antidesertion squad commander in Podgornoe intended to execute these men publicly as a warning of the serious intentions of the antidesertion squad. There remained the far more numerous group of young men who simply did not want to serve through personal disinclination or the pressure from family members.

The squad commander forbade all villagers to leave the village while the squad conducted its searches. Included in the ban were all children, to prevent them from running out to the fields to warn their brothers and fathers of the presence of an antidesertion squad. The squad machine gun would be trained on the nearest open field, where it was suspected young men were hiding in the tall grass. Each evening of their stay in Podgornoe, the squad commander would order the soldiers to open fire on the fields. "In the last instance," explained the commander over the protestations of the soviet chairman, "everyone will at least know that we are not here playing some sort of joke, but that we intend to deal with these deserters and with those who hide them."[92]

The crackdown on deserters in the countryside of central Russia truly began when the attentions of the Red Army shifted from the eastern front and the armies under Admiral Kolchak to the offensive launched from the south of Russia by the White and Don armies. The resurgence of the Whites in the south of Russia had gained considerable momentum by mid-May 1919, at a time when Red Army forces were concentrated in the Urals and western Siberia.[93] With the Whites pushing toward the heart of the Soviet Republic along an expansive front line, the formation of military reserves continued in a chaotic manner, as local military officials in the provinces patched together units from recently mobilized men and their brethren apprehended by antidesertion patrols. These recently formed units were not, in the words of one Red Army inspector reporting to Trotsky, "composed of trained, politically conscious people banded together around common ideas, but are instead dubious squadrons composed of every imaginable social element."[94] As the drive to form reserve units intensified, military commissariats eased the restrictions on eligibility for military service, filling garrisons with individuals who did not belong to conscripted age groups, those who had previously served in the tsarist army, and those who had earlier been apprehended as deserters. The latter were, according to one commander, an "invaluable resource" for military commissariats in the provinces confronted with orders to form reserve units in short order.[95]

As the threat from the approaching front intensified, the major towns of the rear were declared "fortified" regions by the Revolutionary Military Council (RVSR), creating a line of defense just south of the southern front command headquarters in Kozlov.[96] In Tambov, the Red Army was to attend to the formation of a single brigade-strength force, transferring units from other garrisons to secure defenses in the provincial capital. Workers were to be mobilized to prepare defensive positions within the newly formed region, digging trenches alongside the growing contingent of Red Army soldiers.[97] Soon after, the southern uezds of Tambov were placed under martial law, and provincial authorities were issuing appeals for calm alongside calls to vigilance.[98] The public stance of the provincial authorities was to express faith that the people, particularly in the countryside, would rally to the defense of the Soviet regime and especially that erstwhile deserters would return to the fold. An amnesty was announced in June for deserters precisely to encourage such a response to the impending threat by the Whites, and in the province of Tambov the amnesty was extended well into July.[99] By the beginning of that month, uezd-level administration was handed over to extraordinary three-person revolutionary committees (*revkomy*), and one of the first acts of these revkoms was to intensify the struggle against desertion. Sanctioning the seizure of hostages among the village population, threatening to confiscate all household property of known or suspected deserters, and levying massive fines on entire villages for concealing deserters, the uezd officials authorized the increasingly numerous antidesertion patrols and Red Army units in the territory to resolve the desertion problem by any means necessary.[100]

Officials in the province began noting a "massive" return of deserters as soon as June, when the first amnesty was announced, and while they preferred to cast this change in fortunes as a sign of authentic support for the Soviet government in its hour of need, the truth of the matter is much less clear. In the month of June alone, antidesertion patrols succeeded in apprehending 44,000 deserters. In the same month, over 156,000 men voluntarily surrendered to military officials. The situation continued to improve in July, with an increasing proportion of deserters surrendering to military commissariats as distinct from those apprehended by antidesertion patrols.[101] The massive influx of deserters soon overwhelmed local commissariats, who were once more facing an overstretched transport system and overcrowded garrisons. Telegrams to the Revolutionary Military Council and to Supreme Headquarters complained of overcrowding and of the fear of public order problems caused by food shortages and poor security for the growing numbers of deserters returning to the army. Food riots threatened garrison towns, where, as in the case of Kaluga, recently processed deserters numbering in the thousands were kept corralled under armed guards on the street, due to the lack of space in the barracks.[102]

Except in extraordinary cases, deserters who surrendered or were apprehended in the summer of 1919 were assigned to reserve units, rather than to front-line duty.[103] What is more, according to instructions dated 7 July from Red Army Supreme Headquarters, individuals were not to be assigned to reserve units in their native regions nor were they to receive assignments in the area where they had been captured, especially if those regions were near the front lines.[104] When the dividends of the recent crackdown on desertion began to appear, local military commissariats were able to process the returnees and dispatch them to areas where either reinforcements were required or where men were needed to fill reserve garrisons. Officials in Tambov predominantly directed new inductees to the right flank of the southern front (Fourteenth Army group), as well as to areas on the western and southeastern fronts. These units of deserters were often dispatched in groups of several hundred. Redesertion remained a problem for these hastily dispatched reinforcements, especially considering that many were sent with (at best) a bare minimum of supplies, and often without guns.[105]

As in the beginning of the year, many former deserters simply deserted once more after being loaded onto transports.[106] In addition, disorganization contributed to this problem, as the troops were often transferred with a minimum of coordination between military commissariats. Areas near the western front, such as Smolensk, and to the immediate north of Tambov, such as Riazan', found themselves the unexpected recipients of new deserters. Already facing difficulties with their own swelling garrison populations, the military commissariats in these areas pleaded with Red Army Supreme Headquarters to reconsider its policy of transferring these groups of deserters out of their native territories at all costs. Likewise, they urged the army not to press on with plans for further conscription of younger age groups.[107] Local commanders in charge of the garrisons were allowing many of these recent arrivals effectively to redesert, as they were unable to provide them with adequate food or shelter.[108] Military officials in Tambov noticed the same behavior, so overwhelming was the supply crisis during the summer of 1919.[109] Desertion rates began to climb almost immediately after the crisis on the southern front had passed.[110]

Reports such as these moved Red Army officials to reconsider their initial instructions regarding the transfer of deserters. Originally intended as a pragmatic measure designed to limit desertion—distancing young men from their native regions as a means of diminishing localist tendencies—the effort of moving units composed of former deserters was found to exacerbate the problem. Hoping to reduce the congestion on the railways and to defuse antagonisms between provincial and regional military commissariats, Red Army Supreme Headquarters accepted the advice of the Antidesertion Commission and on 4 September 1919 rescinded the instructions regarding the transfer of deserter units. Processed deserters designated for service in the reserves could be assigned to units in their native territory.[111]

Following this decision, further chaos with the coordination of reinforcements and reserves behind the front lines was especially unwelcome, as the Red Army prepared to launch a major counteroffensive on the southern and southeastern fronts. In Tambov, the provincial administration was just surveying the damage caused by the two-week raid into its territory by a force of White cavalry and infantry, during which this force of Don Cossacks, led by General K. V. Mamontov, briefly occupied the provincial capital and the town of Kozlov, the base of the Red Army Southern Front Command.[112] While causing extensive damage to the transport and communications infrastructure, as well as committing countless atrocities in the towns and villages, the White cavalry raid did not significantly delay the Red Army counteroffensive, and the White armies encroached no further into Tambov Province.

Provincial officials, like their superiors in Moscow, desperately wanted to believe that the return of deserters in the summer of 1919 to fill the ranks of the Red Army was an indication of the true political sympathies of the Russian peasantry. In particular, following the direct experience with the harsh conduct of the White forces in Tambov, provincial officials spoke often of having reached a *perelom*, or turning point, in relations between the Soviet government and the peasantry. This sort of rhetoric was certainly informed by local experience, but it was characteristic of official discourse throughout the Soviet republic at this time, which sought to "emplot" the phenomenon of the massive return of young conscripts into the revolutionary narrative. The government in the last ten months had altered its policies toward the rural population in significant ways by abandoning the *kombedy* and voicing commitments to the "middle" peasantry, and the return of former deserters in 1919 constituted an important dividend derived from this alteration in the party line.

For provincial officials, the brief experience of White rule in Tambov meant that the expected *perelom* had been reached.[113] Officials began to speak of the imminent prospect of resolving the desertion problem once and for all.[114] Such talk caused them to turn a blind eye to the many attendant problems that complicated the picture for provincial government, notably, the violence provoked in the countryside both by intensified antidesertion efforts and the virtually simultaneous escalation of panic in local administration, faced with the prospect of evacuation as the threat from the White offensive from the south grew more tangible.[115] In response to both these developments, bands of village men, mostly deserters themselves, began to take matters into their own hands, attacking local soviet administrations and railway stations and issuing cries of defiance to both the Soviet government and the advancing White forces. The "greens," as they became known, imperfectly filled the void being left by the Soviet government in certain parts of the countryside during the summer of 1919, asserting a measure of agency on the part of a village population facing occupation by counterrevolutionary forces, yet the roving bands of "greens" never managed to improvise any effective authority among that same population during the height of their activities.

It would be impossible to deny that the organization of "green bands"—reported in some cases to number in the thousands during June and July in Tambov Province and in many other provinces of Soviet Russia—was a response to the security situation confronting both village men of mobilization age and the village population as a whole. But the rapid disappearance of the "greens" as a mass phenomenon in the autumn of 1919, as the security situation in Soviet Russia once again improved, meant that the influence of the "greens" on the outlook of Soviet officials was correspondingly temporary. In the wake of the military crisis in Tambov, some officials emphasized the continuing need to address popular, particularly economic, grievances if any substantive progress in peasant-state relations was to be achieved and any *perelom* was to be secured.[116] However, in the wake of the Whites' summer offensive, officials in the province were more likely to understand the *perelom* in relations with the village communities as the consequence of the popular practical experience with White "rule" in Tambov in August 1919 and the common Soviet citizen's recognition of a higher calling in defense of the revolution. What is more, experience with the counterrevolution effectively legitimized the conduct and policies of the Soviet government's revolution.

TESTING THE Perelom: REQUISITIONING GRAIN, 1919–1920

The turning point, or *perelom*, was tested almost immediately after provincial officials had declared its achievement. The disruptions brought by the encroaching front line, and the chaos and destruction visited upon the province by White cavalry forces particularly hit the system of food procurement that had been the focus of government administration in Tambov since before the revolution. This fact was made more damaging by the timing of the cavalry raid, which concluded at harvest time, when food procurement should have been entering its most intense period of activity. While soviet officials from the lower levels of administration— particularly in the uezds—appealed for a reform of administration and for more effective decentralization of authority as a means of consolidating the support of the village communities in the wake of Mamontov's raid, provincial authorities demanded precisely the opposite. While publicly declaring the achievement of a *perelom* in peasant-state relations, provincial officials demanded more extensive centralization to counter the influence of the kulaks and of "parochial" officials whose actions only undermined the state's efforts. At the forefront was the state's critically important campaign to procure grain under the policy of the razverstka, whereby collection targets were set in a top-down manner, from the central government to the province, and all the way down to the individual household. The food commissar in Tambov, Iakov Gol'din, addressed his critics from the uezd administrations at the Fifth Congress of Soviets in Tambov in mid-November 1919:

> The food question is the most important one in Tambov Province. Up until 25 October, the rate of grain collection was on average only 8,000 poods per day, but now it has risen to 50,000–60,000 poods. The most important month, November, is passing by, and we have until the first half of February [to complete the campaign]. After this, the intensive period will have come to an end. If we have failed to raise collection rates massively by then to make up for lost time, we will find ourselves saying that our food campaign has been a complete failure.[117]

The Food Commissariat in Tambov Province assumed an ultra-hard line following Mamontov's raid, conducting requisitions in the manner of a military campaign and systematically ignoring the dissent of local soviet officials—in the uezds and districts, as well as the villages—with the assumption that such complaints were fundamentally parochial and thus illegitimate.[118] Working on the assumption that "the food question is exclusively a question of force,"[119] Gol'din personally monitored the progress of requisition agents, urging them to disregard complaints from any quarter, as well as to make liberal use of punitive measures such as arrests and the full confiscation of grain stocks. In an exchange with one such agent, Badaev, who had encountered resistance from local Communist Party officials in Kirsanov concerned about damage to the local economy and to relations with the peasantry, Gol'din demanded that no thought of concessions be entertained:

Either you didn't understand [my earlier instructions] or you're going soft—my orders are: (1) Not one head of cattle is to be given over to the poor; transfer all confiscated livestock as well as sufficient feed to the state farms [*sovkhozy*]. Horses are also to be given over to the state farms, with some reserved for our use; confiscate carts from those who haven't fulfilled the razverstka; (2) Make a list of all those who participated in the Kirsanov Conference and draw up an order for the Cheka to confiscate all their property and to arrest each and every one of them. . . . I am giving you a top-priority order to break this kulak sabotage immediately, do this by any and all means, and at first only in one volost [as an example to other districts]— no mercy, no retreat. The uezd party committee and the executive [in Kirsanov] will pay for their indiscipline.[120]

Outside inspectors, as well as other individuals who witnessed the requisitioning campaign in 1919–1920, filed reports and wrote appeals that backed up the complaints of local officials and village representatives, claiming that the militarized effort to procure grain was severely damaging the local economy as well as the morale of the village communities. Any systematic effort to assess grain harvests, evaluate grain stocks, and distribute contribution burdens either on the basis of class or on the basis of simple means, had been discarded in order to raise the collection rates that Gol'din demanded to meet the targets set by Moscow. The result was overrequisitioning. This problem, together with the wholesale confiscations of draft animals and other moveable forms of property that were often carried out as punishment for even the mildest form of protest, made the prospects for the next season already a source of extreme anxiety. One Red Army official, E. Artamanov, who witnessed a portion of the campaign unfold in Kozlov uezd, wrote to authorities in Moscow that they should heed the complaints about the economic impact of the latest requisition campaign. They needed to make the effort to "understand the internal life of the peasant villages here, lest the peasantry perish by starvation or at the hands of the requisition squads."[121]

The early warning signs of hunger in the villages were already visible after the end of the campaign to requisition grain. Because the vast majority of grain stocks were concentrated in the southern two-thirds of the province, the Food Commissariat's efforts to procure grain were naturally concentrated in that area. And it was here, as well, that local officials began to report the sight of malnourished children wandering the dirt tracks of the large villages, begging for handouts.[122] One militia member, reporting to his superior in the Tambov uezd militia organization, noted similar sights during his rounds in late February 1920:

Now it is already evident in Ekstal'ka, Bogoslovsko-Novinkovka, and in Kun'evska districts, the beginnings of a dangerous ferment due to the onset of hunger in the area; there have been large groups of peasants gathering outside local soviets, literally clamoring for grain. In Bogoslovsko-Novinkovka volost, there was even one case in which a single peasant drove his only cow to the nearby *sovkhoz* and pleaded with them to take his cow in exchange for a mere five measures of millet, saying that he and his entire family will certainly starve to death unless he is able to make a deal for the cow. The last razverstka severely affected the population, and many do not have the ability to meet another razverstka due to a clear shortage of grain.[123]

The immediate onset of starvation, no matter how widespread, was overshadowed by a greater anxiety regarding the next harvest.[124] With substantially diminished amounts of seed grain, which had been requisitioned or confiscated during the procurement campaign, village households feared for their survival even without another round of grain requisitioning in the autumn.[125]

CLOSER TO THE HOME FRONT: DESERTERS AND DESERTION IN 1920

If provincial authorities imagined, along with their superiors in the central government and Red Army, that the desertion problem had been overcome when the tide definitively turned against the White armies in the summer of 1919, the new year brought a strong dose of reality. Whereas desertion in the first year of mass conscription to the Red Army essentially involved the mobilization of recalcitrant young men intent on evading conscription, after the summer of 1919 and the intensified efforts to round up draft dodgers and the threat of victory for Denikin and the Whites with their "drive on Moscow," the problem for military officials became one of managing the Red Army's swollen ranks. Maintaining stability within the ranks on the front lines was only a small portion of this problem, as the main challenges involved control over the large garrisoned population of former deserters and reserve soldiers, which numbered in the tens of thousands in some major provincial towns, and which were a considerable element in any uezd town in provincial settings such as Tambov. Controlling overcrowded garrisons required a strong measure of administrative virtuosity in the best of times, and it was a challenge significantly complicated by the critical economic situation of the final year of the civil war, both in the towns and in the countryside.

Weak local administration continued to hamper efforts by the provincial Military Commissariat to carry out conscription drives, but the final major round of mobilizations in March and April 1920 in Tambov did produce results that surprised commisariat officials. The campaign to call up the single age group born in 1901 was informed by the mistakes made in the previous year, when the mobilization of five separate age groups in the spring of 1919 had coincided with both the Easter holiday and the muddy spring thaw, which presented both moral and practical complications.[126] Awareness of the importance of proper timing for the 1920 campaign, combined with the more limited objectives represented by the call-up of a single age group, appeared to produce far greater success. By the end of March 1920, officials in Tambov reported that of the 23,010 young men considered eligible for conscription, nearly 14,000 had appeared at muster points, and of them, over 8,000 had been enlisted and assigned to units. By the end of the mobilization campaign in May 1920, the gap between those registered as eligible and those actually appearing for mobilization had narrowed considerably, with 24,230 having appeared at muster points.[127] Nearly all of those actually enlisted—14,855 men, according to the final count—were given assignments in reserve garrisons, principally in two of the larger towns, Tambov and Lebedian.[128]

The success of the 1901 call-up was attributed to practical innovations in the process of military mobilization rather than to any general improvement in relations between the state and the village peasantry. One reason for the restrained reception was the continued problem of desertion, particularly from the reserve garrisons that were the final destination for the majority of those recently called up for military service in 1920. Early in 1920, the rate of desertion from reserve garrisons had exceeded 60 percent throughout the Orel military sector, to which Tambov Province belonged, and the rate declined only marginally as winter gave way to spring.[129] The garrisons were filled not only with recent call-ups, but also with those already classified as deserters—those who had either previously deserted from their units or recidivists who had surrendered to military officials or had been apprehended by antidesertion squads.

Those who carried the stigma of deserter and were stationed in reserve garrisons were principally used by the provincial administration to perform various labor duties. In the winter of 1919–1920, the then chairman of the Tambov Soviet Executive Committee, V. A. Antonov-Ovseenko, reported that an ongoing fuel crisis in the southern half of the province was being partially alleviated by assigning over 22,000 deserters to timber-cutting duties.[130] Beyond concerted campaigns to address particular problems, such as clearing transport lines after heavy snowfall, those branded deserters were given other noncombat tasks, such as employment in the state-operated bakeries, state farms, telegraph and postal services, at grain collection points, on railways, and in a variety of sentry and guard duties required by the provincial administration.[131] In addition, as already described, deserters accounted for a large number of grain requisition agents and were also assigned to the antidesertion patrols. Such sustained assignments, however, were the exception. Despite the efforts of the Military Commissariat to utilize the labor of the massive soldier population systematically in 1920, the vast majority of apprehended deserters were effectively incarcerated in the garrisons of the main towns of Tambov Province, as they were elsewhere in Soviet Russia.[132]

The continued desertion problem from garrisons and from compulsory labor duties throughout 1920 was caused by the continuing food crisis throughout Soviet territory. In the garrisons themselves, military authorities struggled to maintain a swollen population of reserve soldiers, deserters, as well as cavalry horses. Problems primarily concerned food supply, but also involved basic hygiene and acceptable quarters for soldiers. As one Military Commissariat report on the situation in Kirsanov put it in 1920: "The garrison does not receive any monetary allowances, its soldiers are ill-clad, ill-shod, and often malnourished; there is no proper barracks facility, barely any cots or bunks, no kitchen facilities whatsoever, and all sit in the cold without any artificial light. As a result of all this, we have epidemics, desertion, a diminishing cavalry stables, and many other disasters besides."

In the same garrison in Kirsanov, nearly 70 percent of the horses kept in the stables had already starved to death by the late summer of 1920, and as for the garrisoned soldiers themselves, according to the same report, "in the past, [the provision of food] has limped along on both legs, and it continues to limp along to this day."[133] Securing enough food for the garrisons, as well as safeguarding against outbreaks of infectious diseases, left local commanders and military commissars often struggling to manage rising levels of visible discontent among the soldiers. It was not unknown for officials to look the other way as soldiers absconded to their home villages, especially if those villages were within the province, as this would help alleviate the supply problem in the garrison.[134]

A second facet of the connection between food supply problems and desertion surrounded the villages communities themselves, with diminishing conditions under the pressure of the grain procurement campaigns. Certainly soldiers were not without incentives to leave their garrisons, given the lack of food and general conditions. Moreover, there was tremendous pressure from family to return home. Concerns about leaving the homestead at such a vulnerable time certainly weighed on the minds of soldiers and prospective soldiers alike. Promises that the Communist Party and the Soviet state were protecting the welfare of the serviceman's family formed a vital part of the "political education" of the Red Army soldier, an innovation in large part informed by the growth of the desertion problem in 1919.[135] The propaganda campaigns aimed at deserters intensified in the second half of 1919, complemented by the development of welfare provisions for the families of Red Army servicemen, intended to reassure prospective and existing soldiers who had left their families and villages behind. Recent historians have placed considerable emphasis on this modern approach to the connection between martial and civil society by the Soviet government, both to explain the phenomenon of desertion during the civil war and especially as a means of understanding the nature of the Soviet state itself following the revolution.[136]

Yet despite promises from the Soviet government and its Military Commissariat that soldiers' families would be protected and provided for by the local communities and soviet administration, such promises were quickly compromised, both by the severe demands placed on rural communities by the state, and by the limited capacity of local soviets to manage such welfare provisions. Much depended upon local circumstances. The wife of a Red Army serviceman (a *soldatka*), without the support of her blood relatives, could find that the village community and local administration was unwilling to extend promised welfare provisions, as a letter intercepted by military censors demonstrates:

> Dearest husband, I have received from you three letters, and from these I have learned that you are alive and well, for which I am very thankful. I have written three letters to you, as well as a telegram and a correspondence from our local soviet. Dearest husband, Daniil Vasil'evich, do you receive my letters or not, and why do you not show any concern for my situation here, it is as if you have tossed me off into the muck. I went recently to your family's house, but your brothers refused to receive me, they would not even allow me to approach the home; I also went to your local soviet regarding the plot of land—but there they also refused to hear me and would not give me any land. What am I to do now? My dear husband, Daniil Vasil'evich, how am I to survive, when I write you letters asking what to do and you pay no attention whatsoever. Unless, that is, you have not received any of my letters. In that case, I write to you all, my dear comrades [apparently an address to the censors], take pity on my inescapable predicament, grant my husband leave, even if only for three days, as my situation here is extremely poor. Believe me, I am not amongst my own here, having arrived here, I do not have my own family, no one who will help me get by, and everything that I had the child and I have now eaten. Most important, I am unable to work in the fields, and I do not receive any help from the family here, it is useless to even ask. My dearest husband, come back, even if for only three days, or I shall surely be done for.[137]

Unable to depend upon the goodwill of the local community or even village administration, the Soviet government established a special commission that oversaw the protection of Red Army households. The Pomoshch' Commission established affiliates in the provinces and uezds of Soviet Russia over the course of 1919, particularly to coordinate the delivery of direct aid to such households, or to provide assistance to homesteads during the periods of intensive field work. However, the responsibilities of the local affiliates of the Pomoshch' Commission far exceeded their capabilities, and for some localities, assistance was provided on paper only.[138]

In practice, assistance and relief to Red Army households was delivered by the antidesertion patrols that were active in the countryside.[139] Typically, there was one antidesertion patrol of 50–100 members operating in each uezd, and it was part of their responsibility to ensure that the antidesertion message came through in their punitive actions against the households of deserters by distributing confiscated property directly to the households of Red Army servicemen.[140] The scope for corruption in such an arrangement was extensive, and investigations into the activities of antidesertion squads were a constant source of tension within the provincial administration.[141] While far from being uniformly corrupt, the antidesertion patrols, like the food procurement squads, were more often considered exemplary of Soviet power when their actions belied the words and policies of the Soviet government, not when they conformed to those policies.[142] As such, the powerlessness of Red Army families, and the anxieties they shared with other community members about the worsening situation in the villages in 1920, came through to the men in the garrisons, either through letters or by word of mouth.[143]

Concerns about material conditions at home and dissatisfaction with the privations endured by the Red Army were only two of the burdens on servicemen.[144] While the provisions crisis prompted some military officials to turn a blind eye when soldiers absconded from their units, this did not make desertion an easy option. Garrisoned soldiers were concerned with their reception in their native villages. Being branded a deserter had practical consequences for households, so that individuals and families appealed against the stigma in terms that must have been gratifying for officials in the Antidesertion Commission. The vast majority of cases heard by the Antidesertion Commission involved men who either claimed medical exemption from service or who had been ill and granted a leave of absence to recover. Staying at home past the designated recuperation time was formally considered desertion. Documentation was vitally important, not only for those who claimed exemption, but for any man of mobilization age who was approached by antidesertion agents in the countryside.[145] Many who had their cases reviewed were brought before the local commissions by antidesertion patrols. Effectively apprehended under suspicion of desertion, many men were left in holding cells at local soviets and offices of the Military Commissariat until authorities reviewed their cases. For those who claimed medical exemption, it could be a matter of days and even weeks before their cases were resolved and they were released.[146] "For the second time," wrote Aleksei Gorin, a village schoolteacher from Rudovsk volost (Kirsanov uezd), "I request that the Antidesertion Commission lift from me this shameful label of 'deserter,' take pity on my large, orphaned family, help me and my family out of our impossible situation, and release me from the detention house and hand back my papers, so that I can appear before the medical commission— as is my right—in order to set this matter straight once and for all."[147]

Men who protested their innocence often did so out of fear that their families would suffer. Although Gorin's status was as yet unresolved, he was classified as a deserter, and his family could be made to suffer for this in the village, where food procurement agents, in particular, targeted the households of known deserters. It is unsurprising, then, that many appeals protesting the innocence of suspected deserters were issued by their wives. Often these women were aided by sympathetic and, most important, literate members of their local soviet, and their appeals focused on the hardships facing the family in the absence of the husband.

Moreover, men who were actively serving in the Red Army submitted appeals protesting official classification as a deserter. Because so many of the soldiers in the army were, as one historian has highlighted, "second-chance men,"[148] for some the status as a deserter was difficult to overcome even after reintegration into the ranks. The files of the Antidesertion Commission are filled with appeals by Red Army soldiers who had initially been apprehended as deserters. They appealed (in the words of one such soldier) against the "disgraceful stain" of being classified as a deserter.[149] In many cases, men felt genuinely aggrieved because they had been away from their units for medical reasons and had either overstayed their leave of absence beyond an acceptable limit or had failed to produce adequate documentation for antidesertion officials. These men, too, were deserters in the eyes of state authorities. The issue, once more, was of genuine importance for the families of these men, not simply an issue of pride or honor for the soldier.[150] Their status as deserters placed their families in a delicate situation, especially when the drive to requisition grain in the countryside became more intense.

The "deserter," as we can see, occupied an ambiguous place in the political world of the villages. Very few, if any, would have embraced the label with pride. Men may not have been ashamed of having deserted the army as long as they could rely upon the local community for implicit support and approval. As long as the local soviet chairman was willing to look the other way and the majority of the village population did not protest, men who had evaded the draft or actively deserted could realize their ambition—to live the quotidian lives they had known before the war. There was no dishonor in such a situation.[151]

Soldiers were known to ask pointedly in their letters home whether the situation there would enable them to return. As one soldier wrote from his garrison: "Please write to me again, which of my buddies [*rebiata*] has already run back home, and is it possible to live at home as a deserter, because for us here things are really bad." Despite the best efforts of state censors, such letters did get home and received replies. "Dearest brother, Serezha, we miss you so much, all your friends are now home, and only you are missing." "All your friends are home. Whoever is a deserter just gets on with his life, and now folks are beginning to joke [about people who enter the Red Army], 'Well, there goes another one to serve in the army, obviously refused to volunteer for work at home.'" "Comrades from our regiment are almost all home. I would really like to see you home, too, and even though comrades here don't live entirely peacefully, it is still a whole lot better than in the city." "Mitia, in our village no one serves in the Red Army—everyone is home now."[152] The clear intention behind such letters was to encourage the soldier to desert and not to fear the reactions of fellow villagers, or indeed of the local soviet administration and agents of the state.[153]

This did not mean that desertion carried a positive connotation in the villages. However much the campaign to discourage desertion may have permeated the countryside through propaganda posters on the trains or by the antidesertion patrols, the negative label *deserter* was wielded strategically by villagers just as frequently as it was by the agents of the Soviet state.[154] Distrusted or despised local soviet workers or Communist Party members were described by villagers as deserters, since so many had been exempted from military service in order to work in the countryside administration and party organizations.[155] Many who joined the party in 1918 and early 1919 were seeking a more secure life, rich with perquisites and power, but also risks. However, the increasing number of mobilizations of Communist Party members to the Red Army tested the political loyalty of such individuals, and party officials noted with some alarm and dismay the vast numbers who resigned from the party just when military mobilization appeared imminent.[156]

In most cases, such state and party officials were already distrusted by locals, and their exemption from military service only sharpened the disdain felt by villagers. Likewise, those who worked in state collective farms and who formed small farmsteads outside the communal system (*artely*), were accused of being nothing more than self-serving deserters interested only in evading military service.[157] Once more, this was not a principled stand against desertion, as local villagers were never short of grievances against the state farms and *artely*. Villagers were frequently required to contribute their labor and machinery, as well as seed grain and live-stock, to collective farms. And because of its proximity, such farmland was always under the covetous gaze of village farmers, who were often appalled at the misuse —and, frequently, *disuse*—of the fields controlled by these collectives.[158] A common expression of anger against these farms was that they were operated by "deserters," people whose only interest was not in cultivating the land but in obtaining an official exemption from military service. Villagers were acutely aware of who among their neighbors was evading military service, just as they were watchful of those among their enemies who could be so accused.

The general context for desertion drew in several considerations—conditions at home, conditions in the garrisons and units, the receptivity of the local community, and the question of security both in the villages, where local authorities and antidesertion agents were a factor, and in the garrisons, whence the young men absconded. The fact that so many in the garrisons of Tambov were themselves natives of the province lowered the risk felt by soldiers, and the draw of the home village was strong. But many factors contributed to the general problem of desertion, none of which was unique to Tambov Province. The provisions crisis, the weakness of soviet administration and the Communist Party in the countryside, and a strong war weariness that had been in evidence at least since the days of the revolution in 1917—all these were outstanding characteristics of provincial life in Soviet Russia, and all encouraged desertion in 1920.

The problem of desertion and redesertion from reserve garrisons in 1920 provoked a major cleavage in the provincial administration, in which the Antidesertion Commission and the Military Commissariat each blamed the other for the continuing problems.[159] Authorities in the Antidesertion Commission in Tambov, when held to account for the large number of deserters still believed to be at large in the countryside, pointed the finger of blame at the Military Commissariat, which had not only been unable to support the soldier population in the province, but also guilty of providing inadequate security in garrisons.[160] They pointed to the high levels of infectious disease in the garrisons, which often resulted in leaves of absence that would be exceeded by soldiers, thus earning the status of "deserters," and the rates of redesertion, creating a cycle that appeared to be effectively tolerated by Military Commissariat officials.[161] Sensing that their institutional autonomy was under threat, authorities in the Antidesertion Commission, like so many bureaucrats in the Soviet Republic during the civil war, raised the intensity of the dispute in the hope that a compromise might be achieved:

The continuation of this type of life for the deserters and soldiers of the Red Army is inconceivable. The Military Commissariat's efforts toward reducing desertion, as well as the purely internal work of the commissariats [in the local administrations], is completely ineffective and, what is more, it is criminal. The entire range of work by the commissariats is intended to reinforce the Red Army, but with such conditions in the garrisons, and given the slipshod work of the military commissars, there will be no effective reinforcement and desertion will continue to grow. If the responsible military commissars are not removed, and if present conditions continue into the future, then the Antidesertion Commission will have no choice but to recommend to Moscow that official criminal charges be brought against the provincial Military Commissariat.[162]

Such threats, however, were not enough to preserve the commission's autonomy, and on 1 June 1920, it was officially made subordinate to the Military Commissariat.[163] Maintaining that the desertion problem was chiefly attributable to the failings of the antidesertion officials active in the localities, the formerly independent commission was now made the subject of intense internal reviews that found its organization and operations to be corrupt and incompetent. The new head of the Antidesertion Commission in Tambov, Shikunov, reported his shock at the state in which he found the organization in the summer of 1920:

In the first place, the provincial commission had no effective contact with the local commissions, such that in the course of an entire year they had not once undertaken to provide instruction for the uezds, and the uezd commissions likewise made no such effort to train those in the districts. Thus, antidesertion work was carried out at all levels in the manner of a cottage industry, without any systematic coordination of efforts. Second, working as they were for nearly eighteen months without any formal contact with the military authorities, not being answerable to the Military Commissariat, the antidesertion commissions naturally became infected with an ethic of haphazardness, which was quickly revealed for all to see over the course of their formal subordination to the commissariat. Third, judging by the available reports and estimates found in the possession of the Antidesertion Commission, the commission actually had very little idea as to how many deserters there actually were in the province, let alone where to find them.... Fourth, the local antidesertion commissions at the village and volost levels were most often composed of only one member, and in the most exceptional cases there were up to two members. Obviously, to talk of productive, effective work, given these circumstances, is impossible.[164]

These conclusions were written in August 1920, at a time when the provincial administration was once more facing the prospect of renewed instability in the countryside as another campaign to procure grain from the villages was about to be initiated. The weakness of local administration remained a problem that threatened to compromise the state's ability to meet its targets for the procurement of food, and the continued failure to control desertion remained an important indication of that weakness. Estimates at the time placed the number of deserters still at large in the countryside at just over 27,000, with the highest concentrations being in Tambov, Kirsanov, and Morshansk uezds.[165] Deserters still at large in the villages represented a potentially volatile element within the communities, and they were a particular focus of anxieties as the confrontation between the peasantry and the state resumed.

Yet as we have seen, while weak administration and the "reach" of the state into the villages was a real problem, the phenomenon of desertion was a complex one that did not necessarily reflect the fears of many Soviet officials in Tambov and Moscow. Desertion was certainly resistance to military mobilization, and it was also a response to the severe conditions of crisis, particularly the food crisis, that affected Soviet society as a whole. Desertion in its provincial context was often a pragmatic response conditioned by both desperation and realism. Young men serving in the reserve garrisons often deserted precisely because they could, and they did so on the basis of individual circumstances rather than out of political principle. Deserters did not constitute a natural collective actor mobilized, or primed for mobilization, in a movement of resistance to the Soviet state. Desertion was, if anything, a symptom of the weaknesses of state authority in Tambov, one that Soviet officials were all too aware of and yet limited in their ability to redress.

THE MAKING OF
A CIVIL WAR BANDIT

Aleksandr Antonov

POPULAR GRIEVANCES AGAINST the Soviet state in a province where local administration and authority was weak did not by necessity translate into focused resistance and opposition to the Soviet government. While the civil war history of Tambov had been turbulent and violent, punctuated by rural uprisings, the only source of sustained opposition in the province came from forces that moved freely within the village milieu yet were outside of it. Banditry—violent criminality, often opportunistic—was a persistent problem in Tambov, but the province was hardly unique in its reporting of incidents involving armed groups of men raiding villages and state farms. Many of these groups were highly localized and isolated from village communities, as well as transient in the disturbances they caused. Far more troubling by 1919 and 1920 was the presence of established groups of armed men who proudly announced their opposition to the Soviet government both in word and deed, targeting state representatives and officials in a campaign of terror waged in the name of the "people."

No other civil war era "bandit" in Tambov Province achieved the fame and prominence of Aleksandr Stepanovich Antonov. As an anti-Soviet rebel, Antonov appears to be rather typical. Like many others who emerged to oppose the Soviet government during the civil war period, he had devoted much of his adult life to underground revolutionary politics. And like other rebels of the era, he had briefly worked with the Bolsheviks following the October 1917 seizure of power. The details of his biography, however, make it far from obvious that he was the kind of man to build a peasant army and lead a large-scale insurgency against the government of the day.[1]

Antonov had been involved with local radicalism as early as his sixteenth year. Born in Moscow on 26 July 1889, Aleksandr Antonov was the third child of Stepan Gavrilovich Antonov and Nataliia Ivanovna Sokolova. Nothing is known of the Antonov family during their time in Moscow, as the interest of historians and, during Antonov's life, policemen and security agents, has been focused on uncovering the sparse details of his life. His time in Moscow could have been brief, for the family moved to Tambov Province soon after Aleksandr's birth. Stepan, a former noncommissioned officer in the Russian army, was a native of Tambov, and he may have been returning home with his family after the birth of their first son. Stepan moved the family to the small but thriving uezd town of Kirsanov, then a bustling regional center of the grain trade, located on the Riazan'-Urals rail line.[2]

Parish documents that record Aleksandr's christening in Moscow in 1889 list the Antonovs as lower middle class, or of the legal estate known as *meshchanstvo*.[3] After their move to Kirsanov, the details of this status were realized in full. Having to support a wife and three children (soon joined by a fourth child, Dmitrii), Stepan set up shop as a tinker, while Nataliia sought to earn money as a seamstress and milliner. In the last years of the nineteenth century, the Antonovs lived and survived in Kirsanov. While Stepan's business did not thrive, Nataliia was able to establish a professional reputation and secure a steady amount of work, effectively supporting the family. The three eldest children received elementary education in Kirsanov, although Aleksandr failed to advance as far as his elder sisters, Valentina and Anna. In his early teens, Aleksandr began to work as an assistant to a local grain trader.

There is no obvious moment that one can pinpoint as the time when Aleksandr Antonov became involved in radical politics in this provincial setting. Certainly there were radical groups operating in Tambov Province, and specifically in Kirsanov, and their prominence would have only increased during the first years of the twentieth century. It is known that the younger daughter, Anna, was involved in radical politics—enough to earn her a prison sentence in Penza Province—but the evidence for this is from 1910 and could have been the result of only a fleeting and superficial involvement or association with radical circles. It is not known whether Anna introduced Aleksandr to revolutionary underground politics and parties or vice versa.[4] According to Anna, Aleksandr was—as a child at least—very much engrossed by family life, with a particularly strong bond with his mother. Physically small and fair in complexion, Aleksandr left few strong impressions upon those who were able to recall him as a child. Nothing remarkable about his childhood, even down to the sensitivity identified by his sister, could have foretold his extraordinary fate. His mother's death when Aleksandr was sixteen or seventeen signaled many changes for the Antonov family, and especially for Aleksandr.[5]

Antonov's elder sister Valentina noted in her testimony given to Soviet investigators that she effectively became the mother of the family following the death of Nataliia Ivanovna. This was especially true for Aleksandr and Dmitrii.[6] However, Valentina soon married, and Anna left home not long after. Stepan, perhaps no longer able to make an adequate living in Kirsanov, moved to the growing village of Inzhavino after his wife's death. Inzhavino was the terminus of a recently built railway feeder line that linked the farms of the south of the uezd to Kirsanov. It is not known if he made this choice in order to be nearer to relatives in the area or if it was a business decision, to provide needed services to a growing village. Either way, Stepan moved to Inzhavino with his son Dmitrii in 1907 or 1908. By this time, Aleksandr had already left home.

Aleksandr was now well on his way to establishing himself within radical political circles as a man of action. It is not known whether he was attracted to revolutionary activity by the strength of ideas or by the lure of high-risk political violence. But by 1908, Aleksandr's name first appears in the police ledgers for Tambov as an eighteen-year-old with an established identity within the Socialist Revolutionary (SR) group in Kirsanov. He is described as a ruddy-faced youth with fair brown hair and of average to smallish build. His reason for traveling to the provincial capital in the summer of 1908 was evidently to establish contact between the SRs in Tambov city and those in Kirsanov, a group described in police reports as independent of the main SR party organization. At a time when there was a strong degree of fluidity and, indeed, disarray in the Russian revolutionary underground, such fractures were both commonplace and difficult to resolve. Given the heightened vigilance of the police and Ministry of Internal Affairs (MVD) amid the sporadic violence in the countryside and nascent "legitimate" party politics of the main towns, a young man such as Antonov, effectively on his own and without immediate prospects, could find opportunity and purpose in revolutionary politics. His first appearance on the police diary of the local newspaper concerned an incident in June 1908 in which a policeman was shot in Tambov while pursuing two suspected revolutionaries, one of whom was Antonov. His in-volvement in this event, which was taken up by the Special Prosecutor's Office in Moscow some weeks later, made it unlikely that he could ever extricate himself from the revolutionary underground.[7]

Aleksandr's calling, however, was not bound up with the realm of ideas and ideology. His was the dirty work of radical politics in Russia—robbery and extor-tion for the purpose of financially sustaining the movement. Antonov was an "expropriator" rather than a revolutionary terrorist. He was enlisted to commit acts of mundane criminality in the name of the revolution, rather than spectacular acts of assassination that constituted the front-line volleys of the revolutionary terrorists. Yet he was easily distinguished from the average criminal, even if he kept the company of individuals whose only interest was in personal profit and securing their own share of the takings. Two of the more prominent "expropria-tions" that are linked with Antonov's name took place in Inzhavino and in the smaller Borisoglebsk settlement of Kaninskii. In each case, unnamed men perpe-trated robberies. However, each was explicitly linked with revolutionaries. When the railway station in Inzhavino was held up at gunpoint, the robbers left a note that read: "4,302 rubles and 85 kopecks taken by the party of anarchists-individualists." It was signed simply: "A member of the party." Likewise, in Kaninskii, where the Peasant Bank was raided at gunpoint, the robbers left a similarly precise account, entering into the accounts book a record of the amount taken, confiscated by "the Volga Union of Independent Socialist-Revolutionaries."[8]

In each case, Antonov worked with fellow SR-Maximalists and with ordinary men from nearby villages, drafted in at short notice to assist in the robbery. The less these men knew about the instigators of the plots the better, and they were re-warded for their help (directly participating in the robberies, providing transport, securing safe hideouts) with a share of the takings. In the case of the Inzhavino "ex-propriation," police investigators that descended upon the village were able to im-plicate four other local men, three of whom were found to have between 147 and 496 rubles each, suspected to be a portion of the 4,302 rubles stolen from the safe at the railway station. The two men believed to have organized the robbery, Antonov and Gavriil Ivanovich Iagodkin, had both fled the scene, leaving their local ac-complices to pay for their self-seeking participation in the crimes.

A similar robbery one month later at the office of the Peasant Bank located on the Kanin farm settlement (*khutor*) yielded 2,296 rubles.[9] In the bank's account books, the robbers, identified later as Antonov and a man named Zelenov, left their customary record of the amount stolen, noting that the money had been confiscated by the Volga Union of Independent Social Revolutionaries. This entry was signed simply "Medved" ("The Bear"). Once again, the two principal robbers were assisted by local men from the nearby village of Uvarova; police made eight arrests in all, none of which yielded detailed information about Antonov or his accomplice beyond some vague ties they had to a schoolteacher in the town of Balashov in neighboring Saratov Province.

But it was not long before the police in Tambov would be able to piece together a more detailed picture of the young man, Aleksandr Antonov. They soon had his photograph, probably secured from his family in Inzhavino, although, as a report at the time notes, they did not possess any of his "anthropometrical measurements." His worth to the authorities in Tambov, as measured by the reward offered for his capture, was 1,000 rubles, and information regarding Antonov—whose code names in underground circles were "Shurka" or "Shura" (common diminutives for Aleksandr) and "Osinovyi" (aspen leaf)—was distributed to regional MVD offices. The first evidence of his whereabouts came from Saratov Province, where an intercepted letter, originating from Kozlov in Tambov Province, inquired of Saratov comrades about "Shura" and others.[10] Officials in Saratov were at the time on a heightened state of alert, owing to the discovery of a plot to assassinate the commander-in-chief of the Kazan region, one General Sadetskii.

When Antonov was finally captured, it was in the dragnet of the Saratov police connected with this assassination plot. It is unknown whether Antonov was involved in this particular plot; police records place him as only a peripheral figure at best. Nevertheless, on 20 February 1909 he was apprehended during an early morning raid on a house where suspects connected with the assassination plot were living in the town of Saratov. Three others were apprehended in the raid. Antonov was caught in the possession of a firearm and a fake passport. Knowing that Antonov was wanted in connection with robberies in Tambov Province, the Saratov officials began to arrange for his transfer to Tambov, although this process was slow and the actual return did not occur until 14 April.

In the Tambov jail, Antonov joined several other "politicals" attached to the PSR. Contact between these jailed party members and the regional organization was fairly regular, and the fact that structural repairs were being made to the prison in Tambov kept the prospect of escape foremost in the minds of prisoners. One of the party leaders, Konstantin Nikolaev Bazhenov, was entreated to visit the prison to learn more about the security situation and to report to the party leadership on opportunities for freeing their comrades behind bars. Prison officials learned of this and other details when they intercepted and decoded a letter sent by PSR inmates to the party organization in Tambov. The letter also contained a request for several hundred rubles by Antonov ("Shurka"), who evidently felt confident, after only a couple of months in prison, that he could bribe his way to liberty. Interestingly, Antonov promised to repay the money with funds he retained from some of his "expropriations," opening the possibility that his revolutionary activities were not exclusively for the sake of the cause. This particular overture failed, however, as did other reported escape attempts involving tunnels and severed window bars. This letter was enough to earn Antonov a regular space in an isolation cell and eventually, following his conviction at a court martial in 1910, a transfer to a prison outside Tambov Province. Eventually, after a spell in a Moscow prison, he was placed in the main prison in the city of Vladimir, where he remained until immediately after the revolution in February 1917. (Once again, there are few details about his term in prison in Vladimir, except for records of six separate periods spent in isolation cells for unspecified transgressions.)

According to his sister Valentina, when Antonov was finally released, along with all political prisoners in early March 1917, he first sent a telegram to announce his release and his intention to return to the city of Tambov, where Valentina and her family were living. After eight years of incarceration, he was emaciated, and it took him nearly a month of rest at Valentina's apartment to regain a healthy disposition. As a member of the PSR, and a former political prisoner, Antonov had both connections and cachet in the immediate postrevolutionary context. With senior PSR members now assuming leadership in the provincial and municipal administration (V. P. Izheev, who had been Antonov's defense lawyer in March 1910, was then the chairman of the municipal Duma in Tambov), Antonov was able to secure a paying position as an assistant to one of the district militia chiefs in the municipality. This was far from being a high-profile post, but in the inverted world of revolutionary Russia, a term in a tsarist-era prison was proof of Antonov's reliability and loyalty. His party code name may have been "the thief," but Antonov now stood on the other side of the thin blue line.

Antonov's moment in the revolutionary summer of 1917 arrived when newly elected members of the municipal Duma in Kirsanov declared the town an autonomous republic—the "Kirsanov Republic"—on 13 May. The event was not an upheaval as such, and it bore no relation to the similar declarations of small "republics" later in the summer by radical groups of politicians and soldiers in other provincial towns. Nor, it would seem, did it resemble the occasions when individual villages or even land communes declared their autonomy following the seizure of property from a local estate.[11] Shortly after having been selected to the municipal Committee of Public Safety, A. K. Trunin, a small businessman of some variety and a member of the PSR, appointed himself "Procurer-General" of the municipality, already declared to be an autonomous republic. Trunin was joined in his adventure by other local businessmen who had recently become members of the municipal Duma, and they were supported by certain individuals attached to the local militia.[12] The declaration of the Kirsanov Republic was far from being the product of a popular movement, even if its instigators later sought to court popular support with all-day orchestra concerts and noticeably prolonged ringing of church bells.[13] The political character of the cabal that assumed control over Kirsanov's affairs, however, remains enigmatic. Variously called "bourgeois," "anarchist," "bolshevik," and "blackhundred," the conspiracy launched by Trunin and his supporters was more than anything a challenge to the authority of the provincial capital and to the Provisional Government.[14] As a man with close ties to Kirsanov, Aleksandr Antonov was chosen to lead a contingent of militiamen to the uezd town to arrest Trunin and the other "republicans."

The operation proved to be more complicated than provincial officials anticipated. The militia detachment led by Antonov was greeted by a large crowd outside the municipal Duma in Kirsanov, and when their initial effort to arrest Trunin was met with defiance from within the building, the situation quickly escalated to an exchange of gunfire and general panic in the market square. When the men inside the Duma building finally succumbed, the problems for the militiamen from Tambov did not cease. Awaiting transportation back to the provincial capital, Antonov and his men were confronted by an angry crowd that once more freed Trunin and simultaneously arrested Antonov.[15] The tables were again turned after the local army garrison was enjoined to restore order and to rearrest Trunin and his associates. The whole episode was over by 23 May, but at the cost of some eight lives.[16]

Antonov's militia activities in the provincial capital in 1917 must have been eventful, given the mounting public disorder surrounding the issues of food supply and the growing political radicalism of the local military garrison, in particular.[17] Antonov's chance for advancement, however, would again be associated more with personal connections than a particularly distinguished record of service. In October, uezd officials in Kirsanov—evidently still attempting to reconstitute a reliable militia organization, particularly following the events of May 1917 —requested that Antonov be made militia chief for the entire territory. This was a significant step up in responsibility for someone with only six months' experience as the assistant to a municipal district militia chief. But those who issued the request were not unknown to Antonov; they were long-time acquaintances from the revolutionary underground. The representative of the Provisional Government in Kirsanov, Konstantin Bazhenov, had been a significant figure in regional PSR circles and was familiar with Antonov's earlier activities as a party "expropriator."

Antonov would be returning home, surrounded by familiar faces, but confronted by an entirely different context.

Before assuming his appointment to Kirsanov, Antonov married his Tambov girlfriend, Sofiia Vasil'evna Orlova-Bogoliubskaia. The couple could not have known one another for very long, since Aleksandr had been in the provincial capital for only a short time. When he informed his sister Valentina of his intention to marry, she had not even known her brother had a girlfriend.[18] Sofiia, a small, dark-haired girl, was the sister of one of Antonov's colleagues in the municipal militia organization. Also named Aleksandr, Sofiia's brother had a background somewhat similar to Antonov's. Both had strong ties to Kirsanov, both were SRs, and both had been involved in "expropriations." (Indeed, both shared the nickname "Shurka.")[19] The only major divergence was the young Bogoliubskii's service in the army during the First World War, suggesting that he was not so fully involved in the revolutionary underground prior to the revolution. Regardless, their fates would become closely tied after the civil war began in Russia.

Leaving his new wife behind in Tambov, Antonov assumed his post in Kirsanov at the beginning of November 1917. The uezd administration in the province was still firmly in the hands of fellow members of the PSR, joined by Menshevik-Internationalists. Despite the uniform appearance of the political scene in the uezd, there was still room for antagonisms and professional rivalries. Soon after Antonov's arrival, one of his colleagues complained to the country administration authorities that he refused "to work under such a crude and uneducated man." Having just been replaced as the assistant militia chief by Antonov, P. N. Kalinin complained further that "by his education he does not meet the required qualifications set for the militia to serve as an assistant to a volost militia chief, let alone assume the post of militia chief for an entire uezd and town [Kirsanov]."[20]

In Kirsanov, the political situation showed signs of change in late 1917. The October seizure of power in Petrograd by the Bolshevik Party was a distant event that had had little immediate bearing on politics in Kirsanov. The uezd soviet remained very much in the hands of Mensheviks and SRs, and the zemstvo administration was similarly dominated by liberals and moderate socialists. In the town of Kirsanov there was as yet no Bolshevik Party organization at the beginning of 1918, although in the first weeks of that year the party began to make noticeable gains in the newly organized volost soviets, as hundreds of former soldiers, proclaiming their allegiance to the Petrograd "party of power," returned to their native villages from their garrisons and units. Their presence in the countryside of Kirsanov had the potential effect of shifting the balance of power in the uezd, although Bolshevik activists in the town were hesitant at first to exploit this rural

Aleksandr Antonov, 1917 or 1918. Detail from a group photo, possibly taken when Antonov assumed his post as Chief of Militia in Kirsanov uezd. This is the only photograph of the adult Antonov that exists, with the exception of those of his corpse taken in 1922. *Photograph courtesy of the Tambovskii Kraevedcheskii Muzei*

base of support, seeing these soldiers and village men as of questionable reliability and temperament.[21]

The relatively peaceful suppression of the municipal Duma and the corresponding declaration of "Soviet power" in Kirsanov were finally completed in February 1918, but not on the strict terms set by Bolshevik Party members in the uezd. The executive committee of the uezd soviet was still made up of Mensheviks, SRs, and Bolsheviks, and the last remained very much a minor force in the early weeks of 1918. But as outside Bolshevik activists arrived, the Kirsanov Bolshevik Party grew assertive in its dealings with the executive committee, turning up the pressure on Menshevik and PSR members, in particular.[22] Some SRs, in order to remain at their posts and work alongside their Bolshevik colleagues, switched their affiliation to the Revolutionary Communists, while others would eventually claim affiliation with the Left SRs, even though the LSR Party was not formally organized in the uezd until April 1918, when the Soviet organization in Tambov finally assumed control over the provincial administration with the significant assistance of outside LSR activists.[23] Antonov would eventually identify himself as a LSR, although one of the founding members of the Kirsanov LSR organization claimed that

Antonov never participated in their meetings, suggesting that this was an affiliation of convenience more than anything else.[24] Antonov remained pragmatic in his politics, but he, like so many others, could not have failed to notice how the balance of power in Kirsanov was shifting. Former close associates of Antonov's, such as Bazhenov and V. N. Mikhnevich, began to defect from the PSR or were dismissed from their posts. The organization of a local branch of the Cheka in Kirsanov in April 1918 accelerated this political transformation in the uezd.

Antonov's position was undeniably vulnerable, and it is reasonable to understand his next significant action in that light. Nearly every biographical sketch of Aleksandr Antonov paints May 1918 as a turning point for him and his closest associates in the militia. The order issued on 29 May 1918 calling for the immediate disarmament of the troops of the Czechoslovak Legion throughout Russia—some of whom were located along the railway that ran through Kirsanov between Tambov and the large junction at Rtishchevo in Saratov Province—had the effect of transforming a tense standoff between certain forces of the legion and Soviet authorities into a violent conflict, one that changed the political landscape of Russia in 1918 and presented a vital opportunity for political opponents of the Bolsheviks. However, unlike other parts of Soviet territory, principally to the east of the province, Tambov had not seen any serious disturbances involving the Czechoslovak Legion. Similarly, no serious incidents were associated with the disarmament order in Kirsanov, although it is unknown how many Czech and Slovak legionnaires were on this particular stretch of the railway.

The opportunity created by the situation for political opponents of the Bolsheviks in Kirsanov was not to be found in any immediate disruptions and clashes, however. Instead, the prominent claim was that Antonov and his associates in the militia pilfered the bulk of the confiscated firearms taken from the Czech and Slovak troops within their area of authority. Antonov's principal accomplices in this operation were two militiamen, I. S. Zaev, a former noncommissioned army officer, and V. K. Lashchilin, who had once been a schoolteacher. Both were appointed by Antonov, each responsible for sectors of the rural southern portion of the uezd. Both were allegedly instrumental in transporting the confiscated firearms and ammunition to the area south of Kirsanov and hiding them in designated spots along the banks of the Vorona River between the villages of Inokovka and Chernavka. Other militiamen close to Antonov were similarly involved, such as P. M. Tokmakov and N. G. Gridchin.

Although the pilfering of arms appears to have represented a fundamental break for Antonov, the actual significance of this development—about which, predictably, there is no detailed documentation—is difficult to assess. This is not simply a matter of quantification, although little is known about the actual scale of the theft. Assuming that they were involved in the pilfering of arms in May and June 1918, it is also difficult to state with any confidence what the plans of Antonov and his associates actually were. Did they have designs for an immediate armed seizure of power in Kirsanov, to be completed before the Cheka in the uezd arrested all of their socialist comrades and removed them from power? Were they stockpiling arms for some future action, as yet undetermined, simply because a large source of firearms had become available when the convoys of the Czechoslovak Legion were stopped? According to a senior agent in the Kirsanov Cheka, the PSR in Tambov had developed concrete plans for an armed seizure of power involving Antonov and his Kirsanov militia, plans that came to light when a mysterious briefcase containing documents detailing the conspiracy was "discovered" by agents. The Cheka agent in question, G. T. Men'shov, made the claims in his published memoirs in 1923, stating that the Kirsanov Cheka organization reviewed the incriminating documents on 15 August 1918, and immediately dispatched agents to arrest Antonov, Lishchilin, and Zaev, the militia officials identified in connection with the plot. Lishchilin and Zaev were apprehended by Cheka agents, brought back to Kirsanov, and, according to Men'shov, shot within twenty-four hours after their capture. Antonov, who had been on leave from his militia post and living with his wife for over a fortnight in a village north of Inzhavino, was somehow alerted of the danger and went into hiding. His wife returned to Tambov. For the next ten days, the Cheka kept a watch on Antonov's apartment in Kirsanov, but he never returned.

The scenario outlined by Men'shov, based on the documents allegedly discovered in the briefcase, may or may not be authentic. No such documents have ever been uncovered, nor any contemporary evidence relating to the discovery of such a briefcase. It is clear, though, that in mid-August 1918 the Cheka did arrest Zaev and Lishchilin, and that they also sought to arrest Antonov. Zaev and Lishchilin had already been under investigation by the Cheka for accusations of professional improprieties such as corruption, and Antonov had personally intervened on one occasion to defend his trusted colleagues. But, according to Men'shov, the intercepted documents, containing plans to "destroy the [Kirsanov] uezd soviet" and to "carry out a campaign of terror against senior officials," provided the immediate pretext for the pursuit of Antonov and his militia colleagues. Given the severity of such charges, it appears strange that, when official documentation of Antonov's dismissal as Kirsanov militia chief in August 1918 was processed by uezd administration authorities, the grounds for his dismissal, as described by the MVD commissar in Kirsanov, T. A. Klimov, was "failure to return from annual leave of absence."

Returning to an underground existence that had become so familiar, Antonov was joined by several known and trusted faces, including some from his underground days nearly a decade before. Although it is unclear if he immediately linked up with them, Antonov's brother and brother-in-law were already on the run from Soviet authorities in connection with a failed uprising in the provincial capital, where both had been members of the municipal militia. Dmitrii Antonov had gone into hiding almost immediately after events in Tambov on 17–19 June 1918, the riots by recently mobilized young men that had so destabilized the Bolshevik-controlled soviet administration in the provincial capital as to allow their opponents in the PSR and Kadet parties to very briefly assume control of the municipal government. Just when the Bolshevik Party was reasserting control with the assistance of recently arrived Red Army troops, Dmitrii Antonov appeared at the door of his sister's apartment. Dmitrii was very much the youngest sibling, and according to Valentina he was understandably anxious, as he had been a reluctant and peripheral participant in the uprising in Tambov and was unsure of his next move. Aleksandr Antonov, when his sister told him of Dmitrii's involvement, called his brother an "idiot" for having been caught up in the doomed affair.[25] Bogoliubskii's role in the June 1918 events in Tambov is less concrete, but his disappearance largely coincides with the immediate aftermath of the failed uprising when the Cheka in Tambov carried out sweeping arrests of known or suspected political opponents.[26]

The two Antonov brothers and Bogoliubskii would certainly have been aware that the others had gone into hiding, but it is not immediately apparent that they found one another during their first weeks on the run. While the activities of the other two remain obscure, there is much speculation as to Aleksandr Antonov's initial moves in the autumn of 1918. Most prominent are claims that Antonov left Tambov Province, drawn to developments in the Middle Volga, where former members of the Constituent Assembly had improvised a rival government initially based in the town of Samara. The Komuch government contained a significant number of SRs, including some with connections to Tambov. There is, however, no evidence to place Antonov among the precious few popular supporters of the Komuch government, and in any case that government's fall in November 1918 would have cut short any flirtation Antonov may have planned with the defenders of the Constituent Assembly in the Volga region.[27]

Other accounts try to place Antonov at the heart of the violence in the villages along the border between Morshansk and Kirsanov uezds in late October and early November 1918.[28] This was one of the most serious rural uprisings that plagued Tambov Province that autumn. Claims that Antonov was involved, however, emerged only well after the event, by sources that demonstrate a tendency to involve Antonov in such incidents of antigovernment violence from the very moment the Bolsheviks assumed control in Tambov. Contemporary reports on the violence in Pichaevo, Rudovka, and other districts along the Morshansk-Kirsanov border make no mention of Antonov as a participant, even a minor one, despite extensive investigations into the disturbances there conducted by Soviet officials in the immediate aftermath.[29]

By the end of 1918, the circle of outlaws had found one another and, without any prospect of returning to peaceful life in a provincial society that was being drawn irrevocably into civil war, resolved to forge for themselves an existence defined in opposition to the Soviet authorities in Tambov. Aleksandr and Dmitrii Antonov were joined by Aleksandr Bogoliubskii and a group of former militia members, including Petr Tokmakov. In all, the group numbered between ten and fifteen—a small squad (*druzhina*) of vigilantes whose first activities recalled the armed "expropriations" of Antonov's formative years conducted in the same area of southern Kirsanov uezd where he most likely continued to maintain strong ties with locals. But the attacks on the village and volost soviets in such places as Zolotovka (Kirsanov) and Utinov (Borisoglebsk) in February 1919 were limited in nature and relatively low-risk. These were, first and foremost, robberies that helped to sustain the druzhina, and there were no attempts to court popular support or entreat community members to rebel. The assault on the soviet in Zolotovka not only relieved the volost treasury of its cash resources, but also left four Communist Party members dead. Despite the violence and instability that had characterized the countryside since the spring of 1917, such a deadly attack by outside vigilantes was highly uncommon, and even if the Communist Party was the target of popular derision and dissatisfaction, the murder of four people must have given the villagers of Zolotovka pause.

As the first months of 1919 passed, the number of bodies continued to mount in Kirsanov. The targets continued to be Communist Party members, but these acts of assassination broadened to target anyone who served the Soviet state and was likely to be associated with unpopular policies or practices in the countryside. Food supply workers and requisition agents, local military commissariat officials, and agents of the Cheka and militia were among those who perished in ambushes over the course of 1919. In late June, a member of the Kirsanov soviet executive committee, Butovskii, and a senior official in the uezd Cheka organization became the most high-profile victims of Antonov and his druzhina. By the end of 1919, Antonov and his men were allegedly responsible for the murder of over 100 Communist Party members in Kirsanov uezd. Their exploits inspired a fear that permeated the Kirsanov Communist Party organization and attracted the attentions of other outlaws in the area who sought safety and purpose outside the typical context of the village community. The druzhina expanded in the first half of 1919, from possibly a dozen to somewhere in the region of 100–200 men. The fluctuating numbers seem to indicate that the druzhina attracted a combination of locals whose involvement was entirely temporary and who could rejoin their communities, and others who found themselves detached from their native communities and wanted by Soviet authorities.

Few of the men who joined would have had the sort of experience in revolutionary activities possessed by Aleksandr Antonov. One who did share a similar background was Ivan Egorovich Ishin, who became involved with the druzhina in early 1919 and later played a central role in the insurgency in Tambov Province. Only slightly older than Antonov, Ishin was a native of Kalugino, in the southern half of Kirsanov uezd. He was born into a peasant family and remained in his native region, eventually settling in the large market village of Kurdiuki. Like Antonov, his involvement with revolutionary politics and the PSR dates from the 1905 revolution. It is not known whether their paths crossed at this time, but it is highly likely that they did, even if Ishin's police record is far less substantial than Antonov's.[30] He was arrested in 1907 in connection with rural disturbances in his native Kalugino, charged with inciting locals to defy public order decrees, and was arrested on subsequent occasions in connection with his involvement with the PSR.[31] However, Ishin never incurred the severe punishments reserved for Antonov, and he remained in his native area until the revolution in 1917. At this time, Ishin surfaced as the chairman of the volost zemstvo in Kurdiuki, a position of some standing, although one that would quickly command less authority as the summer of 1917 passed.

Ishin's involvement with Antonov and the druzhina in 1919 came about as a result of circumstances similar to those surrounding Antonov's own descent into an underground existence. In the months following the Bolshevik assumption of control over the provincial administration in Tambov in 1918, Ishin was the head of the main consumers' cooperative in the village of Kurdiuki, the most recent of several "civic" posts he had held since the 1917 revolution. He was also the head of a growing family, with three young children. However, he regularly found himself in conflict with the local members of the Communist Party, who controlled the volost soviet and, subsequently, the Committee of the Poor in the village and volost.[32] Disputes over the distribution of rare consumer goods, as well as available cash resources, were informed by broader political allegiances and opinion, with Ishin's formal "nonparty" status only thinly veiling his hostility to the Communist Party and marking him as someone who could not be relied upon to "submit to

Soviet authority."[33] Ishin was consistently linked with the episodes of violence in the area that occurred in the autumn of 1918. Between December 1918 and late March 1919, Ishin was twice detained by local officials on charges of corruption and speculation, and on both occasions he was released on the order of uezd officials due to a lack of evidence produced by his opponents in Kudiuki. It is difficult to evaluate whether he was a victim of harassment and intimidation, or was simply more careful and elusive in his subversive activities than his rivals. Then, in late March 1919, he disappeared. No one—particularly members of his large extended family in the area, who evidently closed ranks—was able to offer any information regarding his whereabouts. Later Soviet investigators tried to implicate him in violent disturbances in Nikol'skoe volost in Tambov uezd, but no evidence has been produced. According to a former family friend, it was rumored that he had "joined the White Guards." In fact, Ishin had decided to take flight from increasingly difficult circumstances in his home village, and the fact that an old associate like Antonov was thriving in the area no doubt drew him into an underground existence. In so doing, he abandoned his wife and children in Kurdiuki.[34]

Ishin's unique contribution to the growth and character of Antonov's druzhina emerged in the summer of 1919. His history as a radical in the Kirsanov countryside was quite possibly tied to his talent for oratory, for his name features most prominently in connection with the first efforts of Antonov and his men to communicate a political message to the communities of southern Kirsanov. During the height of their campaign of terror in 1919, targeting the rural cells of the Communist Party and other agents of the Soviet state in the Tambov countryside, Antonov and his group called meetings in areas deemed safe enough to address crowds, particularly young men of conscription age. At these meetings, Ishin would urge resistance to service in the Red Army as a means of protest against the Soviet state. There were no calls for open rebellion against the state, and there was evidently no attempt to recruit these young men to join Antonov and his druzhina in an effort to forge a wider resistance movement in the province. At one such meeting, which drew people from four districts in southern Kirsanov uezd (Treskino, Kalugino, Zolotovka, and Bogdanovka), several thousand were said to have heard the words of Ishin, Antonov, and perhaps others.[35] The circumstances surrounding this particular meeting may have been uniquely convivial for the members of the druzhina, but it is not unreasonable to assume that similar meetings took place on a smaller scale in areas considered less safe.

Nevertheless, the activities of Antonov's druzhina remained limited, and contacts with other groups of antigovernment rebels are difficult to substantiate. Alleged contacts made with Denikin's army in the summer of 1919 were dramatic in quality but, like so many other such allegations articulated in 1920 and 1921—when Antonov's insurgency was at its height—they were either baseless or thin on detail and documentation.[36] At its height in the summer of 1919, the druzhina numbered an estimated 150 armed men. This was a sizable but restricted group—hardly a private army, but a stable armed and mounted force that was easily distinguished from the typical "bandit" groups that roamed the countryside during the civil war period. The druzhina's size contracted, however, the further it strayed from its extended base in southern Kirsanov, and activities were likewise more limited beyond this area. Officials in Saratov Province, for instance, reported that Antonov and his men were attempting to provoke disturbances in Balashov uezd in early August 1919, but these efforts did not directly produce significant disturbances for Soviet authorities.[37] The group was also involved in supplying weapons to other rebels in Saratov Province, but these transactions were similarly small in scale and it is difficult to assess their impact.[38] Somewhere between the elaborate allegations assembled by Cheka and Communist Party officials and the actual documentary record lies the truth about the direction and ambitions of Antonov and his druzhina in 1919 and early 1920. There may well have been tension within the group itself, as the necessity of self-preservation and the need for political purpose came into conflict as the months passed.

The survival of the group was itself a product of the context within which it operated. Antonov's druzhina not only exposed itself to minimal risk in its "expropriations" of collective farms and its attacks on government agents and Communist Party members, but also operated in an area where they could rely upon a network of personal contacts in the villages to provide needed information and occasional shelter and supplies. Another factor was the limited extent to which the provincial government and uezd administration in Kirsanov were willing or able to exact pressure on the druzhina. At the height of the Volunteer Army's advance on Moscow in July 1919, the Kirsanov revolutionary committee (revkom), an extraordinary body formed during periods of heightened alert, was less able to assign security or military units to deal directly with the threat posed by rebels such as Antonov, and the revkom was instead limited to public appeals: "It is time to say to all vile bandits: enough, lay down your guns, the revolution is in danger."[39] Faced with being overrun by counterrevolutionary forces, provincial authorities in Tambov authorized local soviet and Communist Party officials to take hostages from among the local population to be punished in case of further attacks and disruptions caused by "bandits" such as Antonov and his men. Such methods for controlling "bandit" attacks remained the practice of the overstretched provincial administration until the autumn of 1919, when the revkom in Kirsanov uezd finally mobilized local Communist Party personnel to form a special armed unit that would be charged with the capture or elimination of Antonov's druzhina. No sooner had this unit of Communist Party "volunteers" been formed and issued rifles and equipment than provincial Military Commissariat officials in Tambov mobilized the Kirsanov antibanditry unit for service on the southern front. The hunt for Antonov and his druzhina was once again grounded.

The hunt regained impetus two months later, when in October 1919 Antonov claimed the most significant scalp of his ten-month-old campaign. The former chairman of the Tambov Soviet executive committee, M. D. Chichkanov, had only recently been relieved of his administrative responsibilities after the damaging raid by White cavalry forces into Tambov Province in August. Initially accused of partial responsibility for the failure of Red Army forces to hold the provincial capital of Tambov, Chichkanov was first relieved of his post during investigations into the affair. Although he was later vindicated by an official tribunal, Chichkanov nevertheless remained on leave from his post as executive committee chairman, during which time he was officially recuperating from "nervous disorders," which, if not a convenient euphemism to permit Chichkanov's graceful exit from provincial politics, presumably arose from the tense controversy surrounding recent events. While hunting with friends on 14 October, Chichkanov was brutally murdered, along with a companion, another senior administration figure and Communist Party member. The murder was immediately attributed to Antonov, both because it was perpetrated at the heart of Antonov's area of operations, just south of Inzhavino, as well as the testimony by the lone survivor of the attack, a local pharmacist named Kliushchenkov. That Kliushchenkov, who was not a Communist Party member, was left untouched suggested that the murder was carefully planned and executed. Antonov never claimed responsibility for the assassination, nor did he ever deny it in his few known public pronouncements.

The response by provincial officials to the assassination was dramatic and decisive in light of their previous unwillingness to confront the threat posed by Antonov. The head of the Special Section of the Tambov Cheka organization, M. S. Kedrov, was dispatched to the Inzhavino area along with V. M. Volobuev, chief of internal security forces in Tambov. Their investigations into the murder contributed to the momentum behind the campaign to deal once and for all with the Antonov problem in southeastern Tambov. Unable to call on necessary resources in Tambov Province, they appealed for outside assistance. By the end of October, the head of the Internal Security Administration in Moscow, Valabuev,

ordered a special unit of over 200 men with experience in "antibanditry operations" from Saratov Province to concentrate on the elimination of Antonov's
druzhina.[40] The efforts of this special unit, along with the attempts of Tambov
Cheka agents to locate and assassinate Antonov, continued for several weeks, yet,
despite their occasional success in eliminating individuals known or suspected to
have ties with Antonov, no decisive blow was delivered by state agents. Capturing
or killing Antonov, in particular, was "fiendishly difficult," in the words of the
Tambov Communist Party chairman, B. A. Vasil'ev—especially, he noted, when
"he has his people everywhere, even in the party committees and the organs of the
Cheka."[41] This last detail may have been a convenient excuse, especially when incompetence was frequently taken for subversion, but the frustration was likely to
have been palpable, neverthless.

Regardless of their failure to capture or kill Antonov, or indeed any of his closest
colleagues, provincial officials did force the druzhina and its leader to call upon all
its contacts and confidants in order simply to survive. While the state of siege,
which had been declared in Tambov in June 1919 as Denikin's forces threatened,
was rescinded in the province in January 1920, in Kirsanov the local administration
remained concentrated in the revolutionary committees, and curfews continued
to be enforced, as the effort to combat the "antonovists" demanded the continuation
of martial law in the uezd.[42] The Cheka and Internal Security agents continued
their operations until March 1920, during which time Antonov's group shrunk
considerably and their activities were likewise reduced. They remained within a
safe radius of Inzhavino, occasionally staying in villages with trusted individuals
or setting up camp in the wooded areas and swamps that characterize that stretch
of the narrow Vorona River valley.

Antonov was now established as the most prominent antigovernment political
figure in the province, although he had made few substantial calls for popular
support. Despite fears that he was preparing a major uprising against the Soviet
government in Tambov, no such direction was evident in the observable activities
of the druzhina in the first weeks of 1920. When the efforts to hunt down Antonov
were scaled back in early 1920, this was in proportion to the perceived threat he
represented to the Soviet government in the province. Attempts to capture and
kill Antonov were left to quickly organized posses of Communist Party members
in Kirsanov responding to reports of his presence in one locality or another. While
he remained a threat to the safety of government agents, he never truly threatened
to derail state operations in the countryside. It is only in hindsight that the provincial administration's efforts to track down Antonov and kill him could be consid-

ered passive, for by all appearances in early 1920 Antonov conformed neatly to the bandit stereotype that featured prominently in the rare occasions when his name appeared in the official press in Tambov.

~

IT IS ENTICING to examine what is known of Antonov's personal history for clues that can help us understand his fate as a rebel leader. Within the span of such a short life that would end so dramatically, it is tempting to chart those thirty years along a single vector culminating in a spectacular end that was part idealism and part violence. So much of this trajectory, though, was determined by circumstance and in response to rapidly changing conditions that Aleksandr Antonov could hardly have anticipated its course at any point. As we shall see in chapter 3, even when Antonov and his druzhina appeared to have accurately read the political context and their activities projected a sense of direction and purpose, their efforts were far from being an unmitigated success, and the group was forced to rely upon a variety of contingencies that favored their cause.

In this, Antonov's personal history provides an interesting parallel with the vectors of popular grievance and political mobilization that animated and sustained his followers. For there was nothing inevitable about the *antonovshchina* as a popular movement of violent protest against the Soviet government; such grievances had been evident from the very first days of the revolution in Tambov's village communities, as elsewhere in rural Russia, and while the character of these grievances had changed, they remained consistent enough to make localized outbursts of violence in the countryside a regular occurrence. Those grievances were complex and diffuse, and although intense, they were insufficient to create a movement like the *antonovshchina*. The type of collective identity required to sustain a large-scale popular movement had to be forged in the course of rebellion itself. Only through the practical demonstration and experience of rebellion would the insurgent leader truly find his feet, and only through practical experience would the partisan identity emerge as a basis for participation and solidarity among the villagers of the Tambov countryside.

CONSPIRATORIAL
DESIGNS

THE EVENT MOST COMMONLY IDENTIFIED as the starting point in the history of the Antonov insurgency involved government grain procurement agents and the villagers of the volost township of Kamenka, in the southeastern corner of Tambov uezd, a short distance from the railway line linking the provincial capital to the town of Balashov, in Saratov Province. Owing to its proximity to the railway, Kamenka emerges as a typical sort of village that would have suffered the full weight of state demands throughout the civil war period for grain and other obligations, as state agents were often reluctant to venture too far afield from their strongholds tied to the transport system.

When, in mid-August 1920, state procurement agents were attacked by locals upon leaving the village of Kamenka, the incident would not, at first glance, have appeared extraordinary to provincial officials. The beginning of the procurement campaign had been anticipated by grain producers and state officials for several weeks, as targets had been announced in July, before the harvest. The announcement of these targets aroused a storm of protest, from village communities and local officials alike, who protested the basis for such obligations in a year when bad weather had dimmed the prospects for a healthy yield from an area of fields already suffering from three years of civil strife.[1] These fears were voiced in town and country alike and were the source of regular comment in the provincial newspapers.[2] As early as May, when a particularly dry spring season had stunted the growth in the recently sown fields, the state newspaper, *Izvestiia*, attempted to dampen the anxiety shared throughout the province:

> At the present time, it is clearly noticeable that the fields are suffering from a lack of moisture, as there has yet to be a single good rain since the very beginning of spring. Some are already prepared to put the blame on the "godless" Bolshevik government, while others explain the dry soils by pointing to the heavy winds that dried out the fields early in the season. Obviously, the latter explanation is the most plausible, rather than the one which carries the "political theme." With a good sprinkle of rain, everything will quickly be revived. As yet, we have no reason to declare it a bad harvest.[3]

Even though the concerns over the harvest served as a backdrop to all protests against the planned procurement campaign, the experience of similar campaigns during the harvest months of the previous two years instructed state officials to expect resistance, often violent resistance. The autumn of 1918 had seen a wave of uprisings overtake the countryside of nearly every uezd locality in Tambov, which did much more to upset the development of local soviet administration in the province than to upset the procurement campaign for 1918–1919. In the following year, the campaign had been severely compromised by a major incursion by the counterrevolutionary White Army into the province. As a result of the destruction and destabilization caused by Mamontov's raid, the 1919–1920 procurement campaign was delayed for several weeks, then pursued with a ruthless haste that did much to scar relations between the state and village communities of Tambov. While resistance to the procurement efforts in the countryside was not nearly on the scale seen in the previous year, the 1919–1920 campaign was instructive for provincial authorities, particularly in the local offices of the Food Commissariat. The needs of the state during times of civil war must be satisfied over and above the "localist" concerns of individual grain producers and rural communities; and in the end, cooperation could not be expected when state demands were made.

These two experiences—the wave of uprisings in Tambov (and in several other Soviet provinces at the time) that blighted the autumn of 1918, and the experience of Mamontov's raid—had a considerable influence on the response of provincial administrators when events in August and September 1920 began to unfold. Already in August, before the incident in Kamenka, serious rural disturbances had been reported in Morshansk uezd, where agents of the Food Commissariat and the Communist Party were attacked by locals, and where the village communities had proven especially resilient in their defiance to the state. Memories of 1918 could hardly be avoided, as the disturbances arose in localities that had played a central role in the disorders and violence of that autumn season.[4]

Likewise, when further disturbances broke out in Kamenka, to the south of the provincial capital, by all appearances they were of a sort with the 1918 events. The attack on the requisition squad outside Kamenka forced government officials to retreat to the village once more, so soon after having carried out a sweep through the community for reserves of grain. In this retreat to Kamenka, they were joined by another government patrol engaged in antidesertion measures. The combined government force, within the village of Kamenka, was attacked once more, this time by an overwhelming number of villagers and locals. Only a small number managed to escape, the remainder falling victim to the wrath of the crowd that quickly assembled around the spectacle of violence. The spirit of the crowd carried over, it was reported, into speech making and declarations of radical defiance to the Soviet state, and the uprising immediately spread to neighboring communities.[5]

Perhaps with a view to the developing situation, and most certainly recalling the experience of 1918, provincial authorities sought to take decisive measures to contain the insurgency, particularly in Kamenka, at the heart of the grain-growing region in Tambov. On the evening of 21 August, soon after the events in Kamenka had been reported, a temporary military command was organized to plan and coordinate the state response. One of their first measures was to isolate a fourteen-volost area around Kamenka—a sort of containment zone—to be placed under a state of siege (*osadnoe polozhenie*). A modest military force, primarily composed of cadets from the local Tambov Twenty-first Reserve Regiment, was sent to Sampur, the major railway station nearest the insurgency, to reinforce the government troops already at the station, composed of Red Army regulars, requisition squad members, and village militia. The cadets of the Twenty-first, led by V. M. Vorob'ev, were instructed to continue along the rail line until the station at Rzhaksa, while the local Sampur force, under the command of one Nikol'skii, was told to move directly on Kamenka. It was hoped that an initial attack by the Nikol'skii group would force the insurgents in Kamenka southward, where they would be intercepted by the second Red Army force under Vorob'ev.

The initial attack on Kamenka, though, was thwarted, as Nikol'skii's men were met some twenty versts north of Kamenka by insurgents and were forced to retreat to their base in Sampur. Vorob'ev's men also fell back toward Sampur when the news of the initial failure reached them. The following day, after receiving another sixty men on horseback as reinforcement, Vorob'ev's force again tried to enter Kamenka, but once more they were rebuffed and took shelter in the village of Chakino, where they were subjected to periodic sniping throughout the night from armed insurgents located on the outskirts of the village. The Red Army force under Vorob'ev was only able to leave Chakino the following day, after the timely arrival of government soldiers armed with mounted machine guns on railcars.

The government's efforts proved meager in the short run, and the insurgency began to spread from village to village, as armed men traveled to neighboring communities to sound the tocsin of rebellion. More soldiers to strengthen the state force in the region of Kamenka were difficult to find. In Kirsanov, one of the uezds whose border was quickly being engulfed by the insurgency, local officials reported that they were unable to mobilize a force to contribute to the counter-insurgency and that such a move would compromise the security of the town of Kirsanov itself. In Borisoglebsk, another uezd bordering the conflict, a force of just over 100 was dispatched north to the region of Kamenka. While this infantry company was a mixture of Red Army reservists and recently armed Communist Party members, the Borisoglebsk force was able to enter Kamenka on the evening of 24 August and encountered very little resistance in occupying the village.

While a certain peace may have descended over Kamenka, the insurgency continued to engross the fourteen-volost region of containment initially designated by the military command. The Tambov military commissar, P. I. Shikunov, traveled to Sampur, where he sought to establish a command post nearer to the area of the insurgency. He was joined by P. P. Gromov, a senior official in the provincial Cheka organization. That same evening, Gromov's superior, Traskovich, was in Tambov, attending a meeting of the Presidium of the Tambov soviet executive committee and the Communist Party at which the Cheka chief was openly criticized for his organization's failures. In light of the stubborn resilience of the insurgents, the Cheka was faulted for not having yet established the identity of the rebels, who their leaders were, and what they were demanding. It was precisely this type of investigative work that Traskovich's colleague, Gromov, was to carry out in Sampur, and Traskovich subsequently admitted that the Cheka, and by implication the entire administration, had not concentrated on such intelligence work. It was only after nearly a week, following the government's failure to be resolute in responding to the insurgency, that state officials recognized a potential qualitative difference in the character of the present disturbances.

Following the meeting with his colleagues of the Tambov Presidium, Traskovich traveled to the Kamenka region with another group of armed reinforcements to inspect the situation. While confirming that all was secure in the immediate vicinity of Kamenka, Traskovich nevertheless warned his colleagues in Tambov on 27 August that the insurgency was far from over.[6] His colleagues were in little need of such a warning, as Traskovich learned the following day. Soviet employees and Communist Party members from the volost of Kniazhe Bogoroditskoe, only some twenty versts to the south, began to arrive in Tambov, having decided to evacuate following sustained attacks by rebel gangs. These attacks, so near the provincial capital, had seen the murders of the secretary of the volost soviet, a local agronomist, and an official from the uezd food commissariat. The same day, there were reports of new uprisings in northern Borisoglebsk uezd, expanding the scope of the disorders and destruction.[7] The inexorable spread of the insurgency inspired the military commissar, Shikunov, to draft an order intended to dampen the enthusiasm of village communities for contributing to the rebellion. "Order no. 5" identified twenty-two villages to be targeted for harsh retribution by government forces. Mass arrests of the adult male population, wholesale confiscation of private possessions, and the eventual burning of houses and buildings—effectively the destruction of these villages—constituted the creative response of the Military Commissariat in Tambov to the rebellion.

Traskovich told Shikunov on 28 August that it was unlikely that this order calling for such retribution and terror—"an order composed in such a spirit," as Traskovich put it—would be sanctioned by the provincial administration.[8] The military authorities on the scene went ahead and advanced the order for sanction but altered it to exclude specific reference to burning the designated villages. But the option remained open, and the will to do so remained. When the Cheka secretary in Tambov, Kulikov, asked whether retribution could be limited only to the insurgency's known "sympathizers" in the villages, the state official in Rzhaksa explained: "It will affect the entire population to a man, because in these villages everyone has participated and continues to participate in the insurgency. These villages must be wiped off the face of the earth."[9]

As the insurgency moved closer to the provincial capital, there was an emergency mobilization of Communist Party members to defend the city of Tambov. In particular, the murders of agents of the Food Commissariat in Kniazhe Bogoroditskoe volost, so near to the provincial capital, served as the impetus for the chairman of the Tambov soviet executive committee, A. G. Shlikhter, to travel to the volost to inspect for himself the nature of the disturbances, with "a clear focus on the interests of food supply." Accompanied by a small contingent of military cadets on horseback, Shlikhter set off on 30 August, to execute "food-supply terror" (*prodovol'stvennyi terror*), a curious choice of words that nevertheless communicates with a certain eloquence the chairman's conviction that the disturbances were wholly connected to the onset of the procurement campaign.

Traveling from village to village, Shlikhter and the unit of cadets encountered constant reminders of the instability and the air of defiance in the countryside. Advance parties of cadets would return with reports of small groups of rebels moving in and out of gullies and wooded areas, while the main unit was seemingly never out of the sight of villagers on horseback, taken to be "enemy scouts" shadowing the government force. The sound of church bells accompanied the unit's progress through the volost, warning of their approach. On their first day outside the provincial capital, occasional shots were fired at Shlikhter and his men, and they had brief confrontations with small groups of rebels. But these incidents were never beyond the ability of the government unit to control. The first night was spent in the large village of Koptevo, where they took shelter in the local church. After rising the next morning and crossing the bridge over the river that bisected the village, Shlikhter and his men met a significantly more serious group of insurgents. Evidently, as word had spread of the presence of the government force (which was relatively small at 50 men), local insurgents had coalesced into a large group estimated by Shlikhter at 500–600 men. The machine gun in the possession of the government unit was no longer a sufficient deterrent; Shlikhter and his men beat a hasty retreat back to the provincial capital, having managed to avoid any casualties.[10]

To provincial and military authorities in Tambov, the cadets represented the only reliable and capable armed force available to combat the rebellion. Despite the fact that the main garrison force in Tambov city numbered over 15,000 and the composite military force available in the province numbered over 33,000, only a small number of cadets were considered capable of fighting with any effectiveness against the rural insurgents. This much was brought home by the recent capitulation by a small garrison force in the Kirsanov village of Inzhavino, which was occupied by rebels after the garrisoned Red Army soldiers fled without firing a single shot, abandoning their guns and ammunition (including a machine gun) to the rebels.[11] It was precisely this type of behavior that was expected of most of the reserve Red Army soldiers available in Tambov, for they were either "deserters" or "natives of Tambov," as the Cheka chief, Traskovich, explained in a telegram to Red Army regional command in Orel.[12] This was particularly true of the large Twenty-first Reserve Rifle Regiment in Tambov, which contained some 11,000 "professional deserters," and where, in the estimation of the Military Commissariat, "the deserters regularly discuss the shortcomings of Soviet power, especially in the countryside."[13]

The suspect Twenty-first Regiment was one of those earmarked for transfer out of Tambov Province when Traskovich sent his telegram to Orel on 29 August requesting significant reinforcements, in the form of two battalions, to combat the uprising.[14] Requests for reliable troops, with a corresponding concern with removing potentially unreliable garrisoned forces, recalled the lessons learned from the brief and tragic experience with General Mamontov in August 1919, when the White cavalry corps unexpectedly attempted a raid behind the Red Army front lines in neighboring Voronezh Province. The triumph of the White cavalry was made simple by the capitulation of local Red Army units, composed (like most reserve forces) of one-time deserters. The most spectacular case was in Tambov city itself, which was occupied after the commander of the Fourth Rifle Brigade (and temporary commandant of the city) went over to the Whites with many of his officers and the defense of Tambov never materialized. Following the White cavalry raid into Tambov, many local officials were placed on trial for "defeatism" and other such charges, alongside the treacherous commander of the Fourth Rifle Brigade. While these local officials were spared a guilty verdict, the experience was fresh in the minds of many who remained in Tambov when confronted by the insurgency in August 1920, and this helps to explain their concern with securing reliable military units and sufficient firepower to deal with the situation.[15]

An essential part of the memory of Mamontov's raid in August 1919 was the sense shared by provincial officials that Tambov had been abandoned by the Red Army and by central authorities in Moscow. When Traskovich sent his initial telegram demanding military reinforcements, he included a request to have Red Army artillery stores in Tambov city and Morshansk opened up for use by the provincial Military Commissariat. The local Red Army officials controlling the artillery stores initially refused the requests of Traskovich and Gromov in Tambov, claiming that they had no authority to do so without sanction from Moscow.[16] While the Cheka was quick to act on his demand to have units from Tula, Riazan', and Saratov transferred to Tambov, they were silent on the request for artillery guns, shells, and rifle ammunition that were already located in Tambov but were outside the mandate of provincial authorities. After waiting nearly two days for a response, Traskovich and other officials in the Tambov Military Commissariat demanded that the arsenals be opened to combat the insurgency without the sanction of Moscow or Orel. In addition to seizing several hundred artillery shells and some 80,000 rounds of ammunition, provincial officials commandeered artillery guns from the local state repair works in Tambov. Informing Orel of his decision, Traskovich stated that the insurgency was nearly out of control and implied that the insurgents were threatening not only the strategically important gunpowder works located near Tambov city, but also the provincial capital itself.[17]

Orel, while granting Traskovich formal permission to access the Red Army arsenals, nevertheless remained critical of the provincial authorities as they confronted their latest crisis. At first Orel questioned whether Tambov actually had anyone sufficiently trained to operate artillery guns (there were a few, Traskovich pointed out), then insisted that the forces available in Tambov were sufficient to deal with a rural insurgency of such proportions: "Experience teaches that all that is required is one or two salvoes from the artillery guns, and all the bandits will scatter without putting up a fight."[18]

Such an understanding of the insurgency was difficult to square with reports coming from the countryside. From Kirsanov, military authorities were issuing reports claiming that the patchwork of units traversing the countryside had lost control of the entire southern half of the uezd. In Morshansk, it was reported, grain procurement work had come to a virtual halt, as village communities refused to cooperate with government agents, awaiting the "outcome" of the uprisings in Sosnovo, Pechaevo, and Zametchino regions. In Borisoglebsk uezd, a local official reported to Traskovich that there were two main insurgent groupings in the north of the uezd and that "the initiative is entirely in the hands of the rebels." The problem, in part, was coordination among the scattered military units the government had deployed. In Morshansk, for instance, the uezd center had completely lost contact with its military forces in the insurgent area, causing Traskovich to threaten Morshansk authorities with arrest if the situation was not corrected in short order.[19]

The problem confronting officials in Tambov developed in large part because of their initial belief that the disturbances were typical rural uprisings based largely in individual villages. With so many reports of rebels groups appearing in a variety of locations, and with a conviction that a corresponding show of force by the government would quickly dispel the threat, it was inevitable that the longer the insurgency lasted, the more scattered the government units on the ground would become. The commander of the Twenty-first Reserve Regiment, K. V. Brimmer, at the time in the Rasskazovo region of Kirsanov uezd, tried to press this point on officials in Tambov. In a conversation with Traskovich on 2 September, Brimmer stated: "Our experience in the struggle with banditry tells us that the more dispersed our forces across districts, the more frequent will be our misfortunes. . . . I would take another tack and concentrate all our forces to form a single fist and move to occupy one specific point, where we could destroy one enemy group with overwhelming force." The process would then continue, he explained, and the force would move to a second point on the map and concentrate on destroying the enemy there.[20]

Another problem, as in Borisoglebsk and Kirsanov, was a simple shortage of armed men. The arrival of reinforcements from Riazan, Tula, and Saratov was either delayed or simply disappointing. The Riazan unit had been hastily assembled just days before transport to Tambov, and according to Traskovich the unit was composed almost entirely of former deserters, with a distinctly "suspect" look. When Traskovich asked the unit's commander if he could vouch for the dependability of the soldiers, the commander reportedly answered: "I will make no such guarantees, it is possible they will refuse to fight peasants."[21] Borisoglebsk authorities claimed that they had only 135 men to handle rebels groups totaling nearly 600, while in Kirsanov the uezd military officials had only further Red Army capitulations to report following the brief occupation of Inzhavino by rebels. Even nearer to the uezd center, the significant village of Inokovka, located on the railway line connecting Kirsanov and Tambov city, was also occupied after rebels easily overwhelmed the government forces stationed there, reportedly killing seventeen soviet workers and Communist Party personnel.[22] Uezd officials began to sound the alarm as the rebels drew to within fifteen versts of the town of Kirsanov. In a telephone exchange with Nikolai Raivid, the secretary of the provincial RKP and a member of the recently established military soviet, officials in Kirsanov expressed their desire to begin preparations for an evacuation of the town, which only served to set off a heated altercation:

> *Tambov* [N. I. Raivid]: Comrade, you are only in a state of panic. How few forces do you have in Kirsanov that you are moved to begin fleeing from some simple bandits?
>
> *Kirsanov* [Sevostoianov et al.]: We have literally no forces. There are 120 armed security guards (*karaul*), but these are guards and are not reliable.
>
> *Tambov:* How many armed Communist Party members do you have, how many rifles, bullets, and bombs, and what does the cavalry regiment have?[23]
>
> *Kirsanov:* There are 60 armed Communists, rifles are either inoperative or without bullets, and we have no bombs. The cavalry regiment has nothing, and one squadron that was sent on Saturday to Inzhavino, armed with 30 rifles and the remainder with sabres, has disappeared following the occupation of Inzhavino. We have lost contact with all military units in the field.
>
> *Tambov:* What about the unit that departed Inokovka for Kirsanov?
>
> *Kirsanov:* No such unit bound for Kirsanov existed. The Inokovka unit has been acting entirely autonomously. Send troops immediately.

Tambov: What are the enemy's forces?

Kirsanov: One group of 500–600 men, the majority of whom are armed with rifles, bombs, and revolvers, and also have cavalry.

Tambov: OK, [Military Commissar] Shikunov has just arrived here, and we will consider the situation together. Two hours ago an infantry battalion set off for Inokovka, and if possible we will instruct them to continue on to Kirsanov. Brace yourselves, and don't allow yourselves to fall into a panic.

Kirsanov: Nobody here is panicking, but this type of situation requires all our courage. You should spend less time talking and making demands, because now it is the bandits who have taken control of events, and I am telling you now about what is going on with those bandits, about how this has been going on for nearly twenty days, and the bands are growing more and more confident while our units are only gradually pulling themselves together.

Tambov: Enough of this panicky conversation, the insurgency is not spreading. I am through here. All that is required has been done.

Kirsanov: Fine.[24]

Indeed, Raivid stated on the same day, in another conversation, that he was "convinced" that the government's efforts were satisfactory and that the rebels were isolated to two definable regions of the southeast of the province, Sampur-Rzhaksa (Tambov uezd) and Inzhavino-Inokovka (Kirsanov uezd). No new forces were required, he insisted, only ammunition, which was in desperately short supply.[25] His confidence, though, was unique amid reports of regular insurgent attacks and widespread violence—often of an alarming cruelty—that arrived from government agents and local administrations.[26]

While the local uezd officials may have felt abandoned by their superiors in Tambov, provincial authorities felt that the situation confronting them was being similarly dismissed by officials in Moscow and Orel. This was almost a perfect re-creation of the bureaucratic divisions that emerged during and immediately after the White cavalry raid in 1919. One man who was not a member of the provincial administration at that time but was now the chairman of the soviet executive committee, A. G. Shlikhter, traveled to Moscow to communicate directly to Lenin the seriousness of the situation. Shlikhter had sent telegrams reporting to Moscow about the insurgency, but Moscow's continued silence on the matter moved him to travel to the Soviet capital, recalling the regular visits made by provincial governors to Petrograd during the tsarist era.[27] Despite this long tradition in Russian public life, Shlikhter's decision to travel to Moscow on 8 September was no less extraordinary.

Before Shlikhter's departure, the provincial authorities sent a telegram to Moscow, explaining their situation and announcing the imminent arrival of the provincial soviet chairman:

> Tambov Province. For the past three weeks, an intense rebellion of peasants and deserters, orchestrated by the right SRs, has been ongoing in Kirsanov, Borisoglebsk, and Tambov uezds. Because of the acute shortage of troops, guns, and ammunition in the province, the recently organized military soviet has been unable to deal expediently with the insurgent movement, which has now reached a massive scale and threatens to continue its escalation and to overrun new territories. There have been instances in which state forces have been forced to retreat due to a shortage of rifles and ammunition. Thus far, the bands have killed upwards of 150 rural Communists and provisions workers, and they have seized from our small state military units up to 200 rifles and two machine guns. Four soviet farms have been sacked. All state grain procurement work has come to a halt. More than once, we have informed the regional military authorities in Orel, as well as the Cheka and Internal Security administration in Moscow, but to this date we have not received sufficient troop reinforcements or, most important, shipments of rifles. Therefore, we come to you as a measure of last resort.[28]

Several themes are condensed into this brief report, themes that were to continue to influence events for the remainder of the year. For the time being, we shall focus on the initial claim, in which Shlikhter communicates to Lenin and the All-Russia Soviet Executive Committee (VTsIK) that the rebellion has been created and orchestrated by the opposition socialist party, the Socialist Revolutionaries (PSR).

THE OUTBREAK OF THE INSURGENCY AND THE PSR

It is perhaps ironic that, at the same time Shlikhter departed for Moscow to deliver his report and to brief VTsIK and the Military Council (Revvoensovet), representatives of the Tambov PSR were taking part in a clandestine party conference in the Soviet capital. During the one-day conference, attended by only nineteen party members (nine of whom were based in Moscow itself), the Tambov delegates reported on party activities during 1920, including a description of their role in the ongoing insurgency.[29]

The reemergence of the PSR as an organized opposition in Tambov Province during the civil war was described by the Tambov delegates as arising when the PSR Central Committee, in the spring of 1920, called on local organizations to abandon exclusively "legal" work within the Soviet system.[30] In sanctioning the possibility of underground, clandestine opposition activity—a decision made with an eye to the imminent end of the White counterrevolution and the passing of the illusion that the Communist Party would be willing to tolerate rival socialist parties—PSR activists moved from their previously "nonpolitical" work in the consumer cooperatives and trade unions and embarked on openly contentious activities courting mass involvement. They signaled their intentions on the May Day holiday when they sent to the Tambov soviet executive committee a written protest concerning the treatment of industrial workers and peasants. A second written protest followed, again signed by the Tambov PSR organization. The provincial soviet authorities had no clear idea of the extent of the PSR organization in Tambov, for the once powerful party, which had clearly taken the lion's share of ballots in the 1917 Constituent Assembly elections and with such a history in the province in the early twentieth century, effectively melted away once the Bolsheviks took over the reins of government in Tambov in April 1918.

The prospects of an SR revival were made slightly more tangible during the failed "Week of the Labor Front," one of a long number of soviet-led shock campaigns to boost industrial production, held in June 1920. The outbreak of a strike in the city of Tambov, at the railroad car repair works (the largest employer in the city), marred the government's campaign, as did further demonstrations of opposition sentiment during rallies organized to mobilize support for the Labor Front in other uezd towns. "Shady individuals," wrote the uezd officials in Borisoglebsk during the campaign, "have begun their counterrevolutionary work, and they are finding stable footing among the masses."[31] At the September 1920 PSR conference, the Tambov delegates also reported having published two issues of the local party gazette, *Land and Freedom*, printed on the hectograph, the tried and true instrument of the underground political party. Two local party conferences had been successfully convened in 1920: one for Tambov uezd, with seven members participating, only four of whom were representing a local cell; and a second for the province as a whole, but which included representatives from only four organizations —three uezd PSR groups and one from Tambov city.[32] These organizational accomplishments must be considered modest at best and demonstrate the limited extent to which any PSR organization had survived the previous two years of Soviet rule in the province.

But alongside these traditional party activities were the novel pursuits of party activists in the countryside, the PSR's traditional base, particularly in a province such as Tambov. The PSR delegates reported to the September 1920 conference that they had been active in organizing party "brotherhoods," small and exclusive associations akin to the basic party cell that recalled the nascent rural associations organized by the PSR leader Viktor Chernov during his brief period of internal exile in the 1890s spent in Tambov Province.[33] The progress made with these brotherhoods was limited, as the delegates admitted they numbered "no more than ten" at the time of their report.

The real progress, it was believed, was being made in a second line of activity, the organization of "Unions of the Toiling Peasantry" (STKs) in the villages of Tambov Province. The project of organizing such unions was set out in a 13 May 1920 party circular, written by Viktor Chernov.[34] In describing their progress in promoting these new institutions, the Tambov representatives of the PSR were buoyant. Village STKs had been established in Kirsanov, Borisoglebsk, and Usman uezds, as well as in the northern uezds of the province. In Tambov uezd they were particularly successful, with the SR representative claiming that "one-half" of the volosts possessed an STK. (At the time, Tambov uezd was composed of fifty-eight volosts.) Evidently, this success in Tambov uezd encouraged the representatives to convene a regional conference of the STK, although with only four volost organizations participating.

As detailed to the delegates at the September conference, these organizational developments appeared impressive. But what was the intended purpose of the STKs? In their explanation, the Tambov delegates in Moscow specifically identified the two primary tasks for the STKs:

> [First,] removal of the Communist Party from power and placement of power in the hands of a new provincial government, which will be composed of representatives of the peasantry, the [trade] unions, workers' organizations and socialist parties, and which should work toward the convening of all-Russian congresses of the laborers, which will resolve the matter of the future form of government; second task—the full realization of the law on socialization of the land.

With the PSR officially banned by Soviet authorities in Russia, and with its leaders either in prison or on the run, there was little hope that legal work would be allowed to resume under the Communist regime. In its occasional pronouncements in the first months of 1920, the PSR Central Committee acknowledged this fact but never went so far as to endorse direct action against the Soviet government, preferring instead to stick to the policy of "organizing the masses" that had been settled upon at the party's Ninth Conference. This policy was the product of the idealism of many senior officials, who maintained a firm commitment to the idea of democratic socialism and a corresponding fear of the spontaneity of Russian popular movements, which were compromised by a significant strain of the violent and antidemocratic tradition in Russia. Thus, the STKs were envisioned as institutions that fostered democratic ideals and practice among the masses, ideals that would in time give rise to opposition strong enough to topple the Bolsheviks and principled enough to engender a democratic and socialist successor state.

But such a position failed to check several of the PSR's professed followers from charting their own course, some even going so far as to support avowed counterrevolutionaries as long as their program remained exclusively anti-Bolshevik.[35] The official line on the STKs, as reported in the PSR press, was that these "nonparty" institutions would facilitate a *prigovornoe dvizhenie*, that is, generally to focus popular opposition to the Soviet regime by orchestrating a petition campaign similar to that undertaken vis-à-vis the monarchy in 1905, in which village communities expressed their grievances. The description of the STKs offered by the Tambov delegates certainly went further than this, but the delegates underscored their conviction that these initiatives were in keeping with the spirit of the party, even recalling their commitment to the party's policy on socialization of the land.[36]

Still, these words offered by the PSR delegates referred to organizational activities through the summer of 1920. By the time of the conference in Moscow, the rebellion in Tambov Province was entering its fourth week. What tied the Tambov PSR to the rebellion, as the Soviet authorities now alleged? Certainly the conference delegates were true to their words when they urged party support for the rebellion in Tambov and for other such popular insurgencies against the Soviet regime. They defended the practice of terrorism against the Communists, in light of the Soviet government's use of such methods in suppressing the insurgencies. What they called "counterterror in defense of the peasantry" had already in fact been threatened in Tambov. On the same day as the conference in Moscow, Traskovich was informing his colleague, Raivid:

> The SRs have sent to the presidium of the soviet executive committee an anonymous letter in which they demand that the red terror be halted, and they give us a three-day deadline. If their demand is not met, they are threatening their own terror against Communists and Jews, particularly targeting Shlikhter, me [Traskovich], you [Raivid], Zbruev, Shikunov, and all the other comrades, and they express their confidence that nothing and no one will help us [in fighting the insurgency], not the cadets, the recently arrived soldiers, nor the machine gun–mounted automobiles. What do you have to say about this?

Raivid replied curtly, quoting a Russian proverb: "If it's wolves that scare you, then stay out of the forest."[37]

Such actions by PSR members in Tambov city, though, were seemingly in response to the ongoing clashes between government forces and village communities. So what of the rural STKs organized during the summer of 1920? The PSR delegates at the September conference are curiously silent on this matter. In fact, only one contemporary source mentions the activity of these STKs following the outbreak, and that source contends that they were quickly "liquidated" by the provincial Cheka in the weeks following the first clashes. This claim was made by Iurii Podbel'skii, a Tambov native and senior SR activist, who at the time of the outbreak was living in Moscow while maintaining regular links with colleagues and friends in Tambov. Podbel'skii made his claim in a letter to the chairman of the Moscow Soviet Executive Committee (Lev Kamenev) in July 1921, as Podbel'skii was being held on charges of conspiracy, charged with being among the PSR leaders of the Tambov rebellion.[38] In protesting his innocence, Podbel'skii, who had written an article on the Tambov rebellion for the main PSR journal published in Prague,[39] claimed that his party had nothing to do with the insurgency. More important, while not contesting the notion that the STKs were intended to lead a movement against the Soviet government, Podbel'skii claimed that the provincial Cheka had efficiently dispersed the peasant unions which had been organized in the summer of 1920—that is, before they could even react to the violent events that were consuming the southern half of the province. Therefore, any notions that the PSR had instigated, let alone been the leaders of, the rebellion were mistaken.

Leaving aside questions about the veracity of an account formed as part of a protest of innocence produced while in jail, there are two points worth raising about Podbel'skii's claim about the STKs. First, Podbel'skii is the only source that makes this claim. There are no contemporary documents from the Soviet side, let alone from the provincial Cheka itself, that attest to the dismantling of a network of PSR unions. What is more, and this is the second point, it is doubtful that the provincial Cheka in Tambov would have been up to the task, even if they knew that such a network existed.[40] As we have seen, the head of the Tambov Cheka, Traskovich, had come under heavy criticism early on for his organization's inability to pinpoint the nature of the insurgency and the identity of its leaders, and the Cheka was also subsequently criticized for having done nothing to prevent the rebellion. In fact, the future Moscow plenipotentiary who would take over the counterinsurgency effort in February 1921, Vladimir Antonov-Ovseenko, called the Tambov Cheka organization an "utter disgrace," a judgment echoed by others as they reflected on the rebellion from the perspective provided by the passage of several months.[41]

All these doubts point to a central problem with evaluating the involvement of the PSR in the first period of the insurgency: to what extent can the PSR in Tambov be considered a cohesive organization? The point has been made before with regard to the Socialist Revolutionaries. While enjoying huge popularity and recognition among the majority of the people (particularly in an agrarian country such as Russia), it had lacked a viable organization, especially at the local level, throughout nearly all of its history in mass politics. This critical insight explains how the most popular party in the country, as evidenced by the Constituent Assembly elections in November 1917, could turn into a "nonfactor" through much of the civil war. Theirs was a popularity based more on association than on allegiance, particularly in a place such as Tambov, where the PSR had never experienced the type of competition for sympathies and votes that would have stimulated the development of a viable organization in the villages and volosts.[42]

This is partially demonstrated in the first weeks of the insurgency by a letter addressed to Lenin and Sovnarkom, sent by Ivan Gaevskii—"and comrades"—who claimed to represent the Kirsanov uezd organization of the PSR. In this letter, Gaevskii and (presumably) the other Kirsanov SRs attempted to speak for the insurgency, explaining the goals and demands of the rebels. The result is a confusing document, not least because its audience is evidently intended to be Soviet authorities in Moscow. They wrote to Lenin,

> We are fighting not on behalf of individual factories, nor for land, but for our beloved freedom. There lies the essence of our wishes. In order to defend this, we must maintain strict discipline at the present moment. Everything we do should work in support of our general interests, and disgraceful behavior and drunkenness must not be tolerated. If drunkenness is to set in, then it is better to abandon now our war for beloved freedom. At present, we are gathering together deserters, but these same deserters do not see how we are now conducting ourselves worse than hooligans.[43]

Gaevskii's letter, seemingly criticizing and celebrating the insurgency in equal measure, demonstrates how the PSR in Tambov cannot be considered an organization at the heart of a conspiracy that gave rise to the rebellion. While there may have been individuals with PSR affiliation or sympathies who emerged as active participants in the rebellion, the majority of party members were responding to the outbreak of the conflict. The result, in part, were responses such as Gaevskii's, whereby individuals or groups of SR members and sympathizers sought to interpret the seemingly elemental insurgency and to articulate a set of legitimate goals or ideals to be paired with the grievances animating the violence. Such a variety of responses reveals a PSR organization in the province that was hardly in the midst of coordinating an elaborate conspiracy to overthrow the Soviet regime in Tambov.

If we can discount the direct role of the PSR organization—not only in a conspiracy, but in the creation of a significant network of STKs—we are still left with the persistent allegation of a connection between the PSR and the insurgency. This charge centers upon the man who links the party to the rebellion in all versions of the events. This is Aleksandr Stepanovich Antonov, the rural terrorist of the Tambov countryside through much of the civil war period.

EVALUATING ANTONOV'S ROLE

According to Iurii Podbel'skii, Aleksandr Antonov had claimed throughout much of the summer of 1920 to represent the PSR. In claiming this association, Antonov was leading a campaign to organize groups of villagers for an imminent insurgency against the Soviet state. The implication of the information provided by Podbel'skii, of course, was that Antonov may have been easily linked to the PSR, but his activities were not directly connected to the party and its efforts in the countryside. Going even further, Podbel'skii asserted that any and all who later claimed an affiliation with the PSR after the outbreak of the rebellion in Tambov had no formal connection to the party, thus absolving the organization from any responsibility for the violence against the Soviet state.[44]

In the version of events elaborated by Podbel'skii, Antonov assumed a significant role in the actual uprising only after the provincial organization of the STK (and by implication the Tambov PSR organization) had refused to sanction the uprising that began in Kamenka. Meeting with a group of local villagers in Khitrovo, a village located not far to the north of the Kamenka area, a regional committee of the STK, under the influence of two senior members of the Tambov PSR who were present, declared that the organization would not support the insurgents in Kamenka, owing to their clearly hopeless situation. The declaration by the regional STK, though, did nothing to halt the escalation of the conflict. According to Podbel'skii, the real force of the rural insurgency was focused on a growing "peasant march" on the provincial capital, Tambov.[45] Gaining speed and strength like a tumbling snowball, local villagers from the Kamenka area began moving north toward Tambov, taking in new insurgents all the time until, not fifteen versts from the city, they were forcibly repelled and dispersed by reinforced government troops.

In this way, according to Podbel'skii's version of events, the "spontaneous" phase of the uprising came to an end as the defeated peasant rebels retreated to their native districts. It was at this time that Antonov emerged onto the scene, together with loyal and organized units of local deserters and villagers, to assume the mantle of the insurgency, in spite of the recommendations of the Tambov PSR and the provincial STK organizations.[46] In Podbel'skii's words: "Antonov . . . arrived on the scene only after the elemental peasant movement had been suppressed by Soviet forces, thus beginning the partisan phase of the Tambov rebellion."[47]

In actual fact, Antonov had been rallying anti-Soviet sentiment in the villages of Kirsanov and Tambov uezds for nearly two years, focusing particularly on the ever-increasing pool of young men who had evaded military mobilization to the Red Army, or who had grown disaffected with military service in the reserve garrisons and labor units found throughout Soviet territory. While Antonov's core group of active followers (his druzhina) remained small during these early months, they nevertheless did court popular support as early as the summer of 1919. Statements taken in 1921 from arrested participants in the rebellion attest to occasional gatherings of villagers that were addressed by Antonov and members of his cohort urging young local men not to serve in the Red Army and to resist the demands of the Soviet state, such as for grain.[48]

One of these meetings in mid-1919, according to many eyewitnesses, was attended by several thousand local villagers from a four-volost area in Kirsanov uezd. There, one of Antonov's closest associates and a native of the region, Ivan Ishin, addressed the crowd, urging them never to agree to serve in the Red Army, despite the encroachments of the counterrevolutionary White armies from the south. Such an extraordinary meeting was made possible, according to these eyewitnesses, by the local soviet administration, headed by men known to be SRs, or at least anti-Bolshevik sympathizers, who turned a blind eye to the proceedings.[49] But even if the complicity of known or suspected SRs was required, we should not conclude that the PSR as an organization was intimately connected to Antonov's activities. Indeed, in some cases, the soviet officials who effectively worked with Antonov were former members of the uezd militia in Kirsanov, suggesting that a shared personal history with Antonov was more significant than a strict party affiliation. While these two factors are not mutually exclusive, the fact that such activities went against the prescribed policy of the PSR Central Committee again illustrates the independence of rural and local PSR members.[50]

Antonov's activities in 1919 had little to do with organized conspiracy, at least concerning the outbreak of the rebellion in 1920. According to one Soviet source, Antonov and his druzhina were calling such meetings to encourage deserters to organize their own "self-defense" units for the villages.[51] This may well have been the case, even if none of the eyewitnesses mentions such concrete initiatives. While Antonov and the druzhina continued their terrorist activities through 1919, their attacks on Communist Party personnel, requisition squads, and antidesertion patrols remained largely free of involvement from the surrounding community. And while the size of the druzhina fluctuated, it never sought to assume a mass form, remaining a limited but effective nemesis for government agents in southeastern Tambov Province.[52] But this hardly excludes the possibility that other *druzhiny*, in part inspired by Antonov, were similarly active in the region. The work of government agents in the countryside was structured, in large part, by a continual stream of information relating to "green" attacks in the region, or rumors of Antonov's possible presence in the vicinity.[53]

The turn of the year 1920 brought a change in direction. This was signaled by a letter, postmarked 18 February 1920, sent by Antonov and his druzhina to the offices of the Kirsanov uezd militia. In the letter, Antonov addressed the "Comrade Communists" about what he considered to be slanderous treatment of himself and his men. With words steeped in irony, Antonov taunted the Kirsanov militia— few of whose members would have known Antonov during his days as militia chief—and, perhaps unwittingly, revealed that a change in the orientation of his activities had been gestating:

> It has been brought to our attention, Comrade Communists, that in wishing to slander myself and my comrades before the toiling peasantry and all of free-thinking Russia, we have been labelled "bandits," ascribing to us participation in the robberies that have plagued the volosts of Treskino, Kalugino, Kurdiukov, and other volosts contiguous to this region. Such impertinence is worthy of the bureaucrats of the old regime. I am more than certain that, if you are indeed veritable democrats, and that if you look deep into your souls, glistening as they are with the sacred blood of the toilers, you will say to yourselves: "Motivated by weakness and spite, we sling unmerited accusations, slurring the names of citizens we know full well to be undeserving of such disgrace, indeed, are not even capable of such crimes." Insofar as we know of the desire of the Communists to tarnish our names before the toiling population, desires that have by no means been realized, I hope that in the future they persist. For this acts as a further guarantee that the politically conscious toilers of Russia will continue to gravitate toward us. As evidence that we are not among those bands that engage in looting, we direct your attention to the following facts: the Karavain band, under the leadership of Berbeshkin, a man well known to you, has now been liquidated by us. The troops under Berbeshkin and his lieutenant Artiushko can be found in the area of Kenzar', 100 *sazhens* to the right off the road

that connects the villages of Kurdiukov and Rasskazovo. Other such bands, if you ask, can be delivered to a specific location, or can simply be revealed to you; moreover, we consider it our duty to inform you that in the struggle against criminality, we are always ready to extend to you our assistance. Concerning this offer, you can communicate your reply via *Izvestiia,* or by some other means.

Concerning the above, I ask that the uezd committee of the Bolshevik Party be informed. Sincerely, Antonov.[54]

As mentioned in chapter 2, officials in Kirsanov had devoted much attention to the elimination of Antonov before the arrival of this letter, extending martial law in the uezd and assigning a Cheka unit exclusively to the pursuit of the rural terrorist. In one instance, at the end of 1919, they had come tantalizingly close to killing Antonov in the village of Inokovka, a fact that may have only strengthened Antonov's reputation.[55]

It may have been as a result of such pressure that Antonov turned to a more assertive stance, as signaled by the letter reproduced above. There is also, to be sure, a measure of mockery in the letter, as Antonov informs the Kirsanov officials of his own measures taken in the "war on banditry." As the Kirsanov Cheka conceded, the above-mentioned Karavain band had been "liquidated," as Antonov claimed. Nothing is known of this incident, but it suggests the likelihood of Antonov's organizational work among deserters, creating "self-defense *druzhiny,*" and the further possibility that one of those *druzhiny* devoted itself to robbery. On the other hand, it is similarly likely that the Karavain band was simply another gang like hundreds of others throughout the civil war countryside. Although less likely, the Karavain band may have even been a rival gang to Antonov's, thus falling victim to a sort of civil war–era turf war.[56]

If the full intent of the letter were to taunt local authorities, it would explain why it was sent to the uezd militia in Kirsanov rather than to a more senior or prominent office within the province. Yet, revealed in the letter are more profound claims signaling that the rural terrorist was looking to assume a more significant role for his activities. Consistently belittled in the local press and in official pronouncements as a "bandit," Antonov directly addresses the question of his worthiness. Questioning the credentials and conduct of the Soviet authorities—whether they are "veritable democrats"—and invoking the legitimacy of the "toiling masses" who support them, the letter asserts Antonov's own revolutionary credentials at the expense of the claims of the Communist Party. To that question of worthiness, the letter adds the assertion that the people are "gravitating" toward the opponents of the Communist Party, such as Antonov, and that that movement is gaining momentum all the time. Finally, in announcing the liquidation of the Karavain gang, and cheekily offering to perform similar policing measures in the future, Antonov and his group are demonstrating the extent to which it is they, and not the Soviet authorities, who are in control of the Tambov countryside.

It would be wrong to suggest that these were more than just assertions. Antonov was ultimately an outlaw who, for all his contacts within the government apparatus and his popularity in the villages, was still a local terrorist whose activities were losing relevance as the civil war progressed. On the national scale, the anti-Bolshevik movement was retreating further and further. There was little in the way of organization or vision offered by the opposition parties, both within the province and nationwide, and the longer Antonov's band remained a small-scale enterprise engaged in terrorism, the more the "bandit" label would gain credibility.[57] And this would be damaging to Antonov's standing in the countryside, as well as injurious to his pride as a veteran of the Russian revolutionary movement. Even those members of Antonov's band without similar credentials would have to question the trajectory of their activities, especially as pressure from the authorities was mounting.

In April 1920, an uprising occurred in the Kirsanov village of Ramza, an event that failed to set off another round of rural disturbances but is often considered an early attempt by Antonov to raise a popular insurgency in the province. A moderate-sized village in the center of the uezd, Ramza had played host to multiple attacks by rural gangs and was located in the heart of the territory frequented by Antonov's druzhina whose forest, lakes, and marshland provided them ample cover. Even though rural rebels were a common feature in this part of the province, armed bands had never entered the villages of central Kirsanov and made direct overtures to the local population.[58]

Over the Easter holiday, a band of such armed men entered Ramza, led by six primary figures, of whom Mikhail Parkin was identified as the leader, dressed as he was in the long black leather overcoat typically associated with the Cheka and one of the preferred trappings of certain opponents of the Soviet state.[59] The Easter holiday was a particularly favorable time to attempt to incite rebellion, being not only a period of religious ritual and community celebration, but also a peak period for desertion by military conscripts, as Red Army soldiers (particularly those from nearby reserve garrisons) returned to their native villages to help with the spring sowing as well as to participate in the festivities. Without any clear explanatory circumstances, such as the presence of a requisition squad in the village, a band of some twenty rebels entered Ramza and assembled a crowd of villagers. There they explained that they had "secret" government documents regarding a planned

"Week of Death," during which the Communist Party had ordered wholesale killings in local communities to coincide with the "counterrevolutionary" religious festival of Easter. Passing out rifles to some of the villagers at the meeting, Parkin and his colleagues urged the crowd to rise up and strike out against their local Communist Party members.[60]

The crowd gathered around the volost soviet, and Parkin's men, supported by thirty or forty armed villagers, set upon the soviet offices and archive, destroying documents and murdering the Communist Party members inside. In all, nine were killed, as Parkin's men and the villagers also attacked the families of the party members, murdering two children, aged two and eight. A small group of villagers were dispatched to the neighboring village of Burovetsina, with the aim of spreading the uprising. Burovetsina did not respond to this overture. By nightfall, a squad of sixteen men, led by the uezd militia chief, Maslakov, entered the village, and found the band of rebels gone and the village in an anxious, but passive, state.[61] The next morning, Maslakov convened an assembly at which he explained the absurdity of the rumored "Week of Death." Allegedly, the villagers responded by surrendering twenty-three men who had taken an active part in the violence.[62]

A separate militia detachment conducted a search for the rebels, which led them to a nearby lake (presumably either Chernets or Il'men' lakes), and a lake island suspected to be a base for the rebels. When the militia patrol set off on small boats to reach the island, they came under a barrage of rifle shots and small explosives, during which two militiamen were severely injured and the group was forced to retreat. The arrival of an artillery cannon and machine gun improved the situation for the government forces, and an extended bombardment, as if laying siege on a medieval fortress, subdued the resistance from the rebels on the island. The landing party found the bodies of eight men killed as a result of the siege, as well as a small arsenal of bombs and firearms. The actual leaders and members of the armed band involved in the Ramza incident, though, were not among those killed. Instead, they were caught in separate searches in the surrounding countryside over the following days. In all, nineteen men fell into the hands of the uezd militia and the Cheka, the last of whom was Fedor Makarov, killed in a shoot-out with authorities in the village of Kabrinskoe.[63]

Investigations and interrogations of those caught found that the uprising were not part of a coordinated attempt by the so-called Green Army to spark a general rebellion against the Soviet government in the province. Despite the fact that the violence occurred in the heart of the territory dominated by Antonov and his druzhina, investigators found no evidence to connect the instigators of the Ramza uprising to Antonov.[64] Instead, according to their testimony, the actions by Parkin's men were prompted by the desire to exact revenge on the local Ramza Communist Party cell, whose members had killed three men associated with the band in a raid on the group's hideout.[65] Inciting the local population to violence was the tactic chosen by this group of rebels for vengeance, although it was maintained by later investigations that the majority of the killings were done by members of the band, and not by locals. On 22 July, all nineteen rebels were executed by firing squad.[66]

Having had nothing to do with the failed uprising in Ramza, it was found, Antonov and his activities remained largely unknown to Soviet authorities in the province during the summer of 1920. Reports from agents concerning the organization of a "green army" by Antonov in the region of southwestern Kirsanov uezd were as detailed as certain sources could offer, and it was subsequently appreciated that the "bandit movement" had entered a subdued phase following the Ramza uprising.[67] Yet, as members of the PSR in Tambov were aware, the terrorist Antonov was active, invoking the authority of the party in his efforts. According to Podbel'skii, Antonov began organizing "party cells" just as the PSR was rejuvenating its own network of contacts in the countryside, and Antonov had succeeded in creating such cells in Tambov and Kirsanov uezds, although it was reported that these numbered no more than ten. In doing so, he claimed to be working on behalf of the PSR, even identifying himself as a party member. For this transgression, senior PSR representatives in the province offered Antonov a choice: either stop invoking the authority of the PSR in his activities, or submit to the party line and continue with "'peaceful' organizational and cultural work" among the peasantry. To be sure that Antonov was safely marginalized if he agreed to submit to the party line, the representatives also insisted that he confine his organizational work to the northern uezds of the province, well outside his established base of activities. This, though, was never an issue, as Antonov rejected the ultimatum.[68]

A later source confirms that the Tambov PSR had confronted Antonov during the summer of 1920. Following his investigation into the outbreak of the rebellion in October 1920, the Tambov Communist Party chairman and member of the provincial military soviet, Raivid, concluded that the PSR had revoked Antonov's party membership during the summer owing to his activities in organizing a conspiracy.[69] Raivid and Podbel'skii could have been touching on the same incident, but each had separate assumptions regarding Antonov's formal political affiliations, with Podbel'skii insisting that Antonov was not a party member and Raivid assuming that he always was an SR. According to individuals who witnessed Antonov's efforts in organizing a conspiracy, he traded heavily on his personal history as an SR activist.

In the Kirsanov volost of Kalugino, one of the villages in the heart of Antonov's area of activity, the first meeting arranged by Antonov took place in July 1920. The meeting was an extremely limited affair, in which Antonov, Ivan Ishin, and Antonov's brother, Dmitrii, met with four locals who were known to be in sympathy with the opponents of the Communist Party. Among them was Pavel Egorevich Akimov, a forty-eight-year-old villager from Novoe Kalugino. According to his testimony after his arrest in 1921, the first meeting was first addressed by Ishin (a native of Kalugino), who spoke of the Communists' treatment of the peasantry and the need to depose the Communist-dominated Soviet government. The legitimate authority remained with the Constituent Assembly, which must be reconvened. Following this, Aleksandr Antonov rose to speak, concentrating on his own involvement in the political struggle, both against the Communists and as an SR activist working underground since 1905 against the imperial regime. Concluding this first meeting, the conspirators assured their small audience that "throughout Russia everything has already been arranged, and only Tambov Province remains to be organized."

Two weeks passed before a second meeting with the rebel leaders in Kalugino. During this time, two local schoolteachers, Belugin and Anikin (both later accused of having connections with the PSR), began propagating rumors of an imminent insurrection against the Communist government, to begin with a signal from the "center." As to what this "center" represented, Akimov's testimony is unclear. But at the second meeting Ivan Ishin was more concrete about their designs. According to Akimov, "Ishin told us at this meeting that there remains only a little time before the rebellion begins, first in the center and at the front, and that we have three days to speak with hiding deserters, in order to prepare them for the rebellion." So over the next three days (the actual dates are unknown), the local conspirators in Kalugino worked on gathering together known deserters and other volunteers, organizing them into small groups, and distributing weapons.[70]

This same story was repeated in other localities in the weeks leading up to the outbreak of the insurgency, primarily in villages where Antonov and his associates already had established firm contacts among prominent members of the community. Podbel'skii contends, in his article on the insurgency, that many of these cells organized by Antonov quickly broke with the rebel leader when they learned that, in fact, the PSR was not preparing for an insurgency.[71] There is little evidence to support this claim. It seems possible, instead, that Antonov believed he was acting according to the designs of the PSR and that his influence was formidable enough, particularly in southwestern Kirsanov uezd, to see his voice carry the authority of

PSR intentions. Antonov's activities in organizing an armed conspiracy against the Soviet government could well have been undertaken with the confidence that he was acting in accordance with the designs of the PSR Central Committee, which had recently called on its local organizations (in fairly ambiguous terms) to abandon strictly "legal" work under Communist rule. Thus, according to this interpretation, senior PSR officials in Tambov, in rejecting the prospect of armed insurrection in the near future, were themselves misreading the intentions of the PSR Central Committee. If Antonov's statements concerning the leadership role of "the center" remained vague, as recorded in statements from eyewitnesses, it bears remembering the indications given in his February 1920 letter to the Kirsanov militia that the rural terrorist held a fine-tuned sense of his own revolutionary credentials and that he harbored ambitions for his activities. If, as seems likely, Antonov was the one misreading the intentions of the PSR Central Committee in undertaking preparations for an armed insurgency, it is not difficult to understand why he did so.

One area where Antonov's influence was most robust was along the border of Kirsanov and Tambov uezds. In this region, his contacts among former PSR activists were particularly strong, although these individuals were not among those serving in the soviet administrations, as in the Kalugino and Treskino area. Instead, in the region of Kamenka, Aleksandrovka, and Verkhotsen'e, the local Communist Party cell, which filled the vital posts in the local soviet administration, had been under a constant threat from their opponents in the local community. These included individuals with whom Antonov had close and long-standing ties, such as Grigorii Naumovich Pluzhnikov and Efim Ivanovich Kazankov. Over the months previous to the outbreak of the uprising, the Communist Party cell in this area had suffered considerably at the hands of these local opponents, enduring multiple assassination attempts (some of which were successful) and living under the constant threat of violence.[72]

According to a former member of this local Communist Party cell (Toporov), such acts of terror on the part of opponents combined with the despotic activities of the various "agents" of Soviet power in the countryside—the grain procurement squads and antidesertion patrols—to leave his part of the province virtually without local soviet government. This permitted the likes of Antonov to cultivate a safe "nest" in the area of Kamenka.[73] According to most accounts, the uprising in August 1920 effectively began in Kamenka. Most single out opponents of the Soviet regime in Kamenka as having begun the uprising, declaring the initial clash between grain procurement agents and local peasants to be the first event of a major

anti-Soviet insurgency.[74] In his October 1920 report on the outbreak of the uprising, Raivid advances much the same story, adding that the conspirators in Kamenka
were inclined to declare the rebellion, in part, because of mounting pressure in the
area from the local agents of the Cheka in Sampur.[75] Once again, such claims involving the provincial organization of the Cheka are likely to be false. According
to Toporov, the Kamenka Communist Party member, provincial officials had shown
no interest in local warnings about the activities of political opponents in the
Kamenka region, warnings that had been made repeatedly during the summer of
1920.[76] This claim aside, Raivid's picture of the beginning of events and the reaction of the PSR, in particular, jibes well with the version advanced from the other
side by Podbel'skii. Both see the Tambov PSR-sponsored STK (at its gathering in
Khitrovo) quickly deciding, when confronted with the developments in Kamenka,
that the uprising of the Kamenka peasants should not be endorsed, in large part
because it had attained such a degree of seriousness owing to the influence of
Antonov and his supporters.

However, these two versions of events differ in how the events unfolded, and
in their relationship with Antonov, in particular. In calling the Kamenka insurgents to discipline, according to Raivid, the STK in Tambov was asserting its own
authority over these developments. For him, the fact that the insurgency continued
was enough to ascertain the true intent and will of the STK, and thus of the PSR.
For Podbel'skii, the decision of the Tambov STK not to endorse events effectively
absolves that organization, and by association the PSR, from any responsibility
for the continuation of hostilities. In this, the key factor was Antonov, for it was
he, in defiance of the provincial STK, who continued to fuel events.

Judging by the way the events unfolded, it is entirely plausible that the initial
clashes in Kamenka were unplanned and, most important, unknown to Aleksandr
Antonov.[77] The circumstances that surround the initial clash, involving a local
requisition squad and, later, an antidesertion patrol, were unremarkable in the
context of the civil war countryside. But the forceful showing of the local community in the course of this first clash, which saw both government forces beaten and
bloodied, indicates the extent to which the conspiratorial machinations of the
regime's opponents in the villages of Tambov had placed the countryside on a
hair trigger and perhaps boosted the confidence of average village communities
in the area. Given the extent of Antonov's contacts in the Kamenka region, it is safe
to assume that his efforts to organize local deserters, among others, had progressed
substantially, possibly including the distribution of guns to those who had already
volunteered. When the Kamenka villagers set upon the requisition squad that had

only just completed a sweep through the village and was en route to the local railway station, the organizational foundations for concerted defiance were already in place.

If the Tambov PSR and its peasant union organization refused to "sanction" the uprising that began in Kamenka, Antonov most certainly did, and the groups that he had organized in other villages and regions quickly followed suit, attacking village and volost soviets, Communist Party cells, and state farms. It was in these first days following the events in Kamenka that the conspiracy arranged by Antonov, involving multiple small forces of local villagers, was revealed to be either still in its infancy or simply poorly organized. There was never a plan behind the actions and movements of these rebel groups, nor was there any communication among them. On the one hand, as reported by Red Army soldiers who had been briefly captured, some groups of rebels (in northern Borisoglebsk uezd) believed the insurgency had begun prematurely, and these rebels were considering abandoning the struggle and returning to their native villages, possibly to wait until plans were more advanced. Meanwhile, other groups were busy declaring the great victories already won by rebels, some of which were as yet unverified, such as the claim that the rebels had occupied the gunpowder mill outside Tambov city, one of the most important strategic military assets in the province.[78] Antonov himself, it was reported, announced to a crowd in the village of Ramza, briefly occupied on 5 September, that the rebels would soon attack both Kirsanov and Tambov city.[79] The fantastic claims made by rebel groups, such as those in south-central Kirsanov uezd, where government troops had been outnumbered and outmaneuvered, was a direct expression of their growing confidence.

Reports such as those from Ramza, which suggested a sense of unity and purpose among active insurgents, gave further evidence of an elaborate conspiracy at work. The idea that a degree of organization lay behind the disturbances was also suggested by reports that detailed some of the symbols that accompanied rebel activities.[80] The quick appearance of recognized slogans, although often misreported (perhaps with the undeclared aim of discrediting the insurgents), both alarmed government authorities and confirmed to them that simple popular grievances were not the sole explanation for the disturbances. According to one military operations report, filed on 5 September from the area of Sampur station (not far from the Kamenka region), the observed rebel groups included men of all ages from the local villages who brandished flags with embroidered or painted slogans, such as the PSR motto, "In struggle you will secure your rights," as well as "Long live the Union of the Toiling Peasantry," and "The true path to freedom is away from Bolshevik repression."[81]

For government officials, there was no apparent distinction between Antonov's involvement and the involvement of the PSR, nor any incentive to indulge such a possibility. For all intents and purposes, the two strains of the conspiracy behind the insurgency were indistinguishable. The first reports of Antonov's participation in the disturbances—which would have been anticipated—only confirmed the overall implication of the PSR organization.[82] But neither Antonov nor the PSR was directly responsible for the outbreak of the insurgency, even if both parties were quickly drawn into the rapidly developing events.

SHLIKHTER'S REPORT

While invoking the name of the PSR, or of Antonov, may have contributed to the credibility of local reports to the central Soviet government in Moscow, the involvement of the PSR would hardly raise the eyebrows of officials in the capital, given that the party was such an important feature of the real and imagined world of anti-Bolshevik counterrevolution. And the involvement of the PSR could only have been expected in a rural insurgency, especially in a central Russian province such as Tambov, where the Soviet government was itself weak and where the PSR could claim a long tradition of involvement in local politics. Thus when Aleksandr Shlikhter arrived in Moscow in the second week of September 1920 to deliver his report on the insurgency in Tambov Province, it should come as no surprise that the pernicious involvement of such usual suspects as the PSR played a central role in the provincial soviet chairman's pitch for more substantial help in quelling the disturbances.

A summary of Shlikhter's report, copies of which were delivered to Lenin and to the Military Council secretary, E. M. Sklianskii, detailed point by point the situation confronting the provincial administration and the measures local officials believed would be required to regain control over the Tambov countryside:

1. The rebellion has overtaken the three most grain-rich uezds of the province: Tambov, Kirsanov, and Borisoglebsk.

2. The forces currently available to suppress the rebellion stand at 3,500 men. Included in that number are: units of Tambov military cadets, grain procurement squads, and Cheka units sent as reinforcement, at our request, from Riazan, Riazhska, Tula, and Saratov.

3. Given these forces, the Tambov Military Council considers it *possible* to suppress the rebellion, but only under the following conditions: (a) the liquidation of the rebellion will require no fewer than 3–4 weeks; (b) surrounding and destroying

the bandits, including those who have appeared in the south, in Novokhoper uezd [Voronezh Province], is *not possible* with the troops now available. The bandits can be driven away and dispersed, but they will be able to once again regroup and recommence a partisan war.

4. Because of the military operations, procurement work throughout the massive region of the rebellion has *for the time being* been halted; a continuation of the rebellion for a further 3–4 weeks will result in the abandonment of procurement work, and the razverstka will be impossible to fulfill.

5. The fulfillment of the Narkomprod razverstka for Tambov province (11.5 million pood of various foodstuffs) can be secured only after an immediate liquidation of the rebellion.[83]

While Shlikhter detailed the number and types of reinforcements required to suppress the rebellion in Tambov, including the need to transfer potentially unstable garrisoned units out of the province (which had already begun in spite of the formal request made here), the provincial soviet chairman's report focused on the cost of the present disturbances to the ongoing campaign to requisition grain.

It will be recalled that the original telegram sent by Tambov, informing Moscow of Shlikhter's imminent arrival, was composed in large part with the participation of a senior Narkomprod official, A. I. Sviderskii. The real cost of the insurgency was to be counted not so much in the bodies of Communist Party members and soviet personnel, nor was it considered an alarming indication of mass discontent with Soviet power in the countryside, or even of a new plot by opposition groups to topple the regime. The most direct threat highlighted by Shlikhter, a food supply specialist in his own right, was the potentially vital threat posed by the rebellion to the campaign to requisition grain. The overarching concern with procuring grain for the army and the cities, both critical to the survival of the regime itself, was the continuing factor that shaped the Soviet government's strategy in dealing with the insurgency in Tambov for the remainder of 1920.

THE COLLAPSE OF SOVIET AUTHORITY IN TAMBOV

J UST DAYS BEFORE Chairman Shlikhter's meeting with officials in Moscow, there were clear indications that the Soviet government was aware that the situation in Tambov was worsening. From their perspective, there was an obvious need for practical improvements in the efforts of authorities to reimpose order in the countryside. On 9 September 1920, Iurii Aplok, a senior commander in the Internal Security Forces (VOKhR) administration tied to the Southern Front Command in Orel, was notified of his appointment as head of the armed forces in Tambov Province, taking over from the local military commissar, Shikunov. Aplok's appointment was announced to officials in the Tambov administration by the head of Internal Security Forces in Moscow, Vasilii Kornev, whose organization would assume the leading role in the state's armed activities in the province in the following months.[1] The armed forces at the disposal of the provincial government in Tambov were principally oriented toward the procurement of grain, and their inability to mount sustained operations against organized rebels had been clear from the very beginning of the violence in the countryside in August and early September. With the task of imposing a stronger measure of structure and organization upon the armed forces in Tambov, in addition to augmenting those armed forces, the announcement of Aplok's appointment to the province was accompanied by the following instructions for Tambov officials issued by Kornev in Moscow:

1. Draft a plan of action and follow it consistently and steadily.

2. Do not disperse units too sparsely, but conduct operations only with overwhelming force.

3. Take concrete measures to improve coordination and communications between units.

4. Place the provincial Cheka in charge of reconnaissance and intelligence.

5. Ensure that active units are well supplied with arms and ammunition, as well as other necessities.

6. Give attention to rearguard troops and ensure that there are no instances of looting.

7. Conduct thorough searches of "liberated" villages, rounding up deserters and collecting concealed firearms.[2]

These were practical measures, as well as general principles, that focused attention upon the necessity of conducting sustained operations that remained constructive. As such, there was no mention of punitive measures in Kornev's instructions. There was instead an emphasis upon the systematic and consistent conduct of government forces, basic to any counterinsurgency effort.

Further insights into the nature of the rebellion would be offered by concerned individuals much closer to the ground. Following the announcement of the directing role to be played in the province by Internal Security forces, a Communist Party member and journalist for the local newspaper in Kirsanov sent a letter to Kornev offering observations on the mainsprings of the rebellion and the strategy the government should follow in putting an end to the violence. The journalist, identified only as Vodkin, prefaced his comments with an explanation that he had spent much time traversing the countryside now embroiled in the conflict, conducting dozens of meetings with local communities in the months leading up to the outbreak of hostilities and becoming familiar with the grievances and concerns of the local population. Vodkin began by stating that the people in the districts most affected by the violence were "typical middle peasants, proprietors whose overarching concern for their private property has been undiminished by the revolution, and they are therefore principally conservative and risk-averse." Such people, Vodkin went on, valued order and security most of all, and they appreciated any measures that would protect them from disruptions to their everyday lives.[3]

The implication was that the violence was brought upon the village communities from without. The people in the countryside placed no stock, according to Vodkin, in the slogans of the SRs, Mensheviks, or other political opponents of the regime, and any propaganda that was being conducted by these political opponents and any promises they advanced for a better future under a different government were effectively undermined by their own conduct, which victimized everyone, especially the average villagers in Kirsanov uezd, where most of the rebels' activities had been concentrated. The population of the region saw the rebels as mere bandits, stated Vodkin—consciously preferring the older Russian term *razboiniki* to the relatively modern one, *bandity*, to emphasize just how cynically locals viewed the insurgents and their disjointed political claims. The disruptions and depredations of the *razboiniki* did not, however, enforce allegiance to the Soviet government. The experience of those communities with Soviet rule over the previous three years had taught them that the Soviet government was neither powerful, and thus something to feared, nor willing or able to enforce laws and preserve order in the countryside, which would have made it something to respect and value. The local population was effectively caught by the ongoing insurgency in the countryside without clear allegiance to either side, although there were those who had been willing to support the rebels principally out of a vague hope that things could be returned to the familiar conditions of the old regime. This latter sentiment, while prominent, was dismissed by Vodkin as ill-informed nostalgia, but he nevertheless recognized its potential to effect political behavior in the short term.

Vodkin's recommendations to Kornev were many, and perhaps naturally for a journalist, contained a bias toward the importance of strengthening political work and disseminating information throughout the countryside. But the basic objective, according to Vodkin, was to suppress the insurgency while winning the respect of the local population, assuring them of the state's commitment to law and order in the countryside. Those entrusted with waging the campaign against the insurgency in the region must, according to Vodkin's concluding words, "display firmness rather than cruelty. [A successful conclusion to the conflict] will be achieved only if the comrades assigned to the campaign know precisely who their enemies are and also appreciate what they can and cannot demand of the local population."[4] Such an assessment indicated the low regard of observers of the conflict, such as Vodkin, for the conduct of government troops and counterinsurgency efforts to date.

Aplok arrived in Tambov to assume command of the situation with an air of condescension that would continue to characterize relations between central and regional officials and provincial authorities for the rest of the year. The appointment of a commander from Orel served as a recognition that local officials were not up to the task of dealing with "bandits" and that competent leadership had to be brought in from outside, in a way that had characterized Moscow's relationship with the provincial administration through much of the civil war.[5] After he joined his colleagues in the newly formed Military Council in Tambov on the evening of 10 September, Aplok was made aware of the uncertain tactics local commanders had followed in the first weeks of the insurgency, initially abandoning large force concentrations as too sluggish, then realizing that reliance upon more numerous, smaller units only compromised coordination and multiplied the number of weak targets for rebels to attack. The net effect was to lose the initiative, allowing the rebels effectively to dictate when and where engagements took place.[6] Aplok began the restructuring of active armed forces in Tambov, replacing the small units that had previously sought to counter the rebels with similar partisan-style operations and forming them into more traditional brigades and regiments to establish a unified front to contain the violence within a defined territory.

What was clear to Aplok, however, was that the situation in Tambov was defined by a familiar problem with banditry rather than more organized anti-Soviet elements. Such banditry, which had been characteristic of Soviet provinces throughout the civil war, had been a constant feature of the Tambov countryside for decades, according to Aplok, although the present manifestation was certainly distinguished by its scale. But the important features remained the same—attacks on vulnerable Communist Party members in the countryside, ambushes of small units of government troops, and sacking Soviet state farms were all classic tactics of elemental banditry that at the same time revealed the inability of local officials to manage the situation. Such violence would continue, Aplok stated, as long as certain individuals such as Antonov remained at large, but he confidently declared that a modicum of control over the countryside could be established in a matter of days following his arrival.[7]

The confidence that the violence would soon exhaust itself was informed by the conviction that the rebels did not enjoy the sympathy of the local population— yet another distinguishing characteristic of banditry as understood by Soviet officials. While there were numerous small groups of armed rebels containing up to thirty men, only one or two significant groups were occupying individual villages and making overtures to the local population to support the ongoing insurgency. As a government-published leaflet stated, such overtures to assembled community members typically contained erroneous claims, such as news that the Soviet government had been toppled in Moscow and Petrograd and that Soviet rule truly survived only in the southern half of Tambov, while the remainder of the province, and indeed the country, had been "liberated."[8] Tambov officials received reports that the rebels were not receiving overwhelming support and often relied on coercion in their interactions with communities, such as in their regular need to negotiate with villagers for fresh horses after their high-speed travels between villages had exhausted their animals. The rebels' violence against villagers who did not cooperate became a prominent theme in government propaganda, as did the threat that villages that did provide support or sanctuary to the rebels could expect severe reprisals like those begun in late August, when the provincial administration authorized the burning of entire villages as punishment for acts of violence against government and party personnel.[9] There were indications that these threats were having the desired effect, such as when Kirsanov authorities reported that several villages in the Inzhavino region had been willing to fulfill their quotas for grain procurement as an expression of loyalty to the Soviet government.[10]

Under Aplok, the forces engaged in the counterinsurgency operation were reorganized, and the uezds were placed on a partial war footing with the formation of local military councils (*voensovety*).[11] Internal Security (VOKhR) units were brought in from other provincial centers in September, while further groups of unreliable soldiers were removed from the garrisons in Tambov and reassigned to localities beyond provincial borders. By the end of the month, the number of troops available for the counterinsurgency effort had grown from almost 3,000 to just over 4,000. Government troops, operating in six separate groups, had nearly two dozen machine guns and several artillery guns at their disposal. But the troops available to commanders in Tambov were almost exclusively foot soldiers. The number of mounted troops remained minuscule, considering that the estimated 6,000 insurgents were overwhelmingly on horseback. Mobility remained a problem and inhibited the effectiveness of government troops.[12]

But the improvements in organization and coordination achieved in September did produce practical results, as the six operational groups of government troops worked to contain the spread of the violence and created opportunities for attacks on the identifiable clusters of armed rebels. With the pressure from government forces fairly constant, rebel groups were unable to establish a foothold in any given village, even if they could rely upon superior speed and mobility to frustrate Aplok's efforts to establish a clear front against the bandits. The largest group of rebels remained, however, far superior in numbers to the government's forces, and attempts to engage the rebels at various times in September typically ended in hasty withdrawals by government units.

The opportunity to engage the rebels in sufficient numbers did not arrive for the commanders in Tambov until virtually the end of the month, long after Aplok's optimistic forecast for the end of the insurgency had passed. Having established a base of operations in the village of Shabolovka in Kirsanov uezd, the main organized rebel force was divided into four groups dispersed in villages on both sides of the border between Kirsanov and Tambov uezds. From these locations, the groups conducted small raids in the surrounding countryside for several days, accumulating property looted from state farms and soviet administrations while attracting additional active participants from among the local population. It is impossible to ascertain what the plans of Antonov and his associates were at this particular juncture; they may have treated it as an opportunity to take stock of the situation following the intense and chaotic events of the previous weeks. But the effect of this breathing spell in late September was very nearly disastrous for the insurgents. Weighed down by carts filled with looted goods, when the main rebel group went on the move once more, they were attacked by a much larger government force than they had previously encountered. Over 800 government cavalry and foot soldiers attacked at the village of Kozmodem'ianskoe, and government officers reported around 600 insurgents killed in the engagement, a veritable massacre (if government reports are to be believed) that also destroyed over 130 carts filled with supplies and looted property. While several hundred insurgents either survived this attack or had evaded it, it represented the single greatest success the newly reorganized government forces in Tambov had enjoyed in the six-week-old conflict.[13]

On 30 September, the Soviet administration in Tambov appointed a three-man committee to review the available materials relating to the mainsprings of the rebellion. Included among these were statements taken from captured bandits and from members of the PSR, arrested in September in the provincial capital.[14] Reporting on the committee's findings only five days later at a meeting of the Soviet Executive Committee, the secretary of the Tambov Communist Party, N. Ia. Raivid, described the organization at the core of the rebellion, which he assumed had been defeated in the final days of September. At the heart of the conspiracy were local SRs, whose preparations for an armed insurgency were inspired by the instructions of the PSR Central Committee. At some point, according to Raivid's description of the available intelligence, those preparations were hijacked by individuals such as Antonov and his closest associates—Boguslavskii, Ishin, and Tokmakov—as well as by circumstances in the countryside, where clashes between government requisition squads and villagers pushed events faster and further than anyone anticipated.[15]

Raivid's report on the conspiratorial core of the rebellion was followed by the more reassuring words of the provincial soviet chairman, Shlikhter, who insisted that popular participation in the rebellion was far from universal and that many villages had not only refused to take part in the rebellion, but also actually resisted it by denying the rebels any material support. He suggested that the Food Commissariat reward those villages by delivering various supplies and manufactured goods (but only *after* they had fulfilled a significant portion of their targets for food procurement).[16] In a telegram to Lenin, sent soon after the meeting of the Tambov Soviet Executive Committee, Shlikhter wrote of his personal interrogation of captured rebels in the previous few days, and how all had willingly denounced the rebellion and asked forgiveness for their actions. The vast majority of those captured and sent for interrogation, Shlikhter assured, had been released "in the name of Soviet power and Lenin."[17]

Later investigations into the violence in individual localities completed in late October and November 1920 focused particularly on popular participation in an effort to gauge the sympathies of the wider population of the region toward the insurgents. Many of the conclusions drawn from these reports, produced by the Cheka after surveys conducted in the Inzhavino and Sampur regions, where disturbances continued throughout October, emphasized the separation of the village communities from the active insurgents and underscored the "marginal" or "criminal" character of the insurgents themselves. In the case of the Inzhavino-Rasskazovo region, Cheka investigators emphasized the fact that very few individuals actually joined the rebels and that the rebels at no time conducted formal mobilizations, except insofar as they drove members of the community to perform various duties for them, such as transporting carts of supplies or, in some cases, even digging trenches. No more than 1,000 men—mainly "hardened" deserters, or *zlostnyi*— actually joined up with the rebels in this area of over 20,000 residents. While this was far from insignificant, the course of events in the area had seen the local population grow overwhelmingly opposed to the rebels. Even though the initial wave of violence brought multiple scenes of cruelty against soviet and Communist Party personnel that suggested wider community involvement (albeit prompted by the entry into a locality by an armed group of rebels), and it remained impossible throughout much of the region to reestablish regular soviet administration, the Cheka investigators confidently judged that enthusiasm for the rebellion had quickly evaporated.[18]

The same initial enthusiasm followed rapidly by suspicion and opposition was noted by Cheka agents to characterize developments in the Sampur region over the course of September and October 1920. Giving general figures to illustrate their point, the members of the investigating team reported that at the moment of the outbreak of violence in the area, nearly 80 percent of the local population sympathized with the insurgents. This degree of support was attributable, the agents claimed, to the intense underground political work conducted by the PSR in the weeks immediately preceding the outbreak of violence in late August. The categories employed to measure participation, from the typical division of the regional population into familiar, and politically loaded, socioeconomic terms (kulak, middle peasant, and poor peasant) to the speculative evaluations of the percentage of the local population voluntarily and forcibly mobilized, all reinforced the picture of a wider population in the Sampur region ultimately reluctant to engage with the insurgent, or "bandit," movement.[19]

Such findings reinforced the overall tone set at the October meeting of the Tambov Soviet Executive Committee. The message was generally reassuring—the rebellion had been a narrow conspiracy, it had been defeated, and the regime could rely upon a measure of popular support that the rebels themselves did not enjoy after several weeks of violence in the countryside. The priority for the provincial government now, as ever, was to direct the energies of the provincial administration and available military forces to the requisition campaign. While groups of bandits were still active and continued to thwart the operation of local administration and threaten the activities of government agents in the countryside, the rebellion as an organized uprising had been "liquidated" by October 1920. The bandits had failed to establish popular support and could not be considered a substantial challenge to Soviet authority in the province.

SALVAGING THE RAZVERSTKA

The collection of grain in the southern portion of the province, upon which nearly half of the target for the 1920–1921 campaign in the province had fallen, had been seriously disrupted by the violence of the previous weeks. Collection had largely ceased in Kirsanov, Tambov, and Borisoglebsk uezds, where numerous armed bands had attacked government agents, state farms, and grain elevators. From the first days of the violence, nervous uezd officials had ordered the withdrawal of armed requisition squads to the uezd towns for defense in the case of a rebel attack. Any progress that had been made in the campaign during September and October 1920 had been completed in regions as yet unaffected by the insurgency. While some of this had been accomplished in areas such as northern Tambov and Kirsanov uezds, the bulk of the progress with the campaign had been in the central and northern uezds of the province where agricultural production was notably less intensive, but this was not enough to compensate for the shortfalls being experienced on account of the insurgency.[20] The entire machinery of provincial administration in Tambov had developed around this single task of procuring grain, and the need to regain this focus dictated many of the decisions taken in October, after the worst of the violence seemed to have passed. The chairman of the Tambov Soviet, Shlikhter, communicated to Lenin in the beginning of October that, although he recognized that the insurgents were far from destroyed, he would place Red Army troops stationed in the province at the disposal of the Food Commissariat to reinforce procurement efforts.[21]

While measures had been taken earlier by the Military Council in Tambov to organize the defense of the provincial capital against possible attacks by rebels from the surrounding countryside, Shlikhter admonished officials in the uezds for their independent decisions to withdraw requisition squads to the uezd towns to bolster their own security.[22] Similarly, Aplok undertook measures to form available military forces into two principal groups: one devoted to antibanditry operations in Kirsanov, Tambov, and Borisoglebsk uezds—which he took at this time to be "mopping up" operations—and another that would augment available requisition squads to return grain collection rates to the levels expected by the Food Commissariat before the outbreak of the violence.[23] The use of military and internal security forces for requisitioning was seen as one vital way of making up for the shortfall in personnel committed to requisition work.[24]

Communist Party mobilizations in the broader territories most affected by the violence consistently failed throughout September 1920 to produce the desired number of volunteers. The reluctance of party members to perform requisition duty was understandable in light of the situation in the villages, where it was reported that rebels were maximizing the political effect of their attacks by conducting show trials of captured Communist Party members before executing them publicly. The towns were the main destination of Communist Party families evacuated from the countryside, who often arrived with no possessions following rebel attacks.[25] Nevertheless, the failure of such mobilizations remained a source of great frustration for provincial administrators, whose reassurances about the progress being made by the government produced little effect on party morale. Often the only Communist Party personnel who could be relied upon to assist military forces in the area of the insurgency were those who were originally based in the countryside and whose families had been safely evacuated.[26]

The provincial administration would need to overcome the anxiety shared by uezd-level officials and rank-and-file Communist Party members to succeed in restoring the campaign to procure grain in the southern half of the province. With much of the network of soviets in the villages and districts operating irregularly, if at all, because of evacuations and persistent rebel attacks and threats, the reliance upon armed squads and military personnel was even more pronounced than in previous procurement campaigns, which had themselves been "militarized" as part of an effort to centralize the affairs of local government and, in particular, those of the Food Commissariat.[27] But, as commissariat officials in the uezds complained in October and November 1920, the continued disruptions caused by the remaining rebel groups active in the countryside made any systematic conduct of procurement duties impossible. Requisition squads were regularly being recalled to the towns and large villages in response to warnings of a rebel attack, and requests by local representatives of the Food Commissariat for soldiers to be assigned to the requisition campaign were regularly ignored or refused by local military officials. While many of these attacks never materialized, particularly when the uezd towns were reportedly under threat, they intensified the continued nervousness of local officials outside the provincial capital and were one more manifestation of the tensions that characterized relations between the organs of the Food Commissariat and those of local administration in grain-producing provinces such as Tambov.[28] The net effect was to undermine Aplok's earlier commitment to bolstering the food procurement campaign with regular military forces not required for antibanditry operations. In addition, the demands of the requisition campaign, as well as security in uezd towns and at strategic points in the countryside, further undermined the confidence of military and civilian authorities in the manpower resources at their disposal.[29]

The food commissar in Tambov, Shugol', employed the same bullying tactics perfected by his immediate predecessor in the provincial administration, Gol'din, to press uezd-level administrators to accept the circumstances and get on with the task of grain procurement. His words to his colleague in the Food Commissariat in Borisoglebsk, who had complained of difficulties in getting other uezd officials to shift their focus to the requisition campaign, are typical:

> What I am saying, and you can explain this to the uezd executive committee, the uezd party organization, and any other authorities in [Borisoglebsk], is that you are the food dictator for the entire uezd, and the razverstka must be fulfilled. The Antonovist, kulak element in Borisoglebsk should feel your power. Demand of the others in the uezd administration, on the basis of this, that they must give you their support.[30]

Despite the intentions of the military and civilian officials in the provincial capital, the requisition campaign remained a dead issue for as long as the bandits were allowed to operate in the countryside. What authority the Soviet government enjoyed was being daily compromised and challenged by the menacing presence of armed opponents. Food Commissariat officials in the uezds reported that the production of moonshine (*samogon*) had made a dramatic return during the weeks when the requisition squads were unable to operate freely. The consumption of available cereals, vegetables, and meat was on the rise, as households responded to the troubled material conditions and heightened insecurity with partial abandon. And, of course, the rebels were playing their own part, conducting their own requisitions of supplies in the villages they occupied.[31] The results as reported for the end of October spoke for themselves. Despite the intentions of provincial officials to shift the focus back to the procurement campaign, the rates of collection were woeful for the uezds most affected by the violence. The targets for the procurement of cereals in Kirsanov, Borisoglebsk, and Tambov were 16.4–23.3 percent completed, and local officials contested even these low figures. In Borisoglebsk, they claimed that many districts had contributed virtually nothing to the procurement campaign; collections in Zapalotovsk volost were a meager 19 pood from a target amount of over 25,000 to have been collected by November.[32]

Collection rates were much better the further north one traveled from the epicenter of the violence. This was not only a product of fewer disruptions in the countryside. It was also the result of a conscious decision by Food Commissariat officials to concentrate their efforts in the center and north of the province to make up for shortfalls in collection suffered in the southern portion of Tambov. Spassk and Shatsk uezds were the worst, with collection far exceeding the allocated targets for those territories by November 1920.[33] The exploitation of the farming peasantry in these areas predictably antagonized local officials, who feared that the long-term consequence would be widespread hunger, with the short-term consequences of political instability and a possible northward spread of the insurgency.[34] The specter of the rebellion intensifying and engrossing new territories on account of the short-sighted actions of provincial Food Commissariat officials narrowly pursuing the achievement of procurement targets was one that critics of the policy of razverstka had raised since the beginning of the violence in the southern half of the province.[35]

Such concerns only intensified as the disturbances continued in the final months of 1920. Despite the efforts of the Food Commissariat to prompt their subordinates in the uezds to pursue requisitions in a decisive manner, the atmosphere in these localities only grew more despondent, as those in the soviet administrations at the heart of the insurgency felt powerless to effect any constructive change in the strategic situation. The secretary of the provincial soviet executive committee,

Meshcheriakov, having reviewed the political situation in Kirsanov in late October, strongly criticized the Food Commissariat for the unreasonable pressure it tried to exercise upon the beleaguered uezd administration:

> I cannot continue [my report] without raising the extremely rude behavior of the provincial Food Commissar [Shugol'], who is fully aware that it is impossible to conduct a procurement campaign when there are no available requisition units. He clearly knows that military units have no obligation to obey the orders of an uezd food commissar, but he nevertheless demands, and in the most decisive terms imaginable, that the razverstka be fulfilled at any cost. Strict and direct orders are issued [to individuals in the localities] to go and take grain with your bare hands in the midst of a bandit uprising. (I am enclosing copies of these telegrams.) The provincial food commissar is literally ordering the uezds: "Don't talk, don't argue, don't offer me excuses—just get the grain."[36]

Yet the pressure being exerted upon provincial officials from Moscow, particularly those in the Food Commissariat, was likewise severe and uncompromising, affecting their own relations with local officials.[37] The issue of suppressing the insurgency in Tambov remained inextricably linked in the minds of central government authorities in Moscow to that of the food crisis facing the Soviet Republic.

ANOTHER FALSE SUPPRESSION: OCTOBER 1920

Provincial officials would later deny, in the face of criticism from central authorities at the close of 1920, that they had diverted actual armed forces from the antibanditry campaign in October and November to concentrate efforts on the procurement of grain. Aplok's eventual replacement as overall commander in the province (from late October 1920), K. V. Redz'ko, reported to the provincial Military Council that he had considered on more than one occasion reassigning available military forces to supplement the armed squads working under the control of the Food Commissariat, but he felt that these would be of little practical utility for the requisition campaign, and so never took the decision.[38] From the perspective of officials in provinces bordering the area of the insurgency in Tambov, the situation in October and November was indicative of either the incompetence of authorities in Tambov or the inexplicable restraints placed upon the antibanditry effort by Moscow. The heavy blows suffered by the rebels in Tambov in late September 1920 had relieved the situation somewhat, with the main rebel groups no longer presenting a significant problem for military authorities in early October. However, their relief was gained at the cost of severe disruptions suffered by officials in the neighboring provinces of Saratov and Penza.

In the first week of October, officials in Serdobsk uezd, Saratov Province, reported that armed rebels from Tambov had occupied the village of Makarovo, killing soviet and Military Commissariat personnel while also taking possession of soviet property, such as official document stamps.[39] At the same time, to the north in Penza Province, Military Commissariat and Cheka officials in Chembar' uezd reported the appearance of rebels close to the border with Tambov.[40] The numbers reported were at first unimpressive, but as more details emerged, the estimates increased to indicate that the rebellion that had afflicted provincial authorities in Tambov in August and September had been far from liquidated and had instead crossed provincial borders. Cheka and Military Commissariat officials in Saratov quickly established their own headquarters in Rtishchevo, the large railway station on the line connecting the provincial capitals of Saratov and Tambov, and they mobilized armed forces for assignment to the affected regions of the uezd. Likewise in Chembar', Penza authorities worked to clarify the situation along their borders and to mobilize two armed Cheka battalions to force the rebels back over the border into Tambov. But complications prevented these initial actions from producing any decisive effect. In Saratov, state farms, some of which were principally staffed by refugees from the "hungry" cities of Petrograd and Moscow (as they were regularly identified in contemporary publications), found themselves largely defenseless as rebels crossed over into the bordering uezds of Serdobsk and then Balashov. In some cases they began to empty the farms of all livestock and agricultural implements, distributing them to nearby village communities in the hope that they would be kept safe from rebel looting.[41]

While provincial authorities feared that the incursion into Saratov territory would usher in a damaging period of elemental violence against state targets and village communities alike, information received soon after the appearance of insurgents from Tambov suggested that a far more elaborate conspiracy and organization was at work. A rebel scout, captured in the first days of the incursion, informed Cheka officials in Saratov during interrogations that the groundwork had been laid long in advance for rebel activities across the border in Balashov and Serdobsk. The conspiracy that had been organized by Antonov and his men incorporated dozens of contacts in neighboring provinces, including Saratov, and they had every intention of establishing their insurgency in a wider region encompassing parts of Voronezh and Penza.[42] There was strong evidence of the looting of state farms and violence against soviet and Communist Party personnel, and the rebels had reportedly accumulated a vast amount of stolen property reflected in the number of carts they kept in tow, carrying out their activities with a measure of organization that worked to cultivate their popular appeal. The same show trials of state and party personnel that had been among the features of their activities in Tambov Province were reproduced in the villages of Saratov, but in a way that only suggested more elaborate intentions. Few native villagers joined the rebels during their incursion into the province, and beyond the sloganeering and familiar calls for communities to rise up against the state, the presence of the Tambov rebels in Saratov bore the hallmarks of a military raid rather than attempted occupation.[43]

In Penza, a Cheka official closest to the area most affected by the appearance of the Tambov rebels, Karpov, reported to his superiors that their actions had done little to dislodge the rebels from the region:

> Requisitions and all soviet work [in Chembar' uezd] have come to a complete standstill. The situation confronting the Chembar' soviet executive committee is simply idiotic. The citizens are themselves begging for protection from the bandits, and they are blaming Soviet power for its failure to do so. . . . Antonov has resided in the territory of Chembar' uezd for two days, robbing the peasants, and no one has lifted a finger against him. . . . The armed forces in Tambov, Kirsanov, and Saratov do absolutely nothing, and this is just playing into Antonov's hands. They could be closing in on him now, as Antonov and his cavalry, with their huge collection of carts filled with goods, are just sitting there.[44]

Officials in Penza expressed their dismay at the incompetence of provincial authorities in Tambov, but they, like their counterparts in Saratov, were more critical of the formal circumstances that inhibited their own ability to deal decisively with the incursion.[45] Stationing available forces in the larger villages along the border, military and Cheka commanders on the ground grew increasingly frustrated with their superiors in the uezd town of Chembar' and in Penza itself. Rather than rely upon the initiative of local commanders, those who assumed control over operations demanded that any troop movements be the result of formal orders from provincial headquarters. Likewise, there was common frustration because forces in Penza had no authority to cross over into Tambov or Saratov in pursuit of armed rebel groups.[46] While they sought to contain the spread of the insurgency into their territories, they felt they could do nothing to contribute to a concerted effort to eliminate the rebels as a source of instability in the wider region. There had been virtually no contact among the respective authorities in the four provinces now affected by the insurgency originating in Tambov, and while there were several reasons for this state of affairs, the lack of central guidance was the most glaring. The Cheka commander, Karpov, was once again a strong spokesman for this shared sense of frustration after his military forces had endured nearly a month of disturbances along the border with Tambov:

> I believe that if Antonov once again appears on the borders separating Tambov, Saratov, and Penza provinces, and we do not want to fail again on account of coordination problems, then we should establish a single center [of command] to control all armed groups operating in Tambov, Saratov, and Penza, providing clearly defined objectives for each group and maintaining close communications with each while granting individual group commanders a measure of autonomy, such that if the enemy appears in his region, he will be able to move his forces from one village to the next as he requires, crossing borders if need be, and maintaining constant contact with the command center, which would be located near the heart of the action, and not in some office located in Simbirsk, Penza, or some other town a hundred versts away, trying to follow the movements of the partisan bands on a map as if there were an unbroken front line that could be discerned.[47]

With Soviet government forces in the region unable to achieve a sufficient degree of coordination, circumstances played into the hands of the rebels.[48] While officials in Saratov were able to mobilize enough trained soldiers and Communist Party volunteers to force the insurgents from the Serdobsk region and then, eventually, from Balashov uezd, their efforts to warn authorities in Voronezh of the rebels' intentions to travel to the Novokhoper region in the north of that province only met with silence.[49] Voronezh officials had already had difficulty maintaining order in that area, and their apparent indifference to reports of over 2,000 Tambov rebels heading for the forests of Novokhoper provoked disbelief in neighboring Saratov.

SOVIET AUTHORITY UNRAVELS

While authorities in Penza had to contend with continuing problems along the border with Tambov, in the form of armed rebels as well as unarmed groups of villagers exploiting the compromised security situation to plunder timber resources, their neighbors in Saratov had faced a much more coherent force of rebels from Tambov and had managed to deal with them in the first two weeks of October.[50] Returning to Tambov via Borisoglebsk uezd, the rebels—quite probably including Antonov himself—arrived with renewed intent to continue the campaign of violence against the Soviet regime in the province. The return of the rebels betrayed any declarations by provincial officials and Internal Security Service (Voiska vnutrennei sluzhby, or VNUS, which subsumed VOKhR) commanders that the insurgency had been suppressed and that Soviet authority in the Tambov countryside was being restored. In the second half of October, the uezd officials in Tambov admitted defeat in their effort to reconstitute the system of soviet administration and opted to concentrate administrative functions in five regional committees. Recognizing that the system of local administration in the uezd had not been particularly strong even before the outbreak of violence in the autumn, Tambov uezd officials now reported that the rebels had managed to dismantle the soviet administration and Communist Party cells in forty-one of the fifty-six districts in the uezd. "On account of the cruelties committed by the bands against Communists and soviet personnel," they explained, "as well as the destruction of the entire apparatus of the volost soviet executives, including the destruction of documents, printing facilities, archives, and so on, the situation with the soviet executives is now completely catastrophic."[51]

When the rebels successfully launched a brief raid on the manufacturing center Rasskavozo, only a few kilometers from the provincial capital, and managed to inflict significant damage on a number of the medium-scale enterprises there, the news grabbed the attention of Lenin, who angrily demanded that Kornev, head of the VNUS, be formally reprimanded for the evident failure to establish control over the situation in the province. Kornev's reply in early November touched upon many of the themes that would become familiar over the following weeks, as the search for an effective solution in Tambov gave way to finger pointing and recriminations. Kornev explained that there had been a noticeable shift in the character of the conflict in Tambov and that the activities of the rebels were growing more conventional in terms of organization. They nevertheless operated with limited objectives and avoided direct confrontations with government troops. Kornev explained that in the final days of October, the forces in Tambov had managed to deal successive blows to the larger rebel groups, and for this reason, he assured Lenin, "in the broadest sense, the rebellion can be considered suppressed." The remaining task for government forces involved the final stage of "liquidation," rounding up known participants in the insurgency at the village level and "isolating the criminal element" from the wider peasant population. For this purpose, and also to safeguard against the rebellion flaring up once more, Kornev explained that he had ordered significant troop reinforcements, involving a full battalion and two motorized squadrons. The figures he provided in his report further reinforced his claim that the situation was under control: 3,000 insurgents killed (and a mere 300 wounded), 1,000 insurgents taken prisoner, and vast amounts of weapons, ammunition, and supplies, including a military field kitchen and telephone apparatus, seized. Losses for the government had been modest, with just 90 men killed and less than 200 wounded.[52]

Kornev's assessment of the actions of his own VNUS forces and commanders, and of the wider situation in Tambov, was almost immediately challenged by developments on the ground. On the day Kornev sent his report, armed rebels once again attacked the railway station at Inzhavino, where government troops failed to offer any resistance. Then, on 5 November, a coordinated action by armed rebels, involving two separate groups attacking from the north and south, occupied the important railway station at Sampur in Tambov uezd. Overwhelming the small local garrison at Sampur were between 2,000 and 6,000 insurgents (estimates vary), mostly on horseback, and possessing a small number of machine guns and at least one light artillery gun, in addition to rifles and revolvers carried by individuals.[53] It was the largest organized mass of insurgent forces to date, but the occupation of Sampur was short-lived. Having failed to sabotage the railroad on the northern approach, the rebels were soon met by artillery and machine gun fire from government forces on armored railroad cars arriving from the provincial capital. The resistance mounted by the insurgents was minimal, and their flight from Sampur was rapid. It was another important victory for Soviet troops and a debilitating defeat for the rebels, if government reports are to be believed, but also a reminder that the rebellion as an organized phenomenon was far from over.

The search for solutions to the escalating problem of the insurgency was growing more desperate, and that desperation was nowhere stronger than in the uezd towns, where the sense of vulnerability was most pronounced. The only troops considered even remotely effective in countering the rebels were those at the disposal of the central command in Tambov, and uezd officials continued to rely upon reservists, requisition squad workers, and temporarily mobilized Communist Party members to defend the towns and strategic points in their territories. As the secretary of the Tambov executive committee reported following an inspection tour of Kirsanov uezd in early November: "Bands now cover practically the entire uezd. Soviet authority has ceased to exist. One ventures five kilometers outside of the town of Kirsanov, and state authority is already absent." The author of the report, Meshcheriakov, noted that the conduct of Red Army troops under the command of Tambov was contributing to this situation rather than correcting it, highlighting their "disgraceful conduct" as the most "fundamental evil," antagonizing the local population in the villages with uncontrolled looting and often random acts of violence that were pushing average villagers closer to open support of the rebels.[54] But he did not spare local officials, who had themselves abandoned any control over the situation from their secured base in the uezd center. "All the basics," Meshcheriakov wrote of the recently formed Military Council in Kirsanov, "such as communications, scouting reports, profiles of the rebels, are completely lacking. The Military Soviet is completely in the dark about what is happening in the countryside and is therefore serving no purpose whatsoever."[55]

A basic problem facing the local administrations as they confronted the degenerating situation in the territory was the loss of control over the armed forces at their disposal. Government units stationed outside the uezd towns were increasingly abandoning their posts without a fight when confronted by groups of armed rebels, and desertion was on the rise from the garrisons located in the towns and major villages. Whereas the anticipated rate of desertion from reserve units for October and November was a minimal 1–2 percent, the recent worsening of the political situation in the south of the province had seen the rate of desertion increase sixfold at the main garrison in Tambov. Similar increases were noted in other garrisons throughout the province, not only in the area most affected by the instability.[56] Military Commissariat officials in Kirsanov, recognizing the problem with desertion and the fact that men who had already been considered deserters formed the core of support for the rebels, had been calling since mid-October for the provincial administration to send reliable cavalry troops to the uezd to round up deserters in the villages before they fell in with the insurgency. The most they could muster for such a task, given their resources at the time of writing—early November 1920—was fifty men (without horses), a force that was too small and vulnerable, given the circumstances, and one that could be sent out only at the expense of security in the main garrison in Kirsanov town. At every instance when a request for such troops was made, commissariat officials in Kirsanov either received a negative reply, they claimed, or no reply at all.[57]

Yet senior military commanders openly recognized that the struggle with desertion was central to the counterinsurgency campaign, for removing the deserters in the villages would deprive the rebels of active recruits.[58] The connection between deserters and insurgents was more practical than political; such young men were not necessarily opponents of the regime, but being able-bodied and available, they were the logical targets of rebel overtures for support, either voluntary or coerced. As the countryside was abandoned to the rebels in the final months of 1920, such overtures grew increasingly difficult to resist. Provincial authorities attempted to provide an outlet for those young men not naturally drawn to the insurgency, declaring (in accordance with VTsIK instructions from Moscow) a one-week amnesty for deserters in November. The amnesty was extended by two weeks when the results proved disappointing. At the conclusion of the amnesty, the military commissar in Tambov, Shikunov, reported what virtually everyone else already knew: that it was pointless to expect results when the principal areas targeted by the amnesty were effectively outside government control.[59]

The desertion problem in the uezd towns was certainly connected with the degenerating political situation in the countryside, but it was also a product of the worsening material conditions that affected the garrison and town populations alike. With the rebels growing more systematic in their attacks and acts of sabotage, the uezd towns found themselves partially cut off from their sources of supply. With railroad traffic falling to a minimum throughout the area, and in and out of the towns in particular, the problem of desertion from the garrisons was increasingly difficult to contain. In Borisoglebsk, the food supply crisis by early December 1920 had forced local officials to try to illegally commandeer shipments of grain from across the border in Saratov Province in an effort to alleviate the situation.[60] In Kirsanov, where food procurement had come to a standstill, desperation quickly turned to anger among provincial and central officials alike.[61] As the same Military Commissariat officials made clear in yet another report filed toward the end of the year, local uezd authorities felt that they were effectively under siege, a situation their superiors seemed not to appreciate:

> It seems clear that the military forces in Kirsanov have been left to fend for themselves and that the provincial authorities are not willing to pay any serious attention to their plight. We do not have any active armed forces in Kirsanov, and we have no stockpiles of weapons. The railroad could today be repaired, but tomorrow it would only be severed once again; yet both Tambov and [military commanders in] Orel appear to believe that everything is going just fine for us [in Kirsanov].

Only a token number of forces that had been sent to reinforce local units, according to the commissariat officials in Kirsanov, and those reinforcements had been wholly unsuited to active participation in either antidesertion work or counterinsurgency operations. While these "barefoot Red Army soldiers" sent by commanders in Tambov could be assigned to railway stations or villages in the Kirsanov countryside, they explained, there were no guarantees that those same posts would not be guarded the next day by Antonov's men instead. Lamenting the fact that over 600 of "our best comrades" had perished already at the hands of the insurgents in Kirsanov, commissariat officials pointedly questioned whether such a state of affairs was sustainable. "No, comrades," they wrote, "we cannot go on living like this, and further victims will not serve to strengthen our revolution but will only weaken our defences further."[62]

THE PARTISAN ARMY OF THE TAMBOV REGION

An appraisal of the situation in Tambov Province by Cheka officials in Moscow on the basis of agent reports and available assessments at the end of November, began with the following description:

> Dissatisfied with Soviet policy concerning the countryside, incited by the seditious agitation conducted by whiteguardists, assorted dark figures, agents of the Entente, as well as incited by the underground work of the right SRs, and encouraged by the recent successes of Baron Wrangel [on the Crimean peninsula], the strong kulak population of this region has joined with the deserters to form the core of the Antonovist bands. Drawn to them have been various elements from among the White officers, arriving from the Don, Kuban, Ukraine, and elsewhere.[63]

The portrait of a deepening crisis, significantly fueled by the involvement of a variety of outside conspirators and agents of counterrevolution, remained a fixed idea in the assessments of central and provincial authorities alike. While there were elements of popular support, in the villages of southern Tambov support came from expected quarters, from among the kulaks and deserters whose participation could have been expected from the very start of the violence in the province. The growth of the Tambov insurgency was best understood in terms that elaborated the conspiratorial qualities that gave rise to the conflict in the first instance, drawing participation from outside the province and forging further links with known anti-Soviet elements representing a variety of interests and designs.

The rapid dismantling of local administration in the territory of the insurgency in the first two months of the conflict had not produced any noticeable changes in the organization of the insurgency or in the quality of its activities. The swift movement of identifiable rebel groups, led by known individuals with a long-standing record of opposition to the Soviet state in Tambov (such as Antonov, Boguslavskii, and Tokmakov) remained the source of defiance and prevented the Soviet government from reestablishing a foothold in the countryside that would allow its Communist Party members and soviet personnel, as well as requisition squads, to return to work. The entry of an armed rebel group into a given locality was the occasion for grand speech making and gun toting that bolstered the image of strength and viability needed to promote a spirit of defiance, but when those same rebels left, there was little in the way of local organization to take the place of the deposed soviet administration.

Calls for local men to organize their own rebel groups to continue the acts of sabotage and ambush so as to prevent a return of Soviet rule in the area had an effect, but there was an improvised quality to these overtures in the first months of the conflict indicating that very little guidance or organization connected these local bands—who often had to arm themselves—to the established rebel groups moving between villages and districts under pursuit by government forces. Despite the fact that officials in the uezd administrations reported a complete loss of control over significant portions of their territory, there were few signs that the rebels' growing confidence was translating into popular authority in those same territories, creating the impression among government officials that the rebellion would soon exhaust itself. Cheka officials expressed their belief that the enthusiasm for the rebellion fluctuated with the weather and that support for the insurgents would melt away as the winter snows began to accumulate in December.[64]

The attack on Sampur, however, had confirmed that the individual groups of rebels were capable of coordinating their activities and that their growing confidence conveyed a corresponding ambition for greater organization. A network of contacts remained in the countryside and had been expanded in the previous weeks of feverish activity, although to what extent remained obscure to government officials, who had initially believed that they had dismantled the conspiratorial network put in place before the outbreak of the violence in the province. There were worrying reports that numerous Communist Party members and soviet personnel, caught in the violence in the countryside, were actually joining the rebels, welcomed into the ranks of the insurgents rather than killed outright, like so many of their comrades.[65] Such developments were considered problems of discipline and resolve, and it was especially a problem with armed government troops stationed in the major villages and railway stations in the countryside. As with the reports concerning party and soviet personnel, it was becoming increasingly clear to government officials in Tambov that the rebels were not exclusively attacking and slaughtering government troops in acts of demonstrative vengeance, or *rasprava*; they were effectively taking prisoners and enlisting the participation of the young men they vanquished in raids and ambushes.[66]

According to the operational diary kept by military headquarters in Tambov, 14 November was a distinctly quiet day, with no major engagements or attacks to report.[67] Only two weeks before, Kornev had reported to Lenin his conviction that the defeats suffered by the main rebels groups in late October had splintered the insurgency to such an extent that its final suppression was near. However, 14 November stands out as a watershed in the history of the Tambov conflict, the moment when the rebels led by Antonov, Tokmakov, and others sought to forge an organizational structure that would sustain the insurgency for months to come. That a meeting was arranged at all indicated that a substantial level of organization and competence already existed. Nevertheless, the outcomes of the meeting of rebel leaders in the village of Moiseeva-Alabushki in Borisoglebsk uezd on 14 November had independent significance.

The actual discussion at this meeting in northern Borisoglebsk, not far from the original epicenter of the rebellion, remains obscure, and what is known about the proceedings is derived only from Soviet government and Red Army intelligence reports. Apparently the principal outcome, though, was the creation of a unified structure for the rebel groups that had been active for the previous months in Tambov. While identifiable groups of rebels had already attained a measure of stability in their ranks, several smaller groups of armed men needed to be either formally integrated into the organization or, perhaps more important, excluded from the ranks of the rebels led by Antonov et al. on account of their activities, if they were considered contrary (or detrimental) to the objectives of those leaders.

Initially, four armed "regiments" were recognized, each eventually bearing a designation drawn from its main base of operations, and from which the majority of its participants were drawn. For instance, the Third Borisoglebsk Regiment would be composed of individuals drawn from the area where the group had initially formed. The overall commander of the rebel regiments was recognized as Petr Tokmakov, an individual with some practical military experience under the old regime, but most significantly a long-standing and trusted friend of Aleksandr Antonov. Antonov himself would be the overall leader of the insurgency, the commander of its "headquarters," which would travel with him through the countryside and be accompanied by its own armed guard. The earliest available document produced by the insurgents regarding this new structure is dated one month later (16 December), and the name given to the rebel military force is the Armed Militia of the Tambov Region (Boevaia Druzhina Tambovskoi Kraia).[68] This was, however, only a transitional name, indicative of the rebels' own cognitive adjustment to the task of expanding and sustaining their movement as it moved from its underground origins to its above-ground ambitions. The insurgents soon adopted the more impressive title, the Partisan Army of the Tambov Region.

The Partisan Army set up a hierarchy of command through which orders and operational plans could flow. Presenting a unified organizational front marked a constructive step in the effort to cultivate legitimacy and authority in the countryside, and central to that objective would be to instill discipline within its recently formalized ranks. Almost immediately, independent-minded rebels challenged the discipline that lay at the core of the project to form a unified army. Soviet authorities learned of the organization of the Partisan Army in Moiseeva-Alabushki through reports of a schism in the ranks whereby a certain Kazankov and his group of armed rebels refused to submit to the authority of Antonov and the newly formed Partisan Army command. Whatever the source of the disagreement—personal ambition, "principled" objection to the organization of the new army, or something else—the development was a serious one for the rebel leaders. Kazankov and his men hailed from the Kamenka region, at the heart of the rebellion's territory, and the presence of a rogue insurgent leader in such a location was understandably intolerable to Antonov, Tokmakov, et al. An ultimatum was issued by the Partisan Army leaders, one eventually backed with a call to disarm the rogue unit and to hunt down and even kill Kazankov if he refused to submit to the authority of the Partisan Army.[69]

Having received word of this disagreement, Soviet officials quickly recognized an opportunity. Sustaining or deepening the schism could fatally break the back of the insurgency just as it appeared to be consolidating its authority. The senior Cheka officials in the sector drafted and, by all indications, delivered an appeal to Kazankov, "the rebel fighting against the Soviet workers' and peasants' republic." Given the tone of the document and the heavily loaded language used, the appeal appears to be intended more for the eyes of the wider public than for the rebel Kazankov and his men. Although the principal aim of the document is to entice Kazankov and his men to "come over to the side of the Soviet government, which will receive you as a repentant son and guarantee the lives of you and your men," every opportunity is taken to belittle the insurgency and emphasize the strength of the Soviet state and its counterinsurgency effort. Although the appeal makes sensible observations regarding the difficult situation that must have confronted Kazankov and his men, who were now a target for not one, but two warring parties, little or no effort is made to entice Kazankov beyond assurances that he and his men would not be punished by Soviet authorities if they surrendered: "Anyone who does not repent of his crimes and who fails to appreciate that he is committing dark deeds that only serve the interests of the West, for such people there will be no mercy shown, and the repressive arm of the Extraordinary Commission [Cheka] will come down on the head of the guilty with all its force."[70] Such language was understandable in that it underscored the limited options available to individuals such as Kazankov, but it hardly represented a positive enticement, revealing that Cheka officials appreciated the possible propaganda value of an open act of "repentance." Instead, the "appeal" to Kazankov appears to have been drafted under the influence of an overarching insecurity, with Soviet officials needing to proclaim once more the fortitude and capability of the Soviet state in contrast to the hopeless struggle of the bandits. Despite the concluding words about respecting the safety of the envoy delivering the document, this private communication bears all the hallmarks of a public declaration.

It is almost as if the Soviet authorities in Tambov did not expect Kazankov and his men to surrender and that the only propaganda benefit they felt could be harvested would come from this open appeal. Whatever their intentions, the brief crisis within the ranks of the rebel movement was soon resolved, with Kazankov and his men returning to the fold of the Partisan Army, not to the forces of the "Red republic." Three basic possibilities bear brief consideration here. One is that the Soviet promises of amnesty were not considered genuine by the rebels and therefore did not represent a realistic option. A second is that the rebels collectively felt that the threat from the Partisan Army was more substantial and therefore submitted to its authority rather than suffer the consequences. A final consideration is that the rogue group led by Kazankov may have reevaluated their decision in light of principle and joined the cause of the rebellion as closest to their own true sympathies. If any one of these explanations is correct, the overall implications for the Soviet government in Tambov were not positive. It is impossible to determine whether the Soviet appeal to Kazankov had any substantive bearing on the ultimate decision, but there were no apparent reprisals visited upon Kazankov and his men for their initial refusal to submit to the authority of the Partisan Army leadership; Kazankov's unit was integrated into the structure of the army, and Kazankov himself retained command of the "Kamenka" regiment until his apparent death in battle in January 1921.[71]

RECRIMINATIONS AND INVESTIGATIONS

Judging by parallel developments, however, the Kazankov episode did not dominate the period immediately following the organization of the Partisan Army. Attacks by rebel units on government targets continued in the second half of November, and the resolve displayed by Red Army troops in these episodes appeared to commanders to be diminishing. An unbroken series of capitulations finally culminated in the second week of December, when a Red Army garrison numbering over 400 men abandoned their posts in the village and railway station of Inzhavino in Kirsanov uezd after the appearance of a smaller group of armed and mounted rebel fighters. The events provoked an angry assessment by a local military commander:

On the night of 13 December in Inzhavino there took place a bandit attack. The Inzhavino garrison, numbering 433 armed men with two machine guns, not only failed to offer resistance, but shamefully took flight, abandoning their machine guns and tossing their rifles and ammunition behind them in the street. There were no other mitigating circumstances to explain this cowardice. Well clothed, very well armed, and well fed, these soldiers nonetheless fell into a panic and fled when confronted by a gang of bandits. We know now what sort of discipline there was at the Inzhavino garrison, when Red Army soldiers run away like a frightened flock of sheep and trained machine gunners abandon their weapons. I have no need for such men who only carry the Red Army name and do not want to fight, those who take the first available opportunity to run away and indirectly supply the bandits with arms and ammunition.[72]

Several of the men who had abandoned their posts in Inzhavino were sentenced to death by a military tribunal the next day. But this was only the most spectacular such incident involving Red Army forces, as the continuation of the insurgency drained what resolve had existed among rank-and-file government troops as the year drew to a close.

The problem with discipline and the general quality of available troops featured prominently in the report issued by the overall commander in Tambov sent to the provincial military council on 14 December 1920. Konstantin Redz'ko lamented the fact that the reinforcements that had arrived in the province since he assumed the post in late October had been uniformly substandard, requiring extensive re-organization and training for those who were not simply returned to their previous assignments outside the province. For all the thousands of soldiers available on paper for work in counterinsurgency operations, Redz'ko estimated that he had only 1,200 fit and capable (*prigodnye*) troops at his disposal. Only half of these were mounted troops, and the area of operations spanned nearly 20,000 square kilometers. According to the Red Army commander, the number of rebel fighters active in this same area could be estimated at 18,000, with 5,000–7,000 possessing their own firearms. The rebels held the balance of power in the southern half of the province, and incidents such as those at Inzhavino only served to strengthen the authority they enjoyed in the eyes of the wider population.[73] Simply deploying more government troops, regardless of their reliability and preparedness, would be "like pouring grease onto the fire," in Redz'ko's words, and promote the standing of Antonov and the rebels in the countryside. According to Redz'ko, even the occasional defeats the government forces had been able to inflict had done little to diminish Antonov's popular authority. "They believe him," reported Redz'ko, a simple insight that made the (admittedly meager) propaganda efforts of the government fruitless as long as the strategic situation was so unfavorable.[74] .

Maintaining that the problem regarding the quality of troops available for the counterinsurgency effort was well established and known to military and government officials concerned with the conflict, Redz'ko bemoaned the failure of central officials in Moscow to act so as to change the situation on the ground for the better. In particular, he held the commanders in the Internal Security Service (VNUS) principally responsible:

> It is agonizing to recognize that the officials in VNUS have yet to establish a clear view on this question [of inadequate forces deployed in Tambov]. It is even difficult in light of the fact that in two and half or three months we will have the thaw of the spring season, a time when military operations will, whether we desire it or not, cease, and if we do not liquidate the rebellion entirely, at its roots, before that time, then we are going to have a major conflagration on our hands, one whose flames could link up with other fires in neighboring provinces, consuming and destroying all the hard work and progress [the revolution has] made in the recent past.[75]

Redz'ko's words appear to be a dose of realism designed to force the provincial and central government to confront the rapidly degenerating situation in Tambov. But his report, written for the Tambov military council, harmonized with the tenor of provincial reports and correspondence directed to Moscow regarding the insurgency.

In September and October, the provincial authorities had regularly sought to assure officials in Moscow that the situation in Tambov was under control and that the insurgency did not, and could not, enjoy popular support. However, the renewal of the conflict with the return of the large insurgent groups from Saratov, Penza, and Voronezh in November saw those reassurances transformed into accusations. On two occasions, the commander of VNUS, Kornev, had visited Tambov with his assistants to assess the situation, and both times he had come away convinced that the provincial military officials had sufficient forces to deal with the insurgents. Dealing with a manpower shortage that generally affected Soviet forces in 1920 owing to the Polish campaign and the final clashes with the Whites in Crimea, in addition to other rural disturbances in provinces of Soviet Russia, Kornev had only been able to supply reinforcements to Tambov that were clearly not prepared to combat the insurgency. His actions in this regard, combined with his own criticism of provincial military and civilian officials in mishandling the campaign against Antonov, signified for local authorities an incompetence and a dangerously dismissive attitude toward the situation in Tambov.

For provincial officials, Kornev was the man in Moscow most clearly to blame for the failure of the counterinsurgency.[76] Two days after Redz'ko's report, the Presidium of the provincial soviet added its own voice in blaming Kornev directly, passing a resolution that explained that he had "always demonstrated a clear in-difference toward the concerns and demands made to the headquarters of VNUS by the Military Council and the Soviet Executive [in Tambov], concerns and de-mands that were communicated in reports, by telegraph, and in person, as well as before every commission which was sent to Tambov by Comrade Kornev, some of which he himself led." They concluded their resolution with what was by this time a customary remark: that if substantial commitments were not made to improve the situation in the province, they would wash their hands of any responsibility for the consequences.[77] Redz'ko likened the dispirit that pervaded the provincial ad-ministration at all levels to that of August 1919, when the White cavalry of General Mamontov swept through the province. This represented the previous low point for morale among local administrators and officials, who felt abandoned by mil-itary and civilian authorities in Moscow when confronted with an armed chal-lenge. Redz'ko himself did not want to endure such a climate a second time; he and others had been sensationally placed on trial following the debacle of August 1919, and he understandably did not want a repeat of that experience, even if he had been acquitted.[78] Instead, Redz'ko requested to be relieved of his command, as he felt "powerless," in his words, to improve the situation in the province.[79]

Such a request by the head of military forces in the province only reinforced the danger signals coming from Tambov. Continued setbacks at the hands of rebels, particularly at the village of Inokovka in Kirsanov uezd, which was twice occupied by the Partisan Army in mid-December, prompted yet another delegation to be sent from Moscow to investigate the situation and to make strategic recommen-dations. It was the fifth time in four months that central government investigators had visited Tambov to assess the troubles in the province. Arriving on 25 Decem-ber 1920, the delegation officials from VNUS met for three days with provincial officials and military commanders and surveyed available correspondence and documentation relating to the development of the insurgency and the govern-ment's efforts to suppress it. On 28 December, the day before completing their in-vestigations, the officials were joined by Kornev, making his third visit to the provincial capital in the latter half of the year. The reports produced at the end of the month were notable for their vigorous defense of the conduct of officials in

Moscow and VNUS. Yet they also drew commonsense conclusions that helped invigorate the state's subsequent efforts to control the situation in the province.

The main report was the work of Petr Andreevich Kameron, a senior investigating official with VNUS.[80] Kameron and his colleagues reviewed summary reports prepared by members of the Military Council in Tambov and evaluated the origins and progress of the conflict over the previous five months. Many of the points made in the final report had been recognized much earlier by provincial officials. In particular, the report highlighted the antagonistic role played by the Food Commissariat and its agents in the countryside in arousing popular discontent in the grain-growing regions of the province, particularly the commissariat's pursuit of collection targets without regard for local political stability or even the economic sustainability of requisitioning. The report referred to the "abnormal character" of the procurement targets in Tambov, although Tambov was far from alone among Soviet provinces suffering political instability as a consequence of the razverstka policy. But it was a judgment that did, in typical fashion, direct attention onto local officials and their conduct, rather than on the faults of the policy *tout court.* The failure to realize other centrally directed policies according to Moscow's intentions—notably the overarching effort to court the middle and poor peasantry in an effort to weaken the irredeemable kulaks—was also counted among the faults of provincial officials, but this failure too was not unique to Tambov.

The main insights contained in Kameron's report pertain to the course of the insurgency itself. Regarding the provincial government's efforts to suppress the violence, Kameron provided a broad characterization of the local officials' failure to appreciate the quality and potential of the resistance led by Antonov and his armed supporters: "Regrettably, even up to the present time, local authorities have failed to understand the character of the movement, preferring to label it 'banditry,' and even an authoritative governmental organ such as the provincial Cheka clung to such a characterization throughout August and September and, as a consequence, was unable to address the situation adequately." Explaining that the insurgency had revealed itself to be remarkably systematic in its choice of targets and tenacious in dismantling the Soviet government institutions in the countryside of, particularly, Tambov and Kirsanov uezds, Kameron described the inability of local officials to respond adequately:

> The active struggle with the insurgency suffered throughout from a shortage of effective armed forces, and local commanders, unaware that the *antonovshchina* enjoyed deep roots in the countryside, operated on the assumption that they were dealing with simple "banditry" and that liquidating the insurgency was as straight-

forward as destroying the main armed enemy groups. On occasion, when the local command enjoyed genuine victories over the insurgents, and the Antonovist bands appeared to scatter, then those same local authorities would quickly dispatch telegrams to the center declaring that the liquidation of the insurgency was imminent. But again and again the bands reformed, increasing in number and effectiveness with each passing day.

The report then proceeded to evaluate the response of central authorities to the situation in Tambov. Not surprisingly, it took as its starting point the "misleading" characterizations provided by officials in Tambov. Recognizing the limited availability of combat troops, in light of the ongoing operations in Poland, Crimea, and Ukraine, it was not surprising that the conflict in Tambov received relatively low priority when provincial officials downplayed the seriousness of the situation by consistently referring to it as banditry and even provided occasional reassurances about their ability to handle the situation.[81] When there were requests for reinforcements, according to Kameron, these would be issued alongside countervailing assurances that the rebellion was nearly liquidated and that Soviet authority was being reasserted in the countryside. And officials in Moscow, those attached to VNUS in particular, regularly gave greater credence to those optimistic assessments from Tambov rather than the pessimistic ones. In this, Kameron noted a failure in professional judgment by VNUS officials.

However, Kameron's report had much more to say about the failings of provincial military and civilian authorities in their organization, evaluations, and judgment during the course of the insurgency to date. Local officials had not only been naïve with their sweeping, optimistic assessments made on the strength of ephemeral successes against the rebels, but also failed to organize the counterinsurgency effort. Local commanders and Communist Party officials were too quick to resort to demonstrative reprisals against entire village communities while neglecting political work both among the government troops and the wider population caught in the area of the violence. The Military Council established to oversee operations in late October 1920 failed to impose coherence on the campaign against the rebels and was aloof from other government and party institutions, irregularly attending to minor details (*vermishel'nye voprosy*, in the words of the report) while neglecting many broader operational and tactical issues.

The consequence of these and other failings was that the rebel movement in Tambov had assumed a "catastrophic character." In his recommendation, Kameron began with the broad necessity of "occupying" the three uezds of the province most affected by the conflict, an objective that was as much directed to imposing effective organization on the counterinsurgency effort as to bringing in enough reliable reinforcements. Regarding the latter, Kameron did not dwell on the actual level of armed troops required to suppress the insurgency, but he did highlight the need to bring in capable reinforcements for the Tambov Communist Party, which had lost up to 800 of its members at the hands of the "bandits" (note that Kameron himself found it difficult not to fall back into a familiar idiom, even in this document), and the provincial Cheka, which had similarly lost a significant number of its agents (here estimated as 40 percent) in the conflict. While these recommendations enjoyed broad support among officials familiar with the situation in Tambov, the report taken as a whole, with its detailed critique of provincial leaders, also salvaged the reputation of V. S. Kornev (who had received a personal reprimand from Lenin earlier in the month) and the Internal Security Service at a time when the protracted conflict in the province had become the most prominent component of a general political crisis for the Soviet Republic.

Kornev himself submitted a brief report to the Central Committee and RVSR alongside Kameron's detailed assessment. He took up many of the same themes in explaining how the situation in the province had reached this critical point. In particular, he provided a precise characterization of the Tambov conflict, one obviously intended to harmonize with the evaluation contained in Kameron's more extensive report.

> The Antonov rebellion is a partisan rebellion that engrosses a single territory covering three uezds of Tambov Province and is well organized, planned, and led by the SRs; it has displayed a resilient character (of the partisan variety noted in the case of Makhno) and it requires that we employ a strategy of occupation, something that local command is overseeing at present.[82]

With this brief description, Kornev articulated the "correct" evaluation of the insurgency in Tambov. It was a "partisan" movement, and not a case of "banditry." Following detailed investigation by VNUS, the precise military terminology had been discerned, enabling the appropriate response.

But there was no authentic precision behind this change of descriptors. For all the amateurishness displayed by officials in Tambov when confronted with the rebellion, and for all the false suppressions promised or declared over the previous four months, they could not be faulted for continuing to use the term *banditry* in reference to the violence in the countryside of their province. *Bandit* continued to be a normative label used by power holders to denigrate and devalue violent opposition, and Soviet government officials used it no less frequently than tsarist authorities had done before them, even if Soviet officials preferred the more modern expression *bandit* to the older expression *razboinik*. Indeed, *bandit* was much less ambiguous in this regard than the term preferred by Kornev in December 1920. *Partisan* had initially carried a positive connotation among Communist Party members as the rightful descendent of Friedrich Engels's volunteer "militias" of 1848–1849, and early Soviet officials and Communist Party members initially held to the principle of a volunteer workers' militia as the basis for the Red Army in the first months of the civil war. But the decentralizing and destabilizing influence of these formations rapidly forced a reconsideration of the primacy of Communist principle as the party bowed to the necessity of establishing a Red Army that was more traditional in organizational and operational terms in 1918.

Further examples of "partisan" activity in the civil war only reinforced the suspicion of such armed groups held by Soviet officials. Kornev, in his memo, cited the Red Army's experience with Nester Makhno in southeastern Ukraine as an example of a typical partisan-style movement, and the complications caused by Makhno's force for both the Red and White armies in that region served as evidence for a qualified negative assessment of partisan warfare. In Siberia, the Soviet government had largely been the beneficiary of guerrilla, or partisan, activity behind the front lines of Admiral Kolchak in 1918–1919, but there, too, the Red Army had difficulties maintaining control over many of the more successful anti-White guerrillas.[83] *Partisan,* in Soviet usage, was a term that contained no less rhetorical baggage than *bandit,* but it was also caught between assessments informed by political ideals and military realism.

As such, in late 1920, *partisan* was a far more ambiguous term than *bandit.* *Partisan* had certain positive connotations, while in the case of *bandit,* the connotations were only negative. But *bandit* had few precise military meanings in 1920. It was a weapon in the arsenal of political rhetoricians. Kornev, however, was not calling for an end to the use of the expression *banditry* in describing the resistance in Tambov, for in political terms, it remained a useful and powerful characterization. The point of his memo, and of much of Kameron's own report, was that for strategic purposes, a military required a measure of terminological precision in order to conceptualize the enemy. One of the faults attributed to the officials in Tambov was that they had failed to recognize the necessity of maintaining a strict, conscious division between public rhetoric and private, or internal, language, and that this failure had resulted in the ineffective conduct of counterinsurgency operations, as well as a breakdown in communication between military authorities in Moscow and local officials in the province.[84]

In a meeting with Communist Party leaders in Tambov on 29 December, Kornev reemphasized his conviction that the forces available to commanders in

Anti-Antonov propaganda poster. Antonov is presented as a giant in peasant garb laying waste to villages, bearing not only weapons, but also buttons that connect him with the 1917 Provisional Government minister, Aleksandr Kerensky, and the White General, Petr Wrangels. The verse is presented in the style of a Tsarist decree, proclaiming the destructive intentions of "Antonov the First" as the "All-Thief and All-Bandit Autocrat." *Photograph courtesy of the Tambovskii Kraevedcheskii Muzei*

Tambov should have been entirely sufficient to establish control over the situation and deal with the insurgency. Estimating these forces at 9,000 infantry and 1,700 cavalry, Kornev once more compared the situation to that confronted by the Red Army in southeastern Ukraine against Nester Makhno's rebel army in which the Soviet government enjoyed a comparable advantage in armed force. He faulted the provincial leaders for their inability to deploy these forces effectively against Antonov, as well as for their inability to mobilize support from among the wider population, particularly local workers.[85] His words were indirectly supported by the Tambov uezd Trade Unions Congress, which met in mid-December 1920 and passed a resolution condemning the conduct of the counterinsurgency effort, finding particular fault in the secrecy under which provincial officials pursued the state campaign against the insurgents. The provincial government had, according to the union delegates, maintained a public silence on the rebellion, refusing to involve the "the working and Red Army masses," inadvertently creating a situation that saw the propagation of rumors "promoting the legends of the victories and 'escapades' of Antonov, of his extraordinary abilities, and of the impossibility of catching him, such that panic has set in among the workers and the general population." In the words of the resolution, the delegates openly recognized that "in spite of its protracted nature the bandit movement led by Antonov has not declined, but has, instead, escalated and intensified into a full-scale war against Soviet power."[86]

The damning critique of provincial leaders in Tambov spread throughout the state and military infrastructure, and despite indications that Moscow was paying closer attention to the situation in Tambov, complete with the prospect of greater involvement by the Red Army in the conflict, morale continued to sink as the year drew to an end. The chief of the Southern Military Sector, O. A. Skudr, who would be Redz'ko's temporary replacement during the fortnight between the latter's resignation and the arrival of his replacement, reported to one of his officers in Orel on the situation in Tambov on 1 January 1921:

> The struggle with the rebellion has, until this time, been conducted in the most shameless fashion. If it is true that the force arrayed against Antonov numbers up to 8,000 infantry and 1,500 cavalry, then the leadership of that force has been nothing short of murderous in its conduct. Even in the last days [before my arrival], the commanders in Tambov were micromanaging the activities of individual armed groups, sometimes consisting of up to twenty separate units, and it was not uncommon for the reach of the central command to extend all the way down to the level of individual brigades and companies. There is virtually no scouting or intelligence gathering conducted by military groups, and what scouting reports do occasionally arrive at the offices of the provincial military headquarters are effectively worthless. But more important, one cannot speak of a provincial military headquarters at all, unless one counts Redz'ko, who tries to manage everything in his head. There has been no political work conducted among the troops stationed here. There is no effective midlevel leadership for the military groups. The end result is that our 8,000 men freely engage in looting and pillaging and work more to promote banditry than to suppress it.

Skudr added, wryly: "From what I have stated here it should be obvious that I have landed for myself an excellent assignment."[87]

5 THE PARTISAN COUNTRYSIDE AT WAR

THE COLLAPSE OF THE Soviet government in the south of Tambov Province was largely the consequence of its long-standing weakness, which was manifested in several ways, most significantly in the low level of preparedness of the armed forces under its control and in the profound insecurity and division displayed by state and party officials at various levels of administration once the disorders began. The sustained violence in the countryside had revealed this weakness and deepened it, and in turn the rebellion itself had begun to change, as the chaotic events of the first weeks of the uprising gave way to the more systematic and organized activities of an antigovernment insurgency. This transformation could not have been achieved without the active efforts of the emerging rebel leadership to control the violence any more than it could have been without the effective abdication of control over the countryside by the divided provincial government.

There had already been clues to the political contours of the rebellion provided by reported slogans and suggested by the known participants and emerging leaders. These offered few surprises for Soviet state observers, for whom the long-standing tradition and strength of the PSR in Tambov, as well as in the wider region, represented an obvious and expected source of political instability. As the history of the rebellion to date demonstrated, however, the rural population of Tambov was not an SR army in waiting, poised to respond to the signal from the "center" to rise up against the Soviet provincial government. Instead, for the leaders of the nascent insurgency, consolidating control over the violence and asserting mastery over anti-Soviet sentiment meant articulating and communicating a coherent political message, as well as laying the organizational foundations for sustained engagement and participation in the resistance.

This chapter examines the politics of the Antonov movement by focusing on the relationship between efforts to project a collective political identity and the practical experience of the insurgency in the countryside. By concentrating on the micromobilizational aspects of the insurgency, it highlights the degree to which rebel organizers struggled to normalize collective resistance while maintaining a broader sense of the extraordinary required to sustain commitment and solidarity.[1]

PROJECTING A CENTER: THE STK PROGRAM

Soviet government officials reported the range of slogans and rallying calls that accompanied the activities of the rebels in various regions and villages with some interest. They were inclined to highlight those slogans that indicated either sympathy or support for established figures of the "counterrevolution" or betrayed a seemingly elemental thirst for vengeance and violence. Either the politics of the rebels could be positioned into an established category, or the slogans that animated the resistance could be understood as "pre-" or "subpolitical." Identifying the mainsprings of the insurgency, however, remained of minor interest to officials in Tambov, who, while increasingly worried about the insurgency and its seriousness, nevertheless focused on acquiring the military means of suppressing it rather than understanding it.

The same array of rebel slogans that accompanied their many clashes with government troops were of greater concern to the newly established leaders of the insurgency in Tambov. Having survived four months of often chaotic violence, and having managed to capitalize on mistakes by government and military officials in Tambov to finally begin consolidating and organizing their support, particularly among the groups of young men carrying rifles and riding on horseback, formulating a political message for supporters assumed priority status for those in the STK and Partisan Army. With nearly all of the main leaders of the rebellion having an active or past affiliation with the Socialist Revolutionary Party (PSR) or its leftist offshoot, the LSR, it was little wonder that these two parties were the principal source of inspiration and guidance in formulating a program of political objectives that the rebels hoped would become the animating center of the continued insurgency in Tambov and beyond.

The "Program of the Union of the Toiling Peasantry," which emerged in the final weeks of 1920, is both a conventional and curious document. It lists sixteen objectives that range from statements of abstract principle to specific statements of policy. The document also contains two points that address practical considerations following the triumph of the anti-Bolshevik movement. Its most striking passage is the preamble, a vivid statement of intent that overshadows the eighteen points that comprise the bulk of the document:

> The Union of the Toiling Peasantry makes as its first objective the overthrow of Communist-Bolshevik power (*vlast'*), which has taken the country to the edge of destitution, death, and disgrace, and to achieve the destruction of this hated power and its methods [*poriadok*], the Union has organized voluntary partisan units that are carrying out an armed struggle in order to achieve the following aims:
>
> 1. The political equality of all citizens, regardless of class.[2]
>
> 2. An end to the civil war and the return to peaceful life.
>
> 3. Full cooperation with all foreign powers to achieve a stable peace.
>
> 4. Summoning of the Constituent Assembly according to the principle of equal, direct, and secret balloting, without any attempt to predetermine its will in the creation of a new political order, and respect of the right of the voters to remove representatives that fail to respect the will of the people.
>
> 5. Until the convocation of the Constituent Assembly, a provisional authority in the localities and in the center will be formed following voting among the unions and parties that participated in the struggle against the Communists.
>
> 6. Freedom of speech, press, conscience, unionization, and assembly.
>
> 7. Bring into reality the law on land to its original extent, as drafted and passed by the Constituent Assembly.
>
> 8. The supply of products of first necessity, food in particular, to the populations of the towns and villages via the cooperatives.
>
> 9. Regulation of workers' wages and the prices of manufactured goods produced in factories and workshops controlled by the government.
>
> 10. Partial denationalization of workshops and factories, with heavy industry, mining, and metallurgy enterprises remaining in the hands of the government.
>
> 11. Workers' control and government oversight over production.

12. Acceptance of Russian and foreign capital for the reconstruction of economic life [*khoziaistvennaia i ekonomicheskaia zhizn*] in the country.

13. Immediate resumption of political and economic/trade relations with foreign powers.

14. Free self-determination for national groups of the former Russian Empire.

15. Provision of extensive government credit for the assistance of small rural households [*melkie sel'skie khoziaistva*].[3]

16. Unfettered production for cottage industries.

17. Independent (*svobodnoe*) instruction in schools and mandatory education in literacy.

18. Currently organized and active partisan voluntary units shall not be disbanded in advance of the convocation of the Constituent Assembly and its decision on the issue of a standing army.[4]

The program was signed by the Tambov provincial committee of the Union of the Toiling Peasantry. The composition of the program, which appears at times to toggle together slogans and ideas raised in previous such political programs, combined with the inclusion of explicit instructions rather than statements of objectives (such as points 5 and 18), leaves one to conclude that the program, rather than being a document composed by senior PSR activists in Moscow or elsewhere, was in fact the work of local members of the STK and Partisan Army in Tambov Province.[5]

To what extent, though, was this list of objectives a document designed to appeal either to a base of support among the village communities of southeastern Tambov, or to a wider audience of possible sympathizers in the countryside and beyond? The specific objectives cited in the document appear calculated less to appeal to particular grievances held by people under Bolshevik rule than to demonstrate the broad base of support the rebel leaders believed they represented. This included the short- and long-term concerns of industrial workers as well as members of the intelligentsia and professional classes. It also, of course, included the peasantry, both farmers and those involved in small-scale rural enterprise. In addition, there was the point concerning national self-determination and the breakup of the Russian Empire, words that had been the stock and trade of leftist parties for over a generation. But the document as a whole appears to have little in the way of a systematic delineation of goals as a considered political program. The ideas contained in it are far from random, but to identify the program and its goals as a clear representation of rebel ideology would be to overinterpret the document and its significance. This was an example of the political program being produced to advance a claim to legitimacy. It was an effort by rebel leaders to project their insurgency beyond the limited confines of the rural provincial setting and to present their movement as a challenge to the central Soviet government on behalf of the people as a whole.

Indeed, in their spirit, the goals and objectives listed in the document would not have been out of place in any political program advanced by leftist political parties, particularly after March 1917.[6] However, one wonders how those who drafted this particular program could have believed that advocacy of renewed trading links with foreign governments could aid them in their immediate task of creating a centerpiece for political mobilization in the expanding territory of the insurgency. For this reason, it does not warrant detailed consideration except when taken in its entirety as representing the aspirations and ambitions of the rebel leadership.

If any details of the program achieved true resonance in the immediate context of the ongoing insurgency itself, it was the impassioned call for the overthrow of the Soviet government and the familiar advocacy of reconstituting the Constituent Assembly. The Communist regime was considered to be the source of all the problems that afflicted Russia during the civil war, especially the coercive policies that had been most influential in provoking the periodic violence that characterized the countryside of Tambov for most of the previous three years. Perhaps for this reason, such specific policies as forced grain requisitioning and labor and carting obligations are not mentioned in the program itself; these were policies that stemmed from the fact of Communist rule. Elimination of the Communists in government would also mean an end to their "methods," which invariably meant the dictatorial conduct of appointed agents and commissars who ruled by decree and without consent. The shape of Russia following the victory of the anti-Bolshevik movement would be determined by a democratically elected Constituent Assembly—presumably newly elected rather than restored in some way to its original composition. Although there was mention of a temporary, or "provisional," government, there is no indication either in the program itself or in other political pronouncements by the rebels, that the October revolution that overthrew the Provisional Government in 1917 was illegitimate and that the clock should be turned back to March 1917. Indeed, despite the influence of the PSR within the STK and Partisan Army, there was no evidence of nostalgia for the Provisional Government in their materials. In this, at least, they were responsive to the sentiments of the village communities such as those in Tambov, for whom October continued to signify the beginning of their own revolution in the countryside.[7]

The place of the Constituent Assembly in the slogans and program of the rebels represented a middle ground that maintained the legitimacy of the agrarian revolution while at the same time denying legitimacy to the Communist government. Citing the forced dispersal of the Constituent Assembly as the moment of betrayal, rather than the overthrow of the Provisional Government two months earlier, the rebels in Tambov remained consistent in their objectives while at the same time drawing upon slogans invoking the Constituent Assembly that were familiar to citizens of Russia, both in the countryside and towns. What did the Constituent Assembly represent to average people in the Tambov countryside that its defense could be made the centerpiece of the insurgents' political program? In one sense, proclaiming support for the Constituent Assembly had by 1920–1921 become shorthand for opposition to the Communist government. Beyond signifying an alternative to Communist dictatorship, popular understandings of the Constituent Assembly did not run deep.[8]

In another sense, the Constituent Assembly represented an alternative that, for all its vagueness, held out the hope for a better government that would reflect the ideals of democracy that had been so central to discussions of politics immediately following the abdication of the tsar in 1917. It represented the opposite of dictatorship—the experience of which was consistently emphasized in rebel political pronouncements and propaganda—and as an institution, albeit an interim institution, the Constituent Assembly held out the promise of democratic elections and representative government.[9] In either sense, the Constituent Assembly was most important as representing an alternative to the dictatorship of the Communist Party rather than as the embodiment of popular aspirations. It was a project, at best, and would not on its own rally support for the rebellion among the civilian population. The overthrow of the Communist dictatorship and the tangible alternative of the Constituent Assembly were complementary goals, and they represent the most important facet of the STK program in its contribution to the Tambov insurgency. It was in these most basic elements that the STK program contributed to the ideology of the rebel movement.[10]

ENLISTING A PARTISAN POPULATION

The articulation of a political program was a part of the larger project of providing structure and organization to the insurgency. Copies of the program would be distributed and read out as political workers entered villages accompanying Partisan Army units. The program provided an introduction to the insurgency that would develop into a longer-term relationship with the creation of local institutions that would formally tie a village community to the rebel movement. Setting up individual STK committees in the areas of strongest support for the rebels had already been under way before formal instructions on the creation, structure, and function of these local institutions had been printed and distributed. STK committees had already been formed for the three uezds where the rebels had achieved a foothold, all likely to have been relatively close to the base of the provincial committee in Kamenka.[11] Extending the network down to the village level required a higher degree of organization and control to ensure that the process would contribute to the cohesiveness of the insurgency rather than splinter it. With both the provincial and uezd STKs issuing orders and instructions, a link in the hierarchy was required to ensure the proper execution of orders as well as to maintain communications between the central leadership and the localities.

Intermediate control was to be exercised by the regional STKs, composed of five persons, four of whom would head a particular "department," with the fifth serving as the STK chairman. The responsibilities of the regional STKs were the most critical to the functioning of the entire network and to maintaining support for the Partisan Army. These included duties that related to the local economy and supply for the rebels, mobilization of new rebel units, coordination of political work among the local population, and maintaining up-to-date information regarding the village communities and the local STKs. While the members of uezd committees were evidently appointed by the provincial STK, regional committees were formed and sanctioned by gatherings of local committees in the villages and volosts. When a sufficient concentration of local STKs had been reached in a given area—three or four volosts typically constituted a region—then a regional STK would be selected. Likewise, on the lowest level of the hierarchy, members of village and volost STKs were to be selected by a popular vote of a general assembly of individual communities. Not only would the decision to organize a village or volost STK be decided by a general assembly, but also fellow community members elected the STK chairman and his two fellow members.[12]

The great expansion in the system of STKs occurred in the first three months of 1921. While some committees were already in existence before the provincial STK issued instructions on their formation, these had been formed either before the outbreak of the insurgency and had reemerged once security conditions allowed or had been rather haphazardly created by rebel units in villages where they had conducted mobilizations or had received support from the local community.[13] Creating a network to support the insurgency and participate in sustaining the movement required the enlistment of village communities on a much wider scale and on a more organized footing. The appointment of political agi-tators by the provincial STK to travel throughout the territory of the insurgency, often alongside Partisan Army units, set a process in motion that would see the network of STKs expand to nearly 300 by March 1921. This was accomplished through a fairly standard routine, although variations can be attributed to the style and manner of the individual political organizer involved.

The entrance of a Partisan Army unit into a given village during the winter of 1920–1921 became the occasion for the assembly of all community members to hear speeches on the efforts of the insurgents. The political program of the STK played a prominent part, as it was read out and elaborated upon by the political activist attached to the given rebel unit.[14] Sheer curiosity was often enough to bring people out into the streets to hear these speeches and observe the display, although sometimes fear of reprisals by government troops kept villagers in their homes, refusing to be implicated in the resistance.[15] In those villages where an assembly gathered to hear the speeches and pronouncements of the political ac-tivists, the village community was invited to effectively join the rebellion and form their own committee of the STK. The presence of rebels—particularly well-armed ones—would certainly have played an important part in influencing vil-lagers, either by impressing locals with their strength and organization, or sheer intimidation. As with the initial appeals made by Antonov in the first weeks of the insurgency, the rifle and machine gun played an exceptional role in rebel propa-ganda. Still, despite the presence of armed rebels and the rhetorical flourishes of the political agitator, some villages rejected the overtures or simply asked for time to deliberate in private. In Tokarevka volost (Tambov uezd), one village asked for twenty-four hours to consider the offer made by the agitator attached to the Thirteenth Bitiugov regiment, a request that was granted and later rewarded by a decision to join the insurgency.[16] In another case, further from the epicenter of the insurgency, activists working in Usman uezd noted in their report on activities in Kaz'minka volost that "Bolshe Danilovskoe commune [*obshchestvo*] absolutely refuses to consider joining the Green Army organization," possibly the only ref-erence to the "greens" to be found among materials of the STK and Partisan Army in Tambov.[17]

Such refusals, however, were not common, and the next stage in the process of organizing local STKs was to draft a resolution to be voted on by the assembled villagers.[18] There were common elements to the rhetoric and themes of all the surviving declarations, but for the most part, their composition seemed to depend most on the political agitator at the center of these general assemblies, who was often identified in the declarations themselves:

We, the citizens of Maksimovka village, have unanimously agreed to give our promise at this critical [*goriachii*] moment to support the report of the [political] organizer, [Sergei Ivanovich] Belousov, on the struggle with this pack [*svora*] of Communists in order that we can finally uproot the power of these evil dogs and quickly place it in the hands of the Toiling Peasantry and the Constituent Assembly. We heartily answer the call to strangle this entire pack of dogs and unhesitatingly commit our support until final victory is achieved.[19]

Each declaration was unique, even if the same agitator was behind the composition, which would appear to indicate that the individual villagers made their own contribution, however small, to the content. Besides words regarding Communist "dogs" and "vampires," as well as positive references to "partisans" and "comrades," the declarations were also characterized by reference to "our civil war" or "our revolution." However confused these statements may have been in a technical sense, the "we" in such statements was clearly the "toiling peasantry," and the points of reference remained the 1917 revolution and the civil war conflict that had followed.[20] Specific reference to the Constituent Assembly in declarations conjured up images of revolutionary promise that predated the Bolshevik takeover in the autumn of 1917.

The former chairman of the Tambov Soviet Executive Committee, V. A. Antonov-Ovseenko, who would later return to the province as VTsIK's plenipotentiary charged with overseeing the counterinsurgency effort in 1921, wrote in an expansive report that anti-Semitism was an animating force behind the rebel movement. This was so much the case, Antonov-Ovseenko wrote, that the Tambov rebellion was as much the creation of the PSR as of the blackhundreds.[21] Certainly identifying the Communist Party, particularly its leaders, with the Jews was a long-standing charge familiar to all since 1917. Government and party officials were understandably inclined to report any instances in which anti-Semitic references arose in connection with the insurgency.[22] Likewise, any incidents in which Jewish persons who were not members of the Communist Party had suffered at the hands of the rebels were likely to be taken as evidence of rebels targeting Jews in the area of the conflict.[23] Such incidents were quite rare, however, owing to the small number of Jewish families in the countryside at the time of the conflict.[24] In one notable incident that took place in the region of Tokarevka (Kirsanov uezd) in January 1921, four Jewish families were evacuated from the area of the insurgency by fellow community members, helped by members of the STK militia (to be discussed below).[25] While confirming that anti-Semitism was in strong evidence during the course of the insurgency, whose violence was

evidently feared by community members, this particular incident also compli-
cates the picture often painted by Soviet officials and historians about the place
of anti-Semitism in the rebellion. There is no doubt that anti-Semitism was a familiar idiom in appeals for support in the struggle against the Soviet government
(and before October 1917, in the case of the Bolshevik Party), but the language of
anti-Semitism was not central to appeals made by the rebels in Tambov.[26]

While the Communists, whether regarded as Jews or not, were certainly identified as being outsiders and usurpers of the revolution, the insurgency itself,
judging from the village declarations produced during the formation of the STKs,
was presented to citizens as a movement that emerged from the village milieu
but, at the same time, came from without. The relationship between the "partisans" and the "people" was emphasized, but the partisans were never portrayed
as the people. The partisans had a corporate identity all their own. Here is an
example from Bolshe-Lazovka volost (Tambov uezd):

> We, the citizens of Novo-Matveevka village, called together for a meeting by comrade
> Ostroukhov and having listened to several reports, unanimously state: "That we
> declare from this moment forward a merciless and cruel war against our sworn
> enemies—the Communists. With all the strength in our indignant souls we declare
> to our cursed bolshevik enemies: on Russian land there will not remain one single
> Communist. We send a brotherly welcome to all partisan units and to all those
> comrade peasants who have risen up or are presently rebelling, and we promise to
> assist you and support you until we have no more strength, and no more food."[27]

The role of the outside agitator, as well as of the active rebels, in leading the village
communities and mobilizing them for participation was stressed in many declarations. Such words effectively framed the experience of the years of civil war
and, especially, the previous several weeks of chaotic fighting in the countryside,
as both formative for the village communities and dependent upon the initiative
of the partisans, who would place the village communities on the righteous path
of open rebellion:

> We, the citizens of two villages [Chicherino and Malyi Burnak], brought together
> at a meeting led by Comrade Ostroukhov and having heard several reports by him
> and others, declare that we have always been enemies of the Communist regime, but
> until now we have not been organized, until now have been unable to break the
> shameful chains of slavery, unable to overcome the pitiful fear which pervaded our
> souls and froze our hearts—fear which we ourselves allowed to grow and which
> was used by the blood-sucking Communists to bleed us of the laborer's blood. Now

we have broken the chains of fear, and have begun to dismantle the enmity, sown among us by the Communists, which divided us and allowed them to survive and reap many fruits. Now we stand organized, strong, and powerful [*strashnye*], proclaiming a merciless struggle against the regime of the vampire-Communists.[28]

The partisans were a vanguard that had struggled to incite the countryside, which for so long had been politically impotent, to rebel in defense of their own interests and those of Russia as a whole.

Village communities were asked to vote on these declarations and to commit themselves to "joining" the insurgency by forming their own local STK committee. In some cases, the declarations were passed around as citizens were asked to sign the document. In other cases, the document was taken from household to household, beyond the scope of the meeting, and heads of household were asked to read and sign the declaration. Households that refused to sign were noted down separately, an obvious disincentive to anyone considering breaking with the majority.[29]

The manipulation of community pressures was similarly evident in the selection of members for the new STK committee. Often, village assemblies were asked by the STK organizer whom they wanted as their committee chairman. Because most of the statements we have from such individuals who served as chairmen of STKs were taken during government interrogations, the extent of voluntarism is nearly impossible to gauge. No one wanted to admit to having served in the STKs, and if forced to do so, they claimed that their service was provided under duress. The STK organization itself did not have extensive selection criteria.[30] The main requirements for a committee chairman were to have the trust of the local population and not to be a Communist Party member. Other desirable attributes for a committee chairman were literacy and experience with customary bureaucratic routines. This already narrowed the pool of candidates considerably in the rural villages of southern Tambov Province.[31] Those who had previously served in the soviet administration, particularly in more senior roles, were the most clearly qualified, especially given the exceptionally low level of enlistment in the Communist Party among village soviet functionaries in the province. It may come as some surprise, however, that so many of those who served in the local committees of the STK had held similar positions in the soviets being replaced within the territory of the insurgency.

Men who were selected to serve on the STK committees during the initial approaches by rebel agitators touched upon one aspect of this. Many insisted that they had little choice in the matter, and they suspected that, in effectively forcing the men to assume these positions of authority in the local STK, members of the community were protecting themselves from possible retribution by government forces should the village be occupied by the Red Army.[32] In other cases, however, the decision to serve came as a result of strong appeals by their fellow villagers that moved them to assume the post. Such appeals, judging from statements taken during interrogations, were fairly uniform and suggest that the STK agitators may have played a role. The key question posed during these exchanges was this: "Why are you willing to serve for the soviet, and yet you are not willing to serve us?" This must have been an effective appeal on the part of the village community, for many found it impossible to keep up their resistance. "In this way," wrote Fedor Matiukhin, who served as STK chairman in Krasivka volost, "I was *compelled* to serve *voluntarily* on the committee."[33]

If the organizers of the STK committees were not reluctant to enlist the involvement of former soviet functionaries, their attitude toward members of the Communist Party could not have been more different. The depletion of the countryside of Communist Party members, either through murder or flight, was nothing short of spectacular in the first months of the insurgency, but nevertheless some unfortunates remained in the villages at the turn of the new year.[34] Long before an STK political organizer entered a village during the first violent months of insurgency, rebel soldiers would have visited and demanded that local Communist Party members be turned over to the Partisan Army.[35] However, it was not unheard of for Communist Party members to join the STK, alongside others attached to the local soviet organization, once their village was asked to form such a committee. There was probably a strong element of self-preservation in such decisions, and Communist Party members would have relied on their fellow villagers to protect them.[36] For this reason, it is more likely that Communist Party members would have "joined" the insurgency in smaller villages, where greater trust and familiarity could be expected within the community.[37]

THE STKS AND THE PARTISAN ARMY IN THE VILLAGES

In what appears to be a pattern in the formation of local STKs in the first weeks of 1921, a community's willingness to organize a committee by publicly declaring support for the insurgency and selecting local STK representatives was followed by a further deepening of ties between the village community and the rebels. In many cases, the first task of the STK in a given locality was the organization of some act of sabotage, to be performed by villagers, typically against railway lines or bridges.[38] For obvious reasons, such activity was limited to villages situated near such infrastructure points. But these acts of sabotage, as with other deeds orchestrated by the new village and volost STKs, were relatively low-risk activities that could involve a larger range of people in the insurgency.[39] Not only did the attacks on the railways considerably damage the efforts of state authorities to maintain the meager volume of rail traffic that passed through the central provinces, but also they represented a first level of involvement by average villagers in the ever-expanding insurgency.

Getting people involved at an early stage prepared them for what was intended to be the rapid introduction of ordered relations between the villages and the units of the Partisan Army. Instructions formulated in December 1920 conceived of the local STKs regulating village economic and social relations in ways that would maximize the effectiveness of the insurgency rather than actualizing any social or political arrangements that may have counted among its goals.[40] In the villages and volosts, only STK members and the militiamen acting under their authority were to be armed, and their activities were focused on maintaining vigilance in the countryside and assuring that the villages would serve effectively as a base of support for the Partisan Army. Every village STK was supposed to have at least two active militiamen who performed a range of duties, from common policing functions to participating in Partisan Army operations.[41]

The variety of militia activities may explain why there was such a range of names for the militia found both in rebel documents and interrogation records. In addition to the general titles of militia referred to in several STK orders and instructions, what appear to be the same bodies are referred to as "internal security troops" or "military security" through the adaptation of the Soviet government acronym "VOKhR." (The acronym was rarely, if ever, presented in capital letters, thus forming the noun *vokhr*.) This borrowing of the Soviet expression was particularly noted by government investigators and officials, and the regular appearance of the word *vokhr* in reference to the rebel militia may have reflected the government's own interest in the mirror-image organization of the insurgency than a true "reflection" of the summarized rebel documents. On the other end, in the villages, the militia and its members were frequently referred to by tsarist-era terms, such as *sotniki* and *desiatniki*, the colloquial names for prerevolutionary local police and armed forces of public order.[42] These expressions had probably not died out with the fall of the tsarist regime, however, and locals would have identified militiamen operating in the countryside as *desiatniki* and *sotniki*, regardless of whether they were serving the 1917 Provisional Government, the Soviet government, or the insurgency. While at times the use of three different ways of identifying the militia suggests a specificity and precision behind the appearance of these terms, a close examination of the functions and prerogatives of the militia reveals a much more fluid organization that could, at any time, have recalled earlier precedents or represented something entirely novel.

Attending to the security of the village largely meant guarding against government spies or other potential internal enemies of the rebellion in villages with STKs. Many of the duties of the village and volost militias dealt with maintaining vigilance among the local population and rooting out any Communist Party members and suspected sympathizers with the Soviet regime.[43] In rebel-held areas, STKs issued passes to individuals that permitted travel between villages, although how extensive this system was is impossible to determine. Controlling all movements between villages was well beyond the capacity of the STK network, even at its height, but issuing official documents was certainly instrumental to maintaining communications between rebel units and the Partisan Army headquarters, and between STK committees. The delivery of correspondence and official "packets" of instructions and directives was accomplished by villagers mobilized for the task by the STK committees.[44] At the same time, the village and volost STKs and militia were instrumental in arranging security for Partisan Army units resting in a given village, setting up rotas involving villagers taking shifts atop bell towers or along roads on the lookout for Red Army patrols.[45]

The STKs and Partisan Army also enlisted the participation of the village population to feed the network of intelligence that kept them informed of Red Army troop movements more generally, as well as other developments that would clarify the dynamic context for the insurgency. This especially meant utilizing those villagers who traveled between town and country and even across uezd and provincial borders.[46] The village STKs communicated information regarding the location and movements of Red Army troops in the countryside, the forces that were being garrisoned in the towns, as well as the general political "mood" of the military and civilian populations in the towns—information that could be learned through simple observation or "innocent" conversation with other civilians. Women, children, and the elderly were enlisted in this type of activity, and even men in disguise were sent out to learn about affairs in the towns, as confirmed by Soviet government reports of villagers dressed as monks, or even as women, engaged in intelligence gathering for the Partisan Army near Morshansk.[47]

The Partisan Army and STKs exploited a range of contacts both within the countryside and the towns to further advance their knowledge of the government's counterinsurgency efforts, with individuals serving in the soviet administration providing information to STK contacts, and even sympathetic individuals in the government commissariats in the towns supplying details on the Red Army and the government to the rebels. In one case, three men in the uezd military commissariat in Kozlov were arrested by Cheka agents for supplying briefing papers on Red Army activities in the province to contacts in the Partisan Army.[48] In Saratov Province, according to a former member of the local Cheka organization, Partisan Army agents had been cultivated in a variety of government institutions, including the militia, the Food Commissariat, and the local soviets. According to the Cheka agent, Georgii Vedeniapin: "Our counterintelligence efforts were then very poor, and we never suspected that Antonov and his commanders at that time knew so much [about our activities]."[49]

Ignorance of the rebels' efforts to collect intelligence eventually gave way to what Vedeniapin labeled "spy-mania," the overcompensating vigilance by government officials and Red Army leaders in the summer of 1921.[50] To an extent, their fears were valid and vigilance was long overdue, even though the situation in the countryside proved to be delicate and complicated, as officials sought to distinguish between everyday activities and rebel reconnaissance. One Red Army officer was reprimanded after an incident in which a woman came to his headquarters trying to learn the location of her son, whom she claimed was a member of the newly formed Red Army cavalry brigade commanded by V. I. Dmitrenko. He told her the brigade was located in the village of Bolshe Lipovitsa, and when she inquired whether she could travel to Bolshe Lipovitsa to meet him without encountering other Red Army units, he answered: "Go ahead, love [*tetka*], you won't encounter anyone on your way there."[51] Was she a spy, collecting intelligence on Red Army troop locations, or simply a concerned mother? Such exchanges lost their air of innocence as the extent of the rebel intelligence network grew clearer to state authorities.

That network placed priority, as well, on pooling information regarding developments outside the province and the immediate context of the insurgency. News of political developments in other parts of the former Russian Empire that could be connected to the broader anti-Bolshevik movement extended the frame of reference for rebel leaders engaged in seemingly small-scale guerrilla attacks on Red Army patrols, and that widening frame of reference drew on the information collected via villagers and "noncombatants." Individuals who traveled beyond provincial borders, either on personal business or at the urging of the STK and the Partisan Army, were regularly "debriefed" on the situation in those localities, whether in nearby Voronezh, or as far away as the Urals. Demobilized or captured Red Army soldiers were a source of information regarding other "fronts" against the Soviet regime.[52] As the rebellion in Tambov grew stronger in the first months of 1921, the importance of this information regarding the wider context for their activities grew accordingly, and as the fortunes of the rebels declined by the summer, that same interest in the developments in other fronts continued and possibly even grew in importance for the remaining active insurgents.

THE STKS AND REBEL RECRUITMENT

As indicated by the rapid changes in the Partisan Army structure in the first weeks of 1921, one of the most important activities involving the STK committees at the local level during their first weeks of existence was the mobilization of young men for service in the rebel army. Each new committee, from the regional level down to the village, was to have one member to lead a "military department," which would draft and maintain lists of young men of mobilization age, set at eighteen to forty years. Initial appeals for volunteers could be followed by orders from the regional STK for men to be conscripted into service. In the case of such an order, according to the Cheka investigator who summarized captured STK materials, a local partisan unit was to be formed in three to five days.[53] This newly formed unit proved its viability by conducting some sort of minor operation, such as an act of sabotage like those described above, or a more direct confrontation with a small Red Army squadron or an attack on a nearby soviet or Communist Party cell. Following this, the local unit would likely be ordered to join an established Partisan Army regiment in the area.

The emphasis on voluntarism in the instructions and orders of the Partisan Army and STK was complicated by the fact that the vast majority of young men who were available for service were either Red Army recidivists, rejects, or demobs. Many had managed to avoid service in the Red Army by securing exemptions, and regardless of the validity of their claims to exemption, and regardless of how they secured it, the documents they had obtained to validate their exempt status in the face of Soviet antidesertion measures were understandably valuable to them. Therefore, confiscating or destroying exemption documents left many young men with little choice in response to appeals by the STK for service in the Partisan Army.[54] However, coercing young men into service with the Partisan Army was recognized as potentially counterproductive, and as long as the rebels enjoyed success in their clashes with Red Army troops, and as long as there remained targets for rebel attack that promised material gain as well as catharsis for young men whose hatred of the Soviet regime was likely at its peak, enlistment was not a problem for either the STKs or the Partisan Army. Unlike the situation in the first weeks of the insurgency, when poorly organized rebel groups criss-crossed the countryside and engaged in often random acts of violence and intimidation at a time when farmers were still busy with some of the most intense field work of the agricultural calendar, the response of villagers, and young men in particular, to the overtures of the organized Partisan Army and the STKs was more favorable in the first weeks of 1921. At this time the rebel organization was reaching its peak, and countervailing domestic responsibilities were at a minimum.

Groups of village men, organized by the local STKs and agitators, even appealed to the Partisan Army to recognize their improvised military unit or militia as a full Partisan Army regiment; these requests were not always approved, however, either because of doubts regarding reliability and the ability of Partisan Army headquarters to control the armed rebels or concerns that the Partisan Army could not sufficiently arm the new regiment. As such, many such groups of village men enjoyed a somewhat fluid existence, joining and leaving established Partisan Army regiments with some regularity, as circumstances and conditions changed.[55] But the success of the rebels in recruiting supporters in the early weeks of 1921 saw the structure of the Partisan Army grow considerably, divided into two distinct and largely independent "armies" commanded by Ivan Gubarev and Petr Tokmakov. The "First Partisan Army" consisted of several more regiments than the "Second Partisan Army" throughout the first half of 1921, although the "Second" shared its command headquarters with the Supreme Headquarters of the Partisan Army led by Aleksandr Antonov, which was accompanied by the "Special Regiment," a sort of praetorian guard that enjoyed many advantages regarding supply and equipment over other regiments with territorial designations. In all, there were fifteen regiments of the Partisan Army at the height of the rebellion in the first quarter of 1921, including the "Special Regiment," and over the course of the insurgency others would be organized to replace regiments that had, for one reason or another, ceased to exist. In addition, smaller brigades of insurgents operated on the margins, most likely outside the control of the Partisan Army but potentially ready for integration into the rebel movement.[56]

At this juncture in the history of the insurgency, STK appeals for active fighters grew more selective. The earliest instructions of the STK attest to the active targeting of local individuals with military experience. The consistent claim by Soviet propagandists that the rebels courted the support of former tsarist officers was certainly correct, but this was also true of the Red Army itself.[57] More important for the capabilities of the Partisan Army were the young men who had experience in the Red Army and had received rudimentary military training and perhaps combat experience.[58] Such men were immediately targeted in STK instructions, issued

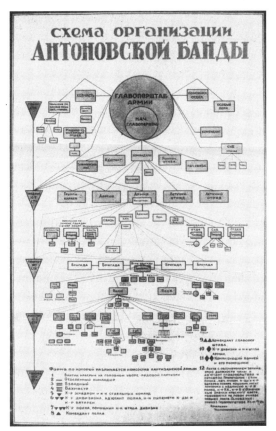

Organizational scheme of the Partisan Army of the Tambov region. This is a flow chart by the Special Department of the Tambov Cheka, which began reviewing seized rebel materials systematically in April 1921 and produced this chart by mid-June. It illustrates how governments often project familiar structures and levels of organization onto non-state challengers. The reality of the rebel organization was much more fluid. *Photograph courtesy of the Tambovskii Kraevedcheskii Muzei*

in December 1920, when the Red Army was beginning its long process of demobilization.[59] Likewise, any Red Army soldier who appeared in his native village, whether following demobilization or on official leave of absence, was targeted by STK officials for enlistment into the Partisan Army.[60] One young man, Grigorii Kolobenkov, told investigators that he fell in with the rebels quite early into the conflict in 1920. When his brother, Fedor, returned from Red Army service in January 1920, he and five of his friends joined the Partisan Army near their native village of Grushevka (Treskino volost, Kirsanov uezd). Grigorii told investigators that he had been allowed to quit the rebels and return home once his brother had joined.[61]

Kolobenkov's release from the Partisan Army may have been the result of official rebel policy limiting mobilization to no more than one young man from a single household.[62] Although no records exist detailing such a practice, it would have mirrored the Red Army's own official policy regarding the weight of military demands upon a given family. It was not the only parallel with government policy regarding military servicemen and the "home front." Local STK committees were instructed to privilege the households of partisan soldiers in ways that recalled the policy commitments of the Soviet regime to the welfare of servicemen and their families. Committees were charged with distributing among the local population any property that had been confiscated or seized by rebel units in the course of their operations. This included grain that had been taken from government collection points or railcars following rebel assaults, the property of state and collective farms looted by the Partisan Army (often with the assistance of nearby village communities), or items confiscated from the families of known Communist Party members. Distribution regularly favored the families of Partisan Army soldiers, although the STKs were also instructed to return any items recovered from government stores that had been confiscated from village households (provided that a household could prove ownership of the property).[63] Other households were similarly favored in the new status hierarchy of the rebellion. STKs maintained lists of households generally regarded as "favorable" to the partisan cause, just as they kept lists of families that had "suffered at the hands of red bands," referring to those who had been the targets of government reprisals or the victims of self-provisioning (*samosnabzhenie*) by Red Army units.[64]

Control over items confiscated and seized by the Partisan Army and other agents of the insurgency was only one facet of the STK's involvement in the local economy. During the winter months, regulation of the food supply to ensure that the needs of the rebel soldiers were met required the control of local mills.[65] According to the instructions issued by the provincial STK, local committees were to require local millers to effectively "tax" grain that they milled for local farmers, taking a cut of one-fifteenth for standard wheat or rye flour, and one-twentieth for flour that contained nongrain filler (*surrogat*), such as pigweed. Similarly, the STKs were instructed to obtain a portion of all sunflower oil produced at local presses.[66] During the height of the insurgency in the winter months of early 1921, delivery of foodstuffs to the rebels typically took place in the village itself, as local STK representatives would be informed in advance of the arrival of a Partisan Army unit, and they would be expected to have food and fodder available for the soldiers and their horses, as well as adequate quarters.[67] Keeping records of the number and type of livestock, including riding horses, was similarly a part of the responsibility of the STKs to both regulate the local economy and support the Partisan Army.[68] If a community agreed to organize an STK committee and "join" the insurgency, their village was many times more likely to be visited regularly by active rebel forces, and the demands placed upon them were apt to be heavy, especially during the difficult season during which Partisan Army numbers increased so dramatically.

The encroachment of the actual fighting between the Partisan and Red armies on the village communities must have been similarly heavy, although it is difficult to gauge this for the period when the rebels were dominant in the countryside. One statement left by a villager from Tsarevka volost (Kirsanov uezd), describes the intense interest of villagers when clashes between rebel and government forces occurred nearby. Young and old alike in the village of Ledovka would climb to the roofs of the houses to get a good vantage point, enjoying the spectacle despite the risks this entailed.[69] Such curiosity, however, was unlikely to have been the norm, even at the peak of the insurgency's strength. There were many more reasons for villagers to seek the relative safety of their houses when violence broke out in the vicinity.

MANAGING PARTISAN RELATIONS

The dependence of the rebels upon the local population for horses, food, and fodder left vast opportunities for abuse of authority by partisan units, particularly those operating outside their native areas. While certain targets, such as soviet collective farms and state grain collection points, were considered legitimate for rebel looting—all of which fed Soviet characterizations of the self-styled "partisans" as "bandits"—the possibility of rebel abuses against the local village communities meant that the Partisan Army had to consistently combat the damaging label of "bandit" in order to maintain its authority among the rural population. This became particularly the case when the rebels tried to impose structure and discipline upon the movement in the new year. A proclamation to Partisan Army soldiers in January or February 1921 sought to remind rebels just how far the movement had progressed:

> Comrade partisans! Already six months have passed since we partisans launched our struggle for the complete liberation of the peasants and workers from oppression and violence and against the bloodthirsty aggressors [*nasil'niki*]—the robber-Communists. In the space of six months we have accomplished much, and from all quarters of the working population hundreds and thousands of honorable fighters are joining us, standing in the ranks of our army and fighting for the achievement of our common goal in the interests of the entire working population and oppressed population. We remember, comrades, when we launched into the first days of our

uprising with only twenty rifles, each with a mere five bullets to fire, and now what do we see before us: a large and well-equipped army, which has already delivered a mighty blow to our enemy and forcing them to reassess their position [*zastavila ikh prizadumat'sia*]

These words of encouragement for the active partisans—an effort to situate their weeks and months of limited fighting into a narrative context of growing strength and dominance—were tempered by reminders of the commitment to a partnership with the local population that had to be maintained for the movement to thrive: "But always remember, comrades, that the population will only support the modern [*peredovyi*] soldiers who strive with all their strength and ability to respect and help them with their needs and who do not allow into their ranks the thugs [*nasil'niki*] and looters who will violate [villagers'] rights and [steal] their hard-earned property." Recognizing that incidents had become common in which rebel soldiers were stealing from villagers and making excessive demands upon them, often for nothing but personal gain and gratification, the proclamation (signed by the Supreme Headquarters of the Partisan Army and its political instructors) appealed for discipline in the ranks of the rebels:

> This type of activity in our army is completely impermissible because it will only place us at odds with the working population and force us to abandon all our sacred visions of the liberation of the oppressed. We, the members of the Supreme Operational Headquarters and your political leaders, appeal to you, dear comrade partisans, with an urgent call to be honorable fighters and defenders of the rights of workers, to present yourselves before the population as the most discreet and veritable sons of our peasant revolution, and then people themselves will understand that we are truly not bandits, as the robber-Communists have labeled us, but are instead honorable fighters for the ideals of the oppressed.[70]

The authors of this proclamation called on partisans to police their fellow rebels and to report any who committed abuses against the local population. But the problem remained throughout the course of the insurgency, regularly compromising the authority of the rebels.[71] "Order no. 1" of the First Partisan Army, issued on 1 January 1921, dealt precisely with the issue of "banditry," although it was mainly concerned with the activities of STKs and village-based guard detachments. It threatened those who engaged in illegal activities, especially theft and looting, with arrest and trial before a "revolutionary army court."[72] While the Partisan Army had established procedures to deal with such crimes earlier in the year, documents detailing the punishments for specific infractions that related to the STKs and to the insurgency effort did not emerge until February 1921.[73]

The sparse document that was distributed to Partisan Army units listed thirty-seven separate crimes and abuses, and it sought to regulate the conduct of rebel soldiers as well as civilians, both of which had a bearing on the military struggle. It lists such crimes as the black market trade in horses and guns by civilians alongside acts such as cowardice (flight from battle) and illegal confiscations carried out by Partisan Army soldiers. The list of crimes was most likely informed by immediate experience, as many such acts had been reported by Partisan Army units and STKs; thus it constitutes a code of punishments governed by contemporary circumstances rather than indicating more popular, deeply held notions of justice. Punishments were principally corporal, although there were exceptions. For lesser offenses, such as the acquisition and consumption of moonshine (*samogon*) by rebel soldiers, the punishment (upon the second violation) was demotion to sentry, which presumably carried with it lower status (an interesting consequence that is difficult to evaluate) and possibly lower benefits for one's family. In cases of severe crimes and repeat violations, the punishment could be death. A soldier who fled battle for a second time could expect to lose his life, as could one who killed in the course of robbery. The most common form of punishment, however, was flogging, and the number of lashes ranged from fifteen to fifty according to the seriousness of the crime and the number of repeat offenses. Corporal punishment was both traditional and logical: while the use of the lash was familiar to rural communities from the (hated) practices of the old regime, it was also one of the few forms of punishment available to Partisan Army leaders hoping to instill discipline within the ranks. And while inflicting corporal punishment and the threat of execution provided fodder for later Soviet propagandists, these practices had more recent antecedents than the modi operandi of state officials serving the tsar.[74]

The courts of the Partisan Army were composed of three judges, each devoted to this sole responsibility, and they were assisted by three others in charge of investigating individual cases and documenting decisions. It is difficult to determine to what extent the population in rebel-held territory had confidence in the army courts, but the Partisan Army was evidently responsive to the complaints of villagers raised against individuals and groups who abused power or engaged in sustained criminal activity.[75] Yet despite evidence that village communities had some confidence in the capacity of the Partisan Army and the STKs to regulate the conduct of its soldiers and members, the struggle with corruption and abuse of power was constant. The corresponding struggle to protect these same communities against the abuses by Red Army "bandits" may have contributed to the effort to stay on the right side of public opinion, but it also underscores the extent to which village communities continued to suffer depredations throughout the course of the insurgency.

LIFE WITH THE PARTISAN ARMY

Cultivating the confidence of the partisan population extended beyond pure material concerns. Ritual and symbolic elements featured in efforts to instill discipline within the rebel units and to tie them more closely to the defense of their communities. Reclaiming the revolutionary high ground went beyond propaganda pronouncements to include the everyday trappings of revolutionary culture. Partisan Army units were reported as entering villages with banners containing familiar words, such as the PSR's long-standing slogan, "In struggle you will secure your rights." In one case, government agents reported that PSR representatives had managed to transport from Moscow an elaborate banner bearing this slogan embroidered with gold thread and other flourishes that distinguished it from the more improvised banners typically displayed to village communities.[76] More mundane designations of revolutionary principle included the red ribbons that Partisan Army soldiers were reported to wear, as well as the singing of the "International" by soldiers as they entered villages.[77] Such symbolic elements were in particular evidence at funerals for fallen rebel soldiers. It was reported by STK members that entire communities turned out to participate in these rituals and that lengthy orations dwelled on the noble qualities of the anti-Bolshevik struggle, something that situated the sacrifices made by individual families.[78] Such displays were as much for the rebel soldiers in attendance as they were for the community, and once again, there are parallels with the Red Army, which conducted similar funerals for soldiers killed during the counterinsurgency and which were also occasions to involve local communities in the broader campaign against the rebels.[79]

The symbolic elements of the rebel movement went beyond those that emphasized the bond between the rebels and the communities and the legitimacy of the struggle with the Soviet regime. The establishment of authority and hierarchy also drew heavily upon symbolic projections of power. As in the first weeks of the rebellion, the display of firearms was vital, both to achieve specific aims and more generally to establish an air of authority. While a machine gun or light artillery gun was vitally important for rebel units in their interaction with village communities, rebel leaders and commanders were proud to brandish personal firearms, particularly pistols kept at the hip. Aleksandr Antonov himself had two revolvers, one on each hip, which he was said never to be without.[80] Likewise, the trappings of authority were found in the clothing worn by senior rebel leaders, especially the black leather jackets that had been the signature of the Cheka agent since that organization's formation.[81] Uniforms were less common, and there was no established display of rank, although one contemporary described in his memoirs a sort of sedan chair that Antonov insisted upon traveling in with his personal guard that would clearly identify him as the grand leader of the partisan movement.[82]

While this last claim appears dubious, there was nevertheless acute attention paid to the projection of authority and power by leaders of the insurgency. There was a strong element of self-indulgence to this, as well as personal gratification accompanying the projection of power always threatened to undermine the authority and legitimacy of the rebel leadership. Providing for the Partisan Army meant supporting the excesses of individuals such as Aleksandr Antonov and Petr Tokmakov, whose entrance into a village brought with it long nights of music and dancing. This may have created a mystique that contributed to their authority, or it may have "personalized" the rebel leaders as honest muzhiks. Either way, a carnival atmosphere frequently accompanied their entourage.

One Siberian woman, Anastasiia Apollonovna Drigo-Drigina, a would-be actor and singer who had suffered multiple misfortunes before and after the revolution and had been imprisoned on three separate occasions, traveled with the rebel leadership in Tambov in the first months of 1921. Having been on a train in January 1921 that was stopped and raided by rebels near Rtishchevo in Saratov Province, she was left without any money or belongings; thus with nothing to lose, she appealed directly to the rebel commander on the scene, Petr Tokmakov. Tokmakov allowed her to travel with his entourage, and their relations quickly progressed: according to an autobiographical statement left by Drigo-Drigina in late 1921, Tokmakov asked her to marry him soon after. Although she refused, she continued to travel with the rebels and performed at their parties when they stopped in villages or set up camp for the night. This continued for over three months in 1921, after which Drigo-Drigina was "released" by Antonov personally (some weeks after Tomakov had died of wounds) and placed in the custody of an elderly couple in the village of Kareevka, near Inzhavino, whom he trusted to keep her safe.[83]

Drigo-Drigina was one of several women who either traveled with the rebel leadership or were invited to their soirees during the height of the insurgency.

One Cheka investigator, surveying the collected testimonies of village women who claimed to have had relations with Antonov but who could provide little useful intelligence about him while he was still at large, commented sardonically in the margins of the testimony of one such woman: "It is obvious that Antonov would not be able to speak in confidence with each and every one of his lovers, seeing as he had at least one in practically every village in the region."[84] It was a measure of the extent to which these men lived for the moment, while at the same time leading a movement that struggled to project hope for the future.

PARTISAN ARMY PROPAGANDA

If the arrival of a unit of the Partisan Army brought with it demands for fresh horses, food, and quarters, as well as an element of excitement and even carnival, communities were also frequently subjected to the political work of Partisan Army members whose task it was to sustain the message of the insurgents. STK committees in the countryside were most frequently involved in practical matters relating to the insurgency and maintenance of the Partisan Army's operations. They were less involved in propagating the message of the insurgents. This was the work of the Partisan Army itself, particularly the political workers that accompanied its constituent regiments and battalions. The goals of the insurgency, summarized in the STK program, remained the centerpiece of interactions between these political agitators and the village communities, but as the insurgency established itself in the countryside of southern Tambov Province, the necessity of providing information for village communities that justified their continued involvement and assumed enthusiasm for the rebel movement grew more important. Progress reports, not only on activities in the province itself, but also on other fronts in the popular struggle against the Soviet regime, became a prominent component of rebel propaganda in 1921, when the insurgency was its height and support was at its peak.

The materials of the Partisan Army regiments attest to the attention paid to political work among the population, as repeated visits to villages within the area of operations for a given regiment brought successive speeches by rebel agitators on familiar themes, such as the Constituent Assembly, the end to grain requisitions and the restoration of free trade, and the end of the arbitrary and abusive rule of the commissars and Communist Party members that would be achieved when the Soviet government was toppled.[85] One summary of seized Partisan

Army materials produced by the Tenth Volche-Karanchan regiment confirmed that many of the documents concerned the "political work conducted by the political bureau of the regiment, including the organization of mass meetings of partisan soldiers as well as among the village population." As an example, the summary cited one such meeting in the area of Novo-Vol'skii on 15 March 1921, in which "a majority of the local population participated." The Cheka investigator described the meeting:

> Orators who delivered speeches included Luchinin [Aleksei Gavrilovich—adjutant in the regiment], "Bat'ko," Parshin [the political chief of the regiment], "Shuba" [another political worker], and others, all of whom described for the assembled citizens the difficult situation that the homeland [*rodina*] finds itself in thanks to the three-year rule of the Communists, who have brought the country to the point of death and destruction, and they called upon the peasants to overcome this situation through concerted and effective organization, which will hasten the moment of victory over the usurpers of the people, the Communists-Jews.[86]

In repeated visits to villages, rebels continued to underscore these basic themes as part of the basic routine of Partisan Army units in the countryside. Articulating and reinforcing popular grievances and defining the objectives of the insurgency were central to interactions between the Partisan Army and the village communities.

Just as the Partisan Army leadership displayed a thirst for information regarding developments in other parts of Russia to provide a context for their own rebellion, that same quality of information became central to the sustained overtures to the partisan population in the spring of 1921:

> Comrade peasants! The Bolsheviks seized power at the point of a rifle . . . then began their vile and bloody rule . . . in which they oppressed us and stole from us from every angle, leaving us without food and without livestock. . . . The Communists never talk about freedom anymore, except insofar as the Communist levelling of all classes has left everyone without freedom and equally at risk of oppression and execution, and this has left us peasants with few options, yet a great many peasants have already begun [to rise up], as the Communists themselves write in their newspapers that rebellions have broken out in seventeen provinces.[87]

Appeals to the rural population and to active rebels integrated the "intelligence" regarding events in other parts of Soviet Russia (and beyond), feeding back the information the people in the villages had themselves gathered. The message was one of progress in the anti-Soviet struggle, of vitality in a movement that extended beyond the province, situating events in Tambov within a wider picture of violent opposition to the regime:

> Comrade partisans! The turning point has been reached. Our strength grows with each passing day. The power of the Communists is melting away like the snow. Every day new villages, towns, and even entire provinces, are breaking away from Communist rule. It was not long ago that the authority of the Communists had spread throughout the central provinces and other places, such as the Ukraine, the Volga, a portion of the Caucasus (a large part of the Caucasus had never known, and never would know, Communist authority), and, as if this were not enough, Siberia. But now the entire south of Russia, including the Caucasus, has been engulfed in a general uprising, the Ukraine is routing the Bolsheviks, and in Siberia, according to the accounts of these same Communists, Semenov is once again up to no good. In the central provinces, it has been almost one year and Communists everywhere have not found themselves respite, and, according to official information, once Communist cities, such as Kronstadt and Petersburg, have chased away the Communists and have established their own rule, the same type of rule for which we have fought for more than seven months, and for which we will continue to fight.[88]

Such claims were the subject of speeches, proclamations, and "circulars" distributed among the STKs by the Partisan Army.[89] One political worker told investigators, following his capture in February 1921, that he had been involved in many such meetings in villages in which he would describe the range of opposition to the Soviet regime, from worker demonstrations to rural insurgencies, and that "without question, these [popular] armies would soon be unified with our very own Partisan Army."[90] Such descriptions tapped into a narrative understanding of collective resistance, one that not only identified the worthiness of similar rebellions ongoing against the Soviet state, but also drew upon a continuity with the revolution of 1917 and the inherent value of its popular, "partisan" defense against the "Communist usurpers."[91]

The veracity of such claims would have been at their peak in the first months of 1921, when the rebellion was at its strongest in the province and popular opposition to the Soviet regime, particularly in Moscow and Petrograd, had provoked a crisis for the Communist Party and the Soviet leadership. One of the many women to have left statements regarding their personal encounters with Aleksandr Antonov and his headquarters noted that one of Antonov's closest companions was a Communist Party member who was sympathetic to the rebels and who frequently spoke with authority regarding events in Moscow, describing them as signaling the imminent collapse of the Soviet government. Partisan Army leaders similarly received communications from the Soviet capital, keenly following developments there.[92] Given the political circumstances in January and February 1921, it is not difficult to appreciate just how short a step it was for rebel commanders, soldiers, and civilians alike to place their own insurgency at the heart of these events, serving as an inspiration for others just as it legitimized their own continued campaign against the regime in Tambov Province. The invocation of outside developments served as an indication of strength—that the movement continued to move and that sacrifices and risks would produce the promised result—and it had yet to emerge as an indicator of weakness.

SOVIET INVESTIGATORS, after the insurgency had ended, would attest to the strength of the STK network—how elaborate it was, how it interacted with the Partisan Army, and most important how much support the committees enjoyed among the local population. Despite the formal responsibilities that the STK committees possessed, the key to the confidence that they and their members enjoyed was probably attributable to their local character and their popular selection, much as many of the early soviets enjoyed popularity and legitimacy before the Communist Party sought to make those institutions reliable instruments of central administration. In a similar way, the STKs, like the early soviets, enjoyed legitimacy and confidence in large part because they made a minimal imposition upon the everyday lives of village communities. Their responsibilities were principally oriented toward the support of the Partisan Army, and the most onerous demands that were made upon villagers—such as those for fresh horses and for food—were occasioned by the arrival of rebel units, rather than a constant feature of life in the partisan countryside.[93] Such arrivals were more frequent in some villages than in others, and as the conflict wore on, maintaining popular support for the insurgency would demand new strategies of the rebel leadership, both in its practical interactions with the village communities, and in the message it brought regarding the status and direction of the anti-Bolshevik movement.

Creating a context for understanding the experience of collective resistance was a dynamic process, one that involved pragmatic and practical elements of integration, as well as symbolic and ritual ones. Solidarity, and the "partisan" collective identity that broadened the appeal of the movement, could not be assumed by Partisan Army and STK leaders, as the struggle to manage relations with village communities and with rebel soldiers demonstrates. Instead, sustaining the movement involved a constant negotiation of material and environmental constraints, popular perceptions, and subjective experiences that promoted the primacy of the rebellion and its objectives in the experience of village communities. What is more, the process involved an adversary that was emerging from its own transitional phase to engage the struggle with the rebellion on all fronts.

CLAIMING
THE INITIATIVE

*Anxiety, Opportunity, and
Seasonal Change in Early 1921*

ALEKSANDR VASIL'EVICH PAVLOV, an experienced career military officer and former divisional commander in the Red Army, arrived in Tambov on 5 January 1921 to assume overall command of the counterinsurgency effort. Following the investigations conducted by the VNUS senior staff in late December, in which the local Tambov leadership was chastised once again for their mismanagement of the military resources at their disposal, as well as for their overall incompetence in confronting the challenge of armed rural rebels, Pavlov entered the scene with the full backing of Moscow to establish state control over the strategic situation in the province.[1] Mindful of the complications that the Russian spring would pose for the government's effort to regain control over the territory—not only the effects of the thaw on roads used by state troops but also the improved cover to be exploited in the forests and swamps by armed insurgents—Pavlov was promised significant armed reinforcements to replace the patchwork force already active in the province, and the Tambov commander was permitted a direct line of communication with Moscow and Red Army headquarters (*glavkom*), rather than answering first to regional headquarters in Orel. The deployment of combat-ready and adequately supplied troops to the province was acknowledged as critical, as even the most savage critics of the provincial authorities acknowledged that the forces at their disposal in the final months of 1920 had been less than expedient.

Having been familiarized with the challenge that confronted him in Tambov, Pavlov offered his reflections on the situation in the province to his Red Army colleagues in Orel less than a week after arriving. Beginning with the now customary acknowledgment that the rebel Antonov and his army of followers had to be taken seriously as a military foe, Pavlov elaborated on the theme with a certain indulgence:

> The latest information processed by the [Red Army] command indicates that in terms of scouting, organization of defense, and other measures developed by the bandits, what we are dealing with is an organization that is operating in a customary military fashion, and without doubt the bandits have in their midst a variety of specialists familiar with military affairs. They possess an excellent knowledge of the terrain, their command center stays on top of developments through a network of informants, and the region provides them with rich resources that have facilitated the bandits' success, and with each passing day the movement expands, reaching a threatening scale.[2]

Explaining that in major portions of the province Soviet power existed only in administrative centers where significant numbers of troops were permanently stationed, Pavlov condensed his list of priorities to two basic points: "First, destroy the individual armed bands, and second, take measures toward the ultimate military occupation of the region, to last for as long as necessary, because at the moment Soviet power in the districts does not possess a strong and close connection with the population."[3]

The notion of occupation as an objective of the counterinsurgency effort in Tambov had grown in currency since December 1920.[4] It was the first of Petr Kameron's recommendations in his report for VNUS in late December, and the word also featured prominently in Kornev's accompanying report to the Central Committee of the Communist Party.[5] Occupying the region dominated by the rebels at the turn of the year meant flooding it with government troops and establishing a stable military presence in major villages and strategic points; this would deprive the rebels of any safe haven in the populated areas, as well as deny them the kind of low-risk attacks they had thrived upon during the preceding months. The shortage of reliable troops during the second half of 1920, and their poor deployment by local authorities, had effectively abdicated authority in the countryside of southern Tambov to the Partisan Army, an observation repeatedly made in communications from the local administrations in the uezds of the province during the final weeks of 1920. Attempts to reorganize soviet administration in individual localities had been brief, as such efforts, without accompanying armed security, only provided easy targets for rebel units or even armed groups outside the purview of the Partisan Army. Restoring control over the strategic situation in the province meant creating conditions in which military operations and a stable armed presence facilitated and complemented the reestablishment of local government and, with that, Pavlov's "strong and close connection" between "Soviet power" and the civilian population.

Recognition of the complementary relationship between local administration and military counterinsurgency was the underlying message of the "occupation" strategy as articulated by military commanders. It was as much a recognition of the "weakness" of administration in Tambov as of the inadequate quality and quantity of troops fighting the rebels. The first step toward the realization of "occupation," as emphasized in Pavlov's report, was to deploy more, and more effective, troops to the province as the struggle against the rebels was reconfigured once again. Steps in this direction had already been taken. Battle-tried Red Army infantry and cavalry brigades were assigned at the end of December, and over 300 Communist Party members from units of the Tenth Special Army joined 300 other Communist Party members drawn from the Red Army's Political Department to augment discipline within the units assigned to the anti-Antonov front. Armored train units, with multiple mounted artillery and machine guns, were also earmarked for deployment to Tambov at the end of 1920, part of the effort to improve the Red Army's ability to respond quickly to threats from a secure base in the administrative centers of Tambov as well as to secure the major railway stations in the south of the province.[6]

Such deployments, by the end of January, nearly trebled the available armed government forces in Tambov. At the beginning of the year, the Orel commander, Skudr, arranged for the creation of distinct military sectors to divide up the territory of counterinsurgency operations.[7] Eventually, as the Red Army presence in Tambov grew, there would be eight military sectors, each with its own command headquarters and occupation forces distributed within the territory. The creation of discrete military sectors within the zone of the insurgency imposed a measure of structure on Red Army operations at the time, but the effects of this restructuring were slow to become manifest, given the general state of disarray in Soviet military forces during the chaotic process of demobilization set into motion at the end of 1920.[8] Troop increases in the province in the first weeks of 1921 were partially offset by the number of Red Army soldiers who, in the course of a hasty demobilization campaign in December and January, fell in with the Partisan Army upon returning to their native villages. The deployment of more units to the province may have promised rapid results on the ground for observers within official circles in Tambov, but the shift in the balance of forces in the conflict with the Partisan Army remained a development very much confined to the paperwork of the Red Army command staff in Tambov, Orel, and Moscow. The same problems that had plagued the counterinsurgency effort in late 1920, namely, troops of questionable reliability and small, poorly defended deployments, continued to plague government forces in Tambov at the start of the new year.[9] While some regular Red Army troops were brought to the province, many of the forces that were assigned to Tambov in early 1921 were former VNUS units, which were frequently filled with "second-chance men" who had previously deserted and who were undertrained, poorly supplied, and unaccustomed to counterinsurgency operations.[10]

Occupation as a guiding strategy enjoyed currency outside military circles principally because of the implication that it would signal a political and material commitment by Moscow to resolve the conflict in the province once and for all. This was the meaning of occupation for many in the local administration and the Tambov Communist Party, who had felt either abandoned by the central government or betrayed by those officials in the provincial capital who repeatedly supplied the Kremlin with misleadingly reassuring assessments of the situation in Tambov in the final months of 1920. From quite early on, officials in Tambov expressed their conviction that the insurgency would be suppressed once regular Red Army forces were deployed to Tambov in adequate numbers. The failure of such a decisive deployment to the province provoked a strong mixture of anger and genuine fear, particularly among state and party officials closest to the fighting. At the turn of the year, local government and party officials in the uezd towns continued to produce damning critiques of the conduct of the counterinsurgency campaign, and these were accompanied by alarming reports of conditions in the towns and villages that were isolated or overrun by the insurgency.

In Borisoglebsk, in the southernmost tip of Tambov Province, uezd officials found themselves effectively blockaded and under siege by rebels in early January 1921, preventing the delivery of any food supplies and threatening an assault on the town at a time when government defenses were understood to be woefully inadequate. Officials there had been composing telegrams and reports to provincial and central governmental offices since the final weeks of 1920, demanding that "real forces" be sent to the uezd, and to the province generally.[11] Reinforcements were promised in early January by Red Army commanders in Tambov, including one armored train group that, upon its approach to Borisoglebsk, encountered intense fighting that may have caught the attention of the bulk of organized rebel forces in the region. When the assault on Borisoglebsk was made on 23 January by the Partisan Army's Sixth Volche-Karachan Regiment (reportedly numbering a paltry 250 men on horseback), the limited armed forces at the disposal of the town, formed around highly motivated Red Army cavalry cadets, was sufficient to defend Borisoglebsk.[12] While almost completely lacking in coordination and planning, this was the first attempt by the rebels to storm one of the uezd towns in the province that represented the last redoubts of the Soviet government in southern Tambov.

Fear of being overrun by the rebels was a constant preoccupation of government and party officials in vulnerable uezd towns such as Kirsanov and Borisoglebsk, where the insurgency had already established effective control over most of the countryside.[13] Even if this level of distress was not replicated in other uezd towns affected by the insurgency, the degenerating material conditions at the height of the Russian winter combined with the instability in the countryside to create a shared anxiety among uezd officials that defined their assessments of the political situation in the towns.

PANIC IN THE UEZDS

If the insurgency had accomplished one of its objectives by the end of 1920, it was the de facto cessation of state grain requisitioning in the territory of the conflict. While the need to terminate the provocative activities of the requisition squads was widely recognized, the true underlying reason for the effective cessation of procurement efforts in southern Tambov was the insecurity of local uezd officials, who withdrew procurement squads from the countryside to help defend the towns against attack by the insurgents. Requisition efforts did not come to a complete halt in the province, however. In the north, unaffected by the violence of the *antonovshchina*, procurement efforts were intensified to compensate for province-wide shortfalls, but the yield from such intensified efforts was minimal as grain production was truly concentrated only in the south of Tambov.[14] The drive to collect grain from the villages in the areas that constituted the periphery of the conflict—parts of Morshansk, Kozlov, and Usman uezds—was unevenly pursued by government officials who were concerned about their own safety as well as the long-term stability of the countryside they administered. The same tensions that had plagued procurement efforts in earlier campaigns, between the Food Commissariat on one side and the local soviet administrations and Communist

Party organizations on the other, continued in early 1921, although the objective difficulties of conducting requisitioning in areas contiguous to the insurgency prompted caution even among the target-obsessed authorities in the Food Commissariat.[15] Frequently, however, this caution was easily overcome, particularly in areas that had previously been under rebel control and where the continued demand for grain collection combined with an evidently strong desire to punish villages that were believed to harbor pro-rebel sympathies. In such cases, the requisition squads served as the first agents of occupation, after a given village had been "liberated" by the army.

The material situation in the towns—particularly the larger ones on the periphery of the conflict, such as Kozlov and Morshansk—had understandably degenerated rapidly as the reserves of food were quickly consumed in the early winter of 1920–1921. In Kozlov, with its relatively large population of railroad workers and substantial military garrison, the government had abandoned its effort to ration bread in recognition that the black market had become the only reliable source of food for townspeople. Local Communist Party members saw that the marginalization of the municipal government because of the challenges confronting its administration and the population was linked to the increasing defiance of government-imposed curfews and other public order measures, particularly by railroad workers. Rather than witnessing heightened tensions between the town and country as the provisions crisis took hold, Kozlov officials reported widespread recognition that the situation in the villages—where grain was in short supply and where bloodshed was always threatened—was much worse.[16]

In Morshansk the same recognition of grain shortages in the countryside prompted uezd officials to cease efforts at requisitioning grain, opting instead to seek relief from the food crisis by confiscating livestock, including draft animals, from the surrounding countryside for slaughter.[17] As in Kozlov, a hungry municipal population was becoming increasingly difficult to manage in Morshansk. Both towns were reporting problems containing desertion from local garrisons when food shortages, rumors of the rebellion in the surrounding countryside, and low temperatures cut into the morale of the reserve soldiers.[18] Efforts continued to transfer Tambov natives from the garrisons to assignments outside the province, and local Military Commissariat officials also attempted to "dilute" the potential for disruptions by forming mixed units of Tambov natives and non-natives in the hope of breaking up the solidarity that was believed to intensify the "pull" exercised by the Partisan Army and the rebellion in the countryside.[19] But the potential for serious disruptions among the soldier population, as with prisoners and other discrete groups that suffered the material shortages even more acutely, remained a prominent concern expressed in the regular updates drafted by the Communist Party organizations from Morshansk and Kozlov.[20]

While reports of outright "counterrevolutionary" organization within the towns were rare, insulating the town population from the restive countryside and limiting their familiarity with the works of the Partisan Army, the STK, and the man Antonov would be far more difficult if civilians were forced to venture out to the villages for food.[21] More important, however, the fact that people in the towns were forced to supplement their diet with the dreaded "surrogates" baked into the bread or boiled in the soup forced local officials to worry about the preservation of order in the towns. Having already endured one attack by the Partisan Army, Borisoglebsk remained in many ways the most isolated of the towns caught in the territory of the insurgency, and the fact that this translated into a de facto siege that cut off food supplies produced a continued stream of telegrams to Tambov and Moscow demanding action. There, officials in the uezd soviet executive committee and local Communist Party reported that all the orphanages had been shut in the new year, as had all the public cafeterias. Rations had ceased in January as the town had no reserves of grain, and all reports pointed to the appearance of hunger and starvation in the surrounding villages, as well:

> At the present time any talk of systematic work in the uezd is impossible and will remain impossible so long as only some sixteen villages can be said to fall under our influence. In light of the threats that face us, we find it necessary to declare that unless [the Tambov provincial soviet] takes decisive measures to save Borisoglebsk from hunger and, following from this, takes quick and decisive steps to end the rebellion, then we will be forced once again to send a delegate to deliver a report directly to the center and to Sovnarkom and to appeal for help regarding these issues.[22]

When the deployment of more troops to the Tambov front in 1921 was accompanied by the assignment of scores of Communist Party members to the province, this was as much to control discipline problems in the army as to control the growing panic being expressed in the local administrations caught in the territory of the rebellion. The level of dispirit is understandable, owing to the strain of the constant threat of armed assault by rebels and the sense of abandonment by authorities in the provincial capital and Moscow; the pain of seeing party colleagues and soviet workers fall victim to often extreme violence committed by a significant portion of the population with a profound hatred of the Soviet regime; and the difficulty of being unable to assist Communist Party refugees from the countryside suffering the food shortages that were shared by nearly the entire town population.

The sense that this situation was not of their making and beyond their control affected virtually every local administration and Communist Party organization in southern Tambov Province. Needing to defend their own decisions and reputations, officials in the provincial administration and Tambov Communist Party organization continued to deflect attention from such protests, and in the first half of January 1921 a party committee was formed in Tambov to deal with the "hysteria" that had come to afflict the party membership and soviet administrations in the localities.[23]

In fact, this constituted one of the rare initiatives taken by the Communist Party in the province to manage the political situation. There had been only limited efforts channeled into propaganda, and the job of combating the Partisan Army and STK on the military *and* political fronts was left to the Red Army and VNUS commanders.[24] By the end of 1920, the involvement of officials from Tambov in the counterinsurgency effort was largely marginal, as military officials appointed by Orel and Moscow assumed direct control over operations. The only branch of the provincial government that was not fully marginalized during this period was the Food Commissariat, whose own operations in the past had been carried out with a controversially strong measure of autonomy, and which was now becoming more closely integrated with the Red Army as the troop presence in the southern uezds of the province was dramatically increased.[25]

THE PLENIPOTENTIARY COMMISSION AND THE END OF REQUISITIONING

The marginalization of provincial officials was not, however, entirely a result of the logic of centralization that lay at the heart of the escalating counterinsurgency campaign in 1921. The provincial administration had, since at least the spring of 1920, been politically divided, with a strong clique of native officials standing in opposition to a small cohort of "outsiders" assigned to positions of responsibility in the province. This basic tension had isolated the two high-profile apparatchiki in the province, the chairman of the Tambov soviet executive committee, A. G. Shlikhter, and his close associate, V. N. Meshcheriakov, who had served as Shlikhter's assistant (*zamestitel'*) on the soviet executive and as head of the Tambov Communist Party organization in late 1920. The "intrigues, machinations, and virtual blood feuds" that Vladimir Antonov-Ovseenko had described following his first spell in Tambov in late 1919 and early 1920 had been brought to the surface as a consequence of the prolonged insurgency and had rendered the provincial government and party organization ineffective and functionally paralyzed as the insurgency entered its sixth full month.[26]

The essential conflict between local officials and centrally appointed outsiders was one that broadly characterized relations between Moscow and provincial governments throughout the latter stages of the civil war, but more generally the themes of centralization and democracy came to dominate a range of center-periphery tensions within the Soviet Republic, from relations between Moscow and non-Russian territories of the former empire to those between Moscow and the trade unions. Ironically, high-profile outsiders had arrived in Tambov in the second half of 1920 in an effort to defuse center-periphery tensions within the province itself. The extended fallout from the calamitous cavalry raid in August 1919 by the White General Mamontov included a bitter conflict between party officials in Tambov with those in the uezds, particularly the party organization in Kozlov, which had been briefly occupied during the White cavalry raid and suffered heavily in terms of lives lost and property destroyed.[27] In the second half of 1920, the two main antagonists were removed from the province: the head of the Communist Party organization, B. A. Vasil'ev, was dispatched to serve in the Smolensk party organization, and the Kozlov party chief, Vitolin, was reassigned to the military front against the last White forces in the South. Shlikhter, an old Bolshevik and party expert in agricultural matters, was brought into the province along with Meshcheriakov, another specialist in rural affairs, to serve (in the popular phrasing of the day) as a "buffer" between uezd-level party organizations and the provincial party committee.[28]

Although the Kozlov party committee was broken up, with eleven of its members reassigned to other organizations within the province, the man chosen to head the Communist Party in that uezd nevertheless emerged as the primary "intriguer" against the newly arrived Shlikhter and Meshcheriakov. In this, N. M. Nemtsov was joined by other party leaders from the uezd organizations, as well as by the new secretary of the provincial party organization, B. Ia. Pinson. Their dispute followed the contours of internal party debates about the feared "bureaucratization" of the Communist Party and the restrictions on internal party "democracy"; at the Tenth Party Conference in Tambov in late January 1921, one of their number from the Morshansk organization, Lotikov, expressed his desire to see all members of the "intelligentsia" removed from party and government posts and enrolled in trade schools to learn a practical craft. In a manner that echoed the ideas being expressed by members of the Workers' Opposition in the central party organizations, like-minded officials in Tambov at the same conference called for replacing party professionals with simple workers in the leading party organizations in the province.

In Tambov, such opposition to "bureaucratization" was focused principally on individuals such as Shlikhter and Meshcheriakov and what they represented to local officials. As such, the opposition could assume many forms as long as its principal targets remained in the crosshairs. The Tenth Party Conference in Tambov coincided with a period of open factional struggle within the party regarding the "governmentalization" of the trade unions and the "militarization" of labor.[29] The open campaigning by leading members of the factions involved in this controversy in the first months of 1921 brought distinguished visitors to Tambov in a way the province had not enjoyed since the first days of "Soviet power" in 1918.[30] The star guest at the Tenth Party Conference in Tambov was Nikolai Bukharin, who arrived to lobby members of the provincial party committee and conference delegates to support the centralizing policies advocated by the "Trotskyist" faction. Bukharin was not only permitted to read a speech on the subject to the assembled delegates (a rebuttal was offered by the much less famous local trade unions leader), but even given the privilege of delivering the closing address. But in spite of these advantages, the delegates were not sufficiently swayed to advocate the leftist platform, voting by a considerable margin to adopt the more moderate "Leninist" approach to the trade unions question.[31]

However, Bukharin's presence in Tambov did galvanize the localist clique in the provincial party committee, whose own deliberations with Bukharin on the trade unions question produced a majority in favor of the Trotskyist line, with the defeated moderate platform represented, most significantly, by the party chairman, Meshcheriakov. The actual vote was exceptionally close (six votes to five), but the ramifications were considerable, for the new party committee elected at the time of the Tenth Conference did not include Meshcheriakov. He was ousted as party chairman, replaced by one of the prime movers in this minor palace coup, Nikolai Mikhailovich Nemstov.

The open campaigning by the factions engaged in the trade unions controversy saw leading faction members from Moscow dispatched to the provinces in time for local party conferences and congresses to convene, and it was only through a complication involving delays on the railway line that one of the main representatives of the Leninist faction was not present at the Tenth Conference in Tambov to offer a high-profile rebuttal to Comrade Bukharin. Instead, A. V. Lunacharsky arrived in Tambov one day after the conference and was relieved to learn that the damage to their campaign caused by this delay had not been as significant as feared. Lunacharsky's was the second visit by a prestigious Communist Party

member to Tambov in only a matter of days, yet the reception he received was noticeably different from that extended to Bukharin. In his report on his brief stay
in Tambov, Lunacharsky noted that the members of the new Tambov party leadership were outwardly warm in their welcome to the commissar for public education, although the sincerity of their welcome he believed to be paper-thin. In his
first formal encounter with the new leadership at the Communist Party fraction
meeting on the eve of the provincial Congress of Soviets, Lunacharsky reported that
he was treated to an "onslaught" of abuse and "heretical broadsides" by Nemstov
and Pinson, and to a lesser extent from Vasil'ev, who had returned to Tambov just
before the Tenth Conference in January.[32] The opinions expressed by these individuals were largely in keeping with the antibureaucracy, antistate line that had animated party opposition in the provinces since 1919 with the emergence of the
Democratic Centralists. Lunacharsky wrote that the experience of the meeting
with the Tambov Communists demonstrated "what is undermining our party in
certain corners: specifically, the disdainful attitude of some toward soviet work,
which is considered on the whole to be morally and politically inferior to the 'pure'
work of the party."[33]

Despite making some progress in his efforts to promote the Leninist platform
on the trade unions issue, Lunacharsky nevertheless left Tambov with a distinctly
negative opinion of the local leadership. In the wake of the factional meeting attended on his first day in the province, Lunacharsky described the new chairman
of the Tambov party organization, Nemtsov, as being "in no way suitable for the
position of chairman due to his extreme partisan opinions, awkward conduct,
and his muddled and ignorant mind."[34] At the time of the Seventh Tambov Congress of Soviets, held almost immediately after the provincial party conference,
Lunacharsky met with Shlikhter, a long-time acquaintance, who further briefed
him on the political climate in the province.[35] Understandably, Shlikhter provided
a downbeat characterization of his situation, emphasizing how, when he first arrived in the province nearly one year before, he had been greeted as a minor
celebrity (Shlikhter had served, very briefly, as a people's commissar in 1917), yet
now, mainly owing to the intrigues of particular individuals in the party organization, his situation was growing difficult to endure. Shlikhter told Lunacharsky
that his close associate, Meshchceriakov, had already been lobbying for some time
for a transfer out of the province, a request that looked increasingly likely to be
satisfied in light of recent developments in the provincial party organization.[36]

Lunacharsky sought to reassure Shlikhter, emphasizing that those seeking his
ouster were men of limited abilities and intellect. Yet in answer to this, Shlikhter
pressed for Lunacharsky to recommend to Moscow that civilian authority in the

province be suspended and all administration handed over to a revolutionary committee or some form of local dictatorship that would not only put an end to political intriguing, but also place the administration of the province back on a stable footing. In his report on this exchange, Lunacharsky fell short of giving his wholehearted endorsement of such a plan, and in so doing acknowledged that Shlikhter was not above making his own share of errors and misjudgments. Shlikhter's words on the benefits of suspending local, civilian control over provincial administration in Tambov are not likely to have been private, incidental thoughts. Given the speed with which such developments took place, they were more likely to have been shared with other senior party and state officials. They were still not enough, though, to prevent Shlikhter from losing his post as chairman of the Tambov soviet executive committee after his opponents managed to orchestrate a reelection for the post, which was secured by Andrei Sergeevich Lavrov, one of Nemstov's allies.

Lunacharsky left Tambov on 2 February 1921. However, his train was forced to return briefly after it was learned that rebels had attacked the railway station at Rtishchevo, blocking Lunacharsky's path to Saratov, the next destination on his whistle-stop tour. The setback served as a reminder of the fact that outside the provincial capital, and beyond the political infighting that had paralyzed the state administration and party in Tambov, there was an anti-Soviet insurgency raging. In fact, it is remarkable that, judging from his own account, the only moment at which Lunacharsky received a briefing on the conflict with the Partisan Army was when the commissar for enlightenment visited Commander Pavlov at the army headquarters in Tambov to conduct a telegraphic exchange with Stalin in Moscow to report on the outcome of the provincial congress. Lunacharsky admitted to having little interest or expertise in military affairs, and he did not relay much information on Pavlov's impromptu report except to say that Pavlov struck him as a capable and intelligent individual, "although not without a certain measure of melancholy." This final impression was most likely informed by Pavlov's words regarding the state of affairs in Tambov in which he emphasized the complications caused by the political wrangling within the provincial administration. Still, he nevertheless expressed some confidence in the ability of the Red Army to defeat the rebels.[37] Yet the fact that the insurgency had been relegated to the background during the intense round of political intriguing that accompanied the conference season in Tambov not only indicates the degree to which local politics had become distorted and blinkered in the province.[38] It can also be taken as evidence that the state and party in Tambov had effectively lost control over the political situation.[39]

In fact, at the time of Lunacharsky's departure, Moscow was already engrossed in discussions regarding strategies for resolving the problems surrounding the campaign in Tambov. When Bukharin returned from his own brief visit to Tambov, he delivered a report to the Communist Party Politburo on the situation in the province in which he highlighted several issues that required action, particularly regarding relations with the rural population in the province and the evident tensions that were preventing the local Communist Party and administration from playing a constructive role in resolving the conflict. Regarding the latter, the Politburo resolved to establish, under the authority of VTsIK, a plenipotentiary commission that upon arrival in the province would assume overall control over civilian government and the local Communist Party organization. This was, broadly speaking, the kind of arrangement that Shlikhter had recommended to Lunacharsky, but the most important facet of the Politburo plan was the appointment of a trusted "outsider" to take control of provincial affairs and assure that the operations of the party and state administration were effectively geared toward the speedy resolution of the conflict in southern Tambov. As such, the Politburo turned to a trusted hand who had previously assumed somewhat similar responsibilities in the wake of Mamontov's raid in Tambov, Vladimir Antonov-Ovseenko.

When he received the telegram from the party secretariat regarding the posting in Tambov in early February 1921, Antonov-Ovseenko was assigned to the seemingly unglamorous task of organizing networks of sowing committees in Perm Province, part of the Soviet government's final attempt to reverse the downward trend in agricultural production within the context of the civil war grain collection (razverstka) policy.[40] But Antonov-Ovseenko's familiarity with the operations of the sowing committees project may have been seen as another advantage in addition to his familiarity with the province and its tangled local politics. One of the main objectives set in the course of the Politburo deliberations on the situation in Tambov was to revive the local economy and appeal to the civilian population

Concerns over the upcoming harvest were shared by both government officials and village communities as the spring sowing season approached, and those popular concerns were understood as an opportunity for the government to grant concessions and utilize the resources at its disposal to undermine support for the rebels. Not only was Tambov to receive a new "dictator" in Antonov-Ovseenko, accompanied by a number of other trusted party activists, to oversee the administration of the province; the Politburo also instructed senior members, including Bukharin, Preobrazhenskii, Kamenev, and Tsiurupa, to consider measures to alleviate the difficult economic situation confronting the rural communities of Tambov and to draft a declaration regarding concessions to this effect. Following the nearly unanimous condemnation of the Food Commissariat and the razverstka policy at the Tenth Party Conference and Seventh Congress of Soviets in Tambov in late January and early February, it was reasonable to assume that the concessions would concern the pursuit of the razverstka in Tambov.[41] Although the minutes of this Politburo session do not contain details of suggested measures to this effect, the Politburo's intentions behind such concessions were no doubt significant, for their instructions specified that the declaration must somehow be restricted to Tambov Province and not publicized in the central press, lest those outside the conflict area take it to stand as general state policy.[42]

One week later, the cessation of grain requisitioning was announced in Tambov.[43] The declaration was composed in such a way as to preserve state legitimacy while at the same time offering public recognition of popular grievances and an acknowledgment of objective hardship. This was not a public apology nor, naturally, was it presented as a concession forced upon the government by the rebels:

> Owing to the recent possibility to receive grain supplies from the South and from the Urals, acknowledging the general difficulty of the present situation which confronts the Tambov peasant while also recognizing that a large portion of the present razverstka campaign has been completed and that the remaining grain supplies held by kulaks are likely to be minimal, the People's Commissariat for Food Supply has responded to the report of the Tambov Communist Party committee by declaring the cessation of continued razverstka completion in Tambov Province.

The declaration emphasized that this was the realization of the grand "bargain" that had been an explicit component of the razverstka policy from the beginning. "Comrade peasants [*krest'iane i krest'ianki*]! Through tremendous hardship, but with honor, you have fulfilled your great obligation to the worker-peasant government. Now your beloved [*rodnaia*] and hard-won worker-peasant government shall in due course pay you back a hundred times over." Promising to provide whatever assistance was necessary to revive household economies and, particularly, to ensure that the fields were sown with summer crops, the declaration was possibly the first time the Soviet government appealed for popular support rather than resorting to threats—and without, interestingly, even a single mention of "bandits." Instead, as if to underscore the desire to effect the transition to peacetime and to establish a "normal" relationship with the villages, the declaration promised that "nonparty conferences" would be organized at which local people would meet with state officials and be given the opportunity to voice their concerns and grievances. "Openly and directly identify your needs and grievances," instructed the declaration. "Soviet power seeks only to defend you."[44]

The declaration certainly appeared to be the result of an emerging consensus regarding the viability of the razverstka and the need for the Soviet government to appeal for popular support in conflict areas such as Tambov. On 8 February, Commander Pavlov reported to the Tambov Communist Party Committee, expressing his belief that they should not be overly distracted by the task of capturing or killing Antonov; something needed to be done to address the grievances of the rural population if they were to overcome the insurgency.[45] Lenin, on the same day, was also reflecting on the scale of unrest and violence in the Soviet countryside and was similarly settling on the opinion that the razverstka policy had outlived its usefulness and had, as several critics had contended for many weeks in early 1921, become detrimental to maintaining state authority in the countryside. Lenin's "draft theses on the tax in kind" presented to the Politiburo on 8 February may not have been an original formulation for replacing the razverstka—the idea of replacing the requisition policy with some form of tax had been muted by others within the party for many weeks, even months—but it does represent one of the earliest, and certainly the most high-level, documented moments in which the VTsIK chairman acknowledged the necessity of ending the hated policy of forced grain requisitioning.[46]

It is possible that the decision to declare an end to requisitioning in Tambov had been taken independently by provincial officials, in effect prefiguring the official suspension of the razverstka one month later with the introduction of the "tax-in-kind" policy at the Tenth Party Congress in Petrograd.[47] Certainly the idea had been circulating within party and state circles in Tambov in January, during the party conference and congress of soviets, and by this time it was public knowledge that other provinces in Soviet Russia had already suspended requisitioning before the official end of the razverstka, although for varying reasons.[48] On 8 February, the new party chairman, Nemtsov, spoke before the Presidium of the party and soviet: "We have changed our opinion and have come to the conclusion that, in order to uproot the banditry problem, we must end the razverstka throughout the province."[49] Indeed, even if the decision to end requisitioning had been taken independently, the fact that it aroused no significant controversy served as further indication, if any was needed, of just how widely the damage being done by the razverstka policy was acknowledged by this time.

A member of the central organization of the Revolutionary Military Tribunal, Vasilii Vasil'evich Ulrikh, a future presiding judge in the Moscow purge trials of the 1930s who had been in Tambov since late January 1921 to oversee the organization of an investigative and judicial tribunal system in the province, saw the discontinuation of requisitioning work as critical to the consolidation of Red Army and government authority in those areas "liberated" from the rebels. In Ulrikh's words: "There is nothing more they [the requisition squads] can achieve other than to arouse more animosity and provoke more bursts of rebellion." He highlighted the fact that many reports from Commander Pavlov and from the provincial Cheka had cited incidents in which requisition squads had come under attack in areas previously thought to be "cleaned" of insurgents. Instead of provoking or even punishing village communities by persisting with the practice of forced requisitioning, Ulrikh (with the backing of Pavlov and the new chief of the Tambov Cheka, Iankin) recommended that many more resources be devoted to alleviating the material shortages that were affecting the rural population and rewarding those villages that demonstrated loyalty to the regime. This way, he hoped, the government could "silence those SR agitators who claim that Soviet power only takes from the peasant without ever giving something in return."[50]

In subsequent instructions regarding the declaration, provincial officials persisted in invoking the authority of the Food Commissariat.[51] It is improbable that local officials would assert independence on such a vital matter. The principal evidence for this conclusion derives from a meeting of senior Politburo officials with representatives from Tambov soon after the declaration had been made. The trip to Moscow was made by the new Tambov party chairman, Nemtsov; the military commissar and former commander of counterinsurgency operations, K. V. Redz'ko; and the Tambov uezd soviet chairman, Mikhail Beliakov. Nemtsov had prepared a report on the situation in the province for the Politburo and even met with Lenin to review the situation on 14 February. Redz'ko was present at the meeting of the Politburo during the visit to the Soviet capital at which Nemtsov's report was considered, and the new provincial party chairman was soon after able to telegraph back to Tambov: "Redz'ko reports that Lenin and [L. P.] Serebriakov have endorsed my line, and it [the declaration] is to remain in force."[52] The extent to which the policy was Nemtsov's "line" is difficult to determine. However, if Nemtsov believed that the confirmation of the change in policy was in effect a personal confirmation of his senior role in the provincial party, he would soon be disappointed.

The visit to Moscow in the second week of February was more distinguished by another meeting with Lenin by representatives from Tambov Province. Provincial officials were accompanied by an unknown number of military cadets (Redz'ko had been instrumental in the organization of the first Red Army academy in Tambov Province in 1918, and the cadets were growing more important to the counterinsurgency by 1921); most important, they were joined by five villagers from Tambov and Kirsanov uezds who were scheduled to meet with Lenin on 14 February 1921 to discuss the insurgency and the position of the Soviet government regarding relations with the peasantry. The origins of this unusual meeting go back to December 1920, when a delegation of party officials from Tambov, including Beliakov and Shlikhter, attended the Eighth Party Congress in Moscow and sought to bend the ear of the VTsIK chairman regarding the ongoing conflict in their province.[53] Catching a moment during a break in Congress activities, the men from Tambov —perhaps inappropriately, given the circumstances—asked Lenin to deploy a full Red Army division to the province to help fight the insurgents. Lenin demurred but did agree to meet with the delegates from Tambov at a later time. At this later meeting, during a recess on 25 December 1920, Lenin displayed an extraordinary interest in Tambov Province. Questioning the three men from Tambov—perhaps equally inappropriately—about a range of technical issues, from the distribution of grain held by individual rural "classes" in the province (kulaks, poor peasants, and so forth), to the state of animal husbandry and livestock, Lenin appeared entirely focused on issues pertaining to agriculture. Taken aback, the Tambov delegates admitted that they were unable to answer any of his formulaic questions regarding such issues, with the sole exception of Lenin's query regarding the number of tractors currently in operation in Tambov. (Beliakov replied that there were only two tractors, both confiscated from former gentry estates, one of which was being used to haul rubbish in the provincial capital.)

Although it would have been unthinkable for Beliakov, whose memoirs supply us with details concerning this meeting, to describe Lenin's questions as both inappropriate and condescending (can people from Tambov have interests beyond agriculture?), one still suspects that the delegates were slightly bemused by the great leader's initial round of questions. Seeking to move on to more vital matters, the delegates repeated their request for Moscow to deploy a full Red Army division to the province. "I certainly sympathize with you," Lenin replied, "and your request is legitimate and carries obvious conviction, but at the present time it is impossible for us to send a whole division to Tambov Province. We can help with guns. But you will have to make do for the time being with your own [human] resources. Mobilize for this purpose all [Soviet] sympathizers."[54] However, Lenin's next suggestion truly surprised the officials from Tambov. Lenin, according to Beliakov, told them to send five or six civilians who were known to sympathize with Antonov (and who were preferably "middle-aged and authoritative" in their communities), and that he would speak with them personally. Shlikhter, evidently taken aback at the suggestion like the others, asked: "Vladimir Il'ich, what need do you have for such people?"[55]

The meeting, when it finally took place some seven weeks later, would provide the basis for one of the most widely distributed pieces of propaganda produced by the Soviet government in Tambov during the period of the insurgency. Preparations had been made well in advance, including the selection of the peasants to be taken to the Kremlin and the drafting of short biographies of each one to be reviewed by Lenin before their meeting. But the meeting itself was hardly fashioned to appeal to the peasant delegates as individuals. The discussion conformed broadly to past encounters between power (*vlast'*) and the people (*narod*), between the tsar and his subjects, even if the Soviet leader made an overt attempt to appear personable and approachable. According to Beliakov's brief description of the meeting, Lenin emphasized from the outset the interests held in common by the Soviet state and the peasantry. The fight against the landlords had been endorsed and facilitated by the Bolsheviks in 1917, and the peasants' and workers' Red Army had fought to prevent the return of the gentry during the civil war. Somehow the peasants of Tambov Province ("dark, illiterate people" according to Lenin, offering a scripted excuse for wayward behavior) had lost sight of the common interests they shared with the Soviet government and had been led astray onto the path of violent resistance. The exceptional nature of the insurgency in Tambov was a prominent theme. "Did you see on your journey through Riazan' and Moscow provinces anything like what is going on in Tambov?" Lenin asked, referring to the provinces traversed by the delegates en route to Moscow. "Nowhere else do we find such disturbances as in Tambov Province," he added, answering his own question.[56]

One of the peasant delegates rose to challenge this assertion, stating that he had understood that there was resistance to the Soviet state everywhere and that even in Moscow Soviet power had ceased to exist. Here Beliakov may have taken some artistic license, for the latter claim would have been absurd in light of the circumstances surrounding this meeting (although not entirely misplaced given the brewing discontent among workers in the capital), but it did permit the memoirist from Tambov to underscore what was obviously a theme identified as of major importance. Lenin, in this case, only threw up his arms in an assured and avuncular fashion and calmly explained to the Tambov peasants that this was clearly not the case and that they had allowed themselves to be easily misled by the former landlords and their devious agents, the SRs. Tambov was an isolated and exceptional case, according to Lenin, for nowhere else did the Soviet state experience resistance of this sort. The claims being made by the rebels, either about other major rural insurgencies or regarding urban disturbances in Moscow and Petrograd, were all lies. At the conclusion of the meeting, Beliakov recalls that Lenin asked the peasants whether he needed to order Red Army units to Tambov to suppress the

Unnamed portrait of one of the Tambov villagers to meet with Lenin, February 1921. While carefully stage-managed, this meeting was not entirely a publicity stunt, as the villagers brought to the Kremlin were drawn from areas at the heart of the insurgency. More than one of the peasants were said to have suffered physical attacks upon return to their villages. *Photograph courtesy of the Tambovskii Kraevedcheskii Muzei*

insurgency there. "No, it is not necessary to do so," answered one. Nodding approvingly, Lenin nevertheless added: "Still, unless you are able to deal with this Antonov yourselves before the beginning of the spring sowing season, then the Red Army will have to come and help you get the job done." And with that, Comrade Lenin sent the peasants from Tambov on their way.

Redz'ko related in a letter to a friend that he spoke to the five peasant delegates from Kirsanov and Tambov during their return journey on 17 February and reviewed with them what they had heard and seen during their extraordinary visit to the Kremlin. Redz'ko made each of them promise that he would discuss the meeting with fellow community members at village meetings and describe what had been seen both in Moscow and on their journey.[57] The impact of these five men upon wider popular opinion, however, could only be limited, so the meeting provided the topic of a pamphlet published soon after entitled, "What Comrade Lenin Told the Peasants from Tambov."[58]

Composed by a member of the Tambov uezd party organization, and ostensibly based on descriptions of the meeting provided by two of the peasant representatives, "What Comrade Lenin Told the Peasants from Tambov" was one of the major propaganda pieces produced during the counterinsurgency operation. The obvious intention of the pamphlet was to cast the peasant communities as the innocent victims of both the agents of the state and the rebels, as well as to re-emphasize that the Soviet government was responsive to the needs of the people, a broad objective of any popular revolution and a principle that had grown ob-scure over the course of the civil war. The Soviet leader in the pamphlet asks, "What is this I hear of some Antonov band, and what are they doing?" One of the peasants answers with a brief description of the robbery and looting of village communities carried out by the rebels. But Lenin also inquires about the razver-stka and the difficulties experienced by communities in fulfilling the demands for grain. Here, interestingly, the parallel with the carefully cultivated dichotomy of the "good tsar–bad boyar" is most clear in his response to the Tambov peasants' complaint regarding the conduct of the requisition squads, which "only demand and take" grain, and yet the grain is frequently left to rot rather than delivered to the needy. Accepting that "local authorities" were to blame for this conduct and many more ills, Lenin told the men from Tambov:

> If the peasants are still unhappy with their local representatives, then you must inform the provincial authorities, and if the provincial authorities fail to pay any attention, then inform Moscow, the Kremlin, me [Lenin]. You may address your problems to me by post or in person. . . . Together with the workers you have spilt your own blood for the sake of freedom, for your own government. Hold this prize firmly in your hands together with the workers. You will soon see what kind of power it will be.[59]

"What Comrade Lenin Told the Peasants," in the context of Tambov, represented a significant contribution to the Soviet state's growing awareness of the necessity of recognizing legitimate grievances held by the rural population and speaking to those grievances. It constituted an overture to village communities that sought to open a dialogue on important questions that, in the experience of those commu-nities during the years of civil war, had been non-negotiable in the policies and conduct of the Soviet state.[60]

Engaging the propaganda war constituted one of the priorities for the Pleni-potentiary Commission and Antonov-Ovseenko, who arrived in Tambov two days before Nemtsov and the others returned from Moscow.[61] But the first order of business for Moscow's new man in Tambov involved enforcing "party discipline" in the province through personnel changes and public demonstrations and dec-larations of unity. Although it is difficult to know how Nemtsov evaluated the security of his own position following the meetings in Moscow in mid-February, after his return to Tambov on 18 February his days as party chairman were numbered. He had incurred the suspicion of several state and party officials, and despite being one of the champions of the decision to end the razverstka in Tambov, and despite being popular among uezd-level party organizations, his removal was deemed necessary if harmony was to return to the provincial party organization.[62]

It was just as well, perhaps, that Nemtsov fell ill upon his return to Tambov and took a two-week break from his duties, for it spared him the public humiliation of seeing B. A. Vasil'ev replace him as party chairman at a hastily organized "extraordinary" Eleventh Tambov Communist Party Conference in early March 1921.[63] The conference gave the new leadership of the Plenipotentiary Commission an opportunity not only to explain the organizational changes being made to the administration of the province and to the counterinsurgency effort, but also a chance to end the political infighting that had characterized the previous weeks.[64] With resolutions denouncing "bourgeois individualism" and "indiscipline" within the local party organization, the conference, under Antonov-Ovseenko, sought to draw a line under the previous regime in Tambov that had been pulled apart under the strains of the conflict with the insurgents.[65]

Even though the soviet executive committee and the provincial party committee continued to meet and the Plenipotentiary Commission was obliged to report to both on a regular basis, the commission assumed control over the day-to-day affairs that were important to the counterinsurgency campaign, the scope of which was expanding with each passing day. Still, the commission included as members both Vasil'ev, the new provincial party chairman, and Lavrov, chairman of the Tambov soviet executive committee. But, as if to underscore the fact that the commission was above the local politics of the province, the Presidium of the Plenipotentiary Commission—the group that would meet most frequently and decide the most pressing issues—was composed only of Antonov-Ovseenko, Commander Pavlov, and A. I. Zhabin, who had arrived with Antonov-Ovseenko to assume control of the political department of the armed forces in the province.[66] Excluded were both Lavrov and Vasil'ev. This highly centralized arrangement was to replace what was labeled the "amateurish" conduct of the counterinsurgency campaign by the previous provincial regime at the first meeting of senior Tambov officials with Antonov-Ovseenko and the future members of the Plenipotentiary Commission.[67]

That first meeting of local officials with the Plenipotentiary Commission team covered several issues that had been identified as "nonmilitary" priorities. These principally fell into two categories. The first was intelligence and the support for the armed effort to be provided by the Cheka (discussed in chapter 7). For present purposes, the second category is of particular importance, for it indicated a change in orientation that arrived with Antonov-Ovseenko and the establishment of the Plenipotentiary Commission. This broadly concerned public relations. Discussing a range of initiatives and tasks on 27 February, the new leadership delegated responsibility for investigating the pursuit of many lines of action that would demonstrate not only the resolve of the Soviet state to suppress the insurgency but also that the state's policies and practices had substantively changed regarding the village communities and peasant households. As such, members of the party and state administration were instructed to review the procurement personnel of the Food Commissariat, not only to remove "suspicious" elements but also in special cases to arrange for the public investigation and trial of those who had committed abuses against villagers in the course of their procurement duties. Likewise, local state and party personnel suspected of activities that "discredited" Soviet power were to be placed on public trial. Such public demonstrations of the state's intention to discipline its agents in the countryside extended to the army, whose soldiers and officers were similarly to be tried publicly for improprieties committed against civilians. Such measures were intended to underscore the developing claim that the Soviet state was changing its practices along with its policies as it made the transition to peacetime.

Making a public show of resolve was not limited to demonstrations of justice targeting the state's own agents. The revolutionary tribunals were also to direct their attentions to the rebels and to organize public trials of captured bandits. A point was even made regarding the possibility of trying captured rebels alongside arrested agents of the Food Commissariat and soldiers suspected of abusing civilians, thus appropriating and undermining the rebels' claims regarding "red bandits" and channeling popular grievances through the state's own institutions of justice, the revolutionary tribunals.[68] Placing the Soviet state at the center of popular demands for justice was accompanied by a plan to boost the profile of the organized counterinsurgency effort through the mass distribution of all orders and decrees issued by the army leadership in individual military sectors. Such orders and decrees were thus to serve an immediate purpose while also reaping a potential public relations benefit by establishing and sustaining an image of the Soviet state as in control of the developing strategic situation and public order in the south of the province.[69]

Mobilizing local communities for public demonstrations of support for the state and the counterinsurgency also featured in the plans of the Plenipotentiary Commission. Provincial officials had already taken a step in this direction with the promise to organize "nonparty" conferences, which would be state-sponsored forums for the open expression of grievances. The Plenipotentiary Commission, however, intended to conduct a campaign that had its nearest equivalent in the rebels' own practices of organizing local cells of the STK on the consensual basis of a signed declaration of support for the insurgency. In late February, Soviet state representatives began planning for a sentencing campaign [*prigovornaia kampaniia*], whereby village communities would be mobilized to sign public condemnations of the insurgents and declarations of support for the Soviet state. It is difficult to determine the authenticity of such declarations after they began to appear in March 1921. Certainly it is impossible to discount them out of hand, given the fact that many village communities harbored serious grievances regarding the conduct of the insurgents, especially after so many months of conflict and concomitant demands placed upon them by the Partisan Army. In the end, as we shall see, what undermined the *prigovornaia kampaniia* was not the questionable authenticity of the *prigovory*, but the practical complications that limited the reach of the *kampaniia*.

Facilitating the transition to "normality"—that is, demobilizing the rural population and prompting them to return to peacetime routines—involved much more than addressing the grievances of village communities. The Soviet state had to speak to the anxieties of the rural population. Even if the prospect of the spring thaw raised fears of operational complications for the Red Army and promised improved natural cover for the insurgents, the rhythms of the agricultural calendar represented a greater challenge to the rebels than to the state. The Partisan Army and STK had to show sensitivity to genuine concerns about hunger and famine shared among the village communities while maintaining the state of emergency that sustained participation in and sympathy with the cause of the insurgency. In essence, the rebels had to acknowledge "ordinary" concerns while working to preserve a general atmosphere of the "extraordinary" in the Tambov countryside.

For the Soviet government, urging peasant farmers back to work in the fields in the springtime should have been akin to moving with the flow of the tide and was appreciated as an important weapon against the insurgents. Government reports regarding popular anxieties about the completion of the upcoming sowing campaign were filed alongside reports of hunger and starvation in the countryside.[70] While such anxieties had been a fixture since the previous summer, the continuing conflict between rebels and state troops only served to diminish the prospects for the harvest. Village communities had to contend with the demands for grain made by Partisan Army regiments and Red Army groups, but it was more the disruption of field work by the insurgency that fed the unease pervading the countryside. Soviet propaganda distributed within the territory of the insurgency and published in the provincial press capitalized on these concerns, seeking to separate the rebels from their partisan base in the villages by amplifying the fears for the sowing season and the harvest.[71]

The newpaper *Krest'ianskaia Bednota* was revived in February 1921, and its content was largely given over to information regarding the introduction of sowing committees to Tambov Province. The legislation regarding the sowing committees, introduced in December 1920, was intended to maximize grain production at a time when it was widely acknowledged that famine was threatened in many parts of the Soviet republic. There were two parts to the legislation. The first involved the pooling and protection of seed grain in individual villages and regions, and the second concerned the improvement of efficiency and techniques by repairing agricultural machinery and implements, as well as teaching more effective methods of cultivation and crop management.[72] Each village was to have its own committee (*selkom*), to be managed by volost and uezdwide sowing committees (*posevkom*). The available seed grain in a given community was to be registered with the sowing committees, possibly even removed for safe storage before the actual sowing campaign commenced, and to maximize the sown acreage in a given locality, seed grain was to be redistributed where possible among capable, "industrious" farmers.

However, in areas where seed grain was perceived to be in such short supply, whether lost to over-requisitioning by state agents or by rebels, such plans for redistribution of seed aroused little reaction, enthusiastic or not. Instead, in most areas affected by the insurgency, the introduction of the sowing committees was taken as a promise of direct assistance by the state in the form of seed grain. The provincial government had already nourished such expectations, perhaps deliberately, with its announcement of the end of requisitioning, which included words regarding the ability of the Soviet government to provide direct aid to communities suffering shortages. When the first Congress of Uezd Sowing Committees convened in early March, few if any concrete accomplishments were discussed. But there was uniform enthusiasm reported in those areas where the sowing committees were only just being introduced or discussed, albeit predicated on the expectation of state deliveries of seed grain.[73] While the sowing committees were very much a work in progress, and in areas affected by the insurgency it was nearly impossible to organize them at the village level,[74] the initial receptivity of village communities to the campaign did represent both a profound anxiety about the economic situation on the immediate horizon and a willingness to accept a role for the Soviet state in alleviating the impending crisis. That the hopes for extensive deliveries of grain were misplaced was a concern for the long term. In the short term, the sowing committees served as an excellent instrument for focusing attentions on "ordinary," everyday concerns and anxieties, and the few supplies available for the government to distribute among "loyal" villages helped to promote the Soviet state as the focal point for hope.[75] The impact could not be measured in purely material terms, as the dividends were sought in the demobilization of the partisan countryside.

Nowhere is the use of economic policy for political purposes clearer than with the introduction of the tax in kind at the Tenth Party Congress in mid-March 1921. The decision to end the razverstka and the policy of requisitioning grain surpluses throughout the Soviet Republic was a response to popular pressure on the Soviet government by countless workers, peasants, and members of the armed forces. From the perspective of the Kremlin, the intensification of disorders throughout the republic by such a broad spectrum of social groups was unmistakably uniform, which necessitated a major change of policy rather than individualized and piecemeal responses in different localities. The question of food supply dominated the agenda of strikes that crippled industrial centers in January and, especially, February.[76]

Cuts in rations aroused even greater discontent with a rationing system that had long been recognized as corrupt and inefficient, and tighter restrictions on unofficial channels of access to food accompanied intensified, objective shortages of grain. Many plants and factories, only recently reopened in the new year, were shut down both because of supply problems and growing unrest among the workers. Attempts to placate the urban population and to alleviate the shortages were limited by the breakdown in the transportation system (to which the conflict in Tambov made a significant contribution) and by more recent flare-ups of rural rebellion in grain-growing regions that the state heavily relied upon, notably western Siberia.[77] The strike wave reached its apex in the final two weeks of February, seeing demonstrations by thousands of workers on the streets of Moscow and Petrograd, as well as later in other industrial areas.[78] There were not only calls for practical measures to alleviate the grain crisis but also openly hostile demands for the removal of the Communist government and the introduction of "people's rule" (*narodovlast'*).

While certainly connected with broader demands for civil rights and democratic elections to the soviets, such overtly political aims and slogans were never as clear as the practical measures advocated by workers' groups for relieving the food supply crisis. But the "political" aims of demonstrators nevertheless found strong resonance in Petrograd, in particular, where demands for an end to the Communist Party's monopoly on power and for "people's rule" animated the spectacular mutiny of sailors at Kronstadt in early March 1921.[79] Famously, the height of the mutiny coincided with the opening of the Tenth Party Congress, at which Lenin presented the legislation replacing the razverstka with the tax in kind as a means of alleviating the grain crisis. The urban disorders in Moscow and Petrograd had been contained by the beginning of March through the imposition of martial law and the extensive use of the Cheka's power to arrest and detain suspected political opponents. And the Red Army was set to launch its first assault on the Kronstadt fortress on the very day that the Tenth Congress opened on 8 March 1921. But neither of these uncompromising tactics to crush political opposition and civil disorder could remove the connection in the minds of congress delegates between the need to appease popular discontent throughout Soviet territory and the proposed replacement of the razverstka with the tax in kind. Force and coercion could not exclusively be relied upon to subdue resistance and rebellion on the scale now reached, especially when the political and economic failure of the razverstka continued to be the bedrock of Soviet policy toward grain producers in the countryside.[80]

The end of the razverstka was followed soon after by a Sovnarkom decree of 27 March liberalizing trade restrictions, opening up possibilities for the exchange of goods and produce between town and country, and recognizing much of the black market economy that had become a lifeline for countless persons suffering under the weight of food shortages in the cities and towns. If introducing the tax in kind promised that producers could retain their after-tax surpluses, the decree on trade opened possibilities for the free dispensation of those surpluses. Both the razverstka and the state's efforts to restrict private trade had been major grievances of both the rural and urban populations, although for workers involved in strikes in the major cities, free trade and the prospect of rampant speculation was far from an ideal resolution to their peculiar hardships.[81] Such a measure regarding trade was bound to favor the farmers and private speculators in foodstuffs, and it addressed one of their most prominent grievances while at the same time acknowledging the state's limited ability to manage the procurement and distribution of food.[82]

The elimination of the razverstka was also widely greeted in the provinces. In Tambov, the burden of implementing the razverstka policy had been instrumental in tearing apart any unity that the provincial leadership had enjoyed after the municipal soviet in Tambov assumed control over affairs in 1918. The decision to end requisitions in February was, in part, a triumph of the provincial leadership, as many local party and state officials had been urging for a suspension of the razverstka since the autumn of 1920. But the announcement of the official end of the razverstka and its replacement by the tax in kind was greeted with a much more tangible sense of relief throughout the party and administration, from the provincial capital to the uezd towns. As the food commissar in Tambov, Shugol', explained to assembled uezd soviet executive committee chairmen at their annual congress in early April, the decision of the Tenth Party Congress to replace the razverstka was a political decision meant to begin the process of repairing relations with the farming peasantry. "These few measures [implemented in March regarding provisions policy] should, of course, have a decisive role in influencing the psychology of the peasant mass and drawing it closer to Soviet power."

Of course, state officials had said similar things about a whole variety of policy changes and circumstances that arose during the civil war. However, the change to the tax in kind permitted even loyal Food Commissariat officials such as Shugol' to disown the razverstka and to distance themselves from its troubled history. "No one here can fail to recognize," he told the uezd chairmen, "that over the course of the last two years we eliminated any and all incentives for the peasant producers with our predatory policy [*grabitel'skaia politika*] [of razverstka]."[83] Shugol' promised that the days of arbitrary arrests and corporal punishment had come to an end (even promising that the food "army" would be replaced by a more acceptable-sounding food "militia") and that the new system of the tax in kind promised not only a reduction in the burden on communities, but also a new ethos in the conduct of provisions work.[84] He was supported by the Tambov party chairman, Vasil'ev, who spoke of the political benefits of the new policy, in particular regaining the trust and confidence of village communities. He promised a complete overhaul of Food Commissariat personnel to accompany the introduction of the tax in kind, removing those individuals whose association with the abuses of the razverstka policy had become fixed in the minds of villagers and farmers: "The simple, primitive mind of the peasant, when he sees in front of him a familiar requisitioning agent [*prodovol'stvennik*], will never trust him, even if he is singing a new tune."[85]

However, beyond these promises of a new ethos and of extensive personnel changes within the commissariat, senior officials admitted that they knew very little of what the new policy entailed, as they still awaited formal instructions on the execution of the new tax-in-kind policy. However, in Tambov the promise that food policy would no longer be divisive and a source of antagonism, both between the Soviet state and the peasantry and within the Soviet state and Communist Party, dominated considerations of the policy change announced at the Tenth Congress.[86] It allowed officials in the provincial government and party to draw a line under the previous policy and provided them with belief that a new start could be made after years of conflict culminating in the ongoing insurgency in southern Tambov.

POPULAR RECEPTION OF THE NEP AND THE NATURE OF PARTISAN RESOLVE

To judge the initial reception of the announcement of the end of requisitioning in Tambov in February, and then the decision to end the policy nationwide and replace the razverstka with a tax in kind, is to depend in large part on the reports provided by agents and officials of the Soviet state. As noted, there was a palpable relief that permeated the provincial administration upon hearing the news of the end to requisitioning, and this relief no doubt informed many early assessments of the public mood. So great was the desire for the conflict to end and for the province to return to normality in the wake of the civil war, those hopes could not but have influenced reports on the popular reception of the news. Certainly the Soviet state had every reason to propagate positive assessments of the end to requisitioning and of the tax in kind, hoping that the published resolutions of support passed by loyal villages—whether legitimate or not—would create a momentum behind the measures being introduced by the state to restore the agricultural economy and with it relations with the rural population.

In the absence of an established network of local administration and Communist Party cells, the organization of nonparty conferences in major villages and towns in late February helped spread the news of the provincial administration's decision to end requisitioning.[87] Despite their nonparty status, the conferences gave Soviet authorities an opportunity to distribute literature and make announcements, and, significantly, to gauge the public mood. It was through direct contact at such gatherings that the showpiece meeting of Lenin with peasants from Tambov became fairly well known, as it was unlikely that state and party officials would rely upon the initiative of those five men from Kirsanov and Tambov to spread the news themselves; in fact, all five became the targets of threats and attacks from rebels and rebel sympathizers upon return to their native villages.[88] The gatherings could be derailed by outspoken opponents of the Soviet government, as in the large village of Rasskazovo, home to several small textile mills and other minor enterprises, where a suspected SR party member incited other participants to make bold denunciations of the Communist Party.[89] Some officials worried that providing public forums for open discussion and criticism could weaken the authority of the Soviet government, and even when the public declarations that emerged from nonparty conferences were supported, the sincerity of such declarations could not be taken at face value. As with the corresponding sentencing campaign (*prigovornaia kampaniia*), there was no small measure of self-protection behind the willingness to sign such declarations and resolutions, and some officials warned colleagues not to get carried away with the few initial pronouncements of loyalty and enthusiasm.[90]

If there was a common feature to early reports regarding the reception of the news of the end of requisitioning and, particularly, of the tax in kind, it was that the news aroused tremendous interest and spread very quickly from village to village.[91] As with provincial state and party officials, townspeople and villagers alike had many questions regarding the practical application of the tax in kind, questions that could be answered only as these considerations were resolved by Sovnarkom and Food Commissariat officials after the initial decision of the Tenth Congress. Similarly, the easing of trade restrictions provoked considerable interest and early initiative, although, once again, the details of the decree had not been entirely worked out at the time it was published in late March 1921, meaning that enthusiasm was tempered by uncertainty. Still, enthusiasm on both sides of the so-called town-country divide for the decree was tangible, and not long after its publication individuals were venturing out from places such as Kozlov and Tambov to purchase foodstuffs from nearby villages.[92]

The spread of the news of the tax in kind naturally provoked distrust as well as curiosity and enthusiasm. On the strength of experience, it was much more likely that village communities would approach the decree with caution if not hostility. "No sooner than the crops are ready for harvest than the state will take them just as before" was one reaction from Tambov uezd recorded in Communist Party reports from the countryside. "The Soviet state will take more from the peasants than the decree on the tax permits" was another voiced at a nonparty conference in Kozlov.[93] That the tax was just a piece of legislative sleight of hand on the part of the Soviet state was a theme regularly voiced at such conferences, one that no doubt was discouraging for authentically enthusiastic state and party officials engaged in political work in the Tambov countryside. Such reactions reinforced stereotypes regarding the "dark" Russian peasantry.

However, the tax in kind undeniably generated interest and prompted individuals and communities to assess its meaning. Certainly the news forced the Partisan Army and STK to engage the NEP as a Soviet offensive on the propaganda front. Leaving aside apocryphal stories of Antonov declaring that the game was up now that the state had abandoned the razverstka, the decrees and initiatives launched by the Plenipotentiary Commission and the Soviet government prompted the political agitators and rebel commanders of the Partisan Army to spend time and effort containing the potential political damage.[94] Not only were Partisan Army units instructed to show greater sensitivity to the needs of the farming peasantry and the economic health of the countryside during the sowing season, they were also prompted to assist the village communities directly in a way that mirrored the Soviet state's own initiatives. Many of these instructions had emerged in the spring but were not necessarily out of character for the Partisan Army, such as for regiments to avoid traveling across newly sown fields or the STK's order banning the distillation of moonshine as a waste of resources when seed grain was in short supply. Others were clearly direct responses to Soviet initiatives, such as the rebels' own attempts to establish sowing committees in villages where STKs had been organized, and in corresponding instructions from the Partisan Army headquarters for rebel soldiers to assist where possible with field work.[95] Using armed soldiers to help villagers during this intense period of the agricultural calendar would become one of the crucial initiatives of the Red Army and Soviet state during the summer when the number of government troops stationed in Tambov had increased considerably.

Of course, the rebel response to the state's initiatives was not confined to institutional innovations. The sowing committees that proliferated in March and April 1921 quickly became easy targets for insurgent attacks, and just as with assaults on state and collective farms, the official press reported these as rebel attacks on the innocent peasant population of Tambov.[96] At the time of the sowing campaign, this was taken as evidence that the Partisan Army sought to sabotage the 1921 harvest and starve the local population along with the urban supporters of the Soviet government. According to one official report on such incidents, the Partisan Army's activities presented the Tambov peasantry with a clear choice "between two evils" [*sic*]—Soviet power or the bandits.[97] Clearly the rebels were not willing to conduct sabotage to such suicidal ends, but it was similarly clear that they had lost the initiative, even if they enjoyed many advantages in the propaganda war.[98] Red Army soldiers, the state's main force on the ground in both the military and political struggles with the insurgency in Tambov, were themselves unclear regarding the new decrees of the Soviet government, and one of the major tasks set for the Plenipotentiary Commission was to improve the political work among their own soldiers as a necessary complement to agitation among the civilian population.[99]

In a protracted conflict such as the rebellion in Tambov had become, the Partisan Army and STK were forced to walk a very fine line to sustain participation in and sympathy with the cause of insurgency. In balancing the need to maintain a heightened level of mobilization and engagement among the rural population of southern Tambov, the rebels were forced to recognize that "normal," everyday life had to continue in the countryside. This was, most important, a product of the passage of time and the nature of the agricultural calendar, but the Soviet state's concessions in February and March only accentuated this pressure on the Tambov rebels. Certainly the reaction to the NEP and the sowing committees belied, in part, the assessment of Shugol', the Tambov food commissar, who contended that peasants had grown so dispirited and despondent following the years of civil war and insurgency that they had ceased to take interest in their fields.[100] In fact, quite the opposite was true, and this proved much more of a challenge for the Partisan Army and STK in Tambov. If an order issued on 20 February by the staff commander of the First Partisan Army, Ivan Gubarev, is any indication, maintaining a required sense of urgency and commitment had become a serious problem for the rebel leadership:

> Following the tremendous strength exhibited by the people throughout the struggle with the tyrants . . . a weakening of the fighting spirit has been noted recently among the partisan units, manifesting itself in selfishness and cowardice. We no longer find the courage that first lifted the partisan heart and compelled the partisans forward to destroy all enemies. No longer do we find those courageous revolutionaries who in August and September threw themselves first into open, honorable battle, not knowing retreat, and who exacted horrible defeats from the communist bands and who grabbed victory after victory. These men somehow and for some reason have left the ranks of the Partisan Army and have secured for themselves safe places in the rearguard administration. The remaining courageous fighters are growing lost in a mass of self-seekers.[101]

The expansion of the STK network and the influx of new recruits in the new year as the Red Army demobilized had changed the composition and character of the Partisan Army. But perhaps more important, the wear of a conflict that had lasted for more than six months had depleted the reserves of motivation and commitment that had been in evidence earlier in the insurgency, something underscored both by the approaching sowing season and the Soviet government's concessions relating to the razverstka. If they had not already secured "noncombat" responsibilities, as Gubarev's order indicates, weary fighters were tempted to view the Soviet government's policy retreat as a victory and thus an excuse to lay down their guns and return to their homes.[102] This temptation would only grow greater as the pressure exercised by the Red Army in Tambov increased.

Minimizing the appeal of accepting promised and partial gains, rather than "victory" over the Soviet government and Communist Party, assumed central importance in the rebels' management of public opinion in the Tambov countryside. Having succeeded in articulating and even broadening the ambitions of the partisan population of the province during a period of regular victories over government troops and gathering momentum in the organization of the insurgent army and its political wing, the STK, the Tambov rebels now confronted the task of keeping the movement moving. For them to do so, and to prevent the demobilization of an exhausted rural population amid strong pressures for self-preservation, the symbols and maximum objectives of the Partisan Army and STK had to remain relevant and realistic in the eyes of potential supporters. The insurgents had to demonstrate progress in their enterprise to sustain support, and as their ability to do so within the confines of Tambov Province diminished, the frame of reference for evaluating success extended to incorporate the broad canvas of anti-Soviet, anti-Communist resistance.

When Pavlov assumed command in Tambov in January, one of the operational priorities was to contain the conflict in Tambov. This was informed by an appreciation of the growing number of insurgencies and rebellions throughout much of the grain-growing regions of Russia and Ukraine. The scenario in which a partisan leader such as Antonov was able to expand his insurgency by linking up with another established rebel figurehead was in the forefront of planning considerations as Red Army officials assembled intelligence regarding the array of identifiable anti-Soviet rebels that had emerged in late 1920. Every rumor regarding a possible link between Antonov and, for instance, the rebel leader Nester Makhno in eastern Ukraine, or the newly emerged Kirill Vakhulin in southern Saratov, commanded the attention of Red Army officers engaged in the struggle with banditry. And these rumors frequently shaped strategic deployments, for while Soviet authorities frequently spoke in public of an "internal front," the prospect of a coherent, unified front engaged by anti-Soviet rebels represented a veritable nightmare scenario. Reports of Makhno's Ukrainian rebels seeking to move into Voronezh Province just south of Tambov in January, and possibly linking up with local rebels in that territory, informed the conviction that Antonov's Partisan Army was more likely to concentrate its activities in the south of Tambov with the intention of establishing operational contact with Makhno. Officials believed that rather than setting their sights on Moscow, as had been feared earlier in 1920, the rebels in Tambov projected their ambitions southward in the hope of expanding the range of the anti-Soviet movement. As such, new troop deployments in January were prioritized for Borisoglebsk uezd in southern Tambov, and the military sector based in Borisoglebsk was expanded to incorporate northeastern Voronezh Province to facilitate operations that extended across provincial borders.[103]

The new year did bring another round of rebel forays across provincial borders, and while these incursions into Saratov and Penza provinces appeared to confirm that the Partisan Army maintained ambitions to expand the territory of the insurgency after consolidating a base in southern Tambov, the actual course of these incursions leaves their military and political utility open to question.[104] Armed insurgents from Tambov had entered Saratov territory in significant numbers on four separate occasions, although only the first such foray in October lasted more than a couple of days. The attack on Rtishchevo on 2 February, in which several rail cars were looted and then burned, was notable in part because it had delayed Lunacharsky's departure from Tambov following the Eighth Tambov Congress of Soviets. But this raid, according to S. S. Kamenev in Moscow, was carried out by a small group of only 150 armed men—hardly a major incursion into the neighboring province and a sad comment on the defense arranged for this significant railway station by officials in the Saratov Military Commissariat.[105]

Only two days later, however, a much larger Partisan Army force entered Saratov in Balashov uezd. According to local reports, the rebels numbered somewhere in the region of 8,000–12,000 men.[106] Local security forces opted to fall back to Balashov and Rtichshevo rather than remain dispersed and vulnerable in the countryside.[107] Rather than simply abandoning the territory to the Tambov rebels, however, officials in Balashov collected a number of hostages from the major villages in the uezd and kept them in the town as insurance against any collusion with the rebels, a similar tactic employed—successfully, they believed—during the first major incursion in October 1920.[108] And while there was evidence that the local peasantry was, at worst, indifferent to the rebels from Tambov, there were other reports of open cooperation with the insurgents and the exploitation of their arrival in Balashov to attack state and collective farms, as well as to carry out revenge attacks on the few state and party officials who remained in the countryside. However, these were largely opportunistic in nature.

The Partisan Army did seek to mobilize the local population of Balashov, both with the organization of village STKs and the formation of a "Saratov" regiment of the rebel army, which according to one member numbered some 500 men on horseback.[109] According to Naum Iul'tsov, an eighteen-year-old who was briefly a member of this regiment, the Partisan Army encountered only distrust and hostility from the local population in Balashov, and it was only when they returned to Tambov territory that they could rely upon support from the village communities.[110] Another eyewitness to the events in February, G. V. Vedeniapin, an agent in the Saratov Cheka organization, similarly recorded only scenes of looting and violence rather than the varieties of political agitation that had accompanied the earlier period of consolidation in Tambov territory or even earlier incursions into Saratov in 1920.[111] While estimates vary of the number of armed men who crossed the border into Saratov, most sources agree that the train of carts carrying supplies and looted goods numbered in the hundreds (one source claims 2,000 carts).[112]

Despite the organization of at least one village STK and the formation of a local Partisan Army regiment in Saratov, the incursion in February 1921 by the rebels from Tambov represented a military raid much more than a genuine effort to expand the insurgency. Much would have depended upon the receptivity of the local population in Balashov and Serdobsk uezds, and here the evidence is mixed, possibly a reflection of the uneven conduct of Partisan Army units in Saratov territory. In villages where STK and Partisan Army agents had prepared the ground by establishing contact with sympathetic locals and distributing information regarding the events in Tambov and the wider struggle against the Soviet government, the arrival of rebels from Tambov who maintained discipline and displayed the honor and dignity (*chestnost'*) so valued in partisan propaganda would likely have been welcomed. However, if the character and discipline of the partisan units was growing compromised, as some rebels leaders evidently feared, then the work of political agitators in Saratov territory would have been quickly undone by rebel soldiers.

Fears that the Partisan Army was seeking to establish links with insurgents in Saratov were not realized in February.[113] Nor were fears that the rebellion would grow to encompass parts of neighboring Penza Province, despite similar raids conducted across the border in late January and early February by the rebel leader in Kozlov uezd, V. F. Selianskii. Once more, provincial authorities struggled to determine where the true sympathies of the local population lay, with some sources reporting the receptivity of the village communities to the overtures of the rebel leaders, and others only detailing the occasions on which similar communities were the chief victims of rebel deprivations.[114] Regardless of the questionable popular appeal of the rebels, officials in both Saratov and Penza provinces reiterated to Moscow earlier complaints regarding the conduct of the antibanditry campaign in Tambov. Once again, the disruption caused to both territories bordering Tambov provoked demands for greater attention to border security, improved coordination between military authorities, and extending the operational jurisdiction of the Red Army command in Tambov to adjacent provinces. The Partisan Army continued to use the neighboring provinces as escape routes following partial defeats inflicted by Red Army forces in Tambov, and officials in Penza and Saratov feared that Antonov could quickly be made their problem at a time not only when they had their own native insurgents, but also when the onset of spring would complicate counterinsurgency operations.[115] The response was to create in March and

April 1921 two new military sectors (the Seventh and Eighth) under Tambov Red Army command, based in Rtishchevo and Penza.

The other outlet across provincial borders for Partisan Army regiments was south into Voronezh, where rebel groups from Borisoglebsk had previously disrupted local administration and tied down Soviet security forces in the Novokhoper region. These incursions continued in January and February 1921, although not in significant numbers and not as part of what might be termed an "operation" conducted by the Partisan Army. Unlike in Saratov, or even Penza, the rebels at no time succeeded in organizing village committees or local armed groups. However, in February and March 1921 the province of Voronezh featured prominently in the renewed political and military activities of the Partisan Army through the arrival of another anti-Soviet army led by Ivan Sergeevich Kolesnikov.

Like many other anti-Soviet rebels during the civil war, Kolesnikov was once an officer in the Red Army before he deserted in the summer of 1920 amid suspicious circumstances involving money and theft and returned to his native region in southern Voronezh (Ostrogozhskii uezd). He rose to prominence in conditions that, once more, were fairly typical of the time, assuming the lead in a localized uprising against requisition squads in November 1920 and distinguishing himself by organizing local men into a coherent armed force and sustaining the insurgency throughout the month. By December 1920 over 5,000 men had been organized into five regiments that combined to form a single rebel division commanded by Kolesnikov himself. They had managed to seize artillery and machine guns from the small government forces assigned to the region to restore order, one of which was commanded by a young Grigorii Zhukov, future marshal of the Soviet Union.[116] The rebels' disintegration over the course of December was nearly as rapid as their rise the month before, however, and Kolesnikov's rebel division was reduced to a mere 150 men on horseback by the time they were forced from Voronezh territory across the southern border into Kharkov Province. Traveling through Kharkov and the Don region, the rebels led by Kolesnikov were able to build up strength once more, and in February 1921 they returned to Voronezh, occupying Kolesnikov's native village, Staraia Kolitva, on 5 February.[117]

Kolesnikov's force caused considerable disarray in Voronezh, where regional Red Army commanders had sought to institute a variety of the occupation strategy by stationing small armed units in strategic locations. This occupation was geared more toward maintaining stability rather than counterinsurgency and relied upon reserve military units to provide a visible presence rather than active defense.[118] Kolesnikov's arrival in Voronezh being the first major challenge local military commanders had been forced to address, not only was coordination between dislocated government forces found wanting, but also the provincial command lacked any viable cavalry force with which to pursue Kolesnikov's rebel army, as nearly all local cavalry units had been transferred to Tambov in January.[119] Attempts to organize a Red Army pursuit force encountered persistent difficulties over the course of February, and the consequence was a string of successes by Kolesnikov, occupying the uezd towns of Kalach and Novokhopersk as the force traveled northward toward the Tambov border.[120] Eventually, a pursuit force on a smaller scale than originally intended was formed under the command of I. N. Mikhailov-Berezovskii, although this "flying cavalry squadron," as it was known, engaged the insurgents under Kolesnikov too late to enable the Voronezh authorities to deal with the rebellion within their own borders. Only a couple of days after the formation of Mikhailov-Berezovskii's pursuit force, Kolesnikov crossed into Tambov Province with a contingent of some 1,500 men on horseback.

It is not known if Kolesnikov's original intention had been to link up with the Partisan Army. Certainly the Partisan Army had no apparent plans in this regard. But when, on 26 February, Kolesnikov's men cooperated with the Third Partisan Brigade of the Tenth Volche-Karachan Regiment in an attack on the railway station at Ternovka, the event was heralded as a major watershed. Gubarev, the chief of the First Partisan Army headquarters, wrote an announcement of the development for all partisan units, explaining that "Kolesnikov's purpose in our region is to link up with the armies of the Tambov region in order to resolve some common military objectives."[121] The same day, the provincial committee of the STK announced that Kolesnikov's arrival in Tambov represented "a historic turning point" for the anti-Soviet movement that demanded heightened urgency and commitment from partisan representatives and village communities so that the moment was not wasted. In a circular instruction, the provincial committee ordered all committees

> to take all decisive measures in the pursuit of our revolutionary work, and in particular to maintain communications [between STKs, Partisan Army units] on an exceptionally high level such that not one hour or one minute is wasted. This includes attention to the time required to receive and deliver packets, as well as to ensure that materials are delivered in their entirety. In order to maintain this high level of communications, all committees are ordered to mobilize the healthiest and fastest horses from civilian owners, as well as to mobilize the most reliable and energetic persons for communications duties. Execute these orders in accordance with the needs of revolutionary times. Those suspected of incompetence and negligence in this connection will be punished in accordance with revolutionary justice.[122]

Kolesnikov's arrival was not simply expedient for the leaders of the rebellion in Tambov, providing circumstances in which renewed appeals for militancy and commitment could be delivered to the rural population of southern Tambov. By every indication, they genuinely believed that Kolesnikov's appearance in Tambov constituted a chance to join two major constituents in the broad popular movement against the Soviet regime. The importance they ascribed to Kolesnikov and his rebel army was quickly manifested in the decision by the senior commanders of the First Partisan Army to appoint Kolesnikov overall commander of the army, replacing Boguslavskii, who was made chief of staff of the First Army, with Gubarev yielding his post to become Boguslavskii's lieutenant. Kolesnikov's men from Voronezh were integrated into the Partisan Army as the First Boguchar Regiment.[123]

On the surface, the decision of Partisan Army leaders to embrace Kolesnikov to this extent appears puzzling. Although the rebels had their scouts throughout the extended region, including Voronezh and northern portions of the Don territory, there is little evidence that the Partisan Army was very familiar with Kolesnikov before his sudden appearance in Tambov in February. Kolesnikov was, in fact, forced out of Voronezh by the intensified pressure applied by the Red Army once it managed to organize effectively in the latter part of February. Yet Kolesnikov was greeted as more than an equal when he finally made contact with rebel commanders of the Partisan Army in Tambov. Despite their continued success with the guerrilla tactics adopted by the Partisan Army and with the rapid expansion of the STK network, the insurgents in Tambov desperately needed indications that concrete progress was being made, and Kolesnikov's arrival was taken as a harbinger of precisely such progress in the partisan movement.

Kolesnikov's personal credibility was augmented by claims he and his men regularly made regarding their links with other anti-Soviet rebels, most significantly, that they were active members of the insurgent army led by Nester Makhno, possibly the most famous anti-Soviet rebel of the civil war period.[124] It is not known if Kolesnikov had had contact with Makhno during December and January before his return to Voronezh Province, but it is not unreasonable to assume that some contact had been made, for Makhno at this time was himself seeking to establish contact with other anti-Soviet rebels to the north of his base in eastern Ukraine.[125] Regardless, the alleged contact with Makhno, even if indirect, proved to be a valuable morale-boosting development, as the legend of Makhno and his exploits in Ukraine was already established in the popular mythology of the revolutionary era. Certainly the leaders of the Partisan Army pinned considerable hope on future contact with Makhno, and if one of Antonov's many girlfriends can be considered authoritative in this regard, even the overall commander of the Partisan Army spoke openly of his faith that the insurgents in Tambov would soon be joined by the Ukrainian rebels led by Makhno.[126] The appeal of association with Makhno's name finds further evidence in the very STK circular announcing Kolesnikov's arrival in Tambov in which the rebel commander from Voronezh is introduced as an "emissary from Makhno."[127] This appeal endured throughout the final months of the Tambov insurgency and grew in prominence as the rebels became more and more desperate.[128]

"Desperate," however, did not yet characterize the circumstances surrounding the insurgents in Tambov in February and early March. Their awareness of the developments in Moscow, Petrograd, and Kronstadt was fed by an intelligence network that was not exclusively focused on rumors and reports of mysterious Ukrainian anarchists.[129] Established contacts with PSR activists and civilian travelers between Moscow and Tambov kept the insurgent leaders informed of the worker demonstrations and the sailors' mutiny at Kronstadt, and information regarding the other "fronts" of the anti-Soviet movement remained the focus of Partisan Army interrogations of captured Red Army soldiers and Communist Party members.[130] What is more, their interrogations of captured government troops forged confidence that the Red Army's counterinsurgency campaign could falter on the crumbling morale of their own troops. Red Army soldiers were the main target group for rebel propaganda in the spring of 1921. It had already become standard practice for the Partisan Army to recruit captured Red Army servicemen, who were not only interrogated by rebel intelligence agents but also exposed to presentations by Partisan Army and STK agitators on the current political and strategic situation, as well as the grievances and objectives that animated the insurgency. If the prisoners still desired to return to their units rather than join the Partisan Army, they were allowed to do so, but only if they gave their word to distribute rebel propaganda among their fellow Red Army servicemen.[131] In a very real sense, the Partisan Army's treatment of prisoners contributed significantly to their cause.

Appeals to "Red Army conscripts" emphasized the natural solidarity such soldiers should have felt with their peasant brethren in the Partisan Army, and it pointedly countered state propaganda that sought to marginalize the rebels:

> Comrade conscripts! It is time for our shared indignation to find a common voice and to unite behind the common slogan: "Death to the Communists, and long live the general armed struggle of the laboring peasantry and all the oppressed against the Communist-aggressors!"

We the peasants have already done this and have taken to arms. The hypocrite-communists call us bandits, hoping to degrade us in the eyes of our brothers and to drive the laboring people into the struggle against us.

Do not believe the scoundrels, as they unscrupulously lie like a Yid lies to swindle a lady of her last kopeck. We are not bandits, but are instead the armed rebellious people—the people's army. This is why we appeal to you now, our conscript friends.[132]

The appeals also sought to capitalize on the known hardships endured by Red Army soldiers, both during the civil war generally and, in particular, on the front against the insurgents. In asking conscripted soldiers to "turn away for a minute from the nightmare and the feast of horrors" of civil war, rebel propaganda drew attention to the material conditions of the Red Army units and how the soldiers were being driven to sickness and hunger by the state while their own families were being similarly victimized by the Soviet government.[133] Such appeals were informed both by intelligence drawn from the partisans' network of "spies" sent to investigate Red Army morale in the active units and garrisons and by the increasing incidence of Red Army looting and "self-provisioning" that victimized the civilian population of Tambov.[134]

Supplying Red Army units with provisions had been a problem for state and army officials from the very beginning of the counterinsurgency effort in August and September 1920, but as the army presence increased, those problems only grew more acute and created major complications regarding discipline within those units and relations between the state and the village communities in the conflict zone. Almost immediately after provincial officials announced the end of requisitioning, with the evident backing of military commanders in Tambov, those same officials began voicing concerns regarding the consequences of this political decision on the practical necessity of supplying armed troops with food and fodder. On 11 February, the Tambov Presidium telegraphed Moscow explaining that the province did not have the resources to sustain a soldier population—active and reserve—that had swelled to exceed 108,000 men. Claiming that hunger had already been reported among the units, it demanded that the central government find adequate reserves of grain to deliver to Tambov.[135] (This was despite the claim in the 9 February announcement that deliveries were assured.) It had already become commonplace for official updates on the political situation in the province to combine reports of rebel looting and destruction of property with details of similar abuses perpetrated by Red Army units suffering shortages of food and supplies.[136] On 13 March, Commander Pavlov was forced to issue an order threatening any soldier who looted civilian property with summary execution.[137] This order, however, had little effect on the conduct of military units facing extreme shortages and hunger.

With regular demands from both sides, the net result was the exhaustion of the civilian population. While not necessarily an entirely negative development for the Soviet government, this was not part of anyone's strategy for pacifying the insurgency in Tambov. Certainly members of the provincial administration hoped that the decision to end requisitioning, followed by the announcement of the tax in kind, would soften peasant attitudes toward the Soviet regime. That hope was quickly extinguished once it became obvious that the military would have to rely upon local resources to supply its men. To build up some reserves of grain, the provincial Food Commissariat was forced to disregard its much vaunted public announcement and to continue grain requisitioning in certain areas throughout much of February and March.[138]

By April, it became official policy to permit the Red Army Supply Commission to conduct requisitioning within the burgeoning zone of the occupation, albeit not to levels above the original procurement targets of the razverstka.[139] This proviso was of little value to Red Army units facing what was universally described as a "catastrophic" situation regarding food supply.[140] The continuation of sanctioned requisitioning was politically damaging enough in the eyes of local officials but was still insufficient to meet the needs of the occupying forces, who were forced to carry out their own ad-hoc procurement operations outside the control of the Red Army Supply Commission and the Food Commissariat, undermining sincere hopes for peace even further.[141] Eggs and dairy products, which were still subject to official state procurement despite the announced end of the razverstka, were a prime target for hungry Red Army units because they could be consumed immediately. Other easy targets were perhaps even more damaging to the local economy and to the counterinsurgency campaign, such as when Red Army units sought out villages that were known to have established sowing committees from which reserves of grain could be more easily confiscated.[142] Antonov-Ovseenko, writing in early April, complained to Moscow that looting as a practice was "entrenched" among Red Army troops that, in his words, had been "put out to pasture" in the Tambov countryside.[143] An attendant phenomenon was open indiscipline, as hungry soldiers ignored the demands for restraint issued by their commanders. But just as often commanders turned a blind eye to the looting or even openly engaged in it themselves as a necessary evil.[144] The developing food supply crisis for the occupying forces in Tambov recalled the comment about Napoleon's armies during the Peninsular War of the early nineteenth century: "Spain is a place where small armies are beaten and large ones starve."

Certainly the Partisan Army and STK sought to make as much political capital as possible from the frequently abusive conduct of government forces in the countryside. Efforts to organize aid for households that suffered at the hands of "red bandits" could only be on a limited scale, however, especially as the Partisan Army itself suffered many of the same hardships—albeit on a less critical level—occasionally producing similar abuses by partisan soldiers against the civilian population of the villages.[145] The number of raids for food that could be made on state and collective farms by the Partisan Army was finite and provided diminishing returns, and as the regionwide provisions crisis grew more critical, the political principles of even the most "honorable" partisan could be compromised as the burden shifted entirely onto the village communities. The overall consequence, however, favored neither side in the short term. The practical complications created by an increased (and increasing) Red Army presence in Tambov eliminated the immediate prospects of a transformation (*perelom*) in the attitudes of the village communities toward the Soviet state following the announced end of requisitioning and the decisions of the Tenth Party Congress in Petrograd. The conduct of Red Army soldiers belied the state's public pronouncements that conjured up images of the forces of order rounding up bandit outlaws. And the continued practice of requisitioning foodstuffs, both through official and unofficial channels, betrayed the claims of government authorities that the Soviet state now recognized the legitimate grievances of the beleaguered civilian population and had changed course in order to redress those grievances.

Yet, for the rebels in Tambov, the initiative was rapidly slipping from their grasp as the context for their insurgency changed. The onset of spring had predictably brought practical anxieties into focus for village communities facing the real prospect of hunger and starvation. The state, recognizing the need to address these anxieties on a much larger scale, had shown a measure of flexibility and, in significantly changing its policies, sought to speak for the grievances of the rural population while also recognizing their anxieties about the future in a manner that only intensified the challenge facing the rebels. To sustain support for their rebellion against the Soviet state, the partisan leaders in Tambov would need to convince their own active followers and the broader civilian population that the movement continued to progress. Although the Partisan Army had managed to survive intensified efforts in March by the Red Army to encircle and destroy its main forces, there were clear signs that mere survival was not enough to maintain support or even sympathy for the movement. There were already worrying signs, such has when an entire Partisan Army regiment surrendered to Red Army authorities in mid-March, that the rebellion was in danger of "demobilizing" unless it could adapt to the changing seasonal context and the initiatives of the Soviet government.[146] Certainly the themes that emerged from rebel pronouncements at the time—emphasizing the wider context for the rebellion and the "concrete" links being established with other fronts of anti-Bolshevism—indicated that the Partisan Army and STK recognized the need for movement and progress as spring approached. However, rhetoric alone could go only so far in managing public opinion while the balance of forces in the countryside was shifting irrevocably to the government's favor.

BETWEEN AMBITION AND NECESSITY

Insurgency and Counterinsurgency,
April–June 1921

A FEBRUARY 1921 APPEAL issued by the Soviet government in Tambov to active insurgents asked supporters of the insurgency a series of questions highlighting the discrepancy between the inflated claims of the rebel leaders and the "facts" on the ground. "Is it possible that you don't understand," it asked insurgents, "that if this war continues a further two or three months then all the local working folk will be threatened with poverty, hunger, and death?" The costs of continued resistance were set alongside an image of the leaders of the rebellion that emphasized manipulation and lies. "Could it be that you still fail to understand that Antonov and all the bandit chieftains [*vozhaki*] have fallen into utter confusion and do not know themselves what to do further and where to take their insurgency, and that they seek comfort only in gluttony and alcohol[?]" But after several months of conflict, during which time the Partisan Army had effectively controlled the countryside of the southern portion of Tambov Province but had singularly failed to expand beyond its borders, perhaps the following question would have achieved some resonance among the rural population and the active insurgents: "Is it not clear to you that Antonov does not have a mighty army (for if he did, wouldn't he long ago have seized a major town such as Tambov or Kirsanov, instead of just marking time for the last five months)?"[1]

This question may have hung in the air during the following weeks. After an intense period of engagements with Red Army units in March, the Partisan Army was seemingly exhausted and fractured into smaller units, as well as considerably low on ammunition. But having survived, sometimes narrowly, the Partisan Army continued to boast confidence in their strength and in the prospects for ultimate victory.[2] One of their proclamations insisted in March 1921:

> Now, comrade partisans, it should be clear to you all that the hated Communists are living through their final days. Therefore in these last few days of the struggle, in giving assistance to our comrades to the north, south, and elsewhere, we should energetically follow the activities of the Communists, stay always on the alert and coolly await the time when we are able to deliver the decisive blow to the impudent Communists. Always be prepared for the moment when we must deliver such a blow, because for them it will ultimately be fatal. This blow will force them to reconsider their approach to the peasant movement and will force them to realize that they are ultimately powerless to suppress the insurgency.[3]

This promise was joined with further news from "other fronts," particularly Moscow, Petrograd, and Kronstadt. But the promise of some sort of breakthrough was not entirely focused on these other fronts. Recent developments that had been publicized widely within rebel territory had not proven as substantial and lasting as had been claimed. A prime example was Ivan Kolesnikov's arrival in Tambov from Voronezh, which was hailed as a significant development in the unification of major anti-Bolshevik forces. Yet, despite early indications that the unification was authentic and that the event would invigorate rebel activities, Kolesnikov's arrival on the scene was disruptive for the Partisan Army, and his stay in Tambov was short-lived.[4] Another setback for the Partisan Army came in late March 1921, when the government in Tambov confirmed the claim of its first scalp from among the original conspirators behind the rebellion. Petr Tokmakov, who had not only served in the Kirsanov militia with Antonov, but was one of the founding members of the famous druzhina of 1919–1920, had finally died on 23 March from a head wound suffered the previous day in a battle with Red Army soldiers in the village of Belomestnaia Dvoinia (Tambov uezd).[5] It is impossible to evaluate the impact of the loss of Tokmakov, the commander of the Second Partisan Army, for the rebel movement and its leaders. It was undoubtedly a setback, however, not only a personal loss for Aleksandr Antonov and others who had known Tokmakov for some time, but also a tangible blow to the Partisan

Army's credibility. At a time when the Partisan Army appeared to be struggling to survive, they required a demonstration of their own capabilities and resolve, at the very least to revive a spirit of defiance that had been flagging in the face of mounting pressure from the Red Army and Communist Party in Tambov Province.

TWO BATTLES: RASSKAZOVO AND KIRSANOV, APRIL 1921

Believing that the operations against the main Partisan Army forces in March had significantly weakened the rebellion, provincial officials received a damaging reminder of the rebels' renewed ambitions. Having regrouped in southwestern Kirsanov uezd, once more exploiting the tendency of military officials to abdicate responsibility when the enemy was possibly located outside their formal juris-diction, Antonov was able to amass over 5,000 fighters from among the fractured units that survived the battles of the previous month.[6] A series of raids in early April against Red Army units in the area brought limited rewards but further aided the rebels by attracting more locals to the ranks of active insurgents.[7] Then, on 10 April, came a major attack on Rasskazovo—one of the larger villages in the province and the home of some of the more sophisticated cottage industries, no-tably textiles, that operated in Tambov.

The "Tambov Manchester," as Rasskazovo was rather fancifully called by provin-cial notables,[8] had never before been occupied by the rebels, largely owing to the strong presence of armed government forces garrisoned there to protect the range of enterprises still operating in the village.[9] But Rasskazovo was far from being a pro-Soviet stronghold, even if it was home to a proto-working-class population employed in several small mills, tanneries, and distilleries. Workers had repeatedly expressed their discontent with Soviet authorities, particularly regarding food supply, and strikes had recently been broken up by agents of the Cheka in Rassk-azovo, with sixteen people arrested.[10] Recent attempts to hold nonparty conferences in the village had degenerated into chaos, as individuals identified by government officials as PSR supporters virtually took over the assemblies with anti-Soviet speeches and predictions of the demise of the regime.[11] It was likely that Antonov and his associates were aware of the situation in Rasskazovo, both the disposition of the local population and the state of the Red Army forces in the village.[12]

Rasskazovo was the base for the Volga Infantry Brigade that had arrived in January from Saratov. It also had one further infantry company from the Second Cheka Regiment, a platoon of machine gunners, and one unit of armed Commu-nist Party members. When the Partisan Army began to move on Rasskazovo on

10–11 April, they undertook a diversionary attack on the village of Nizhne-Spasskoe, to the southwest. This attack, carried out by a small number of Antonov's men, prompted the military commanders in Rasskazovo to scramble one unit—the Communist Party members—to reinforce the Red Army in Nizhne-Spasskoe. One hour later, the Partisan Army attacked Rasskazovo from the west and south. The forces in the village almost instantly gave up on a defense, with many abandoning their weapons and positions, first finding safety in a nearby forest before retreating and regrouping at the railway station of Platonovka to the east. The alarm had been sounded by the time the government forces had quit Rasskazovo, and Red Army airplanes were already in the air to scout the situation while armored cars were preparing to leave Tambov.[13]

For three hours, the Partisan Army occupied Rasskazovo. A Cheka bulletin written several weeks later described what took place:

> On the night of 11 April [in Rasskazovo], as a matter of first priority, he [Antonov] ordered his men to begin pillaging the factories and mills, and joined by the local kulaks and other anti-Soviet elements they succeeded in looting completely the local tannery, and then they set upon the Orzhevskii distillery (*vinzavod*), where the bandits drank themselves drunk and began to fire their weapons in wild celebration, killing two local guards in the process.[14]

However, the evaluation of senior officials in both the Red Army and the provincial administration was quite different. According to both Antonov-Ovseenko and the Red Army officer Ivan Trutko, the raid on Rasskazovo had a very specific purpose—to replenish the Partisan Army's supply of arms and ammunition. While the figures for the losses differ in each account, they represent the largest single seizure of military supplies by the rebels: one artillery gun and between 200–300 shells, 11 machine guns, and nearly 400 rifles with over 100,000 rounds of ammunition. In addition, the rebels seized nearly 80 telephones with over 50 *verst* of cable. And, of course, there was all the food, clothing, and drink they could carry—either in their carts, on their backs, or in their bellies. Such a haul would have been possible only if Soviet authorities in the province had believed Rasskazovo to be a village safe from rebel attack.[15]

Despite this setback, provincial officials still expressed confidence that the rebellion was only further discrediting itself with these raids—that in spite of the material gains represented by the seizure of munitions the rebels were only "marking time" with continued attacks on weakened rural outposts. In a small detail that is suggestive in this regard, a Partisan Army protocol, dated 14 April,

Crash site of a Red Army airplane with local onlookers in the background, 1921. The use of airplanes by the Red Army against the rebels in Tambov was mainly restricted to scouting operations. Such operations proved of limited value to the Red Army, however, and these exceptionally fragile airplanes frequently drew fire from the rebels. At least one senior army officer (Tishchenko) was captured and killed by insurgents after his plane was shot down. *Photograph courtesy of the Tambovskii Kraevedcheskii Muzei*

describing a meeting of senior figures behind the rebellion contains the issue of the continued overall command of Aleksandr Antonov. The protocol notes that after a vote, confidence in Antonov's leadership was reaffirmed.[16] It is impossible to know whether this reflected the apparent overall direction of the insurgency or was instead a matter of personalities or even physical health. But the issue of the current legitimacy of the insurgency appeared to be of growing importance. "Among the peasantry," wrote one Cheka evaluation, "there is much talk of the ultimate impotence of the Antonovist army, and in conversations one regularly hears 'that that Antonov is always just found in the heart of the countryside, where he can carry on knowing he has nothing to fear from us peasants, but in the towns and in other places where the real Red Army forces are located, he is totally afraid to show his face [*on tuda i nosa boitsia pokazat'*]."[17]

Using guerrilla war as a long-term strategy to weaken and ultimately discredit an enemy government was a principle not entirely lost on the Partisan Army rebels, whose instructions refer to the relative advantages of "partisan" warfare against the more conventional "positional" warfare in a struggle with superior state forces.[18] Yet it is clear that in the spring of 1921 Partisan Army leaders felt a strong pressure to "progress" with their insurgency in a way that is not uncommon for those who must both maintain military effectiveness and popular legitimacy.[19] The Soviet government and Red Army had possessed the initiative for many weeks, on both the military and political fronts, and rebel leaders were pressed to reassert themselves in the conflict. In this regard, the success of the raid on Rasskazovo was likely to have boosted their confidence and prompted them to target more ambitious objectives.[20] Within days of completing the raid on Rasskazovo, the Partisan Army under Antonov was planning its first major attack on a provincial town, the uezd seat of Kirsanov.[21]

However, the decision to strike on Kirsanov was not an act of hubris on the part of Antonov and his fellow rebel commanders.[22] They remained well informed, as in previous raids during 1921, of the defensive capabilities of the town. Kirsanov was not nearly as vulnerable as it had been in the first weeks of the insurgency in August and September 1920, when there were only some forty armed Communist Party members in the town scrambling to resist an expected assault by peasant insurgents and anxious officials were pleading with recuperating Red Army soldiers in the local hospital to get out of their beds to shore up the town's defenses.[23] Since that period of apparent helplessness at the start of the insurgency, Kirsanov had acquired a siege mentality that was only heightened by the influx of Communist Party refugees from the surrounding countryside who had evacuated their posts in the villages and volosts of the uezd and arrived with their families and possessions. As in other major towns caught in the territory of the insurgency, such refugees were an object both of pity and concern (but sometimes utter indifference) for state officials, who could hardly provide for them. There was little or no provision made for housing these refugees, and little food or employment could be found for them.[24] For many of the men, one of the only outlets for activity was rudimentary military training and volunteer service in the growing number of Communist Party defense militias and "Units of Special Assignment" (known by the acronym ChON).[25] Regular Red Army units previously assigned to garrisons in towns such as Kirsanov were steadily being given active duty patrolling the countryside, leaving the towns to organize their own defenses from among local Communist Party members and others loyal to the government.[26]

Preparations for an assault on Kirsanov began soon after the success of the Partisan Army in Rasskazovo. Following their raid for supplies on Rasskazovo, rebel forces once again amassed north of the Kirsanov-Tambov railway line, moving between Morshansk and Kozlov uezds to avoid engagements with the Red Army cavalry forces in the region. Antonov's main force was joined by two other major rebel groups—that led by the Kozlov uezd rebel named Karas' (identified later as V. V. Nikitin-Korolev), and another led by the rebel V. F. Selianskii, also from the central part of Tambov Province.[27] According to a summary report of a month later by Antonov-Ovseenko, this meeting in the village of Kamenka (Tambov uezd) secured the integration of Selianskii's "northern" army and the "western" army of Karas' with Antonov's own force in preparation for a major operation. According to Antonov-Ovseenko, the rebels had for the first time abandoned the limited territorial basis for individual rebel activities in favor of large strategic amassments for specific operations.[28]

One of the rebels, a twenty-one-year-old from Tambov uezd named Petr Ivannikov, later told Red Army interrogators that the meeting in Kamenka formally involved six of the surviving Partisan Army regiments. Ivannikov himself was in the Kozlov-based force led by Karas', although he had joined the insurgency in his native region of Abakumovka in December 1920. Ivannikov's regiment, along with the others assembled in Kamenka in April 1921, underwent a brief "inspection" by Antonov and other Partisan Army commanders, after which they were treated to rousing speeches about the political objectives of the insurgency and the nature of the present strategic situation. Antonov himself evidently spoke of the plans to attack Kirsanov, and he made each unit of insurgents vow that they would fight to the bitter end. Supplies of guns and ammunition were distributed among the soldiers before they broke up into three "columns" to undertake the assault.[29]

As in the attack on Rasskazovo, the Partisan Army sought to employ diversionary tactics to draw Red Army forces out of the region of the intended target. This involved two columns of rebel soldiers traveling north across the main Tambov-Kirsanov railway line toward the northern border of Tambov uezd.[30] The intention was to draw the attention of government forces toward Morshansk uezd. The movement of such large rebel forces in this direction appeared to have worked, as the alarm was raised in scouting reports filed on 22 April of an imminent attack by the Partisan Army on the town of Morshansk—within two days, according to one report.[31] After the column led by Antonov met up once more with Selianskii's group near the village of Pakhotnyi Ugol, they changed their tack dramatically and quickly moved southeast in the direction of Kirsanov. In the village of Kobiaki, only some ten kilometers from the town itself, all three groups of Partisan Army forces converged to launch their assault.[32]

It is difficult to determine with any accuracy the strength of the Partisan Army force that ultimately assembled at Kobiaki on 24 April 1921. Red Army prisoners attested to the fact that Antonov's force that attacked Rasskazovo only a fortnight before was somewhere in the region of 5,000–6,000 strong.[33] Added to this would be the two regiments under the leadership of Karas', estimated by observers at nearly 1,500 men, and the force under Selianskii, for which there are no contemporary figures.[34] Estimates by eyewitnesses many years later describe the overall numbers of the Partisan Army in Kobiaki as between 5,000 and 10,000.[35] Not all, however, would take part in the assault on Kirsanov.

Leaders of the Partisan Army forces in Kobiaki were possibly aware of the fact that the main garrisoned unit in Kirsanov, an infantry brigade from Saratov, was being transferred to Rasskazovo as part of a standard change in assignment. However, the Red Army unit assigned to take over the Kirsanov garrison (another infantry brigade, this time from Moscow) had only just left Tambov on 23 April and was no more than halfway to Kirsanov on the eve of the assault as they marched to their new assignment.[36] What the Partisan Army commanders did not know was that the authorities in Kirsanov were fully aware of the presence of rebel forces and that they were quickly setting up the town's defenses as well as calling on whatever Red Army or government troops were available to the east of the town.[37]

Municipal officials sounded the alarm on the evening of 24 April, calling all available Communist Party and trade union members to arm themselves and to take up positions in strategic points within the town. One party member, Sergei Pomazov, later wrote that he and others feared that the Partisan Army and its supporters had a kind of anti-Communist "St. Bartholomew's Night massacre" planned for Kirsanov, set to coincide with Palm Sunday on 25 April.[38] They must have felt vulnerable when they saw that their fate rested on the defense mounted by the 500 or so Communists who turned out for the emergency mobilization, reinforced only by the local mounted militia force and a single Cheka infantry unit. That evening another infantry unit arrived in Kirsanov, just hours before the assault. The numbers, however, remained unimpressive. Their real advantage was in the weapons at their disposal. The government possessed two machine gun–mounted armored cars and several more machine guns with a plentiful supply of ammunition. Every progovernment fighter was supplied with a rifle and bullets. According to one source, the defenders in Kirsanov also possessed an airplane, although how this would be of use is difficult to ascertain, and it played no active part in the events that followed.[39] They concentrated their defenses at four points in the town—at the entry from the north, within the grounds of the cathedral, at the cemetery, and on the street along the riverfront on the western edge of town. Believing that the rebels could attack from any of three different directions, the men in Kirsanov felt they had to distribute their forces across these four points.[40]

When the attack commenced, it became apparent that the rebels had decided not to throw all their forces at Kirsanov. Instead, only the two regiments under the leadership of Karas' took part in the assault when it began in the middle of the night on 25 April 1921.[41] Evidently not anticipating organized resistance, the rebel soldiers charged toward the center of the town on horseback (many riding bareback, with others using ordinary pillows for saddles) and armed with rifles and sawed-off shotguns. According to nearly all the memoirists who wrote about the assault, the result was a massacre, with most damage being done by the machine guns at the cemetery. An initial charge was thrown into confusion by the machine gun fire, and after a brief retreat, a second assault similarly fell into disarray when the two armored cars emerged from the municipal fire station to reinforce the machine guns at the cemetery. When the rebel soldiers under Karas' finally retreated, less than two hours after the start of the fighting, they were chased by the mounted Kirsanov militia, joined by the commander of the armored cars, Vas'kin, who took up the pursuit on a motorcycle. According to Gavril Zaitsev, "after the battle practically the entire field that stretches out toward Kobiaki was covered with the bodies of people and horses."[42]

According to both eyewitnesses from the government side and from the rebel side, Antonov himself did not take part in the assault, preferring to stay behind in Kobiaki to "oversee" the attack. When news arrived of the defeat, the rebels quit Kobiaki, and it was only then, after Kirsanov officials had raised the alarm, that the Red Army forces patrolling the countryside appeared on the scene to pursue the rebels toward their stronghold of southwestern Kirsanov uezd. While the pursuit force under the cavalry commander Dmitrenko inflicted no further significant damage, the losses sustained by the rebels in the failed assault were, by all accounts, substantial. According to Antonov-Ovseenko, the rebels left behind some twenty machine guns and one light artillery gun, but the number of dead and wounded sustained by the Partisan Army on 25 April is unknown.[43] The great victory the Partisan Army leaders had desired—one that would have brought the seizure of another cache of arms and munitions, the "liberation" of rebel prisoners, and the prestige of having actually occupied one of the administrative centers of the province, one that many people, especially those in the Tambov Communist Party and administration, believed would be the turning point in the armed conflict—had ended in a significant defeat.[44]

CONTINUED RECRIMINATIONS, APRIL 1921

The successful defense of Kirsanov had been fortunate for the Soviet government. The town could well have been taken if the Partisan Army had attacked with the full strength of what was reported to be their amassed forces. Antonov-Ovseenko had underscored the need for a coherent strategy in dealing with the insurgency in March, and while significant advances had been made in formulating such a strategy, the now familiar problem of overstretched military and political resources only gained further clarity.[45] Since January 1921, the deployment of Red Army forces under General Pavlov in Tambov had increased dramatically, far outstripping any of the estimated gains made by the Partisan Army during the period.[46] But the demands of pursuing an effective and balanced counterinsurgency operation—one that sought to separate the rebels from the partisan population, as Antonov-Ovseenko desired—required more troops in higher concentrations to provide safety for the village communities in the territory of the insurgency.[47] The shortcomings were revealed in the case of Kirsanov, where the local garrison was severely reduced in size in order to deploy more troops to strategic locations, effectively spreading the available forces thinly across the countryside and leaving the task of pursuing rebel forces to the limited mobile forces under the Red Army command in the province. The response of the Partisan Army—to concentrate their forces into larger amassments for more ambitious operations—had overwhelmed the Red Army in Rasskazovo and could very well have done so in Kirsanov. More troops would be needed for the oft-mentioned occupation to be effectively realized in Tambov.

The consequences for the Red Army in April 1921 were a series of defeats of military units by much larger rebel forces, at a time when provincial officials and members of the Plenipotentiary Commission were optimistic that political reforms would quickly have a positive impact on the popular standing of the Soviet government.[48] Such vulnerability bred considerable dissatisfaction among commanders and political officials alike. One of the most bitter episodes involved the arrest of Georgii Russov, brigade commander with the Third Infantry Regiment, based in the First Military Sector. Following the surrender of one of the battalions under his authority in the area of Inzhavino, Russov was relieved of his command and arrested for defeatism and suspected ties with the rebels.[49] Not only had Russov allegedly failed to respond to warnings from local Communist Party members that the battalion would be attacked by rebels, but also the Red Army men under his command had failed to put up satisfactory resistance, indicative of a weak "pro-Soviet spirit"—a failing attributed to correspondingly weak leadership. Besides the circumstances of the surrender of the battalion—which took place on 9–10 April, when the Partisan Army attacked Rasskazovo—the fact that Russov had previously been an officer in the tsarist army was central to the investigation by tribunal officials.

Russov's attempt to defend himself against the allegations revealed much about the difficulties facing Red Army units in the field in the spring of 1921 and many of the frictions that were developing between the army and the provincial administration and within the Red Army itself. In a long letter to tribunal investigators, Russov explained the circumstances surrounding the battalion's surrender and the rationale for his decisions at the time. Russov stated that he was skeptical of the warnings from the village of Parevka given by local Communist Party members that the battalion was under threat, since these warnings claimed that a force of over 9,000 rebels was descending on the battalion. Russov believed that this was a gross overestimate, something he and other Red Army commanders had come to expect of local party members, whose own heightened sense of insecurity had repeatedly prompted them to "cry wolf," wasting the military's time and resources.[50] Making his own adjustments to the alarmist reports and estimating that the rebel force probably numbered 1,000–2,000 men, Russov believed that his battalion of some 700 soldiers would be able to overcome them, given that most previous clashes had been short-lived and in keeping with the hit-and-run tactics of the Partisan Army. (Intelligence available to Russov stated that there were no more than 200 rebels in the Inzhavino region, and most recent clashes in the sector had involved only between 40 and 100 rebel fighters.) He also gave other reasons for not responding to the warning, such as the threat that diverting forces away from the headquarters in Inzhavino would have left it vulnerable (in case the attack on the battalion, or simply the warning itself, was part of a diversion orchestrated by the Partisan Army), and also the lack of cavalry at his disposal, making the regiment's reaction time relatively slow.

Most offensive from Russov's point of view was the charge that he and his fellow commanders did not do enough to cultivate a fighting spirit among the soldiers:

> As concerns the level of political education of the Red Army soldiers, the [investigating] commission did not even bother to question the soldiers of the First Battalion themselves, all of whom fell prisoner to Antonov and all of whom, after being exposed to strong political agitation on the part of Antonov, returned to the fold with an even more intense hatred of the bandits than before. Did the commission even bother asking if a single one of these soldiers went over to the side of Antonov after falling prisoner? Not one of them did so.[51]

Sensing that he was being made a scapegoat for the failure of the Red Army to master the strategic situation in March and April, Russov launched into his own bitter attack on his fellow officers. He stated that only two elements could possibly have a vested interest in prolonging the war—the enemies he identified as the "international bourgeoisie" and "careerists" in the Red Army. His invective was particularly focused on two of his fellow officers—Petrovskii and Chaikovskii (the latter of the Volga Infantry Brigade)—but he was generally scornful of all those soldiers who saw the rebellion in Tambov as an opportunity to reap decorations and commendations for heroism.[52] As an example, Russov contended that younger officers (in a way not unknown in armies the world over) routinely inflated the casualty figures for rebels following battles with Red Army soldiers they themselves had led, sometimes by as much as ten times the actual number:[53]

> Those individuals who collect their medals and who are promoted to high-profile posts hardly grow more intelligent as a result, but on the contrary they only eventually bring more grave difficulties upon themselves and upon the exhausted proletariat. No medals or promotions are going to solve the banditry problem, but instead they only serve to make it worse, as was seen before we arrived, when some commander or other was awarded a gold decoration for the nonsensical boast that the insurgency was defeated, when in fact it was only beginning to lay down its roots.[54]

Russov's lengthy appeal communicated a strong sense of indignation, as well as a note of betrayal, as he had made a conscious choice in 1918 to join the Red Army and support the Soviet government, only to be continually suspected and victimized for his past service in the tsarist army as a staff captain.[55] The defeats suffered by the Red Army in Tambov, he believed, were owing to the unsound policies of the Soviet government and the lack of strong commitment by the Red Army.[56] Individuals such as he were not to blame, for they were being placed in an impossible situation. And the demands on the troops in Tambov were increasing all the time, as the designs for an effective counterinsurgency effort grew more and more ambitious.

Casting Russov as a possible counterrevolutionary and defeatist revealed more than a conflict of personalities and ambitions within the ranks of the officer corps in Tambov. It fit in with a larger effort by government agents to uncover possible sources of treachery believed to explain the recent and long-term failings of the counterinsurgency effort. It was a widely held view that there was a degree of complicity in the behavior of provincial administrators that would explain why the insurgency had grown to such a degree of seriousness. The view was well expressed by a Red Army officer cadet, Fedor Liubkin, who returned to Kirsanov in the spring of 1921 and was moved to write directly to Lenin about what he saw in his native uezd:

I went home for the holiday to find that all the forces in our Kirsanov uezd are being dominated by the bandits, and that they are simply unable to be done with the rebellion. A band of criminals simply cannot raise an army of 30,000 without some sort of sabotage going on. Many of our Communist brethren have died, and all there is to answer for their sacrifice is the fact that Antonov's following has grown from no more than 10,000 to no fewer than 30,000. . . . Moreover, it has become clear in recent times that local authorities even cooperate with the bandits, issuing them travel passes and identification papers and giving them passwords. People from among our own Soviet military servicemen are working with the bandits to return the proletariat to slavery. . . . It would be impossible for me to write about everything I have seen here, so let me leave you, Comrade Lenin, with this one request: pay serious attention to what I have written and to the need for us to uncover who among those sitting in the various departments and commissariats is a true defender of the working people and who is a traitor.[57]

The existence of "spies" and informants was by now well known, for rebel documents appeared to confirm that the Partisan Army and STK had sympathizers within government circles, including the military commissariat and the Cheka.[58] Information such as this welcomed Antonov-Ovseenko when he arrived in Tambov in February 1921 to take control of the provincial administration and to oversee the counterinsurgency effort.

Vladimir Antonov-Ovseenko always had a special interest in the secret police, the Cheka. While serving as provincial governor for a period after the brief occupation of parts of Tambov by the Whites in 1919–1920, he devoted considerable energy and attention to reorganizing the provincial Cheka at the cost of attending to the pressing demands of economic reconstruction and establishing popular political faith in the Soviet government.[59] Arriving in Tambov in the wake of a defeat at the hands of the Cossack General Mamontov, Antonov-Ovseenko addressed his duties as soviet executive chairman as a Chekist himself—the defeat, in his estimation, was a signal of the failure of the Soviet rearguard to hold, and the cause was not military disorganization but the failure of political resolve. The instrument of political fortification for the Soviet Republic, especially in the provinces, was the Cheka.

Similarly, when Antonov-Ovseenko arrived in Tambov for a second spell, this time as chairman of the Plenipotentiary Commission, he was resolved to focus once more on the insurgency in the province as a fundamentally political problem. In this, he eventually received the support of Moscow and the Communist Party leadership, especially following their decisions in March to end forced requisitioning and to loosen restrictions on private trade. A vigor that had been sorely lacking was brought to the government propaganda campaign, with the fundamental link between economic and political questions as its centerpiece. But as in 1919–1920, Antonov-Ovseenko also devoted considerable energy to the operations of the Tambov Cheka organization and its role in the counterinsurgency effort.

Earlier assessments had highlighted the need to strengthen the provincial Cheka organization that had suffered considerably in the first months of the rebellion, losing upwards of 40 percent of its staff in rebel attacks by the end of 1920.[60] While the manpower shortage remained an issue in early 1921, the principal concern for Antonov-Ovseenko and his associates on the Plenipotentiary Commission was the degree to which the Tambov Cheka had become infected with either fatalism or outright corruption. An initial inspection in late February 1921 revealed an organization in which "it was not at all rare to find incompetent and criminal elements. The situation called for a fundamental purge of the Tambov Cheka, and this is what was initiated and is still being pursued. Many arrests have already been made, for crimes such as counterrevolution, sabotage, contact with bandits, and all matter of other criminal infractions."[61] The purge of the surviving Cheka membership occurred in February and early March, when Moscow assigned a young Chekist with extensive experience both in the rearguard and at the front lines of the civil war, Mikhail Davidovich Antonov, to assume control over the Tambov provincial Cheka organization.[62] This was possibly the first time Mikhail Davidovich regretted his decision, taken in the early months of the civil war, to change his surname from the original (more clearly Jewish) "German" to "Antonov."[63]

What could be termed the "traditional" activities of the Cheka intensified markedy. Reporting on rumors overheard in markets and cafeterias was stepped up, and reports on possible opposition party activity also showed a demonstrable rise. Surveillance was complemented by increased activity, particularly along the railways and within the towns. In March and April there were regular roundups of individuals living in the major towns with known ties to opposition socialist parties, such as the PSR or the Mensheviks. Despite widespread arrests, very little substantive political activity was uncovered.[64] As the Cheka organization in Kozlov uezd reported following a similar roundup of members of the local "intelligentsia": "their attitude in relation to politics is wholly internalized—concerns about their stomachs are what possess them now."[65] Similarly, the Cheka in Tambov became increasingly active within working-class circles, seeking to sabotage any plans for strikes that were taken to be indicative of opposition politics but were also principally dictated by fundamentally prosaic concerns.[66]

The reinvigoration of the Cheka in Tambov in March and April 1921 was not limited to the traditional duties of suppressing independent political and oppositional activity. The Cheka was also to play a central role in the counterinsurgency. For the previous three months of 1921, most intelligence gathering had been completed by Red Army units, particularly the interrogation of rebel prisoners and the debriefing of Red Army servicemen who had been temporarily taken captive. Many Partisan Army and STK materials had fallen into the hands of the Red Army and the provincial government over the course of the insurgency, but little systematic effort had been made to develop either a composite picture of the organization of the insurgency or of the depth of the support enjoyed by the rebels. Addressing the first issue was a long-term project, involving the analysis of all materials seized from the Partisan Army and STKs, as well as information gleaned from prisoners and civilians in the countryside. The second project was, for the counterinsurgency effort, far more pressing. The newly reorganized Cheka and Special Department, assisted by the arrival of several agents brought in by Antonov-Ovseenko, began to compile lists of rebel villages and families with known connections to the rebels. Such lists would be compiled on the basis of information contained in interrogation records, but the task was made much simpler because the Partisan Army and STKs maintained their own lists of supporters in the villages as well as lists of active rebel soldiers. In addition to these ready-made intelligence materials, the Cheka also relied upon materials in the village and volost soviets, as well as those of the short-lived Committees of the Poor, which contained records that identified kulak families among the local population. All these sources informed the project of drawing up lists of known or suspected rebel supporters.[67]

According to Antonov-Ovseenko's report, the lists would be instrumental in the next phase of the counterinsurgency effort. Separate lists would be compiled that distinguished between villages that actively joined the rebellion and those that were drawn in "from without" by units of the Partisan Army. Other lists would identify villages that were either actively or passively "pro-Soviet." In addition to helping Red Army units chart and predict the movements of rebel units from one "safe" village to the next, Antonov-Ovseenko also outlined how lists of individual community members "will assist us in the selection of hostages from each village, who will be shot on the occasion of a repeated flare-up of bandit activity in that particular village." Antonov-Ovseenko ordered that officials in surviving local institutions and in the Cheka compile lists of suspect inhabitants in the rural communities. This way, according to Antonov-Ovseenko, government forces can "check on the local inhabitants of suspicious villages, determining who among those counted absent has a valid reason and who is likely to be participating in the rebellion, so that they can then take hostages from the families of those likely to be bandits."[68]

"OCCUPATION" AND THE ARRIVAL OF TUKHACHEVSKII

Such designs assumed an adequate amount of local knowledge, which could only truly be gained by establishing a permanent foothold in the villages. Since the start of the insurgency, however, this was precisely what had been lost to the government. The dismantling of the network of rural soviets by the rebels had occurred fairly rapidly in the final months of 1920, and efforts to reestablish these institutions had frequently been short-lived, providing only easy targets for rebel units that dominated particular localities. At the beginning of April, for instance, Tambov uezd had only twenty-two of its fifty-six volost soviets up and running, and all but two had been forced to abandon operations at one time or other over the previous seven months.[69] Communist Party members with experience working in the countryside were hesitant to take new assignments in revived village or volost soviets if the Red Army was unable to provide adequate security.[70] The same problem affected the revolutionary committees, extraordinary institutions installed by the military in front-line zones and areas of instability that were intended to function in lieu of civilian soviets.[71] The political wing of the Red Army began installing revolutionary committees (or revkoms) in Tambov in late February 1921, but because they could sustain an adequate troop presence only in certain regional centers, the revkoms only extended to what was called the "regional" level.[72] Attempts to extend the network to the volosts and villages of the territory of the insurgency were unsuccessful, and Communist Party members in the main towns of the province were far from enthusiastic at the prospect of receiving such an assignment without adequate guarantees for their safety.[73]

The shortage of military forces in the area that could provide a stable source of security was affecting nearly all government initiatives to earn the trust of the rural population. The two-week amnesty that had been announced on 20 March was generally considered to be a failure, despite the fact that over 3,000 men surrendered during its course.[74] With only a handful of men surrendering with weapons in order to accept the full amnesty offered by the Plenipotentiary Commission, provincial officials were forced to accept that the amnesty had done little to weaken the insurgency. According to an assessment offered by the Tambov

Cheka, rebel soldiers were confronted with strong propaganda messages to limit the impact of the amnesty, ranging from efforts to suppress information about the offer (such as taking down announcements detailing its provisions), deliberate misinformation (such as warnings that the Cheka planned not to honor the amnesty), and provisional acceptance of the soldier's desire to take up the offer (for example, permitting rebels to accept amnesty but without surrendering their weapons).[75] Most who took up the amnesty were not directly connected with the rebellion but were classified as deserters and had managed to avoid involvement in the conflict on either side.[76] For those who served in the Partisan Army in the heart of the insurgency, amnesty offered few real assurances if they had to surrender in defiance of the rebel leaders and if postamnesty freedom in one's native village meant extreme vulnerability to rebel reprisals.[77]

The plans to draft lists of villagers that could be used by military and Cheka forces to separate the "bandit" from the "nonbandit" families were similarly limited by the government's inability to provide a stable presence and security for village communities. There were some encouraging signs of a will to cooperate with government agents in this regard, but these were found on the periphery of the conflict zone and thus were not a sound basis for generalization by members of the Plenipotentiary Commission.[78] The shortage of armed forces affected nearly every aspect of the work initiated by Antonov-Ovseenko and his Plenipotentiary Commission as part of the occupation system. By mid-April, Antonov-Ovseenko was compelled to lament the situation in terms that echoed the outrage voiced by provincial and local officials in late 1920 when they confronted their own "powerlessness" to affect a positive change in the strategic situation: "All our work among the peasantry has been ruined—the bandit elements have returned and have begun to punish the members of the peasantry loyal to us. The peasants, who had begun to come over to our side, are being bled on account of our own weakness, for when our forces depart, the bandits once more find themselves masters of the situation in a particular region."[79]

Antonov-Ovseenko requested that Moscow make a major commitment to resolving the situation in Tambov by assigning seasoned Red Army troops in large formations, rather than transferring the odd battalion of irregulars to raise troop totals to what appeared to be an overwhelming number. Antonov-Ovseenko asked for no fewer than two divisions of three brigades each, including armored or motorized units. This was nearly double the request he had sent to Moscow only a few days before via the provincial party chairman, Vasil'ev.[80] He also made several recommendations that would guarantee that Moscow maintained a close interest in the rapid "liquidation" of the rebellion in Tambov. This surprisingly included making the Red Army command in Tambov directly subordinate to Red Army Supreme Headquarters in Moscow and not to the Southern Regional Headquarters in Orel, which had previously been assured for Commander Pavlov when he arrived in January 1921.[81] Four months on, and the same requests and recommendations were being made to effect a transformation of the counterinsurgency effort, and the same themes were being repeated by senior officials stationed in Tambov. "Occupation is the prerequisite condition for all of our work," Antonov-Ovseenko wrote in April, confirming that, after several months, "occupation" remained aspirational rather than operational.[82]

Antonov-Ovseenko, having recovered from illness in the final week of April, traveled to Moscow to report directly to VTsIK's Antibanditry Commission on the situation in Tambov and to recommend a significant intensification of the counterinsurgency operation. His recommendations were hardly novel, but Antonov-Ovseenko returned to Tambov with new confidence that Moscow was finally focused on resolving the situation in the province.[83] In response to Antonov-Ovseenko's report before the Antibanditry Commission, E. M. Sklianskii (a member of the commission and of the Revolutionary Military Council) wrote a brief memo to Lenin: "I would think it beneficial to send Tukhachevskii to suppress the rebellion in Tambov. Things there have not improved in recent times, and in some areas the situation has even grown worse. If we were to make such a decision, there will be a considerable political effect. Especially abroad. Your opinion on this?" Lenin agreed to Sklianskii's proposal, adding: "Take this to Molotov for a decision tomorrow at the Politburo meeting. I propose we appoint [Tukhachevskii] without any publicity in the Center [Moscow], without any notices in the press."[84]

Mikhail Nikolaevich Tukhachevskii had joined the Red Army in 1918 after escaping from a POW camp in Germany following the conclusion of the Brest-Litovsk Treaty. He had been a lieutenant in the tsarist army but was almost immediately awarded the rank of general in the Red Army, which had been so desperately short of experienced commanders from the time of its foundation. He had been an army group commander on the eastern front of the civil war, then became overall commander of the Caucasian front in early 1920, followed by a similar tenure as commander of the western front during the invasion of Poland in the summer of 1920. He was the most celebrated of the Red Army's commanders and the most recognizable and respected such figure on the international stage.

Lenin's wariness of attracting attention to the appointment of Tukhachevskii was possibly more informed by the general's most recent assignment as the organizer of the suppression of the Kronstadt mutiny near Petrograd. Nearly all persons living in Moscow and Petrograd were aware of the uprising in Tambov and the protracted conflict between the rebels and the provincial government. But the seriousness of the insurgency and the escalating commitment of the Red Army and Soviet state to suppressing it remained the subject of rumors rather than communicated through the press organs of the party and government. An official announcement of the appointment of Tukhachevskii—the general who oversaw the bloody suppression of Kronstadt—would have raised both popular anxieties about the seriousness of the insurgency in Tambov and the prospect of yet another brutal "liquidation" of popular resistance in the manner of Kronstadt. In addition, the seriousness of internal disorder in the Soviet Republic would have been signaled to international governments by the appointment of the celebrated general.

Tukhachevskii's appointment, however, was a clear indication that Moscow had accepted Antonov-Ovseenko's recommendations, something further indicated by the decisions made at the Politburo meeting on 28 April that approved the appointment.[85] The Politburo gave Tukhachevskii full authority over military operations in Tambov, making him answerable only to Red Army Supreme Headquarters. Tukhachevskii was given a one-month deadline for the complete "liquidation" of the rebellion. On the day of the Politburo meeting, the Plenipotentiary Commission met in Tambov to discuss in detail the measures approved by the Politburo and by the special Antibanditry Commission in Moscow. With the understanding that the internal situation was on the whole improving for the Soviet state, with the singular exception of the conflict in Tambov, officials initiated a wide range of measures in addition to appointing General Tukhachevskii.[86] Most important, two infantry brigades were to be assigned to reinforce the Tambov sector, along with the cavalry brigade led by General Grigorii Ivanovich Kotovskii, a force with extensive experience fighting under similar conditions in Ukraine.[87] These mobile forces were to be complemented by a strengthened contingent of armored and motorized units and aided by intensified aerial reconnaissance. Perhaps most important for the realization of state objectives in Tambov, the Revolutionary Military Council and Red Army Supreme Headquarters were instructed to transfer senior command staff and reliable officers to the region, with the hope of adding structure and responsiveness to the chain of command in a conflict zone plagued by poor communications and coordination between military units and commanders. As for the military units themselves, nearly 1,000 political workers tied to the Red Army were designated for assignment to Tambov to maintain discipline among the troops engaged in the counterinsurgency operation and generally to ensure a suitable "political consciousness" among them.[88]

Tukhachevskii brought not only the full backing of the RVSR and the Politburo. He brought with him an uncommon energy and commitment to effective organization, qualities that had been lacking in the recent efforts to deal with the insurgency in Tambov. Although Antonov-Ovseenko had been sent to Tambov in February to take control of a worsening situation, he was not only hampered by illness, but also much more focused (despite his military background) on issues of civil administration and government than strictly military matters. His efforts had been mainly in trying to set the political side of the counterinsurgency campaign on an effective footing and to revive the functions of state administration in the province. When Tukhachevskii arrived on 6 May 1921, he was installed as a member of the Plenipotentiary Commission with particular focus on the military suppression of the insurgency. He was made overall commander of the "Tambov Army" (a change of designation that corresponded to the expanded powers of the new commander) and given direct control over the military conduct of the counterinsurgency effort. Whereas in the previous months intermediary officials (such as Red Army command in Orel) and independent bureaucracies (VChK and NKVD) had represented complicating and crosscutting lines of communication and decision making, Tukhachevskii was now the sole intermediary with Moscow on matters pertaining to the conflict in Tambov, controlling all armed forces deployed in the region.

Tukhachevskii established his base outside the city of Tambov at the fortified settlement thirteen kilometers to the south where the strategically important gunpowder works were located.[89] Taking a week to familiarize himself with the situation, he took the concept of occupation and, with the knowledge that significant reinforcements were on their way to Tambov, gave the idea shape with an instruction to all military and political officials in the province issued on 12 May. Identifying the rebellion as an "epidemic" that infected the villages of the province, he insisted with his opening words that what was required was not some sort of long, drawn-out program of treatment for the people of the villages in Tambov, but rather a shock campaign, "or even a war," to annihilate the disease: "Operations against the bandits should be unfailingly methodical, because banditry will come to an end only when it is morally defeated, when the very character of the suppression is one of consistency and brutal persistence. Simply undertaking a small war against groups of bandits will never succeed in uprooting banditry and, as experience demonstrates, it only manages to fuel the criminal and partisan flames."[90]

Tukhachevskii's description of the occupation strategy comprised two essential strands. The first was the tireless pursuit of the active rebel formations. This was to be undertaken by mobile forces that would enjoy independence of maneuver across the designated borders of individual military sectors, which had themselves been extended across provincial borders into parts of Penza and Saratov following Tukhachevskii's appointment.[91] With an emphasis on constant scouting, the objective of mobile forces should be to attack rebel groups as soon as they appeared, and those attacks should be maintained until the rebels were destroyed—"Pursuit should not cease until the band is completely extinguished. . . . In a word, that [Red Army] unit should attach itself like a leech to its band and should not allow it sleep, rest, or the opportunity to compose itself." In Tukhachevskii's later writings on the subject, he explained that this constituted a critical break with the past strategy of the military commanders in Tambov. No longer was the objective of the Red Army in the province to maneuver troops to encircle the rebel forces. This strategy was excessively static (owing, in part, to the predominance of infantry troops at the time) and allowed the rebels to make the most of their superior mobility in order to escape.[92]

The second aspect of Tukhachevskii's plan was the establishment of a constant presence in the villages previously dominated by the rebellion. This was to cut off the rebellion from its mainsprings and to force the active rebels out into the open and away from their most important sources of supply and support.[93] It was also to provide an opportunity for military forces to oversee the establishment of government institutions once more in those villages and volosts in the area of the conflict. "Liberation" was not to be extended to a given village unless sufficient forces were available to "occupy" it effectively.

On the whole, Tukhachevskii's plan was very much what local commanders and government officials had themselves wanted to do many weeks before the general arrived in Tambov. But with Tukhachevskii's arrival, these designs all appeared to be feasible because of the promise of new and better armed forces. Many of his recommendations were predicated on this knowledge, even if they appeared to be informed by the mistakes of the previous months. "Occupying forces in the military sectors must never, under any circumstances, take the decision to break up into small units," Tukhachevskii wrote, but government forces had previously been unable to realize this luxury, as they were stretched so thinly across the territory of the conflict. He continued: "Every individual unit within a military sector should be capable of carrying out autonomous actions against any given gang of bandits; therefore, the known size of the bandit gangs in a given occupied sector will determine the size of the individual government units located there."[94]

While these direct actions against rebel forces were the first measures to be described by Tukhachevskii, the guiding concerns of the occupation system were

to recover a safe environment in the villages, an environment in which administrative institutions could be reestablished. Tukhachevskii noted that available
army units would also have to provide guard detachments in any village in which
they settled during the course of operations. But the real source of security would
have to be the militia, composed of nonlocal individuals and Communist Party
members, which would be a permanent armed security detachment in any village
where the state sought to establish a revolutionary committee. Reassuring the
local population was to be critical to the stability of the counterinsurgency effort,
and this, according to Tukhachevskii, was to be achieved principally by a demonstration of the firmness of Soviet power. Military occupation, in Tukhachevskii's
plan, was to enable the pacification of the civilian population and to allow for
the restoration of civilian administration, a process he called "sovietization."[95]

The first significant measure taken by the Plenipotentiary Commission following Tukhachevskii's arrival was meant to signal precisely this type of resolve
to the rural population as a whole. "Order no. 130," issued on 12 May 1921, was designed to project a image of force and resolve to the rural population and to signal
to the rebels that a turning point had been reached: "The Workers' and Peasants'
government has decided to eradicate the banditry problem in Tambov Province
in short order, taking the most decisive measures to achieve this result." The
Plenipotentiary Commission then listed eight orders and ultimatums:

1. All military forces in Tambov Province will be joined by reinforcements and
are to take the most decisive and rapid actions to destroy the bandit gangs.

2. All peasants who have joined bands are to surrender without delay to Soviet
authorities, giving up their weapons and turning in their leaders so that they can
be handed over to the courts of the military revolutionary tribunal. Voluntary surrenders will not be threatened with the death penalty.

3. Families of bandits that fail to surrender are to be arrested, with all their property confiscated and redistributed among peasants that truly support Soviet power.

4. Arrested families are to be resettled to distant territories of the Soviet Republic
if their family member does not give himself up.

5. Bandits that do not surrender are to be considered outside the protections of
the law.

6. Innocent peasants must not permit the mobilization and formation of bands
in their own villages and must inform Red Army forces of all bandit activity.

7. All Red Army units without exception must give the peasants full support and
provide full protection for them against bandit raids.

8. The present order is the final warning in advance of decisive and severe operations, and it will be carried out harshly and methodically.[96]

Tukhachevskii explained in his adjoining instruction to Soviet forces and government officials that these threats had to be carried out with exceptional severity, for the intention was to drive a significant wedge between the civilian population and the active rebels. "[Banditry] is both ruinous and wearying for the peasantry," he wrote, and he believed that genuine efforts to bring stability to the villages could not but create allies for the Soviet government among the rural population.[97] Punishing rebel families would drive that wedge further. Thus, confiscated property would be redistributed among members of the same community, and arrested families would be removed from the villages, threatened with exile.[98] Redistribution would immediately give other community members a material interest in the identification of rebel supporters and thus would stamp other community members as supporters of the regime.[99]

While Tukhachevskii's designs may not have been entirely original and may have relied upon the arrival of armed reinforcements that had been denied previous commanders in the province, he did succeed in communicating and instilling precisely the need for decisive measures that had inspired authorities in Moscow to assign him to Tambov in the first place. Order no. 130 and the accompanying instructions truly signaled a break with past experience and conduct for officials in the province, for it took the systematic struggle with the rebellion to the villages themselves rather than remaining focused on the rebel armies.[100] Knowing that the rebels were severely weakened by recent defeats (especially as a result of the failed attack on Kirsanov), and knowing that the farming communities had grown increasingly impatient and antagonized by a continuation of the conflict far into the agricultural season, the Plenipotentiary Commission and the Red Army began to make the transition to a concerted campaign of pacification, with all the enticements and punishments that this entailed.[101]

DEMOBILIZATION AND OCCUPATION

New units began to arrive in Tambov even before Tukhachevskii's own arrival in the province. On 3 May, the cavalry brigade under General Kotovskii reached its assignment in the Fifth Military Sector, in Morshansk uezd, consisting of just over 1,300 men.[102] During the first two weeks in May, some 15,000 Red Army officer cadets would assemble in Tambov from all over Russia and Ukraine, reinforcing existing cavalry, artillery, and infantry groups as well as forming their own units that would play a significant role in the First Military Sector that encompassed all of Kirsanov uezd.[103] If the arrival of three full battalions, two infantry and one cavalry, in addition to other armored and motorized units, allowed Tukhachevskii to believe that the one-month deadline handed down by the Politburo could be achieved, other factors that had previously complicated the efforts of commanders in Tambov would similarly be resolved after his arrival in the province.[104] The realization of the occupation scheme still rested upon the state's ability to establish a permanent administrative presence in the villages. Troops could occupy major villages and establish modest garrisons capable of defending these localities, but a motivated contingent of civilian administrators would be required to staff the revolutionary committees that were to act in the capacity of local government until the election of new village soviets. The strongest source of support that the government was able to tap for the restoration of civilian administration and self-defense came with the demobilization of the multimillion-strong Red Army in the spring of 1921.

The issue of demobilization was of particular importance, for the release of soldiers from active duty could be as influential in the effort to pacify the countryside as it had been in inflaming the situation during an earlier round of demobilization begun in January 1921.[105] Then, abruptly demobilized older soldiers had been released into a rural environment dominated by the insurgency and its burgeoning organization and confidence. It was at a time when the provincial government had all but abandoned southern Tambov Province to the rebels. Many of the estimated 4,000 soldiers native to Tambov who were demobilized from local garrisons and from other locations in January 1921 were quickly integrated into the ranks of the Partisan Army, either voluntarily or through compulsion. Since that experience, government and military officials had been intent on preparing the demobilization process in such a way as to minimize the possibility of former soldiers falling into the Partisan Army's ranks.

Soldiers were to go through a filtering process to assess their political reliability and whether or not they were likely to join the rebels. In the wake of the landmark decision of the Tenth Party Congress in March to introduce the tax in kind and liberalize free trade, Red Army political workers believed they had new ammunition with which to appeal to soldiers scheduled for demobilization and to arm them as they returned to their native villages. Instruction in the new policies of the Soviet government and the long-term benefits to the peasantry became an integral part of the demobilization process as conceived by provincial officials in April and May 1921, and soldiers were given explanatory materials to take home to help them spread the word.[106] The extra precautions and care taken in the grooming of soldiers scheduled for demobilization indicated that the government recognized their potential influence on the political situation in the countryside.[107]

The main failing of the previous round of demobilizations in early 1921 was not that soldiers were unprepared upon their release. It was in large part that they had no protection or institutional ties once they arrived in their home districts. To correct this error, demobilizing soldiers after April 1921 entailed a type of reenlistment, as soldiers were encouraged to serve in the fledgling network of revolutionary committees being promoted within the territory of the insurgency. The first choice for service in these committees remained members of the Communist Party with experience in administrative affairs, but the experience of work in the soviets and Communist Party cells over the previous two years, and especially during the first months of the insurgency in late 1920, had left many Communist Party members in Tambov disillusioned and unwilling to return to work in the rural milieu. Party membership had declined drastically since mid-1920, and while there were still Communist Party members based in Tambov who were willing to work in the revkoms and other rural institutions—as much out of desperation, often, as of commitment—there were nevertheless serious shortfalls to be made up if the system of local government was to be restored.[108] The Antibanditry Commission recognized this, and it ordered the transfer of 300 party members to Tambov to assist in the counterinsurgency operation. Demobilized soldiers, however, represented a more stable and long-term option. Lists were prepared as soldiers were processed for demobilization of men native to the villages of Tambov Province who were considered suitable for service in the revkoms. On the lists were those who responded positively to the overtures of the political instructors or who expressed a strong antipathy for the rebels in Tambov and in other parts of the Soviet countryside.

The impact of demobilization, however, was not immediate. While captured and surrendered Partisan Army soldiers revealed that demobilization in the Red Army had made an impact on the morale of the rebels, its contribution to the occupation and to Tukhachevskii's counterinsurgency campaign was minimal in the first month.[109] The demobilization process truly began only in May, when the Plenipotentiary Commission and provincial government received assistance from Moscow in the form of more experienced political workers to prepare the ground and manage the undertaking. In addition, the organization of local revolutionary committees only began in earnest in the same month, as the military forces exercised considerable pressure on the larger remaining groups of rebel forces in the territory. Coordinating the work of the army with that of the Communist Party and provincial administration to facilitate the establishment of revolutionary committees in the individual military sectors were the sector political commissions (*uchastkovye politicheskie komissii*, or *upolitkomy*). Appointed by the Plenipotentiary

Uezd	Released from Local Garrisons	Demobilized Soldiers Returning to Uezd	Total Registered at Railway Stations	
			Trains	*Demobilized Soldiers*
Tambov	7,485	33,863	50	26,387
Kozlov	4,505	1,086	133	66,807
Borisoglebsk	4,030	3,019	64	28,094
Kirsanov	1,239	33,456	59	31,980
Usman	5,732	n.d.	n.d.	n.d.
Lipetsk	4,398	73,808	17	86,789
Lebedian	261	2,624	n.d.	n.d.
Morshansk	1,084	2,543	12	23,630
Shatsk	2,565	n.d.	n.d.	n.d.
Spassk	1,439	113	n.d.	n.d.
Temnikov	21	302	n.d.	n.d.
Sosnovka/Elat'ma	n.d.	4,013	n.d.	n.d.

Demobilization Activity in Tambov Province, 24 December 1920–1 June 1921

Note: n.d. = no data

Source: TsDNITO f. 840, op. 1, d. 1043, l. 24.

Commission and intended to serve as the local embodiment of this institution, each political commission typically consisted of senior political and military officials who enjoyed the confidence of Tukhachevskii and Antonov-Ovseenko. Their purpose, according to the instruction issued on 15 May, was to oversee the reestablishment of state administration in the individual sectors, a task that began with the execution of punitive orders such as no. 130 and ended with the installation of revolutionary committees and soviets in the villages and volosts.[110]

The execution of Order no. 130 proved to be the most pressing and challenging task for the newly formed political commissions. In May, however, a number of changes, both in the military forces deployed in the province and in state and party personnel, complicated the effective implementation of the order. For instance, in the Second Military Sector that encompassed Tambov uezd, one of the first major targets selected by the political commission led by the uezd Communist Party chief, Ia. L. Smolenskii, was the village of Pichaevo. The village had long been considered a rebel stronghold, where Red Army detachments had been attacked and disarmed on more than one occasion during the winter of 1920–1921, and where local Communist Party and soviet workers had been killed. Entering the village on 20 May, representatives of the sector political commission took hostages from among those identified on their lists of rebel families, held a general meeting of community members at which the terms of the order were read out, and the assembled villagers were required to agree on a resolution condemning the rebels and recognizing the authority of the Plenipotentiary Commission and Soviet armed forces.[111]

That same night, however, locals attacked and killed four persons identified as "sympathizers of Soviet power," prompting the sector political commission to request permission from the Plenipotentiary Commission for a second entry into Pichaevo to take further hostages and oversee the confiscation of more property from those on the list of prorebel families.[112] This request brought a critical reply from Antonov-Ovseenko in Tambov, who warned against any more sudden punitive operations without adequate preparation for security in the village after the departure of the political commission's representatives. "Never leave our sympathizers defenseless," said Antonov-Ovseenko to the commission chairman, Smolenskii. He insisted that better coordination was needed with military officials, for such an operation could not succeed without the military being able to devote a garrison force to protect villagers in Pichaevo. In reply to this criticism, however, Smolenskii found it difficult to look beyond the fact that Pichaevo was a "bandit" village and that they had a list of villagers associated with the insurgency that numbered over 100 names, among them three known rebel leaders. "At the same time," Smolenskii told Antonov-Ovseenko in their telephone exchange, "they killed eleven Communists there in addition to the volost party chairman, and it is a fact that they have now, in reply to our taking hostages and ordering the confiscations of property, spilled blood once again." It was difficult for local officials to resist the urge for vengeance, but Antonov-Ovseenko in this case emphasized the need for a dispassionate commitment to the strategy set out by Tukhachevskii. "If there are no forces available to commit for an adequate amount of time," he wrote, "then it is better to simply wait until such forces are available."[113]

In the weeks following the issue of Order no. 130, the assembly of troops to serve in the garrisons at the heart of the occupation scheme, as well as the organizations of the militia that would provide long-term security in the villages, was only just beginning. Every military sector had begun operations associated with Order no. 130, but few reported anything more than sporadic success. By the end of the month, in the First Military Sector (Kirsanov) only seventeen volost revolutionary committees had been established, and the number of rebels who had surrendered in connection with the execution of Order no. 130 had been disappointingly small. The main cause for the slow progress was, predictably, the shortage of military units to provide security.[114] But there were other difficulties. In the Second Military Sector, operations relating to the same order had been complicated by the refusal of individuals to reveal their true surnames, thus making a match according to the compiled lists a matter of speculation and reliance upon third-party information. The same phenomenon was reported in other sectors, as was the fact that households were hiding their belongings with neighbors or with friends in other villages or towns, so as to minimize the impact of threatened confiscation.[115] Added to these concerns was the report that the STK had issued its own order in reply to the recent punitive approach of the Plenipotentiary Commission, threatening a campaign of terror against the families of Communist Party members, thus bringing the war to the so-called innocents, just as the Soviet government had done with its Order no. 130. Notably addressing its local STK committees as "revolutionary committees," at a time when the Soviet government was seeking to organize its own such revkoms, the Tambov provincial STK threatened reprisals against the families of Communist Party members in response to every instance of punitive measures being taken against families of rebel soldiers and "party workers," that is, members of the PSR.[116]

The news on the progress with Order no. 130 was not all disappointing; in the Fourth Military Sector (Kozlov and Lipetsk uezds), the attitude was upbeat, with up to 1,700 persons arrested, of whom 540 were taken as hostages. There had been fewer problems here in deploying available soldiers and Communist Party members to the occupied volosts to establish revkoms and a garrison presence, but then only eleven volosts had been targeted for occupation in the entire sector, all of them in Kozlov uezd territory.[117] For the other sectors, principally those that included the traditional "nests" of the rebel movement, the tactics would have to be altered, just as more troops would need to be brought in.

BREAKING THE PARTISAN ARMY, MAY–JUNE 1921

The new units introduced to the province to serve as pursuit forces had taken some two weeks to assemble and acclimatize before full-scale operations could begin, and this period constituted a brief breathing spell for the beleaguered forces of the Partisan Army. On the whole, clashes in May were relatively few. One incident on 11 May involving Dmitrienko's cavalry brigade and one of the units of the Second Cheka Regiment produced the claim that "the core of Antonov's band is defeated and they have fled with the bulk of their forces to the north. . . .

Prisoners and deserters inform us that Antonov is planning to take his army across the railway in the region of Platonovka-Lomovis [the Kirsanov-Tambov railway] and cross over to the northern part of the province."[118] It is unclear if this report does, in fact, describe an engagement with the "main force" under Antonov, but the belief that the rebels had been thrown into flight to the safety of the north was misplaced. By the end of the month, both rebel armies—the First Partisan Army under Boguslavskii and the Second Partisan Army under Antonov—were still settled in the region where Kirsanov, Borisoglesk, and Tambov uezds meet.[119]

There are even indications that the Partisan Army and its leaders were far from exhibiting the desperation that some Red Army reports attribute to them. A young woman identified only by the surname Garshineva testified that she was stopped on the road to the village of Pushino by a group of rebel sentries. She and her sister were told that "martial law" had been declared in the region, and they were "arrested" and taken to rebel headquarters. Her account of what she saw was far from what one might expect of rural rebels under severe pressure from government forces:

> When we arrived in the headquarters, I did not have much time to inspect the surroundings, as one of the rebel commanders with his bodyguard approached us and took us over to a man they said was their leader, Antonov. Antonov made a good impression on me, and I let him hold my hand. Then, while I was still there, they called in the barber, and Antonov suddenly declared: "Better have a shave, so that the ladies will love me!" When he finished with his grooming [*svoi tualet*], he sat down next to me and we began speaking, but after a while I gave him my hand and explained that he must be tired and in need of rest, and I asked him to allow me to leave. He answered by saying that it was not a problem—we are typical people and not brutes, he said—and he allowed me to go home. When I got myself ready to depart, he spoke to me again, inviting me to a party they were having that very night. I thanked him for the invitation and left. I got home at around midnight, but even so, I decided that I would go to the party. When I arrived back at the house [where the rebels were], they allowed me in and Antonov and I danced many times around the room, but after a while I stopped and told him that I was not able to dance any longer, as it was too hot and sweaty for my liking, and so we stopped and Antonov then asked me if I would like to go for a walk instead. I agreed, and we went walking for nearly an hour and a half before he stopped and said that he had to leave and have his dinner. I grabbed hold of him and asked him not to go, but he insisted that he could not stay with me, after which I finally left once more for home and never saw him again.[120]

Besides being yet another testament to the apparent charms of the Partisan Army leader, Garshineva's description is also one of a rebel headquarters that continued to maintain a sense of security at its base in southwestern Kirsanov uezd. This remained rebel territory, where rebel guards patrolled the streets enforcing their own "martial law" and where partisan leaders continued to dance to their own music.

By the end of May, however, this breathing spell would come to an abrupt halt. Knowing that the rebels forces were concentrated in a limited area, and leaving to one side the lesser rebel force under Boguslavskii, the new military leadership in the province planned an orchestrated attack on the Second Partisan Army that would force Antonov out of the base territory where he enjoyed such security and possibly push him out of Tambov Province into areas where he could no longer rely upon the familiarity and support of the local population. The object of their plan was not to carry out an overwhelming assault on the Second Partisan Army, but rather to spur it into a flight that would eventually wear it down and finally defeat it. While the Red Army was aware of the rebels' superior mobility, their intelligence assured them that Antonov could truly rely on the effectiveness of only two of the remaining Partisan Army regiments currently under his command—the Fourth and the "Special." These accounted for what was believed to be only one-third of the 3,000 men under arms in the Rzhaksa region. What is more, the rebels were low on ammunition, it was believed, and only some 40 percent rode with saddles or cushions.[121] A prolonged and intense pursuit would wear down the rebel horsemen, both mentally and physically.

Positioning three cavalry groups to the north, northeast, and northwest of Rzhaksa, the Red Army in Tambov sought to cut off lines of escape for Antonov that would draw him deeper into Kirsanov uezd and in the direction of Morshansk and Kozlov uezds.[122] As expected, upon learning of the advance of Red Army troops, Antonov's men hastily set off due north, but after realizing that they were moving directly toward Kotovskii's brigade, the rebels turned sharply in the direction of the Kirsanov-Saratov border. Their progress was too swift to allow the Fourteenth brigade to cut them off, but the Fourteenth did move eastward in order to take up a position along the border to prevent a possible return into Tambov along the same route Antonov had taken. Red Army and other government troops in Saratov were then ordered to move toward the rebels' positions near the Khoper River. The intention was evidently to force the rebels northward, as troops in Penza were similarly instructed to take up positions along their border with Saratov, to cut the rebels off should they advance that far north. Kotovskii's men were moved to a similar position, as was Dmitrienko's cavalry brigade. The speed of the rebel horsemen, however, meant that the Red Army cavalry was slow in moving into position. Able to change horses two or three times daily, the rebels had a distinct advantage in such chases. One of the participants in this operation, Ivan Trutko, wrote later that Antonov's army could cover between 120 and 150 versts per day—a speed of movement "unprecedented in history," he wrote.[123]

The clear alternative for the Red Army was the use of motorized units to maintain the pressure on the rebel horsemen. These had recently been organized by commanders Fed'ko and Uborevich. The former's motorized unit consisted of seven vehicles, six heavy trucks, and one smaller car, all outfitted with machine guns.[124] It was the first to engage the Partisan Army in Saratov, which was the first time the rebels had been confronted by such motorized units. The initial encounter occurred in the village of Dve Sestritsy, where the Second Partisan Army —still nearly 3,000 strong—had paused following two days of travel into Saratov territory. On 31 May, the seven vehicles of Fed'ko's unit converged on the village. Taken by surprise and believing themselves to be surrounded, the rebels were thrown into a panic, with many taking cover in the houses and huts of the small village, while the bulk of the group managed to escape to a nearby woods. Few casualties were reported, and this first confrontation between the rebel horsemen and the government's armored vehicles was written off by Red Army commanders as a missed opportunity. Limited by the lack of cavalry support, the motorized unit under Fed'ko opted to take up the chase of the larger group of rebel cavalry, which quickly left the woods after regrouping and headed for the village of Elan', only twenty-five versts south of Serdobsk.[125]

On the following day, Fed'ko, with the support of both Kotovskii and Kovalev's cavalry brigades, initiated an attack on Elan'. Some 3,000 followers of Antonov had occupied the small village during the night, and they remained there in the morning as the Red Army planned its assault. At noon on 1 June, three of the heavy vehicles were sent into the center of the village, while the remaining four took up positions on the periphery. Again, the appearance of the trucks with their mounted machine guns prompted a scramble among the rebel soldiers, but this time around they provided sterner resistance as they fired their rifles at the vehicles from inside the houses of Elan'. This resistance, however, did not last once the cavalry of Kovalev's brigade entered the village. The appearance of Red Army troops in greater numbers inspired the rebels to take flight once more, managing to regroup again in a nearby woods before continuing their progress northward closer to Serdobsk.[126]

By 2 June, the men still with Antonov were able to rest in a forest just to the east of Serdobsk, while the Red Army motorized forces were concentrated to the north of the same town, in the village of Baltinka. In moving further east during the day, Antonov ordered his men to destroy all bridges passed to slow the pursuit of the motorized units. However, Fed'ko's vehicles were further north, following a parallel route in the hope of getting ahead of Antonov and attacking from the east. The cavalrymen under Kotovskii continued to pursue Antonov as well, following in the tracks of the rebel force. Both units eventually encountered the rebels once again on the evening of 2 June in the village of Bakury, on the banks of the river Serdoba. The appearance of the Red Army's trucks and the firing of the cavalry brigade's artillery once again surprised the rebels, who had stopped to rest in Bakury in part because of the sympathy they met from among the local population. Their flight from the village was even more hasty and chaotic than in previous encounters, evidenced by the significant amount of munitions and other supplies left behind as the rebels sought to cross over to the other side of the Serdoba to make their escape. They abandoned some nine machine guns with stockpiles of ammunition and over 300 horses. More important, scores of rebel soldiers were left for dead.[127]

The surviving rebels continued on course up the Serdoba River as it followed an easterly path, eventually bending northward. The Red Army forces, however, did not continue their chase. It was widely accepted that Antonov, after suffering such debilitating defeats, would seek a return to home territory at the earliest possible moment, so military forces were concentrated along the railway line that traveled north-south between Penza-Rtishchevo-Balashov.[128] In addition, the motorized units in Bakury lacked fuel and were unable to continue. Upon refueling, both the motorized unit under Fed'ko and the cavalry commanded by Kotovskii traveled in a northwest direction to sit in ambush for the remaining Partisan Army forces when they attempted to recross the Khoper River toward Tambov Province. However, neither the armored trains dispatched from Penza nor the soldiers under Kotovskii were able to pick up the rebels when they crossed the railway and the Khoper on 5 June. Less than 100 versts from the provincial border, Antonov and his remaining followers could have been excused for thinking that their nightmare turn through Saratov and Penza provinces was coming to an end.

With the remnants of what had been six regiments, including the "Special" regiment that had always traveled with Antonov, the Second Partisan Army (now numbering about 1,000 men) reached the confluence of the Vorona and Chembar rivers, only ten versts from the Tambov-Penza border, on 6 June. There, near the village of Chernyshovo, they were attacked for the fourth time in one week by

Fed'ko's armored vehicles. The encounter followed a familiar pattern, with the rebels taking refuge in the nearest forest (Shiriaevskii Forest, through which the Vorona River cuts a swath), after having suffered some 200 casualties. Antonov himself famously received a head wound at Cheryshovo, the first time he had been known to suffer a serious wound since the beginning of the insurgency.[129] The Red Army forces now assembled in the immediate vicinity appeared to have the rebels trapped in the Shiriaevskii Forest, having taken up positions near all of the main villages on either bank of the Vorona River and across the border in Peresypkino volost (Kirsanov uezd). An attempt by Antonov's men to break out of the forest confirmed their predicament, as they immediately encountered Red Army troops and suffered dozens of casualties before retreating to the safety of the woods. On 7 June, however, the small core of rebel fighters and their leader, Antonov, encountered a stroke of good fortune that allowed them to escape with their lives. A severe thunderstorm that night forced the Third VChK infantry regiment to withdraw from its position guarding the banks of the Vorona to the south of Shiriaevskii Forest to seek cover in the nearby village of Ol'shanka. The withdrawal of this regiment enabled the rebels to escape under the cover of darkness, rain, thunder, and lighting. With a mere 200 men, Antonov traveled south along the banks of the Vorona toward the region of Kirsanov uezd that he called home.

The path home brought a second stroke of good fortune. Along the railway that extends east from Kirsanov toward Rtishchevo, the Red Army had placed an armored train group (the open-platform type, called a *broneletuchka*) to patrol the stretch covering the perpendicular crossing of the Vorona River. But on the evening of the thunderstorm and Antonov's escape south in the very direction of this stretch of railway, the patrol was forced to move from its position to allow General Uborevich's personal train to pass. Because of the complications caused by this unexpected traffic incident, the remaining rebels with Antonov reached the southern half of Kirsanov uezd unscathed.[130]

DESPITE THE MINOR FARCE that concluded this intense series of clashes between the Red Army and the Second Partisan Army, there was no doubt that the beginning of June had witnessed a debilitating defeat for the Partisan Army and for the cause of the insurgency.[131] Not two months had passed since the brief occupation of Rasskazovo had caught the attention of Soviet officials in Moscow, when the Partisan Army appeared to have reached a watershed in their organization and strategy that confirmed their ambitions after a winter of effectively uncontested supremacy. However, their failure to realize those ambitions only strengthened the claims being advanced by the Soviet government in the province.

The insurgency was adrift, without goals and without purpose, during a time when the survival of individual communities relied upon the restoration of "normal" life.

"Normal" life, however, was far from being realized. While the Soviet government continued to press local communities to return to the fields and to place faith in the promised concession of the tax in kind, the Plenipotentiary Commission in Tambov simultaneously raised the stakes, bringing the conflict closer to the villages than it had previously been. The strategy of occupation ushered in by Tukhachevskii escalated the intensity of the conflict, making the war against banditry both more "total" and more "mundane." With the Partisan Army under pressure and significantly destroyed, the counterinsurgency effort in Tambov became increasingly focused on the villages and the managed transition to a new life under Soviet government.

FACETS OF "SOVIETIZATION"

Repression, Countermobilization, Occupation

T HE OPERATIONS COMPLETED by the Red Army pursuit forces in the first week of June had inflicted losses on the Partisan Army from which it was unlikely to recover. Antonov's personal wound was emblematic of the wounded spirit of the rebels, who found the strategic and moral context for their insurgency to have irrevocably changed, making continued resistance to the Soviet state a nearly hopeless cause. Less than two weeks after Antonov and his men had completed their torturous circuit across provincial borders and back again, the First Partisan Army, led by Boguslavskii, experienced a similar, albeit less epic, encounter with the motorized and cavalry pursuit forces of the Red Army. Attacked from three directions while near Kamenka in Tambov uezd, the estimated 2,000 rebel soldiers narrowly escaped annihilation in an area that had been a rebel stronghold for much of the previous ten months. The region along the border between Tambov and Kirsanov uezds was now virtually flooded with Red Army infantry and cavalry forces, and as Boguslavskii's men traveled south from Kamenka they had no time to recompose, and each pause in their flight brought another assault by Red Army pursuit forces and more casualties. By the third week of June, the rebel army was composed of only some 200 survivors whose desperation and panic was tempered only by vague assurances by commanders that their journey would eventually conclude when they joined up with Don Cossack rebels, in accordance with instructions from the PSR Central Committee.[1] The end came on 18 June, at the village of Trukhtanskaia, where Voronezh-based Red Army cavalry trapped the remnants of the First Partisan Army on the banks of the Khoper River some twenty versts south of Novokhopersk, firing their machine guns into the water as the fleeing rebels attempted to swim to safety. Boguslavskii himself was captured and killed during this engagement, bringing to an end nearly three years to the day his personal struggle against the Soviet regime in Tambov, one that had begun with his participation in the uprising in the provincial capital in the summer of 1918.[2]

Intelligence reports based on the statements of captured rebels, as well as the information provided by cooperative villagers, attested to the fear felt by the surviving rebel units, where discipline and group cohesion were rapidly declining as supplies of food and ammunition became harder to secure and the pressure exercised by the Red Army intensified.[3] Many small groups of rebels, holed up in the woods following the final operations of the organized Partisan Army, lived from day to day focusing upon mere survival. Government commanders reported with satisfaction on the desperate state of those who ultimately surrendered after being unable to endure the material conditions and especially the insecurity in their forest hiding places.[4] Short of options, reliable information, and leadership, these men faced the worst of dilemmas.

As senior commanders had anticipated, the military operations against the Partisan Army were completed with only minor setbacks once the required armed forces were brought to bear on the rebellion in Tambov. These were elite, mobile forces—motorized and cavalry battalions and divisions—whose speed of movement was a greater asset than their superior numbers. Yet the military defeat of the main Partisan Army forces was only one aspect of the pacification of the region. Red Army commanders had recognized this at the start of the year, and Tukhachevskii had similarly emphasized the twin goals of military victory and the demobilization of resistance in the countryside when, upon assuming overall command, he spoke of the overarching objective of the "sovietization" of the region. The most violent period of the conflict was only beginning after the military defeat of the Partisan Army, as the Plenipotentiary Commission and Red Army took the counterinsurgency to the villages with the full weight of the armed forces at their disposal. Yet "sovietization" involved much more than state repressions directed at village communities caught within the zone of the conflict. Demobilizing resistance to Soviet authority in the countryside and distancing local communities from the memory of rebellion involved the entire complicated experience of occupation, which combined extraordinary elements involving extreme risk and danger with more mundane, quotidian interactions and concerns that worked to underscore the shared desire for a return to normality.

ORDER NO. 171 AND THE "OCCUPATION OPERATIONS"

While the one-month deadline given to Tukhachevskii by VTsIK for the final liquidation of the insurgency was unlikely to be met, recent developments appeared to produce results that represented substantive steps in that direction. The defeat of Antonov's Second Partisan Army was a particular breakthrough, one given widespread publicity within the province to boost the morale of government loyalists who had endured such a prolonged period of setbacks and hardships.[5] The confidence of leaders in Tambov was articulated further in an order to the five main political commissions of the military sectors, issued on 11 June. "Since the 1 June," read the preamble, "the decisive struggle with banditry has begun to produce the rapid pacification [*uspokoenie*] of the region. Soviet authority is steadily being established, and the laboring peasantry is making the transition to peaceful and undisturbed work. The Antonov band has been broken up by the decisive actions of our forces, and the remainders have been reduced to functioning in isolation."

The remainder of the order contained instructions that appeared to run contrary to the triumphal tone of the preamble. Order no. 171 built on the recent successes against the remaining forces of the Partisan Army by shifting attention once again to the villages and to the task of "definitively uprooting SR-banditry" by elaborating on previous instructions to this effect, notably Order no. 130, issued soon after Tukhachevskii's arrival in Tambov in May 1921. The new order read:

> 1. Civilians who refuse to provide their true names [to Soviet authorities] will be summarily shot.
>
> 2. Hostages will be taken by the sector or regional political commissions from villages believed to be secretly holding weapons, and in the event that hidden weapons are not surrendered, those hostages will be summarily shot.
>
> 3. In the event of hidden weapons being found in the possession of a given household, then the eldest working member of that family is to be summarily shot.

4. Any family who has allowed their home to be used to hide a bandit will be placed under arrest and deported from the province, with all their possessions confiscated and their senior working member executed.

5. Any families who assist in hiding either the family of a bandit or a bandit family's possessions will be looked upon by the state as a bandit family themselves, and the eldest working member of that family will be executed.

6. In the event of a bandit family taking flight from their village, the possessions of that family will be redistributed among peasants loyal to the Soviet state and the house of the bandit family either burned or dismantled.

7. The present order must be carried out rigorously and mercilessly [*surovo i besposhadno*].[6]

This was obviously an escalation of the campaign to eradicate the "disease" of banditry that Tukhachevskii had identified when he assumed command the previous month. Isolating the bandits meant intensifying the pressures placed on the village communities that had previously formed the backbone of the Partisan Army and still provided security to individual rebels and the remaining leaders of the insurgency.

This much was clear from the experience over the previous weeks with operations mandated by Order no. 130. The main condition that had complicated efforts to carry out this measure was the rebellion itself, which made it difficult for Soviet authorities to enter many of the most "bandit-filled" villages to check names against lists and take hostages from among the civilian population. But even in areas that Red Army units and government agents were able to penetrate in late May and early June, the refusal of individuals to provide their true surnames was only one complication that limited the effectiveness of the order. In some cases where lists were maintained by surviving local soviet officials, rebels or villagers had managed to seize and destroy the lists to prevent officials from carrying out Order no. 130. In one village in Kirsanov uezd, according to the head of the sector political commission, fifty-two of the fifty-six families on the list of "bandit" households had already abandoned their homes and the village. Some had taken their possessions, while others had left them behind. Many of these families moved to "nonbandit" villages within the province that would not be targeted by the political commissions, while others went into self-imposed exile outside the province to avoid the consequences of having been implicated in the insurgency. In other villages, it was suspected that "bandit" households had given their possessions to neighbors to keep them safe from confiscation, while still other families had buried their possessions, to be collected after the risk of confiscation had passed.[7]

It was no surprise that village communities would work to complicate punitive orders such as this, but the extreme nature of the state's response that came in the form of Order no. 171 must have startled even those frustrated by the willingness of certain communities to protect "their" bandits.[8] But an element of fear lay behind the order. Despite the intelligence reports of an "ammunition famine" that debilitated the remaining insurgents, the countryside was believed to be awash with weapons. In addition, Soviet officials were convinced, not without reason, that many one-time rebels had managed to escape detection and had returned to "normal" life in the villages. Declarations that preceded Order no. 171 urged rebels to surrender, even threatening those who hid in the forests that they would be burned out, but such declarations had been made before without significant effect.[9] Recent amnesties had attracted many individuals to surrender, but a significant number admitted to having been deserters or draft dodgers rather than active Partisan Army soldiers, and most who sought amnesty appeared before Red Army or political commission authorities without "weapons in hand," that basic provision of all such amnesty offers to reassure state officials that a renewal of hostilities was less likely as a result of an offer of amnesty.[10] Order no. 171 conveyed a strong suspicion that the remnants of the Partisan Army, following the defeats of the previous fortnight, would melt away with their weapons, only to reemerge at a more auspicious moment when the occupation by Red Army troops was ended.

Red Army and Cheka intelligence reported on rumors of an order issued by Antonov after the defeat of the Second Partisan Army for rebel soldiers to hide their weapons and seek to reintegrate into their native communities for precisely this reason.[11] Although the existence of such an order has never been confirmed, the rumor was so widespread as to provide sufficient confirmation for Red Army and Plenipotentiary Commission officials, who cited the rebels' plans when justifying their intensified efforts to round up suspected bandits and bandit sympathizers.[12] The first public report of this so-called order appeared in July 1921, when the local press carried the following story: "From the interrogations of rebel prisoners, it has been established that Antonov issued an order to the bandit gangs to break up into small groups and to hide in the forests until the reds have left. Bandit leaders are to bury rebel weapons in the ground themselves, so that the average bandits will not be able to locate them and hand them in when they seek amnesty."[13] While the propaganda value of such a report is clear, the actual content of this story, in particular the final detail regarding "bandit leaders" and "average bandits," is subtle enough to bolster the veracity of the account and to make it less likely that it was the invention of Soviet propagandists, whose work during

the insurgency had largely been short of nuance. Regardless of whether this instruction came from Antonov and the Partisan Army, the propagation of the
rumor itself revealed the diminished morale within the rebel camp and among the
erstwhile partisan population, just as the attention given to the rumor by Soviet
authorities said much about their own fear that the "disease" of banditry might
fall into remission only to return and inflict more harm.

The ability of military and state authorities in Tambov to enforce the provisions of orders no. 130 and 171 improved as the occupation of population centers
within the military sectors grew.[14] The network of revolutionary committees increased dramatically in June 1921 following the major Red Army operations, and
the network effectively extended down to the volost and even village level in certain areas, rather than remaining limited to the regional level, as it had before the
Red Army's successes of late May and early June.[15] Critical to this expansion was
Red Army demobilization, as noted in chapter 7. If they did not already hold
strong pro-Soviet political convictions, former Red Army soldiers were often
drawn into service in the revkoms after viewing the destruction visited on their
homesteads by the rebels, and more generally when faced with the catastrophic
economic situation that affected all families in the Tambov countryside. Service
in the revkoms not only gave them an institutional authority within their native
village, it also represented a source of income—factors explaining both the growth
of the revkom network and its compromise through corruption and other abuses.
Government officials maintained lists of demobilized servicemen who had expressed a willingness to serve in local institutions such as the revkoms, and in some
regions, over 80 percent of revkom members were Red Army demobs.[16] The committees also provided an outlet for refugee members of the Communist Party,
those who had been forced to evacuate their homes during the first months of the
insurgency when the system of village and volost soviets was destroyed by the
rebels and by angry village communities. They were joined by several hundred
Communist Party members mobilized from other provinces to participate in the
occupation of the insurgent territory of Tambov.

Having an institutional base in the countryside made it easier to enforce orders
no. 130 and 171, as information regarding the local population could be collected
in advance and individual villages or districts could be targeted on the basis of
more recent intelligence. The operations, however, were conducted as they had
been with Order no. 130, by a five-man commission (or *piaterka*) that could include members of the uezd soviet executive and Communist Party organization,
the local revolutionary tribunal, the Red Army, and the Special Department of the
Cheka. A *piaterka* would be appointed by the Plenipotentiary Commission for a

given operation, although the same five-man group could be involved in multiple operations within a military sector. An example is the *piaterka* appointed to enforce Order no. 130 in the volost of Parevka.[17] On 14 June, the political commission of the First Military Sector issued a "sentence" condemning Parevka, stating that the volost "finds itself on the <u>black list</u> as a village [*sic*] of bandits and traitors of the laboring people." All adult members of the volost communities were considered "guilty before the Revolution" of involvement in the insurgency.[18] Following this declaration, the *piaterka* was charged with enforcing the provisions of Order no. 130 within forty-eight hours, and at 3 A.M. on 16 June the following notice was posted in the volost township:

1. Parevka volost will be placed under martial law as of 4 A.M. of 16 July 1921.

2. No one is to leave the volost without the formal permission of the commandant of the Plenipotentiary Commission.

3. All movement within the volost between 9 P.M. and 7 A.M. is forbidden, except for those given special permission by the PIATERKA.

Failure to observe these conditions will be punished in accordance with the norms of revolutionary times.[19]

Having served notice of their presence and intention to conduct a sweep of the villages in the volost, members of the *piaterka* would return with armed support after dawn with a second order, this time read aloud. The details were as follows:

The population of Parevka is given <u>3 hours</u> to fulfill the following:

1. Hand over all bandits and deserters hiding in the volost.

2. Surrender all hidden firearms and other weapons, as well as any ammunition, that have been acquired from the bandits over the course of 1920–1921, as well as those firearms acquired from the Fifty-sixth Division in June 1919.[20]

3. The population must surrender all equipment and uniforms that have been given to them for safekeeping.

4. Hostages will be taken from among the local population to ensure that these orders are fulfilled.

If after three hours the orders have not been fulfilled in their entirety by the population of Parevka volost, then the hostages will be executed and the punishments outlined in the sector political commission's order of 14 June will be carried out.[21]

Parevka was the first test case for the new hard-line practices sanctioned by Order no. 171.[22] Not believing that the *piaterka*'s threats would be carried out, the first three-hour deadline was not met, as villagers refused to hand over bandit suspects and the weapons and supplies they were alleged to possess. Some eighty hostages were then publicly executed, and another group of hostages were taken. It was then that this new batch of hostages immediately began to point out community members who were either rebels, the family of rebels, or were known to be hiding items from the state authorities.[23]

Word of the success of the Parevka operation spread rapidly, and when the *piaterka* moved on to other volosts following this operation, the ground was already well prepared by rumor and by fear. Kamenka and Inokovka were similarly targeted with "sentences" and orders posted at dawn. In both places, hostages were shot following resistance from local communities, but as with Parevka, resistance quickly turned to cooperation as principle yielded to self-protection and survival. Soviet officials in the First Military Sector proudly reported that in Inokovka, one old man marched his son out to the members of the *piaterka* and said, "Here's another bandit for you."[24] The method introduced at Parevka quickly became the standard for such operations in all the military sectors, and officials claimed, perhaps with some exaggeration, that in the first three weeks of June over 11,000 suspected rebels had been rounded up in the course of these "occupation operations," most of whom had been apprehended only since the Plenipotentiary Commission sanctioned the extreme methods of Order no. 171 on 11 June.[25] The impressive results reported in the sector that experienced most of the special operations since the publication of the order give an indication of the breakdown of such grand totals. In the First Military Sector of Kirsanov uezd, operations in the month of June saw the capture of 665 rebels (only 10 with weapons) and 777 deserters. The operations also prompted the surrender of 246 rebels (36 with weapons). One hundred and five families were taken hostage in the course of these operations, a total of 565 people. The total number of bandits, deserters, and hostages taken over the previous weeks was 2,254. Some fifty-five homes were burned as part of the punitive measures, although curiously it was claimed that only five hostages were killed.[26]

The destruction of an entire community was not unheard of in cases where a village was deemed to have had strong links with past and current rebel groups. Such was the case with a small village in Kurdiuki volost (Kirsanov uezd), which had the misfortune to play host to a small group of rebels (reportedly led by Ivan Ishin) while a government *piaterka* was conducting operations elsewhere in the same volost. The punishment for the village community of Kareevka-2, composed of some eighty families (over 300 people), was swift and comprehensive. With the exception of Red Army households, families were arrested en masse and sent to concentration camps. Their possessions were confiscated, as was all other moveable property in the village, such as church valuables. The families of Red Army servicemen were resettled in the volost township of Kudiuki and given the homes of rebel families there, while the village of Kareevka-2 was torched, reportedly destroying some seventy homes. Officials who oversaw this operation justified it on political and strategic grounds, not only because the village had consistently demonstrated support for the insurgents and thus deserved punishment, but also because the location of the village made it strategically valuable for the Partisan Army. Removing the village was thus expedient militarily as well as politically. The same officials expressed confidence that the example made of Kareevka-2 was having a considerable impact upon the population of the surrounding villages and that this severe punitive exercise had even prompted groups of local rebels to surrender.[27]

It is impossible to know how many hostages were killed or homes destroyed. While the activities of the sector political commissions were highly organized and documented, operations carried out by individual military units in the countryside were not. The same holds true regarding the families and communities that were banished from the province and deported to far-flung parts of the Soviet Republic. There had been concerns from the very start when provincial officials in March 1921 raised the possibility of exiling rebel families as means of ensuring against further disturbances.[28] The new chairman of the provincial Cheka organization, M. D. Antonov, reported on these suggestions in early May 1921, highlighting the practical difficulties of transporting hundreds, even thousands, of families at a time when the rail system was in a chronic state of chaos. He also described the potential long-term implications of exile and deportation:

> Those who are uprooted and resettled to various locations would preserve the spirit of banditry that infects the peasantry of Tambov Province, and they will prove to be effective agitators for the SRs and kulaks. Tales of the bandits, of the forced deportations, and of the insults and deprivations suffered, would travel far and wide and find a healthy echo in the psyche of the peasantry in other parts [of the republic]. What is more, those members of the families that are participating in the bandit gangs will not simply give up any connection with their families. They will hold onto those connections, will learn of the deprivations their family members have suffered, and it will strengthen their resolve and even spread the sympathy that is felt for them among the peasant population.[29]

Whatever the validity of these concerns, the practical complications involved in managing deportations repeatedly compromised plans for large-scale operations of this sort. The issue was raised before the Plenipotentiary Commission in Tambov and the Antibanditry Commission in Moscow in June and July, and on each occasion was sent back for review.[30] There was evidently a persistent confusion regarding the ambitions of officials in Tambov for such a practice, particularly if they meant to conduct mass deportations of "bandit" villages or simply the exile of individual families.[31] Thus no decisive policy on deportations ever emerged in the summer of 1921, even if exile featured prominently in public pronouncements, and the ad hoc use of the practice meant that families and even entire villages were exiled from the province in punishment for involvement in the insurgency.[32] Indeed, the only time provincial administrators settled on a clear policy concerning the relocation of entire communities, it was in response to food shortages and the emergence of hunger in the autumn of 1921, which was partially alleviated by sending hundreds of families to parts of Siberia.[33] This scheme, however, was voluntary rather than punitive.

Order no. 171 had an undeniable impact, although results were certainly achieved with a much larger loss of life than some reports would concede.[34] Indeed, despite the open acknowledgment that the rural population had suffered considerably at the hands of both sides throughout the conflict, within certain circles there appeared to be an easy acceptance of the utility of demonstrative violence against villagers that bordered on enthusiasm. The sense that results were being secured with the new hard-line methods had an intoxicating effect on officials, many of whom had endured many weeks and months of frustration and varying degrees of fear while the rebels enjoyed free reign in the countryside of southern Tambov. The chairman of the Fourth Military Sector political commission explained in a report in late June that the methodical conduct of "occupation operations" eventually would encourage the local population to participate in the counterinsurgency effort:

> My tasks not only included clearing the area of bandits, seizing their families, and confiscating property and weapons, but also dividing up the population into bandit and nonbandit groups and enlisting the latter in the struggle with local bandits, and to accomplish this, I settled on the following method: if the population refused to surrender local bandits and weapons (and it did refuse), then hostages were taken by the hundred and the community members were given thirty minutes to reconsider their position, and if they still refused to cooperate, then we began to shoot the hostages, until such a time as the locals agreed to cooperate. As hostages we took men as well as women, who were also executed. This method brought us satisfactory results, not only in terms of bandits and weapons that were handed over, but also

in that the local population was brought into direct contact with the hunt for bandits throughout the region. In addition, the nonbandit element was immediately alienated from the bandit element in a village, and they quickly grew supportive of our activities.[35]

Reliance upon public executions of hostages to overcome the hesitation of local communities was mainly attributable to the continued threat of reprisals from the rebels. As certain officials explained, villagers had grown accustomed to the flying raids of Red Army units and the brief visits of government authorities who promised rewards for cooperation with the Soviet state in its effort to suppress the insurgency. But for the previous several months, the only consistent presence had been that of the Partisan Army, and in the circumstances of June 1921 that meant a strong possibility of reprisals against those who cooperated with Soviet authorities. The remaining rebel groups and surviving STKs had already signaled their intent to punish the families of Communist Party members and Red Army servicemen if the operations under the authority of orders no. 130 and 171 continued, and in some areas, such reprisals had already claimed the lives of some families.[36]

Judging by the reports of such announcements, punishing the families of Communist Party members and Red Army men represented an escalation for the Partisan Army and STK, even if those groups had already suffered violence at the hands of rebels over the course of the previous months. Still, the response of the rebel leadership showed that the policies adopted by the Plenipotentiary Commission in Tambov in May and June 1921 had tangibly raised the threshold of violence, even if the rebels' ability to realize their threats was minimal in comparison with that of the Soviet state.[37] But it was the threat that the rebels would turn to punishing the civilian population that caused so many to hesitate before meeting the demands set by the Soviet government during the occupation operations. As the chairman of the political commission in the First Sector wrote at the end of June 1921:

> In the majority of cases the peasantry approaches our operations with tremendous caution, preferring to remain aloof and avoid any activities that relate to banditry. As should be clear from my reports, the peasantry is exhausted, broken, ruined, and they fear the representatives of the Soviet state and Red Army as much as they do the local bandits. An illustrative example involves a peasant from Kaban'-Nikol'skoe, who begged with tears in his eyes that we whip him in public so that the bandits would no longer consider him a communist.[38]

The tragedy of such hesitation was that only punishments by the state could over-come the fear of rebel reprisals. In the words of a revolutionary committee chair-man in the Second Military Sector: "Without executions, nothing can be achieved. Executions in one village have no demonstrative effect unless we are willing to carry them out in every village."[39]

These operations were most effective in dismantling the network of rebel STKs in the major villages and volosts that had supported the insurgency.[40] In June and early July the Special Department of the Cheka compiled an impressive dossier on the activities of the STKs in the province, from the provincial and regional committees down to the individual village STKs. In a landmark of the counter-insurgency campaign, at the end of June seventeen members of the Kamenka STK organization were captured by the Red Army, several of them senior mem-bers of the provincial committee that was also based in Kamenka. This coup not only removed a key component of the rebel organization in the countryside, but also provided investigators with a wealth of information regarding the extent of that organization and the inner workings of the Partisan Army.[41] However, the task of understanding the inner workings of the rebel movement was secondary to the practical task of uncovering its extent and arresting those who had partici-pated. As such, the focus of Special Department investigators working with seized STK and Partisan Army materials, as well as of revkom members and Cheka agents involved in interrogating captured or surrendered STK members, was very much on building up the database of names that would guide future operations in the villages.[42]

While there was no open controversy surrounding orders no. 130 and 171 that rivaled that regarding the continuation of requisitioning at the start of 1921, it is difficult to believe that the hard-line methods and the strict centralization of de-cision making that had accompanied Tukhachevskii's arrival in Tambov would have sat well with provincial officials who had frequently shown themselves to be jealously protective of local prerogatives and occasionally protective of rural com-munities. While no vocal protests erupted in Tambov itself, the punitive orders of the occupation regime did provoke controversy in Moscow several weeks after they had already begun. In early July, the text of Order no. 171 came to the atten-tion of Politburo members who had not been privy to the deliberations of the Antibanditry Commission, which had originally sanctioned the measure, and apparently after some days of background discussions, there was enough oppo-sition for the Politburo to reconsider the operation in Tambov and demand the annulment of the order.

The principal agent behind these developments in the Politburo was apparently A. I. Rykov, and it may not have been a coincidence that he had learned of the contents of Order no. 171 from the local Kozlov Communist Party newspaper, *Nasha Pravda*, whose 4 July issue reproduced the text of the punitive order. That Rykov was sent an issue of a local newspaper from the uezd Communist Party organization that had been at the heart of most of the political controversies in Tambov for the past three years is only suggestive of local moves to undermine the policies being pursued by the Plenipotentiary Commission and the Tambov Army Command. On 18 July, Rykov informed Trotsky of the majority decision of the Politburo to annul Order no. 171 and to recall both Tukhachevskii and Antonov-Ovseenko from Tambov. He was evidently concerned that the decisions of these two men, while producing results for the counterinsurgency campaign in the short term, would damage relations with the peasantry in a way that was incompatible with the new orientation of the Soviet government following the decisions of the Tenth Communist Party Congress in March. With a clear eye for repairing relations with the rural population in Tambov, Rykov recommended that the Plenipotentiary Commission make a public show of annulling Order no. 171.[43]

Rykov's memo to Trotsky appears to be the culmination of a quiet campaign to rein in the hard-line approach being taken by Red Army officers in Tambov since May. Before the Politburo decision regarding the annulment of Order no. 171, army officials were already providing detailed reports on the results of the Tambov occupation regime that in effect justified the very hard-line policies pursued in previous weeks. S. S. Kamenev of Red Army Supreme Headquarters weighed in on the situation just two days before the Politburo meeting on that topic, emphasizing the decisive impact of General Tukhachevskii's arrival in the province. Concentrating on the results of the counterinsurgency operation—bandit surrenders, captures, and kills—rather than the methods used to achieve those results, Kamenev's report was full of praise for Tukhachevskii:[44] "On the whole, since the appointment of Comrade Tukhachevskii to the command in Tambov, all the measures that have been undertaken have proven entirely appropriate and effective, just as they had been successful in their application in the Minsk region."[45]

Tukhachevskii's summary report, submitted personally to the Antibanditry Commission in Moscow on 17 July, provided further evidence—presented in a concise and dispassionate manner—of the results achieved during his term in command of the Tambov counterinsurgency operation, results that only slightly exceeded the one-month target given by the Politburo in May. The general emphasized that his main objective upon assuming command was to make the counterinsurgency a single, coherent campaign, to treat it "even as a war," in his words. While the long-term objective was the "sovietization" of the insurgent countryside, in the short term the rebellion had to be broken militarily and politically using methods that differentially targeted the entire population. To those on the Antibanditry Commission, this approach was already familiar through progress reports filed by Tukhachevskii in previous weeks. The net effect for the province was that the Partisan Army was reduced from a force estimated to be over 21,000 strong in the beginning of May to only 1,200 in mid-July. Nearly all the main rebel leaders had been killed, according to Tukhachevskii, thus minimizing the prospects for a revival of the insurgency in the short term.[46]

The general's summary report recommended maintaining current troop levels and command staff, as well as the number of Communist Party members mobilized for work in the province, to sustain the occupation until the end of the year. He also recommended that no additional taxes be imposed upon the peasantry above those already anticipated on the current crop.[47] Upon consideration of Tukhachevskii's recommendations, the Antibanditry Commission agreed to extend the occupation system until October 1921, and it appealed to the Central Supply Commission to ensure that the current troop numbers were adequately supplied for the duration of the operation.[48]

Planning for the future of the occupation regime in Tambov, as well as reviewing the progress made in the past six weeks against the rebels, were integral to the rapid changing of the guard in the province and Tukhachevskii's departure from the scene. In a sense anticipating the disquiet in the Politburo surrounding the methods of the Plenipotentiary Commission and military command in Tambov, but also following a prearranged schedule for the counterinsurgency campaign in the province, S. S. Kamenev and Tukhachevskii himself sought the general's release from command in Tambov and a return to his previous duties as commander on the western frontier. The Antibanditry Commission agreed to this on 17 July, but it did not defuse the situation surrounding Order no. 171. The same commission met again two days later, this time with the participation of Trotsky, who chaired a session of this body for the first and only time in following up on Rykov's memo and the Politburo's resolution on the annulment of the order the day before. With no known critics of the Tambov command present, and indeed with Tukhachevskii himself to provide whatever further explanation might be required, the commission predictably confirmed the necessity and effectiveness of the methods pursued by Tukhachevskii and the Plenipotentiary Commission, stating:

The order was intended above all to demonstrate to the majority of the peasantry the full seriousness of the situation that had been created by the above-mentioned elements ["anarcho-SR-bandit elements"] and demonstrate the resolve of the Soviet state to pursue those elements by any means necessary in order to preserve the security of the republic and in order to restore its economic health. In addition, the Soviet state sought to put an end to the brutal tortures that the bandits regularly carried out against the defenseless workers and peasants who loyally supported Soviet power.[49]

With this strongly worded justification on record, the commission nevertheless agreed to the Politburo's demand that Order no. 171 be withdrawn, although on the grounds that it had effectively achieved its objectives. The following day, 20 July 1921, the Plenipotentiary Commission in Tambov publicly announced the withdrawal of Order no. 171 and the termination of the "occupation operations" conducted under its authority.[50]

However, this announcement—officially issued as Order no. 234—was accompanied by a secret instruction to sector political commissions qualifying the discontinuation of occupation operations. The secret instruction stated,

> As a general directive, Order no. 234 can only be enforced in those areas where a *transformation* [*perelom*] *can be clearly discerned* in the attitudes of the peasantry, where it is manifested by *the voluntary surrender of bandits with guns in hand, the surrender of firearms, handing over bandit leaders, and so on.* On the other hand, where such a transformation is not in evidence, where the reports to the sector political commissions instruct that a withdrawal of Order no. 171 will be taken by the bandit elements as only a sign of weakness or hesitation by Soviet power, then Order no. 171 must remain in force and be pursued as before, in all its severity.

In addition, in those areas where the discontinuation of occupation operations produced a return of bandit attacks and an end to local cooperation, the political commissions were "*obliged to intensify immediately the severity of the terror*" in that locality. "*Order no. 234 does not abrogate Order no. 171*," the Plenipotentiary Commission "clarified" in its secret memorandum.[51]

THE OCCUPATION SYSTEM AND THE CONCENTRATION CAMPS

Over the course of May and June, the conduct of sweeps for bandits and bandit families under the authority of orders no. 130 and 171 quickly expanded both in the number of villages identified for "occupation" and agents empowered to conduct these operations. Known rebel strongholds were designated for special operations orchestrated by the *piaterkas*, but regular military units and armed Cheka units engaged in the counterinsurgency were also involved in rounding up bandits and deserters that entailed punitive measures such as taking hostages, confiscating household property, and burning homes. As the occupation system developed, the newly formed regional militias became increasingly involved in these operations, as well.[52] One of the many consequences of this stands out both as emblematic of the counterinsurgency as a whole and as an indication of how these two significant orders inspired contemporary criticism. This was the rapid and unsustainable expansion of the "concentration camp" (*kontsentratsionnaia lager'*) system in Tambov in 1920–1921 in which the number of makeshift internment camps for hostages and prisoners grew from three to seven and then finally to eleven. The expansion of the camp network was directly linked with the realization of the occupation system and the use of civilians as hostages in the effort to uproot the insurgency.

It is enlightening to look at a snapshot of the camp system in Tambov Province before this tremendous expansion in the summer of 1921. When the rebellion broke out in the autumn of 1920, there were three camps in operation in Tambov. Of these, the largest and oldest was in Tambov uezd. According to its records, from the time of its opening in July 1919 to the beginning of November 1920, it had held a total of 2,066 detainees, of which 916 had been released and 117 had escaped (only 12 of these were reapprehended). The largest categories of detainees held at the camp were those convicted of banditry (23 percent) and speculation (22 percent). Many of the detainees had short sentences of one year or less (40 percent), while just over one-fifth had slightly longer sentences of one to three years (22 percent). A number of the detainees were held as hostages, such as members of the registered "bourgeoisie" in the town of Tambov, particularly during the period when the front lines threatened the province in 1918 and 1919, or hostages taken in the ongoing struggle with banditry. Both of the other camps in Tambov before the outbreak of the rebellion were much smaller. In Morshansk, the local camp was distinguished by the large number of POWs—65 percent of the 490 detainees in Morshansk were Polish prisoners of war brought to the camp when it opened in July 1920. In the camp in Borisoglebsk, a significant portion of the detainees were suspected or known to have fought for the Whites. Most would presumably have been transferred to the camp in Borisoglebsk, for by the time it opened in May 1920, the threat from the Don and Volunteer armies had already retreated.[53]

In essence, the camps were prisons, containing a wide variety of detainees who, for one reason or another, were not considered to be violent criminals. Military POWs were placed alongside kulaks and *burzhui*, speculators and thieves.[54] The provincial Department of Forced Labor, a part of the soviet executive's Department of Administration (Otdel upravleniia), operated the camps, although other institutions, notably the provincial Cheka, the Revolutionary Tribunal, and the Food Commissariat, were empowered to commit individuals to the camps. In the Tambov camp, there was even a concert hall and a library (containing over 600 "items," most likely political-agitational brochures). In the inflated rationalizations of the camp directors, their purpose was not exclusively related to the short-term security of the republic; their objectives were informed by more "progressive" conceptions of reform and redemption through hard work. Class enemies and "agents of international imperialism" would be transformed into honest Soviet citizens during their months of hard labor in the camps. According to Skubakov, the camp director in Borisoglebsk,

> The main difference between the concentration camps and the tsarist-era bourgeois prisons is the following: tsarist prisons only further corrupted and demeaned the fallen, while the guiding objective of the concentration camps in our great and free republic is not humiliation but rehabilitation through service in these schools of labor in our republic, such that upon release these citizen prisoners will have overcome their wicked [*durnye*] instincts and will be able with confidence to engage in honorable work.[55]

This was to echo the comments on penal servitude contained in the Communist Party program adopted in March 1919.[56] Toward the objective of rehabilitation, prisoners would be paid for the work they performed, to be settled upon their release. According to the same camp director in Borisoglebsk, the daily cost of the upkeep for each individual prisoner was thirty rubles and seventy-two kopecks. Each working prisoner would receive a daily wage of forty-two rubles, leaving a daily take-home pay (or "surplus") of eleven rubles and twenty-eight kopecks. The wage evidently was a significant indication of the Soviet state's respect for the dignity of the individual prisoner.[57] Camp directors, playing their part, kept accounts like good factory managers, calculating overall work days and economizing in areas that displayed an unsatisfactory level of efficiency.[58]

If this represented the typical functioning of a camp, as the directors in Tambov Province contended, then conditions at the end of 1920 made such normal operations impossible. Security had been a constant problem, especially when guards were natives of the province, but the number of prisoners was rarely overwhelming.[59] The growing strength of the rebellion in the province, however, made security a major concern, especially for the Borisoglebsk camp, which was located a fair distance from the town of Borisoglebsk and almost completely cut off from the uezd town when the rebels effectively "blockaded" it in January 1921.[60] At this time, the fear of escapes was certainly at its height and there was little or no stability within the guard detachments.[61] The shortage of military personnel in the first months of the rebellion meant that internal security (VOKhR and VNUS) troops that served as guards were very likely to be transferred to assignments patrolling the countryside, meaning that new, inexperienced soldiers would be assigned to guard duty at concentration camps. According to the Borisoglebsk director, a guard recently assigned to duty at his camp could expect less than a week of service before being reassigned to active patrol duty.[62] The lack of adequate security, especially in light of the increasingly threatening situation in the region, meant that prisoner work routines had to be abandoned. Even before the massive influx of detainees in the summer of 1921, the character of the camps was changing, as the camp directors had to contain an increasingly restless population of prisoners.[63]

The first response to this growing problem with camp security was to find spaces for inmates in camps outside Tambov Province. A small committee led by the new chief of the Tambov Cheka (M. D. Antonov) and the head of the provincial Commissariat of Justice (Kizilov) was able to secure some 1,500 spaces in camps located in Saratov, Eletsk, Viatka, and Astrakhan.[64] But this was only a stopgap measure, new prisoners continued to arrive. With orders no. 130 and 171, the number of detainees increased dramatically, as hostages were taken from villages and held in camps until their sons and fathers surrendered. When Order no. 130 was published on 12 May, there were no plans to expand the camp system, and no preparations had been made to accommodate a large influx of people—not just adult men and women, but entire families—in the existing three camps in Tambov Province.[65] Within a fortnight of the publication of the order, Tukhachevskii was already reporting the seizure of a "massive" number of hostages from the villages occupied by Red Army forces.[66]

Tukhachevskii's assessment may have been exaggerated, given the technical problems the Red Army forces were encountering in putting his occupation scheme into practice.[67] Nevertheless, on 1 June 1921 the decision was made to "militarize" the system of camps in Tambov. This meant placing them entirely at the disposal of the Plenipotentiary Commission and the Red Army command in Tambov and establishing seven more camps to cope with the rising number of hostages and prisoners associated with the counterinsurgency effort.[68] With the publication of Order no. 171, which significantly radicalized the enforcement of Order no. 130 on hostage taking, there was a marked increase in the number of people being delivered to the established concentration camps in Morshansk, Tambov, and Borisoglebsk. The prison camps of 1919 and 1920—and the ethic of rehabilitation through labor, so cherished by established camp administrators—were being rapidly transformed into the concentration camps of the counterinsurgency operation.

To prepare for the expected increase in the number of hostages and prisoners, two camps were quickly established in Kirsanov uezd and another in Kozlov in June. A fourth was built near the railway station at Sampur (Tambov uezd). These four new camps were very basic; in the words of a state official attached to the Department of Forced Labor, they were not much more than "army-issue tents surrounded by wire fencing."[69] Soon after, camps were created in Tambov, Morshansk, and Borisoglebsk uezds, thereby bringing the overall number for the province to ten. One of these new camps, "No. 8" in Kirsanov, was inundated with prisoners and hostages as soon as it became operative. A progress report filed by the camp officials on 21 June stated that the total number of detainees in the Kirsanov camp was 1,013, of whom 318 were hostages taken under the authority of Order no. 130. Another camp in the Second Military Sector reported 796 hostages out of a total camp population of 1,605 in June 1921. Because the policy of hostage taking entailed placing entire families in camps, the Kirsanov camp in the second half of June had 75 children between the ages of one and five under its care.[70] Officials in the provincial administration warned that the camp facilities were hardly suitable for the care of children. One official pointed out on 22 June 1921: "Keep in mind the fact that these camps are built as temporary structures (tents on bare ground), and this could lead to serious health problems for children."[71]

While hostages were taken and held in other facilities, the ten camps in the province became the dumping point for the vast majority of those taken by authorized units of the Cheka and Red Army.[72] Further instructions that accompanied the emendation of Order no. 171 on 20 July 1921 addressed the problem of the indiscriminate taking of hostages, especially the elderly, pregnant women, and mothers with small children. According to these instructions, the practice of hostage taking was not to be discontinued, only regulated and controlled. While on the one hand acknowledging that particular practices had to be refined and regulated, while at the same time clarifying (contrary to Order no. 234) that hostage taking must continue in certain trouble spots, the new instructions issued on 20 July emphasized the need to minimize the general disruption of families and communities by the counterinsurgency operations. For instance, in cases where unsuitable persons (such as pregnant women) were threatened with being detained as hostages because of their connection to a suspected or known rebel, they were now to be given the "status" of hostages while remaining in their homes. According to this new practice, if a suspect did not surrender within two weeks, his relatives would become hostages in actual fact, held in concentration camps and with all personal property confiscated.[73] Other, seemingly contradictory, instructions held that children, pregnant women, and mothers with children were not to be arrested as hostages under any circumstances.[74] In any case, the new instructions that accompanied the end of operations under Order no. 171 confirmed that, in the background at least, concern over the uncontrolled practice of hostage taking was arousing skepticism about the conduct of the counterinsurgency effort. Nevertheless, the Soviet government addressed the widely recognized problem of overcrowding in the burgeoning camp network only at the local level of the individual military sector.

Further instructions distributed in late July recommended the "removal from camps of unfit (*netrudosposobnye*) elements, especially children." This meant that women, children, and elderly people held as hostages should be released, with their status preserved and monitored by local revolutionary committees.[75] Obviously, this was to be permitted only in cases where revolutionary committees were in place in a given locality. However, there were other complications. If the property of a given "bandit" household had been confiscated by government authorities, the return of hostages meant that at least a minimum of possessions, such as the house itself, would have to be returned. But what if the confiscated property had already been redistributed among members of the community, as stipulated in Order no. 130, or if possessions had mysteriously "disappeared," as a significant amount of such property did? These problems were more difficult to resolve, especially when hostages were entitled to release because of the surrender of a rebel fighter who was a son, husband, or father. The instructions that accompanied Order no. 234 stated that when the property of hostages had been confiscated, the concerned hostages were not to be released immediately.[76] Likewise, hostages were not to return to their native villages if the community had issued a declaration banishing the family of the suspected rebel. This form of ostracism was sometimes encouraged by Communist Party officials working in the countryside, and it was taken as an indication of loyalty to the Soviet regime. But community members might also have an interest in making such a declaration if the property of a family had already been confiscated and redistributed.[77]

Such complications partially limited the impact of the new regime on the number of detainees in the concentration camps after Order no. 171.

Efforts to limit the number of children held in the camps were similarly inhibited by the incapacity of the state infrastructure. The problem was all the more pressing, given the unsanitary conditions in the overcrowded camps, about which alarmed inspectors regularly informed provincial officials.[78] A special commission was formed to monitor the welfare of children in the camps, and each camp administration was to provide regular reports on the plight of child hostages. Attempts were initially made to place them under the authority of the Commissariat for Education and to place them in orphanages rather than the camps.[79] But the small number of such homes had already exceeded their capacity well before the rebellion in Tambov reached its height.[80] Children who had to stay on in state custody as hostages remained in the care of the camp administrators and the Department of Forced Labor. At the beginning of August 1921, there were 1,155 children under the age of five still in the camps.[81] Administrators in the more established camps in Tambov, Morshansk, and Borisoglebsk sought to deal with the situation as best they could, using scarce resources to set up crèches and schooling for the child hostages under their care.[82] But the main sources of concern were the recently constructed camps that had been formed amid the insurgency. They had few permanent structures and were administered by individuals lacking an outlook that extended beyond the context of a counterinsurgency campaign.

Similarly, regarding the general welfare of detainees, the camps established in the prerebellion period were much more willing and able to cultivate the "ethic" of rehabilitation so dear to some camp commandants. In Borisoglebsk, this translated into a concern for the cultural life of the camp. The political department maintained contacts with Communist Party workers in the town of Borisoglebsk to organize concerts, theater performances, and public readings for detainees over the course of 1921. In his report, the camp commandant (Skubakov) curiously noted with pride the fact that not all the plays and readings were of a purely political character—they were standard dramas, comedies, and farces, in addition to productions that could be categorized as "agitprop."[83]

This approach did not have unanimous support among Communist Party members, who believed that the hostages held in camps were effectively prisoners, not innocent victims of the rebellion. Reporting to a party conference in the Third Military Sector in July 1921, an official from the Borisoglebsk camp, Rychkov, spoke of the efforts to improve the cultural life of the camp inmates:

In the concentration camp, reeducation has been pursued on a wide scale. We have brought the bandits to understand what Soviet power is and what it seeks to achieve. Political enlightenment work is being undertaken. We have organized a [political discussion] circle. So far we lack a [Communist Party] club. We already have a choir in which the inmates take part. The choir performs whenever we have meetings. In the camp we have more than 2,000 inmates. In our library there are more than 100 visitors every day. Our librarian is very experienced and is, in fact, one of the inmates.[84]

At this report, the chairman, appearing to represent the voice of the average party member in attendance, interrupted Rychkov: "You there appear to be fussing over your bandits, organizing little sing-alongs and plays for them. An enemy must be destroyed—you don't make a military concentration camp into a nice little holiday resort for them." A voice from the hall agreed: "A concentration camp is a concentration camp—it's not supposed to be like a visit to your auntie's house!" Then accused by the same voice of being a "hidden stooge of the bandits," Rychkov tried to defend himself: "Comrades! This kind of criticism we have heard more than once, telling us that while we [Communists] are suffering one shortage after another, you are there busily caring for that vermin [in the camps]." Another voice then interjected: "Correct! Why are we fussing like this?—I say up against the wall with the lot of them and be done with it." Rychkov, evidently exasperated and offended, replied to the angry participants:

This is just an unbelievable delusion, one that we have heard over and over again. "Put them up against the wall—get it over quickly—our bullets are not just for show." But to turn our erstwhile enemies into good, solid friends—this is what we should really be doing. Of course, I could understand if some [old regime] aristocrats or rich men were to observe what we are doing, then they would not agree with our goals. And, of course, if some clear bandit-murderer does not submit to political reeducation and continues to go his own way, then he won't be long for this world. But for those who got involved [in the rebellion] by mistake and who repent—their fate should be a very different one.

Another participant identified as Zakharov interrupted Rychkov once more. "Comrade Rychkov, you forget that we came here to talk with our guns and not with words—empty phrases have no place on the field of battle." Ever more on the defensive, Rychkov again tried to justify his approach: "Who here is planning to enter the field of battle to carry on a conversation? No one! What has to be done in the battlefield is clear to everyone. But when the enemy surrenders or is wounded and becomes our prisoner in the camp, then the situation is completely different. You simply must not beat a man when he is down!" Once more, an angry voice from the assembly: "They would beat our man if he were down. They would try and beat our man to death, wounded or not. They would strangle the life out of our man with their bare hands if given half the chance."[85]

Rychkov was not winning any converts among the Communist Party members assembled at the conference, all of whom were too close to the "field of battle" to appreciate the outlook Rychkov and the other camp administrators were trying to preserve amid the counterinsurgency. The dispute, though, was also part of larger tension that characterized Soviet attitudes to penal servitude and toward designated "enemies of the people." The administrators of camps that had been in existence in the province since 1919 had been inclined to view their detainees as subjects of possible rehabilitation, and they sought to maintain this outlook, which they understood to be progressive and modern, when the camps were militarized as part of the counterinsurgency operation and prisoners and hostages began to arrive who either were victims of the rebellion themselves or were misguided and worthy of efforts at reeducation. On the other hand, the Communist Party members who protested the soft line taken by men such as Rychkov saw the hostages and prisoners either as members of a hostile class or as social miscreants who were essentially beyond rehabilitation and were best isolated from Soviet society or placed "up against the wall."[86]

Certainly reeducation and "enlightenment" never truly entered into considerations that informed the decision to employ camps in 1921. Nor, however, did the concentration camp tradition that dictated the *isolation* of class enemies from the rest of society. The camps were of temporary strategic value in the war against banditry, and they permitted the government forces to exercise influence over the native population. Officials were well aware of conditions in the camps.[87] The population of the camps was never constant, although overcrowding was a persistent problem.[88] With shortages of provisions a continual worry for the Red Army during the summer of 1921, it could only be expected that the camps would similarly suffer from lack of food for the inmate population. As with the Red Army, the camps relied upon the local villages for supplies of food, and people taken to camps as hostages were initially instructed to take as much food as they could carry for their own consumption during their internment.[89] After several weeks, villages were called upon to deliver foodstuffs to nearby camps in order to provide for their fellow community members held as hostages.[90]

Transfers were always an outlet for the provincial officials in the Department of Forced Labor to relieve the overcrowding, and thousands of detainees were sent to camps as near as Saratov and as distant as Irkutsk. A move to camps out-

Expansion and Flux of the Camp System, 15 June–24 August 1921

Camp Number (Location)	Detainees, 15 June 1921	Arrivals, 15 June–23 August 1921	Departures, 15 June–23 August 1921		No. of Inmates, 24 August 1921
			Transferred to Camps Outside Tambov Province	Released for Various Reasons	
No. 1 (Tambov)	844	3,885	3,716	237	776
No. 2 (Tambov)	n.a.	1,693	n.a.	812	881
No. 3 (Borisoglebsk)	321	319	242	150	248
No. 4 (Borisoglebsk)	n.a.	4,347	254	303	3,790
No. 5 (Morshansk)	405	580	358	118	509
No. 6 (Morshansk)	n.a.	1,863	n.a.	1,499	364
No. 7 (Kozlov)	908	6,083	4,270	649	2,072
No. 8 (Kirsanov)	345	3,504	2,008	44	1,797
No. 9 (Inzhavino)	56	942	n.a.	727	271
No. 10 (Sampur)	165	4,803	n.a.	2,102	2,866
TOTAL	3,044	28,019	10,484	6,641	13,574

Note: n.a. = not applicable
Source: GATO f. R-394, op. 1, d. 700, l. 41

side the province distanced those groups of people from developments in Tambov, which in the short term may have been to their advantage, avoiding the extreme shortages and insecurities that plagued camps inside the conflict zone. Over the longer term, however, such groups risked being overlooked as provincial state and military leaders sought to wind down the occupation regime and reduce the number of camps and prisoners. Camp administrators outside the province may have questioned continued incarceration for these civilian hostages, as well, as the commandant of a camp in Moscow Province evidently did in encouraging a group of Tambov peasants to petition the Commissariat of Justice for return to their native province:

We, the peasants of Tambov, Kirsanov, and Kozlov uezds, Tambov Province, were arrested in June 1921. It is already now the fourth month that we, who include the aged, pregnant mothers, and children, have had to endure difficult conditions: we are hungry, sick, and among the children there have already been fatalities. As ignorant people, we do not understand why we have been arrested, nor do we understand why we old people, children, and mothers have been placed in camps while healthy members of our families and of other families in our villages remain free. Now the weather is beginning to turn cold, and we are without warm clothes and proper footwear, because when we were arrested we did not take with us such items, as being completely innocent, we never expected to remain incarcerated for such a long time, and we are still uncertain if we are here as hostages in connection with the antonovist bands or if we are here for some other reason.[91]

Such groups of people were often transferred to camps outside the province without any accompanying documentation, and all the commandant of the Kozhukhovskii camp could provide by way of added context to the inmates' petition was the fact that they had arrived at this camp on 24 July, arrested on the orders of the "troika" operating in the Fourth Military Sector. It is impossible to know how many groups of hostages, transferred to camps outside of Tambov Province, fell into a black hole of incarceration and were unable to draw attention to their plight through such petitions.

Typically, those who were transferred out of the province were either captured rebels or "other" inmates, such as Communist Party members or Red Army servicemen who had committed infractions and had, for obvious reasons, to be separated from the vast majority of native camp inmates.[92] And despite limited space and provisions, there were those who requested admittance to the camps for their own personal security. This was particularly the case with rebels who surrendered to Red Army or government officials and who feared reprisal attacks on themselves and their families by other rebels in the locality.[93] For them, the material and moral hardships endured in the concentration camps were insignificant when placed alongside the risks they would court upon reintegration into their native communities.

The camps could not have been anything but tragic, however, even if the few records we have concerning mortality do not approach the kind of death rates witnessed in camps operated by the British during the Boer War, for instance.[94] The camps were unsanitary, overcrowded, and chaotic, problems that individual camp administrators struggled unsuccessfully to contain. But the camps were also undoubtedly successful for the purposes of the counterinsurgency, serving as a real and ominous prospect discouraging villagers against supporting the remaining rebels and forcing them to make the kind of awful and tragic choices concerning their own kin that were ultimately required for a return to peaceful, normal life. Certainly this was how most Red Army and state administrators understood the camps, and while the established camps endured into the 1920s as prisons, as they had been before the insurgency, there was a clear desire to discontinue using them to detain civilian hostages caught up in the rebellion and to dismantle the makeshift structures that had been hastily assembled amid the orgy of hostage taking in the first weeks following the publication of Order no. 171. But the camps were never as controversial as the summary execution of hostages had been. By 1921, detention camps, as well as civilian hostages, were an established feature of Soviet policing and counterinsurgency operations, in a way largely in keeping with customary practices of the European colonial powers in the early twentieth century.

COUNTERMOBILIZATION: THE REVKOMS AND SELF-DEFENSE MILITIAS

Nearly all concerned with the state counterinsurgency effort felt a tension between the need for sustainability and the drive for vengeance, itself partly a product of frustration and extreme insecurity. One of the parting recommendations made by Tukhachevskii in July was to issue broad reassurances to rebels that guarantees of amnesty would be respected by military commanders and state officials. This was emphasized in the pronouncements of the Plenipotentiary Commission, which sought to publicize as widely as possible those cases in which rebel groups had been convinced to surrender en masse.[95] Given the difficulties of the swollen camp population, military sector officials were encouraged to use detained hostages as intermediaries with outstanding groups of insurgents to deliver these reassurances, as well as confronting the rebels directly with examples of the kind of punishment they were destined to suffer if resistance continued.[96]

Part of the problem for military commanders and state officials was that the occupation system was growing increasingly complex, and the principles informing the public pronouncements of the Plenipotentiary Commission were frequently ignored in practice. There was no one culprit, but the expansion of the network of revkoms in the occupied countryside soon became the principal point of interaction between civilians and the state, and these institutions became the focus of efforts by state officials to control abuses of authority that undermined public confidence and support. As already noted, the revkoms had been integral to the counterinsurgency strategy since January 1921, but it was only with the massive reinforcements and other organizational and tactical improvements that accompanied Tukhachevskii's arrival in May that the network truly expanded. The revkoms were staffed in part by Communist Party members attached to local military garrisons, by Red Army soldiers, and by loyal local villagers, principally demobilized Red Army servicemen. As the revkom network expanded and became an alternative system of local administration in lieu of the village and volost soviets, their responsibilities and powers in connection with the counterinsurgency effort grew. In many areas where the Red Army presence was weak or distant, the security of the existing revkoms was understandably tenuous, and reports from such areas described revkom members working during the day and secretly leaving the village at night due to the danger of attacks.[97]

The capacity to antagonize the local community was limited, however, by the muscle a revolutionary committee could call upon in the case of disturbances. In villages situated near a military garrison, revkoms assumed greater responsibility regarding the daily affairs of the local community and grew more involved in the effort to root out the insurgency from the countryside. While earlier instructions had placed the revkoms at the heart of the occupation strategy, setting rigorous standards for membership as well as a timetable for their activities, appointed revkom members rarely met these standards and were frequently unclear as to their own duties and role until the arrival of a stable military presence in the vicinity. Military units could provide instructions on the proper conduct of interrogations of villagers, but frequently it was the simple presence of armed support that inspired the work of the revolutionary committees.[98] As noted, revkom members were to work on the basic intelligence provided by the Cheka's Special Department in creating lists of "bandit" and "nonbandit" households, preparing the ground for the activities of the *piaterka*s and other armed state authorities undertaking "occupation operations." Pressuring local communities to surrender known rebels or identify those who had provided support for the Partisan Army and STK was not limited to these special operations, however. Not every village or volost was targeted, and in those localities the revolutionary committees engaged in a much slower, although by no means more deliberate, process of interrogation and investigation to uncover and remove the "bandit element" from their midst.

Interrogations by revkom officials and the drafting of written statements by villagers came to possess an almost ritual quality in which those called in for questioning provided assured, yet often formulaic, explanations of their attitudes toward the insurgency and their involvement, if any, in known episodes of resistance or cooperation with rebels. A typical statement read:

> I, Kolmakov, do not admit guilt [*vinovnym sebia ne priznaiu*] of participation in banditry, because when our village joined and during those times when the bands were here, I was ill and did not leave home; I did not rob anyone, I did not sabotage any rail lines, and my son, Ivan Kolmakov, was forced at gunpoint by the bands

only one time to go and sabotage the railway, but at no other time did he do this or any other [bandit] activity.[99]

As with Kolmakov's son, young men who were forced to concede some involvement with the rebel bands would rarely admit to traveling with the Partisan Army for more than a week or two, and nearly all claimed to have been forcibly mobilized. Such accounts conformed well to the received understanding of the rebellion and its dynamics that had characterized official thinking since the first days of the conflict. Uncovering the extent of rebel organization and the level of participation in the insurgency in a given village meant following the trail of references that linked one statement to the next, calling anyone mentioned in one statement to corroborate or elaborate on that of another. Young children were called in to verify the claims of innocence made by the parents, and grandparents were prompted to decry the "foolishness" of the younger cohort in the village.[100] Most statements, however, were simple protestations of innocence and ignorance, providing a distinct echo of the theme, repeatedly emphasized in Soviet propaganda, of a "dark peasantry" misled by "bandits" and "counterrevolutionaries."

The authority to question and to arrest people came with the power, under Order no. 130, to confiscate property from "bandit" households—the source of the vast majority of problems encountered by the network of revolutionary committees. There had already been difficulties with undocumented confiscations conducted by Red Army units involved in the execution of orders no. 130 and 171. While shortages and speculation were behind the abuses of the Red Army units, in the case of the revolutionary committees such punitive actions frequently contained an added element of personal vengeance and local justice. This was especially true where Communist Party members returned to their villages to serve on the revolutionary committees, for they frequently found that their own households had suffered considerably during the months in which the STK and Partisan Army had dominated. The same held for demobilized Red Army servicemen who became members of the local revkom.

But in truth, the political background of an individual revkom member made little difference when the shared circumstances of hardship and shortage met with opportunity. Household property confiscated under the authority of Order no. 130 frequently found its way into the hands of friends and family of those who served on the revkom. In many cases, including those in which the Red Army was behind confiscations, seized property—including firearms—went directly onto the market, in part fueling the revival of private trade in the province as more and more items were channeled to the market towns of Tambov.[101] While the redistribution of confiscated property to loyal households, particularly to the needy, did proceed, there were also several cases in which confiscated items were given to former "bandit" households rather than to the poor, if the revkom chairman was friendly with the family of the known rebel. In Pakhotno-Ugol (Kirsanov uezd), six confiscated cows grazed in the field adjoining the offices of the regional revolutionary committee, whose members had denied repeated requests from the local orphanage for some of the livestock to be given over for the benefit of the children.[102]

Records were rarely (if ever) kept of confiscations carried out by the revolutionary committees, just as they were rarely documented by any other acting authority ostensibly carrying out the provisions of Order no. 130. The Plenipotentiary Commission and provincial administration in Tambov were well aware of this, principally through the work of the three-man inspection teams, or "troikas," that had been in operation since February.[103] The troikas involved in inspecting all levels of local administration, from the surviving volost soviets to the newly organized revolutionary committees and regional militias, regularly visited these institutions or followed up on complaints. They were empowered to take immediate action against local authorities found to have committed abuses or were proved incompetent. Most often, such individuals were summarily dismissed, while in rare cases, such as those involving collusion with rebels, dismissed individuals were also handed over to the prosecutors of the Revolutionary Tribunal. In part, the administrative troikas were designed to boost popular confidence in the system of local administration and policing installed by the occupying authority.[104] But the work of the troikas was also very much a part of the effort to uproot the rebellion, in that it was strongly believed that the new institutions of local administration would provide cover for those with strong ties with the insurgency, especially those who had served in the village and volost STKs.[105] The fear that the revkoms were being infiltrated by former Partisan Army rebels and STK members colored the interpretation of troika reports regarding illegal confiscations and corruption within the revkom network.[106] Examples of this certainly existed, but such cases of infiltration were nearly always about the exploitation of local possibilities and ties within a community to ensure individual survival rather than part of a concerted strategy to sustain the rebellion.[107]

While provincial state and military officials were concerned that revolutionary committees might protect rebels and rebel families, much as local soviets frequently protected young men from military conscription, the context by the summer of 1921 had changed so radically that such incidents were exceptional. Troika inspectors were more likely to investigate reports of overzealous revkom members

summarily executing surrendered rebels than they were to investigate local officials working in cahoots with known insurgents, even if the Plenipotentiary Commission was prompted in late July to issue an instruction to all revolutionary
committees clarifying that they did not have the authority to independently try
and execute surrendered or captured bandits.[108] In a broadly similar vein, the
Plenipotentiary Commission was prompted to consider the problem of revolutionary committees rearresting former rebels who had been granted amnesty by
government authorities. Such activities may have been the result of corrupt motives, or may have been the innocent consequence of misinformation, but the
overall effect was to generate uncertainty regarding state amnesty offers and to set
back timetables for the complete pacification of the territory.

The Tambov Communist Party had sought to facilitate the integration of surrendered rebels back into their village communities by requiring individuals to
sign a ten-point public oath of loyalty to the regime, declarations that drew on religious motifs of sin and forgiveness:

> 1. I acknowledge the full severity of my crimes committed against the Soviet
> government during my time with the band.
>
> 2. I fully recognize the plunder and robbery that was committed under the mask
> of the false Union of the Toiling Peasantry, led by that scoundrel Antonov and his
> followers.
>
> 3. I repent for all the blood that has been spilled on account of my ignorance and
> foolishness, I repent for the fires that I have set, for the thefts of peasant property
> that have been committed by my own hand.
>
> 4. I repent for the tremendous crime that I have committed against the workers'
> and peasants' government.
>
> 5. I vow never to sin before Soviet authority in word or in deed, never to bring
> upon Soviet power any distress or injury, but instead I will work only to strengthen
> Soviet power and help it flourish.
>
> 6. I swear to defend Soviet power against any attacks by bandits and brigands
> [*banditov i razboinikov*].
>
> 7. I promise never to allow myself to be deceived by Antonov, Vas'ka Karas', or
> any other former bandit leaders.
>
> 8. I promise to hand over any bandit that appears in my village, for there is no
> place for such black sheep in the Soviet flock.
>
> 9. I give the solemn word of a mistaken and repentant laborer to use all my pow-
> ers to help other misled comrades see the error of their ways.
>
> 10. I was once a bandit, a thief, and a brigand, a vagrant living in the swamps and
> forests like a savage who had rejected the workers' and peasants' motherland, unable

to expect forgiveness—Soviet power gave me back my life and my family, forgave me my crimes, and restored me as an honorable Soviet citizen and son of the Great Revolution—Long Live Soviet Power![109]

Such oaths formed the ritual basis for reintegration into the community for rebels who had surrendered and been granted amnesty. For the pardoned bandit, however, return to the native village was not always straightforward. It was not uncommon for village communities to protest against the planned return of a certain individual, especially if that former insurgent had harmed locals directly by participating in acts of violence or theft, or indirectly as a consequence of the harm visited upon the village by government authorities conducting occupation operations.[110] As already mentioned, communities did occasionally "banish" rebel families that had been taken hostage by state agents, preventing them from returning to their homes and, not insignificantly, retaking possession of their private property. In the case of former insurgents, however, the revolutionary committees were at the forefront in seeking to manage relations with the native community in order to facilitate peaceful reintegration. In some cases, revkom authorities assigned local "caretakers" for amnestied rebels who would work to minimize any antagonism toward the man who had now publicly repented for his "sins" against the Soviet state.[111]

Public protest against the return of former rebels and "bandit families" was only one way for communities to express loyalty to the regime, even if this may have often been a convenient by-product of genuine antagonism or avarice. The introduction of the revolutionary committees themselves provided the occasion for village declarations of support for the Soviet state and denunciation of the Partisan Army.[112] Providing an organized basis for demonstrations of loyalty was one of the central tenets of the occupation strategy, and the most important institutions in this respect brought to the villages during the summer of 1921 were the self-defense militias, introduced by order of the Plenipotentiary Commission on 17 July.[113] The original order introduced the self-defense militia as an innovation necessary to deal with the rapid transformation of the conflict from one in which the rebels were organized into partisan regiments to one in which small groups of five and ten bandits hid in the forests and survived only by attacking the villages. Self-protection required organization, and each village was obliged to form a militia and to establish lines of communication with the surrounding communities. In the event of a bandit attack, however, the order stipulated that the organized village militia must offer resistance and alert the local state and military authorities. The clear implication was that failure to resist the bandits— indeed, failure to use "all available means" to destroy the bandits—would be taken as an unambiguous indication of support for the insurgents.

By mid-June, when this order was published, some village communities organized self-defense militias independently in order to guard against bandit attacks. This was particularly the case in areas on the periphery of the conflict, beyond the organizational core of the rebellion but where state authority was nevertheless weakened by proximity to the conflict.[114] State and party observers cited such examples of spontaneous mobilization by villagers with approval, but the self-defense militias of the occupation required greater control over personnel and, especially, firearms, and they became active parts of Red Army operations during the period of "mopping up" from midsummer 1921 into the winter. In this case, control began with yet more lists of villagers; men between the ages of seventeen and fifty were considered eligible for service if they had no established connection with the insurgency. Naturally, the group that rose to the fore was demobilized Red Army servicemen, although those who had been too young or too old for military conscription during the civil war were also placed on the lists for the self-defense militia. Revolutionary committees were entrusted to oversee the organization of the militia and instructed to choose only "honorable citizens who are devoted to Soviet authority." In some cases, the organization of a village self-defense militia was preceded by a meeting of demobilized servicemen, who as a block interest group understood their role in the current political situation, part of which was to defend the community and the Soviet regime.[115]

Revkom members who were sent out to the villages to organize these militia groups also encouraged communities to produce declarations of support for the militia as a practical measure of engagement with the government counterinsurgency effort. Such declarations, like those produced at the behest of Communist Party and Partisan Army agitators in the recent past, were formulaic but important devices for communicating a sanctioned context for understanding present developments. In the case of Tokarevka, a village at the heart of the insurgency in Kirsanov uezd, the resolution of support adopted following the organization of a militia on 22 July read:

> We the citizens of Tokarevka, having heard the report of Comrade Stepanov about the organization of fighting brotherhoods [*boevye druzhiny*], have decided without hesitation to organize our own armed brotherhood from among our most trusted and reliable comrades in order to carry on the fight against the bandits, deserters, and criminal elements who refuse to leave us in peace. Down with the bandits, down with the deserters! Long live the fighting unit [*otriad*], long live the Red Army![116]

There was nearly always a surplus of volunteers for the self-defense militia, indicating a genuine enthusiasm—at least, at first—for open engagement with the campaign against the bandits. Part of this enthusiasm was motivated by practical considerations, such as the stipend for those who participated in the self-defense militias, stipends that were paid in kind (typically grain) and would be sorely missed once the militias were discontinued in most areas later in the year.[117] As with revolutionary committees, service in the local institutions of the occupation regime provided an authoritative foothold for newly returned servicemen who often entered into disputes with other villagers regarding land and property that had changed hands or disappeared during the conflict.[118]

The militia attracted participants whose interest in defense was frequently "selfish." Several men who volunteered for the militias were later accused of being *truddezertiry*—people who had been exempted from participation in the work brigades engaged in harvesting, forestry, railroad repair, and so forth, owing to their attachment to a "state institution" such as a self-defense militia.[119] Indeed, in one volost in Kirsanov uezd where enthusiasm for the self-defense militias was initially muted, revolutionary committee members warned local men that if they did not volunteer for the militias, they would likely be reconscripted into the Red Army, which was on the brink (it was reported) of a major conflict with Japan in the Far East.[120] And in one extraordinary case of individual self-protection rather than community self-defense, corrupt revkom officials helped a group of twenty-nine former rebels—survivors of a single Partisan Army battalion—secretly register as a village self-defense unit in Karian volost (Tambov uezd). The crime was eventually discovered, however, but only after the militia had been armed and prepared for antibanditry operations.[121] Because of the importance attached to the self-defense militias, as well as the opportunities they provided for corrupt practices, their membership was constantly monitored by revkom officials at the regional and uezd levels, and as a consequence membership was often quite fluid over the life span of a single unit, as circumstances changed and information about members was acquired.[122]

None of these complications diminished the significance of the self-defense militias as a practical component of the counterinsurgency regime. This much is evident from the number of appeals to village and volost revolutionary committees by volunteers for inclusion in the militia. Providing an outlet for popular involvement in the state campaign against the failed insurgency—what in other contexts has been termed countermobilization[123]—inspired a concern for public displays of loyalty to the regime that became part of the cognitive demobilization of resistance. Appeals for inclusion became an integral part of militia formation, and they were frequently written on the reverse of the paper containing the Plenipotentiary Commission's Order no. 178. As an example:

> I, [E. I.] Avgustov, from a poor peasant background, declare my loyalty to the Soviet regime as the only true authority and the government of all the people, and I sincerely hope to further the merciless struggle against counterrevolution and against the remnants of banditry, and so I therefore ask the Vasil'ev volost revkom to enlist me in the volunteer militia of the Tokarevka region.[124]

Similar appeals were written by individuals who were unable to immediately enlist in the militia and were afraid of how they would be viewed by state officials. Even when not permitted to enlist, some wrote letters to the revkom to prevent negative consequences. Ivan Poliakov felt compelled to explain his nonparticipation for precisely this reason:

> I ask the volost revkom to appeal on my behalf [to the regional revkom] regarding my exclusion from the list of militia members due to illness, as I am required to be in Tambov for medical treatment and therefore am unable to participate in the militia, but I nevertheless declare that I remain a steadfast defender of the people against the bands.[125]

Such appeals were frequently commented on by local Communist Party members or revkom officials, providing background information on the applicants regarding their known or suspected ties with the rebels and even their political activities before the outbreak of the insurgency.[126]

All was part of the practical experience of reviewing and demonstrating loyalty among the village communities that had previously been at the heart of the rebellion. The active resistance by self-defense militias to the incursions of local bandits, however, was a much less scripted and choreographed exercise. Obviously, disarming the countryside in the wake of a ten-month rebellion ran contrary to the task of distributing firearms to the self-defense militias that were quickly being formed under the auspices of the revolutionary committees, and those that had been formed faced an uphill battle to have the state authorities release guns and ammunition at all, not to mention enough for all militia members.[127] Red Army authorities in the military sectors were reluctant to arm the militias, arguing that they were not necessary to defeat the remaining rebel groups, and therefore releasing weapons back into the villages was unlikely to improve security and stability in the countryside.[128] Lack of firearms did not prevent village militias from organizing lines of intervillage communication called for in the original Plenipotentiary Commission order, nor did it prevent them from organizing round-the-clock guards against bandit incursions. Lightly armed but organized communities could overwhelm small bandit groups and march them to nearby Red Army headquarters, successes that state officials believed only fed enthusiasm for the counterinsurgency effort.[129]

Objections regarding the distribution of firearms to the militias were overcome in certain cases where officials were sufficiently assured of the reliability and capability of a given unit. In the late summer and autumn of 1921 the militias became active participants in several of the mopping-up operations conducted by the Red Army. Frequently, however, their involvement was limited to the highly risky but noncombat tasks of reconnaissance and scouting in the forests and swamps, searching out rebel locations and alerting Red Army units that would then proceed to "flush out" the rebels.[130]

RETURN TO THE FORESTS: FROM COUNTERINSURGENCY TO ANTIBANDITRY

By the end of July 1921, the days of partisan supremacy in southern Tambov Province were already a memory becoming ever more distant, and the maturing occupation of the region had a growing influence over that memory. The efforts by the Red Army, Communist Party, and Cheka to divide village communities and identify rebel supporters and their families had been a violent and painful process that nevertheless worked to instill a new solidarity in the villages, one that on the surface appeared artificial in light of the previous spirit of defiance demonstrated during the height of the insurgency but nevertheless provided the basis for a genuine transformation in popular attitudes toward the Soviet regime. Reinforcing this transition were the actions of surviving rebel groups who, no longer able to rely upon the support of local communities and uncertain of their survival, rapidly came to depend upon the very banditry that Soviet officials had consistently and publicly ascribed to them from the start.[131] Deprived of their major leaders and with their slogans and ideals sounding ever more hollow and irrelevant, the one-time partisans quickly became desperate bandits who preyed upon vulnerable communities.

In mid-July, the last major active rebel leader had been defeated by mobile Red Army forces. Vas'ka Karas' and his Kozlov-based insurgent army had been reduced to only a couple of hundred by the time the squadrons from the Third and Fourth Red Army Cavalry Regiments engaged pursuit, driving the former commander of the "western" group of the Partisan Army away from his operational base in Kozlov into the region along the eastern border of neighboring Usman uezd, reportedly Karas's native area.[132] The homecoming was brief for the rebel chieftain, however, as repeated skirmishes with Red Army cavalry diminished the number of men under his command and, finally, on the morning of 17 July, Karas' (whose real name was Vasilii Vasil'evich Nikitin-Korolev) was killed in battle.[133] Other groups still remained, particularly in Borisoglebsk and Kirsanov uezds, but were finding it virtually impossible to prevail against government forces. Many were being led by individuals who had only emerged during this final, desperate period. While large amassments of rebels could still provide stern resistance to the Red Army from their forest and ravine strongholds, such occasions were few and only briefly forestalled what was regarded as the inevitable conclusion to the Tambov insurgency.[134]

The surviving rebels were desperately short of supplies and ammunition. Red Army forces traversing the countryside had regularly discovered caches of rebel guns and ammunition during the early weeks of the occupation in May and June, but by the late summer they increasingly discovered hidden machine and artillery guns without bullets and shells, indicating that the guns would be retrieved once these supplies were secured.[135] Nevertheless, there were continued fears that the remaining rebels were intent upon surviving through the upcoming winter, in accordance with Antonov's alleged "last order," and then resuming the struggle once the Red Army forces had been withdrawn. Such suspicions were reinforced by occasional pieces of intelligence, and they provided a new gloss to the regular reports of the hit-and-run attacks by rebels, who were targeting forestry workers and fishermen, among other vulnerable parties, who were not held to ransom nor often harmed, but had their equipment and stocks stolen at gunpoint.[136] The conditions made forestry work impossible, in particular, leaving the woods open for local peasants to exploit freely and at their own risk.[137] While the decline in the rebel activity in the summer had permitted the resumption of rail traffic, the chaos that surrounded forestry meant that needed shipments of wood for fuel in the cities to the north had not resumed, and the fuel crisis in the towns of the province itself continued throughout the summer and autumn of 1921.[138]

Although there were isolated incidents in which larger groups of armed rebels were caught in firefights with Red Army and Cheka units in the late summer, the military task of the occupying forces was largely limited to cleaning out the forests, swamps, and gullies (*ovragi*) of the remaining small groups of desperate rebels. Rarely, however, did the occupying forces directly move into these domains and risk an ambush. Instead, most who were engaged in rounding up rebel groups focused on isolating the surviving rebels and maintaining or creating conditions that would force surrender. Bleeding the rebel groups that had dug themselves in and established hiding positions in the forests and swamps meant encouraging a steady flow of defections and surrenders, a process that could achieve a certain momentum as former rebels were enlisted in the effort.[139]

In the Sixth Military Sector (covering southern Kirsanov, northern Borisoglebsk and southeastern Tambov uezds), which had been created following Tukhachevskii's arrival in the province in May and encompassed the true heartland of the insurgency, the occupation included a significant force of officer cadets. This force numbered over 15,000, with infantry, cavalry, and artillery cadets brought in from twelve Red Army academies in European Russia and Ukraine. The force had been organized for the single purpose of occupation in Tambov, for officer cadets were expected to be disciplined and reliable in a way that many regular Red Army units were not (over 75 percent of the cadet force were Communist Party or Komsomol members).[140] Moreover, conditions in Tambov were considered ideal for training Red Army officers in the necessary skills of counterinsurgency, which they were likely to need often as the Soviet government looked to consolidate its control over the territories of the former Russian Empire. In effect, the Sixth Military Sector, based in the important village of Inzhavino, was to become a training ground in fundamental combat skills for a young generation of Red Army officers.[141]

The Sixth Sector included the slow-moving, forested section of the Vorona River and its branching streams, with dozens of small swamps, adjoining lakes, and tenuous marshy islands that had long been a virtually secure and unapproachable hiding place for outlaws. It included unusually deep and extensive ravines, overgrown with vegetation and difficult to penetrate. Whereas much of the land encompassed by the rebellion in Tambov was flat and dominated by farmland and moderate-sized villages, southern Kirsanov was ideal terrain for guerrillas and outlaws, and it was in this region that the Soviet occupying authorities faced their most difficult challenges in returning political stability and security to the countryside. For this reason, the military commissar in Tambov, Shikunov, referred to the cadet force deployed in the Sixth Sector as his "lions," for they faced the greatest danger of any of the occupying forces.[142]

The cadets suffered the same practical complications that all occupying forces encountered following their deployment in the province, when the organization of supply lines was slow in taking shape, and the first weeks of their assignment were spent settling in and even gathering whatever food they could secure, including fishing for carp and crayfish in local waters.[143] They did not participate in military operations during this initial period, and because of the partially pedagogical nature of their assignment, Red Army commanders sought to delay their participation in active operations until adequate support structures and training staff were set up. In addition, the cadets were initially left in larger formations and groupings that were unsuitable for active operations but were nevertheless safer in the short term.[144] By June, following the defeat of the Second Partisan Army, the cadet force underwent reorganization and redeployment to realize the occupation of the region, dispersing across the sector with single units (*otriady*), composed of multiple infantry battalions and a cavalry regiment that were garrisoned in major villages and had an operational reach of five to six volosts each. Throughout June and July, the cadet units were involved in much the same antibanditry activities as other Red Army units, including the conduct of "occupation operations" and day-to-day involvement in the activities of the revolutionary committees.

By the end of July, however, attention turned to the task of cleaning the rugged countryside of the Sixth Military Sector of surviving rebel groups. The garrisoned forces were regularly assembled for single operations to clear individual forests or discrete areas, operations that were typically well planned and informed by regular intelligence regarding the size and morale of rebel groups provided by local villagers, surrendered rebels, or scouting parties, including airborne reconnaissance. The size of the cadet forces assembled for individual operations was typically determined by the area that needed to be encircled rather than the suspected size of the rebel contingent within. The typical procedure involved an initial sustained artillery bombardment of the forest where rebels were hiding. If all went according to plan, this would be enough to throw the rebels into a panic and attempted flight, after which they would be caught by the Red Army forces arrayed along the periphery. With some experience, sector commanders recognized the need for cavalry troops to participate in the encirclement, as foot soldiers were incapable of coping with mounted rebels.[145] Where the Vorona River provided a natural barrier, local Red Army commanders arranged for machine gun–mounted pontoon boats to patrol the waters and intercept any rebels who attempted to swim to safety.[146]

The final stage of these operations was always the most dangerous, for no infantry battalion relished the opportunity to enter a forest or ravine to flush out the remaining rebels, even after a prolonged artillery or machine gun barrage.[147] Sector commanders sought to mitigate the soldiers' natural unease by promoting a competition whereby the unit that captured or killed the greatest number of rebels would be rewarded.[148] But the fear of ambush always cast a pall over soldier morale during these mopping-up operations, and because of the risks involved, military officials sought every possible way to encourage the voluntary surrender of recalcitrant rebels.

The difficulty and danger of these operations also prompted military commanders to use more dangerous and controversial weaponry. A subject still lacking full detail is the use of chemical weapons in the counterinsurgency campaign under Tukhachevskii. Certainly poisonous gas was used by Red Army forces, and the use of gas was probably intended to be much more extensive than circumstances permitted. Only the lack of trained specialists, and a certain degree of restraint exercised by local commanders, prevented Tambov becoming yet another training ground for the Red Army seeking to master techniques and practices that had been demonstrated on a much wider scale in the First World War. Part of the thinking behind the decision to introduce chemical weapons to the Tambov conflict concerned the psychological impact of such weapons, but an added factor was the commitment of senior commanders, such as Tukhachevskii, to the potential that these weapons represented for the Soviet armed forces.[149] Not only did senior Red Army commanders share an enthusiasm for chemical weapons, but they also showed a highly selective sensitivity to the dubious ethics of employing such weapons, particularly against one's own people.[150]

The announcement of the intention to introduce chemical weapons came on 12 June 1921, in an "operationally secret" order signed by Tukhachevskii and his chief of staff, N. E. Kakurin. Like Tukhachevskii, Kakurin was a veteran of the First World War with command experience. Their familiarity with poisonous gas was quite possibly intimate, given that the Russian Army suffered more than any other belligerent from the effects of chlorine and mustard gas.[151] The 12 June order explained that the remaining rebel groups were now effectively isolated from the villages and from the partisan population by the measures undertaken since Tukhachevskii's arrival in Tambov. But with the longer-term problem of rounding up the remaining rebel groups from dangerous and difficult terrain, Tukhachevskii and Kakurin announced that they would distribute poison gas canisters and artillery shells to field commanders in each military sector to place rebel strongholds under a cloud of "asphyxiating gas" that would "kill all who hide within."[152]

Despite the measured and confident tone of the 12 June order, the decision to introduce chemical weapons into the conflict in Tambov was an acknowledgment of failure. At the 9 June meeting of the Plenipotentiary Commission, Tukhachevskii led with a statement recognizing his failure to meet the one-month deadline he had been given by his political superiors in Moscow, and which he himself had stated was to begin on 6 May, when he felt he had established himself and his staff in their headquarters outside the provincial capital.[153] After hearing of the difficulties experienced by local commanders in the military sectors in bringing Order no. 130 to fruition and in setting up institutions deemed essential to the occupation strategy outlined by Tukhachevskii, at the 9 June meeting the commission agreed to intensify efforts at subduing the rural population. Among the measures accepted was the use of gas against rebel groups in forested areas.[154]

Briefed on Tukhachevskii's 12 June order on the use of gas, at their 20 June meeting the Antibanditry Commission in Moscow counseled restraint, advising commanders in Tambov to use gas only when success was assured and the appropriate technical expertise was available. With official approval secured, Glavkom informed Tukhachevskii that five teams of chemical specialists would be transferred to Tambov, and that they would transport supplies of E-56 chlorine gas in sufficient quantity for use in the province against the rebels. The chief of the artillery inspectorate in Orel Military Sector headquarters received orders that same day to begin assembling teams of specialists for operations in Tambov. [155]

A 1 July 1921 report written by the chemicals specialist, V. Pus'kov, to the artillery commander in Tambov confirms the arrival in the area of 250 canisters of chlorine gas.[156] By this time, commanders attached to the cadet force in the Sixth Military Sector had received instructions on the use of chemical weapons, specifically the firing of artillery shells armed with poisonous gas rounds. The artillery inspector in Tambov, S. Kasinov, stipulated that shells should be used as a delivery system only when conditions made the release of gas from canisters impossible, such as when the wind was too weak to carry the gas to the desired target, or when the target was in an inaccessible area, such as deep gullies. Likewise, the instructions warned against the use of artillery shells when the wind was too strong and would disperse the gas too quickly, or if the target was located in swamp or marshland (as was the case in the Sixth Military Sector), where the ground was too soft and a fired shell would likely sink below the surface. Cool conditions were also optimal for the use of such chemical rounds, which were less predictable in hot temperatures. As the summers in Central Russia were exceptionally warm, with temperatures regularly topping thirty and occasionally thirty-five degrees Celsius, this meant that night was the best time for using poisonous gas.[157] Instructions argued against using chemical weapons as a means of flushing out rebels, for while they would be driven out by gases that were irritants, they would be more likely to escape capture under cover of darkness. For this reason, *lethal* chemicals, such as the green chlorine gas, were more likely to be used at night, allowing Red Army soldiers to enter a rebel stronghold such as in a forest with a degree of con-

fidence that only corpses would be left behind. At any rate, this was the theory behind the use of such weapons in a conflict such as the one in Tambov.

Despite these detailed instructions and the extensive supply of chlorine gas and
specialist personnel, it remains difficult to assess the degree to which poisonous
gas was used in Tambov in the summer of 1921. There are very few references to
its use and no detailed reports on the effectiveness of chemical weapons in the
fight against the rebels. There are no records of chlorine gas canisters being
opened upwind of forest strongholds, enveloping the rebel fighters in a cloud like
the one Tukhachevskii warned of in his 12 June order. There are records of individual Red Army units firing artillery shells or throwing grenades that contained
chemical rounds. In two instances, both in the Sixth Military Sector, Red Army
cadet artillery groups recorded the use of such weapons. One took place near the
village of Kipets (near Karai-Saltykovo), where some fifty-nine chemical-filled
artillery shells were fired at an island in a lake only one and a half versts from the
village.[158] The island was no doubt a hideout for local rebels, and the chemical
weapons were used in combination with conventional artillery rounds. But because the artillery groups were not involved in the mopping-up operations, there
was no specific mention of this in the field diary, let alone a report of the effectiveness of these chemical shells. In another incident, the field journal of the artillery division in the Sixth Military Sector notes that 47 chemical-filled shells
were fired in combination with over 220 other conventional shells in an incident
(no location is given) on 13 July. Once more, there is no specific mention of the
effectiveness of the chemical shells, but it is unlikely that the gas had much impact, for the concentration of fire was quite low, and thus the concentration of the
gas charges would have been low as well.[159]

The other side of the coin was, of course, the propaganda value that such
weapons represented. While Tukhachevskii's 12 June order was classified as secret,
political and military officials wasted no time in publicizing the threat in order
to press rebels to surrender. Even before the use of poisonous gas had gained
sanction from Moscow, the Plenipotentiary Commission released an appeal to
insurgents that warned: "If you hide in the forests, we will smoke you out. The
Plenipotentiary Commission has decided to use poisonous gas to smoke bandits
out of the forests."[160] Military and political commissars in the Fourth Sector
(Kozlov) issued their own Order no. 5, which repeated many of the ultimatums
and threats relating to the consequences of continued resistance and defiance by
villagers and active rebels alike, only this order concluded with the explicit threat
that "POISONOUS GAS" would be used against those bandits who continued to

hide in the forests.[161] Possibly the first published reference to the use of such weapons by the Red Army in the Russian civil war, by V. Mokarev, who was a regional chief in the Sixth Military Sector in Tambov in 1921, questions the actual military effectiveness of chemical artillery rounds, but Mokarev is less doubtful about the overall value of such weapons. In describing the operations of one cadet artillery group near the village of Parevka, Mokarev writes: "Regrettably, the cadets as well as the other military units in the area were not equipped with chemical rounds, the use of which would likely have produced much more favourable results, even if only as concerns morale."[162]

What is unclear from Mokarev's words is whose morale he means, that of the rebels or of the Red Army soldiers? The answer is very likely to be both. Chlorine gas was seen as both a threat and as a battlefield weapon. For the rebels still holed up in the forests and other hideouts, the sight of a gas charge from an artillery shell would certainly have been frightening, but the Red Army was unlikely to have ever built up a lethal concentration of gas. The fear of gas would have been high, both for those who had known chlorine, phosgene, and mustard gases in World War I, and for those who had not served in the Russian imperial army but had only heard of such episodes. But for the Red Army soldiers charged with rounding up the remaining bandits in Tambov Province in 1921, the prospect of entering a dark forest or other overgrown area in which enemies waited in ambush was similarly terrifying. While conventional artillery would have "softened up" a target as well as chemical shells, something recognized by British commanders following World War I, the faith in chemical weapons could very well have been as inflated for the soldiers as it was for their commander, General Tukhachevskii.[163]

While chemical weapons featured more in the thoughts of commanders than in the fields and forests, the forest clearance operations continued into the autumn and winter of 1921, although on a diminishing scale as greater numbers of rebels surrendered under the pressure of the Red Army presence and with the desperation that came with basic exposure as the seasons changed. Red Army force levels, however, remained largely constant, and the assignment of the cadet force in the Sixth Military Sector was extended until the end of 1921.[164] Although antibanditry operations continued until the end of the year, the occupation of Tambov came to be characterized not by combat missions and forest clearances but by the daily interaction between the Red Army forces garrisoned in the countryside and the village communities they were meant to protect. This was a peculiar occupation of Russians by Russians (for the most part); indeed, it was largely an occupation of Russian peasants by Russian peasants in uniform. The essential foundations for trust were already there, although the practical difficulties of sustaining a large conscript army in the province did much to test those foundations and compromise the transition back to normality for the villages of Tambov Province.

THE DAILY FACE OF OCCUPATION

Forest clearance operations were less common in other sectors of the occupation of Tambov Province, both because there were fewer concentrations of former rebels outside of this core region of the defeated insurgency and because the terrain elsewhere was marginally more accessible and open. Active operations against identifiable rebel groups largely relied upon the motorized units that had proven so effective in early June during the decisive pursuit of the Second Partisan Army, and Red Army cavalry numbers remained quite small relative to infantry for the occupation as a whole.[165] As summer gave way to autumn in 1921, the main challenges that confronted the vast majority of Red Army servicemen assigned to garrisons in Tambov during the occupation concerned their own maintenance, given the shortage of basic provisions and the struggle with boredom.

The growth in the Red Army presence in Tambov had produced misgivings among local officials from the early months of 1921, and the continued expansion of the occupation in the summer prompted the Plenipotentiary Commission to lobby Moscow to recognize Tambov as a "grain-deficit" or "hungry" province and for central military and state authorities to assume responsibility for maintaining the army. Antonov-Ovseenko reported that the province could simply not sustain a military presence of "130,000 eaters," a figure that no doubt included the permanent garrison population of Tambov as well as forces assigned to the province since the start of the year.[166] Balancing a concern with reviving the local economy and avoiding starvation in the coming winter with the need to establish political stability and security, Antonov-Ovseenko's recommendations were largely ineffective in forcing a resolution to the army's supply crisis.

While the Red Army had been allowed to provision the occupying forces by requisitions in Tambov, within the territory of the conflict, this did not sanction autonomous requisitioning, or "self-provisioning," by individual army units. The Tambov military command had arranged for food brigades to operate in conjunction with the provincial Food Commissariat, but these official channels were unable to satisfy the needs of the dozens of garrisons and mobile units deployed in the southern half of Tambov, giving rise to a plague of "self-provisioning" in the summer of 1921 that became the norm among all Red Army forces in the province.

Just as local officials had feared, such conduct only undermined the trust and faith of village communities in the occupation forces. Commanders in the field regularly reported instances of self-provisioning and what they did not hesitate to identify as "looting," detailing the damage being done to peasant-state relations in the hope that improvements would be made to the army supply apparatus.[167] Similarly, commanders that reported healthy relations with local village communities attributed their successes to adequate supply lines that permitted interaction between soldiers and villagers that would win hearts and minds rather than filling stomachs.[168]

The image of the occupying authorities was damaged by the sight of Red Army units begging for handouts from rural households, as was the case with one infantry group arrived from neighboring Penza Province, but the greater problem was indiscipline among soldiers, which was often manifested more broadly than mere looting.[169] Hungry and bored soldiers could take out their frustrations by firing live rounds into villages to scare locals, just as they fired their rifles into the air to protest a reduction or delay in rations.[170] Communist Party agitators attached to military units felt powerless to influence the conduct of Red Army soldiers who were hungry, and incidents of looting were rife in even the elite brigades and divisions assigned to the antibanditry front in Tambov.[171] Indeed, the mobile pursuit forces were frequently the worst offenders in this regard, as it was far more difficult to maintain supply lines to autonomous motorized and cavalry groups, and they generally relied on local resources for sustenance, especially foods that could be consumed immediately, such as eggs and dairy products.[172]

The Plenipotentiary Commission sought to control self-provisioning by Red Army forces by drawing in the participation of revolutionary committees, which were instructed to liaise with local military commanders and provide information regarding available food resources and arrange for collections.[173] Yet, as with the village and volost soviets before them, revkoms were always suspected of a narrow parochialism if they sought to limit the demands placed upon local communities, and the revkoms were frequently bypassed as military commanders sought to satisfy the needs of their soldiers. Countless instances of undocumented confiscation occurred under the authority of Order no. 130, in some cases even leading to hostage taking and public executions in villages where hungry Red Army units had only been searching for food.[174] It is mainly owing to the persistent supply crisis that affected the Red Army that the true cost of orders no. 130 and 171 will never be known.

However, within the occupation zone, the presence of Red Army garrisons was not entirely a force for antagonism. Military units were regularly called upon to participate in agricultural work, a development in the summer of 1921 that was viewed as both a welfare measure that could strengthen public confidence in the Soviet state and Red Army, as well as providing a necessary outlet of activity for the thousands of soldiers assigned to the south of the province. Groups of service-men were assigned to assist in field work as a means of helping the households of Red Army soldiers who were away on assignment or were dead or disabled. Similarly, occupying garrisons were mobilized to assist loyal villages and even to ensure that the fields left unattended by bandit households held in the camps were utilized as effectively as possible.[175] Along with the *subbotniki*—Communist Party members and townspeople mobilized to work one day per week or month for the "public good"—the Red Army's involvement in agricultural field work could at times be significant, such as with the repair and provision of tools, and especially the provision of draft animals that were in such desperately short sup-ply at the end of the civil war and following the rebellion.[176] The involvement of the Red Army in local agricultural work continued until the harvest, and while such assistance brought the occupying forces into regular and practical contact with vil-lage communities, a measure of disquiet lingered among those who suspected that this assistance was only a Trojan horse for a return of the requisitioning squads. Having Red Army soldiers involved in working the fields would make it harder for peasant farmers to underestimate harvest yields and conceal distant fields from tax collectors of the Food Commissariat, and it was even feared that the army would demand a portion of the harvest in return for their beneficence.[177]

The experience of occupation was not dominated by limited acts of welfare as-sistance, however. Only during the harvest period from August to October was the interaction between village communities and garrisoned soldiers centered on agricultural work. While some Red Army commanders did seek to insulate their soldiers from local communities as a means of focusing on security matters as well as preserving discipline, for the majority of village communities in the south-ern half of the province the occupation was characterized by quotidian economic and social interaction with soldiers.[178] For example, Red Army soldiers became the energizing force in the revival of market activity in the province following the partial decriminalization of private trade in March 1921. This was just as true for the markets in the large garrison towns as it was for the smaller market villages in the countryside, where Red Army soldiers eagerly sold and traded military-issue equipment and even their rations. As noted earlier, property confiscated by Red Army units during "occupation operations" frequently found its way onto local markets, and for all the unease surrounding "speculation" voiced by local state and party officials, who were slowly adjusting to the new possibilities under the NEP, the realization that Red Army men were at the heart of this activity tempered the zeal for a crackdown on markets in Tambov Province in 1921.[179]

The sheer boredom that most units had to cope with, though, sometimes dominated the concerns of average soldiers, as well as those of the political commissars and Communist Party agitators attached to the garrisons. The need to provide outlets for soldiers, whether by stocking libraries, organizing team sports, or scheduling musical and theater events, became more vital in the final stages of the conflict, when less manpower was required for operations against rebel groups and the vast majority of soldiers stationed in Tambov were intended to provide a visible and reassuring presence within the zone of occupation.[180] Even before the occupation achieved its peak in May and June 1921, Red Army servicemen were independently organizing underground social clubs that provided an opportunity to drink, play music, and—most important—meet local girls.[181] In a sense, the stationing of a Red Army garrison had parallels with the arrival of a Partisan Army unit, which sometimes occasioned long parties that involved entire communities, particularly young single women.[182] While the carnival atmosphere may not have been the same, such social events became important for Red Army soldiers in the countryside and could acquire importance for local households, as well. Women who had had relationships with known rebels could partially remove themselves from suspicion and possible persecution if they socialized or struck up relations with occupying soldiers.[183] The same was true for the families of former STK members. The only documentation relating to such cases involves those who were discovered, but it stands to reason that many villagers and rural households would have found a degree of security from investigation and persecution by cultivating personal relationships with occupying soldiers and state officials.[184]

The social interactions between occupying soldiers and village communities were not necessarily determined by considerations of self-protection. But in a region where the multiple levels of participation in the insurgency meant that the vast majority of households were compromised to some degree by the rebellion, relations with occupying authorities could never be entirely divorced from such concerns. As such, even the starry-eyed romances that sprung up between Red Army soldiers and village girls—such as the first love of the future Soviet children's author, Arkadii Gaidar, who was stationed near Morshansk during the summer of 1921—could not be entirely innocent of the charged political context created by the occupation and the facilitated transition to normality in the province.[185] Regardless of the motivations—conscious or unconscious—that lurked behind such relationships, they became a factor in that transition, albeit a complicated one. Instances of rape by Red Army soldiers were not uncommon and, while the data are only suggestive, several military units reported rises in venereal disease among troops during the occupation in the summer and autumn of 1921.[186] But the ease with which most village communities adjusted to the presence of Red Army garrisons, even amid terrible material conditions and shortages, is testament to the unusual nature of the occupation of Tambov. Although senior commanders sought to underscore the seriousness of the operation by likening it to the occupation of enemy territory, there were no defining national or ethnic distinctions that could form the basis for strict social division between occupying forces and rural communities.[187] The presence of large Red Army units in the province underscored the extraordinary nature of the conflict and the stakes involved, but the fact that these were predominantly Russian peasants in uniform providing security and helping to restore political stability facilitated the demobilization of the resistance to the Soviet state in the Tambov countryside by blurring the concepts of "civil-military relations" and "fraternization" that typically accompany foreign occupation.

THE OCCUPATION OF southern Tambov Province during the summer of 1921 was characterized by conditions that encouraged a return to normality while preserving a sense of the extraordinary for village communities. In this, the occupation was the converse of life under the Partisan Army and STK, in which it was an extraordinary atmosphere was promoted while a sense of everyday normality was, by necessity, preserved. The task of mobilizing the rural population for resistance to the Soviet state, like the task of demobilizing that resistance in the summer of 1921, was primarily to create conditions for the desired individual and collective interpretation of events and context. The facets of the occupation regime described here highlight the extent to which pacification was a multitudinous process that divided local communities and pushed them in different directions, punishing resistance while providing opportunities for collaboration, requiring interaction with state institutions and agents while encouraging a return to "peaceful work" and normality. While government officials frequently reported on the "pro-Soviet" sympathies of the rural population, no one truly hoped for such a complete transformation in the short term. Instead, the task of distancing the village communities from the experience of rebellion, of undermining and supplanting that memory, became the essence of "sovietization" during the second half of 1921.

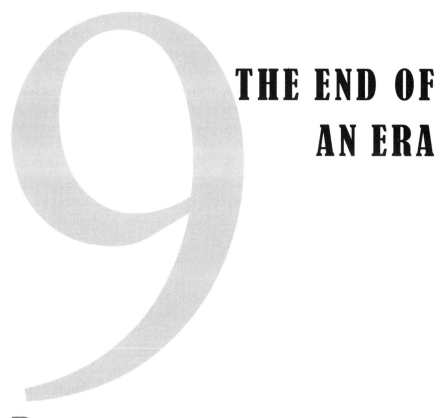

THE END OF
AN ERA

BY THE END OF the summer of 1921, most of the important figures in the Partisan Army and STK were either dead or in Cheka prisons. Tokmakov, Boguslavskii, Karas', Selianskii, and other Partisan Army commanders had been killed in battle. "Bat'ko" Pluzhnikov and his son, Dmitrii, had been found dead soon after the hub of the STK organization was discovered by the Red Army and Cheka in Kamenka, and a wave of arrests ensued. The political wing of the movement had been decapitated just as the Red Army was breaking up the main forces of the Partisan Army. The STK had ceased to function in any meaningful way by July 1921, and like the surviving rebel groups holed up in the forests and swamps, those who had participated in the administration of the partisan countryside through the network of village and volost STKs, were principally concerned with escaping discovery and returning to their everyday lives once the revolutionary committees began their own steady and systematic investigations.

In early 1921, following the organization of the VTsIK Antibanditry Commission in Moscow, as well as the overhaul of the provincial Cheka organization Tambov by Antonov-Ovseenko and the new Cheka chief, M. D. Antonov, the VChK chairman (and member of the Antibanditry Commission), Felix Dzerzhinskii, arranged for provincial Cheka organizations in the central agricultural region to collaborate on the investigation of the wider rebel network and its ties with anti-Soviet political parties and groups.[1] While few sustained and concrete ties between the rebels and opposition groups were established, pooling the efforts of Cheka agents across the wider region—including Tambov, Voronezh, Penza, Orel, and the Don territory—resulted in more organized counterintelligence operations and the arrangement of regular efforts to infiltrate the Partisan Army in Tambov. While the provincial Cheka had successfully broken up the organizational core of the PSR and LSR parties in Tambov itself, arresting dozens of senior PSR members (including Aleksandr Antonov's brother-in-law, Aleksandr Bogoliubskii), there had been few efforts if any to penetrate the rebel camp in 1921, and operations one might classify as counterespionage were few during the early months of the new year, when the provincial administration in Tambov was afflicted by so much disorganization and division.[2]

Despite the relative coherence of the rebel organization and the interactions between the Partisan Army and the STK network, the Cheka in Tambov was nevertheless able to infiltrate both organizations with some regularity in the summer of 1921, mainly capitalizing on the rebel movement's strong desire to forge contacts with anti-Soviet movements and groups in other parts of the former Russian Empire. While the information garnered from the infiltration of the rebel camp by Cheka agents rarely proved of immediate value to the operations of the Red Army in Tambov, these activities did manage to disrupt the rapidly fragmenting organization of the rebel movement and undermined the fragile confidence of the rebel soldiers and leadership. On at least two occasions, undercover agents managed to lure senior rebel leaders to Moscow and into the hands of Cheka.[3] Included in this number were Ivan Ishin and Pavel Ektov, the former possibly the most visible propagandist under Antonov both before and during the rebellion, and the latter a former cooperative worker who established himself as a senior figure attached to Partisan Army headquarters. These two were drawn to Moscow by Cheka agents posing as PSR members seeking to coordinate armed opposition movements by arranging a summit of anti-Soviet political and rebel leaders in Moscow. While at first glance, the story of such a summit in the Soviet capital appears preposterous, especially insofar as it formed the basis of a Cheka counterespionage operation. However, the rebels did have regular, if unsystematic, contact with individuals in Moscow who were attached to the PSR or were sympathetic to the anti-Soviet cause, and control over opposition political activity in the city was far from comprehensive.[4] Still, the story of a planned gathering of anti-Soviet

forces resonated with the worldview of rebel leaders in Tambov, who always sought
to contextualize their own activities in relation to similar rebellions and opponents
of the Communist Party and who frequently channelled their energies accordingly.
Most important, such a story also fed their hopes of eventual success in toppling
the Soviet government precisely when their own movement was in such dramatic
decline.[5]

Each success for the Cheka fed into the next such operation. While Ishin, as a
long-standing opponent of the Soviet regime who had severed all ties with his
family, was most likely shot quickly after his capture and interrogation in Moscow,
Ektov turned informer for the Cheka after his family was taken hostage by state
agents.[6] He even agreed to cooperate in the most famous and elaborate undercover
operation carried out by the Red Army during the final months of the insurgency:
he returned to Tambov and escorted the men of Kotovskii's Red Army cavalry
brigade, posing as Don Cossacks who had come to join forces with the Partisan
Army, into the forests of Tambov uezd to ambush one of the few remaining Partisan
Army regiments. The story of Kotovskii's destruction of the rebel unit led by Ivan
Matiukhin quickly entered into the folklore of the Red Army and the Cheka, appearing several times in memoirs, children's fiction, and on film and stage.[7]

Yet just as in the months before the outbreak of the insurgency in the autumn
of 1920, the Red Army and Cheka still found it (in the words of B. A. Vasil'ev)
"fiendishly difficult" to pin down and capture Aleksandr Antonov himself, as well
as his younger brother, Dmitrii. In the late summer of 1921, following the defeat
of the Second Partisan Army and the discovery of Antonov's alleged "final order"
for rebels to suspend armed activities until the occupation of southern Tambov
ended, both organizations had launched operations in response to intelligence regarding Antonov's location, but none had succeeded in securing his capture or
confirmation of his death.[8] The provincial administration had been hasty in the
past to announce the death of rebel leaders, often on the basis of unconfirmed intelligence and unreliable statements by captured Partisan Army soldiers, and it
was feared that as long as Antonov continued to be at large, the capacity for a revival of hostilities in the province would remain.[9]

Quite early in the conflict, in October 1920, the Cheka in Tambov had sought
to trap Antonov by using his wife, Sofiia, to lure the rebel leader into their hands.
But Antonov had long since cut any close ties with his wife, having gone into hiding in Kirsanov uezd less than a year after they were wed, and the effort to capture
Antonov ended in disappointment; nevertheless, the Cheka honored their promise
to release Sofiia if she cooperated with state officials in the plot.[10] She was arrested
a second time in late March 1921, soon after the reorganization of the Tambov

Cheka organization, and sent to Moscow, where she joined her brother, Aleksandr, in prison. But no further efforts were made by the Cheka to utilize Sofiia Bogoliubskaia in efforts to capture Antonov, nor were Antonov's two sisters arrested for this purpose, even though both had been detained during earlier investigations regarding Aleksandr and Dmitrii before the outbreak of the rebellion in 1920. While Antonov had been the main target of the Cheka operations during the summer of 1921, in each case, agents had to settle for marginally lesser game, as Antonov himself proved elusive. The failure to locate and capture Antonov fueled the belief in Cheka circles that Antonov had withdrawn from participation following the head wound he sustained in early June 1921, or even that he had become the victim of a schism in the Partisan Army leadership, leaving him isolated and excluded from the rebel organization.[11]

In early October 1921, the Plenipotentiary Commission in Tambov was dissolved, and despite the continued presence of Red Army troops in the southern half of the province and the continued functioning of the sector military commands that formed the basis of the occupation system, the counterinsurgency campaign was rapidly drawing to a close. Scouting reports at the beginning of October placed the number of active rebel groups in the six military sectors at no more than fifteen, comprising an estimated 363 "bandits."[12] In the winter of 1921–1922, the search for Antonov fell to the Tambov Cheka, and specifically to the Antibanditry Department of the Criminal Investigations Unit, headed by Mikhail I. Pokaliukhin. While Pokaliukhin was able to cultivate many contacts who had been close to Antonov and to the rebel leadership, particularly among those who had surrendered and taken amnesty in 1921, the flow of information concerning the health and whereabouts of Antonov and his brother had dried up by the end of 1921, a state of affairs that persisted for the first months of 1922.

It was entirely by luck that the Cheka, now known by the acronym GPU, was alerted in late May 1922 to the possible location of the Antonovs when a pharmacist by the name of Firsov, in the village of Uvarovo in northeastern Borisoglebsk uezd, reported a visit to his pharmacy by a young woman who requested a supply of quinine expressly for the ailing Aleksandr Antonov, then in hiding in the woods near the small village of Nizhnii Shibriai. Her willingness to surrender such information to a stranger is explained by the fact that medicines such as quinine were in short supply and she evidently knew the pharmacist had once been a member of the PSR and personally knew Aleksandr Antonov. She was likely sent to Firsov on Antonov's instruction in hopes that he would help him cope with the malaria he had contracted after long months in the mosquito-infested forests and swamps of southeastern Tambov. After supplying the needed medicine, however, Firsov alerted the Tambov GPU and Pokaliukhin, who quickly organized surveillance of the village.

It transpired that the Antonovs had managed to cultivate a limited number of safe contacts in the village of Nizhnii Shibriai and had been in hiding in the area since at least Easter 1922. While they spent much of their time in the neighboring forest—a place they had previously used as a hiding place long before the outbreak of the insurgency[13]—in the evening they frequented the house of thirty-five-year-old Natalia Ivanovna Katasonova, a woman of limited means whose husband had died and whose brother was a former rebel, serving a term in a nearby camp. She had one boarder, the local schoolmistress, Sofiia Gavrilova Solov'eva, the young woman who had visited the pharmacist for quinine. Solov'eva had also run other errands for the Antonovs, such as traveling to the provincial capital to acquire newspapers. In fact, both women were quite close to the Antonovs, with Aleksandr having an intimate relationship with Katasonova, and the twenty-one-year-old Solov'eva allegedly taken with Dmitrii. The Antonovs' other main contact in the village was Katasonova's neighbor, the local miller, Vasilii Vladimirovich Ivanov, who provided the Antonovs with food and, in maintaining regular contact with them, also conveyed information from other close associates in the region. There were others who knew of the presence of the Antonovs near Nizhnii Shibriai and who safeguarded this secret, such as the local forestry official, Gerasim Ivanovich Lomakin, but none had such regular and close contact with the former partisans as the miller, the schoolmistress, and the widow.

The end for the Antonovs came on the evening of 24 June 1922. Taking a team of Cheka colleagues and trusted informants who had previously known and worked with Antonov in the Partisan Army, Pokaliukhin approached Katasonova's house after agents confirmed that the Antonovs were inside and placed his men around the perimeter of the four-room wooden home. Katasonova herself was found in the small adjoining barn after Pokaliukhin's knock on the locked door was unanswered. When asked who was in her house, she admitted that two armed men—unknown to her—were inside. Asked to tell the men to come out peacefully, she refused, fearing they would kill her.[14] Pokaliukhin approached the door and knocked a second time, and when the door began to open slightly, he was greeted by pistol shots.

The shoot-out that ensued between the Antonov brothers and the nine-man team assembled by Pokaliukhin lasted for over an hour without either side suffering casualties. Five of the eight men working with Pokaliukhin were former Partisan Army rebels, including Iakov Vasil'evich Sanfirov, who had been the commander of the "Special Regiment" that accompanied Antonov's Partisan Army headquarters.[15] They were the only ones who knew what Aleksandr Antonov looked like, although Pokaliukhin claimed to have a vague memory of Antonov from his time as chief of the Kirsanov uezd militia.[16] According to one memoirist, the brothers quickly learned that they were under fire by their erstwhile comrades and pleaded for them to show some loyalty. Instead, one threw a grenade at the house that started a fire. The flames quickly reached the roof, and it was only a matter of time before the Antonovs were forced out by the smoke. By this time, virtually the entire village of Nizhnii Shibriai had come out and assembled at a safe distance to watch the spectacle.

The moment the Antonovs leapt out of the windows of Katasonova's burning home, their assailants were temporarily thrown into a panic, but without a clear plan of escape, Aleksandr and Dmitrii ran aimlessly through the crossfire before reaching the street. By this time, Pokaliukhin and his men had composed themselves and two bullets fired from their pistols hit the brothers, with Dmitrii suffering the most serious wound, leaving him scarcely able to move. They continued their flight, however, onto the property of the miller, evidently hoping to reach the forest's edge, but their wounds brought them to a halt in Ivanov's garden, where they were discovered by their one-time trusted comrade, Iakov Sanfirov, who shot them. Pokaliukhin and his men hesitated before approaching the bodies, but after some ten minutes, they were reassured that the two former partisan leaders were finally dead.

Pokaliukhin recalled in his memoir of the event that the curious villagers who had gathered to investigate the shooting and smoke were all supportive of the government agents once they learned that Antonov was inside the house. When the bodies of the Antonov brothers began their journey back to Tambov, to be buried on the grounds of the seventeenth-century Kazan Monastery, now the headquarters of the GPU, residents of the villages they passed along the way would gather along the streets and cheer the deaths of the former rebel leader and his brother. Still, despite such reassuring expressions of popular support for the Soviet government, the provincial administration and Communist Party in Tambov nevertheless arranged for photographs of the lifeless bodies of Aleksandr and Dmitrii to be published in the local press, one of the first times photographs appeared in the newspapers of Tambov Province. The obvious intention was to reach as wide as audience as possible with evidence of the death of the famous bandits, suppressing any lingering hope that the former leader of the Partisan Army was still alive and capable of a return.

Whatever plan the Antonovs may have had about resuming their campaign of resistance to the Soviet state is impossible to determine, but such an event would have been highly unlikely, judging from reports of the popular reaction to the

The Antonov brothers following the shoot-out with Cheka agents, 22 June 1922. This image was distributed widely in Tambov province to confirm the deaths of the former rebel leaders. *Photograph courtesy of the Tambovskii Kraevedcheskii Muzei*

news of their deaths. While the rebellion had temporarily inspired a certain hope that the Soviet government could be overwhelmed by the vast yet disjointed wave of popular rebellion and protest throughout the former Russian Empire at the end of the civil war, suppression of the movement in Tambov had been achieved at tremendous human and material cost to the village communities of the province. The weight of the occupation of southern Tambov was felt in virtually every village and town of the region, for even households and families that had no significant connection with the insurgents were forced to make sacrifices to support the thousands of Red Army troops assigned to the province in 1921. As a member of the provincial soviet executive committee, G. Z. Zanegin, explained at the Eighth Congress of Soviets in Tambov in early December 1921:

> If you consider that the entire phenomenon of banditry in Tambov has had a singularly destructive character, then we on the soviet executive committee must also include in this the role played by the cadre of Red Army units that flooded Tambov Province. Leaving to one side the anarchical activities in which some of these units indulged during individual clashes with bandits in the villages, activities that resulted in colossal damage for the peasants and the local authorities, the huge wave of military forces that came into the province had a generally destructive character. Each town, village, and hamlet can support only a limited number of

people. Tambov and other towns were so overwhelmed by military personnel that one could barely even breathe, and there was absolutely no possibility that they could be adequately housed, and as a result we now find extensive damage everywhere. Tambov suffered much less as a consequence of Mamontov's raid [in 1919] than it has as a result of the military occupation of the past year.[17]

Zanegin had in mind the constraints on the food supply and the spread of infectious diseases as much as the broken windows and toppled street lamps left behind by the Red Army in the provincial capital.[18] In fact, it was the burden of the military occupation of the province on all public and private resources that was such a matter of controversy at the Eighth Congress, an occasion that was intended to forge a measure of political unity in the wake of the insurgency's defeat, but which proved to be as divisive and ill-tempered as its predecessor earlier in the year.

The first tax collection campaign under the NEP had been only a very qualified success, as the ongoing counterinsurgency operations throughout the summer and autumn complicated the organizational efforts of the Food Commissariat as much as the Red Army presence compromised the relations with village communities that the same commissariat was so desperate to repair.[19] While the tax in kind had initially captured the imagination of village producers, this quickly turned to anxiety as the harvest approached and so much about the functioning of the new system remained unclear. Part of this was attributable to the understandable difficulty of being required to completely alter the system, as well as the entire "ethic," of food procurement, but material shortages in the countryside and uncertainties regarding present and future harvests further complicated the transition to the tax in kind, as the commissariat was flooded with appeals from individual villages in response to the first publication of tax assessments in May 1921. Commissariat officials were under no illusions regarding their ability to conduct reliable assessments of the upcoming harvest yields, and the wave of angry appeals from individuals and communities only prompted them to revert to the same hard-line methods they had been accustomed to using in the face of local appeals regarding unfair procurement targets under the razverstka.[20]

In practice, however, when the tax campaign began in the autumn, commissariat agents proved much more flexible in their approach to collection, and this combined with an acknowledged lack of solid information concerning the harvest to generate a high degree of uncertainty within the Commissariat regarding the progress of the collection campaign.[21] Indeed, the Food Commissariat and Sovnarkom in Moscow also proved flexible to a certain degree, for despite demands by central officials that the tax burdens for individual provinces be met in full, they were willing to make allowances for provinces burdened by major military operations that had disrupted preparations for the tax campaign.[22] This was sensible, as it quickly became clear that the uezds that had suffered during the rebellion and under the burden of the Red Army occupation were unlikely to make significant contributions to the 1921 campaign. This was particularly true of Kirsanov and Borisoglebsk, where the estimated decline in sown acreage was the most dramatic.[23] As such, the final tax levied on cereal grains for the province was less than half of the razverstka set for 1920–1921, although it was roughly on a par with the revised target authorized by the Food Commisarist in January 1921.[24] By the end of 1921, the commissariat in Tambov had managed to collect nearly two-thirds of the tax on cereals, and tax revenues on other products, such as potatoes, climbed even higher after collection agents were authorized to accept "equivalent" products from producers in the place of scarce cereal grains.[25]

That Kirsanov and Borisoglebsk uezds contributed relatively little to the first tax campaign did not mean that these areas had escaped material hardship. In fact, these were the two areas where food supply concerns and fears of hunger and starvation generated the most volatility in the winter of 1921. Although the revolutionary committees had been withdrawn from much of the former territory of the insurgency, replaced by newly elected village and volost soviets and reports were encouraging regarding the reception of the tax in kind and more generally regarding popular attitudes toward the Soviet government, the problem of banditry persisted in these uezds through the end of the year.[26] Much of this involved former rebel outlaws who raided villages for food and supplies. But grain shortages were so severe that some village self-defense militias attempted to conduct forced food requisitions in other villages; in one case, a militia had to be arrested and disarmed by a nearby Cheka battalion, but only after an extended firefight that resulted in the death of one militiaman and the wounding of several others.[27] Such episodes increased as the year drew to a close, but in early December 1921 the provincial government in Tambov remained convinced that the banditry problem could be still be managed by the local Cheka and militia, and that the Red Army would not need to return to restore civil order.[28]

That same month, however, officials in Kirsanov uezd were given a fresh reminder, if any was necessary, of how rapidly low-level disturbances could transform into all-consuming chaos. Only a few weeks after complaining in reports about how village communities under the NEP were exclusively concerned with restoring the household economy, and thus indifferent to politics, the Communist Party in Kirsanov was confronted with a round of armed village uprisings that rapidly dismantled the newly restored network of village and volost soviets, occupied railway stations, and destroyed valuable infrastructure. In the area around Inzhavino, the garrison force of nearly 300 soldiers was overcome by an estimated 4,000 peasants bearing firearms and more "agricultural" weapons, and the entire personnel of the Cheka station in Inzhavino was, to a man, killed by insurgents. Over forty Communist Party members lost their lives, and officials in the uezd town of Kirsanov reacted much as they did in the autumn of 1920, by withdrawing all available armed forces and state agents in the countryside to the town itself and issuing urgent appeals to Moscow for military support. It seemed as if the worst fears regarding the Partisan Army and Antonov's "last order" were being realized, and the thousands of former rebels who had been granted amnesty and released back to their native villages were responding to a single call to rise against the Soviet state once more. But the crisis, so spectacular in its appearance in the second half of December, produced no slogans, no leaders, and no identifiable organization. The appearance of Red Army troops in Kirsanov quickly extinguished the outburst of rage that briefly consumed the uezd, although local officials in Kirsanov nevertheless felt compelled to justify their appeals to Moscow for armed assistance, no doubt sensitive to accusations of panic that had tarnished them a year before.[29]

This violent episode had its roots, first and foremost, in the anxieties over the food supply. While the tax in kind had been unevenly organized and irregularly collected in Kirsanov, shortages were most acute in this area following the destruction and displacement brought by the insurgency and the burdens imposed during its suppression. The fear of hunger and starvation were made more tangible by reports of real famine in the neighboring Volga region, for which appeals were being issued and collection drives organized in order to relieve what was already a human catastrophe.[30] The disturbances in Kirsanov were no doubt connected with the final push to meet the targets for grain procurement set for the 1921 tax campaign, but their severity is best understood against the backdrop of popular anxiety regarding famine and the vulnerable self-confidence of local party and state officials in a province that was only just emerging from a full year of rebellion and occupation.[31]

While the outburst of violence in Kirsanov in December 1921 demonstrated the fragility of state institutions and Soviet authority in the area, the episode also served to demonstrate just how far the region had become distanced from the rebellion that had dominated the political landscape for so many months. There was no return of Antonov on the strength of popular anxiety and anger, nor were there even rumors of a revival of the Partisan Army that could be invested with hopes for the future. Instead, those same hopes that rebel leaders had sought to

promote alongside participation in the insurgency had given way to resentment
of the experience of rebellion, an experience that had cost families and communities so much, and a resentment that was frequently directed at former rebels
who similarly sought to return to the lives they had led before the outbreak of the
civil war. Whereas popular grievances remained high while shortages and material
conditions were so oppressive, the brief outbreak of violence in Kirsanov in December served to demonstrate just how important Antonov and his co-conspirators
had been in actively transforming disorder and violence into organized rebellion.
The nature of the violence in December also demonstrated just how rapidly village communities had moved to distance themselves from the experience of the
antonovshchina.

If the memory of Antonov and the insurgency was kept alive at all, it was the
Soviet state that sought, in the short term, to provide reminders of the partisan
leader and his responsibility for the destruction that had been inflicted on the Tambov countryside. The trial of the Socialist Revolutionary Party (PSR), a drawn-
out process that began early in 1922, was accompanied by a nationwide propaganda
campaign in which civilians were enlisted to participate in drafting condemnatory
proclamations, encouraged to discuss the accusations against the PSR and its leadership, and even to attend screenings of the filmed proceedings of the trial once
it began.[32] The insurgency in Tambov, and the conspiracy that was attributed with
its creation, comprised an important facet of the case against the PSR, although
the accusations concerning the direct involvement of the PSR in the Partisan Army
and STK were given greater prominence in the trial itself and in the coverage by the
central press than they were in the accompanying campaign in Tambov Province.[33]
Instead, the coverage in Tambov principally concerned the damage and destruction caused by the rebellion, and any shortfalls in agricultural production and appearances of hunger and material shortage were laid directly at the feet of Antonov
and his co-conspirators. While the prosecutors in Moscow branded Antonov a
"political illiterate" and sought to portray him as a tool of the PSR Central Committee, Communist Party agitators in Tambov worked on the assumption that the
PSR—as an idea as much as an organization—continued to enjoy a certain measure
of authority and respect among the rural population, and the propaganda campaign
in the province that accompanied the trial became as much about Antonov as the
personal embodiment of the rebellion and the destruction it brought to Tambov
as it was about the PSR as a "counterrevolutionary" political party.[34]

It would be facile to claim that the propaganda campaign against Antonov and
the PSR in the first months of 1922 helped convince the people of Tambov that the
former partisan leader was responsible for the hardships that so many communi-

ties had endured and continued to suffer as they emerged from the civil war. In fact, Antonov, and the movement that he had led, had long since abdicated the role of speaking for the grievances, as well as to the hopes, of the beleaguered rural population. Amid the chaos, destruction, and deprivation that characterized the Soviet countryside in late 1921 and 1922, no person, party, or movement successfully spoke for those grievances, let alone articulated those hopes. The civil war period of risk, uncertainty, and possibility—when disparate political ideas, and even occasionally ideals, could be entertained and briefly inform individual and collective identities—had come to a close for the villages of Tambov, ushering in a period of desperate reconstruction and healing for so many families and communities. The Antonov rebellion had formed the final chapter in the history of the revolution and civil war in Tambov Province, but any legacy of the event was quickly lost as the occupation regime was wound down. The next few years saw the event consigned to history as communities sought to distance themselves from the experience and the memory of their involvement. Only when the peasantry was under assault once more at the end of the decade did the name Antonov creep back into circulation, although even then the memory of the rebellion did not provide a stable basis for the rallying of resistance to the Soviet state during its chaotic efforts to push village households into a system of collective farms.[35]

The story of the *antonovshchina* is, perhaps inevitably, a tragic one, and it would be incorrect to place the name of its leader, Aleksandr Antonov, in any imaginary pantheon of popular rebels against the state whose names live on in myth and folklore. Emelian Pugachev and Stenka Razin belonged to the long era of serfdom and autocracy, an era that consumed both of them, and Nester Makhno, while a contemporary of Antonov, assumed a peculiar status as a symbol of Ukrainian national identity rather than attaining a broader and lasting cultural resonance. Yet Antonov could boast no such legacy, and it was only with the fall of the Soviet Union that certain groups struggled, without success, to recover the memory of the rebellion and establish a place for the partisan leader in local and national culture. The Antonov movement, no less than the rebellions of Pugachev and Razin, belonged to a particular era, but in the case of Antonov, this era was the unusual and brief time of revolution and civil war in Russia. The history of the movement can teach us much about this particular era, about the anxieties and sense of the possible that make revolutions and civil wars such chaotic and fascinating periods. But it was an era that ultimately came to an abrupt end even before Aleksandr Antonov fought his last, desperate battle.

NOTES

Preface

1. The first work in English was Oliver H. Radkey, *The Unknown Civil War in Soviet Russia* (Palo Alto, CA: Hoover Institution Press, 1976). The first study of the Antonov rebellion examined the few primary source materials that existed in the West at the time. See Seth Singleton, "The Tambov Revolt (1920–1921)," *Slavic Review* 25 (1966).

2. See Donald J. Raleigh, *Experiencing Russia's Civil War: Politics, Society, and Revolutionary Culture in Saratov, 1917–1922* (Princeton: Princeton University Press, 2002). A detailed local study of politics in revolutionary Russia (published after this manuscript was completed) is Sarah Badcock, *Politics and the People in Revolutionary Russia: A Provincial History* (Cambridge: Cambridge University Press, 2007).

3. Peter Holquist, *Making War, Forging Revolution. Russia's Continuum of Crisis, 1914–1921* (Cambridge: Harvard University Press, 2002); Joshua Sanborn, *Drafting the Nation: Military Conscription, Total War, and Mass Politics, 1905–1925* (DeKalb: Northern Illinois University Press, 2003).

4. John Dickie, "A Word at War: The Italian Army and Brigandage 1860–1870," *History Workshop Journal* 33 (1992): 4.

5. As an example, see Vladimir Brovkin, ed., *The Bolsheviks in Russian Society: The Revolution and the Civil Wars* (New Haven: Yale University Press, 1997).

Chapter 1: Revolution and Recalcitrance

1. "Konets esero-bandita Antonova," *Izvestiia VTsIK*, 2 July 1922, 4.

2. V. I. Lenin, *Sochineniia*, 4th ed. (Moscow: Gosudarstvennoe izdatel'stvo politicheskoi literatury, 1941–1955), 32:160.

3. A. A. Sobol'eva, *Krest'ianskoe vosstanie v Tambovskoi gubernii (1920–1921 gg.): Bibliograficheskii ukazatel'* (Tambov: MINts, 1993); V. D. Dement'ev and V. V. Samoshkin, "Vosstanie krest'ian na tambovshchine v 1920–1921 godakh (obzor literatury)," *Istoriia SSSR* 6 (1990).

4. S. P. Klishin, "Tambovskie volki (razmyshleniia o geroiakh zemli tambovskoi)," *Tambovskie izvestiia*, 22 June 1999, 12. Klishin has written a historical novel on the Antonov rebellion, available for download from Russian white supremacist Internet sites.

5. Official cultural links between Tambov and the Vendée region in France, site of a broadly similar historical tragedy, were initiated after Aleksandr Solzhenitsyn addressed a bicentennial commemoration of the Vendée rebellion in September 1993 and spoke of the events in Tambov in 1920–1921, which he had researched in the 1960s. See Aleksandr Solzhenitsyn, "Slovo pri otkrytii pamiatnika Vandeiskomu vosstaniiu," *Vestnik russkogo khristianskogo dvizheniia* 168 (1993); Lev Lazarenko, "IMKA-Press i dni vandei na tambovshchine," *Vestnik russkogo khristianskogo dvizheniia* 170 (1994).

6. A succinct statement of the charge that deserters formed the core of anti-Soviet opposition was made in the summer of 1921, when Red Army officers surveyed the wreckage following the suppression of the Tambov insurgency: "Many obligations [during the civil war] fell upon the peasant, but the thrifty *muzhik* does not believe in obligation. As a consequence, opposition to the proletariat grew, . . . peasants hid their surplus grain by burying it in the ground, and they refused to send their sons to serve in the Red Army. Such evasion of military service, rejecting the call of the revolution, assumed significant proportions; . . . nearly nine-tenths of the service-age population in Tambov was deserters. Desertion possesses a political character, it is a protest against the revolution." Quoted in N. V. Fatueva, *Protivostoianie: krizis vlasti—tragediia naroda* (Riazan': Rus', 1996), 252. See also the article by the same officer, A. Kazakov, "Obshchie prichiny vozniknoveniia banditizma i krest'ianskikh vosstanii," *Krasnaia Armiia. Vestnik voenno-nauchnogo obshchestva pri voennoi akademii,* no. 9 (1921), 32–33.

7. M. A. Molodtsygin, *Krasnaia Armiia: rozhdenie i stanovlenie, 1917–1920 gg.* (Moscow: IRI RAN, 1997), 106–08. Trotsky never ruled out conscription, and in March 1918 declared that the regime was forced to rely on the "voluntary principle" of enlistment by the organizational shortcomings of the Soviet state, which made conscription unlikely in the short term. See Leon Trotsky, *How the Revolution Armed,* trans. Brian Pearce (London: New Park Publications, 1979), 1:43–44.

8. V. P. Portnov and M. M. Slavin, *Pravovye osnovy stroitel'stva Krasnoi Armii, 1918–1920 gg.: istoriko-iuridicheskoe issledovanie* (Moscow: Nauka, 1985), 109–11.

9. Small units mobilized from Tambov to engage Czechoslovak legionnaires at Rtishchevo in Saratov Province were defeated. Two captured Red Army soldiers were released with the instructions: "Go and tell the Russians that they are idiots. What do they want from us? We don't want any bloodshed, we just want to get out of Russia as quickly as we can." Quoted in V. V. Kanishchev and Iu. V. Meshcheriakov, *Anatomiia odnogo miatezha. Tambovskoe vosstanie, 17–19 iiuniia 1918 g.* (Tambov: Tambovskii gosudarstvennyi universitet, 1995), 59. See also *Bor'ba rabochikh i krest'ian pod rukovodstvom Bol'shevistskoi partii za ustanovlenie i uprochenie Sovetskoi vlasti v tambovskoi gubernii (1917–1918 gody): sbornik dokumentov* (Tambov: [s.n.], 1957), 157.

10. Kanishchev and Meshcheriakov, *Anatomiia,* 59; L. M. Spirin, *Klassy i partii v grazhdanskoi voine v rossii (1917–1920 gg.)* (Moscow: Mysl', 1968), 342–43. The original decrees setting out this first conscription campaign were not published until June. See *Dekrety sovetskoi vlasti* (Moscow: Izdatel'stvo politicheskoi literatury, 1957–1989), 2:428–29, 438–40, 507–08.

11. Iurii Meshcheriakov, "Ul'timatum [1]," *Gorod na Tsne,* 12 August 1997, 7.

12. In the elections to the Constituent Assembly in November 1917, the PSR won over 75 percent of the rural vote in Tambov Province, and the Bolsheviks 20 percent. This was a respectable showing for the Bolsheviks in a province with only 6.5 percent of its population officially categorized as urban, but the Bolsheviks evidently fared better in areas close to a substantial military garrison. In some cases, "herd voting" was evident. For instance, in Morshansk uezd, one of the five voting districts within Kulikov volost unanimously supported the Bolshevik Party. In two neighboring districts, the Bolshevik Party received only 98 votes out of a possible 3,000. See L. G. Protasov, *Vserossiiskoe uchreditel'noe sobranie: istoriia rozhdeniia i gibeli* (Moscow: ROSSPEN, 1997), 232–36.

13. The first uezd soviet to assert control over local administration was in Usman, in November 1917. In this town, where soldiers outnumbered townspeople, the military garrison

was the prime mover in events leading to the declaration of Soviet power. Other towns with large garrison populations—Lipetsk, Borisoglebsk—declared soviet power before the end of 1917. Kozlov, another such town, had both a large soldier population and many railway workers. See V. Andreev, "Vozniknovenie i razvitie Sovetskoi vlasti v Tambovskoi gubernii," *Kommunist*, no. 11 (1923). On the political activity of garrisoned soldiers in the Blackearth region of Russia in 1917, see also L. G. Protasov, *Soldaty garnizonov tsentral'noi Rossii v bor'be za vlast' sovetov* (Voronezh: Izdatel'stvo Voronezhskogo universiteta, 1978).

14. Kanishchev and Meshcheriakov, *Anatomiia*, 69.

15. Similar demands were made by French villagers during the mobilization for war with Prussia. See Bertrand Taithe, *Citizenship and Wars: France in Turmoil, 1870–1871* (London: Routledge, 2001), 23.

16. The Soviet government was just beginning to grapple with the problem of disarming the rural population. According to Trotsky, the soldiers demobilized in 1917 left with their firearms, and the village communities guarded these weapons fiercely against attempts to repossess them. Similarly, a problem for the new Red Army was that the cavalry reserves of the former tsarist army had melted away with the demobilization of soldiers in 1917. These became serious issues when the Red Army was taking shape in the summer of 1918. See V. V. Ovechkin, "Iz"iatie loshadei u naseleniia dlia Krasnoi armii v gody grazhdanskoi voiny," *Voprosy istorii* 8 (1999); Trotsky, *How the Revolution Armed*, 1:427–28; Sanborn, *Drafting the Russian Nation*, 179; S. V. Starikov, *Demobilizovannye revoliutsionnye soldaty i oktiabr'skaia revoliutsiia v derevne* (Saransk: Izdatel'stvo Saratovskogo universiteta, 1989), 41–42.

17. Kanishchev and Meshcheriakov, *Anatomiia*, 67–68. The demand for firearms and for general military training was strong in other parts of the Soviet territory, as well. See Alexis Berelowitch and V. P. Danilov, eds., *Sovetskaia derevnia glazami VChK-OGPU-NKVD, 1918– 1939: dokumenty i materialy* (Moscow: ROSSPEN, 1998), 1:71; Starikov, *Demobilizovannye*, 150–51. There are parallels with efforts by the French republican officials to mobilize peasants, as one community's response from 1793 makes clear: "You speak of enemies who threaten our homes; it is there that we shall be able to push them back if they come to attack us; it is there, against them and against all others, that we shall defend our women, our animals, our harvests or else we shall perish together." Quoted in Yves-Marie Bercé, *Croquants et nu-pieds: les soulèvements paysans en France du XVIe au XIXe siècle* (Paris: Gallimard, 1991), 185.

18. V. V. Kabanov, "Oktiabr'skaia revoliutsiia i krest'ianskaia obshchina," *Istoricheskie zapiski* 111 (1984).

19. P. S. Kabytov et al., *Russkoe krest'ianstvo: etapy dukhovnogo osvobozhdeniia* (Moscow: Mysl', 1988), 114.

20. Portnov and Slavin, *Pravovye osnovy stroitel'stva Krasnoi Armii, 1918–1920 gg.*, 112.

21. John Bushnell, *Mutiny amid Repression: Russian Soldiers in the Revolution of 1905–1906* (Bloomington: Indiana University Press, 1985); A. B. Berkevich, "Krest'ianstvo i vseobshchaia mobilizatsiia v iiule 1914 g.," *Istoricheskie zapiski* 23 (1947); Joshua Sanborn, "The Mobilization of 1914 and the Question of the Russian Nation: A Re-examination," *Slavic Review* 59, no. 2 (2000).

22. On the early organization of local military commissariats, see E. G. Gimpel'son, "Iz istorii organizatsii mestnogo voennogo upravleniia (1918–1920 gg.)," in *Grazhdanskaia voina v rossii: sobytiia, mnenii, otsenki*, ed. N. A. Ivnitskii (Moscow: Raritet, 2002).

23. Mikhail G. Kolosov, quoted in Kanishchev and Meshcheriakov, *Anatomiia*, 60.

24. On the uprising in Tambov, 17–19 June 1918, see Kanishchev and Meshcheriakov, *Anatomiia*.

25. Raleigh, *Experiencing Russia's Civil War*, 55–56.

26. The settled balance of the coalition upon its assumption of control over the Soviet executive committee in Tambov Province in April 1918 was fifteen Bolshevik members and ten LSRs. This provincial coalition took shape after the LSRs had walked out of the Sovnarkom in March 1918 in protest of the Brest-Litovsk Treaty. The LSR central committee urged its members to remain in local government and other bureaucratic posts, but by June 1918, there would be no LSRs on the Tambov soviet executive committee. Still, the LSRs maintained a strong presence in local administrations, and an outright exclusion so early in the development of Soviet administration in the province would have been unworkable, owing to the organizational weakness of the Bolshevik Party in the province. Following the failed uprising in Moscow in July 1918 and the formal collapse of the coalition, LSRs in local administrations were tolerated in Tambov, so long as individual LSRs formally denounced the actions of their central committee. See N. A. Okatov et al., eds., *Sovety Tambovskoi gubernii v gody grazhdanskoi voiny, 1918–1921 gg.* (Voronezh: Tsentral'no-chernozemnoe knizhnoe izdatel'stvo, 1989), 74–75; V. V. Shelokhaev et al., eds., *Partiia levykh sotsialistov-revoliutsionnerov, 1917–1925: dokumenty i materialy* (Moscow: ROSSPEN, 2000), 1:183. Reactions by regional LSR party organizations and the local soviet administration are surveyed in Ia. V. Leont'ev, "6 Iuliia 1918 goda: regional'nyi aspekt," in *Grazhdanskaia voina v rossii: sobytiia, mnenii, otsenki*, ed. N. A. Ivnitskii (Moscow: Raritet, 2002).

27. Village communities facing the demands of state food procurement agents in June 1918 were emboldened by news that the provincial soviet administration had been overthrown on 17 June, and for a brief time many clung to this received information to justify continued defiance. See Iurii Meshcheriakov, "Ul'timatum [2]," *Gorod na Tsne*, 19 August 1997.

28. In the consecutive mobilizations between June and August 1918, the Red Army conscripted some 560,000 soldiers, but most were from the major industrial centers and areas immediately threatened by military conflict. See S. M. Kliatskin, *Na zashchite oktiabria* (Moscow: Nauka, 1965), 201.

29. The Red Army experienced major setbacks in conscripting the general population in 1918, but enjoyed success in the cities, broadening the scope of mobilization in Petrograd and Moscow to offset shortfalls in provincial centers. See Molodtsygin, *Krasnaia Armiia: rozhdenie i stanovlenie, 1917–1920 gg.*, 121; David Footman, *Civil War in Russia* (London: Faber and Faber, 1961), 158.

30. Membership of the RKP(b) in Tambov was 2,700 in August 1918. See *Perepiska sekretariata TsKa RKP(b) s mestnymi partiinymi organizatsiiami* (Moscow: Gosudarstvennoe izdatel'stvo politicheskoi literatury, 1957–), 4:173.

31. Kanishchev and Meshcheriakov, *Anatomiia*, 249. If the Bolshevik Party leadership in Tambov was considered weak, this was not reflected in an independence of mind that made other provincial organizations troublesome for central party leaders. In an August 1918 report, the Moscow regional party committee listed Tambov as having one of the best party organizations in the region. See *Perepiska sekretariata*, 4:254–55.

32. Orlando Figes, *Peasant Russia, Civil War: The Volga Countryside in Revolution, 1917–1921* (Oxford: Clarendon Press, 1989), 64–66.

33. When the organization of kombedy was made the first priority of the Tambov Communist Party, no fewer than six party activists from Petrograd assumed positions on the provincial party committee. See A. Ia. Pereverzev, *Sotsialisticheskaia revoliutsiia v derevne chernozemnogo tsentra rossii* (Voronezh: Izdatel'stvo Voronezhskogo universiteta, 1976), 111–12, 116–17. One survey of kombedy revealed that the organization of only one-third of local committees had been initiated by local cells of the Communist Party in Tambov Province. Similar results were reported for neighboring provinces. See T. V. Osipova, *Rossiiskoe krest'ianstvo v revoliutsii i grazhdanskoi voine* (Moscow: Strelets, 2001), 179.

34. In Morshansk uezd, four out of five party workers sent out to organize kombedy were sailors from the Black Sea fleet. This contingent, in Morshansk ostensibly for a Bolshevik Party conference, were unusually influential in establishing Soviet power in the uezd in the late summer and autumn of 1918. See N. N. Azovtsev, *Grazhdanskaia voina v SSSR.* (Moscow: Voenizdat, 1980), 1:207–09; S. F. Tylik, "Komitety bednoty v Tambovskoi gubernii," *Vestnik leningradskogo universiteta: seriia istorii, iazyka i literaturii* 18, no. 8 (1963): 43; Pereverzev, *Sotsialisticheskaia revoliutsiia,* 118. Roughly one-third of the village-level committees in the province were organized in Kozlov uezd, another major center for garrisoning and assigning Red Army troops. See Fatueva, *Protivostoianie,* 35.

35. Some 20 percent of local kombedy in Tambov Province were organized on the initiative of volost soviet organizations. Osipova, *Rossiiskoe,* 182.

36. Figes, *Peasant Russia,* 193–94; Tylik, "Komitety," 44; Okatov et al., *Sovety Tambovskoi gubernii,* 123; V. P. Antonov-Saratovskii, ed., *Sovety v epokhu voennogo kommunizma (1918–1921): sbornik dokumentov* (Moscow: Izdatel'stvo kommunisticheskoi akademii, 1928), 1:357–58.

37. S. F. Tylik, "Vedushchaia rol' rabochikh Petrograda, Moskvy, i drugikh tsentrov v revoliutsionnykh preobrazovaniakh v derevne v 1918 g. (po materialam tambovskoi gubernii)," in *Iz istorii Velikoi Oktiabr'skoi sotsialisticheskoi revoliutsii i sotsialisticheskogo stroitel'stva v SSSR,* ed. V. A. Ovsiakin (Leningrad: Nauk, 1967), 157.

38. At the beginning of October 1918 there were just over 4,800 requisition agents in the province. By the end of 1918, there would be 5,546 such agents, organized into forty-eight squads—more than in any other province in Soviet territory. See G. A. Belov, ed., *Iz istorii grazhdanskoi voiny v SSSR: sbornik dokumentov i materialov v trekh tomakh* (Moscow: Sovetskaia Rossiia, 1960), 1:297; Alessandro Stanziani, "La gestion des approvisionnements et la restauration de la *gosudarstvennost'*: le *Narkomprod,* l'armee, et les paysans," *Cahiers du Monde russe* 38, nos. 1–2 (1997): 87. According to another source, the number of requisition workers in Tambov was much greater in August and September—11,325—at a time when such workers were intended to be aiding with the harvest and registering the quantities of grain. (This figure seems inflated.) See A. Ia. Pereberzev, *Velikii Oktiabr' i pereobrazovanie derevni* (Voronezh: Tsentral'noe-Chernozemnoe knizhnoe izdatel'stvo, 1987), 61. Also Aleksei M Chernykh, "Rol' gubernii chernozemnogo tsentra v reshenii zadach prodovol'stvennoi politiki v Rossii (1918–1920 gg.)" (Candidate's diss., Moskovskaia gosudarstvennaia akademiia im. Skriabina, 1996), 170.

39. Pereverzev, *Sotsialisticheskaia revoliutsiia*, 147–48. Some procurement agents became members of these local kombedy, just as garrisoned soldiers and non-native Communist Party became members of committees they helped establish.

40. Tylik, "Komitety," 44; Tylik, "Vedushchaia rol' rabochikh Petrograda, Moskvy, i drugikh tsentrov v revoliutsionnykh preobrazovaniakh v derevne v 1918 g. (po materialam tambovskoi gubernii)," 163–64. Tylik gives slightly higher figures in his later essay, but his conclusion that some 95 percent of all local-level kombedy were established in August and September remains unchanged.

41. The plan adopted by the Soviet government in May 1918 called for a Red Army of some eighty-eight infantry divisions, thirty of which would be held in strategic reserve. On 11 September, RVSR scrapped these plans and ordered the formation of only eleven large divisions, composed of nine regiments each, to be held in reserve. See P. Dmitriev, "Sozdanie strategicheskikh rezervov Krasnoi Armii v gody grazhdanskoi voiny," *Voenno-istoricheskii zhurnal* 6 (1974): 66.

42. Molodtsygin, *Krasnaia Armiia: rozhdenie i stanovlenie, 1917–1920 gg.*, 127.

43. Evan Mawdsley, *The Russian Civil War*, 2nd ed. (Edinburgh: Birlinn, 2000), 63, 182; Molodtsygin, *Krasnaia Armiia: rozhdenie i stanovlenie, 1917–1920 gg.*, 165; A. I. Panov, ed., *Ofitserskii korpus v politicheskoi istorii Rossii. Dokumenty i materialy* (Moscow: Eidos, 2002), 2:438–40.

44. G. V. Sharapov et al., eds., *Istoriia sovetskogo krest'ianstva* (Moscow: Nauka, 1986), 1:132.

45. The formation of local military committees (*voenkomy*) was ordered by Sovnarkom on 8 April 1918. According to Gimpel'son, by the end of 1918, there were 7 regional military commissariats in Soviet Russia, 39 provincial offices, 385 uezd-level, and around 7,000 volost-level offices of the commissariat. This contrasts with the statistics for mid-June 1918, on the eve of the first general mobilization and before the introduction of the kombedy, at which time there were only 3 regional, 26 provincial, 190 uezd-level, and a grand total of 13 volost-level offices of the commissariat in Soviet Russia. Gimpel'son, "6 Iuliia 1918," 352–54; E. G. Gimpel'son, *Sovety v gody inostrannoi interventsii i grazhdanskoi voiny* (Moscow: Nauka, 1968), 287–88.

46. See the resolution on "Red Terror" adopted by the Morshansk uezd Congress of Village Kombedy, 13 September 1918. *Bor'ba rabochikh i krest'ian*, 211.

47. Pereverzev, *Sotsialisticheskaia revoliutsiia*, 121–23.

48. RGASPI f. 17, op. 65, d. 67, ll. 4–5.

49. Silvana Malle, *The Economic Organization of War Communism, 1918–1921* (Cambridge: Cambridge University Press, 1985), 338–49.

50. *Bor'ba rabochikh i krest'ian*, 182; Iurii Meshcheriakov, "Stolknovenie [1]," *Gorod na Tsne*, 25 March 1998; Iurii Meshcheriakov, "Stolknovenie [2]," *Gorod na Tsne*, 1 April 1998; Iurii Meshcheriakov, "Stolknovenie [3]," *Gorod na Tsne*, 8 April 1998. The resolution passed by the dissident "extraordinary" congress warned local inhabitants: "At the time of the harvest, there will be merciless requisitioning. We must be united."

51. Following this incident, an officer in the Second Morshansk Aviation Group, Kezhun, requested permission from the chairman of the military-revolutionary council in Morshansk to disperse crowds of marchers with machine guns fired from light aircraft. The uprising began anew a few days later, but it is unknown whether Kezhun's request was granted. See

V. Danilov and T. Shanin, eds., *Krest'ianskoe dvizhenie v Tambovskoi gubernii, 1917–1918. Dokumenty i materialy* (Moscow: ROSSPEN, 2003), 368. See also Danilov and Shanin, *KDT*, 373–76, 383–85.

52. GATO f. R-5201, op. 2, d. 96, ll. 600b, 81; GATO f. R-5201, op. 2, d. 82, ll. 15–150b.

53. *Bor'ba rabochikh i krest'ian*, 229; Okatov et al., *Sovety Tambovskoi gubernii*, 121.

54. *Bor'ba rabochikh i krest'ian*, 240–44. Okatov et al., *Sovety Tambovskoi gubernii*, 121–22; Berelowitch and Danilov, *Sovetskaia derevnia* 1:105. A serious disturbance occurred in Borisoglebsk, where mobilized junior officers were joined by members of the Borisoglebsk Cheka, who were themselves on the conscription list. The insurgents seized some twenty machine guns and two light artillery guns on 4 October 1918 and addressed a meeting in the town center calling for, among other things, the reelection of the soviets, restrictions on the powers of the Cheka, and purging all Jews from the state administration. (As if the call for restictions on the Cheka—by Chekists—was not curious enough, the insurgents also called for the arrest of all former imperial army officers, which probably complicated attempts of Soviet officials to brand this another "whiteguardist" conspiracy.) The uprising was short-lived, however, ending after less than twenty-four hours, and with the municipal soviet chairman, Savin, the only notable casualty. See Danilov and Shanin, *KDT*, 363.

55. Osipova, *Rossiiskoe*, 262; Fatueva, *Protivostoianie*; Spirin, *Klassy i partii v grazhdanskoi voine v rossii (1917–1920 gg.)*, 183. The most severely affected uezds were Morshansk, Tambov, Kirsanov, and Shatsk. (Some description of these events can be found in Osipova, *Rossiiskoe*, 267–70, although the author confuses many details and place names, collapsing several dispersed events into a single uprising.) Possibly the most serious incident occurred in Shatsk, where the town was virtually surrounded by insurgents from the countryside in early November 1918. The local Communist Party and militia and Red Army men braced for a siege, but the uprising was suppressed when reinforcements armed with light artillery arrived on 6 November. See Danilov and Shanin, *KDT*, 380–81.

56. GATO f. R-5201, op. 2, d. 178, ll. 9–10. Parish church bells were traditionally used to sound the alarm in case of fire. On disturbances in the area around Levye Lamki, see Okatov et al., *Sovety Tambovskoi gubernii*, 129–30.

57. GATO f. R-5201, op. 2, d. 178, l. 10.

58. At the Fourth Tambov Congress of Soviets in February–March 1919, the report of the provincial department of administration spoke first of the planned conspiratorial nature of the November uprisings and, second, noted that in November 1918 four state policies—all "painful" for village communities—were introduced: military conscription, collection of an extraordinary monetary tax, requisition of grain surpluses, and the decree on separation of church and state. See Antonov-Saratovskii, *Sovety*, 1:151. Some state officials remained convinced that the uprisings were the work of foreign and domestic enemies of the revolution. See Berelowitch and Danilov, *Sovetskaia derevnia* 1:110.

59. State officials were aware of the variety of causes of uprisings throughout Soviet territory and sought to gain a composite picture in their requests for reports from provincial administration officials. See V. Danilov and T. Shanin, eds., *Krest'ianskoe dvizhenie v Povolzh'e, 1919–1922. Dokumenty i materialy* (Moscow: ROSSPEN, 2002), 33–34.

60. GATO f. R-1236, op. 1, d. 137, ll. 58–59. For contemporary appeals concerning the need to contain panic, see *Bor'ba rabochikh i krest'ian*, 242–43.

61. On "mobilization" of horses by the state in 1918, see Ovechkin, "Iz"iatie"; Sharapov et al., *Istoriia*, 133. The fate of parish churches was also of concern as the government cemented its presence in the countryside. Many uprisings were triggered by incidents that reflected people's concern for the sanctity of their local church. For example, see Danilov and Shanin, *KDT*, 379. Nevertheless, some local officials were convinced that the "people" were being won over to the secularizing principles of the revolution. See *Perepiska sekretariata*, 5:105–06.

62. For research into similar events in the northern provinces, see S. V. Iarov, "Krest'ianskie volneniia na Severo-Zapade sovetskoi Rossii v 1918–1919 gg.," *Krest'ianovedenie: Teoriia, istoriia, sovremennost'* 1 (1996).

63. GATO f. R-5201, op. 2, d. 94, l. 22.

64. Fatueva, *Protivostoianie*, 40.

65. V. V. Britov, *Rozhdenie Krasnoi Armii* (Moscow: Gosudarstvennoe uchebno-pedagogicheskoe izdatel'stvo, 1961), 231. On mobilization of officers and junior officers throughout the civil war, see A. L. Kublanov, *Sovet rabochei i krest'ianskoi oborony* (*noiabr' 1918–mart 1920 g.*) (Leningrad: Izdatel'stvo Leningradskogo universiteta, 1975), 52. For results in Tambov Province, see RGVA f. 25883, op. 1, d. 946, l. 290.

66. *Bor'ba rabochikh i krest'ian*, 205; *Perepiska sekretariata*, 5:349, 354–56; Okatov et al., *Sovety Tambovskoi gubernii*, 128–29; V. P. Portnov, ed., *Partiino-politicheskaia rabota v krasnoi armii* (*aprel' 1918–fevral' 1919*). *Dokumenty* (Moscow: MinOborony SSSR, 1961), 126–28, 292.

67. Mark Von Hagen, *Soldiers in the Proletarian Dictatorship: The Red Army and the Soviet Socialist State, 1917–1930* (Ithaca: Cornell University Press, 1990), 48.

68. The collapse of resistance in Borisoglebsk occurred despite the best efforts of the uezd Communist Party to prepare for the street fighting that they feared would accompany "white-guardist" uprisings. See *Perepiska sekretariata*, 4:315; V. Danilov and T. Shanin, eds., *Krest'ianskoe vosstanie v Tambovskoi gubernii v 1919–1921 gg. "Antonovshchina": dokumenty i materialy* (Tambov: Intertsentr, 1994), 27; E. A. Nakrokhin, *Inogo ne bylo puti* (Voronezh: Izdatel'stvo Voronezhskogo universiteta, 1975), 87–94. Later reports by Borisoglebsk administration and party sources stated that some 300 people in Borisoglebsk were executed by the Cossacks during the occupation. Most were Communist Party members and soviet personnel who failed to evacuate, but one source insists that civilians were often executed for the slightest infringements: "Women and children suffered terrible abuses (*izdevatel'stva*), and the Cossacks shot people for nothing more than [for example] dancing Latin-style dances." See RGASPI f. 17, op. 65, d. 68, ll. 1–20b.

69. The town was retaken by the Red Army on 7 January 1919. Borisoglebsk officials, meeting at the uezd Congress of Soviets in February 1919 emphasized the collaboration of local Menshevik and SR party members with the Don Cossacks during the occupation. What they failed to mention, and which was raised one week later by provincial officials at the Fourth Tambov Congress of Soviets, was that over eighty Borisoglebsk soviet personnel and Communist Party members had defected to the Don Cossacks during the occupation and left town with the Cossacks who managed to escape on 6 January 1919. See Antonov-Saratovskii, *Sovety*, 1:152–53, 428.

70. RGVA f. 25887, op. 1, d. 816, ll. 46, 56, 56ob; d. 819, ll. 23–230b, 24, 25, 117, 155.

71. Likewise, the stability of the Provisional Government in 1917 was seriously compromised by riots involving garrisoned soldiers in provincial cities and towns. See V. I. Kostrikin,

Zemel'nye komitety v 1917 godu (Moscow: Nauka, 1975), 282–84; V. V. Kanishchev, *Russkii bunt, bessmyslennyi i besposhchadnyi: pogromnoe dvizhenie v gorodakh Rossii v 1917–1918 gg.* (Tambov: Tambovskii gosudarstvennyi universitet im. Derzhavina, 1995), 71, 72–73; Kanishchev and Meshcheriakov, *Anatomiia*, 6–9.

72. RGVA f. 25887, op. 1, d. 819, ll. 193–94.

73. "Postanovlenie soveta oborony o bor'be s dezertirstvom," 25 December 1918. See *Dekrety sovetskoi vlasti*, 4:254–56.

74. M. A. Molodtsygin, *Raboche-krest'ianskii soiuz, 1918–1920* (Moscow: Nauka, 1987), 138.

75. Molodtsygin, *Raboche-krest'ianskii soiuz, 1918–1920*, 68–91.

76. Lars T. Lih, *Bread and Authority in Russia, 1914–1921* (Berkeley: University of California Press, 1990), 148. Villagers who participated in the march toward Morshansk in October 1918 demanded a return to the popularly elected soviets, a demand later investigators found far from "counterrevolutionary." See GATO f. R-5201, op. 2, d. 90, l. 163.

77. In one case, violent clashes between villagers and Communist Party officials occurred in Andreevka (Borisoglebsk uezd), where a village assembly proceeded with elections while disregarding the electoral list handed down by party officials that excluded so-called kulaks—identified as more than one in five adults in the locality. When party officials nullified the election results, they were confronted by a mob of villagers. Red Army soldiers were called in after shots were fired by the panicked party members, and over thirty-five arrests were made. See GATO f. R-5201, op. 2, d. 399, ll. 1–2, 5, 71 73; Okatov et al., *Sovety Tambovskoi gubernii*, 162.

78. Antonov-Saratovskii, *Sovety*, 1:153; Portnov, *Partiino-politicheskaia rabota*, 292; *Perepiska sekretariata*, 6:166.

79. Gimpel'son, *Sovety*, 484; Figes, *Peasant Russia*, 211–12, 219.

80. Molodtsygin, *Raboche-krest'ianskii soiuz, 1918–1920*, 254.

81. RGVA f. 25887, op. 1, d. 819, ll. 193–94.

82. Molodtsygin, *Krasnaia Armiia: rozhdenie i stanovlenie, 1917–1920 gg.*, 131–32; V. M. Andreev, *Rossiiskoe krest'ianstvo: navstrechu sud'be* (Moscow: Moskovskii Pedagogicheskii Gosudarstvennyi Universitet, 1997), 130–31. In many cases volost administrations dispatched individuals who were patently unsuited for military service, such as invalids and the elderly. In Iaroslavl Province, over 30 percent of those who were mobilized deserted before they were assigned to units. See Molodtsygin, *Krasnaia Armiia: rozhdenie i stanovlenie, 1917–1920 gg.*, 134.

83. Molodtsygin, *Raboche-krest'ianskii soiuz, 1918–1920*, 129–38; Mark A. Weitz, *A Higher Duty: Desertion among Georgia Troops during the Civil War* (Lincoln: University of Nebraska Press, 2000).

84. Molodtsygin, *Krasnaia Armiia: rozhdenie i stanovlenie, 1917–1920 gg.*, 178.

85. Britov, *Rozhdenie*, 230.

86. RGASPI f. 17, op. 65, d. 67, l. 46; *Perepiska sekretariata*, 7:474, 480.

87. An official from the Ministry of Internal Affairs in Penza wrote of an acquaintance working in Tambov, in his native Morshansk uezd: "[The men in the village of Lipovka] were refusing to enter the Red Army. They had sent a delegation to comrade Lipin [the local soviet chairman], who gave them his word that they would not be forced into the army. I was told about this from comrade Gavrilov, who learned about it from some friends in Solominka who did not know that he was a Communist Party member. It should be pointed out that Gavrilov is the son of a local priest, and therefore people in the area treat him with full con-

fidence, even though he in fact is a very active member of the party and is even an editor of our uezd's Communist Party newspaper." GATO f. R-394, op. 1, 278, l. 400b (15 May 1919).

88. Danilov and Shanin, *KV*, 29–30. The introduction of antidesertion patrols mirrors the introduction of the *colonnes mobiles* under Napoleon, a similar escalation in the French state's struggle with desertion in the early nineteenth century. See Alan Forrest, *Conscripts and Deserters: The Army and French Society During the Revolution and Empire* (Oxford: Oxford University Press, 1989), 211–13.

89. The tactic of lying low in areas previously searched by the antidesertion patrols was extremely common, as state officials quickly learned. RGVA f. 25883, op. 1, d. 283, l. 20b; f. 25887, op. 1, d. 819, ll. 193–94.

90. According to Okninskii, the commander spoke perfect Russian but with a distinctively "foreign" accent.

91. S. Olikov, *Dezertirstvo v Krasnoi armii i bor'ba s nim* (Leningrad: Izdatel'stvo shtaba, 1926), 39–40, 59.

92. Anton Okninskii, *Dva goda sredi krest'ian: vidennoe, slyshannoe, perezhitoe v Tambovskoi gubernii s noiabria 1918 goda do noiabria 1920 goda* (Newtonville, MA: Oriental Research Partners, 1986), 122–30.

93. The lion's share of recently mobilized reservists assigned for active duty as reinforcements were sent to the eastern front. Nevertheless, the Red Army consistently enjoyed a numerical superiority over its enemies on the southern front. See P. Dmitriev, "Ispol'zovanie strategicheskikh rezervov Krasnoi Armii v vesennei kampanii 1919 goda," *Voenno-istoricheskii zhurnal* 9 (1976): 63–64; Mawdsley, *Russian Civil War*, 169.

94. RGVA f. 25887, op. 1, d. 819, l. 390.

95. RGVA f. 25887, op. 1, d. 819, ll. 227, 2270b, 228, 2280b, 229, 577; f. 11, op. 8, d. 232, l. 5.

96. Tambov formed this line of defense with Kursk, Voronezh, and Kamyshin. N. M. Viunov et al., eds., *Direktivy Glavnogo komandovaniia Krasnoi Armii, 1917–1920: Sbornik dokumentov* (Moscow: Voenizdat, 1969), 427, 432.

97. The fortified region (*ukreplennyi raion*) was declared in the press on 18 June 1919. The southern portion of the province was placed under the control of a special council, headed by the provincial military commissar, K. V. Redz'ko. Okatov et al., *Sovety Tambovskoi gubernii*, 171. Tambov Province was also transferred at this time from the Moscow military sector to the Orel sector. V. O. Daines and T. F. Kariaev, eds., *Revvoensovet Respubliki. Protokoly, 1918–1919 gg.* (Moscow: Russkii mir, 1997), 252.

98. Declaration of martial law sent a panic through the city of Tambov, and the provincial Cheka and municipal authorities were prompted to issue a supplementary declaration spelling out the crimes that would invite summary execution as reassurance that "the Communists have no plans to begin slaughtering the people of Tambov city." See Danilov and Shanin, *KV*, 31.

99. Pavel A. Aptekar', "Soprotivlenie krest'ian politike Bol'shevikov v 1918–1922 godakh" (Candidate's diss., Moskovskii gosudarstvennyi universitet im. Lomonosov, 2002), 160; Okatov et al., *Sovety Tambovskoi gubernii*, 215.

100. Okatov et al., *Sovety Tambovskoi gubernii*, 175–77; Danilov and Shanin, *KV*, 33–34. The Communist Party began speaking of a "turning point" in the struggle against desertion as early as July. As explained in the famous circular letter entitled "All Out for the Fight Against

Denikin!" "The reasons [for the mass return of deserters] are, first, the more capable and systematic work of our party comrades; second, the peasants are growing more aware of the fact that a victory for Kolchak and Denikin would mean the establishment of conditions far worse than those suffered during tsarist times—the enslavement of the workers and peasants, flogging, robbery, and abuse from officers and landlords." V. I. Lenin, *Polnoe sobranie sochinenii*, 5th ed. (Moscow: Gosudarstvennoe izdatel'stvo politicheskoi literatury, 1958–1965), 39:94.

101. Osipova, *Rossiiskoe*, 319–20.

102. RGVA f. 11, op. 8, d. 232, l. 132. Riots did occur in Mtsensk, where recently returned deserters overwhelmed guards and searched private houses for food, an ominous development for military officials. See RGVA f. 11, op. 8, d. 232, ll. 37, 400b.

103. K. V. Agureev, *Razgrom belogvardeiskikh voisk Denikina* (Moscow: Voenizdat, 1961), 82. Most of the shortfalls at the front in the autumn of 1919 were made up by mobilizations of Communist Party, Komsomol, and trade union members. See P. Dmitriev, "Ispol'zovanie strategicheskikh rezervov Krasnoi Armii v osenne-zimnei kampanii 1919–1920 gg.," *Voenno-istoricheskii zhurnal* 10 (1979): 46. The Antidesertion Commission filtered apprehended deserters into two basic groups, "malicious" (*zlostnyi*) and "weak-willed" (*po slabosti voli*, or simply *nezlostnyi*). "Malicious" deserters were those who overstayed leave time by fourteen or more days; deserted with army-issue equipment, including firearms; resisted or evaded capture by antidesertion authorities; deserted more than once. Such men were to be tried before revolutionary tribunals, with sentences ranging from reassignment to reserve units, assignment to penal units and prison camps, to (in rare cases) execution. Because of the manpower shortage in the summer of 1919, antidesertion officials were instructed to distinguish between those who had been captured and those who had surrendered. From the latter group, those who had received military training and were deemed dependable could be assigned to active duty. The remainder were assigned to reserve units. See RGVA f. 11, op. 8, d. 232, l. 49; RGASPI f. 17, op. 65, d. 68, l. 91; Orlando Figes, "The Red Army and Mass Mobilization during the Russian Civil War, 1918–1920," *Past and Present* 129 (1990): 199; Hagen, *Soldiers*, 76.

104. RGVA f. 11, op. 8, d. 232, ll. 17, 49, 57.

105. RGVA f. 25883, op. 1, d. 150, l. 114.

106. Daines and Kariaev, eds., *Revvoensovet*, 288.; RGVA f. 11, op. 8, d. 232, l. 147. While the chief of staff at Supreme Headquarters, N. I. Rattel', instructed some military commissariats to send these deserters to portions of the front in need of reinforcement, without regard to their material condition (send them "as they are"), Trotsky complained that local commissariats were simply "dumping" (*brasaiut*) lots of deserters on front-line units. Yet, front-line commanders were requesting reinforcements by asking for "X number of *deserters*," rather than "soldiers" or "reservists." (ibid., ll. 5, 26, 27, 28, 29, 149)

107. RGVA f. 11, op. 8, d. 232, ll. 300b, 61, 86, 87. Military officials in Riazan' complained that Tambov continued to send their deserter transports (*eshelony*) well after Tambov had been transferred to a different military sector (Orel).

108. Garrison commanders were instructed to have a reserve supply of provisions in case of an unexpected arrival of troops, but this made little impact given the general shortages. In a crisis, their only instructions were to intensify political work among the troops to defuse mutinous sentiment. See RGVA f. 11, op. 8, d. 232, l. 49.

109. RGVA f. 11, op. 8, d. 232, l. 23.

298 Notes to Pages 26–32

110. Berelowitch and Danilov, *Sovetskaia derevnia* 1:272.

111. RGVA f. 11, op. 8, d. 232, ll. 132, 133.

112. On "Mamontov's raid," see Erik-C. Landis, "A Civil War Episode: General Mamontov in Tambov, August 1919," *The Carl Beck Papers in Russian and East European Studies*, no. 1601 (2002).

113. Ibid., 22–23.

114. The immediate fallout of the White raid into Tambov territory was the trial of many senior party and provincial administration officials accused of negligence, indecision, and defeatism. While some were found guilty of minor offences, all the senior officials were eventually acquitted. Senior members of the provincial Communist Party organization protested against the coverage of the trial in the national press. While the headline in the state organ *Izvestiia* was "On the Tambov Affair," the article in the Communist Party newspaper *Pravda* was headed "The Trial of the Deserters." This headline particularly offended officials in Tambov, who demanded (unsuccessfully) that *Pravda* editors withdraw it and publish an apology. See RGASPI f. 17, op. 65, d. 67, ll. 133–1330b.

115. On the chaos in local administration, see Okninskii, *Dva goda*, 151–52.

116. Danilov and Shanin, *KV*, 29–31.

117. Okatov et al., *Sovety Tambovskoi gubernii*, 205.

118. See Delano DuGarm, "Local Politics and the Struggle for Grain in Tambov, 1918–21," in *Provincial Landscapes: Local Dimensions of Soviet Power, 1917–1953*, ed. Donald Raleigh (Pittsburgh: University of Pittsburgh Press, 2002), esp. 71–73; Erik-C. Landis, "Between Village and Kremlin: Confronting State Food Procurement in Civil War Tambov, 1919–1920," *Russian Review* 63, no. 1 (2004).

119. Okatov et al., *Sovety Tambovskoi gubernii*, 205.

120. GATO f. R-5201, op. 2, d. 1333, l.34 (25 February 1920).

121. GATO f. R-1236, op. 1, d. 773, l. 9 (6 April 1920)

122. GATO f. R-5201, op. 2, d. 1333, l. 10 .

123. GATO f. R-394, op. 1, d. 515, l. 160.

124. Iurii Meshcheriakov, "O prichinakh volniknoveniia 'Antonovshchina,'" in *Nash krai tambovskii: tezisy, dokladov, i soobshchenii* (Tambov: [s.n.], 1991), 66.

125. Rural soviet officials and Food Commissariat authorities reported villagers going to ever greater lengths to secure seed grain for the sowing season of 1920, with large groups traveling outside the province to barter for seed grain. See GATO f. R-761, op. 1, d. 185, ll. 37–370b; GATO f. R-1, op. 1, d. 234, l. 500.

126. RGVA f. 11, op. 8, d. 1023, ll. 54–55.

127. RGVA f. 11, op. 8, d. 1023, ll. 77–79, 81, 176, 332.

128. This record of men enlisted as a proportion of the pool of eligible conscripts was reported as 58 percent, which placed Tambov near the mean for performance throughout the Soviet Republic in 1920 for this particular campaign. The principal reason for nonenlistment was medical, with many young men with typhus sent home with orders to return after recuperating. RGVA f. 11, op. 8, d. 1023, ll. , 339, 377. In July 1920, the garrison population in Tambov city was 18,656, and in Lebedian the total was 5,633, making it the second largest garrison population in the province. Other significant garrisons were located in Borisoglebsk (3,544), Kozlov (3,533), Kirsanov (2,660), and Morshansk (2,457). The garrisoned population rose and fell

month by month, as many were only temporarily assigned to given garrisons. In the largest garrisons, such as in Tambov and Lebedian, the ratio of permanent to temporarily assigned troops was roughly 50-50, but in the smaller garrisons, the soldier population was almost entirely permanent. RGVA f. 25887, op. 1, d. 217, l. 126ob.

129. RGVA f. 25887, op. 1, d. 211, ll. 1, 3.

130. GA RF f. 8415, op. 1, d. 115, ll. 9–120b.

131. RGVA f. 25883, op. 1, d. 288, l. 23; GATO f. R-1836, op. 1, d. 816, ll. 23–24; GATO f. R-1889, op. 1, d. 34, l. 90; GATO f. R-1889, op. 1, d. 297, l. 9.

132. GATO f. R-1832, op. 1, d. 621, l. 59. On the militarization of labor and the Red Army reserves, see Malle, *Economic Organization*, 485–86.

133. GATO f. R-1837, op. 1, d. 144, l. 287. On the outbreak of infectious diseases in the garrisons of Tambov Province in 1920, see GATO f. R-1, op. 1, d. 233, ll. 133–34; GATO f. R-1889, op. 1, d. 297, l. 8; GATO f. R-394, op. 1, d. 520, l. 3; GATO f. R-1832, op. 1, d. 816, l. 68.

134. GATO f. R-1832, op. 1, d. 836, l. 41.

135. The first major pronouncements on this theme emerged during the autumn mobilization campaigns in 1918, focusing on the financial welfare of households whose members were conscripted into service. See the 8 September 1918 Narkomtrud decree ("O fonde obespecheniia semei krasnoarmeitsev"), in Panov, *Ofitserskii korpus*, 436.

136. The first major treatment of the state's measures surrounding the welfare of Red Army families is Molodtsygin, *Raboche-krest'ianskii soiuz, 1918–1920*. The only other author who treats welfare measures in direct relation to the civil war desertion problem is Sanborn, *Drafting the Russian Nation*. Sanborn also discusses these measures in the context of Soviet state building, developing points about the relationship between the Soviet state and Red Army soldiers made in Hagen, *Soldiers*. These welfare measures in the context of village social and political dynamics are treated in detail in Emily Pyle, "Village Social Relations and the Reception of Soldiers' Family Aid Policies, 1912–21" (PhD diss., University of Chicago, 1997). In *Peasant Russia* Figes touches on the place of the Red Army serviceman and his family during the civil war period.

137. Danilov and Shanin, *KV*, 56.

138. The Kirsanov uezd branch of the commission was investigated and convicted by a revolutionary tribunal in 1920 for precisely such failings. The conclusions of the tribunal read:

> The affairs of the Pomoshch' Commission are in such a chaotic state that it is utterly impossible to establish the extent of its activities. On all requests for aid filed by Red Army households, there is the official stamp stating "fulfilled," but any manifestation of its execution is not found in the survey records of the commission, nor are there any further references to the official number of the filed request. In twelve districts there has yet to be a branch of the commission established, and in those districts where such a branch has been set up, there is no evidence of any assistance being performed. Between the uezd commission and the districts there is no systematic or active contact to be found. The majority of districts have yet to submit reports on the number of Red Army households in their locality and on the needs of those households, and of the nine districts which have submitted such reports, there have yet to be any updates, despite the fact that official guidelines require updates to be filed at least twice a month.

GATO f. R-5201, op. 2, d. 152, ll. 3, 28–31, 38. All members of the Kirsanov uezd commission were officially pardoned on the third anniversary of the October Revolution.

139. Assistance with field work to Red Army families was also accomplished by the *subbot-niki,* Communist Party, Komsomol, and trade union members mobilized for such as tasks as sowing and harvesting. See William Chase, "Voluntarism, Mobilisation and Coercion: Subbotniki, 1919–21," *Soviet Studies* 41, no. 1 (1989).

140. Pyle, "Village Social Relations," chap. 5.

141. GATO f. R-5201, op. 2, d. 1397, l. 18.

142. On the victimization of Red Army households by food requisition squads in Tambov, see GATO f. R-1, op. 1, d. 233, l. 335; GATO f. R-1, op. 1, d. 234, l. 142.

143. See I. Davidian and V. Kozlov, "Chastnye pis'ma epokhi grazhdanskoi voiny. Po materialam voennoi tsenzury," in *Neizvestnaia Rossiia: XX vek* (Moscow: Istoricheskoe nasledie, 1992).

144. On the impact of material conditions on Confederate Army soldiers during the Civil War, see J. Tracy Power, *Lee's Miserables: Life in the Army of Northern Virginia from the Wilderness to Appomattox* (Chapel Hill: University of North Carolina Press, 1998), 236.

145. Identity cards for men of service age were introduced in July 1919, and on 27 August 1919 the Defense Council initiated a campaign to verify such documentation. See Molodtsygin, *Krasnaia Armiia: rozhdenie i stanovlenie, 1917–1920 gg.,* 155, 168–70.

146. GATO f. R-1889, op. 1, d. 36, ll. 238, 240.

147. GATO f. R-1889, op. 1, d. 36, l. 163 (3 March 1920).

148. Sanborn, *Drafting the Russian Nation,* 54–55.

149. GATO f. R-1889, op. 1, d. 36, l. 154.

150. Some protested their status as deserters in defense of their honor. One soldier stationed in Kirsanov uezd complained of being placed in a reserve unit designated for former deserters, even though he had successfully defended himself against the charge of desertion. GATO f. R-1889, op. 1, d. 36, l. 57. On the importance of honor and family obligation in late imperial Russian peasant society, see Jeffrey Burds, *Peasant Dreams and Market Politics: Labor Migration and the Russian Villages, 1861–1905* (Pittsburgh: Pittsburgh University Press, 1998).

151. A historian of the American Civil War writes: "One key to honor is that the community acts as a mirror in which the individual sees himself reflected. When conduct receives community approval, it ceases to be dishonorable." See Weitz, *Higher Duty,* 25.

152. RGVA f. 25887, op. 1, d. 218, ll. 5, 50b, 7, 10, 17.

153. The Central Antidesertion Commission, aware of the impact of reports from home on morale and discipline in the reserve units, tried to orchestrate a campaign in which loyal Red Army soldiers wrote to friends and relatives about the nobility of their service in the military and of how damaging desertion was to the village, the military campaign, and the revolution. See RGASPI f. 17, op. 65, d. 68, l. 34.

154. This was similar to how the most famous word of early "Bolshevik-speak"—kulak—became a weapon in the hands of rival villagers, both during the civil war and beyond. See Stephen Kotkin, *Magnetic Mountain: Stalinism as Civilization* (Berkeley: University of California Press, 1995); Sheila Fitzpatrick, *Stalin's Peasants: Resistance and Survival in the Russian Village After Collectivization* (Oxford: Oxford University Press, 1994); Lynne Viola, *Peasant Rebels Under Stalin: Collectivization and the Culture of Peasant Resistance* (Oxford: Oxford University Press, 1996).

155. For instance, see Davidian and Kozlov, "Chastnye pis'ma epokhi grazhdanskoi voiny," 228, 229.

156. Provincial Communist Party officials noted that many who resigned their membership on the eve of party mobilizations cited ill health, family obligations, bereavements, and other dubious reasons. Even more worrying was that many reapplied for membership after military mobilizations had been completed. See RGASPI f. 17, op. 65, d. 68, ll. 66–660b, 103.

157. Danilov and Shanin, *KV*, 49. Some accusations were not quite true. Many who worked on state farms were one-time deserters who were not trusted with active military service.

158. On the mismanagement of state cooperative farms, and peasant attitudes toward them, see Danilov and Shanin, *KV*, 36–38, 47, 48–49; Okninskii, *Dva goda*, 217–19; "Kommunisty na rabote (Pis'mo krest'ianina iz Tambovskoi gub.)," *Revoliutsionnaia Rossiia*, no. 5 (1921): 28. On the number of such farms in Tambov Province, see V. P. Danilov and E. A. Tiurina, eds., *Kooperativno-kolkhoznoe stroitel'stvo v SSSR, 1917–1922. Dokumenty i materialy* (Moscow: Nauka, 1990), 234–35.

159. Such tensions generally characterized antidesertion efforts from early 1919, when the Antidesertion Commission was created as an independent body, rather than as subordinate to the Military Commissariat. Tensions may have first begun when the intensified campaign to round up draft dodgers in the summer of 1919 led to calls for Red Army units to supplement the efforts of antidesertion patrols, calls initially resisted by Red Army officers. See RGVA f. 25887, op. 3, d. 964, l. 6; Danilov and Shanin, *KDP*, 283–84.

160. The Antidesertion Commission gained the authority to inspect Red Army reserve garrisons in October 1919. See Daines and Kariaev, *Revvoensovet*, 432.

161. The Antidesertion Commission claimed that of the 35,685 deserters handed over to the Military Commissariat between 1 January and 1 May 1920, by 1 June 1920 nearly one-third (10,578) had deserted again and had been reapprehended. Furthermore, of the 4,973 deserters handed over in the week of 23 May–1 June, over 50 percent were alleged to have already absconded once more from the custody of the Military Commissariat. See GATO f. R-1832, op. 1, d. 836, l. 41.

162. GATO f. R-1832, op. 1, d. 630, l. 21.

163. GATO f. R-1832, op. 1, d. 621, l. 59.

164. GATO f. R-1832, op. 1, d. 593, l. 104. This report provoked a reply by the former head of the Antidesertion Commission, Mokhnachev, accusing Shikunov of writing an "illiterate" memo on the basis of minimal familiarity with the commission's work. This reply did not reverse the changes that had been made. See GATO R-1, op. 1, d. 184, ll. 875–76.

165. GATO f. R-1832, op. 1, d. 36, ll. 238, 240. This figure was down slightly from the totals reported in May 1920, which estimated the number still at large in the province as 35,000. See Berelowitch and Danilov, eds., *Sovetskaia derevnia* 1:272.

Chapter 2: The Making of a Civil War Bandit

1. This biographical sketch largely relies upon the following sources, unless otherwise noted: Vladimir V. Samoshkin: "Eser Aleksandr," *Literaturnaia Rossiia*, 2 August 1991; "Aleksandr Stepanovich Antonov," *Voprosy istorii* 2 (1994); "V preddverii miatezha," *Literaturnaia*

rosssiia, 13 December 1991. These have been collected and supplemented in Vladimir V. Samoshkin, *Antonovskoe Vosstanie* (Moscow: Russkii Put', 2005), 145–220.

2. One memoirist whose family, at nearly the same time as the Antonovs, relocated to Kirsanov from the the Pale of Settlement, noted that Kirsanov was "full of Jews," despite being legally off-limits to that group. They were attracted by the opportunities offered by the grain trade, and by the corruption in the local bureaucracy that enabled Jews to stay in the town provided they paid regular bribes. See Michael M. Shneyerhoff, *Recollections of the Russian Revolution* (Berkeley: University of California Regional Cultural History Project, 1960), 10. (My thanks to P. Holquist for directing me to this source.)

3. Danilov and Shanin, *KV*, 264. The baptismal record from the Rogozhskaia church in Moscow was located and copied by investigators in 1908, when Aleksandr Antonov was wanted by the police in Tambov.

4. Ibid., 278.

5. Accoding to police reports, Nataliia Ivanovna died in 1907. However, Valetina Stepanovna recalled for Soviet investigators in 1920 that her mother had died in 1906. Ibid., 267, 273.

6. Ibid., 275.

7. Ibid. 265. The event also compromised Antonov's family in Inzhavino: Stepan Gavrilov was soon identified in police correspondence as "politically suspect" owing to the activities of his eldest son. Ibid., 266.

8. Ibid., 266–67.

9. *Khutors* were settlements or communities of peasant families who had taken advantage of recent legal reforms to leave the village commune to become private farmers. However, there is no clear evidence that the robbery targeted the Peasant Bank in Kanin (Borisoglebsk *uezd*) because of this association.

10. Danilov and Shanin, *KV*, 268.

11. Most people living in Kirsanov were unaware that their Duma representatives had declared the town an autonomous republic until they read it in the central press. "For us, it caused quite a sensation. But soon after, everything in the town was quiet, peaceful and calm," wrote A. O. Belousov in "Kirsanovskaia respublika" (Internet site), www.grad-kirsanov.ru/source .php?id=memory.belousov [accessed 18 September 2006]. On the more radical "republics" of the summer of 1917, see Donald Raleigh, "Revolutionary Politics in Provincial Russia: The Tsaritsyn 'Republic' in 1917," *Slavic Review* 40, no. 2 (1981).

12. Trunin was a salesman of furniture or kitchenware. Small businessmen such as Trunin were a new force in Kirsanov government and politics in 1917.

13. G. Pirozhkov, "Kirsanovskaia respublika," *Tambovskie khroniki* 5–6 (1995): 9.

14. A Cheka report from 1921 advanced the claim that the "Kirsanov Republic" episode was, in fact, an early Bolshevik attempt to seize power in the town and that Antonov's involvement in its suppression indicated his profound hostility to the Bolshevik Party. It was even claimed, without evidence, that Antonov had overseen the burning of party literature in the wake of the episode. Danilov and Shanin, *KV*, 271.

15. Ibid., 269.

16. See Pirozhkov, "Kirsanovskaia respublika."

17. See Kanishchev, *Russkii bunt*; Protasov, *Soldaty*.

18. Danilov and Shanin, *KV*, 275.

19. This is according to Antonov's sister Valentina, who became close friends with Bogoli-ubskii's other sister, Klavdiia. See ibid., 274.

20. Ibid., 270.

21. A. I. Ageikin, "Kak proiskhodila Revoliutsiia v Kirsanovskom uezde i vosstanovlenie Sovetskoi vlasti s 1 fevralia 1918 goda" (Internet site), www.grad-kirsanov.ru/source.php?id= memory.agejkin1 [accessed 18 September 2006]; *Bor'ba rabochikh i krest'ian*, 224.

22. A Bolshevik Party committee in Kirsanov was organized in March 1918, composed principally of outsiders, such as A. I. Ageikin. Links with Bolshevik Party cells in the countryside were established later still, and a uezd party committee was not organized until June 1918. See the reminiscences of the main Bolshevik protagonist in these developments, A. I. Ageikin, "Kak proiskhodila rabota v Kirsanovskom uezde" (Internet site), www.grad-kirsanov.ru/source .php?=memory.agejkin [accessed 18 September 2006].

23. Antonov's long-time SR colleague, Bazhenov, was the first chairman of the Kirsanov soviet executive committee when it assumed administrative authority in February 1918. By that time, Bazhenov had joined the Revolutionary Communists and enjoyed temporary se-curity as a result. On the LSRs in Tambov and Kirsanov, see Danilov and Shanin, *KV*, 282; Kanishchev and Meshcheriakov, *Anatomiia*, chap. 1. On the Revolutionary Communists, see Raleigh, *Experiencing Russia's Civil War*, chap. 5.

24. Danilov and Shanin, *KV*, 271, 282. The personnel form on which Antonov declares himself to be a Left SR is dated 24 July 1918, over two weeks after the LSR Central Committee staged their uprising in Moscow.

25. Ibid., 276; Kanishchev and Meshcheriakov, *Anatomiia*, 195–96. Aleksandr Antonov's skepticism about the uprising in Tambov in June 1918 casts doubt on his continued connec-tions with the PSR in the province. At the very least, it highlights the degree to which the PSR, like other political parties at the time (including the Bolsheviks), was far from a unitary political organization in Russia.

26. Kanishchev and Meshcheriakov, *Anatomiia*, chap. 7.

27. While it is conceivable that Antonov would have been drawn to involvement in the "People's Army" of the Komuch government, no evidence substantiates that involvement. The best circumstantial evidence offered by Samoshkin relates to the involvement in the Komuch Government of V. K. Vol'skii, a long-standing PSR member and Constituent Assembly delegate from Tambov Province whom Antonov evidently knew personally. See Samoshkin, "V preddverii miatezha." One of the more informed summaries of Antonov's early activities, filed by the Kirsanov Politburo in October 1920, makes no mention of Antonov traveling to Saratov or Samara in 1918. See Danilov and Shanin, *KV*, 69. It is tempting, but speculative, to understand the alleged pilfering of firearms from the Czechoslovak Legion as informed by knowledge of the Komuch government and as an intention to support its "People's Army" in a conflict with Soviet armed forces.

28. GA RF f. R-8415, op. 1, d. 127, ll. 2–8.

29. GATO f. R-1, op. 1, d. 138, l. 220b; GATO f. R-400, op. 1, d. 150, ll. 14–150b. Iurii Podbel'skii notes that a regional party conference in Inzhavino in 1918 linked Antonov to events in Rudovka and condemned him to death, even organizing a posse to hunt him down. Podbel'skii claims

that Antonov's first acts of violence in the region were vengeance against those at the conference who had condemned him. See Iurii Podbel'skii, "Vosstanie tambovskikh krest'ian," *Revoliutsionnaia Rossiia*, no. 6 (1921).

30. Ishin is mentioned in the same intercepted letter of 1909 that tipped off provincial gendarmes that Antonov was located in Saratov, where he was arrested. See Danilov and Shanin, *KV*, 268.

31. Ibid., 279.

32. GATO f. R-5201, op. 2, d. 382, ll. 28, 29, 30, 32.

33. Danilov and Shanin, *KV*, 280.

34. GATO f. R-5201, op. 2, d. 382, ll. 20, 22–23, 440b.

35. RGVA f. 34228, op. 1, d. 299, ll. 38–39.

36. These include allegations of Antonov's role in promoting antigovernment violence carried out by (in the words of the report itself) "greens" in June and July 1919, and allegations that Antonov sought contact with Denikin's representatives, who used airplanes to drop propaganda leaflets encouraging support for Antonov in Tambov Province. See Danilov and Shanin, *KV*, 156.

37. Berelowitch and Danilov, *Sovetskaia derevnia* 1:159.

38. GATO f. R-5201, op. 2, d. 1040, l. 12. This was alleged by one so-called bandit in Balashov, Petr Fedorovich Popov, arrested in March 1920 (not to be confused with the more prominent rebel figure from the same province, F. Popov, whose insurgency peaked in March 1921).

39. Dated 26 July 1919, quoted in Samoshkin, "V preddverii miatezha," 21.

40. According to the Tambov Cheka chief, Iakumchuk, provincial military and security authorities did not have a trained force of 200 or more men suitable for such an assignment. Those who were available were largely former deserters. See I. K. Iakovlev, ed., *Vnutrennie voiska Sovetskoi respubliki, 1917–1922 gg. Dokumenty i materialy* (Moscow: Iuridicheskaia literatura, 1972), 432–33.

41. Samoshkin, "A. S. Antonov," 70.

42. Okatov et al., *Sovety Tambovskoi gubernii*, 223, 227.

Chapter 3: Conspiratorial Designs

1. The razverstka target for the province in the autumn of 1920 was later explained away as a mistake whereby the projected harvest was overestimated by some 50 percent. While this was certainly true, accurate harvest projections were never truly achieved by the Food Commissariat, nor was it necessarily in their short-term interest to do so. See Fatueva, *Protivostoianie*, 267. On the controversy raised by the 1920 procurement targets, see Landis, "Between Village and Kremlin."

2. The provincial Cheka organization regularly reported on the fears of hunger expressed by the townspeople, as rumors of the expected harvest raised concerns about food supply during the winter months. See GATO f. R-1, op. 1, d. 197, l. 379.

3. *Izvestiia Tambovskogo gubernskogo soveta rabochikh i krest'ianskikh deputatov*, no. 109 (18 May 1920), 3. The dry weather had also contributed to the dramatic rise in the number of

bush and forest fires in the region, which were difficult to contain because state officials relied upon the assistance of local communities to contain any outbreaks. See GATO f. R-394, op. 1, d. 556, ll. 46, 48, 54, 56–59, 61, 64, 65, 66, 69–72, 83.

4. Disturbances in Morshansk were first reported to Tambov on 16 August and focused on the volost of Aleksandrovsk. These disorders escalated to engross several other localities in western and northwestern Morshansk uezd. See GATO f. R-1832, op. 1, d. 361, l. 37; GATO f. R-1832, op. 1, d. 631, l. 59. Morshansk uezd became a focus for opposition to the Soviet government's declaration of a monopoly over grain surpluses in May 1918 and to plans to requisition food from village producers. Northwest Morshansk, in particular, became the rural base for the violent resistance that occurred in the autumn. See the three-part series by Iurii Meshcheriakov, "Stolknovenie," *Gorod na Tsne*, 25 March 1998 (p. 6), 1 April 1998 (p. 5), 8 April 1998 (p. 11).

5. The accounts of the uprising in Kamenka, dealing with what is considered the origin of the *antonovshchina*, are often elaborate in detail and thin on documentation. Leaving aside the identifiably "political" content of the event, the most important descriptions are I. P. Donkov, *Antonovshchina: zamysl' i deistvitel'nost'* (Moscow: Izdatel'stvo politicheskoi literatury, 1977); Vladimir V. Samoshkin, "Antonovshchina: kanun i nachalo," *Literaturnaia Rossiia*, 8 June 1990, 18–19. Also see Radkey, *Unknown Civil War*, which is largely based on Podbel'skii, "Vosstanie," 24–26. All give slightly different accounts, with different dates.

6. GATO f. R-1832, op. 1, d. 631, l. 84; Vladimir V. Samoshkin, "Miatezh. Antonovshchina: Protivostoianie," *Literaturnaia Rossiia*, 26 October 1990, 18.

7. GATO f. R-1832, op. 1, d. 631, ll. 69, 80; Danilov and Shanin, *KV*, 57.

8. GATO f. R-1832, op. 1, d. 631, l. 23.

9. Danilov and Shanin, *KV*, 57.

10. GATO f. R-1, op. 1, d. 233, ll. 570–72.

11. GATO f. R-394, op. 1, d. 541, ll. 2, 3. The incident occurred on 29 August 1920.

12. Danilov and Shanin, *KV*, 58.

13. RGVA f. 25887, op. 1, d. 217, l. 160; GATO f. R-1832, op.1, d. 630, ll. 117, 140.

14. GATO f. R-1, op. 1, d. 233, ll. 498–99. The initial request to Orel to have portions of the Twenty-first Regiment transported out of the province was made by Shikunov, as early as 22 August, when the insurgency was considered isolated to a three-volost area. Reserves were to be transferred to Voronezh, Karachev, Kursk, and Livna. See GATO f. R-1832, op.1, d. 630, l. 140.

15. See Landis, "A Civil War Episode."

16. The Regional Artillery Administration (OKARTU) possessed authority over these military arsenals.

17. Danilov and Shanin, *KV*, 59–60.

18. Ibid., 60.

19. GATO f. R-1832, op. 1, d. 631, l. 33 (Tambov-Rasskazovo, 3 Sept. 1920), 37 (Tambov-Morshansk, 5 Sept.), 53 (Borisoglebsk-Tambov, 6 Sept.).

20. GATO f. R-1832, op. 1, d. 631, l. 36.

21. Danilov and Shanin, *KV*, 63. The unit arriving from Tula was insignificant in size (only 67 men with horses), but they did possess two machine guns with some 7,000 bullets. See GATO f. R-1832, op. 1, d. 631, ll. 28, 36.

22. Danilov and Shanin, *KV*, 59.

23. Raivid here refers to the Second Reserve Cavalry Regiment, which was billeted in Kirsanov at the time but was off limits to provincial authorities owing to its planned departure for southern Ukraine. See RGVA f. 235, op. 5, d. 63, l. 37.

24. GATO f. R-1832, op. 1, d. 631, ll. 81. Listed in the document as participating in Kirsanov are: Sevostoianov (chairman of the uezd soviet executive committee), Ludil'shchikov (assistant secretary of the uezd militia politburo), and Plastun (title unknown). See also an earlier, more civil exchange between Kirsanov and Tambov officials in Danilov and Shanin, *KV*, 59.

25. Danilov and Shanin, *KV*, 62.

26. Ibid., 73–74.

27. In his telegram of 3 September 1920, Shlikhter addressed the Revolutionary-Military Soviet (Revvoensovet) in Moscow as Tambov's "last resort," in light of Orel's continued silence. See GATO f. R-1832, op. 1, d. 630, l. 117. On the work of provincial governors in the late imperial period, see Richard G. Robbins, *The Tsar's Viceroys: Russian Provincial Governors in the Last Years of the Empire* (Ithaca: Cornell University Press, 1987).

28. The 8 September 1920 telegram was addressed to Lenin and to N. P. Briukhanov, in charge of army and navy provisions. The telegram was composed following a meeting of Tambov soviet officials, provincial Communist Party authorities, and A. I. Sviderskii, a member of VTsIK *en mission* in Tambov Province. See Donkov, *Antonovshchina*, 7–8; Okatov et al., *Sovety Tambovskoi gubernii*, 262–63.

29. Their report is reproduced in Danilov and Shanin, *KV*, 63–64.

30. The delegates date this change in tactics as February–March 1920. It is unclear why such a change would occur at that time.

31. GATO f. R-1, op. 1, d. 234, l. 583; S. A. Esikov, "Tambovskie esery v 1920 godu," in *Obshchestvenno-politicheskaia zhizn' rossisskoi provintsii. XX vek*, ed. S. A. Esikov (Tambov: Tambovskii institut khimicheskogo mashinostroeniia, 1993), 40–41. Perhaps surprisingly, provincial soviet and Communist Party officials were not able to establish substantively the role of the PSR in organizing these disruptions until August 1920, two months later. See Antonov-Saratovskii, *Sovety*, 2:445.

32. A Cheka investigation in 1921 claimed that there was another such uezd party conference in July 1920 in Borisoglebsk, but this is not claimed by the PSR delegates to the party conference in September 1920. See GARF f. R-8415, op. 1, d. 127, l. 4.

33. The genesis of the "peasant brotherhoods" is described in Viktor M. Chernov, *Zapiski sotsialista-revoliutsionnera: kniga pervaia* (Berlin: Izdatel'stvo Z. I. Grzhebina, 1922), 245–339. These activities are briefly summarized in Maureen Perrie, *The Agrarian Policy of the Russian Socialist Revolutionary Party: from its origins through the revolution of 1905–7* (Cambridge: Cambridge University Press, 1976), 23.

34. N. D. Erofeev, ed., *Partiia sotsialistov-revolutsionnerov: dokumenty i materialy, 1900–1925* (Moscow: ROSSPEN, 2000), 3 (pt. 2): 637–40. The composition of the circular appears to be inspired by local organizations of the PSR, perhaps in response to the activities of other socialist opponents of the Bolsheviks, such as the Left SRs. A published protocol of the PSR Central Committee has Chernov being instructed to compose the circular in response to initiatives originating with the PSR organization in the province of Tver'. See ibid., vol. 3 (pt. 2): 636. There are echoes of Chernov's earlier embrace of the land committees in the autumn of

1917, which were authorized initially by provincial governments (notably in Tambov) to assume control of gentry estate properties in the hope of quelling violence in the countryside. See E. A. Lutskii, "Krest'ianskoe vosstanie v tambovskoi gubernii v sentiabre 1917g.," *Istoricheskie zapiski* 2 (1938): 74. For an analysis that links the origins of the STKs to the "nonparty peasant congresses" of 1919–1920, see A. A. Kurenyshev, *Krest'ianstvo i ego organizatsii v pervoi treti XX veka* (Moscow: Gosudarstvennyi istoricheskii muzei, 2000), 157–61.

35. Marc Jansen, ed., *The Socialist Revolutionary Party After 1917: Documents from the PSR Achive* (Amsterdam: Stichting beheer IISG, 1989), 223–24. See also Vladimir N. Brovkin, *Behind the Front Lines of the Civil War: Political Parties and Social Movements in Russia, 1918–1922* (Princeton: Princeton University Press, 1994), 363–66.

36. On the intellectual background to this policy, see Oliver H. Radkey, "Chernov and Agrarian Socialism Before 1918," in *Continuity and Change in Russian and Soviet Thought*, ed. E. J. Simmons (Cambridge: Harvard University Press, 1955), 63–80. If the summary of the conference protocol, found in the published materials from the PSR trial, is accurate, the Tambov delegation was hardly alone among local organizations in pushing for a more radical party line on armed resistance to the Soviet regime. See *Obvinitel'noe zakliuchenie po delu Tsentral'nogo komiteta i otdel'nykh chlenov inykh organizatsii Partii sotsialistov-revoliutsionerov: po obvineniiu ikh v vooruzhennoi bor'be protiv sovetskoi vlasti, organizatsii ubiistv, vooruzhennykh ograblenii i v izmennicheskikh snosheniiakh s inostrannymi gosudarstvami* (Moscow: Izdatel'stvo VTsIK, 1922), 41.

37. Danilov and Shanin, *KV*, 63. Later investigations led by Raivid established that PSR members had sent the letter. See Antonov-Saratovskii, *Sovety*, 2:447–48. Because the actual letter has never resurfaced, it is difficult to evaluate whether Traskovich's description of its content —particularly of threats against Jews—is accurate.

38. The letter is reproduced in Jansen, *Socialist Revolutionary Party*, 551–55.

39. Podbel'skii, "Vosstanie," 24–26.

40. In June 1920, Raivid published an article lampooning recent reports of a LSR plan to initiate a "Trade Union of the Toiling Peasantry." The idea of this trade union (*profsoiuz*) for the peasantry predated the notion of the STKs, and in the original circular relating to the STKs, Chernov noted the LSR idea, instructing local organizations not to discourage them. But the fact that Raivid, in his article, noted the LSR scheme and summarily dismissed it, may indicate the attitude of local officials in Tambov to other such opposition plans for rural unions. See *Izvestiia Tambovskogo gubernskogo soveta rabochikh i krest'ianskikh deputatov*, no. 129 (12 June 1920), 2; Erofeev, *Partiia s.-r.*, 3 (pt. 2): 640; Kurenyshev, *Krest'ianstvo i ego organizatsii*, 157–58. The LSR party had undergone a schism of its own in 1920, and the newspaper in which the "trade union" scheme was published, *Znamia truda*, represented the more radical faction of LSRs. The LSRs in Tambov possibly took their cue from this wing of the party, as it was associated with the LSR Central Regional Committee, which had strong links with other cities in the Blackearth region, such as Voronezh. See "Ko vsem chlenam partii levykh S-R," International Institute of Social History (Amsterdam), PSR Collection, folder 859, p. 1.

41. Jan M. Meijer, ed., *The Trotsky Papers, 1917–1922* (The Hague: Mouton, 1971), 2:506. See also the comments by Gromov in Danilov and Shanin, *KV*, 109.

42. This point is made in Oliver H. Radkey, *The Sickle Under the Hammer: The Socialist Revolutionaries in the Early Months of Soviet Rule* (New York: Columbia University Press,

1963), 277. According to an October 1920 report prepared by Raivid, the local PSR was hardly in the position to direct a mass insurgency: "SR organizations are not capitalizing on their successes among the peasantry because, as has become clear from the statements taken from arrested party members, now in Tambov there are only tens of PSR members, whereas in the past they numbered in the thousands." See Antonov-Saratovskii, *Sovety*, 2:447.

43. GATO f. R-1, op. 1, d. 232, l. 357. Note that the letter identifies the Kirsanov PSR organization having its base in the volost of Rudovka, in the north of the uezd, where the disturbances had yet to reach.

44. Podbel'skii, "Vosstanie," 24–26.

45. Such "peasant marches" (*pokhody*) were a traditional feature of rural resistance in imperial Russia. Often spontaneously mobilized, groups would set off for an administrative center to voice grievances to government authorities, gaining strength and support en route. Often such episodes would turn violent as armed authorities confronted aggrieved groups of subjects. The tradition continued into the Soviet period, most notably, relating to the experience of Tambov soviet officials in Morshansk uezd during the rural disturbances of October–November 1918.

46. Podbel'skii's version of the events in these first days of the uprising has survived in later narratives of the Antonov rebellion, most notably in Samoshkin, "Miatezh. Antonovshchina: Protivostoianie," 18–20. However, there is little evidence that such a decisive event took place. M. F. Beliakov, chairman of the Tambov uezd soviet executive, mentioned such a *pokhod na Tambov* originating in Kniazhe Bogoroditskoe, where villagers were rounded up by insurgents and ordered at gunpoint to set off and attack Tambov. According to Beliakov, this forced march quickly petered out, and the remaining core was easily dispersed by government forces at Koptevo. (If these locations are accurate, then the "march" would have moved eastward rather than north to Tambov city.) Beliakov states that the PSR, as the instigators of the rebellion, nevertheless claimed in the course of efforts to recruit support for the insurgency that Tambov had already been sacked by the marchers. See Mikhail F. Beliakov, "Bor'ba s antonovshchinoi," in *Antonovshchina: Stat'i, vospominaniia i drugie materialy k istorii esero-banditizma v Tambovskoi gubernii*, ed. O. S. Litovskii (Tambov: Biuro Tambovskogo gubistparta, 1923), 40. The truth surrounding the so-called march is difficult to extract. What is often described in contemporary reports is the spread of the insurgency from village to village and the alarm caused by the insurgency's growing proximity to the provincial capital. The spread of the disorders could well have been understood as possessing a greater coherence than was the case.

47. Jansen, *Socialist Revolutionary Party*, 554.

48. RGVA f. 34228, op. 1, d. 299, ll. 38–39.

49. The meeting took place near the village of Treskino. Ivan Ishin was a native of Kalugino volost. See GATO f. R-4049, op. 1, d. 89, ll. 98ob, 109–109ob. Despite the complicity of the local soviet leadership, such meetings did not go unnoticed by the uezd and provincial authorities, who were well aware of Antonov's activities, believed to be in league with the Whites during their advance toward Moscow in the second half of 1919. See RGVA f. 827, op. 1, d. 8, l. 336. See also the more elaborate accusations included in a Cheka report on Antonov, written at the height of the insurgency in 1921, in Danilov and Shanin, *KV*, 156.

50. At the time of Denikin's advance on Moscow in 1919 the PSR, as well as other socialist

parties (notably the Mensheviks), maintained a reserved support for the Soviet state as it was threatened by the counterrevolution. See Brovkin, *Behind the Front Lines.*

51. GA RF f. R-8415, op. 1, d. 127, ll. 2, 3.

52. The size of the druzhina was estimated to be 150 men—by no means a small number for a band of terrorists, as evidenced by an impressive tally of over 100 government agents murdered during the summer of 1919. See Samoshkin, "A. S. Antonov," 70.

53. GATO f. R-5201, op. 2, d. 1395, l. 17; Danilov and Shanin, *KV*, 41.

54. Danilov and Shanin, *KV*, 41–42.

55. See Okatov et al., *Sovety Tambovskoi gubernii*, 227–29; Samoshkin, "A. S. Antonov," 70–71; Danilov and Shanin, *KV*, 34–35.

56. There is little evidence that Antonov had contact with other rebels before the outbreak of the insurgency in August 1920. Still, one source, a captured "green" from Saratov Province, claims that Antonov had been a source of arms and munitions for other similar rebels in the extended region. See GATO f. R-5201, op. 1, d. 1040, ll. 10–13.

57. A report by the Tambov Communist Party to Moscow raised the possibility that Antonov in February 1920 was being urged by native Tambov PSR activists to assume greater ambitions in his defiance of the Soviet state, even to attack the provincial capital. This is the only mention of contact between Antonov and these members of the PSR. See Danilov and Shanin, *KV*, 41.

58. GATO f. R-5201, op. 2, d. 1018, ll. 64–65.

59. GATO f. R-5201, op. 2, d. 1018, l. 1170b.

60. GATO f. R-394, op. 1, d. 520, l. 73. An investigation commission found that the rebels distributed literature identifying the leaders of the Soviet government with the forces of evil and the coming of the Antichrist. See GATO f. R-5201, op. 2, d. 1018, l. 128.

61. M. S. Maslakov was the senior commander of the special unit designated by the Tambov Communist Party and Cheka organization to hunt down Antonov.

62. GATO f. R-394, op. 1, d. 520, l. 73.

63. GATO f. R-5201, op. 2, d. 1018, ll. 26,157.

64. The Kirsanov militia chief, Maslakov, possibly was drawn to the lakes near Ramza because they were a known hideout for Antonov. The clash that took place there in April 1920 may have been between government agents and members of Antonov's druzhina, in other words, not involving the armed men who had incited the uprising in the village of Ramza.

65. GATO f. R-5201, op. 2, d. 1018, l. 157.

66. GATO f. R-5201, op. 2, d. 1018, ll. 128, 157.

67. The phrase "green army" was placed in quotation marks throughout the original source, a report by the Cheka agent, F. A. Sharov. See Danilov and Shanin, *KV*, 45–46, 69.

68. Podbel'skii, "Vosstanie," 25.

69. Antonov-Saratovskii, *Sovety*, 2:447–48.

70. Akimov's testimony is located at RGVA f. 34228, op. 1, d. 299, ll. 32–33. A summary based in part on Akimov's testimony is in Danilov and Shanin, *KV*, 205–06.

71. Podbel'skii, "Vosstanie," 25.

72. RGASPI f. 17, op. 13, d. 1010, ll. 47–470b.

73. RGASPI f. 17, op. 13, d. 1010, ll. 460b, 47. The author of this report is identified only by his surname.

74. Donkov, *Antonovshchina*, 31.

75. Antonov-Saratovskii, *Sovety*, 2:448.

76. RGASPI f. 17, op. 13, d. 1010, l. 47.

77. This is the conclusion given in the most recent account of the uprising, in Samoshkin, "Antonovshchina: kanun i nachalo," 19.

78. GATO f. R-1832, op. 1, d. 631, l. 23.

79. RGVA f. 235, op. 1, d. 63, l. 114; Danilov and Shanin, *KV*, 61.

80. Some reports remained only strictly suggestive, such as the statement taken from a local priest in Ponzar' volost (Tambov uezd), who reported that daily, following mass, locals would hold memorial services for fallen "bandits." See Danilov and Shanin, *KV*, 58–59.

81. Ibid., 61. In the first days of the uprising, there were reports of rebels declaring "Long live Wrangel!" (in reference to the White commander, General Petr N. Wrangel) and the like. Such openly counterrevolutionary slogans, while likely to have been voiced, were hardly representative of the insurgency, and such reports of pro-White slogans quickly disappeared within weeks of the beginning of the uprising.

82. The first report of Antonov's involvement appears to be from a 1 September 1920 exchange between Tambov (Traskovich) and Kirsanov officials, in which the latter state that Antonov and other familiar local "bandits" were assuming a prominent role in the disturbances along the border between Kirsanov and Tambov uezds. The day before this exchange (31 August), Traskovich had informed Red Army regional command in Orel of the uprising, citing the involvement of "Corporal Boguslavskii, Kazakov, Pluzhnikov, Iurin, the SRs and others." Aleksandr Antonov is strangely missing from this list, despite the fact that all the others were known primarily by their association with Antonov. See GATO f. R-1832, op. 1, d. 631, l. 29; Danilov and Shanin, *KV*, 59.

83. Okatov et al., *Sovety Tambovskoi gubernii*, 263–64 (emphasis in original).

Chapter 4: The Collapse of Soviet Authority in Tambov

1. VOKhR had been at the heart of most government efforts against similar rural rebellions throughout Soviet territory during the civil war period. The experience formed the basis of Kornev's summary report on counterinsurgency strategy, "On the Two-and-a-Half Year Struggle with Banditry," published in late 1920. See RGVA f. 33988, op. 2, d. 306, ll. 22, 23. On 1 September 1920, Kornev became the head of a new organization, VNUS, an internal security directorate that incorporated the forces of the VOKhR. VNUS was relatively short-lived as an autonomous bureaucracy, however, and state and military officials were often slow to adjust to the designation and acronym changes, a cause of occasional confusion for (at the very least) the later historian.

2. Iakovlev, *Vnutrennie voiska*, 514–15.

3. GATO f. R-1, op. 1, d. 197, l. 393.

4. GATO f. R-1, op. 1, d. 197, l. 395. Vodkin's letter was forwarded to Shlikhter in Tambov after being reviewed in Moscow and Orel. Shlikhter did not read the letter until November 1920, when he immediately assigned it to the archive (l. 391).

5. On the tense relationship between central and provincial officials in the realm of food procurement, see DuGarm, "Local Politics."

6. Danilov and Shanin, *KV*, 65.

7. RGVA f. 33988, op. 2, d. 306, l. 8; Danilov and Shanin, *KV*, 65–66.

8. Danilov and Shanin, *KV*, 66.

9. Samoshkin, "Miatezh. Antonovshchina: Protivostoianie," 18.

10. GATO f. R-1832, op. 1, d. 631, l. 31; Danilov and Shanin, *KV*, 66.

11. Iakovlev, *Vnutrennie voiska*, 522–24.

12. Ibid., 524–25.

13. Danilov and Shanin, *KV*, 70. Other reports claimed that the rebel commander Tokmakov, as well as another, unnamed figure prominent in the conspiracy had been killed in the clashes at Kozmodem'ianskoe. See Berelowitch and Danilov, *Sovetskaia derevnia* 1:345.

14. GATO f. R-1, op. 1, d. 197, l. 578.

15. Antonov-Saratovskii, *Sovety*, 2:447–48.

16. Ibid., 2:448–49.

17. Samoshkin, "Miatezh. Antonovshchina: Protivostoianie," 19. Provincial officials in the Military Council were later criticized for permitting the release of prisoners in early November 1920 while Red Army commanders were simultaneously enforcing collective punishments (such as burning scores of peasant homes) for rebel villages. See Danilov and Shanin, *KV*, 84–85.

18. Danilov and Shanin, *KV*, 73.

19. Ibid., 74–75. A man named Nasonov involved in the early organization of the state response to the conflict in Kirsanov wrote in March 1921 of his experiences in coming face to face with captured bandits: "Here I found myself confronted not with gentry landlords and bankers, but instead I met with poor peasants who had risen up against the 'Communist tyrants' and who had begun to hunt down and kill them. The captured bandits were dressed in simple peasant blouses and were frequently barefoot and emaciated. As I reflected on what could have driven these men to such a state, I was nearly overcome with shame, as I could not help but think that many of us here were partly to blame." See ibid., 132.

20. When Meshcheriakov, the secretary of the Tambov provincial soviet executive committee, met with Lenin in late September, he presented the following progress report on the procurement campaign: "As concerns the requisition squads, nothing to this day has been forthcoming. No reinforcements have been given. Collection has proceeded at a rate of 20, 22, 25 thousand *pood* per day, at a time when 200–250 thousand is the target." Lenin's response following this briefing represents his first substantive contribution to the drama unfolding in Tambov. His short memo to Sklianskii and Dzerzhinskii read: "Must take the most drastic measures!! Urgently!!" See Donkov, *Antonovshchina*, 10. Soon after this exchange, and evidently after reflecting upon the situation in Tambov, Lenin sent a memo to the head of the Food Commissariat, Briukhanov, in which he asked whether the 11 million *pood* razverstka for cereals assigned to Tambov was too high a target. There is no record of Briukhanov's reply, or of any follow-up on this issue by Lenin.

21. B. A. Shlikhter, "Vospominaniia o V. I. Lenine," *Vorposy istorii KPSS* 9 (1969), 113. Kornev reported on 27 September 1920, after personally inspecting affairs in Tambov, that the provincial administration was too preoccupied with the procurement campaign. Despite his conviction that the rebellion was more or less defeated, he was concerned that of the 4,200 soldiers available in the province for counterinsurgency operations, only 1,200 actually were involved in those operations. The remainder was either assigned to work in grain procurement (1,400)

or general guard duty at railway stations and towns (1,600). In the same report, Kornev acknowledged that reinforcements would be needed (a single infantry regiment, two infantry squadrons, and an armored unit), but that VNUS was unable to provide such reinforcement, given the demands of other ongoing operations. See Iakovlev, *Vnutrennie voiska*, 524–25.

22. GATO f. R-1, op. 1, d. 233, l. 527.

23. Danilov and Shanin, *KV*, 65.

24. See also GATO f. R-1, op. 1, d. 197, ll. 465, 466.

25. Uezd officials in Tambov complained that the families of district soviet personnel and rural Communist Party members suffered terrible material privations, even before the outbreak of the violence in the autumn. Uezd officials claimed that rural soviet employees, often partially clothed, barefoot, and hungry, were held up as emblematic of Soviet rule by the kulaks, who told fellow villagers that supporting the Soviet government and Communist Party could obviously bring no personal or collective benefits if this was the way its faithful servants were forced to live. See GATO f. R-1, op. 1, d. 228, l. 128.

26. TsDNITO f. 840, op. 1, d. 824, ll. 23–230b; GATO f. R-1, op. 1, d. 183, l. 843; Danilov and Shanin, *KV*, 64, 73–74.

27. In his reminiscences, the one-time Narkomprod representative to Orel Province, N. A. Miliutin, recalled a meeting with Lenin in late 1920 during which they discussed the procurement campaign in Orel and the problematic reliance upon coercion by requisition squads. Lenin expanded on the use of force, rather than persuasion and agitation, in grain requisitioning: "Do not make the conclusion from all this that rifles are just for decoration. Struggle is struggle, after all. In the absence of extreme circumstances, then it is better to carry on like that, but when the situation demands, requisition squads must be firm. Look at Tambov, where grannies are going around disarming squads and handing over the weapons to the bandits. And this is going on at our doorstep. The *antonovshchina* can begin to spread, even all the way to Moscow." Miliutin was later involved in the suppression of the *antonovshchina* in 1921, as representative of VTsIK in Tambov and Voronezh. See his "Po zadaniiam Lenina," in *Vospominaniia o Vladimire Il'iche Lenine* (Moscow: Gosudarstvennoe izdatel'stvo politicheskoi literatury, 1956–1960), 2:411.

28. GATO f. R-1, op. 1, d. 184, l. 460.

29. This was particularly a problem regarding VNUS troops, which were more readily deployed in noncombat roles. In neighboring Voronezh Province, where local authorities similarly relied extensively on VNUS troops to quell their own "banditry" problems, the overall commander in the province (Kaufel'dt) complained about the dislocation and fracture within the forces under his overall command: "I have learned that commanders of individual units have absolutely no idea how many men they have or where they are located. A significant number of the VNUS troops are engaged in provisions work, but the regimental and brigade commanders not only do not know how many of their men have been given such assignments, they also have no idea where these men have been assigned or for how long they have been gone." RGVA f. 25887, op. 1, d. 511, ll. 25–26 (February 1921).

30. GATO f. R-1, op. 1, d. 234, l. 951.

31. GATO f. R-1, op. 1, d. 184, ll. 524–25; Danilov and Shanin, *KV*, 71.

32. GATO f. R-1, op. 1, d. 184, ll. 524, 798.

33. In Spassk uezd the collections had reached over 122 percent of targets. See GATO f. R-1, op. 1, d. 184, l. 524.

34. GATO f. R-1, op. 1, d. 181, l. 413; GATO f. R-1, op. 1, d. 184, ll. 664–700b.

35. For examples, see GATO f. R-1236, op. 1, d. 843, ll. 99–103; Danilov and Shanin, *KV*, 75.

36. GATO f. R-394, op. 1, d. 541, ll. 3–30b (telegrams mentioned here not found). Meshcheriakov illustrated his point by assessing the state of the squads ordered to go into the countryside to requisition grain. Because of the severe shortage of firearms, these units (three in all, composed entirely of Communist Party members) were forced to go unarmed, prompting the Kirsanov provisions commissar to call them "miserable workers" (*pechal' rabotniki*). Under such conditions, as Meshcheriakov wrote in his report, "Cowards are not allowed." For similar comments from the Kirsanov uezd Communist Party chief, see RGVA f. 7, op. 2, d. 483, l. 1.

37. See the 23 October 1920 telegram issued by Lenin to provincial soviet executive committees in grain-producing provinces, reproduced in Danilov and Shanin, *KDP*, 586.

38. Danilov and Shanin, *KV*, 77. Aplok vacated the post in Tambov on 16 October, while Redz'ko did not assume the overall command of forces in Tambov until 25 October. In the interim, the commander in the province was V. I. Blagonadezhdin, a local VNUS brigade commander.

39. Berelowitch and Danilov, *Sovetskaia derevnia* 1:347; Danilov and Shanin, *KDP*, 572–74.

40. Danilov and Shanin, *KDP*, 591–92.

41. G. V. Vedeniapin, "Antonovshchina," *Volga*, nos. 5–6 (1997): 222.

42. Danilov and Shanin, *KDP*, 577, 590.

43. Vedeniapin, "Antonovshchina," 224–26.

44. Danilov and Shanin, *KDP*, 579. Karpov often refers to Antonov in metonymic terms, meaning insurgents from Tambov, rather than reporting any reliable information regarding Antonov's personal presence in Chembar' uezd.

45. Danilov and Shanin, *KDP*, 574.

46. Similar frustrations were expressed by uezd Military Commissariat officials in Kirsanov and were also raised by Shlikhter in communication directly with Lenin in mid-October. See GATO f. R-1889, op. 1, d. 34, l. 262.

47. Danilov and Shanin, *KDP*, 593.

48. RGVA f. 33988, op. 2, d. 306, ll. 5, 6, 7.

49. *Gubcheka: sbornik dokumentov i materialov iz istorii Saratovskoi gubernskoi chrezvychainoi komissii, 1917–1921 gg.*, ed. N. I. Shabanov and N. A. Marakov (Saratov: Privolzhskoe knizhnoe izdatel'stvo, 1980), 155; Vedeniapin, "Antonovshchina," 224–25; Danilov and Shanin, *KDP*, 578; Berelowitch and Danilov, *Sovetskaia derevnia* 1:342.

50. On the situation in Penza, see GATO f. R-1, op. 1, d. 234, l. 908.

51. Okatov et al., *Sovety Tambovskoi gubernii*, 279–80.

52. See Donkov, *Antonovshchina*, 41. This estimate of government losses does not include Communist Party and soviet personnel killed or wounded. Danilov and Shanin, *KV*, 72. A summary of the activities of rebels in Kirsanov uezd during the month of October is provided in ibid., 70–71.

53. Berelowitch and Danilov, *Sovetskaia derevnia* 1:352, 367.

54. Despite early efforts by Aplok to reorganize the system of supply to government forces, self-provisioning by troops remained a problem for the counterinsurgency effort throughout 1920 and into 1921. As Meshcheriakov put it in his report on affairs in Kirsanov: "[Our own troops] often conduct themselves worse than do the bandits. They loot whomever they can, pay absolutely no attention to local administration, and effectively erode away what support we enjoy from the local population." See GATO f. R-394, op. 1, d. 541, ll. 2–3 (emphasis in original). See also GATO f. R-1, op. 1, d. 197, l. 483; Samoshkin, *Antonovskoe*, 51. Danilov and Shanin, *KV*, 65.

55. GATO f. R-394, op. 1, d. 541, ll. 2–3.

56. GATO f. R-1889, op. 1, d. 297, ll. 223, 259, 318, 319, 320, 321, 317, 322.

57. GATO f. R-1889, op. 1, d. 34, l. 262.

58. The senior commander in the Orel Military Sector, Skudr, criticized local officials for their failure to address the problem of desertion on 30 October 1920: "According to the information available to me, the rounding up of deserters in the uezds of your province that are currently consumed by the rebellion (Tambov, Kirsanov, Borisoglebsk) is not being pursued with the necessary commitment. You are reminded that these uezds have always been distinguished by the sheer number of deserters present there. These deserters have now become a sensitive issue for us, for they constitute the principal material for the 'ANTONOV' band. The success of our campaign against the bandit 'Antonov' depends entirely upon our ability to deprive him of this material—the hardened deserters." GATO f. R-1832, op. 1, d. 593, l. 261.

59. GATO f. R-1832, op. 1, d. 593, ll. 262, 322; Okatov et al., *Sovety Tambovskoi gubernii*, 241.

60. GATO f. R-1, op. 1, d. 234, l. 968. The insecurity felt in Borisoglebsk, according to the memoirist Anton Okninskii, prompted municipal officials to take villagers from the surrounding countryside into the town as hostages, as a safeguard against a possible rebel attack on Borisoglebsk. See Okninskii, *Dva goda*, 309–10.

61. See the resolution passed by a nonparty conference of garrisoned soldiers in Kirsanov, condemning the conduct of officials in the Food Commissariat in their pursuit of the razverstka policy, in Danilov and Shanin, *KV*, 76. A year-end report by the Kirsanov Military Commissariat described near-starvation conditions in the main garrison, killing off the cavalry stables and weakening the immune systems and morale of soldiers. See GATO f. R-1837, op. 1, d. 144, l. 287.

62. GATO f. R-1832, op. 1, d. 630, l. 123; RGVA f. 7, op. 2, d. 433, l. 1.

63. Berelowitch and Danilov, *Sovetskaia derevnia* 1:367.

64. Ibid., 368.

65. According to the Soviet historian, Trifonov, nearly one-half of all party and state personnel in Kirsanov uezd went over to the rebels by early 1921. One of these, I. V. Belousov, later told Soviet investigators that when he first joined the rebel group led by Tokmakov at Inzhavino in late September 1920 he was not allowed to carry a firearm owing to his previous affiliation. Belousov was eventually allowed to carry a gun after a probation of some weeks, and he stayed with the rebels for eight months. Such "traitors" were later condemned by a government inspector, reporting in early 1921 to the Revolutionary-Military Council in Moscow, when he alluded to "the indiscipline of our party comrades at the Tambov front, those who have sat too long in the localities and grown lazy, those who have become infected with purely parochial and, specifically, petit-bourgeois ambitions, those who have thrown away all restraint and

sold their souls for short-term gain and comfort." See RGVA f. 33988, op. 2, d. 646, ll. 243–44; GATO f. R-5201, op. 2, d. 1683, l. 54; I. A. Trifonov, *Klassy i klassovaia bor'ba v SSSR v nachale NEPa, 1921–1923 gg.* (Leningrad: Leningradskii gosudarstvennyi universitet im. Zhdanova, 1964), 37.

66. Danilov and Shanin, *KV*, 68, 76; Samoshkin, "Miatezh. Antonovshchina: Protivostoianie," 19.

67. GATO f. R-5201, op. 1, d. 22, ll. 6, 7, 8, 21.

68. Danilov and Shanin, *KV*, 79.

69. On the Kazankov episode, see Fatueva, *Protivostoianie*, 117.

70. Danilov and Shanin, *KV*, 75.

71. Ibid., 91.

72. GATO f. R-1, op. 1, d. 184, l. 456.

73. Both the rebels and government troops had to contend with contagious diseases and illnesses, with outbreaks of cholera, in particular, being reported by military commanders and civilian officials in the countryside. Redz'ko contended that he was losing up to 300 every week due to poor sanitary and material conditions, but outbreaks were notable in other areas that were outside government control. See GATO f. R-1, op. 1, d. 184, l. 547; Danilov and Shanin, *KV*, 76.

74. Danilov and Shanin, *KV*, 77.

75. Ibid.

76. Ibid.

77. GATO f. R-1, op. 1, d. 181, l. 220.

78. Landis, "A Civil War Episode," 20–21.

79. Danilov and Shanin, *KV*, 77–78.

80. The report is reproduced in ibid., 82–85.

81. In Kameron's words, "Categorical and definitive demands for reinforcements, containing declarations that the province was in flames and that any delays in sending troops would result in the complete destruction of the province, simply did not arrive from Tambov." See ibid., 83.

82. Ibid., 86.

83. N. Iliukov, *Partizanskoe dvizhenie v Primor'e (1918–1920 gg.)* (Moscow: Voenizdat, 1962); Ia. S. Pavlov, *Narodnaia voina v tylu interventov i belogvardeitsev* (Minsk: Belarus', 1983). On guerrilla warfare and Soviet military doctrine generally, see A. A. Maslov, "Concerning the role of partisan warfare in Soviet military doctrine of the 1920s and 1930s," *Journal of Slavic Military Studies* 9, no. 4 (1996).

84. A broadly similar point, employed differently, can be found in Donald Raleigh, "Languages of Power: How the Saratov Bolsheviks Imagined Their Enemies," *Slavic Review* 57, no. 2 (1998).

85. Danilov and Shanin, *KV*, 81–82.

86. GATO f. R-1832, op. 1, d. 593, ll. 378–79. In Saratov, provincial officials were evidently prohibited from printing material relating to local rebels, provoking protests by trade union representatives similar to those voiced in Tambov. See Raleigh, *Experiencing Russia's Civil War*, 384; Vedeniapin, "Antonovshchina," 220. Anton Okninskii, before his departure from Tambov Province in late November 1920, noticed the state of panic that had beset the towns-

people of Borisoglebsk. There, too, the situation was aggravated by the municipal administration. Even at the vaguest rumor of an attack by rebels on the town (which Okninskii
thought preposterous; it became a reality of sorts in the new year), municipal authorities
would round up innocent civilians believed to have contacts with the surrounding countryside to use them as hostages in case of an advance by rebels into the town. See Okninskii, *Dva
goda*, 309–10.

87. RGVA f. 25887, op. 1, d. 409, l. 5. The idea had been raised in Moscow and supported
by Sklianskii (of the Revolutionary Military Council) and Dzerzhinskii (of VChK) that the
Southern Military Command should be relocated from Orel to Voronezh to be nearer the epicenter of the growing disturbances in the central agricultural region. Skudr rejected the idea
of relocating to what he termed the "geometric center" of events, preferring instead to continue to rely upon the operational authority of provincial commands while Orel oversaw
supply and coordination. See RGVA f. 25887, op. 1, d. 409, l. 9.

Chapter 5: The Partisan Countryside at War

1. Materials of the Tambov STKs and the Partisan Army exist primarily in digest form compiled by the Tambov Cheka in the spring of 1921. (For examples, see Danilov and Shanin, *KV*.)

2. A second version of the program adds that the equality of all citizens, mentioned in
point 1, did not extend to the "house of the Romanovs." This was not the only copy to contain
this added detail, for Antonov-Ovseenko, in a July 1921 report, mentions it in describing the
STK program. The significance is difficult to assess, however. The rest of the program betrays
no sympathy for the autocracy, and these added words could simply be giving rhetorical emphasis to the insurgents' leftist credentials. Unaware of the disparity, Radkey sees the added
words as being a hallmark of Right SR influence, so this copy could have been seized from PSR
members. See Danilov and Shanin, *KV*, 231, 293; Radkey, *Unknown Civil War*, 71.

3. Other copies of the program omit the provision of government credits to small farms
and instead speak of "opening of extensive government credits to individuals." This copy of
the program found its way into the hands of émigré opposition figures and was reproduced
in the PSR journal *Revolutionary Russia*. See the pamphlet "Kak tambovskie krest'iane bori-
atsia za svobodu" (1921), HIA NC, box 630, folder 7; Rex Wade, ed., *Documents of Soviet History*
(Gulf Breeze FL: Academic International Press, 1993), 2:199; Danilov and Shanin, *KV*, 293.

4. Danilov and Shanin, *KV*, 79–80.

5. The PSR member and Tambov native, Iurii Podbel'skii, in a letter protesting his continued incarceration by the Cheka in May 1921, pointed to the "ignorant" wording of the STK
program to argue that the PSR could not have been involved in its composition. As illustra-
tion, he referred in particular to the passage cited in note 3 above on providing government
credits to individuals. Certainly Podbel'skii was correct in that the program was not supplied
by the central organization, nor were senior PSR figures involved in its composition. The arrest of senior PSR members in Tambov in September 1920 deprived the Tambov organization
of whatever close ties it may have had with the Moscow committee. Still, less notable PSR
members from Tambov could have been involved, and the PSR could still have been the principal source of inspiration for the document. See Jansen, *Socialist Revolutionary Party*, 545. For

the continued concern of the PSR central committee for the arrested members of the Tambov organization, see Erofeev, *Partiia s.-r.*, 746.

6. A list of eight points was drafted by the Tambov provincial committee of Left SRs (whose ranks had also been severely depleted by Cheka arrests), but it is unclear as to whether this short document was a work in progress intended as an alternative program for the STK or a draft of goals worked on separately by the LSRs as part of a cooperative effort (with the remaining members of the Tambov PSR) to settle upon a unified political program. Not all points are contained in the final product. Included in the LSR document are:

> 1. General armed uprising for the overthrow of the aggressor Communists.
>
> 2. Realization of the law on the socialization of land.
>
> 3. Temporary administration of the government should be placed with the Revolutionary union of the Committee of the toiling peasantry.
>
> 4. The permanent government must be popularly elected on the basis of equal and direct suffrage of all the working masses.
>
> 5. Freedom of the press, of speech, personal liberty (*svoboda lichnosti*) and freedom of religion.
>
> 6. Government credit available on a broad and open basis for the improvement of agricultural production.
>
> 7. Government credits widely available for the establishment of schools, both rural and urban, and for training (*kursy*) and university studies.
>
> 8. Open, public instruction at all educational institutions, allowing for extensive initiative for commercial manufacturing and agricultural production.

> Signed: Provincial Committee of the Left SRs

While there are differences in wording, the spirit of the LSR list is fairly consistent with the main STK program, but it is not a complete alternative program. It is a separate list, and the fact that it surfaced during the course of the conflict (quite possibly via Cheka agents who had infiltrated the regional LSR organization) indicates that Left SRs in Tambov felt the need to begin drafting their own points for inclusion in a political program for the insurgency. See Danilov and Shanin, *KV*, 80.

7. This is an on-balance conclusion, but not without exception. A village declaration in Vol'naia Vershina (Borisoglebsk uezd), contained words about the revolution in Russia being usurped by the "October Counterrevolution," but in this case the Bolshevik seizure of power in 1917 was identified explicitly with the loss of civil liberties. See TsDNITO f. 840, op. 1, l. 1112, l. 16. Although the slogan "Soviets without Communists!" did not feature as prominently in the insurgency in Tambov as it did in earlier uprisings such as the *chapannaia voina* in Samara province (March 1919) and the later conflict in western Siberia (1920–1921), the continued emphasis on the soviets as decentralized democratic institutions was connected with the land and estate seizures of 1917–1918 that were famously "validated" with the fall of the Provisional Government. See Danilov and Shanin, *KDP*, 103; V. I. Shishkin, ed., *Za sovety bez kommunistov: krest'ianskoe vosstanie v Tiumenskoi gubernii 1921 g.* (Novosibirsk: Sibirskii khronograf, 2000).

8. Agitational literature used by the rebels regarding the Constituent Assembly was supplied by the PSR. See Danilov and Shanin, *KV*, 187. In a small example of how meaning is constructed and ideas are communicated in movements such the Antonov rebellion, one

woman questioned by state officials said that the Constituent Assembly had been described to her as a popularly elected body that would, in turn, elect a new "tsar" for Russia. This "tsar" would have a five-year term, after which the people could freely vote to reelect or reject him. This arrangement was explained to her by none other than Aleksandr Antonov himself. See GATO f. R-4049, op. 1, d. 143.

9. On the experiential background to political claims by insurgents, see Landis, "Between Village and Kremlin."

10. On the relationship between collective actors and ideologies, see Roger V. Gould, *Insurgent Identities: Class, Community, and Protest in Paris from 1848 to the Commune* (Chicago: University of Chicago Press, 1995), 15–16.

11. Kamenka was the confirmed location for both the provincial and Tambov uezd STK committees. Unfortunately, the uezd committees for Borisoglebsk and Kirsanov are not identified in the available materials. Judging by the activities and movements of the Partisan Army, however, as well as by the first volost and village STKs to be organized in January, one may assume that the STK committees for these two uezds were located in the southwest of Kirsanov uezd and the north of Borisoglebsk. It is also possible that the committees in Kirsanov and Borisoglebsk, unlike their counterpart in Tambov uezd, were not able to secure an established base and were forced to move from village to village in 1921.

12. There were no STKs, to my knowledge, that had a woman either elected or appointed to membership. While there are not records for all committees formed during the insurgency, the membership appears to be uniformly male.

13. One villager from Krasivka volost (Tambov uezd) told government investigators in April 1921 that his village had received rebel groups throughout the autumn of 1920, but his community was not asked to join the insurgency with the organization of an STK until January 1921. See GATO, f. R-1979, op. 1, d. 1090. l. 436. A similar case is noted in GA RF f. R-8415, op. 1, d. 127, ll. 46–46ob. As one might expect, there was no true uniformity to those committees that existed before the issuance of STK instructions in January 1921. In Treskino volost, at the heart of the insurgency, the future volost STK chairman stated that before 1921, the volost had only known the organization of "defense headquarters" that would dissolve periodically when Red Army forces took up positions in Treskino. See GATO f. R-4049, op. 1, d. 89, l. 110.

14. According to a summary of activities of the First Kamenka regiment by Cheka investigators:

> Agitation was carried out in the following way: upon the arrival of a rebel regiment in a given village, volost, or hamlet, the political workers and agitators of the regiment would call for a gathering of citizens at which they would make speeches on the inspiration and goals of the partisans as members of a voluntary army, and they would call the citizens to maintain order and calm and to give every assistance to the partisans and to actively join their ranks. In addition, the agitators would read out the STK program, their propaganda declarations, and so on, even posting copies of these materials for people to read throughout the village or volost. At the same time, they would attempt to organize a local committee of the Union of the Toiling Peasantry, if one did not already exist in that locality.

See GA RF f. R-8415, op. 1, d. 127, l. 46.

15. Such reluctance greeted STK agitators in the village of Mokhrovka (Borisoglebsk uezd), which was explained to the agitators with reference to the reprisals villagers had suffered following a small uprising in 1919 in the volost. This initial approach by the STK was made on 3 January 1921. However, some days later, the villagers overcame their reluctance and invited the STK activists back to their village. A similar story was described for the nearby village of Alebukhi:

> On 1 January 1921, during a two-hour stop in Alebukhi, the citizens of the village were called to a general assembly, but despite the church bell being rung to call people out of their homes, only thirty people at most showed up, and the meeting was postponed until the following day. At a later meeting with some of the villagers, it became clear [to STK organizers] that the villagers, despite their clear opposition to Soviet power and sympathy for the uprising of the peasants, were fearful of openly supporting the rebels, as they remembered all too clearly the uprising of the greens in 1919 and how the Soviet government severely punished the rebels. But in private meetings [with the STK organizers], the citizens expressed confidence that on the next day everyone would show up for an assembly to finally agree to the creation of their own [STK] organization.

See GA RF f. R-8415, op. 1, d. 127, l. 460b; TsDNITO f. 840, op. 1, d. 1112, l. 38.

16. GA RF f. R-8415, op. 1, d. 127, l. 75.

17. TsDNITO f. 840, op. 1, d. 1110, l. 174. Likewise, among local STK documents of this type, there are only two references to the PSR. In one, a rebel unit formed under the auspices of the STK in Zolotovka volost (Kirsanov uezd) initially named itself the Partisan Unit of the Party of Socialist Revolutionaries, a designation that was dropped once the rebels were formally integrated into the Partisan Army structure. See TsDNITO f. 840, op. 1, d. 1112, l. 109; also see Danilov and Shanin, *KV*, 199.

18. The size of the assembly depended on the size of the village or the density of settlements in a given area. Assemblies could be of a single village community, one commune within a larger village, or of several small villages in close proximity. Numbers could range from a few dozen to over 1,000, and these figures were often recorded in the protocols of these organizational meetings. Weather must have exercised some influence, as most STKs were formed in the winter of 1920–1921, inhibiting mass gatherings outdoors. STK records reviewed by the Cheka do not describe the venue for organizational meetings.

19. TsDNITO f. 840, op. 1, d. 1110, l. 93. Comparable wording is found in the declaration of Griaznovskie Dvoriki (Vasil'evka volost, Tambov uezd). See Danilov and Shanin, *KV*, 200.

20. The focus on the "toiling peasantry" was not entirely exclusive in the sense of class identity. One early such STK declaration proclaimed "Long live the Union of workers and peasants!" See Danilov and Shanin, *KV*, 207. All other indications are that the insurgents sought to cultivate a broad class identity based on the "working people" as a whole.

21. Danilov and Shanin, *KV*, 126.

22. During the first weeks of the rebellion, the crude nature of the rebels was emphasized both in their alleged support for the White commander, Wrangels, but also calls such as "Down with the Jew-Communists." See Danilov and Shanin, *KDP*.

23. An anecdotal reference to such a case is provided in Vedeniapin, "Antonovshchina," 225.

24. In one town, Kirsanov, with a sizable number of Jewish families, government officials were more worried about the anti-Semitic sentiment among Red Army soldiers stationed there than among the civilian population. See RGVA f. 25887, op. 1, d. 217, l. 172ob (September 1920).

25. GATO f. R-1979, op. 1, d. 1090, ll. 32–37. These materials relate to an investigation into the incident by government officials, who were interested to learn if the Jewish families were arrested by the Partisan Army, rather than evacuated to a safe place. The fact that all members of the families in question were still alive, and all swore to the honorable intentions of their fellow community members, made these investigations a dead end for government officials in 1921.

26. There are only a few anti-Semitic references in the surviving examples of pro-Antonov verse composed during the insurgency. See Danilov and Shanin, *KV*, 293–95. Even the less guarded language of rebel internal correspondence appears to be fairly clean of anti-Semitism. (An example can be found in Danilov and Shanin, *KV*, 99.) One letter, written by a villager from Borisoglebsk uezd to a Partisan Army regiment commander, referring to the abusive activities of "Jew-Communists," is remarkable for its uniqueness, but this did not prevent Cheka investigators from holding it up as typical. See GA RF f. R-8415, op. 1, d. 112, l. 17.

27. Danilov and Shanin, *KV*, 201. While "comrade" was generally used to describe fellow partisans and supporters of the insurgency, it was also fairly consistently used to designate certain activists within the STK and Partisan Army, while others were not. It is likely that, where possible, rebel activists who were also members of the PSR were graced with this title, while those who were not PSR members were simply recorded by their surnames. This would be parallel to the Bolsheviks' strict use of the title "comrade" to designate full party membership in official records, such as protocols of meetings.

28. Village of Malyi Burnachek (Tambov uezd). See TsDNITO f. 840, op. 1. d. 1110, l. 94.

29. GATO f. R-1979, op. 1, d. 1090, ll. 108, 151, 221, 230, 241–43; Danilov and Shanin, *KV*, 200. It is difficult to gauge how widespread this practice of gathering signatures had been. In many later interrogations of villagers in places occupied by the Red Army, people often insisted that they had never signed any documents supporting the formation of their local STK committee.

30. There were instructions regarding membership in the STK as a public organization similar to those regulating membership in a political party or union, but they emerged at a time when rebel political leaders had high hopes for the STK developing into a larger social movement in line with the original conception of the PSR Central Committee outlined in its 13 May 1920 circular letter. The actual functioning of the STK in Tambov in 1920–1921 was something entirely different, and membership criteria were much more pragmatic when it came to the selection for posts in the local committees. See Danilov and Shanin, *KV*, 95–96.

31. GATO f. R-1979, op. 1, d. 1090, ll. 251, 439. One church psalmist from the village of Gromushka (Tambov uezd) stated that he was selected for membership in the local STK because he could read and write, and his professed involvement was restricted to reading STK propaganda and correspondence to members of the committee and community at large and taking minutes at STK meetings. See GATO f. R-5201, op. 2, d. 1690, l. 43.

32. GATO f. R-1979, op. 1, d. 1090, ll. 59, 194, 230.

33. Emphasis added. See GATO f. R-1979, op. 1, d. 1090, ll. 60–60ob, 124, 442. In other STK documents pertaining to the appointment of committee members, the element of voluntarism was specified. See Danilov and Shanin, *KV*, 201.

34. A report to the Tenth Tambov Party Conference in January 1921 stated, perhaps with some exaggeration, that nearly 1,000 party members had been killed since the start of the insurgency. See RGASPI f. 17, op.13, d. 1005, ll. 39–45.

35. A typical statement comes from the village of Chernavka (Tokarevka volost, Tambov uezd):

> I, [Egor Vasil'evich] Klinkov, served for nearly three years as the chairman of the local soviet in Chernavka, and on 11 January [1921] the bandits appeared in our village from Pavlovka [a neighboring village to the southeast], led by Vasilii Kirilov Mistratov [*sic*], and they demanded from me as the soviet chairman for all the Communists to be handed over, but I said that there were no Communists in our village, and so they then took from us all our horses and left, after which bandit scouts returned to Chernavko almost daily, demanding from me fodder for their horses and food for themselves, which I was forced to give against my will. Then on 8 January [*sic*—18 January?] three bandits from Pavloka came into our village—their names were Iurii, Vasilii, and Mikhail, I don't recall the surnames—and they demanded that we come out for a general assembly in order to choose a chairman [of the village STK], and at the assembly the local citizens demanded that I, as the senior chairman [of the soviet], be appointed chairman of the committee, and up until the arrival of the Reds, nearly four months later, I served as chairman of the bandit committee.

See GATO f. R-1979, op. 1, d. 1090, l. 59.

36. Suspicion of Communist Party members remained strong, however. One group of villagers in Petrovskoe (Tambov uezd) appealed to the Partisan Army to protect their former soviet chairman: "Our former village soviet chairman, Nikita Timofeevich Zakhatov, has the full backing of the members of our community, and he has never done anything bad for the local population and as can be seen from his documents he has always been nonparty." See TsDNITO f. 840, op. 1, d. 1110, l. 132.

37. TsDNITO f. 840, op. 1, d. 1112, l. 94. On the dynamics of rebellions in small communities, and particularly the role of intervillage agitators, see Roger Peterson, "A Community-Based Theory of Rebellion," *European Journal of Sociology* 34 (1998).

38. TsDNITO f. 840, op. 1, d. 1110, ll. 84, 108, 110; GATO f. R-1979, op. 1, d. 1090, ll. 1129, 130. The Partisan Army also contained units that appeared to specialize in such acts of sabotage, particularly in areas near significant railway stations, such as Tokarevka. See GA RF f. R- 8415, op. 1, d. 127, ll. 55–560b, 93.

39. Instructions to the newly created STK in Mozhaika (Tambov uezd) are an example of the comprehensive destruction sought by rebel leaders, calling on citizens "to spread out along the rail line with horse-drawn carts, pull up and remove the rails and ties to a far distance from the line. The workers at the station [Rzhaksa] are to be informed that they have two days to leave their posts. Bridges should be burned. Spare rails, ties, points, and switch rails kept at the stations and warehouses should be removed. Warehouses, stations, water tanks, and reservoirs should be either burned or disabled." See TsDNITO f. 840, op. 1, d. 1110, l. 108.

40. For a differing interpretation of this characteristic of the STKs, see S. A. Esikov and V. V. Kanishchev, "'Antonovskii NEP' (Organizatsiia i deiatel'nost' 'Soiza trudovogo krest'ianstva' Tambovskoi gubernii, 1920–1921)," *Otechestvennaia istoriia* 4 (1993).

41. Danilov and Shanin, *KV*, 80–81. According to STK instructions, the regional committees were to have a militia force of ten men under their authority, and district committees were to have five men.

42. On the tsarist-era militias and police force, see Stephen Frank, *Crime, Cultural Conflict, and Justice in Rural Russia, 1856–1914* (Berkeley: University of California Press, 1999).

43. TsDNITO f. 840, op. 1, d. 1110, ll. 56, 76.

44. GATO f. R-1979, op. 1, d. 1090, ll. 59, 194.

45. TsDNITO f. 840, op. 1, d. 1112, l. 106.

46. On rebel scouting, see the official Partisan Army instruction, dated 21 February 1921, at GA RF f. R-8415, op. 1, d. 127, ll. 25–260b.

47. GA RF f. R-8415, op. 1, d. 127, l. 50b; GA RF f. R-8415, op. 1, d. 124, l. 2.

48. GA RF f. R-8415, op. 1, d. 112, l. 2; GA RF f. R-8415, op. 1, d. 127, l. 6; GATO f. R-4049, op. 1, d. 89, l. 35.

49. Vedeniapin, "Antonovshchina," 223–24. For a similar contemporary assessment of rebel "spying," see Danilov and Shanin, *KV*, 155–56.

50. Vedeniapin, "Antonovshchina," 241.

51. GA RF f. R-8415, op. 1, d. 124, l. 24. Another example is provided by the case of a woman, visiting the village of Kochetovka with her young son, looking for a cobbler who could provide the boy with shoes. She was soon arrested by local government officials who suspected her of spying for the rebels because she asked many questions of locals. As the woman explained to investigators, she was only trying to learn where the cobbler lived. Statements were taken from the cobbler and the boy regarding the case, which was eventually dropped. See GATO f. R-1979, op. 1, d. 1090, l. 235.

52. GA RF f. R-8415, op. 1, d. 127, ll. 370b, 450b, 740b.

53. Danilov and Shanin, *KV*, 215–16.

54. This was a typical excuse for young men being investigated for possible involvement in the insurgency. If a man was of Red Army service age and claimed not to have participated in the rebellion, then he was immediately suspected of being a deserter if he lacked the proper exemption documents. However, several STK members admitted confiscating and destroying such documents. See GATO f. R-1979, op. 1, d. 1090, ll. 200, 211, 212, 326, 340, 431.

55. Danilov and Shanin, *KV*, 202. The fluidity of such groups also complicated the efforts of Cheka investigators to form an accurate portrait of the Partisan Army structure and composition in the summer of 1921. See, for example, GA RF f. R-8415, op. 1, d. 127, l. 63.

56. In all, Cheka investigators identified over twenty-one separate Partisan Army regiments following analysis of captured rebel documents. See RGVA f. 633, op. 1, d. 129, ll. 1–12; RGVA f. 7709, op. 1, d. 232, l. 56; Samoshkin, *Antonovskoe*, 65–66, 115–16.

57. GA RF f. R-8415, op. 1, d. 127, l. 76. The mobilization of former officers was evidently in accord with Order no. 78 of the First Partisan Army, 14 January 1921. At the Tambov uezd STK Congress on 5 February 1921, one of the issues on the agenda was the formation of new units composed of veterans of World War 1 and the Russo-Japanese War. See Danilov and Shanin, *KV*, 201, 203. Comparing the mobilization of former officers by the Partisan Army to the same measure introduced by the Red Army is not to say that former officers did not join the rebels out of a well-honed hatred of the Communist regime. But joining was not a reflex response to the insurgency. Mokarev relates the story of one former tsarist officer discovered near the village of Treskino, at the heart of the rebellion. This particular man was found living in a small bunker near the village, where he had been intent on avoiding contact with both the Red Army and Partisan Army. He had been living in this bunker for six months before Red

Army cadets discovered him in the summer of 1921. See V. Mokarev, "Kursantskii spor na bor'be s antonovshchinoi," *Voina i revoliutsiia*, no. 1 (1932): 74. Others went to great lengths to avoid service in both armies. For example, see RGVA f. 235, op. 2, d. 335, l. 27.

58. Partisan Army regiments, in some cases, kept records of the military experience of rebel soldiers, especially those who had been officers or had served in the tsarist army. Contrary to Soviet-era contentions, there is no indication that the keeping of such records was informed by considerations of political reliability. See GA RF f. R-8415, op. 1, d. 127, l. 77.

59. Danilov and Shanin, *KV*, 81; Hagen, *Soldiers*, 129. Later assessments estimated that the number of Red Army men who subsequently joined rebel forces at the turn of the New Year approached 4,000. RGASPI f. 17, op. 13, d. 1010, l. 29. The prominence of demobilized soldiers in the Partisan Army was confirmed in the course of amnesties conducted in the spring and summer of 1921. See GATO f. R-1979, op. 1, d. 1090, ll. 353–54, 357–58, 365–66, 369–71 and *passim*.

60. GATO f. R-4049, op. 1, d. 89, ll. 98ob, 114. In one curious incident in January 1921, recorded in seized Partisan Army materials, a rail convoy of demobilized Red Army service-men (identified as former soldiers of Admiral Kolchak's army in Siberia, who surrendered in 1919 and joined the Red Army) were held up Zherdevka station by Partisan Army forces. They claimed to know nothing of the insurgency in Tambov, and they expressed their desire to continue on their way rather than join the rebellion. Despite reports that the soldiers were in-clined to fraternize with the rebels, they instead asked the rebels to guarantee their safety as they passed through Tambov Province, promising that they would never participate in Red Army counterinsurgency operations, in Tambov or elsewhere. However, all the cars of Red Army servicemen left Zherdevka except one, whose passengers were assumed to have agreed to join the rebels. See GA RF f. R-8415, op. 1, d. 1127, ll. 66ob–67. In a January 1921 protocol of the provincial STK, one member (Cherkasov) reports on fears that such convoys of demobilized Red Army servicemen were being stopped in Tambov by local officials in order to organize and equip them for participation in the counterinsurgency efforts. See Danilov and Shanin, *KV*, 96–97.

61. GATO f. R-4049, op. 1, d. 89, ll. 71–72.

62. The STKs were also charged with making sure that young men in the villages did not fall into the hands of the Red Army. When advance warning was received of an approaching Red Army unit, a local STK was to organize the evacuation of all young men of service age to nearby rebel villages. See TsDNITO f. 840, op. 1, d. 1110, l. 65.

63. This assistance to the families of Partisan Army soldiers included the continuation of welfare provision to the families of rebels who had died in action. See TsDNITO f. 840, op. 1, d. 1110, ll. 81, 159; GATO f. R-4049, op. 1, d. 89, l. 114. On the recovery of previously confiscated property, see TsDNITO f. 840, op. 1, d. 1112, l. 72 (Tugolukovka STK, Borisoglebsk).

64. TsDNITO f. 840, op. 1, d. 1112, ll. 36, 74. A practice that did not favor particular house-holds was the recovery of property confiscated by government agents as punishment for non-fulfillment of the razverstka. In one case described in rebel documents (Tugolukovka volost, Borisoglebsk uezd), the local STK accepted applications from individual households, in which confiscated items were listed, and these items would then be returned to their owners if and when they were recovered from government storage points seized by the Partisan Army. See TsDNITO f. 840, op. 1, d. 1112, l. 75.

65. TsDNITO f. 840, op. 1, d. 1110, l. 159; Danilov and Shanin, *KV*, 203, 211.

66. Danilov and Shanin, *KV*, 81. There were even ideas of holding congresses of millers, meat curers, dairy producers, and so on to coordinate production and supply in the rebel zone. It is unknown as to whether these ideas were brought to life. See ibid., 99.

67. GATO f. R-1979, op. 1, d. 1090, l. 59; Danilov and Shanin, *KV*, 199.

68. Danilov and Shanin, *KV*, 215.

69. RGVA f. 235, op. 5, d. 136, ll. 39–390b.

70. Danilov and Shanin, *KV*, 97.

71. See the words of Fedor Podkhvatilin, who worked both in the STK organization and with the Partisan Army as a political agitator, in ibid., 194. This is a common problem for all armed forces involved in insurgency situations and occupations. A close comparison for the situation in Tambov is that provided by the *chapannaia voina* in the Volga region in 1919, whose leaders issued similar appeals to insurgents discouraging "banditry." See ibid., 107. Another example of insurgents struggling to contain banditry is provided by the army under Emiliano Zapata in the Mexican civil war. See Samuel Brunk, "'The Sad Situation of Civilians and Soliders': The Banditry of Zapatismo in the Mexican Revolution," *American Historical Review 101*, no. 2 (1996). For the counterinsurgency aspects of the same problem generally, see Anthony James Joes, *Resisting Rebellion: The History and Politics of Counterinsurgency* (Lexington: University Press of Kentucky, 2004).

72. Danilov and Shanin, *KV*, 86.

73. GA RF f. R-8415, op. 1, d. 127, ll. 21–22.

74. A. Kazakov, *Partiia sotsialistov-revoliutsionerov v Tambovskom vosstanii 1920–21 gg.* (Moscow: [s.n.], 1922).

75. In one case of sustained criminal activity by a Partisan Army brigade, the three senior members of the brigade were tried and punished after villagers petitioned army headquarters about the black market trading being controlled by the brigade in their area. The two most senior brigade members received death sentences, while a third was punished by fifty lashes, with a threat of execution upon a repeat violation. See GA RF f. R-8415, op. 1, d. 127, l. 390b.

76. GATO f. R-1979, op. 1, d. 89, ll. 143–44. This banner was kept by Antonov's "Special Regiment."

77. According to one contemporary, the rebel army maintained at one time "an entire orchestra" to accompany their renditions of the "International." See Sergei Semenovich Pomazov, "Bor'ba za vlast' Sovetov v byvshem Kirsanovskom uezde" (Internet site), www.grad-kirsanov.ru/source.php?id=memory.pomazov1 [accessed 18 September 2006]. Also Pavel Vasil'evich Romanov, "Vospominaniia" (Internet site), www.grad-kirsanov.ru/source.php?id=memory.romanov [accessed 18 September 2006]; Vladimir V. Samoshkin, "Miatezh. Antonovshchina: Konets," *Literaturnaia Rossiia*, 30 November 1990, 18. Reports of Antonov and his men adorning their "uniforms" with red ribbons emerged in the first weeks of the conflict in 1920. See Danilov and Shanin, *KV*, 69–70.

78. GA RF f. R-8415, op. 1, d. 127, l. 46.

79. RGVA f. 34228, op. 1, d. 49, l. 470.

80. Red Army servicemen who had been held prisoner by the Partisan Army later told investigators that Antonov carried two Nagan system revolvers. This may have been the case in January 1921, when the men were held prisoner, but these were not the monogrammed

weapons allegedly found in the possession of the Antonovs when they were eventually hunted down and killed in 1922. See RGVA f. 235, op. 5, d. 136, l. 30.

81. GATO f. R-4049, op. 1, d. 89, ll. 143–44.

82. Pomazov, "Bor'ba za vlast'." Samoshkin describes Antonov's "Special Regiment" as wearing fairly elaborate uniforms—complete with black leather coats, red breeches and red service caps—as well as being distinctively professional and disciplined in their conduct. See Vladimir V. Samoshkin, "Slovo o krasnykh kursantakh," *Pod'em* 10 (1987): 123.

83. Tatiana A. Liapina, "Ispoved' v podvale GubChK," *Posleslovie* 6 (1993): 3.

84. GATO f. R-4049, op. 1, d. 198, l. 141ob. Despite his desire to make Drigo-Drigina his "wife," Tokmakov too kept several lovers during his time as a rebel commander. GATO f. R-4049, op. 1, d. 89, l. 178.

85. RGVA f. 235, op. 5, d. 136, l. 13; GATO R-1979, op.1, d. 1090, l. 282.

86. GA RF f. R-8415, op. 1, d. 127, l. 66.

87. Vedeniapin, "Antonovshchina," 245–46. Vedeniapin describes how such words were effective, particularly, in feeding the misgivings of Red Army soldiers. He and his colleagues in the Cheka in Saratov had to convince soldiers that the claims of the insurgents were a complete falsehood, and that anti-Soviet rebellions were confined to Tambov Province. See Vedeniapin, "Antonovshchina," 238.

88. Danilov and Shanin, *KV*, 142.

89. TsDNITO f. 840, op. 1, d. 1112, l. 49.

90. GATO f. R-5201, op. 2, d. 2558, l. 48.

91. See Erik-C. Landis, "Waiting for Makhno: Legitimacy and Context in a Russian Peasant War," *Past and Present* 183 (2004).

92. GATO f. R-4049, op. 1, d. 198, l. 141–141ob.

93. See GA RF f. 8415, op. 1, d. 127, l. 46; RGVA f. 235, op. 5, d. 136, l. 39.

Chapter 6: Claiming the Initiative

1. Danilov and Shanin, *KV*, 86.

2. Ibid., 103.

3. Ibid.

4. M. N. Tukhachevskii, "Bor'ba s kontrrevoliutsionnymi vosstaniiami," *Voina i revoliutsiia*, no. 8 (1926): 5.

5. Danilov and Shanin, *KV*, 85, 86.

6. The forces deployed to Tambov in January included: the Fifteenth (Siberian) Cavalry Division, the Tenth (Briansk) Rifle Brigade, one infantry brigade from Samara, three armored train groups, and three motorized armored units. Although VNUS and reserve troops had proven unreliable in the final months of 1920, the January deployments to Tambov included many units to replace those that had been composed principally of Tambov natives. See RGVA f. 25887, op. 1, d. 511, ll. 4, 21; Iakovlev, *Vnutrennie voiska*, 574–77; Danilov and Shanin, *KV*, 103, 306–07; I. Ia. Trifonov, "Iz istorii pazgroma antonovshchiny v 1920–1921 godakh," *Voenno-istoricheskii zhurnal* 9 (1968): 30.

7. Initially, four sectors were established, dividing up the territory of the insurgency in three uezds, Kirsanov, Tambov, and Borisoglebsk. The First and Fourth Sectors were based in Kirsanov and Borisoglebsk towns, respectively, while the Third was situated at the railway station at Zherdevka (by the end of January it was moved to another railway station at Mordovo). The Second Sector headquarters had no fixed location at first, but its area of operations covered the area of Tambov uezd immediately south and east of the provincial capital.

8. Hagen, *Soldiers*, 129.

9. In particular, minor railway stations were often defended only by Labor Army groups, and not by relatively well-trained VNUS or regular Red Army troops. According to an official attached to such a labor unit in Borisoglebsk uezd: "The rebel bands and local population can see how weak we are, and they also continue to suffer the depredations of the requisition brigades, and this not only strengthens the morale of the bandits, it also increases their numbers in real terms, as more and more of the local population are drawn into their ranks." See RGVA f. 25887, op. 1, d. 371, ll. 213–213ob; RGVA f. 25887, op. 1, d. 511, l. 13.

10. On 19 January 1921, largely to compensate for the ongoing demobilization of the Red Army, the armed internal security forces of VNUS were transferred (with some exceptions) to the War Commissariat and placed under Red Army command. VNUS was dissolved and an internal security directorate was created under the auspices of the Red Army Glavkom.

11. Samoshkin, "Slovo o krasnykh kursantakh," 121; Trifonov, "Iz istorii razgroma," 30. For an example, see the letter sent by party officials in Borisoglebsk to the Central Committee, 28 December 1920: "It is left for us here to repeat that local forces are not sufficient to liquidate the banditry problem, and, given the circumstances, just sending firearms will not suffice. . . . We must again emphasize to you that the situation is extremely serious not only in Borisoglebsk, but throughout the republic, and the uezd party committee requests that the Central Committee pay serious attention to the urgent need to take decisive measures, particularly the deployment of regular Red Army troops, especially cavalry and a variety of others weapons, to Borisoglebsk and generally to Tambov Province." Quoted in Donkov, *Antonovshchina*, 46–47.

12. Unlike Red Army documents, STK records date the assault on Borisoglebsk as 16 January 1921. TsDNITO f. 840, op. 1, d. 1112, l. 48; Samoshkin, "Slovo o krasnykh kursantakh," 121; Vladimir V. Samoshkin, "Bronepoezd no. 121," *Zherdevskie novosti*, 3 February 1996, 2. On the day the regiment of the Partisan Army attempted to storm Borisoglebsk, the armored train group "no. 121" sent to defend the town came under attack near the station at Rymarevo, to the north. With the rail lines sabotaged in both directions, the thirty-nine Red Army soldiers on the armored train held out for a staggering twelve days under regular gunfire from rebels before Red Army troops arrived on 4 February to dispel them.

13. As a Kirsanov Communist Party member wrote: "I can still recall terrible, horrifying images from that time. Often our comrades were carried back to Kirsanov missing heads, with the chest or spine slashed, the eyes or ears removed, sometimes completely dismembered." See L. G. Protasov, ed., *Stranitsy istorii Tambovskogo kraia* (Voronezh: Tsentral'noe-Chernozemnoe knizhnoe izdatel'stvo, 1986), 143. See also a Kiranov party report to the Central Committee in Moscow, quoted in Donkov, *Antonovshchina*, 46.

14. The overall fulfillment of the procurement target was well above the national average, but this was achieved only after the target for Tambov was revised in early 1921 and reduced by nearly half. See Chernykh, "Rol' gubernii," 171.

15. The conflict between Food Commissariat officials and other state and party authorities was most pronounced in Kozlov, Morshansk, and Shatsk. See RGASPI f. 17, op. 13, d. 1000, ll. 5, 32.

16. GATO f. R-18, op. 1, d. 62, ll. 82–84, 93–96. In Kirsanov uezd, all food distribution to the civilian population (except for state orphanages) ceased on 20 January 1921. See Donkov, *Antonovshchina*, 52.

17. GATO f. R-1, op. 1, d. 293, ll. 89, 210, 211, 268. The officials in the Morshansk Soviet administration responsible for this practice were eventually arrested.

18. Desertion from Red Army units in Tambov accounted for the loss of 8,362 men in January and February 1921, but it is not clear what proportion deserted from nonactive reserve garrisons. Samoshkin, *Antonovskoe*, 77.

19. GATO f. R-18, op. 1, d. 62, ll. 94, 102–102ob. On this point, see Peter Bearman, "Desertion as Localism: Army Solidarity and Group Norms in the US Civil War," *Social Forces* 70, no. 2 (1991).

20. GATO f. R-18, op. 1, d. 62, l. 91.

21. GA RF f. R-8415, op. 1, d. 124, l. 124.

22. GATO f. R-1, op. 1, d. 317, l. 1. Like officials in Kirsanov, those in Borisoglebsk had first made a display of their decision to send representatives in December 1920 directly to Moscow, bypassing the provincial administration in Tambov. See also Danilov and Shanin, *KV*, 131.

23. RGASPI f. 17, op. 13, d. 1000, l. 2.

24. It was only at the end of November 1920 that the Tambov Communist Party resolved to begin publication of a satirical wall newspaper entitled "The Truth about the Bandits," accompanied by other publications, such as another wall newspaper produced for government troops engaged in the counterinsurgency effort. However, in the estimation of the Tambov ROSTA chief, Evgenev, these limited efforts were not an effort at "mass agitation" to rival that undertaken by the Partisan Army and the STK. See GA RF f. R-8415, op. 1, d. 110, l. 7; Danilov and Shanin, *KV*, 78; A. Nabokin, "Vintovkoi i slovom," in *Parol'—muzhestvo. Ocherki o tambovskikh chekistakh*, ed. G. D. Remizov (Voronezh: Tsentral'noe-chernozemnoe knizhnoe izdatel'stvo, 1986), 101.

25. A 17 January 1921 order established joint control by the Tambov military command and the Food Commissariat over procurement efforts in Kirsanov, Borisoglebsk, and Tambov uezds. See f. R-1, op. 1. d. 293, l. 34.

26. S. A. Esikov, "Rukovodstvo Tambovskikh bolshevikov v 1920–nachale 1921g. (Kachestvennaia kharakteristika)," in *Obshchestvenno-politicheskaia zhizn' rossiiskoi provintsii XX vek* (Tambov: Tambovskii Gosudarstvennyi Tekhnicheskii Universitet, 1996), 59.

27. See Landis, "A Civil War Episode."

28. RGASPI f. 17, op. 13, d. 1005, l. 139. While Skhlikhter and Meshcheriakov arrived in Tambov at different times in May and July 1920, respectively, the two had worked closely together in Ukraine in 1919, where Shlikhter was food commissar and Meshcheriakov commissar for land affairs.

29. William Chase, *Workers, Society and the Soviet State: Labor and Life in Moscow, 1918–1929* (Urbana and Chicago: University of Illinois Press, 1987), 52–53.

30. Kanishchev and Meshcheriakov, *Anatomiia*, 27.

31. *V. I. Lenin i A. V. Lunacharskii. Perepiska, doklady, dokumenty* (Moscow: Nauka, 1971), 482.

32. A later memorandum written by an unidentified Cheka agent described Vasil'ev as an "insufferable intriguer" who preferred positions in which he had maximum influence with minimum responsibility, concluding that Vasil'ev was "an entirely dangerous, yet well-mannered and talented, demagogue." See Esikov, "Rukovodstvo," 60.

33. *V. I. Lenin i A. V. Lunacharskii,* 484.

34. Ibid.

35. Lunarcharsky addressed the Seventh Congress on 1 February 1921. See Okatov et al., *Sovety Tambovskoi gubernii,* 296.

36. See, for example, Danilov and Shanin, *KV,* 111. On Meshcheriakov, see Grigorii Orlovskii, *"Kak dela v tambovskoi gubernii?": sbornik ocherkov* (Voronezh: Tsentral'noe chernozemnoe knizhnoe izd., 1974), 128–35.

37. Pavlov is quoted by Lunacharsky as stating: "Up to this moment, [the campaign] has been conducted with a certain measure of indifference, as in power we have people who are not entirely capable of performing their duties, people I fear who are extremely petty and who are nevertheless in charge of a rich and very complex province." See *V. I. Lenin i A. V. Lunacharskii,* 484.

38. Shlikhter had approached Commander Pavlov about imposing more centralized leadership in the province. He later wrote to S. S. Kamenev at Red Army headquarters in Moscow: "In Tambov there is such a feud taking place between the party and the soviet executive committee that I may be forced to intervene myself in order to settle the dispute. Comrade Shlikhter visited recently and pleaded with me to help save the situation, to help save the party. The suppression of the insurgency can only be achieved with the cooperation of the party, but at present there is no such cooperation. I have spoken with Lunacharsky, and with [L.?] Kamenev, and they share my evaluation of the situation. Therefore . . . I ask for your advice: is it not time for us to apply a strong military hand to the situation and establish a revolutionary military soviet that would allow men such as Shlikhter and Meshcheriakov, whom you know and with whom I can work productively, to concentrate on the important matters at hand [?] I repeat: the situation here is now very critical." Samoshkin, *Antonovskoe,* 81.

39. A June 1921 report by a political commission attached to the Red Army in Tambov held the local politicians largely to blame for the rise of the insurgency in the province, linking their political intrigues to a wider sense of dispirit in the provincial Communist Party. The result was an organization in which "two-thirds" of local party members worked to discredit Soviet authority and indirectly helped fuel the insurgency, although this was as specific as the commission's conclusions on the whole were. See Esikov, "Rukovodstvo," 60.

40. The sowing committees were introduced on 15 January 1921 by VTsIK decree. See E. B. Genkina, *Gosudarstvennaia deiatel'nost' V. I. Lenina, 1921–1923* (Moscow: Nauka, 1969); Lars T. Lih, "The Bolshevik Sowing Committees of 1920: Apotheosis of War Communism?" *The Carl Beck Papers in Russian and East European Studies* 803 (1990).

41. GATO f. R-18, op. 1, d. 62, l. 93. The Tambov Communist Party also sent a detailed report to the Central Committee on the food crisis in the province on 25 January 1921. See I. P. Donkov, "Organizatsiia razgroma antonovshchiny," *Voprosy istorii KPSS* 6 (1966), 66.

42. Danilov and Shanin, *KV,* 109–10.

43. Ibid., 111–12; Okatov et al., *Sovety Tambovskoi gubernii,* 299–300.

44. The first such nonparty conference was scheduled to take place on 20 February. Just

how "nonparty" the conference was could be almost immediately questioned, following the instructions issued on 12 February 1921 for Communist Party organizations in the uezds to begin selecting delegates for the conference. See Okatov et al., *Sovety Tambovskoi gubernii*, 302.

45. Orlovskii, *Kak dela*, 81.

46. Lenin, *Sochineniia*, 32:111. On the long-standing controversy over the razverstka and party debates relating to its termination, see S. A. Pavliuchenkov, *Krest'ianskii Brest, ili predystoriia bolshevistskogo NEPa* (Moscow: Russkoe knigoizdatel'skoe tovarishchestvo, 1996).

47. Citing archival documents, Grigorii Orlovskii claims that the decision had been taken by the Tambov soviet executive committee on the evening of 8 February. See Orlovskii, *Kak dela*, 81–82.

48. Arup Banerji, *Merchants and Markets in Revolutionary Russia, 1917–30* (Basingstoke: Macmillan, 1997), 42.

49. Donkov, *Antonovshchina*, 56.

50. Fatueva, *Protivostoianie*, 232–33.

51. Okatov et al., *Sovety Tambovskoi gubernii*, 302.

52. Quoted in Orlovskii, *Kak dela*, 83.

53. Beliakov offers this version in his memoirs. See Mikhail F. Beliakov, "Na VIII s'ezde Sovetov. Vospominaniia delegata," in *O Vladimire Il'iche Lenine: Vospominaniia, 1900–1922 gg.*, ed. F. N. Petrov (Moscow: Gosudarstvennoe izdatel'stvo politicheskoi literatury, 1963), 580–84.

54. Ibid., 581.

55. Orlovskii claims that it was Pavlov who proposed the idea in February 1921 of sending peasants to meet with Lenin. While it is always best to treat "Lenin-centered" versions of events with caution, such an orchestrated meeting with Lenin had likely been arranged well in advance. See Orlovskii, *Kak dela*, 81–82.

56. Beliakov, "Na VIII s'ezde," 582.

57. Orlovskii, *Kak dela*, 83–84.

58. The piece initially appeared in the first issue of the newspaper *Tambovskii pakhar'*. See Danilov and Shanin, *KV*, 121–22; Okatov et al., *Sovety Tambovskoi gubernii*, 304–05; Donkov, *Antonovshchina*, 61.

59. Danilov and Shanin, *KV*, 122. Lenin is recorded as adding: "I know how difficult life is for the peasant, how all people ever do is take from the peasant while he receives so little in return. I know peasant life, I love it, and I respect it. I only ask that the peasants remain patient for a while longer and continue to assist their government."

60. On local communities' efforts to engage the state regarding the pursuit of food procurement targets, see Landis, "Between Village and Kremlin."

61. The full name was the Plenipotentiary Commission of VTsIK for the Fight Against Banditry in Tambov Province. The first session of the commission did not take place until 2 March, after personnel and organizational matters had been resolved.

62. Ulrikh was particularly suspicious of Nemtsov, and he reported that Nemtsov believed that the first nonparty conference scheduled for 20 February could be used as an opportunity to meet with "representatives of the insurgent regions, including Antonov himself" and for negotiations to be opened between the Soviet government and the insurgents.

> Moreover, Comrade Nemtsov spoke to me of the need to liquidate the revolutionary military tribunals [Ulrikh's own specialism], of the conviction that the Special Department [of

the Cheka] was not needed, and that what was required was for all armed forces deployed on the "so-called front" (his exact words) to be withdrawn, in effect a termination of all military operations.... Nemtsov's plan would bring complete chaos to the fight against kulak rebellions not only in his own Tambov but also in neighboring Saratov, Voronezh, etc.

Questioning Nemtsov further, Ulrikh asked what he would do with Antonov and the other senior rebels if negotiations were to succeed: "They would certainly make excellent agitators," Nemtsov is reported as replying. See Fatueva, *Protivostoianie*, 233–34.

63. Vasil'ev had been made secretary of the provincial Communist Party on 17 February, before his promotion to party chairman two weeks later. See RGASPI f. 17, op. 13, d. 1005, ll. 139–140; RGASPI f. 17, op. 13, d. 1000, l. 17.

64. Antonov-Ovseenko had prepared the ground for the conference with a series of speeches to municipal organizations in Tambov, denouncing the Tambov clique as "demagogic" and labeling their political platform an example of "hooray democracy." See Antonov-Ovseenko's first summary report on his activities as Plenipotentiary Commission chairman, in Danilov and Shanin, *KV*, 127.

65. Donkov, *Antonovshchina*, 61–63.

66. On the army's political department (POARM) at the time of Zhabin's arrival in Tambov, see Trifonov, *Klassy*, 199.

67. Danilov and Shanin, *KDP*, 118.

68. Similar proposals were made regarding the antidesertion patrols accused of corruption and mistreatment of civilians. In the words of the Orel staff commander, A. Azarov: "The population—that is, the peasantry—will see and appreciate the honorable face of Soviet power, and banditry, having been struck in this way at its roots, will be easily liquidated with an energetic and sharp blow." See Fatueva, *Protivostoianie*, 238–41.

69. Danilov and Shanin, *KDP*, 118–19.

70. "In general, this is an anxious moment in time," wrote party officials in Kozlov in mid-February 1921, "in all respects it is difficult, but especially for the peasants. The prospects for famine are clear, not only in the present year but also for the next due to the shortage of seed grain and draft horses.... The overall conclusion is that it is simply impossible to do what is required for the next sowing season. The necessary materials are completely lacking ... and this contributes to a picture of village life that is truly nightmarish." See GATO f. R-18, op. 1, d. 62, l. 99.

71. "Helping the countryside" was added to the masthead of all official publications in the province. See Danilov and Shanin, *KV*, 127; Trifonov, *Klassy*, 199–202.

72. There was debate over the use of coercion to introduce more "modern" techniques of cultivation to peasant communities. See Lih, "Sowing Committees."

73. RGASPI f. 17, op. 13, d. 1010, ll. 31–32.

74. Sowing committees were set up in the conflict area in larger villages where the state could establish revolutionary committees. The expectation of direct assistance also held true in such cases. See GATO f. R-1, op. 1, d. 283, l. 30.

75. While seed grain was in short supply for distribution, other scarce items such as salt and kerosene were available in limited quantities for villages that demonstrated loyalty, as had been done in previous years of the civil war by the Soviet government. See RGASPI f. 17, op. 13, d. 1008, l. 30.

76. Chase, *Workers, Society and the Soviet State*, 49; Jonathan Aves, *Workers Against Lenin: Labour Protest and the Bolshevik Dictatorship* (London: Tauris Academic Studies, 1996), 138–39.

77. V. Moskovkin, "Vosstanie krest'ian v Zapadnoi Sibiri v 1921 godu," *Voprosii istorii* 6 (1998); Shishkin, *Za sovety*; V. I. Shishkin, ed., *Sibirskaia vandeia* (Moscow: "Demokratiia," 2001).

78. V. P. Naumov and A. A. Kosakovskii, eds., *Kronshtadt 1921. Dokumenty o sobytiiakh v Kronshtadte vesnoi 1921 g.* (Moscow: Demokratiia, 1997), 27–29, 34, 36–37.

79. Ibid., 8.

80. This problem was intensified by the ongoing demobilization of the Red Army, a fact highlighted by senior military and state officials in a memorandum to the Central Committee of the Communist Party on 13 February 1921. See Fatueva, *Protivostoianie*, 222–24; Naumov and Kosakovskii, *Kronshtadt 1921*, 24–25.

81. Aves, *Workers*, 160–61.

82. The Sovnarkom decree provided another opportunity for the Plenipotentiary Commission to compose another announcement to the rural population of Tambov. See Okatov et al., *Sovety Tambovskoi gubernii*, 313–14.

83. GATO f. R-1, op. 1, d. 283, l. 36.

84. Shugol' even stated, in sharp contrast to his predecessor as food commissar in Tambov, Gol'din, that he would refuse to conduct tax assessments on the basis of fifteen-year-old zcmstvo statistics on harvcst yiclds, as was customary undcr thc razvcrstka. Shugol's criticism was echoed openly after the razverstka policy was abandoned. See GATO f. R-1, op. 1, d. 283, ll. 36–37, 40–41, 54; GATO f. R-1, op. 1, d. 293, l. 510.

85. GATO f. R-1, op. 1, d. 283, ll. 43–44.

86. The first instructions issued on the new "Methods of Provisions Organs" on 14 April underscored the new ethos of provisions workers to be encouraged under the tax in kind. See GATO f. R-1, op. 1, d. 293, ll. 417–18.

87. Local conferences began in late February 1921 and culminated in a provincial nonparty conference held in the second week of March. See Donkov, "Organizatsiia," 67–68. On the provincial administration's limited capabilities at the time, see Trifonov, *Klassy*, 199.

88. According to Vasil'ev, at least one was nearly killed in an assault soon after returning from Moscow. See GATO f. R-1, op. 1, d. 283, l. 11.

89. GATO f. R-1, op. 1, d. 283, l. 30. Provincial Communist Party and Cheka officials were already aware that the shortages and grievances of workers in Rasskazovo had prepared the ground for such manifestations of anti-Soviet sentiment. See Okatov et al., *Sovety Tambovskoi gubernii*, 303–04.

90. According to Beliakov, the Tambov uezd soviet chairman: "The sentencing campaign is ongoing in the villages and volosts, and the sentences are being collected at volost gatherings. However, one cannot be led to believe that these sentences are sincere and from the heart of the assembled peasants because, in the end, the peasants are scared when the Red Army arrives in their village and calls a general assembly—they cannot possibly reveal their true sentiments. We have so far about twenty of these sentences, but we cannot truly say on the basis of these that there has been some sort of shift (*perelom*) [in peasant sympathies]. What the peasants are really asking is, set up a permanent garrison in our village, and then we will know for certain that Soviet power is strong and we will support it and fulfil all our

duties. But when the garrison is removed, then the bandits will return and call everyone to account, finding those who spoke for Soviet power and who obeyed the orders of the local soviet. The bandits do not only rob these people of their possessions, but they frequently kill them." See GATO f. R-1, op. 1, d. 283, l. 29. In Kirsanov, both the sentencing campaign and the nonparty conferences were limited because the government controlled so little territory. As of April, no "sentences" had been collected and the only nonparty conference to be convened had been held in the uezd town of Kirsanov (l. 120).

91. GATO f. R-18, op. 1, d. 62, l. 82.

92. GATO f. R-18, op. 1, d. 62, ll. 71–710b; GATO f. R-1, l. 1, d. 283, l. 30.

93. These and other opinions are recorded in S. A. Esikov and L. G. Protasov, "'Antonov-shchina': novye podkhody," *Voprosii istorii* 6/7 (1992), 51.

94. RGASPI f. 17, op. 13, d. 1005, ll. 141–42. According to a Red Army intelligence report, when Antonov learned of the decisions of the Tenth Party Congress in mid-March, he told his lieutenants that the rebellion was all but finished with the abandonment of the razverstka. See Samoshkin, *Antonovskoe*, 82–83. In a speech (otherwise filled with unreliable claims) to the December 1921 Eighth Tambov Congress of Soviets, Vasil'ev told delegates that seized STK documents attested to the impact of the tax in kind, which had prompted some rebel leaders to consider supporting the Soviet government if it would continue endorsing points of the STK platform. Danilov and Shanin, *KV*, 262.

95. Assistance included the organization of a rebel "land commission." Once more, the Partisan Army was the main agent in disseminating these instructions (each regiment was supposed to have its own "sowing committee") and their realization in the villages. See GA RF f. R-8415, op. 1, d. 127, ll. 50b, 820b, 84, 840b.

96. RGASPI f. 17, op. 13, d. 1002, l. 71; RGVA f.34228, op. 1, d. 48, ll. 25, 27.

97. GA RF f. R-8415, op. 1, d. 111, l. 5. The Red Army High Command received encouraging reports from Tambov regarding the "peasants' fear that the bandits will not permit them to sow their fields, which has led them to the conclusion that they should work to lure Antonov and other bandit leaders into the hands of the reds." See RGVA f. 633, op. 1, d. 63, l. 75 (6 April 1921).

98. In Kozlov, officials reported in April that the presence of rebel groups destabilized the work of the sowing committees. They were not directly attacked, but locals were less willing to work with them because of the threat that the rebels would occupy the villages and punish those who had cooperated. See GATO f. R-18, op. 1, d. 121, 2–20b.

99. Danilov and Shanin, *KV*, 143–44. Many Red Army and VNUS soldiers, expecting demobilization instead of assignment to Tambov in the spring of 1921, were openly insubordinate, according to army intelligence. See RGVA f. 34228, op. 1, d. 46, ll. 2, 3.

100. GATO f. R-1, op. 1, d. 285, l. 36; Esikov and Protasov, "'Antonovshchina': novye podkhody," 50.

101. Quoted in Nabokin, "Vintovkoi i slovom," 105.

102. The statements of surrendered partisans reveal such reasoning. See GATO f. R-1979, op. 1, d. 1090, ll. 439, 440.

103. RGVA f. 25887, op. 1, d. 409, l. 32; RGVA f. 25887, op. 1, d. 571, ll. 175, 305. The effectiveness of deploying new forces to the south depended upon the cavalry contingent assigned to seal off the border to prevent rebel movement into Voronezh and Saratov. Glavkom in Moscow

asserted in February that the cavalry reinforcements under Pavlov's command were enough for this purpose, but in late February Pavlov himself requested that the territory be transferred back to the Voronezh local command because the Fourth Military Sector (Borisoglebsk) did not have sufficient forces to control it. See RGVA f. 25887, op. 1, d. 511, ll. 4, 11, 12, 51; Fatueva, *Protivostoianie*, 242; Danilov and Shanin, *KDP*, 651–52.

104. Nevertheless, the Partisan Army leadership was aware of the state's fear that the insurgency would spread beyond the borders of the province. As is noted in surviving Partisan Army records, one Red Army officer, Iukhnevich, briefly fell prisoner to the Partisan Army in late January 1921 and surrendered intelligence regarding Red Army tactical deployments intended to create a cordon sanitaire along the southern periphery of the insurgency. Surprisingly, he was not killed, despite being an officer. Iukhnevich was lucky: not only had many of his men been executed by the partisans following their capture, but he had similarly fallen prisoner to anti-Soviet rebels in Tambov in 1919 on the eve of Mamontov's raid and escaped serious harm. See GA RF f. R-8415, op. 1, d. 127, l. 600b.

105. Danilov and Shanin, *KDP*, 651.

106. Ibid., 655, 656.

107. The network of local administration quickly dissolved in much of Balashov, and the conduct of grain procurement came to an abrupt halt. See Vedeniapin, "Antonovshchina," 240–44; Iurii K. Strizhkov, *Prodovol'stvennye otriady v gody grazhdanskoi voiny i inostrannoi interventsii: 1917–1921 gg.* (Moscow: Nauka, 1973), 277.

108. Danilov and Shanin, *KDP*, 656.

109. Another source claims that the Partisan Army succeeded in organizing three separate regiments in Saratov, mainly through forced mobilizations. This is probably too high. The one regiment that definitely was organized, however, had five separate squadrons. See Vedeniapin, "Antonovshchina," 242. The only STK materials from Saratov Province that eventually fell into the possession of the Tambov Cheka were from the village of Malo-Shcherbidino. See TsDNITO f. 840, op. 1, d. 1110, ll. 179–80.

110. RGVA f. 235, op. 5, d. 136, ll. 45, 46, 47, 470b.

111. Vedeniapin, "Antonovshchina," 243–44. Vendeniapin understandably had no inclination to credit the Tambov rebels with any degree of sophistication, political or otherwise. According to his memoirs, his sister was raped by Partisan Army rebels during the February raid into Saratov territory.

112. The Partisan Army forces evidently also attracted the attentions of local Saratov evangelicals who traveled with the armed rebels and proselytized among them. See Danilov and Shanin, *KDP*, 655; Figes, *Peasant Russia*, 347.

113. The armed force led by the Saratov rebel, Vakhulin, remained pinned down in southern Saratov at the time of the Partisan Army's incursion into the province. They made no attempt to link up with Tambov partisans. Vakhulin was killed on 17 February and was succeeded by his lieutenant, Popov, who then sought to travel northwest toward the border with Tambov. He was cut off by Red Army forces in March, bringing to an end another (although not the last) suspected effort to establish contact with Antonov. See Danilov and Shanin, *KDP*, 659, 661, 686–88; Figes, *Peasant Russia*, 344–45.

114. Danilov and Shanin, *KDP*, 714, 719.

115. Ibid., 642–43, 647–48, 666–67, 707.

116. G. K. Zhukov, *Vospominaniia i razmyshleniia*, 10th rev. ed. (Moscow: Novosti, 1990), 1:111.

117. On Kolesnikov, see Samoshkin, *Antonovskoe*, 86–92; R. Litvinov, "V te trevozhnye dvadtsatye gody," in *Voronezhskie chekisty rasskazyvaiut . . .* (Voronezh: Tsentral'noe chernozemnoe knizhnoe izdatel'stvo, 1976), 28–35.

118. RGVA f. 25887, op. 1, d. 511, ll. 21, 24.

119. RGVA f. 25887, op. 1, d. 371, ll. 212–2120b.

120. Danilov and Shanin, *KV*, 117–18.

121. The announcement continued: "Kolesnikov, together with the commander of the Third Brigade [Ivan Makarovich Kuznetsov], carried out an attack on Ternovka station on 26 February in which they engaged enemy forces from nine in the morning until two in the afternoon; the enemy demonstrated stubborn resistance, but the partisans showed exceptional valor and the enemy ultimately yielded and was destroyed. Only under the cover of artillery fire were a mere 10–15 men able to escape, carrying a single machine gun. One hundred men were taken prisoner, and one Maxim machine gun was seized along with carts full of ammunition. The enemy suffered 150–200 casualties. Our losses were minimal." Samoshkin, *Antonovskoe*, 89–90.

122. Danilov and Shanin, *KV*, 212.

123. GA RF f. R-8415, op. 1, d. 127, l. 87; Samoshkin, *Antonovskoe*, 90.

124. One ChON soldier, taken prisoner by the rebels in early March, then released, told Red Army investigators that Kolesnikov's men all publicly identified themselves as *"makhnovists."* See RGVA f. 235, op. 5, d. 136, l. 44.

125. Kolesnikov evidently gave the Partisan Army credible information regarding Makhno's activities. See Danilov and Shanin, *KV*, 116. Red Army scouting reports included details and rumors of Makhno's insurgents operating along the southern border of Voronezh Province in January 1921. In fact, he had dispatched one of his lieutenants, Parkhomenko, to Voronezh to gauge the prospects for expanding their insurgency, but, as he later recalled, this was in March 1921. He made no mention in his writings to Ivan Kolesnikov. See RGVA f. 25887. op. 1, d. 409, l. 32; A. Shubin, *Makhno i makhnovskoe dvizhenie* (Moscow: Mik, 1998), 145–46; Petr Arshinov, *History of the Makhnovist Movement, 1919–1921*, trans. Lorraine and Fredy Perlman (London: Freedom Press, 1987), 200–01.

126. GATO f. R-4049, op. 1, d. 89, ll. 143–44

127. Danilov and Shanin, *KV*, 212.

128. See Landis, "Waiting for Makhno." A minor rebel leader even called himself "Makhno," according to one captured Partisan Army soldier. See RGVA f. 7709, op. 1, d. 253, l. 68.

129. Makhno was also aware of wider developments, such as the Kronstadt mutiny, which his army welcomed with a broadcast transmitted weakly on seized radio equipment. See V. N. Volkovinskii, *Makhno i ego krakh* (Moscow: VZPI, 1991), 206–07.

130. GA RF f. R-8415, op. 1, d. 127, ll. 450b, 740b; GATO f. R-4049, op. 1, d. 89, ll. 141–42; Danilov and Shanin, *KV*, 226. Kronstadt sailors and workers in the capitals were also aware of the insurgency in Tambov, and in the case of the former, at least, the Tambov insurgents assumed greater prominence as their own prospects diminished. See Naumov and Kosakovskii, *Kronshtadt 1921*, 77.

131. RGVA f. 235, op. 6-s, d. 12, l. 9; RGVA f. 235, op. 6-s, d. 136, l. 30. This treatment did not extend to Red Army officers, however, underscoring the Partisan Army's targeted appeal to

rank-and-file soldiers. Ivan Shablov, a Red Army cavalry officer, fell prisoner and was taken, along with his men, to the Partisan Army headquarters, where they met Antonov himself. Knowing the treatment that awaited officers, Shablov consistently denied his true status and even affected camaraderie with Antonov, calling him "Shurka" (Antonov's codename, or *klichka*, from his prerevolutionary underground days) in the rebel leader's presence. Shablov was eventually released. See RGVA f. 235, op. 6-s, d. 136, ll. 27–28ob.

132. Danilov and Shanin, *KV*, 100.

133. Ibid.

134. On the intelligence gathering related to Red Army morale, see GA RF f. R-8415, op. 1, d. 124, ll. 2–4.

135. GA RF f. R-8415, op. 1, d. 110, l. 62. Intriguingly, Commander Pavlov, who was a signatory of the 11 February telegram, had complained to Lunacharsky a week earlier that the province had significant grain reserves that were not being used owing to disorganization and negligence within the provincial administration. Either Pavlov later learned this to be untrue or he changed his view in accordance with political circumstances. See *V. I. Lenin i A. V. Lunacharskii*, 243.

136. For example, see the reports of March 1921 in Berelowitch and Danilov, *Sovetskaia derevnia* 1:387, 388, 390, 393.

137. Pavel A. Aptekar', "Krest'ianskaia voina [part 1]," *Voenno-istoricheskii zhurnal* 1 (1993), 66.

138. As Soviet Chairman Lavrov explained to uezd soviet chairmen in early April 1921:

> We were presented with difficult circumstances surrounding the supply of the army operating in the localities. With our limited reserves, and with our limited transportation system, we were simply unable to provision the army. Thus it was necessary for us to arrange quickly for the collection of foodstuffs by the military itself, bypassing the Food Commissariat authorities, and this meant that collection was conducted in a manner even worse than before, because it is impossible to impress new methods of procurement upon the military. But we had no other options, and this operation is only now being completed. . . . What we have now is a situation in which we have a new policy that enables us to facilitate a positive transition in our relations with the peasantry, but on the other side we are forced to continue a practice that is diametrically opposed to this policy, and this situation has prompted us to appeal sincerely to the center [Moscow] for assistance. Despite the fact that the center knows of our plight through a whole series of considerations and statistics, and via categorical and urgent demands . . . the center simply cannot satisfy our requests.

See GATO f. R-1, op. 1, d. 283, ll. 2–3, 8.

139. Official figures demonstrating only partial fulfillment of the 1920–1921 razverstka do not include the requisitions conducted by occupying Red Army troops. See RGVA f. 633, op. 1, d. 63, l. 76ob; Samoshkin, *Antonovskoe*, 108.

140. RGVA f. 633, op. 1, d. 63, l. 83.

141. For a range of local reports for March and April 1921 that detail the "self-provisioning" activities of Red Army units, see GATO f. R-1, op. 1, d. 183, ll. 318–38.

142. GATO f. R-18, op. 1, d. 63, l. 63; GATO f. R-4049, op. 1s, d. 34, ll. 6–7ob; GATO f. R-394, op. 1, 978, ll. 304–05, 308–10.

143. RGASPI f. 17, op. 13, d. 1010, l. 250b.

144. RGVA f. 235, op. 6s, d. 12, l. 25; Danilov and Shanin, *KV*, 121.

145. TsDNITO f. 840, op. 1, d. 1112, l. 36.

146. These themes figure prominently in the two published propaganda leaflets pertaining to the surrender of the Fourteenth Arkhangel'sk Regiment of the Partisan Army. The event may have occurred in Voronezh Province because its commanders felt more secure seeking surrender at a distance, or it could have been a *consequence* of the regiment being distanced from the stronghold of the Partisan Army. But Soviet propaganda emphasized that the rebels had surrendered as a matter of conscience, making peace with the state so the population could return to field work, also claiming that the surrendered rebels were greeted "not as enemies, but as brothers, with warm words and music." Another piece, signed by the commanders of the Fourteenth Regiment, urged other partisans to surrender, claiming, "During our first meeting [with Red Army authorities] it became clear to us that the aims of our struggle are shared by all principled Communists." See Danilov and Shanin, *KV*, 134–35. The latter appeal was specifically addressing a brigade led by one "Comrade Chumichev" that was operating in western Borisoglebsk uezd and allegedly attacking villages that collaborated with the Soviet government. Judging by reports, the Chumichev unit had always been a "rogue" element, even stealing food and supplies from other Partisan Army regiments. See GA RF f. R-8415, op. 1, d. 127, ll. 50b, 91.

Chapter 7: Between Ambition and Necessity

1. Danilov and Shanin, *KV*, 110.

2. For ten days in March 1921, government forces had the First Partisan Army on the run, and on 19–20 March, they believed to have had the main force led by Antonov encircled in the region between the Tambov-Rasskazovo railway and the major village near the Tambov-Morshansk border, Pakhotnyi Ugol. Some of Antonov's force (est. 1,500 men) was able to escape across the railway to southern Tambov and Kirsanov uezds on 20 March, owing to a major blunder by military and rail officials in which a passenger train was allowed to pass through the conflict zone. Unbelievably, Antonov and his men were able to escape by using this train for cover, crossing the rail line at Platonovka, a station to the east of Rasskazovo. The operation did result in significant losses for the rebels—reportedly over 1,000 killed and masses of firearms and ammunition seized. Antonov's narrow escape raised suspicions of sabotage and treachery, but a special commission concluded otherwise after an investigation. "At the time," wrote Antonov-Ovseenko, "I called this a 'tactical victory' ... but I can now hear the words loudly spoken: 'But a strategic defeat?'" See RGASPI f. 17, op. 13, d. 1010, l. 28; GATO f. R-1, op. 1, d. 283, ll. 8–9; Ivan Trutko, "Primeneniia aeroplanov, kak razervov," *Krasnaia Armiia*, nos. 5–6 (1921).

3. Danilov and Shanin, *KV*, 142.

4. Having been made overall commander of the First Partisan Army in late February, Kolesnikov refused to submit to the authority of the Partisan Army headquarters. This involved both operational matters as well as sharing captured loot and, in particular, seized weapons that were in such short supply among rebel units. Kolesnikov's independence prompted a minor schism within the First Partisan Army in early March 1921 but was not itself decisive for Kolesnikov. Instead, a series of setbacks in late March forced him and the First Partisan Army to withdraw from Tambov to Voronezh Province, where they continued to be pursued by Red

Army cavalry. This evidently provoked a second schism in which the Voronezh natives separated from the majority *tambovtsy*, who returned to Tambov Province and reorganized under the overall command of Boguslavskii. Kolesnikov's fortunes continued to worsen, and on 28 April he was shot dead during a battle with Red Army forces. See Samoshkin, *Antonovskoe*, 97.

5. One rebel soldier (Sergei Vasil'evich Ionov, born 1896, from Treskino volost in Kirsanov uezd), who surrendered after this event, sought to gain a pardon from Red Army interrogators by claiming to have killed Tokmakov by his own hand, after which he fled from his regiment. He told interrogators that he had a grudge against Tokmakov, who had reprimanded him for looting, and that he chose a moment of vulnerability during a battle to strike him, unintentionally killing him. This was not a typical pardon tale, but investigators chose not to believe him. (Such stories from insurgents who claimed to have killed high-profile rebel leaders were not unknown in 1921.) See GATO f. R-4049, op. 1, d. 89, l. 58. However, Tokmakov's "wife," Anastasia Drigo-Drigina, testified that he died of battle wounds. See GATO f. R-5201, op. 2, d. 1717, l. 6.

6. Trutko, "Primeneniia aeroplanov, kak razervov," 41–42.

7. Raids in the village of Treskino (Kirsanov uezd) and Sampur (Tambov uezd) saw the rebels seize and disarm two Red Army squadrons and one battalion-strength force. RGASPI f. 17, op. 13, d. 1010, l. 28.

8. Trutko, "Primeneniia aeroplanov, kak razervov."

9. Some enterprises in Rasskazovo had been attacked by rebels in October 1920, however. See Donkov, *Antonovshchina*, 41.

10. GATO f. R-1, op. 1, d. 183, l. 318; RGASPI f. 17, op. 13, d. 1000, l. 67.

11. GATO f. R-1, op. 1, d. 285, l. 30.

12. The Plenipotentiary Commission in Tambov had suggested in mid-March 1921 rounding up a portion (10–20 percent) of local workers in Rasskazovo—that portion deemed politically suspect—and moving them to other regions. See Esikov and Protasov, "'Antonovshchina': novye podkhody," 51.

13. Trutko, "Primeneniia aeroplanov, kak razervov," 42–43. Only three days before the assault, a senior figure in the Red Army headquarters in Tambov, N. E. Kakurin, suggested using tethered hot air balloons to assist scouting operations in garrisoned villages and towns. See Danilov and Shanin, *KV*, 143.

14. GA RF f. R-8415, op. 1, d. 111, l. 60b.

15. RGASPI f. 17, op. 13, d. 1010, ll. 28, 280b; Trutko, "Primeneniia aeroplanov, kak razervov," 43.

16. GA RF f. R-8415, op. 1, d. 127, l. 4.

17. GA RF f. R-8415, op. 1, d. 111, l. 60b.

18. GA RF f. R-8415, op. 1, d. 127, l. 25. See also Ian F. W. Beckett, *Modern Insurgencies and Counterinsurgencies: Guerrillas and Their Opponents since 1750* (London: Routledge, 2001).

19. A classic example in this regard is the Democratic Army of Greece, whose Communist Party leadership made the fateful decision to switch to "positional" warfare in 1947 in response to the perceived need to cultivate international legitimacy by adopting more conventional tactics. See Charles S. Shrader, *The Withered Vine: Logistics and the Communist Insurgency in Greece, 1945–1949* (Westport, CT: Praeger, 1999), 261–63.

20. A letter from a rural miller from Tambov uezd, I. M. Kazakov, to a relative in Moscow

(and intercepted by censors) cited the recent occupation of Rasskazovo as an indication that the rebellion was far from finished. See GATO f. R-1, op. 1, d. 183, ll. 466–67.

21. Provincial officials saw that a more ambitious attack by the Partisan Army was in the cards, and they believed it was owing to the influence of outside PSR advisors. Following the brief occupation of Rasskazovo, the head of the Tambov Communist Party, B. A. Vasil'ev, reported to Moscow (15 April 1921): "According to our intelligence, eight senior organizers with a special interest in military matters were sent from Moscow by the Central Committee [of the PSR] in order to assist in improving the military capacity of [Antonov's] army. And the latest reports from the field suggest that the resistance offered by the antonovists has radically intensified, and we even have reports that Antonov may be planning an attack on a town. His first experience with such an attack was highly successful when one looks at what occurred in Rasskazovo. You already surely know of the occupation of Rasskazovo by Antonov for a period of a few hours, and at the moment [we believe] he is preparing an assault on the Gunpowder Plant and on Tambov." See Danilov and Shanin, *KV*, 145. While it is difficult to verify the intelligence reports that Vasil'ev cites, the presence of outside advisors could be associated with the 14 April "vote of confidence" in Antonov's leadership. See also Iakovlev, *Vnutrennie voiska*, 609. Officials in the Military Commissariat in Kirsanov had reported an attempted raid by armed rebels on 17 December, but its extent is unclear, and it may have been reported to underscore the vulnerability felt in the town. See GATO f. R-1832, op. 1, d. 630, l. 123. The April attack on Kirsanov involved larger rebel forces and much more planning, in contrast to the earlier "assault" on Borisoglebsk in January 1921 mentioned in chapter 6.

22. This description of the assault on Kirsanov should qualify V. Brovkin's comments regarding the reluctance of the Partisan Army and Antonov to attack towns. See Brovkin, *Behind the Front Lines*, 370.

23. Danilov and Shanin, *KV*, 130. According to Gavril Andreevich Zaitsev, a member of the Kirsanov Communist Party Committee, injured cavalrymen from Budennyi's celebrated brigade being treated in a military hospital in Kirsanov in August 1920 were asked to assist, and thirty of them bravely volunteered, stating that they could do without firearms as long as horses were available and they had knives (*klinok*) for weapons. See Gavril Andreevich Zaitsev, "Za vlast' sovetov" (Internet site), www.grad-kirsanov.ru/source.php?id= memory .zajcev [accessed 18 September 2006].

24. One disillusioned rural Communist Party member named Toropov gives a depressing description of the situation that confronted evacuated comrades in the spring of 1921: "Arriving in the town without having secured even a tiny corner of living space, many Communists were forced to live in abandoned railcars, and they were confronted by the utter indifference of their urban comrades, who sat in their comfortable offices. Rural Communists learned that they did not even share a common language with their urban colleagues, and instead they were despised and driven away. Forced to abandon the party, they were left to their lives in the railcars and to make do as best they could." RGASPI f. 17, op. 13, d. 1010, l. 470b.

25. TsDNITO f. 837, op. 1, d. 456, l. 10b.

26. RGASPI f. 17, op. 13, d. 1010, l. 280b.

27. According to the Red Army report to the Revolutionary-Military Council, Antonov was initially forced north of Rasskazovo, but in Kozlov uezd he linked up with Karas', who had

until this time been "passive" toward Antonov's Partisan Army organization. See Iakovlev, *Vnutrennie voiska*, 608–09. Nikitin-Korolev's *nom de guerre* was taken from the name of a large variety of carp common to local waters and prized by anglers in the region. The Borisoglebsk-based historian Vladimir Samoshkin notes in his biography of Antonov that Selianskii was introduced to him after Antonov arrested Selianskii in 1917 in connection with rural disorders early in his term as Kirsanov militia chief. Samoshkin, "V preddverii miatezha," 20.

28. RGASPI f. 17, op. 13, d. 1010, l. 280b. These designations for Selianskii's and Karas's forces were evidently contained in a Red Army or Cheka report on the Partisan Army, and Antonov-Ovseenko thought they perfectly represented the inflated (and deluded) ambitions of rebel leaders. See Meijer, *The Trotsky Papers, 1917–1922*, 2:502. The village of Kamenka for this "meeting" described by Antonov-Ovseenko is doubtful, given that the main Partisan Army forces were north of this area.

29. RGVA f. 235, op. 2, d. 335, l. 41 (statement taken 16 July 1921).

30. GA RF f. R-8415, op. 1, d. 115, l. 111.

31. RGVA f. 235, op. 6s, d. 12, l. 400b, 43. Morshansk was also believed to be the target owing to the involvement of Selianskii's regiments, which originated from this area. However, another Red Army report claims that Antonov intentionally spread rumors that the Partisan Army planned to attack Morshansk (in addition to Sosnovka and the railway station at Benkendorf). See Iakovlev, *Vnutrennie voiska*, 609.

32. GA RF f. R-8415, op. 1, d. 115, l. 111.

33. RGVA f. 7709, op. 1, d. 232, l. 78.

34. GA RF f. R-8415, op. 1, d. 127, l. 820b.

35. Zaitsev, "Za vlast' sovetov." An otherwise reliable memoir by a former senior political worker with the counterinsurgency effort in Tambov gives a much more inflated figure of 17,000 for the Partisan Army force involved in the attack on Kirsanov. See G. A. Sychev, "Vospominaniia" (Internet site), www.grad-kirsanov.ru/source.php?id=memory.sjchev [accessed 16 September 2006].

36. TsDNITO f. 9019, op. 1, d. 179, ll. 5–6; Zaitsev, "Za vlast' sovetov."

37. Zaitsev, "Za vlast' sovetov."

38. Pomazov, "Bor'ba za vlast'."

39. Romanov, "Vospominaniia."

40. Ibid. According to Zaitsev, troops that arrived late on 24 April set up in the church cemetery with their ten machine guns and dug "shallow" (one would hope!) trenches in preparation for the assault. See Zaitsev, "Za vlast' sovetov." On the grounds of the town cemetery was a church, and in the center of town were the cathedral and a small chapel. In the north of Kirsanov a convent had been commandeered for use by the uezd administration.

41. By all accounts, the attack commenced at three in the morning via the small village of Shinovka on the road entering Kirsanov from the west. A. Ia. Soshnikov, "Ustanovlenie Sovetskoi vlasti i bor'ba s antonovshchinoi v Kirsanovskom uezde Tambovskoi gubernii (1917–1921 gg.)" (Internet site), www.grad-kirsanov.ru/source.php?id=memory.soshnik [accessed 18 September 2006].

42. TsDNITO f. 9019, op. 1, d. 179, ll. 5–6; Zaitsev, "Za vlast' sovetov"; Romanov, "Vospominaniia."

43. GA RF f. R-8415, op. 1, d. 115, l. 111.

44. Nearly all the memoirists cited above expected this to be a turning point. See also GATO f. R-1, op. 1, d. 287, l. 18; GA RF f. R-8415, op. 1, d. 111, l. 60b.

45. Danilov and Shanin, *KV*, 127–28.

46. According to a report by A. I. Zhabin, a member of the Plenipotentiary Commission and also the head of the Red Army's political department in Tambov, the Partisan Army continued to grow in 1921 despite the Red Army's undoubted superiority in numbers.

	Red Army			Partisan Army		
	Soldiers	Machine Guns	Artillery Guns	Soldiers	Machine Guns	Artillery Guns
1 Jan 1921	11,870	136	18	6,660	13	1
1 Feb 1921	33,750	312	44	16,050	10	1
1 Mar 1921	41,846	463	53	17,600	26	5

Source: RGASPI f. 17, op. 13, d. 1010, l. 42.

47. A typical unit deployed to Tambov in early 1921 was the Second Labor Brigade of the Third Special (Osobaia) Army of the Republic. According to a report to Orel by a commissar assigned to the brigade, the further deployment of small units of questionable quality, no matter how many, would only further weaken the state's position in the countryside. "In my opinion, entirely reliable and steadfast troops must be sent [to Tambov] with the greatest of haste (units that are not steadfast simply disintegrate in clashes with bandits) along with commanders that are experienced and stolid. If we continue to deploy units that number only 200–300 men, this will only serve to strengthen the bandits' position." See RGVA f. 25887, op. 1, d. 371, ll. 213–213ob.

48. A concise list of government setbacks in April 1921, based on Partisan Army field diaries, is in Danilov and Shanin, *KV*, 155.

49. TSDNITO f. 840, op. 1, d. 1053, l. 1.

50. This was a typical complaint by Red Army officers about local state and party officials in Tambov. See Danilov and Shanin, *KV*, 141.

51. TsDNITO f. 840, op. 1, d. 1053, l. 320b.

52. It is interesting to place Russov's comments alongside those attributed to Mikhail Tukhachevskii by F. Kasatkin-Rostovskii, Tukhachevskii's contemporary in the tsarist army in World War I and later an officer in the White movement. Kasatkin-Rostovskii recalls him as stating: "For me, war is everything! Where would I be without war? In the best case scenario, I might become a battalion commander after several years, or perhaps become a member of the General Staff. But here [at the front] I can really make my move. If I am not killed, who knows how far I could go during this war! This is my calling! This is my career!" This quotation is questionable, given the White officers' well-known disdain for Tukhachevskii's decision to fight on the side of the Soviet government. See G. P. Verkeenko and S. T. Minakov, *Moskovskii pokhod i krushenie 'dobrovol'cheskoi politiki' generala A. Denikina* (Moscow: Moskovskii gosudarstvennyi otkrytii pedagogicheskii institut, 1993), 28–29.

53. Another whistle-blower, who was similarly arrested, wrote of the casualties reported by Red Army commanders and asked whether all those killed were truly rebel soldiers: "Entirely appropriately, reports [on individual battles] record that many bandits have been killed, but these certainly are not bandits, but are instead just simple peasants. . . . If these are bandits,

then where are their weapons that we should have seized when there are 500 reported killed? Often there are no more than ten or twenty rifles reported as seized [following such battles]." See Danilov and Shanin, *KV*, 129. Rebel commanders were similarly prone to exaggerate enemy casualty figures, although they were much more likely to detail the number of prisoners taken rather than the number of Red Army soldiers killed. Incredibly, Red Army tribunal investigators, to verify the reports of their own commanders and to evaluate the circumstances behind individual clashes, as well as to safeguard against "casualty inflation," would occasionally use captured field reports of Partisan Army commanders to cross-check casualty figures reported by their officers. See RGVA f. 25887, op. 1, d. 362, ll. 9, 11–110b, 12. Rebel and Red Army commanders also shared a propensity to include value judgments in their reports concerning individual engagements, often referring to the actions of their troops and officers as "brave" and "heroic." See the materials of the Twelfth "Takaiskii" Regiment of the Partisan Army, at GA RF f. R-8415, op. 1, d. 127, ll. 70–700b.

54. Russov's letter is at TsDNITO f. 840, op. 1, d. 1053, ll. 31–380b. Russov's replacement as brigade commander, Vasilii Larin, lasted less than a fortnight before he, too, was arrested on suspicion of ties with the rebels. He was arrested on 25 April, the night of the assault on Kirsanov by the Partisan Army, during which he exhibited exceptionally panicky behavior, which investigators feared was intended to divert Red Army forces away from Kirsanov. The issue before the tribunal was whether Larin's actions were attributable to drink or if a certain suspicious village woman (or prostitute) had too significant an influence on him, compromising his pro-Soviet principles. See TsDNITO f. 840, op. 1, d. 1043, ll. 15–150b.

55. Russov also blamed his fellow officers for focusing on his past in the tsarist army, blaming Petrov, in particular, of asking "innocent" questions to investigators, such as: "I wonder how many former officers have surrendered to Antonov so far?" See TsDNITO f. 840, op. 1, d. 1053, l. 36. The suspicion of former tsarist army officers was later brought up to account for the change of fortunes enjoyed by the Soviet government in June and July 1921, when much of the command staff had been overhauled. According to an inspector's report from 13 July: "The former command staff had been largely composed of former tsarist officers, and only with the arrival of Comrade Tukhachevskii, who brought in several other Red staff officers who were assigned to field commands, did we begin to see an improvement." Danilov and Shanin, *KV*, 181. Also rank-and-file soldiers asked senior officers during a Red Army conference in Tambov in July 1921 about "rumors" of treachery by former tsarist officers serving the Red Army raised in relation to the earlier, more difficult phase of the counterinsurgency. See Fatueva, *Protivostoianie*, 270–71.

56. Russov also faulted the Soviet government for failing to honor the announced end of grain requisitioning, which he claimed reversed the political impact of the announcement and resulted in the steeling of rebel morale in Tambov. See TsDNITO f. 840, op. 1, d. 1053, l. 37.

57. RGASPI f. 17, op. 13, d. 1002, ll. 11–110b.

58. Danilov and Shanin, *KV*, 155. The historical strength of the Socialist Revolutionaries in the province—both Right and Left SRs—also contributed to the continued suspicion of their influence reaching as high up as the provincial soviet executive committee. See RGASPI f. 17, op. 86, d. 103, ll. 4–5.

59. See Landis, "A Civil War Episode."

60. Danilov and Shanin, *KV*, 85.

61. According to the same report by Antonov-Ovseenko's point man in the reorganization of the Cheka, Iakov Levin, only eleven "substandard" agents had been assigned to counter-intelligence duties before March 1921. See GA RF f. R-8415, op. 1, d. 111, ll. 1–30b.

62. As part of the overhaul of the provincial Cheka organization, the Tambov Presidium ordered the formation of a Special Department (Osobyi Otdel), extensions of VChK that were tied to the Soviet armed forces. An early attempt to organize such a department in February had been stonewalled by the Tambov Communist Party committee, evidently another consequence of the political intrigues that had reached a boiling point by that time. With the arrival of Antonov-Ovseenko and the organization of the Plenipotentiary Commission, however, the reorganization could be pushed through, with an experienced Chekist, G. N. Chibisov, appointed director of the Special Department. On 19 March, the Plenipotentiary Commission discussed the division of responsibilities between these two organizations, leaving the provincial Cheka to concentrate on the activities of "antisoviet" parties with all other matters tied to the counterinsurgency being the work of the Special Department. See GATO f. R-1, op. 1, d. 287, ll. 7–8; GATO f. R-1, op. 1, d. 285, ll. 7–8; Fatueva, *Protivostoianie*, 232; Danilov and Shanin, *KV*, 135; George Leggett, *The Cheka: Lenin's Political Police: The All-Russian Extraordinary Commission for Combating Counter-revolution and Sabotage, December 1917 to February 1922* (Oxford: Clarendon Press, 1981), 95–98.

63. Antonov-Ovseenko's involvement in Cheka activities in March and April was limited by a bout of typhus that left him bedridden for nearly four weeks after he arrived in Tambov. He nevertheless continued to write and file reports on his progress with the counterinsurgency effort. See RGASPI f. 17, op. 13, d. 1010, l. 30ob.

64. RGASPI f. 17, op. 13, d. 1000, ll. 36ob, 37; GA RF f. R-8415, op. 1, d. 110, l. 19. In April 1921 Mikhail Romanov was rumored to have appeared in the Urals, leading an army marching toward Moscow to restore the Constituent Assembly; another rumor heralded the approach of a massive cavalry force led by former White officers. See GA RF f. R-8415, op. 1, d. 111, l. 6; GA RF f. R-8415, op. 1, d. 124, l. 50b.

65. GATO f. R-18, op. 1, d. 62, l. 88ob.

66. There had already been three strikes (*zaminki*) by workers at the Tambov railroad repair works in March. Danilov and Shanin, *KV*, 128. The Kozlov Cheka thwarted a planned "go-slow" (or "Italian") strike on the railways, but the only evidence of suspicious political activity were some items of vaguely pro-Antonov literature in the possession of a state (Rabkrin) inspector. GATO f. R-18, op. 1, d. 62, ll. 71–71ob.

67. RGASPI f. 17, op. 13, d. 1010, ll. 25–25ob; GA RF f. R-8415, op. 1, d. 127, ll. 2–8, 9. The Cheka was also involved in the type of activity called for by Fedor Liubkin. In late April, for instance, three men working in the Kozlov military commissariat were arrested for regularly passing on sensitive information on political and military developments to the leaders of the Partisan Army. See GA RF f. R-8415, op. 1, d. 112, l. 2.

68. RGASPI f. 17, op. 13, d. 1010, l. 25ob (underlined words in original).

69. GATO f. R-1, op. 1, d. 285, l. 29.

70. GATO f. R-18, op. 1, d. 121, l. 20b.

71. Revkoms appeared in a variety of contexts, but they were typically a way of bypassing civilian administration when the political or security situation made the normal functioning of soviets impractical or impossible. On 23 January 1921, at a session of the Tambov provincial

party organization, preparations were set in motion to establish a network of revolutionary committees as part of the effort to combat the rebellion. They were to be overseen by the political wing of the Red Army in the Tambov region (POARM). By mid-February, a scheme was adopted that saw revolutionary committees organized at the regional level within each of the four military sectors. These were named according to the village that would serve as the revkom base of operations. Between February and April 1921, the network grew as military operations expanded and as government control of territories was consolidated. See GA RF f. R-8415, op. 1, d. 112, ll. 44–45ob. On the revolutionary committees in the civil war generally, see Iu. M. Ponikhidin, *Revoliutsionnye komitety RSFSR (1918–1921 gg.)* (Saratov: Izdatel'stvo Saratovskogo universiteta, 1982); N. F. Bugai, *Organy zashchity zavoevanii oktiabria: problemy i izucheniia* (Moscow: Mysl', 1982); Portnov, *Partiino-politicheskaia rabota*, 286–88.

72. GATO f. R-1, op. 1, d. 287, l. 23; Danilov and Shanin, *KV*, 131.

73. RGASPI f. 17, op. 13, d. 1010, l. 47ob. One community in Tambov uezd wrote to the Second Military Sector headquarters expressing their desire to reorganize their village soviet, but they first demanded assurances that local Red Army forces would protect them. See GATO R-1979, op. 1, d. 1047, l. 8.

74. Okatov et al., *Sovety Tambovskoi gubernii*, 310–11; Danilov and Shanin, *KV*, 136–37. The original amnesty was extended from two to three weeks, owing to disappointing results. In Borisoglebsk uezd (Fourth and Fifth Military Sectors), the amnesty was extended to four weeks for the opposite reason; Borisoglebsk and Usman uezds accounted for most of the results produced during the amnesty period. The Red Army had considerably more success in Borisoglebsk, first in pushing Kolesnikov out of the province, and second in maintaining pressure on the numerous small rebel groups in Borisoglebsk. This pressure and the lack of any larger Partisan Army formations in the uezd produced significantly better results for the provincial government and Red Army. See Danilov and Shanin, *KV*, 145.

75. GA RF f. 8415, op. 1, d. 111, ll. 7–7ob. One former partisan claimed that when he expressed a desire to surrender to Red Army troops, he was shot at by his rebel commander—and injured in three places—and left for dead before Red Army soldiers discovered him. He said the rebel commander was Dmitrii Antonov. See RGVA f. 235, op. 2, d. 335, l. 31.

76. RGASPI f. 17, op. 13, d. 1010, l. 27. The Tambov Communist Party chief, B. A. Vasil'ev, reported to uezd soviet executive chairmen in early April that the proportion of individuals surrendering with weapons in hand to the total of those appearing for amnesty was 1:20. See GATO R-1, op. 1, d. 285, l. 11.

77. Suspicions were mounting that those surrendering as deserters were in fact insurgents who believed admission of this crime was preferable to admission of active rebellion. Such suspicions partially informed the more hard-line approach taken by the Plenipotentiary Commission and Red Army in June and July. See TsDNITO f. 840, op. 1, d. 1053, l. 16.

78. In some cases, local rebels posted warnings to villagers not to cooperate with the authorities, but Cheka agents were encouraged by the fact that occasionally such villagers took them down and gave them to local Red Army commanders. See GA RF f. R-8415, op. 1, d. 111, l. 8.

79. RGASPI f. 17, op. 13, d. 1010, ll. 28ob, 29–29ob.

80. Danilov and Shanin, *KV*, 145.

81. Pavlov had been promised a direct (*neposredstvennyi*) line of communication with Moscow after Skudr's fall from grace, but he continued to be hampered by the range of forces

active in Tambov (including Cheka, Communist Party and Komsomol, etc.), many of which he did not directly control. See RGASPI f. 17, op. 13, d. 1010, l. 290b.

82. RGASPI f. 17, op. 13, d. 1010, l. 270b.

83. Danilov and Shanin, *KV*, 148.

84. Ibid., 147; Meijer, *The Trotsky Papers, 1917–1922*, 2: 460–62. This document has no date, and Trotsky's attempt to date it June 1921 is in error.

85. Danilov and Shanin, *KV*, 147–48. To maintain secrecy, the protocol of the 28 April 1921 Politburo meeting instructs other governmental and army organs, particularly the Revolutionary Military Council, not to mention Tukhachevskii's appointment in their own protocols.

86. While other parts of the Soviet Republic continued to suffer instability, several major flash points that had dominated the political landscape at the start of the year had, by April, been resolved or were steadily being "pacified" by government troops and officials. This includes the urban disturbances in Petrograd and Moscow, as well as the major rural insurgency in Western Siberia (Tiumen province) that had done so much to disrupt grain supply to the Northwest in February and March 1921.

87. Kotovski's cavalry brigade received its orders on 23 April 1921, before the meeting of the Politburo that discussed Tukhachevskii's assignment. This raises some questions about the date of both Sklianskii's memo to Lenin [which has not been determined] and the date of the Antibanditry Commission's meeting in Moscow to discuss Antonov-Ovseenko's proposals. Antonov-Ovseenko's proposals were drafted on 19 April and the Antibanditry Commission met with Antonov-Ovseenko on 27 April. The decision to assign Kotovskii to Tambov was made on or before 23 April, and it is unlikely that Tukhachevskii's assignment would have been made later or separately. Therefore, Sklianskii's memo was likely to have been written between 19 and 23 April 1921.

88. Danilov and Shanin, *KV*, 148–49.

89. This is present-day Kotovsk (named after G. I. Kotovskii in 1940). Until this time, the settlement was only known simply as the "gunpowder works," opened on the eve of World War I in 1912. Despite having a permanent population that grew from eight thousand to over thirty thousand (mainly workers and garrisoned soldiers), it did not officially become a town until 1940. Tukhachevskii's headquarters is now the site of the town's local museum.

90. Danilov and Shanin, *KV*, 163. Another Red Army officer, Kazakov, pursued the infection analogy in 1921: "In Tambov Province . . . all or a significant portion of the population is sick with the same infectious disease: and rather than to engage in treatment of the disease, our first priority had to be to establish a quarantine around the area in order to identify and to localize the infected population. We had to create a quarantine in order to begin treatment of the disease—banditry. This quarantine is what we call the occupation system. All regions overcome with banditry must fall within the quarantine, and the population therein must receive methodical treatment." See Fatueva, *Protivostoianie*, 265–66.

91. At its height in March 1921, there were eight military sectors, including ones in Penza and Rtishchevo (Saratov Province). Tukhachevskii reduced the number to six, eliminating those in Saratov and Penza provinces and extending the operational jurisdictions of the remainder across provincial borders. See Danilov and Shanin, *KV*, 165–66.

92. Tukhachevskii, "Bor'ba [2]," 5. The break was not as complete, perhaps, as Tukhachevskii claimed. The description of the assault on Kirsanov in April suggests that the Red Army in

Tambov gave some autonomy to mobile units, such as Dmitrienko's cavalry brigade in Kirsanov uezd, to pursue rebel forces.

93. Previously, the commanders in Tambov sought to maintain garrisons in strategically important areas such as uezd towns and locations of important manufacturing enterprises. Rasskazovo was one such center, and thus the rebel occupation in early April caused a shock. See Tukhachevskii, "Bor'ba [2]," 5.

94. Danilov and Shanin, *KV*, 164.

95. Tukhachevskii's emphasis on "sovietization" appears to bear the influence of the most famous strategy of counterinsurgency—oil slick (*tache d'huile*), developed by the French army in Indochina at the end of the nineteenth century and then developed further in Morocco in the early twentieth century. According to Ian Beckett: "The analogy used was that of oil spreading slowly over water, the classic exposition of the technique being the article by [Louis-Hubert Gonzalve] Lyautey in the *Revue des deux mondes* in 1900. *Tache d'huile* therefore implied the gradual extension of French administration hand-in-hand with military occupation. Firm military action would be followed by economic and administrative reconstruction of the state by French military administrators. Hearts and minds would be won over by providing the population with protection and such facilities as free medical assistance and subsidized markets. At the same time, the French would work through traditional rulers whenever possible." See Ian F. W. Beckett, *Encyclopedia of Guerrilla Warfare* (Santa Barbara, CA: ABC-CLIO, 1999), 227.

96. Danilov and Shanin, *KV*, 162.

97. For similar counterinsurgency tactics pursued by Union forces during the U.S. Civil War, see Charles R. Mink, "General Orders No. 11: The Forced Evacuation of Civilians During the Civil War," *Military Affairs* 34, no. 4 (1970).

98. Some of these measures had already been put into effect in some areas where the Red Army had established a presence and revolutionary committees were up and running. For instance, as early as March 1921, families in Bolshe-Lazovka volost in Tambov uezd were being interrogated and faced demands to present their sons—suspected rebels—for interrogation on pain of losing their property. See GATO f. R-1979, op. 1, d. 1090, l. 79.

99. Danilov and Shanin, *KV*, 164. Once again using lists of villagers, regional and volost revkoms were supposed to redistribute confiscated property among local households with no known connection with the rebels, who had suffered at the hands of the rebels, families of recently demobilized Red Army soldiers, and the village poor. RGVA f. 34228, op. 1, d. 3, l. 15. M. D. Antonov also expressed misgivings about this policy in his 8 May 1921 memorandum, stating that confiscated property would invariably be distributed among those in positions of authority in the villages, such as members of the revolutionary committees. See GA RF f. R-8415, op. 1, d. 111, l. 24.

100. Tukhachevskii recognized that the previous command in Tambov had been on the right track but had not gone far enough: "When Comrade Pavlov arrived in Tambov the military command then began to put into operation the correct strategy of occupation, setting solid foundations for the restoration of Soviet power. But occupation alone could not truly secure Soviet power, for what was needed was the sovietization of the whole region, for state power to function in those areas occupied by our military forces." RGVA f. 235, op. 5, d. 24, ll. 148–49 (29 July 1921).

101. On the weakened condition of the Partisan Army, see Danilov and Shanin, *KV*, 159. Following the defeat at Kirsanov, Antonov's main force came under severe pressure by the Fourteenth Cavalry Brigade, suffering further defeats that, according to Red Army reports that almost certainly exaggerate the figures, resulted in over 2,000 rebel deaths in the final week of April alone. See Trifonov, *Klassy*, 250–51.

102. L. M. Chizhova and Kh. M. Muratov, eds., *G. I. Kotovskii. Dokumenty i materialy* (Kishinev: Gosudarstvennoe izdatel'stvo Moldavii, 1956), 343; B. Roitman, "Rol' kavbrigady G. I. Kotovskogo v razgrome antonovshchiny," *Voenno-istoricheskii zhurnal* 6 (1981): 72.

103. Mokarev, "Kursantskii," 61.

104. Other forces to arrive were the cavalry brigade led by M. D. Kovalev (joining the Fifteenth Siberian Cavalry Brigade commanded by I. V. Tiulenev in Kirsanov uezd), as well as motorized units organized by General I. F. Fed'ko and I. P. Uborevich, two senior "red" commanders who joined Tukhachevskii soon after he accepted the assignment to Tambov. See Trifonov, "Iz istorii razgroma," 33.

105. S. A. Tiushkevich, *Sovetskie vooruzhennye sily. Istoriia stroitel'stva* (Moscow: Voennoe izdatel'stvo, 1978), 123–24.

106. The designs of the Plenipotentiary Commission in Tambov in this regard were in place well before the decisions of the Antibanditry Commission in late April concerning the conflict in the province. But, without enough qualified personnel to staff the demobilization process in Tambov, plans were suspended until the Antibanditry Commission and the Politburo resolved to support them with reinforcements of party and political workers. See RGASPI f. 17, op. 13, d. 1000, l. 490b; d. 1010, ll. 26–26ob; Danilov and Shanin, *KV*, 149.

107. In addition to political screening and indoctrination, another part of the process was the more literal form of grooming. Demobilized soldiers given a bath and a shave and proper clothing and shoes—amenities often lacking during military service itself, especially in the reserve garrisons. On 25 February 1921, the Council of Labor and Defense (*Sovet trudy i oborony*) sanctioned the release of a fund of shoes and clothing for distribution among demobilized soldiers, as well as adequate quantities of soap. See TsDNITO f. 840, op. 1, d. 1043, l. 17; Tiushkevich, *Sovetskie vooruzhennye sily*, 125. Generally, see E. A. Bechkov, "Voennoe stroitel'stvo i sotsial'naia zashchita voennosluzhashchikh v SSSR v 20-e gody," *Voenno-istoricheskii zhurnal* 6 (1998); I. B. Berkhin, *Voennaia reforma v SSSR (1924–1925 gg.)* (Moscow: Voenizdat, 1958).

108. The Tenth Party Conference in Tambov in February 1921 reported that party membership had declined from 14,200 to 9,100 due to reregistration exercises in the previous year, and in the same period resignations (mainly by workers and peasants) had cut membership by 50 percent. More important, the conference reported that over 1,000 party members had perished in the rebellion and that the membership was characterized by "general dispirit" (*upadnicheskoe nastroenie*). RGASPI f. 17, op. 13, d. 1005, ll. 140, 141. On 15 May, the Communist Party in the five uezds affected by the insurgency was "militarized," and all members were to be made available for service in the occupation system. But the actual mobilization of party members in May 1921 was described as "disappointing" by a Red Army inspector, despite the fact that 75 percent of the set target was met (1,200 of an anticipated 1,600). Many who answered the call, described by the inspector as "weak, sick, shoeless, and poorly clothed," had

obviously suffered since their evacuation from the countryside. See Danilov and Shanin, *KV*, 180; Donkov, "Organizatsiia," 70.

109. Surrendered rebels attested to the impact of Red Army demobilization, reasoning that if the Red Army was permitting soldiers to go home, they could see no reason for the Partisan Army to continue the fight. See GATO f. R-1979, op. 1, d. 1090, l. 440.

110. Danilov and Shanin, *KV*, 166–67. The political commissions were composed of: the commander of sector military forces, the head of the political department in the sector, the chief of the local Special Department (Osobyi Otdel), the head of the uezd Communist Party committee, and the chairman of the uezd soviet executive committee. The head of the revolutionary-military tribunal joined these five as a junior member of the sector political commission. The Plenipotentiary Commission selected an overall chairman and secretary for the individual political commissions.

111. One such resolution was passed in the village of Gavrilovka-1 in the First Military Sector (Kirsanov) on 29 May 1921: "We, the villagers of Gavrilovka-1 declare ourselves united in support of Soviet power and agree to fulfill all directives and orders of the Revolutionary Committees without question. We welcome the measures already taken by the Revkom to eliminate banditry and desertion, and to combat anarchy and ruin, and we therefore declare our continued support for a just authority and offer every assistance to those sent to us to work with the Revkom to help establish a peaceful and tranquil (*spokoinaia*) life." See TsDNITO f. 840, op. 1, d. 1053, l. 27 (see also l. 26); Fatueva, *Protivostoianie*, 249.

112. Danilov and Shanin, *KV*, 168.

113. Ibid.

114. A problem in the First Military Sector was the failure of the large contingent of military cadets, based in the Treskino region, to support the efforts of the political commission. This was not only owing to the difficulties they found in setting up operations and establishing lines of supply for the troops, it was also a simple problem of communications that left sector officials in the dark as to the activities of the several thousand cadets in the region. See Danilov and Shanin, *KV*, 176, 183.

115. TsDNITO f. 840, op. 1, d. 1053, l. 16; Danilov and Shanin, *KV*, 176–77.

116. The STK order was reported to have been signed by Pluzhnikov. GA RF f. R-8415, op. 1, d. 112, ll. 24–25; Danilov and Shanin, *KV*, 212; K. P. Orlov, "K istorii likvidatsii antonovskgo miatezha (1921 g.)," *Istoricheskii arkhiv* 4 (1962), 205.

117. Danilov and Shanin, *KV*, 177.

118. Chizhova and Muratov, eds., *G. I. Kotovskii*, 346–47.

119. Ivan Trutko, "Razgrom bandy Antonova," *Krasnaia Armiia*, nos. 7–8 (1921), 20. The failure of the Red Army cavalry brigades to achieve a breakthrough in the second half of May 1921 prompted calls for more reinforcements and for improvements to the supply lines to the pursuit forces. As Uborevich wrote to Tukhachevskii at the end of May: "The cavalry group has shown itself to be unprepared for serious operations. The brigade under Dmitrienko three times lost Antonov after having him encircled, but this was not down to the failings of Dmitrienko but because the cavalry brigade is effectively operating as infantry with poor quality peasant horses. Kotovskii's brigade is much smaller in size and operates within a much smaller territory, but its horses are nevertheless exhausted." Quoted in Samoshkin, *Antonovskoe*,

106. Both Antonov-Ovseenko and Vasil'ev added their voices to the call for further reinforcements, prompting Lenin to ask E. M. Sklianskii: "How are things going with Tukhachevskii? Hasn't he caught Antonov yet? Have you been pressing him [Tukhachevskii]?" See Orlovskii, *Kak dela*, 66–67.

120. GATO f. R-4049, op. 1, d. 89, l. 88.

121. Trutko, "Razgrom Antonova," 20.

122. The three groups that were moving to converge on Rzhaksa were Dmitrenko's cavalry brigade (2,000 men; moving from the direction of Sampur railway station in Tambov uezd), Kotovskii's cavalry brigade (1,000 men, moving south from Lomovis station in Kirsanov uezd), and the Fourteenth Cavalry Brigade (1,000 men, moving along the path of the Vorona River from Karai-Pushkino in Kirsanov uezd).

123. Trutko, "Razgrom Antonova," 25. This was obviously not the speed typically demonstrated by the rebels during the previous two forays made into Saratov territory, when they trailed a string of carts, filled with stolen goods, numbering in the hundreds.

124. Fed'ko had had previous experience in employing motorized units when he had been assigned to the North Caucasus in 1918, but the experience was limited and the vehicles deployed of questionable reliability. Fed'ko's group in Tambov was composed of six large vehicles that were outfitted with armored siding and emplacements for two mounted Maxim machine guns. These were converted trucks—Fiats—that were named "one-and-a-half tonners." In addition, the same unit had one smaller vehicle, a Packard, that was similarly outfitted with a lighter (Colt-manufactured) machine gun. The group was formally composed of the First and Fifty-second VChK motorized detachments, both of which had been in operation in Tambov since the beginning of 1921. See I. L. Obertas, *Komandir Fed'ko* (Moscow: Voennoe izdatel'stvo MinOborony SSSR, 1973), 142; Iakovlev, *Vnutrennie voiska*, 605.

125. Obertas, *Komandir*, 143.

126. Trutko, "Razgrom Antonova," 22–23; Obertas, *Komandir*, 143.

127. Trutko writes that over 900 rebels were killed in the fighting in Bakury, which would be a veritable massacre if true. His casualty figure is repeated in other sources, but there are reasons to doubt that the losses in this one battle could be so high. See Trutko, "Razgrom Antonova," 23; Trifonov, *Klassy*, 254; Danilov and Shanin, *KV*, 177.

128. Trifonov, *Klassy*, 254. Senior officials in the Saratov Cheka organization later speculated that Antonov had entered Saratov territory in late May because he faced a severe shortage of munitions and hoped to link up with rebels there. See Shabanov and Makarov, *Gubcheka*, 184–85.

129. Captured rebels most likely reported that Antonov had been wounded at Chernyshevo. It was confirmed in June to revkom officials by another of Antonov's female acquaintances, Ol'ga Petrovna Sineleva, from the village of Beliaevka (Treskino volost, Kirsanov uezd). See GATO f. R-4049, op. 1, d. 89, l. 141.

130. According to Trutko, not only was the armored train group forced to move from its position, there was also a minor collision between it and Uborevich's personal train that left the stretch of railway crossing the Vorona unguarded. Such a collision is not mentioned in other sources, however, including Uborevich's final report. See RGVA f. 235, op. 2, d. 77, l. 22; Trutko, "Razgrom Antonova," 24–25.

131. Despite contributing to the failure of the Red Army to rout the rebels and Antonov comprehensively, Uborevich received the credit and a commendation for heroism for having

commanded the overall operation. According to the summary of the operation contained in the Plenipotentiary Commission's 9 June 1921 protocol: "In the space of 9 days Antonov faced 6 battles with the 7 armored vehicles and 47 soldiers commanded by comrade Uborevich. Up to 800 bandits were killed. The band lost all of its machine guns, many rifles, and has been left completely broken. Antonov himself received a wound to the head, and only managed to escape with 100 men, the smallest and most pitiful remnants of his 'army.' Automobiles have proven to be the best weapons in the fight against banditry. Cavalry simply cannot outrun automobiles, and what is more, automobiles have a demoralizing effect on the enemy. Our motorized unit was operated by only 47 men, and it threw into a panic 2,000 of Antonov's most reliable bandits." Danilov and Shanin, *KV*, 177. Trifonov states that Antonov escaped with only ten to fifteen of his closest associates. This claim, however, is not supported by the available documents. See Trifonov, *Klassy*, 255.

Chapter 8: Facets of "Sovietization"

1. This claim comes from Trutko, but the provincial STK did consider reports of extensive preparations for a massive uprising in the Don region in June 1921. See Ivan Trutko, "Unichtozhenie band Boguslavskogo," *Krasnaia Armiia*, nos. 3–4 (1921), 37–38; Danilov and Shanin, *KV*, 213.

2. Trutko, "Unichtozhenie Boguslavskogo," 36–38.

3. GA RF f. R-8415, op. 1, d. 127, ll. 37–370b; RGVA f. 34228, op. 1, d. 49, l. 225; GATO f. R-4049, op. 1, d. 89, ll. 30, 300b.

4. TsDNITO f. 840, op. 1, d. 1053, l. 28.

5. Danilov and Shanin, *KV*, 178.

6. Ibid., 178–79.

7. TsDNITO f. 840, op. 1, d. 1053, l. 16; Danilov and Shanin, *KV*, 197.

8. One old woman interrogated by state agents referred to the insurgents from her village community as "our bandits"—"*nashy bandity,*" echoing state pronouncements calling for villages to surrender "their bandits." See GATO f. R-4049, op. 1, d. 89, l. 158. One rebel in Saratov Province, a former Communist Party member, wrote to officials for reassurances regarding an amnesty offer, referring to himself throughout as a "bandit," even sarcastically signing the letter "Your bandit." See Danilov and Shanin, *KDP*, 724–25. On a similar theme, Cheka agents investigating the provincial administration in Tambov city noted that employees in the commissariats frequently discussed the counterinsurgency operation not in terms of "us" and "them" (or even "bandits")—terminology that would have pleased officials—but of "Reds" and "partisans," indicating no personal identification. See GATO f. R-1, op. 1, d. 183, ll. 466–67.

9. Danilov and Shanin, *KV*, 178.

10. While it had been feared the percentage was much higher, Tukhachevskii later said that only about 5 percent of those who surrendered as deserters had been Partisan Army rebels. See Fatueva, *Protivostoianie*, 284.

11. Antonov's "order" was first discussed by the Plenipotentiary Commission the day after Uborevich reported on the success of the operations against the Second Partisan Army. See GA RF f. R-8415, op. 1, 122, ll. 67, 68; Danilov and Shanin, *KV*, 183.

12. The Plenipotentiary Commission warned remaining units of the Partisan Army against obeying any demobilization order issued by Antonov on the day that Order no. 171 was published (11 June 1921). See GA RF f. R-8415, op. 1, 122, l. 70.

13. Danilov and Shanin, *KV*, 295. Lenin read about the order in a report in *Tambovskaia Pravda*, during his recuperation at Gorkii following his first stroke. Orlovskii, *Kak dela*, 72.

14. According to instructions, the revkom network could only expand as the occupation became established. Of the five members of a regional or district revolutionary committee, two had to be drawn from the occupying military unit. This was not strictly observed in practice, however.

15. By July, the network of revolutionary committees in the uezds affected by the insurgency was as follows: Borisoglebsk (8 regional revkoms, 33 volost revkoms), Kirsanov (5 regional, 35 volost), Kozlov (3 regional, 13 volost), and Tambov (10 regional, 66 district). Ideally, each region was to comprise 3 to 5 volost revkoms, but this was not always the case. See the introductory essay to GATO f. R-1979, op. 1.

16. GATO f. R-4049, op. 1-s, d. 34, ll. 6–70b and *passim*; GATO f. R-17, op. 1, d. 240, l. 2170b; RGVA f. 633, op. 1, d. 341, ll. 92–93 and *passim*; RGVA f. 34228, op. 1, d. 299, l. 43.

17. The members were: Shcherkoldin (head of the sector Red Army political department), Znamenskii (chairman of the Kirsanov soviet executive committee), Sadovskii (secretary of the uezd Communist Party), Ruprekht (chairman of the uezd revolutionary tribunal), and Troianov (chief of the Special Department).

18. TsDNITO f. 840, op. 1, d. 1053, l. 14.

19. TsDNITO f. 840, op. 1, d. 1053, ll. 40b, 6.

20. This refers to the weapons seized from a local Red Army division by "greens" during the summer of 1919. Parevka was the heart of the region where Antonov's druzhina was active in 1919–1920, and also where there were considerable disturbances when the White and Volunteer armies were at the zenith of the "march on Moscow" late that summer. Whether the villagers hid weapons seized from the captured members of the Fifty-sixth Division is not known. See RGVA f. 827, op. 1, d. 13, ll. 229, 336.

21. TsDNITO f. 840, op. 1, d. 1053, l. 5. Also in Danilov and Shanin, *KV*, 184.

22. Danilov and Shanin, *KV*, 238, 239.

23. Ibid., 186.

24. Ibid.

25. Ibid., 187–88.

26. Ibid., 190. The Plenipotentiary Commission issued a clarification warning the authorities carrying out sweeps of villages not to arrest as bandits or deserters those who had been amnestied by the Plenipotentiary Commission in March. See ibid., 196–97.

27. A summary report from Morshansk uezd noted with approval an increased incidence of suicide among active rebels since the implementation of Order no. 171. See RGVA f. 34228, op. 1, d. 49, l. 143; Danilov and Shanin, *KV*, 218–19.

28. RGASPI f. 17, op. 13, d. 1008, l. 30. Tambov officials first raised the possibility of mass deportations, indicating that the counterinsurgency campaign was not entirely characterized by tensions pitting local *moderantisme* against the hard-line approach of central Red Army and government authorities.

29. GA RF f. R-8415, op. 1, d. 111, l. 25.

30. Danilov and Shanin, *KV*, 184, 196.

31. Antonov-Ovseenko noted as much after reviewing M. Antonov's previously cited report on the matter. See his handwritten comments, GA RF f. R-8415, op. 1, d. 111, l. 24.

32. For examples, see RGVA f. 34228, op. 1, d. 49, ll. 133, 163, 167, 172, 194.

33. GATO f. R-1236, op. 1, d. 1121, ll. 790b-80, 120–1200b.

34. Tukhachevskii provided a summary of statistics relating to the effectiveness of orders no. 130 and 171 at the end of July, stating that while authorities had carried out 1,530 public executions between 28 May and 26 July 1921, only 274 of those shot had been civilian hostages. The general may have been speaking only of executions carried out by the *piaterka*s of the sector political commissions, not including executions carried out by military units working under the authority of the two orders. Otherwise, it is difficult to understand how Tukhachevskii arrived at this low figure. See his speech to a Red Army conference in Tambov, quoted in Fatueva, *Protivostoianie*, 284.

35. Danilov and Shanin, *KV*, 188. The results of the operations summarized in this report— five days of operations covering four villages—were as follows: 154 rebels and hostages executed, 227 rebel families taken hostage, 41 homes burned or demolished, and 22 homes (and property) confiscated and given to the poor.

36. GA RF f. R-8415, op. 1, d. 124, l. 26; Danilov and Shanin, *KV*, 187, 190, 191.

37. STK agitators allegedly told assembled villagers that the Red Army was using non-Russian troops—Chinese, Tatar, and Latvian—who would show no mercy in carrying out the punitive policies set by the Soviet government. In fact, there were non-Russian troops involved, such as Chinese and even German POWs, but there is no evidence of the use of such troops for punitive operations. See Danilov and Shanin, *KV*, 187.

38. Ibid., 191. The story of the old man from Kaban'-Nikolskoe became well known and was repeated with satisfaction by other Red Army officials. See Orlov, "K istorii likvidatsii," 204.

39. Danilov and Shanin, *KV*, 197. The effect of public executions on the willingness of villagers to hand over rebels was described by the leader of a *piaterka* who had conducted operations in Kudiuki volost: "Once the shooting ended, the crowd began to murmur, and then the cries arose: 'All because of them, the devils [*prokliatye*], we are made to suffer, well give them up if you know any!,' 'Enough of this silence!,' and then representatives emerged from the crowd and requested from us permission to carry out their own search for weapons and bandits. Permission was granted." See ibid., 218.

40. Military sector officials had noted that communities were much more reluctant to betray STK members to state investigators than to betray local rebels. This resistance, however, was overcome with Order no. 171. See RGVA f. 34225, op. 1, d. 66, l. 27.

41. Orlov, "K istorii likvidatsii," 205; Danilov and Shanin, *KV*, 223. Missing from those arrested in Kamenka was the head of the Tambov STK, Grigorii ("Bat'ko") Pluzhnikov, although his wife and one of his sons were arrested during the operation in late June. "Bat'ko" Pluzhnikov's death in unknown circumstances occurred not long after the Kamenka arrests, and was confirmed to officials in the Special Department in mid-July. See ibid., 195, 226.

42. Instructions regarding interrogations specified that names must be named and that no expressions of ignorance should be permitted. See ibid., 188.

43. Ibid., 226–27.

44. Bukharin may have shared in Rykov's protest. Lenin forwarded his copy of Kamenev's progress report to Bukharin with the note: "To Bukharin. Read this carefully line by line as punishment for panicking." This note could suggest that Bukharin, who along with Rykov now championed the cause of repairing relations with the villages, shared his concerns regarding the damage to peasant-state relations being done in Tambov. The editors of the documents on the Antonov rebellion make much of this, and while it is consistent with Bukharin's earlier contribution to government strategy in January and February 1921, the evidence is only suggestive. See ibid., 16–17, 224. Lenin hardly managed to stay on top of developments in Tambov. The VTsIK chairman had briefly shown a strong interest in the Antonov movement in the beginning of 1921, receiving regular reports on the progress being made by the forces under Commander Pavlov, but by the summer Lenin was recuperating from his first stroke and could not become involved. He forwarded to Bukharin his copy of Kamenev's report only in August, over a month after it had been written and discussed by members of the Politburo.

45. Ibid., 223–24. Kamenev's reference to the experience in the Minsk region is somewhat puzzling, but it may be best understood as a further effort to legitimize the methods used in Tambov. The two "banditry" problems—in Belorussia and Tambov—were dissimilar, and the Red Army's involvement in resolving the disturbances in Belorussia commenced at much the same time as Tukhachevskii's "occupation system" began in Tambov. An early treatment of the topic even contends that the Tambov operation informed strategy in Belorussia, rather than the other way around. See S. Ventsov, "Banditizm v Belorussii i organizatsiia bor'by s nim," *Krasnaia Armiia*, no. 9 (1921).

46. Danilov and Shanin, *KV*, 222.

47. Ibid.

48. Ibid., 226.

49. Ibid., 227.

50. Ibid., 227–28.

51. Ibid., 228 (emphasis in original).

52. The army units involved in such activities typically formed "plenipotentiary troikas," three-man teams that oversaw sweeps in occupied villages. These were also occasionally identified as "political troikas" (or *polittroika*). For example, see ibid., 221–22. These "troikas" were distinct from other three-man teams engaged in monitoring and regulating the local administration in Tambov in 1921, sometimes referred to as "administrative troikas."

53. GATO f. R-394, op. 1, d. 700, ll. 16–17. The camps in Tambov were part of a wider network of camps throughout Soviet Russia. According to the records of the Internal Affairs Commissariat, there were camps in sixty-one provinces and regions of Soviet territory by May 1921, including fourteen in and around Moscow. GATO f. R-394, op. 1, d. 700, ll. 1040b; Leggett, *Cheka*, 178.

54. The mix only proved volatile when former requisition squad workers or Chekists who had been convicted of abuses of authority were detained alongside those they had arrested. See GATO f. R-394, op. 1, d. 700, l. 29.

55. GATO f. R-394, op. 1, d. 710, l. 70. In the camp in Tambov uezd, some two-thirds of the prisoners were engaged in work outside the camp, often laboring on state farms or engaged in snow clearance and road maintenance. See GATO f. R-394, op. 1, d. 700, ll. 16–17.

56. Leggett, *Cheka*, 175–76; Michael Jakobson, *Origins of the GULAG: The Soviet Prison Camp System, 1917–1934* (Lexington: University of Kentucky Press, 1993).

57. According to statutes passed in mid-1920, prisoners in labor camps had to pay for their own upkeep. See Jakobson, *Origins of the GULAG*, 59.

58. GATO f. R-394, op. 1, d. 700, ll. 73, 157ob. Camp directors and commandants strove to demonstrate efficiency and cost-effectiveness in an effort to preserve control over the penal camp system for the Commissariat of Internal Affairs (NKVD). See Jakobson, *Origins of the GULAG*, chap. 4.

59. The director of the Tambov department for compulsory labor reported that security was rarely a problem in Tambov because the guards were all Siberians who had fled Kolchak's army in 1919. Not until the camps in Morshansk and Borisoglebsk opened in 1920 did officials realize how effective they had been. In the two new camps, escapes became more common, as local guards often turned a blind eye to the attempts made by fellow Tambov natives. GATO f. R-394, op. 1, d. 700, l. 280b.

60. GATO f. R-394, op. 1, d. 700, l. 28. The typical locations for prison camps during the civil war were the sites of tsarist-era prisons (usually in the center of provincial towns, as in Tambov) or of closed Orthodox monasteries. The camp established in Morshansk was located in the town itself, then in late October 1921 relocated to the site of a former monastery. GATO f. R-394, op. 1, d. 702, ll. 79, 80.

61. Camp officials discovered that the Partisan Army had managed to establish a "cell" inside the camp in Borisoglebsk in 1921 when a group of inmates who had been apprehended in connection with the insurgency succeeded with an escape plan involving coordination with rebels on the outside. See GA RF f. R-8415, op. 1, d. 127, l. 75. An STK document refers to the return of twenty-eight villagers from Pavlodar in Borisoglebsk uezd after their escape from the local camp, during which they managed to overpower three guards. It is not known if this is the same incident referred to above. See Danilov and Shanin, *KV*, 202.

62. GATO f. R-394, op. 1, d. 710, ll. 12, 13.

63. GATO f. R-394, op. 1, d. 710, l. 112.

64. GATO f. R-394, op. 1, d. 700, l. 13 (April 1921). That the Cheka and Commissariat of Justice would be involved in this decision, without the involvement of a representative of the NKVD and Department of Administration (Otdel Upravleniia) indicates the extent to which the Cheka was beginning to control the operations of the camps in Tambov during the course of the rebellion.

65. Included were the families of individuals summarily executed in the course of occupation operations. These families were taken to camps not as hostages, however, but to remove them from the village milieu "in order to allow for the healing of the village community," in the words of a *piaterka* summary report. See Danilov and Shanin, *KV*, 218.

66. Ibid., 172.

67. Tukhachevskii was confronted with these difficulties at the 9 June 1921 meeting of the Plenipotentiary Commission. See ibid., 176–78.

68. GATO f. R-394, op. 1, d. 700, l. 34.

69. GATO f. R-394, op. 1, d. 700, l. 34.

70. Danilov and Shanin, *KV*, 185–86, 218.

71. Ibid., 186.

72. Hostages could also be held at "special posts," which were smaller in scale and administered by military sectors. See ibid., 251.

73. Ibid., 228. Hostages were also taken as insurance against rebel attacks on railway lines and bridges. According to an initial order dated 9 July, the Plenipotentiary Commission instructed sector officials to take hostages from villages near essential infrastructure, with their lives dependent upon the ability of their fellow community members to prevent rebel attacks. (This was an intensification of earlier orders made in April 1921 regarding the collective responsibility of villages for protecting railroad lines, stations, and bridges.) Because of overcrowding in the detention camps, however, the 9 July order was amended only days later, allowing hostages to return to their native villages while nevertheless maintaining hostage "status" in the event of damage being done to nearby bridges and railroads. See RGASPI f. 17, op. 13, d. 1008, l. 30; Danilov and Shanin, *KV*, 217, 220.

74. Danilov and Shanin, *KV*, 229.

75. Ibid., 246.

76. According to one inspection report of regional revolutionary committees in Tambov uezd (27 June 1921): "Concerning the expenditure of confiscated property we can state the following fact: simple accounting books are completely lacking and all the documents that relate to confiscated items and property are often in a chaotic state, and as such no one can really be given any guarantees relating to their [confiscated] property." See GATO f. R-394, op. 1, d. 692, l. 80b.

77. Danilov and Shanin, *KV*, 228, 246. In August 1921, the uezd political commission in Tambov recommended that the Plenipotentiary Commission acknowledge that confiscated property that had already been redistributed would not be returned to the owners. See ibid., 252.

78. GATO f. R-394, op. 1, d. 710, l. 1940b. With many camps struggling to provide even clean water, let alone facilities for boiling water to purify it, it is little wonder that one doctor who inspected a camp in Kirsanov declared the situation regarding sanitation (especially for children) as "most catastrophic." Danilov and Shanin, *KV*, 247.

79. TsDNITO f. 840, op. 1, d. 1053, l. 7.

80. By the end of 1921, according to the member of the Tambov soviet executive committee responsible for children's welfare, E. A. Vasil'eva (wife of the Tambov Communist Party chief), the provincial government in Tambov was responsible for the maintenance of some 20,000 orphans. See GATO f. R-1, op. 1, d. 250, l. 106.

81. Danilov and Shanin, *KV*, 248, 249.

82. GATO f. R-394, op. 1, d. 710, l. 1940b. The much more extensive system of camps established by the British in 1900–1902 during the Boer conflict similarly introduced schooling, with a particular eye toward indoctrination of subjects to the English language and to British values. See Paul Zietsman, "The Concentration Camp Schools—Beacons of Light in the Darkness," in *Scorched Earth*, ed. Fransjohan Pretorius (Cape Town: Human and Rousseau, 2001).

83. GATO f. R-394, op. 1, d. 710, ll. 196–97.

84. M. G. Nikolaev, "Govoriat uchastniki 'likvidatsii antonovshchiny'," *Otechestvennyi archivy* 2 (1996): 64. According to camp records, the chorus did not sing exclusively political songs, but also folk songs and classic choral pieces by Glinka, Rimsky-Korsakov, and Mendelssohn. See GATO f. R-394, op. 1, d. 710, l. 197.

85. Nikolaev, "Govoriat uchastniki," 65–66.

86. For background, see Leggett, *Cheka*, 171–86. The debate echoes that in the U.S. Civil War in which guerrilla warfare tested and distorted popular notions of acceptable conduct and justice. See Michael Fellman, *Inside War: Guerrilla Conflict in Missouri During the American Civil War* (Oxford; New York: Oxford University Press, 1989), esp. 86–93.

87. On sanitary conditions in civil war era camps in general, and on the bureaucratic tensions that limited improvements in prison health care in particular, see Mary Shaeffer Conroy, "Health Care in Prisons, Labour and Concentration Camps in Early Soviet Russia, 1918–1921," *Europe-Asia Studies* 52 7 (2000).

88. Shortage of tents in the newly established camps was a constant problem. In one case, the chief administrator of the camp located in Sampur was arrested for selling tents to the highest bidder among the hostages. See GATO f. R-394, op. 1, d. 700, ll. 400b–41. Similar problems plagued many of the camps set up during the Boer War. See Elria Wessels, "'A Cage Without Bars'—the Concentration Camp in Bloemfontein," in *Scorched Earth*, ed. Fransjohan Pretorius (Cape Town: Human and Rousseau, 2001), 66–68.

89. GA RF f. R-8415, op. 1, d. 122, ll. 55–550b.

90. GATO f. R-1979, op. 1, d. 1000, l. 48 (8 July 1921).

91. Danilov and Shanin, *KV*, 258–59.

92. GATO f. R-18, op. 1, d. 118, ll. 16–160b, 19. Legget mentions captured rebels from Tambov listed among the prisoners at the infamous Solovetsky camp complex on the White Sea coast. See Leggett, *Cheka*, 180.

93. GA RF f. R-8415, op. 1, d. 111, l. 8.

94. While disease is always a problem in prison camps, during the Boer War the camps were much more affected by potentially fatal infections. See Stowell V. Kessler, "The Black and Coloured Concentration Camps," in *Scorched Earth*, ed. Fransjohan Pretorius (Cape Town: Human and Rousseau, 2001).

95. Danilov and Shanin, *KV*, 226, 227.

96. Ibid., 220.

97. GATO f. R-394, op. 1, d. 691, l. 23.

98. GATO f. R-394, op. 1, d. 693, ll. 360b, 37; GATO f. R-4049, op. 1-s, d. 34, ll. 12–13, 19, 200b, 220b; Danilov and Shanin, *KV*, 171; Mokarev, "Kursantskii," 73; Chizhova and Muratov, eds., *G. I. Kotovskii*, 351–52.

99. GATO f. R-1979, op. 1, d. 1090, l. 129. The first words of this statement are highly typical of those produced by routine revkom investigations.

100. For instance, see GATO f. R-4049, op. 1, d. 89, ll. 78–79, 84.

101. GATO f. R-4049, op. 1-s, d. 34, ll. 2–3, 5, 12–13.

102. GATO f. R-4049, op. 1-s, d. 34, l. 20b.

103. Danilov and Shanin, *KV*, 127.

104. GATO f. R-1, op. 1, d. 293, l. 664.

105. Danilov and Shanin, *KV*, 221.

106. GA RF f. R-8415, op. 1, d. 112, l. 30; GATO f. R-1979, op. 1, d. 726, l. 90.

107. RGVA f. 34228, op. 1, 298, l. 14.

108. GATO f. R-5201, op. 2, d. 2558, *passim*; GATO f. R-1979, op. 1, d. 726, l. 95.

109. TsDNITO f. 840, op. 1, d. 1053, l. 24.

110. Regional revolutionary committee reports attest to the practice of amnestying rebels in the hope that, even if they were to rejoin groups of rebels still in hiding, they would spread word of the government's practice of honoring the amnesty. Such practices upset local villagers, who felt that former rebels were being released too quickly without concern for the damage that might be done to rural communities. GATO f. R-394, op. 1, d. 692, ll. 11–120b.

111. GATO f. R-1979, op. 1, d. 1000, ll. 76, 158, 159, 160, 170.

112. For example, TsDNITO f. 840, op. 1, d. 1053, l. 27.

113. The term used most frequently was *druzhina*, which I have loosely translated here as "militia." See Danilov and Shanin, *KV*, 184.

114. For instance, in parts of Morshansk and Kozlov uezds, village self-defense groups were reported as early as March 1921. See GATO f. R-18, op. 1, d. 62, ll. 83–84. Other notable examples come from northern Kirsanov uezd, also on the periphery of the insurgency. See TsDNITO f. 840, op. 1, d. 1053, l. 10.

115. GATO f. R-1979, op. 1, d. 836, ll. 4–5, 7–8, 23, 26, 32, 49; GATO f. R-394, op. 1, d. 691, l. 23.

116. GATO f. R-1979, op. 1, d. 1097, l. 94. For added respectability, the regional revkom agitator sent to the village, Stepanov, had identified himself as a member of the Petrograd Soviet, and he was so identified in another portion of the quoted declaration by the Tokarevka community.

117. GATO f. R-1979, op. 1, d. 756, l. 73.

118. There were many disputes over horses, which were regularly exchanged or requisitioned by the Partisan Army. See GATO f. R-1979, op. 1, d. 1090, ll. 309–13.

119. GATO f. R-4049, op. 1-s, d. 34, ll. 12–120b; GATO f. R-1979, op. 1, d. 836, l. 61. As with military desertion, accusations of neglect of obligations to the state on the labor front inspired written appeals by many who pleaded that they were of more use on the antibanditry front in their native villages than serving at a sugar refinery or fire station in some far-off province. For example, see GATO f. R-1979, op. 1, d. 1097, l. 204.

120. RGVA f. 34228, op. 1, d. 298, l. 10. This practice was not endorsed by state authorities, however, and the matter was passed to the Special Department for investigation.

121. GATO f. R-5201, op. 2, d. 2316, ll. 2, 3, 9.

122. Revolutionary committees were required to give weekly updates on membership in the self-defense militias. For example, see GATO f. R-1979, op. 1, d. 836, l. 30.

123. This term is taken from Klandermans but used in a slightly different manner. See Bert Klandermans, *The Social Psychology of Protest* (Oxford: Blackwells, 1997), 8.

124. GATO f. R-1979, op. 1, d. 1097, l. 35. Another written appeal (l. 67) made by a fellow villager contained almost identical wording, which could indicate the hand of a revkom official or simple collaboration between villagers.

125. GATO f. R-1979, op. 1, d. 1097, l. 53.

126. For examples, see GATO f. R-1979, op. 1, d. 1097, ll. 135–45.

127. In the words of one appeal for firearms: "Only with weapons in hand can the peasantry be able to work alongside the Red Army to destroy the ignorant [*nesoznatel'nye*] bandits who refuse to surrender to army headquarters." RGVA f. 34228, op. 1, d. 298, l. 3.

128. TsDNITO f. 840, op. 1, d. 456, l. 5.

129. GATO f. R-4049, op. 1-s, d. 82, ll. 19–190b; RGVA f. 34228, op. 1, d. 48, l. 17. Of course, signaling between villages as part of the self-defense scheme not only built upon traditional practices that long predated the revolution, but also were reinforced by the STK and Partisan Army during the insurgency. See GA RF R-8415, op. 1, d. 127, l. 410b.

130. For an example, see the operational reports of a self-defense militia from Belomestnaia volost (Tambov uezd) at GATO f. R-1979, op. 1, d. 898, *passim.*

131. GATO f. R-1832, op. 1, d. 978, ll. 60–67; RGVA f. 34225, op. 1, d. 55, ll. 46, 48, 50, 53, 55, 70, 99. Such activities included entering villages under the pretense of being an official self-defense militia and carrying out requisitions of foodstuffs. See RGVA f. 235, op. 6-s, d. 12, l. 95; TsDNITO f. 840, op. 1, d. 1053, l. 390b.

132. According to a rebel soldier who was taken prisoner on 16 July, Karas' invested more hope in escaping to Poland than returning to his native Usman. See RGVA f. 235, op. 2, d. 335, l. 41.

133. GATO f. R-18, op. 1, d. 62, l. 142; Ivan Trutko, "Unichtozhenie bandy Karasia," *Krasnaia Armiia*, nos. 1–2 (1921).

134. Such episodes in this late stage of the conflict were also prone to embellishment and exaggeration by Red Army officers in the operation and those who wrote about it after the conflict. For example, see the article by N. Domozhirov originally published in *Voennyi vestnik* in 1922, reproduced in Samoshkin, *Antonovskoe*, 297–303.

135. RGVA f. 235, op. 6-s, d. 12, l. 64; Mokarev, "Kursantskii," 32.

136. GATO f. R-394, op. 1, d. 978, l. 95, 131, 160. Anglers even complained of having their pack lunches stolen by bandits. See RGVA f. 34228, op. 1, d. 49, l. 143.

137. One provincial official complained that the workers were refusing to go into the forests out of fear, and that tree felling and wood cutting had now degenerated into a free-for-all in which even state and military officials participated. See GATO f. R-18, op. 1, d. 113, ll. 71–72. Also see GATO f. R-18, op. 1, d. 62, l. 154.

138. GATO f. R-1, op. 1, d. 183, l. 911.

139. Mokarev, "Kursantskii," 84–85.

140. Samoshkin, "Slovo o krasnykh kursantakh," 122.

141. A. V. Pavlov, the former commander of military operations in Tambov in 1921 who had been involved with the Red Army's operations against Makhno in southeastern Ukraine, was assigned to lead the cadet force in the Sixth Military Sector after Tukhachevskii assumed overall command in the province.

142. Mokarev, "Kursantskii," 64–65; Samoshkin, "Slovo o krasnykh kursantakh," 120–21.

143. Crayfish are a great delicacy in contemporary Tambov, but Mokarev notes that the hungry cadets were forced to eat them—and, even worse, without salt! See ibid., "Kursantskii," 68–69; Danilov and Shanin, *KV*, 176–77. The food supply problem colored early assessments of the cadet deployment to the Sixth Military Sector. According to the director of the Red Army military academy, D. G. Petrovskii: "The effort to combine typical academic exercises with the actual struggle against banditry has yielded wretched results on both counts." According to Petrovskii (and contrary to Mokarev's later account), the cadets were soon dependent upon the local population for their meager supply of food. See Petrovskii's July 1921 report, in Danilov and Shanin, *KV*, 183.

144. Mokarev, "Kursantskii," 68.

145. Ibid., 78–81. Mokarev describes the planning that went into these operations and the frustration felt after one operation was undermined when infantry troops refused to enter a forest following an extensive artillery bombardment because they had not received orders to do so from sector headquarters. (ibid., 80)

146. Such boats were first used to patrol the waters of the Tsna River near Tambov city, where a certain paranoia regarding a rebel assault survived into the summer of 1921. The effectiveness of the flotilla was much more limited on the Tsna than on the Vorona, however, owing to the many small dams that restricted traffic. See GATO f. R-1832, op. 1, d. 797a, *passim*.

147. Mokarev describes the lengths some rebels went to in order to avoid capture, including burying themselves in the ground. See Mokarev, "Kursantskii," 86.

148. Ibid.

149. B. V. Solokov, *Mikhail Tukhachevskii: zhizn' i smert' "Krasnogo marshala"* (Smolensk: Rusich, 1999), 220–21. Soviet military officials had been interested in learning directly from the Germans about chemical weapons technology and doctrine as early as 1920, and the grounds for future collaboration were set in the final months of the civil war in 1920–1921. Soviet state and military officials believed, in large part, that chemical weapons represented a rapid means of alleviating the relative technical "backwardness" of the Soviet armed forces, although the Germans did not supply the Soviets with such weapons during this first period of military-economic relations between the two countries. See E. S. Gams, "Sozdanie sovetskogo khimicheskogo oruzhiia (1921–1940 gg.)," *Voprosy istorii* 4 (1997); Sergei A. Gorlov, *Sovershenno sekretno: Moskva-Berlin, 1920–1933* (Moscow: IVI-RAN, 1999), 49–58. Frunze contended that the future of warfare would invariably include chemical weapons, regardless of efforts to ban them by international convention. See Walter Darnell Jacobs, *Frunze: the Soviet Clausewitz, 1885–1925* (The Hague: Martinus Nijhoff, 1969), 121–23.

150. While the context had certainly changed in the years following World War I, Tukhachevskii appeared to have forgotten his own role in using chemical weapons against fellow Russians when he criticized J. F. C. Fuller's *The Reformation of War* for defending the practices of the British Royal Army in fighting "small wars," including the use of chemical weapons against civilian populations. See Tukhachevskii's introduction to the Russian-language version of Fuller's monograph, reproduced in M. N. Tukhachevskii, *Izbrannye Proizvedeniia* (Moscow: Voennoe Izdatel'stvo Min. Oborony SSSR, 1964), 2:154–55.

151. Russian casualties were as much owing to the shortage of effective countermeasures as to the extensive use of chemical weapons by the German and Austro-Hungarian forces on the eastern front. See Ludwig F. Haber, *The Poisonous Cloud: Chemical Warfare in the First World War* (Oxford: Oxford University Press, 1986), 243.

152. Pavel A. Aptekar', "'Khimchistka' po-Tambovskii," *Rodina* 5 (1994): 56; Danilov and Shanin, *KV*, 179.

153. Danilov and Shanin, *KV*, 169.

154. Ibid., 176–77. Many of the other measures agreed upon at the 9 June 1921 meeting were incorporated into Order no. 171, published two days later.

155. Aptekar', "'Khimchistka,'" 56.

156. Documents repeatedly refer to "asphyxiating" gas, which indicates that chlorine and phosgene were the most likely chemicals used, rather than mustard gas, which was a vesicatory agent.

157. Aptekar', "'Khimchistka'," 57.

158. Ibid.; Solokov, *Mikhail Tukhachevskii: zhizn' i smert' "Krasnogo marshala,"* 221–22.

159. Artillery shells, especially for the lighter guns used by the Red Army in Tambov in 1921, had a fairly low capacity for the liquid chemical mixtures required. A tremendous amount of shells would have to be fired to create and sustain a lethal concentration of whatever gas was being fired, such as phosgene or chlorine. See Haber, *Poisonous Cloud*, 96–97.

160. Danilov and Shanin, *KV*, 178.

161. GATO f. R-18, op. 1, d. 116, l. 27 (15 June 1921; emphasis in original).

162. Mokarev, "Kursantskii," 79. Military cadets reportedly were given demonstrations on gas attacks as early as 15 June 1921.

163. Edward M. Spiers, *Chemical Warfare* (Basingstoke and London: Macmillan Press, 1986), 32–33.

164. The cadet force was to remain in Tambov until the beginning of October 1921, but this was extended on the recommendation of Tukhachevskii. See Danilov and Shanin, *KV*, 226.

165. For one Red Army officer, the use of large infantry battalions in Tambov against the remaining rebel groups smacked of overkill: "It can be quite funny for our units to chase after these small bands on horseback, kind of like swatting flies with a sledgehammer." He nevertheless warned that these small bands remained dangerous, representing the hardened core of rebel support. See Orlov, "K istorii likvidatsii," 207.

166. "The province cannot feed itself and feed such an army on the basis of local resources. The goods-exchange program [*tovaroobmen*] produces no results [to this effect]. If we do not want a repeat of peasant uprisings, and if we want instead to revive the peasant economy in Tambov Province, then what we require is: (1) recognition of the province as threatened with severe hunger and the protection of its grain and seed supply (that is, withdraw the recent order to transfer half of its seed resources to Samara province); (2) place the responsibility for feeding the army with the center [Moscow]; (3) similarly make the center responsible for feeding the railroad workers; (4) consider local workers as belonging to that group of workers in the 10 "hungry" provinces (and make them eligible for assistance from the 40-million *pood* aid fund). We must also recognize how exhausted the supply of horses is in the province (due to the bandits' exploitation of local horses, et cetera) and to protect what horses we have here from requisition." Danilov and Shanin, *KV*, 247. As regards this last point relating to requisitioned horses, on 7 September 1921 the Plenipotentiary Commission decided it would be too difficult to return horses requisitioned from village households by occupying forces. See RGVA f. 34228, op. 1, d. 302, l. 16.

167. TsDNITO f. 840, op. 1, d. 1053, ll. 10–100b.

168. TsDNITO f. 840, op. 1, d. 1053, l. 39.

169. On the Penza infantry group, see RGVA f. 235, op. 6-s, d. 12, l. 62.

170. RGVA f. 235, op. 6-s, d. 12, l. 67; Samoshkin, *Antonovskoe*, 106–07.

171. On looting by the Kotovskii brigade, see RGVA f. 235, op. 6-s, d. 12, l. 65; RGVA f. 34228, op. 1, d. 299, l. 7; Nikolaev, "Govoriat uchastniki," 48–49.

172. GA RF f. R-8415, op. 1, d. 124, l. 26. Cavalry units also favored requisitioning oats from local villages for their horses, rather than rely upon open grazing, which was much more time-consuming. See Chizhova and Muratov, eds., *G. I. Kotovskii*, 354, 366.

173. TsDNITO f. 840, op. 1, d. 1053, l. 21.

174. GATO f. R-4049, op. 1-s, d. 34, l. 9.

175. GATO f. R-4049, op. 1-s, d. 34, l. 40; Nikolaev, "Govoriat uchastniki," 53–54.

176. GATO f. R-1, op. 1, d. 406, ll. 1220b-24; Okatov et al., *Sovety Tambovskoi gubernii*, 327–28. The military sector commands issued public declarations and orders promoting the assistance received by cooperative villages and volosts. See TsDNITO f. 840, op. 1, d. 1053, l. 16.

177. GATO f. R-4049, op. 1-s, d. 34, ll. 11–110b; RGVA f. 34228, op. 1, d. 49, l. 218.

178. GATO f. R-4049, op. 1-s, d. 34, l. 6.

179. On the markets in Tambov and the role of Red Army soldiers, see GATO f. R-18, op. 1, d. 62, ll. 141–42; GA RF f. R-8415, op. 1, d. 124, l. 4; RGASPI f. 17, op. 13, d. 1009, l. 7; Nikolaev, "Govoriat uchastniki," 57. Soldiers in Morshansk who were questioned about the wisdom of selling their ration packets explained that they could always get food from the homes in which they were quartered. See Boris Kamov, *Obyknovennaia biografiia* (*Arkadii Gaidar*) (Moscow: Molodaia gvardiia, 1971), 64.

180. A delegate to a Red Army party conference in 1921 explained to Communist Party officials that the soldiers enjoy sing-alongs in the evening, but they much prefer the old songs to the new Soviet ones, such as the "International," which they find too difficult. "Of course, if you don't feed a wolf, he will go back to singing his old songs," explained the delegate, somewhat cryptically. Nikolaev, "Govoriat uchastniki," 49, 51, 57.

181. RGVA f. 235, op. 6-s, d. 12, l. 12.

182. One encounters parallels that are almost beyond coincidence. One Red Army cavalryman described a "ballerina from St. Petersburg" who came to attach herself to his unit, providing regular recitals and even serving as a cook for the soldiers. She quickly established herself as the center of cultural life in the unit and considered herself a full member of the Red Army unit. No name was given, but the description recalls that of Anastasia Drigo-Drigina, the dancer and singer who fell in with the Partisan Army in January 1921 and was asked to become Petr Tokmakov's "wife." Soon after Tokmakov's death in March, Drigo-Drigina was allowed to leave the Partisan Army, and according to her own account she then met a Red Army cavalry officer from the elite Dmitrenko brigade and traveled with them for a month and a half before her arrest by the Special Department. According to Pavel Ektov, a senior Partisan Army operative who informed the Cheka on rebel leaders after his capture, Drigo-Drigina was certainly capable of anything: "To put it bluntly, that woman really got around." See GATO f. R-5201, op. 2, d. 1717, ll. 56–560b; Nikolaev, "Govoriat uchastniki," 54; Liapina, "Ispoved' v podvale GubChK," 3.

183. One of Aleksandr Antonov's former girlfriends stated that her relationship with a Red Army soldier gave her security when she felt vulnerable before local revolutionary committee and Cheka officials. However, her Red Army boyfriend betrayed her after she admitted to her past relationship with Antonov. See GATO f. R-4049, op. 1, d. 89, l. 890b.

184. In one case, the daughter of an STK chairman married a Cheka agent. Similarly, a Rabkrin inspector had similarly planned to marry the daughter of an STK chairman and had arranged to secure amnesties for his future in-laws, only to be betrayed by his flat mate in Kirsanov, a Cheka agent. See GATO f. R-5201, op. 2, d. 1685, ll. 11, 13, 14, and *passim*; RGVA f. 34228, op. 1, d. 298, ll. 11–110b.

185. Kamov, *Obyknovennaia biografiia*, 74.

186. Chizhova and Muratov, eds., *G. I. Kotovskii*, 367.

187. Note an extraordinary exchange between a Red Army soldier (Fediunin), who was evidently drunk and intent upon speaking his mind, and stunned delegates at a Red Army Communist Party conference in July 1921:

Voice from the hall: Tell us about the attitudes of the Red Army soldiers?

Fediunin: What attitudes?

Voice: Well, for instance, how do they view the bandit problem?

Fediunin: They view it like anything else. At meetings and demonstrations, they cast their votes as expected, but outside of these occasions they argue about it, and there is a lot of shouting and punches thrown, asking in what way are these people bandits? How are they bandits? They're not bandits at all, they're our brothers—peasants. They grow grain, and the city folk come in and take it in exchange for . . . shish! That's why they end up as bandits.

Conference chairman: You shouldn't say such things.

Fediunin: I'm only saying what they are saying. They're saying: if they [bandits] didn't bother us, weren't trying to kill us or slash our throats, then we could easily move to their side and join them.

Chairman: If someone ever says such a thing to you, you should smack him right in the teeth!

Fediunin: Yeah, right! Try that yourself, and you'll get more in return. You won't only get your nose broken—they might even kill you. Best keep your bravery to yourself.

Chairman: You'll speak to me with more respect!

Fediunin: And the same goes for you. You can go ahead and throw yourself in with our lot, but there the folks are hardboiled, and if you go in with your head held high, you'll likely return with your head missing.

See Nikolaev, "Govoriat uchastniki," 61.

Chapter 9: Conclusion

1. A. Lobotskii, "V skhvatke s antonovshchinoi," in *Parol'—muzhestvo. Ocherki o tambovskikh chekistakh*, ed. G. D. Remizov (Voronezh: Tsentral'noe chernozemnoe knizhnoe izdatel'stvo, 1986), 72.

2. STK records confirm, however, that government spies had been discovered and apprehended by the rebels. See TsDNITO f. 840, op. 1, d. 1110, l. 76.

3. The first to be lured into a Cheka trap was N. G. Gerasev, reportedly the head of Partisan Army counterintelligence. Gerasev was brought to Moscow under the pretense of meeting with senior PSR officials who had prepared the ground for an armed coup d'etat in Moscow and were willing to supply the Partisan Army with weapons and ammunition. Another casualty of this same Cheka operation was one of the rebels' main contacts in the provincial capital of Tambov, a man named Fedorov whose alleged connections with the Kadet Party and whose professional background provided Soviet propagandists with rich material for linking the rebellion to all variety of "counterrevolutionary elements." See the descriptions in D. M. Smirnov, *Zapiski chekista*, 2nd ed. (Minsk: "Belarus," 1972), 64–67; Danilov and Shanin, *KV*, 261–62; Radkey, *Unknown Civil War*, 83. According to the reminiscences of the foremost agent involved in this operation, some forty other Partisan Army soldiers were drawn to Moscow for the transport of weapons and captured by the Cheka in the Soviet capital. See E. F. Murav'ev,

"Poltora mesiatsa v shtabe antonovtsev," in *Voronezhskie chekisty rasskazyvaiut*... (Voronezh: Tsentral'noe chernozemnoe knizhnoe izd., 1976), 57.

4. GA RF f. 8415, op. 1, d. 124, ll. 22–23; Danilov and Shanin, *KV*, 194.

5. These themes, as well as the Cheka operations in the summer of 1921, are discussed at greater length in Landis, "Waiting for Makhno."

6. Pavel Vasil'evich Ektov is the principal character of the short story "Ego" (1995) by Aleksandr Solzhenitsyn.

7. See Landis, "Waiting for Makhno."

8. Some of these are described in N. Domozhirov, "Epizody partizanskoi voiny," *Voennyi vestnik*, no. 12 (1922); Zhukov, *Vospominaniia*, 1:114–16; M. Pokaliukhin, "Konets banditskogo atamana," in *Parol'—muzhestvo. Ocherki o tambovskikh chekistakh*, ed. G. D. Remizov (Voronezh: Tsentral'noe-chernozemnoe knizhnoe izdatel'stvo, 1986), 109–10.

9. Notable in this regard is B. A. Vasil'ev's report to uezd soviet chairmen in Tambov, April 1921, in which he claims, erroneously, that all major Partisan Army figures except Aleksandr Antonov had been killed in battle or assassinated. See GATO f. R-1, op. 1, d. 283, ll. 9–10.

10. Samoshkin, *Antonovskoe*, 201–02.

11. Lobotskii, "V skhvatke s antonovshchinoi," 79; Murav'ev, "Poltora mesiatsa," 56–57.

12. Danilov and Shanin, *KV*, 261.

13. In 1919, Antonov's druzhina evidently used the forest, and Antonov himself moved freely among the people of Nizhnii Shibriaia, albeit using a pseudonym, Mikhail Petrovich Naumov. See Danilov and Shanin, *KV*, 297.

14. Katasonova may have feared being used as a hostage by the Antonov brothers, although she probably already knew that she was pregnant with Aleksandr's child, even if she had not told him. Katasonova gave birth to a daughter, Eva, in December 1922 while still in a Cheka prison. Eva was registered as the offspring of Katasonova's brother, Fedor, and his wife, but mother and daughter remained together, eventually settling in Cheliabinsk, where Eva had a family of her own and a career as a schoolteacher until her death in 1975.

15. Sanfirov had surrendered to Red Army authorities in early July 1921. See Danilov and Shanin, *KV*, 223.

16. Men who had known Antonov at least since early 1921 would have been aware that he had lost his front teeth, his most obviously distinguishing characteristic (rendering him, in the words of one source, "not particularly handsome [*ne ochen' simpatichnyi*]"). How Antonov lost his front teeth is unknown, but the fact was confirmed both by former partisans and captured Red Army soldiers. See RGVA f. 235, op. 2, d. 335, l. 32; RGVA f. 235, op. 5, d. 136, ll. 27–280b, 30. One of the former rebels now working with Pokaliukhin, Egor Zaistev, had incorrectly identified Antonov when Voronezh Chekists arrested a Ukrainian man, Kovalenko, whom they believed was the former Partisan Army leader. (Serendipitously for the agents, the man had been a small-time anti-Soviet rebel himself during the civil war.) This occurred only one month before Tambov Chekists discovered Antonov's actual whereabouts. While Kovalenko did bear a resemblance to Antonov, most likely Zaitsev did not know Antonov's face as well as he claimed. See Vladimir V. Samoshkin, "Dvoinik," *Literaturnaia Rossiia*, 18 February 1994; Samoshkin, *Antonovskoe*, 210.

17. GATO f. R-1, op. 1, d. 250, ll. 18–19.

18. Zanegin stated that the state of public health in Tambov was even worse than in 1822, when major cholera riots threatened to overwhelm the provincial capital. In fact, the riots Zanegin refers to occurred in 1830. See GATO f. R-1, op. 1, d. 250, ll. 23–24; Protasov, *Stranitsy istorii Tambovskogo kraia*, 52.

19. The Food Commissariat representative at the same Eighth Congress of Soviets in Tambov, Tretiakov, reported on the efforts that had been made to overhaul the commissariat personnel to distance the present tax-in-kind system from that of the civil war razverstka. This included the dismissal of ten uezd food commissars, as well as a major purge of food procurement agents, in which only 256 agents (out of more than 1,000) were retained and all were moved to new localities far from their previous assignments. See GATO f. R-1, op. 1, d. 250, ll. 49–50; GATO f. R-1832, op. 1, d. 1121, ll. 1160b-1170b. While Tretiakov reported this with some pride, his predecessor had condemned the dismissal and arrest of requisition agents begun earlier in the summer of 1921, stating that the old agents associated with the razverstka were being "terrorized." See GATO f. R-1832, op. 1, d. 1121, l. 49.

20. RGASPI f. 17, op. 13, d. 1001, ll. 21, 25; GATO f. R-1, op. 1, d. 293, ll. 714, 858, 881, 882; GATO f. R-1832, op. 1, d. 1121, ll. 1.

21. RGASPI f. 17, op. 13, d. 1001, ll. 35, 55.

22. RGASPI f. 17, op. 13, d. 1002, l. 69.

23. Borisoglebsk, for instance, reported a 68 percent drop in sown acreage, while in some parts of Kirsanov, only 10 percent of arable fields had been successfully planted. See RGASPI f. 17, op. 13, d. 1005, l. 95; GATO f. R-1832, op. 1, d. 1121, l. 138; TsDNITO f. 837, op. 1, d. 658, ll. 31–310b.

24. The original 1920–1921 razverstka on cereals in Tambov was 11.5 million *pood*. The first tax on cereals in the province in 1921 was assessed at 5.4 million. GATO f. R-1832, op. 1, d. 1121, l. 112.

25. GATO f. R-1832, op. 1, d. 1121, l. 112; RGASPI f. 17, op. 13, d. 1005, l. 39; RGASPI f. 17, op. 13, d. 1009, ll. 4–5; Okatov et al., *Sovety Tambovskoi gubernii*, 360–62.

26. The elections of new soviets began throughout Tambov Province in May 1921 and continued into the autumn of that year. The franchise was significantly restricted, with anyone who had been linked in even a minor way with the rebellion being deprived of the vote. See GATO f. R-1, op. 1, d. 248, ll. 12, 53–540b; GATO f. R-18, op. 1, d. 62, ll. 153–54; TsDNITO f. 837, op. 1, d. 456, ll. 10, 12–120b.

27. RGVA f. 235, op. 6-s, d. 12, l. 95; TsDNITO f. 840, op. 1, d. 1053, l. 390b.

28. RGASPI f. 17, op. 13, d. 1002, l. 48.

29. A Kirsanov Communist Party report from January 1922 stated: "If we had not alerted the center immediately (rather than delayed), then the situation in the uezd, and possibly even in the province as a whole, would have been allowed to become critical, and the result might very well have been the complete and irreversible destruction of the party and soviet organization, and many more hundreds of soviet and Communist Party workers would have fallen victim." See TsDNITO f. 837, op. 1, d. 456, l. 13.

30. Okatov et al., *Sovety Tambovskoi gubernii*, 344–47, 359; Berelowitch and Danilov, *Sovetskaia derevnia* 1:556.

31. Okatov et al., *Sovety Tambovskoi gubernii*, 347–48, 356–58.

32. Marc Jansen, *Sud bez suda 1922 goda. Pokazatel'nyi protsess sotsialistov-revoliutsionnerov* (Moscow: Vozvrashchenie, 1993), 163–78.

33. "Protsess pravykh eserov. Dvadtsat' deviatyi den'. Utrennee zasedanie," *Izvestiia VTsIK,* 12 July 1922, 2; *Obvinitel'noe zakliuchenie,* 42–44.

34. TsDNITO f. 837, op. 1, d. 658, ll. 12–13, 19, 97, 104, 108. This variety of reporting on the trial as concerned the Antonov rebellion was not entirely absent, however. See "Banditskie itogi," *Pravda,* 27 May 1922, 3.

35. Former Partisan Army rebels were obviously deeply involved in the resistance to collectivization, although not uniquely so. That the name Antonov and former ties with the 1920–1921 rebellion could form the basis for organized resistance to collectivization was more of a minor preoccupation of local state officials than it was an actual force behind the widespread resistance. For example, see Danilov and Shanin, *KV,* 285–88.

BIBLIOGRAPHY

Materials of the Tambov STKs and the Partisan Army are available primarily in digest form. The Tambov Cheka began to analyze systematically the seized materials of the Partisan Army and STK network in the spring of 1921, compiling digest reports summarizing the activities of individual Partisan Army regiments and armies, as well as those of STKs at all levels of authority. These digests regularly quote directly from the original documents (for examples, see Danilov and Shanin, *KV*), but the original rebel materials have not been found.

Archival Materials

Gosudarstvennyi arkhiv Rossiisskoi Federatsii, Moscow (GA RF)
   fond
   R-8415   Vladimir Andreevich Antonov-Ovseenko
Rossiiskii gosudarstvennyi arkhiv sotsial'no-politicheskoi istorii, Moscow (RGASPI)
   fond
   17   Central Committee of the KPSS (op. 13 – Information and Instruction Department)
Rossiiskii gosudarstvennyi voennyi arkhiv, Moscow (RGVA)
   fond
   7   Red Army Command Headquarters
   11   All-Russian Supreme Headquarters (Vserosglavshtab)
   235   Headquarters of the Commander of Antibanditry Forces, Tambov Province
   633   First Military Sector of Antibanditry Forces, Tambov Province
   827   Headquarters of the Kozlov Fortified Region
   7709   Fifteenth Siberian Cavalry Division
   25883   Administration of the Moscow Military Sector
   25887   Administration of the Orel Military Sector
   33988   Secretariat of the Deputy Chairman of the Revolutionary Military Council (RVSR)
   34225   Fifth Military Sector of Antibanditry Forces, Tambov Province
   34228   Sixth Military Sector of Antibanditry Forces, Tambov Province
Gosudarstvennyi arkhiv Tambovskoi obslasti, Tambov (GATO)
   fond
   R-1   Executive Committee of the Tambov Provincial Soviet (gubispolkom)
   R-18   Executive Committee of the Kozlov uezd Soviet (uispolkom)
   R-394   Tambov Provincial Department of Administration (GOU)
   R-400   Kirsanov uezd Department of Administration (UOU)
   R-761   Tambov Provincial Bureau of Statistics (gubstatotdel)

R-1236   Tambov Provincial Food Commissariat (gubprodkom)
R-1832   Tambov Provincial Military Commissariat (gubvoenkomat)
R-1836   Tambov uezd Military Commissariat (uvoenkomat)
R-1837   Kirsanov uezd Military Commissariat
R-1889   Uezd Anti-Desertion Commissions
R-1979   Revolutionary Committees of Tambov Province
R-4049   Political and Administrative "Troikas" of Tambov Province
R-5201   Tambov Provincial Revolutionary-Military Tribunal
Tsentr dokumentatsii noveishoi istorii Tambovskoi oblasti, Tambov (TsDNITO)
    fond
    837   Kirsanov uezd Committee of the VKP(b)
    840   Tambov Provincial Committee of the VKP(b)
    9019   Tambov Regional Committee (*obkom*) of the KPSS
International Institute of Social History, Amsterdam (IISG)
    Archive of the Socialist Revolutionary Party (PSR)
Hoover Institution Archives, Stanford CA (HIA)
    Nicolaevskii Collection (NC)

Works Cited

Ageikin, A. I. "Kak proiskhodila rabota v Kirsanovskom uezde." www.grad-kirsanov.ru/source
    .php?=memory.agejkin (accessed 22 August 2007).
———. "Kak proiskhodila Revoliutsiia v Kirsanovskom uezde i vosstanovlenie Sovetskoi
    vlasti s 1 fevralia 1918 goda." www.grad-kirsanov.ru/source.php?id=memory.agejkin1
    (accessed 22 August 2007).
Agureev, K. V. *Razgrom belogvardeiskikh voisk Denikina.* Moscow: Voenizdat, 1961.
Andreev, V. "Vozniknovenie i razvitie Sovetskoi vlasti v Tambovskoi gubernii." *Kommunist,*
    no. 11 (1923): 25–49.
Andreev, V. M. *Rossiiskoe krest'ianstvo: navstrechu sud'be.* Moscow: Moskovskii Pedago-
    gicheskii Gosudarstvennyi Universitet, 1997.
Antonov-Saratovskii, V. P., ed. *Sovety v epokhu voennogo kommunizma (1918–1921): sbornik
    dokumentov.* 2 vols. Moscow: Izdatel'stvo kommunisticheskoi akademii, 1928.
Aptekar', Pavel A. "'Khimchistka' po-Tambovskii." *Rodina* 5 (1994): 56–57.
———. "Krest'ianskaia voina [part 1]." *Voenno-istoricheskii zhurnal,* no. 1 (1993): 50–55.
———. "Soprotivlenie krest'ian politike Bol'shevikov v 1918–1922 godakh." Candidate diss.,
    Moskovskii gosudarstvennyi universitet im. Lomonosov, 2002.
Arshinov, Petr. *History of the Makhnovist Movement, 1919–1921.* Translated by Lorraine and
    Fredy Perlman. London: Freedom Press, 1987.
Aves, Jonathan. *Workers Against Lenin: Labour Protest and the Bolshevik Dictatorship.* London:
    Tauris Academic Studies, 1996.
Azovtsev, N. N. *Grazhdanskaia voina v SSSR.* 2 vols. Moscow: Voenizdat, 1980–1986.
Badcock, Sarah. *Politics and the People in Revolutionary Russia: A Provincial History.* Cam-
    bridge: Cambridge University Press, 2007.
"Banditskie itogi." *Pravda,* 27 May 1922, 3.

Banerji, Arup. *Merchants and Markets in Revolutionary Russia, 1917–30*. Basingstoke: Macmillan, 1997.

Bearman, Peter. "Desertion as Localism: Army Solidarity and Group Norms in the US Civil War." *Social Forces* 70, no. 2 (1991): 321–42.

Bechkov, E. A. "Voennoe stroitel'stvo i sotsial'naia zashchita voennosluzhashchikh v SSSR v 20-e gody." *Voenno-istoricheskii zhurnal* 6 (1998): 9–15.

Beckett, Ian F. W. *Encyclopedia of Guerrilla Warfare*. Santa Barbara, CA: ABC-CLIO, Inc., 1999.

———. *Modern Insurgencies and Counterinsurgencies: Guerrillas and Their Opponents since 1750*. London: Routledge, 2001.

Beliakov, Mikhail F. "Bor'ba s antonovshchinoi." In *Antonovshchina: Stat'i, vospominaniia i drugie materialy k istorii esero-banditizma v Tambovskoi gubernii*, edited by O. S. Litovskii, 38–47. Tambov: Biuro Tambovskogo gubistparta, 1923.

———. "Na VIII s'ezde Sovetov. Vospominaniia delegata." In *O Vladimire Il'iche Lenine: Vospominaniia, 1900–1922 gg.*, edited by F. N. Petrov, 580–84. Moscow: Gosudarstvennoe izdatel'stvo politicheskoi literatury, 1963.

Belousov, A. O. "Kirsanovskaia respublika." www.grad-kirsanov.ru/source.php?id=memory .belousov (accessed 22 August 2007).

Belov, G. A., ed. *Iz istorii grazhdanskoi voiny v SSSR: sbornik dokumentov i materialov v trekh tomakh*. 3 vols. Moscow: Sovetskaia Rossiia, 1960–1961.

Bercé, Yves Marie. *Corquants et nu pieds: les soulèvements paysans en France du XVIe au XIXe siècle*. Paris: Gallimard, 1991.

Berelowitch, Alexis, and V. P. Danilov, eds. *Sovetskaia derevnia glazami VChK-OGPU-NKVD, 1918–1939: dokumenty i materialy*. 4 vols. Moscow: ROSSPEN, 1998– .

Berkevich, A. B. "Krest'ianstvo i vseobshchaia mobilizatsiia v iiule 1914 g." *Istoricheskie zapiski* 23 (1947): 3–47.

Berkhin, I. B. *Voennaia reforma v SSSR (1924–1925 gg.)*. Moscow: Voenizdat, 1958.

Bor'ba rabochikh i krest'ian pod rukovodstvom Bol'shevistskoi partii za ustanovlenie i uprochenie Sovetskoi vlasti v tambovskoi gubernii (1917–1918 gody): sbornik dokumentov. Tambov: [s.n.], 1957.

Britov, V. V. *Rozhdenie Krasnoi Armii*. Moscow: Gosudarstvennoe uchebno-pedagogicheskoe izdatel'stvo, 1961.

Brovkin, Vladimir N. *Behind the Front Lines of the Civil War: Political Parties and Social Movements in Russia, 1918–1922*. Princeton: Princeton University Press, 1994.

———, ed. *The Bolsheviks in Russian Society: The Revolution and the Civil Wars*. New Haven: Yale University Press, 1997.

Brunk, Samuel. "'The Sad Situation of Civilians and Soliders': The Banditry of Zapatismo in the Mexican Revolution." *American Historical Review* 101, no. 2 (1996): 331–53.

Bugai, N. F. *Organy zashchity zavoevanii oktiabria: problemy i izucheniia*. Moscow: Mysl', 1982.

Burds, Jeffrey. *Peasant Dreams and Market Politics: Labor Migration and the Russian Villages, 1861–1905*. Pittsburgh: Pittsburgh University Press, 1998.

Bushnell, John. *Mutiny amid Repression: Russian Soldiers in the Revolution of 1905–1906*. Bloomington: Indiana University Press, 1985.

Chase, William. "Voluntarism, Mobilisation and Coercion: Subbotniki, 1919–21." *Soviet Studies* 41, no. 1 (1989): 111–28.

————. *Workers, Society and the Soviet State: Labor and Life in Moscow, 1918–1929*. Urbana and Chicago: University of Illinois Press, 1987.

Chernov, Viktor M. *Zapiski sotsialista-revoliutsionnera: kniga pervaia*. Berlin: Izdatel'stvo Z. I. Grzhebina, 1922.

Chernykh, Aleksei M. "Rol' gubernii chernozemnogo tsentra v reshenii zadach prodovol'stvennoi politiki v Rossii (1918–1920 gg.)." Candidate diss., Moskovskaia gosudarstvennaia akademiia im. Skriabina, 1996.

Chizhova, L. M., and Kh. M. Muratov, eds. *G. I. Kotovskii. Dokumenty i materialy*. Kishinev: Gosudarstvennoe izdatel'stvo Moldavii, 1956.

Conroy, Mary Shaeffer. "Health Care in Prisons, Labour and Concentration Camps in Early Soviet Russia, 1918–1921." *Europe-Asia Studies* 52, no. 7 (2000): 1257–74.

Daines, V. O., and T. F. Kariaev, eds. *Revvoensovet Respubliki. Protokoly, 1918–1919 gg*. Moscow: Russkii mir, 1997.

Danilov, V. P., and E. A. Tiurina, eds. *Kooperativno-kolkhoznoe stroitel'stvo v SSSR, 1917–1922. Dokumenty i materialy*. Moscow: Nauka, 1990.

Danilov, V., and T. Shanin, eds. *Krest'ianskoe dvizhenie v Povolzh'e, 1919–1922. Dokumenty i materialy*. Moscow: ROSSPEN, 2002. [*KDT*]

————, eds. *Krest'ianskoe dvizhenie v Tambovskoi gubernii, 1917–1918. Dokumenty i materialy*. Moscow: ROSSPEN, 2003. [*KDT*]

————, eds. *Krest'ianskoe vosstanie v Tambovskoi gubernii v 1919–1921 gg. "Antonovshchina": dokumenty i materialy*. Tambov: Intertsentr, 1994. [*KV*]

Davidian, I., and V. Kozlov. "Chastnye pis'ma epokhi grazhdanskoi voiny. Po materialam voennoi tsenzury." In *Neizvestnaia Rossiia: XX vek*, 201–50. Moscow: Istoricheskoe nasledie, 1992.

Dekrety sovetskoi vlasti. 13 vols. Moscow: Izdatel'stvo politicheskoi literatury, 1957–1989.

Dement'ev, V. D., and V. V. Samoshkin. "Vosstanie krest'ian na tambovshchine v 1920–1921 godakh (obzor literatury)." *Istoriia SSSR*, no. 6 (1990): 99–110.

Dickie, John. "A Word at War: The Italian Army and Brigandage 1860–1870," *History Workshop Journal*, no. 33 (1992): 1–24.

Dmitriev, P. "Ispol'zovanie strategicheskikh rezervov Krasnoi Armii v osenne-zimnei kampanii 1919–1920 gg." *Voenno-istoricheskii zhurnal*, no. 10 (1979): 45–49.

————. "Ispol'zovanie strategicheskikh rezervov Krasnoi Armii v vesennei kampanii 1919 goda." *Voenno-istoricheskii zhurnal*, no. 9 (1976): 60–69.

————. "Sozdanie strategicheskikh rezervov Krasnoi Armii v gody grazhdanskoi voiny." *Voenno-istoricheskii zhurnal*, no. 6 (1974): 64–73.

Domozhirov, N. "Epizody partizanskoi voiny." *Voennyi vestnik*, no. 12 (1922): 45–48.

Donkov, I. P. *Antonovshchina: zamysl' i deistvitel'nost'*. Moscow: Izdatel'stvo politicheskoi literatury, 1977.

————. "Organizatsiia razgroma antonovshchiny." *Voprosy istorii KPSS*, no. 6 (1966): 59–71.

DuGarm, Delano. "Local Politics and the Struggle for Grain in Tambov, 1918–21." In *Provincial Landscapes: Local Dimensions of Soviet Power, 1917–1953*, edited by Donald Raleigh, 59–81. Pittsburgh: University of Pittsburgh Press, 2002.

Erofeev, N. D., ed. *Partiia sotsialistov-revolutsionnerov: dokumenty i materialy, 1900–1925*. 3 vols. Moscow: ROSSPEN, 2000.

Esikov, S. A. "Rukovodstvo Tambovskikh bolshevikov v 1920–nachale 1921g. (Kachestvennaia kharakteristika)." In *Obshchestvenno-politicheskaia zhizn' rossiiskoi provintsii XX vek*, 57–60. Tambov: Tambovskii Gosudarstvennyi Tekhnicheskii Universitet, 1996.

———. "Tambovskie esery v 1920 godu." In *Obshchestvenno-politicheskaia zhizn' rossisskoi provintsii. XX vek*, edited by S. A. Esikov, 40–42. Tambov: Tambovskii institut khimicheskogo mashinostroeniia, 1993.

Esikov, S. A., and L. G. Protasov. "'Antonovshchina': novye podkhody." *Voprosii istorii*, no. 6/7 (1992): 47–57.

Esikov, S. A., and V. V. Kanishchev. "'Antonovskii NEP' (Organizatsiia i deiatel'nost' 'Soiza trudovogo krest'ianstva' Tambovskoi gubernii, 1920–1921)." *Otechestvennaia istoriia*, no. 4 (1993): 60–72.

Fatueva, N. V. *Protivostoianie: krizis vlasti—tragediia naroda*. Riazan': Rus', 1996.

Fellman, Michael. *Inside War: Guerrrilla Conflict in Missouri During the American Civil War*. Oxford: Oxford University Press, 1989.

Figes, Orlando. *Peasant Russia, Civil War: the Volga Countryside in Revolution, 1917–1921*. Oxford: Clarendon Press, 1989.

———. "The Red Army and Mass Mobilization during the Russian Civil War, 1918–1920." *Past and Present*, no. 129 (1990): 168–211.

Fitzpatrick, Sheila. *Stalin's Peasants: Resistance and Survival in the Russian Village After Collectivization*. Oxford: Oxford University Press, 1994.

Footman, David. *Civil War in Russia*. London: Faber and Faber, 1961.

Forrest, Alan. *Conscripts and Deserters: The Army and French Society During the Revolution and Empire*. Oxford: Oxford University Press, 1989.

Frank, Stephen. *Crime, Cultural Conflict, and Justice in Rural Russia, 1856–1914*. Berkeley: University of California Press, 1999.

Gams, E. S. "Sozdanie sovetskogo khimicheskogo oruzhiia (1921–1940 gg.)." *Voprosy istorii*, no. 4 (1997): 127–37.

Genkina, E. B. *Gosudarstvennaia deiatel'nost' V. I. Lenina, 1921–1923*. Moscow: Nauka, 1969.

Gimpel'son, E. G. "Iz istorii organizatsii mestnogo voennogo upravleniia (1918–1920gg.)." In *Grazhdanskaia voina v rossii: sobytiia, mnenii, otsenki*, edited by N. A. Ivnitskii, 351–61. Moscow: Raritet, 2002.

———. *Sovety v gody inostrannoi interventsii i grazhdanskoi voiny*. Moscow: Nauka, 1968.

Gorlov, Sergei A. *Sovershenno sekretno: Moskva-Berlin, 1920–1933*. Moscow: IVI-RAN, 1999.

Gould, Roger V. *Insurgent Identities: Class, Community, and Protest in Paris from 1848 to the Commune*. Chicago: University of Chicago Press, 1995.

Haber, Ludwig F. *The Poisonous Cloud: Chemical Warfare in the First World War*. Oxford: Oxford University Press, 1986.

Hagen, Mark Von. *Soldiers in the Proletarian Dictatorship: The Red Army and the Soviet Socialist State, 1917–1930*. Ithaca: Cornell University Press, 1990.

Holquist, Peter. *Making War, Forging Revolution. Russia's Continuum of Crisis, 1914–1921*. Cambridge: Harvard University Press, 2002.

Iakovlev, I. K., ed. *Vnutrennie voiska Sovetskoi respubliki, 1917–1922 gg. Dokumenty i materialy*. Moscow: Iuridicheskaia literatura, 1972.

Iarov, S. V. "Krest'ianskie volneniia na Severo-Zapade sovetskoi Rossii v 1918–1919 gg." *Krest'ianovedenie: Teoriia, istoriia, sovremennost'* 1 (1996): 134–59.

Iliukov, N. *Partizanskoe dvizhenie v Primor'e (1918–1920 gg.).* Moscow: Voenizdat, 1962.

Jacobs, Walter Darnell. *Frunze: The Soviet Clausewitz, 1885–1925.* The Hague: Martinus Nijhoff, 1969.

Jakobson, Michael. *Origins of the GULAG: The Soviet Prison Camp System, 1917–1934.* Lexington: University of Kentucky Press, 1993.

Jansen, Marc. *Sud bez suda 1922 goda. Pokazatel'nyi protsess sotsialistov-revoliutsionnerov.* Moscow: Vozvrashchenie, 1993.

———, ed. *The Socialist Revolutionary Party After 1917: Documents from the PSR archive.* Amsterdam: Stichting beheer IISG, 1989.

Joes, Anthony James. *Resisting Rebellion: The History and Politics of Counterinsurgency.* Lexington: University Press of Kentucky, 2004.

Kabanov, V. V. "Oktiabr'skaia revoliutsiia i krest'ianskaia obshchina." *Istoricheskie zapiski* 111 (1984): 100–50.

Kabytov, P. S., V. A. Kozlov, and B. G. Litvak. *Russkoe krest'ianstvo: etapy dukhovnogo osvobozhdeniia.* Moscow: Mysl', 1988.

Kamov, Boris. *Obyknovennaia biografiia (Arkadii Gaidar).* Moscow: Molodaia gvardiia, 1971.

Kanishchev, V. V. *Russkii bunt, bessmyslennyi i besposhchadnyi: pogromnoe dvizhenie v gorodakh Rossii v 1917–1918 gg.* Tambov: Tambovskii gosudarstvennyi universitet im. Derzhavina, 1995.

Kanishchev, V. V., and Iu. V. Meshcheriakov. *Anatomiia odnogo miatezha. Tambovskoe vosstanie, 17–19 iiuniia 1918 g.* Tambov: Tambovskii gosudarstvennyi universitet, 1995.

Kazakov, A. "Obshchie prichiny vozniknoveniia banditizma i krest'ianskikh vosstanii." *Krasnaia Armiia. Vestnik voenno-nauchnogo obshchestva pri voennoi akademii*, no. 9 (1921): 21–39.

———. *Partiia sotsialistov-revoliutsionerov v Tambovskom vosstanii 1920–21 gg.* Moscow: [s.n.], 1922.

Kessler, Stowell V. "The Black and Coloured Concentration Camps." In *Scorched Earth*, edited by Fransjohan Pretorius, 132–53. Cape Town: Human and Rousseau, 2001.

Klandermans, Bert. *The Social Psychology of Protest.* Oxford: Blackwells, 1997.

Kliatskin, S. M. *Na zashchite oktiabria.* Moscow: Nauka, 1965.

Klishin, S. P. "Tambovskie volki (razmyshleniia o geroiakh zemli tambovskoi)." *Tambovskie izvestiia*, 22 June 1999, 12.

"Kommunisty na rabote (Pis'mo krest'ianina iz Tambovskoi gub.)." *Revoliutsionnaia Rossiia*, no. 5 (1921): 25–28.

"Konets esero-bandita Antonova." *Izvestiia VTsIK*, 2 July 1922, 4.

Kostrikin, V. I. *Zemel'nye komitety v 1917 godu.* Moscow: Nauka, 1975.

Kotkin, Stephen. *Magnetic Mountain: Stalinism as Civilization.* Berkeley: University of California Press, 1995.

Kublanov, A. L. *Sovet rabochei i krest'ianskoi oborony (noiabr' 1918–mart 1920 g.).* Leningrad: Izdatel'stvo Leningradskogo universiteta, 1975.

Kurenyshev, A. A. *Krest'ianstvo i ego organizatsii v pervoi treti XX veka.* Moscow: Gosudarstvennyi istoricheskii muzei, 2000.

Landis, Erik C. "Between Village and Kremlin: Confronting State Food Procurement in Civil War Tambov, 1919–1920." *Russian Review* 63, no. 1 (2004): 70–88.

———. "A Civil War Episode: General Mamontov in Tambov, August 1919." *The Carl Beck Papers in Russian and East European Studies*, no. 1601 (2002).

———. "Waiting for Makhno: Legitimacy and Context in a Russian Peasant War." *Past and Present* 183 (2004): 199–236.

Lazarenko, Lev. "IMKA-Press i dni vandei na tambovshchine." *Vestnik russkogo khristianskogo dvizheniia* 170 (1994): 247–54.

Leggett, George. *The Cheka: Lenin's Political Police. The All-Russian extraordinary commission for combating counter-revolution and sabotage, December 1917 to February 1922.* Oxford: Clarendon Press, 1981.

Lenin, V. I. *Polnoe sobranie sochinenii.* 5th ed. 55 vols. Moscow: Gosudarstvennoe izdatel'stvo politicheskoi literatury, 1958–1965.

———. *Sochineniia.* 4th ed. 45 vols. Moscow: Gosudarstvennoe izdatel'stvo politicheskoi literatury, 1941–1955.

Leont'ev, Ia. V. "6 Iuliia 1918 goda: regional'nyi aspekt." In *Grazhdanskaia voina v rossii: sobytiia, mnenii, otsenki*, edited by N. A. Ivnitskii, 362–87. Moscow: Raritet, 2002.

Liapina, Tatiana A. "Ispoved' v podvale GubChK." *Posleslovie*, no. 6 (1993): 3.

Lih, Lars T. "The Bolshevik Sowing Committees of 1920: Apotheosis of War Communism?" *The Carl Beck Papers in Russian and East European Studies*, no. 803 (1990).

———. *Bread and Authority in Russia, 1914–1921.* Berkeley: University of California Press, 1990.

Litvinov, R. "V te trevozhnye dvadtsatye gody." In *Voronezhskie chekisty rasskazyvaiut...*, 28–41. Voronezh: Tsentral'noe chernozemnoe knizhnoe izdatel'stvo, 1976.

Lobotskii, A. "V skhvatke s antonovshchinoi." In *Parol'—muzhestvo. Ocherki o tambovskikh chekistakh*, edited by G. D. Remizov, 65–96. Voronezh: Tsentral'noe chernozemnoe knizhnoe izdatel'stvo, 1986.

Lutskii, E. A. "Krest'ianskoe vosstanie v tambovskoi gubernii v sentiabre 1917g." *Istoricheskie zapiski*, no. 2 (1938): 47–78.

Malle, Silvana. *The Economic Organization of War Communism, 1918–1921.* Cambridge: Cambridge University Press, 1985.

Maslov, A. A. "Concerning the Role of Partisan Warfare in Soviet Military Doctrine of the 1920s and 1930s." *Journal of Slavic Military Studies* 9, no. 4 (1996): 885–94.

Mawdsley, Evan. *The Russian Civil War.* 2nd ed. Edinburgh: Birlinn, 2000.

Meijer, Jan M., ed. *The Trotsky Papers, 1917–1922.* 2 vols. The Hague: Mouton, 1964–1971.

Meshcheriakov, Iurii. "O prichinakh volniknoveniia 'Antonovshchina.'" In *Nash krai tambovskii: tezisy, dokladov, i soobshchenii*, 65–67. Tambov: [s.n.], 1991.

———. "Stolknovenie [1]." *Gorod na Tsne*, 25 March 1998, 6.

———. "Stolknovenie [2]." *Gorod na Tsne*, 1 April 1998, 5.

———. "Stolknovenie [3]." *Gorod na Tsne*, 8 April 1998, 11.

———. "Ul'timatum [1]." *Gorod na Tsne*, 12 August 1997, 7.

———. "Ul'timatum [2]." *Gorod na Tsne*, 19 August 1997, 7.

Miliutin, N. A. "Po zadaniiam Lenina," in *Vospominaniia o Vladimire Il'iche Lenine.* 3 vols. Moscow: Gosudarstvennoe izdatel'stvo politicheskoi literatury, 1956–1960.

Mink, Charles R. "General Orders No. 11: The Forced Evacuation of Civilians During the Civil War." *Military Affairs* 34, no. 4 (1970): 132–36.

Mokarev, V. "Kursantskii spor na bor'be s antonovshchinoi." *Voina i revoliutsiia*, no. 1 (1932): 61–92.

Molodtsygin, M. A. *Krasnaia Armiia: rozhdenie i stanovlenie, 1917–1920 gg.* Moscow: IRI RAN, 1997.

———. *Raboche-krest'ianskii soiuz, 1918–1920.* Moscow: Nauka, 1987.

Moskovkin, V. "Vosstanie krest'ian v Zapadnoi Sibiri v 1921 godu." *Voprosii istorii*, no. 6 (1998): 46–64.

Murav'ev, E. F. "Poltora mesiatsa v shtabe antonovtsev." In *Voronezhskie chekisty rasskazyvaiut . . .* , 42–62. Voronezh: Tsentral'noe chernozemnoe knizhnoe izd., 1976.

Nabokin, A. "Vintovkoi i slovom." In *Parol'—muzhestvo. Ocherki o tambovskikh chekistakh*, edited by G. D. Remizov, 96–109. Voronezh: Tsentral'noe-chernozemnoe knizhnoe izdatel'stvo, 1986.

Nakrokhin, E. A. *Inogo ne bylo puti.* Voronezh: Izdatel'stvo Voronezhskogo universiteta, 1975.

Naumov, V. P., and A. A. Kosakovskii, eds. *Kronshtadt 1921. Dokumenty o sobytiiakh v Kronshtadte vesnoi 1921 g.* Moscow: Demokratiia, 1997.

Nikolaev, M. G. "Govoriat uchastniki 'likvidatsii antonovshchiny.'" *Otechestvennyi archivy*, no. 2 (1996): 34–66.

Obertas, I. L. *Komandir Fed'ko.* Moscow: Voennoe izdatel'stvo MinOborony SSSR, 1973.

Obvinitel'noe zakliuchenie po delu Tsentral'nogo komiteta i otdel'nykh chlenov inykh organizatsii Partii sotsialistov-revoliutsionerov: po obvineniiu ikh v vooruzhennoi bor'be protiv sovetskoi vlasti, organizatsii ubiistv, vooruzhennykh ograblenii i v izmennicheskikh snosheniiakh s inostrannymi gosudarstvami. Moscow: Izdatel'stvo VTsIK, 1922.

Okatov, N. A., I. V. Barinov, I. P. Zhuravlev, V. S. Malinina, V. S. Manuilov, G. I. Sel'tser, and G. I. Khodiakova, eds. *Sovety Tambovskoi gubernii v gody grazhdanskoi voiny, 1918–1921 gg.* Voronezh: Tsentral'no-chernozemnoe knizhnoe izdatel'stvo, 1989.

Okninskii, Anton. *Dva goda sredi krest'ian: vidennoe, slyshannoe, perezhitoe v Tambovskoi gubernii s noiabria 1918 goda do noiabria 1920 goda.* Newtonville, MA: Oriental Research Partners, 1986.

Olikov, S. *Dezertirstvo v Krasnoi armii i bor'ba s nim.* Leningrad: Izdatel'stvo shtaba, 1926.

Orlov, K. P. "K istorii likvidatsii antonovskgo miatezha (1921 g.)." *Istoricheskii arkhiv*, no. 4 (1962): 203–08.

Orlovskii, Grigorii. *"Kak dela v tambovskoi gubernii?": sbornik ocherkov.* Voronezh: Tsentral'noe chernozemnoe knizhnoe izd., 1974.

Osipova, T. V. *Rossiiskoe krest'ianstvo v revoliutsii i grazhdanskoi voine.* Moscow: Strelets, 2001.

Ovechkin, V. V. "Iz"iatie loshadei u naseleniia dlia Krasnoi armii v gody grazhdanskoi voiny." *Voprosy istorii*, no. 8 (1999): 114–24.

Panov, A. I., ed. *Ofitserskii korpus v politicheskoi istorii Rossii. Dokumenty i materialy.* 2 vols. Moscow: Eidos, 2002.

Pavliuchenkov, S. A. *Krest'ianskii Brest, ili predystoriia bolshevistskogo NEPa.* Moscow: Russkoe knigoizdatel'skoe tovarishchestvo, 1996.

Pavlov, Ia. S. *Narodnaia voina v tylu interventov i belogvardeitsev.* Minsk: Belarus', 1983.

Pereberzev, A. Ia. *Velikii Oktiabr' i pereobrazovanie derevni.* Voronezh: Tsentral'noe-Chernozemnoe knizhnoe izdatel'stvo, 1987.

Perepiska sekretariata TsKa RKP(b) s mestnymi partiinymi organizatsiiami. 11 vols. Moscow: Gosudarstvennoe izdatel'stvo politicheskoi literatury, 1957– .

Pereverzev, A. Ia. *Sotsialisticheskaia revoliutsiia v derevne chernozemnogo tsentra rossii.* Voronezh: Izdatel'stvo Voronezhskogo universiteta, 1976.

Perrie, Maureen. *The Agrarian Policy of the Russian Socialist Revolutionary Party: From its origins through the revolution of 1905–7.* Cambridge: Cambridge University Press, 1976.

Peterson, Roger. "A Community-Based Theory of Rebellion." *European Journal of Sociology* 34 (1998).

Pirozhkov, G. "Kirsanovskaia respublika." *Tambovskie khroniki,* nos. 5–6 (1995): 6–11.

Podbel'skii, Iurii. "Vosstanie tambovskikh krest'ian." *Revoliutsionnaia Rossiia,* no. 6 (1921): 24–26.

Pokaliukhin, M. "Konets banditskogo atamana." In *Parol'—muzhestvo. Ocherki o tambovskikh chekistakh,* edited by G. D. Remizov, 109–15. Voronezh: Tsentral'noe-chernozemnoe knizhnoe izdatel'stvo, 1986.

Pomazov, Sergei Semenovich. "Bor'ba za vlast' Sovetov v byvshem Kirsanovskom uezde." www.grad-kirsanov.ru/source.php?id=memory.pomazov1 (accessed 22 August 2007).

Ponikhidin, Iu. M. *Revoliutsionnye komitety RSFSR (1918–1921 gg.).* Saratov: Izdatel'stvo Saratovskogo universiteta, 1982.

Portnov, V. P., ed. *Partiino-politicheskaia rabota v krasnoi armii (aprel' 1918–fevral' 1919). Dokumenty.* Moscow: MinOborony SSSR, 1961.

Portnov, V. P., and M. M. Slavin. *Pravovye osnovy stroitel'stva Krasnoi Armii, 1918–1920 gg: istoriko-iuridicheskoe issledovanie.* Moscow: Nauka, 1985.

Power, J. Tracy. *Lee's Miserables: Life in the Army of Northern Virginia from the Wilderness to Appomattox.* Chapel Hill: University of North Carolina Press, 1998.

Protasov, L. G. *Soldaty garnizonov tsentral'noi Rossii v bor'be za vlast' sovetov.* Voronezh: Izdatel'stvo Voronezhskogo universiteta, 1978.

———. *Vserossiiskoe uchreditel'noe sobranie: istoriia rozhdeniia i gibeli.* Moscow: ROSSPEN, 1997.

Protasov, L. G., ed. *Stranitsy istorii Tambovskogo kraia.* Voronezh: Tsentral'noe-Chernozemnoe knizhnoe izdatel'stvo, 1986.

"Protsess pravykh eserov. Dvadtsat' deviatyi den'. Utrennee zasedanie." *Izvestiia VTsIK,* 12 July 1922, 2.

Pyle, Emily. "Village Social Relations and the Reception of Soldiers' Family Aid Policies, 1912–21." PhD diss., University of Chicago, 1997.

Radkey, Oliver H. "Chernov and Agrarian Socialism Before 1918." In *Continuity and Change in Russian and Soviet Thought,* edited by E. J. Simmons, 63–80. Cambridge: Harvard University Press, 1955.

———. *The Sickle Under the Hammer. The Socialist Revolutionaries in the Early Months of Soviet Rule.* New York: Columbia University Press, 1963.

———. *The Unknown Civil War in Soviet Russia.* Palo Alto, CA: Hoover Institution Press, 1976.

Raleigh, Donald. *Experiencing Russia's Civil War: Politics, Society, and Revolutionary Culture in Saratov, 1917–1922.* Princeton: Princeton University Press, 2002.

———. "Languages of Power: How the Saratov Bolsheviks Imagined Their Enemies." *Slavic Review* 57, no. 2 (1998): 320–49.

———. "Revolutionary Politics in Provincial Russia: The Tsaritsyn 'Republic' in 1917." *Slavic Review* 40, no. 2 (1981): 194–209.

Robbins, Richard G. *The Tsar's Viceroys : Russian Provincial Governors in the Last Years of the Empire*. Ithaca: Cornell University Press, 1987.

Roitman, B. "Rol' kavbrigady G. I. Kotovskogo v razgrome antonovshchiny." *Voenno-istoricheskii zhurnal*, no. 6 (1981): 71–74.

Romanov, Pavel Vasil'evich. "Vospominaniia." www.grad-kirsanov.ru/source.php?id=memory .romanov (accessed 22 August 2007).

Samoshkin, Vladimir V. "Aleksandr Stepanovich Antonov." *Voprosy istorii*, no. 2 (1994): 66–76.

———. "Antonovshchina: kanun i nachalo." *Literaturnaia Rossiia*, 8 June 1990, 18–19.

———. *Antonovskoe Vosstanie*. Moscow: Russkii Put', 2005.

———. "Bronepoezd no. 121." *Zherdevskie novosti*, 3 February 1996, 2.

———. "Dvoinik." *Literaturnaia Rossiia*, 18 February 1994, 16.

———. "Eser Aleksandr." *Literaturnaia Rossiia*, 2 August 1991, 28–30.

———. "Miatezh. Antonovshchina: Konets." *Literaturnaia Rossiia*, 30 November 1990, 18–20.

———. "Miatezh. Antonovshchina: Protivostoianie." *Literaturnaia Rossiia*, 26 October 1990, 18–20.

———. "Slovo o krasnykh kursantakh." *Pod'em*, no. 10 (1987): 120–27.

———. "V preddverii miatezha." *Literaturnaia rosssiia*, 13 December 1991, 20–22.

Sanborn, Joshua. *Drafting the Russian Nation: Military Conscription, Total War, and Mass Politics, 1905–1925*. DeKalb: Northern Illinois University Press, 2003.

———. "The Mobilization of 1914 and the Question of the Russian Nation: A Re-examination." *Slavic Review* 59, no. 2 (2000): 267–89.

Shabanov, N. I., and N. A. Makarov, eds. *Gubcheka: sbornik dokumentov i materialov iz istorii Saratovskoi gubernskoi chrezvychainoi komissii, 1917–1921 gg.* Saratov: Privolzhskoe knizhnoe izdatel'stvo, 1980.

Sharapov, G. V., V. P. Danilov, V. V. Kabanov, V. I. Kostrikin, T. V. Osipova, and Iu. V. Poliakov, eds. *Istoriia sovetskogo krest'ianstva*. 4 vols. Moscow: Nauka, 1986–1988.

Shelokhaev, V. V., Ia. V. Leont'ev, K. M. Anderson, O. V. Volobuev, and A. K. Sorokin, eds. *Partiia levykh sotsialistov-revoliutsionnerov, 1917–1925: dokumenty i materialy*. 3 vols. Moscow: ROSSPEN, 2000.

Shishkin, V. I., ed. *Sibirskaia vandeia*. 2 vols. Moscow: "Demokratiia," 2001.

———, ed. *Za sovety bez kommunistov: krest'ianskoe vosstanie v Tiumenskoi gubernii 1921 g.* Novosibirsk: Sibirskii khronograf, 2000.

Shlikhter, B. A. "Vospominaniia o V. I. Lenine." *Vorposy istorii KPSS*, no. 9 (1969): 111–15.

Shneyerhoff, Michael M. *Recollections of the Russian Revolution*. Berkeley: University of California Regional Cultural History Project, 1960.

Shrader, Charles S. *The Withered Vine: Logistics and the Communist Insurgency in Greece, 1945–1949*. Westport, CT: Praeger, 1999.

Shubin, A. *Makhno i makhnovskoe dvizhenie*. Moscow: Mik, 1998.

Singleton, Seth. "The Tambov Revolt (1920–1921)." *Slavic Review* 25, no. 3 (1966): 497–512.

Smirnov, D. M. *Zapiski chekista*. 2nd ed. Minsk: "Belarus," 1972.

Sobol'eva, A. A. *Krest'ianskoe vosstanie v Tambovskoi gubernii (1920–1921 gg.): Bibliograficheskii ukazatel'.* Tambov: MINTs, 1993.

Solokov, B. V. *Mikhail Tukhachevskii: zhizn' i smert' "Krasnogo marshala."* Smolensk: Rusich, 1999.

Solzhenitsyn, Aleksandr. "Slovo pri otkrytii pamiatnika Vandeiskomu vosstaniiu." *Vestnik russkogo khristianskogo dvizheniia,* no. 168 (1993): 151–54.

Soshnikov, A. Ia. "Ustanovlenie Sovetskoi vlasti i bor'ba s antonovshchinoi v Kirsanovskom uezde Tambovskoi gubernii (1917–1921 gg.)." www.grad-kirsanov.ru/source.php?id= memory .soshnik (accessed 22 August 2007).

Spiers, Edward M. *Chemical Warfare.* Basingstoke and London: Macmillan Press, 1986.

Spirin, L. M. *Klassy i partii v grazhdanskoi voine v rossii (1917–1920 gg.).* Moscow: Mysl', 1968.

Stanziani, Alessandro. "La gestion des approvisionnements et la restauration de la *gosudarstvennost':* le *Narkomprod,* l'armée, et les paysans." *Cahiers du Monde russe* 38, nos. 1–2 (1997): 83–116.

Starikov, S. V. *Demobilizovannye revoliutsionnye soldaty i oktiabr'skaia revoliutsiia v derevne.* Saransk: Izdatel'stvo Saratovskogo universiteta, 1989.

Strizhkov, Iurii K. *Prodovol'stvennye otriady v gody grazhdanskoi voiny i inostrannoi interventsii: 1917–1921 gg.* Moscow: Nauka, 1973.

Sychev, G. A. "Vospominaniia." www.grad-kirsanov.ru/source.php?id=memory.sjchev (accessed 16 September 2006).

Taithe, Bertrand. *Citizenship and Wars: France in Turmoil, 1870–1871.* London: Routledge, 2001.

Tiushkevich, S. A. *Sovetskie vooruzhennye sily. Istoriia stroitel'stva.* Moscow: Voennoe izdatel'stvo, 1978.

Trifonov, I. A. *Klassy i klassovaia bor'ba v SSSR v nachale NEPa, 1921–1923 gg.* Leningrad: Leningradskii gosudarstvennyi universitet im. Zhdanova, 1964.

Trifonov, I. Ia. "Iz istorii pazgroma antonovshchiny v 1920–1921 godakh." *Voenno-istoricheskii zhurnal,* no. 9 (1968): 27–35.

Trotsky, Leon. *How the Revolution Armed.* Translated by Brian Pearce. 5 vols. London: New Park Publications, 1979.

Trutko, Ivan. "Primeneniia aeroplanov, kak razervov." *Krasnaia Armiia,* no. 5/6 (1921): 41–43.

———. "Razgrom bandy Antonova." *Krasnaia Armiia,* no. 7/8 (1921): 20–25.

———. "Unichtozhenie band Boguslavskogo." *Krasnaia Armiia,* no. 3/4 (1921): 35–39.

———. "Unichtozhenie bandy Karasia." *Krasnaia Armiia,* no. 1/2 (1921): 33–35.

Tukhachevskii, M. N. "Bor'ba s kontrrevoliutsionnymi vosstaniiami." *Voina i revoliutsiia,* no. 8 (1926): 3–15.

———. *Izbrannye Proizvedeniia.* 2 vols. Moscow: Voennoe Izdatel'stvo Min. Oborony SSSR, 1964.

Tylik, S. F. "Komitety bednoty v Tambovskoi gubernii." *Vestnik leningradskogo universiteta: seriia istorii, iazyka i literaturii* 18, no. 8 (1963): 41–55.

———. "Vedushchaia rol' rabochikh Petrograda, Moskvy, i drugikh tsentrov v revoliutsionnykh preobrazovaniiakh v derevne v 1918 g. (po materialam tambovskoi gubernii)." In *Iz istorii Velikoi Oktiabr'skoi sotsialisticheskoi revoliutsii i sotsialisticheskogo stroitel'stva v SSSR,* edited by V. A. Ovsiakin, 157–75. Leningrad: Nauk, 1967.

Vedeniapin, G. V. "Antonovshchina." *Volga,* nos. 5–6 (1997): 218–46.

Ventsov, S. "Banditizm v Belorussii i organizatsiia bor'by s nim." *Krasnaia Armiia*, no. 9 (1921): 44–51.

Verkeenko, G. P., and S. T. Minakov. *Moskovskii pokhod i krushenie "dobrovol''cheskoi politiki" generala A. Denikina.* Moscow: Moskovskii gosudarstvennyi otkrytii pedagogicheskii institut, 1993.

V. I. Lenin i A. V. Lunacharskii. Perepiska, doklady, dokumenty. Moscow: Nauka, 1971.

Viola, Lynne. *Peasant Rebels Under Stalin: Collectivization and the Culture of Peasant Resistance.* Oxford: Oxford University Press, 1996.

Viunov, N. M., N. I. Deev, and T. F. Kariaev, eds. *Direktivy Glavnogo komandovaniia Krasnoi Armii, 1917–1920: Sbornik dokumentov.* Moscow: Voenizdat, 1969.

Volkovinskii, V. N. *Makhno i ego krakh.* Moscow: VZPI, 1991.

Wade, Rex, ed. *Documents of Soviet History.* 2 vols. Gulf Breeze, FL: Academic International Press, 1993.

Weitz, Mark A. *A Higher Duty: Desertion among Georgia Troops during the Civil War.* Lincoln: University of Nebraska Press, 2000.

Wessels, Elria. "'A Cage Without Bars'—the Concentration Camp in Bloemfontein." In *Scorched Earth*, edited by Fransjohan Pretorius, 60–85. Cape Town: Human and Rousseau, 2001.

Zaitsev, Gavril Andreevich. "Za vlast' sovetov." www.grad-kirsanov.ru/source.php?id=memory .zajcev (accessed 22 August 2007).

Zhukov, G. K. *Vospominaniia i razmyshleniia.* 10th rev. ed. 3 vols. Moscow: Novosti, 1990.

Zietsman, Paul. "The Concentration Camp Schools—Beacons of Light in the Darkness." In *Scorched Earth*, edited by Fransjohan Pretorius, 86–109. Cape Town: Human and Rousseau, 2001.

INDEX

amnesties: and desertion, 25, 106–7; and rebellion, 112, 208–9, 231, 252, 256–57, 277, 283, 323n59, 343n74, 343n76, 350n26, 356n110, 360n184

Antibanditry Commission, 210–11, 217, 236, 238–40, 266, 274

Antidesertion Commission, 19–21, 27, 36, 38–39, 297n103, 300n153, 301nn159–61, 302n164

antidesertion patrols, 22–25, 32–33, 35, 37, 62, 78, 84–85, 296n88, 301n159, 330n68

anti-Semitism: rebel, 130–31, 320nn25–26; Red Army, 320n24

Antonov, Alexander, 284–85; early years, 40–59, 302n3, 302n14, 303nn24–25, 303n27, 303n29, 304n36; death of, 1–3, 276–79, 280, 362nn13–14, 362n16; and Nester Makhno, 182, 187; and outbreak of rebellion, 76–87, 94, 101, 308n49, 309nn56–57, 310n82, and Partisan Army, 110–11, 136, 138, 145–46, 148, 179, 194, 198–99, 201, 221, 224–25, 227, 231–32, 318n8, 324n80, 332n94, 335n131, 348n129, 348n131

Antonov, Dmitrii, 42–43, 52–53, 83, 343n75; death of, 1–3, 276–79, 280

Antonov (German), Mikhail, 206, 235, 244, 274, 351n31

Antonov, Stepan, 42–43, 302n7

Antonova, Anna, 42–43

Antonova, Valentina, 42–43, 46, 48, 52, 303n19

Antonov-Ovseenko, Vladimir: as Plenipotentiary Commission chairman, 74, 130, 172, 190, 196, 199, 201–2, 205–7, 209–12, 218–19, 239, 269, 274, 316n2, , 336n2, 339n28, 342n61, 342nn42–43, 344n87, 348n119, 351n31; and Tambov Communists, 158, 163, 170–71, 330n64; as Tambov Soviet chairman (1919–1920), 32

Aplok, Iurii, 89–93, 97–98, 100, 313n38, 314n54

Balashov (town), 45, 60, 183, 224

Balashov (uezd), 56, 101, 103, 183–184, 305n38, 333n107

bandits: banditry, 41, 56–59, 67, 91–92, 215, 260–61, 282, 310n1, 324n71, 344n90, 357n136; in political rhetoric, 78–80, 116–19, 141–42, 189, 230, 232, 254, 256, 349n8. See also Partisan Army: discipline; propaganda: anti-rebel; soldiers, Red Army: self-provisioning

Bazhenov, Konstantin, 45, 47, 50, 303n23

Beliakov, Mikhail, 166–68, 308n46, 329n53, 331n90

Bogoliubskii, Aleksandr, 52–53, 275

Boguslavskii, Aleksandr, 94, 108, 187, 221–22, 227–28, 274, 310n82, 337n4

Borisoglebsk (town), 8, 10, 107, 155, 157, 289n13, 293n54, 298n128, 314n60, 316n86, 326n12; White occupation of, 18, 294n68, 294n69

Borisoglebsk (uezd), 10, 18, 63–64, 67–68, 70, 71, 72, 86, 87, 96, 97, 98, 99, 154, 182, 282, 326n11, 343n74, 363n23

cadets, Red Army: and counterinsurgency, 62, 64–65, 87, 155, 166, 215, 263–68, 347n114, 357n141, 357n143, 359n162, 359n164

Cheka, 70, 108–9, 176; and Antonov, 1–2, 50–51, 53, 56–58, 79, 79, 309; and counterinsurgency, 63–64, 66, 74, 87, 90, 95, 111, 116, 118, 136, 139, 166, 206–7, 209, 232, 235, 238, 242–45, 253, 261, 274–75, 329n62, 342nn61–62, 343n81, 353n64, 361n3; in Penza Province, 101–3; in Saratov Province, 101, 136, 325n87; in Tambov Province, 14, 52, 81, 85, 195, 205, 283, 293n54, 296n98, 342nn66–67. See also Antonov, Aleksandr: death of

chemical weapons, 265–68, 358nn149–51, 358n156, 359n159

committees of the poor (kombedy), 9–17, 20, 27, 207, 291nn33–35, 292nn39–40

Communist Party: military conscription of members: 11–12, 18, 20, 37, 97, 105, 301n156, 313n36, 346n108; organization in Tambov Province: 9, 14, 38, 118, 154, 158–163, 171, 208, 217, 298n114, 312n25, 328n39; rebel attacks against, 53, 56–57, 70, 86, 104, 109, 133, 220, 237, 283, 321n34, 326n13; refugees, 64, 97, 157, 198, 232, 338n24

concentration camps, 243–52, 352n55, 352nn57–61, 352nn64–65, 354n78, 354n84, 355n88, 355n92

conscription, Red Army, 5–9, 15, 18–19, 21–22, 32, 290nn28–29; of former Tsarist army officers, 12–13, 17–18

Constituent Assembly: elections, 71, 75, 288n12; in rebel propaganda, 83, 124–27, 130, 146, 317n8, 342n64